The Gospel of Accor ✍ W9-CRC-541

The Gospel of According to St. John

THE SUNDAY SERMONS OF
THE GREAT FATHERS

VOLUME ONE

Dr Toal's work contains what is in effect the spiritual inheritance of every Christian. The four volumes together give, Sunday by Sunday and for the greater festivals and fasts, selected sermons of the great Fathers and Doctors of the Church.

In the framing of the great corpus of Catholic doctrine and theology, the authority and the influence of the Fathers are secondary only to those of the Apostles and Evangelists themselves. To one we owe the true interpretation of facts or phrases, to another the unfolding of a doctrine out of a single word; to all of them the handing on and enrichment of a tradition which runs back to the foundation of the Church. Their homilies on the liturgical Gospels for Sundays and the greater feasts and fasts cannot fail to add clarity and depth to any reader's understanding of these key passages from holy scripture; and this treasury of their commentaries will above all be of constant help to priests whose office it is to preach and expound the Gospel in the continuance of the tradition.

An especially valuable point is the inclusion, after the printed text of each Gospel reading, of the relevant passage of the *Catena Aurea* or *Golden Chain*, the great commentary on the Gospels compiled by St Thomas Aquinas from the writings of all the Fathers and Doctors of the Church. This has not hitherto been available in English.

The four volumes correspond with the four liturgical divisions of the year. This first volume was recently published in a large format under the title *Patristic Homilies on the Gospels* and is now reissued in a small and handy pocket size. The subsequent volumes will appear in the same small format for the individual user and, simultaneously, in a large format for libraries.

Semper redeundum ad divinae revelationis Fontes; quod depositum Divinus Redemptor concredidit authentice interpretandum soli Ecclesiae Magisterio.

Pope Pius XII,

Encyclical *Humani Generis*,

12 August 1950.

THE
SUNDAY SERMONS
OF THE GREAT
FATHERS

VOLUME ONE
*From the First Sunday of Advent
to Quinquagesima*

TRANSLATED AND EDITED BY
M. F. TOAL, D.D.

P.O. Box 612   Preservation Press   Swedesboro, NJ 08085

Library of Congress Cataloging-in-Publication Data

Patristic homilies on the Gospels.
The Sunday sermons of the great Fathers: a manual of preaching, spiritual reading, and meditation / translated and edited by M. F. Toal.
    p. cm.
Originally published Patristic homilies on the Gospels. Chicago: Regnery, 1955-1963.
    Contains Saint Thomas Aquinas' Catena aurea.
    Includes bibliographical references and indexes.
    Contents: v. 1. From the first Sunday of Advent to Quinquagesima—v. 2. From the first Sunday in Lent to the Sunday after the Ascension—v. 3. From Pentecost to the tenth Sunday after Pentecost—v. 4. From the eleventh Sunday after Pentecost to the twenty-fourth and last Sunday after Pentecost.
    ISBN 1-886412-14-6 (set: alk. paper). — ISBN 1-886412-15-4 (v. 1: alk. paper). — ISBN 1-886412-16-2 (v. 2: alk. paper). — ISBN 1-886412-17-0 (v. 3: alk. paper). — ISBN 1-886412-18-9 (v. 4: alk paper)
    1. Bible. N.T. Gospels—Sermons. 2. Sermons, English. 3. Church year sermons. 4. Bible. N.T. Gospels—Commentaries. 5. Fathers of the church. I. Toal, M. F. II. Thomas, Aquinas. Saint, 1225?-1274. Catena aurea. English. III. Title.
BS2555.A2T6 1997
252'.011 —dc21
                                           96-44004
                                           CIP

For information write Preservation Press:
P.O. Box 612, Swedesboro, NJ 08085

TO
THE MOST REVEREND FATHER
MICHAEL BROWNE, O.P.
MASTER GENERAL OF THE ORDER OF PREACHERS

FORMERLY

THE MASTER OF THE SACRED PALACE

THE INSPIRER OF THIS WORK

THIS SECOND EDITION OF THE HOMILIES

OF THE GREAT FATHERS IS

GRATEFULLY AND RESPECTFULLY DEDICATED

FOREWORD

THE author of the present work has had as his purpose to put into the hands of his fellow priests material of incomparable value, in a form easy of access, with a view to aiding them in the sacred ministry of preaching. This apostolic ministry is the one on which all else depends in the mission of the Church for the salvation of souls.

A large portion of it will always consist in homilies on the Gospels of the Sundays and Principal Feasts. Father Toal, in this first volume, has in view this sector of the preacher's work. For the Gospel of each Sunday and Feast he has brought together from the most reliable sources, and translated, all that he thought to be best and most useful in the homilies and expositions of the Fathers and of the Angel of the Schools.

Nothing more suited to his noble purpose could be conceived. The word of God contained in Scripture, and especially in the Gospels, has been given to the Church for the instruction of men. Sacred Tradition guided by the Spirit of God has expounded it in the writings of the Holy Fathers and Doctors.

Father Toal has placed in the easiest possible reach of the busy priest this treasure house of sacred lore, this quintessence of the doctrine of Tradition on each Gospel. What he supplies may, of course, not be all that may be usefully known in relation to it, but it is, and by long odds, the most important thing. A sermon well prepared on the matter here supplied cannot fail to be learned, solid, simple and effective.

What more can be said in praise of the utility of Father Toal's contribution? We shall all be grateful to him, and *his reward will indeed be great.* (Mt. v. 12.)

MICHAEL BROWNE, O.P.

Vatican
24 November, 1954

vii

PREFACE

He opened their minds, and gave them power to understand the Scriptures
(Lk.xxiv. 45.)

The supreme mission imposed by Christ on His Apostles was to preach the Gospel to every creature. In virtue of this mission, they to whom the command was given, and those to whom it descends, speak with authority and power in the things of God: the power being in the word given them (1 Cor. ii. 4). And this alone do men wish to hear from those so commanded: the word of God in the Gospel of Christ. It is now their birthright: that wherein they hope, the source of faith, the bond of charity; "for it is in the Gospel that the form of Catholic faith, and the rule of the whole Christian life, is chiefly laid down."[1]

But it may happen that where the Faith is well established the preaching of the Gospel may no longer be regarded as an urgent task. Indeed it has come about that many, whose duty this is, do not fulfil it; though not as a rule through indifference or neglect. Various immediate reasons for this do arise, through particular circumstances, but there may possibly be a general underlying reason: a deterrent, simple, effective, but not realized, arising from the manner in which the Gospel sermons are prepared.

In training the future preachers of the Gospel there is a fairly general tradition of dependence, as to form, on the great court preachers of the seventeenth and eighteenth centuries, and on their imitators. The acknowledged masterpieces of pulpit oratory of this period, elaborate, sustained, elegant, are widely used as models in seminaries and ecclesiastical colleges. Students are encouraged to imitate them; their first efforts at preaching are invariably formed on them. Afterwards, as priests, they continue to prepare their own sermons on these lines, and come to regard these forms, involving the building of a somewhat elaborate verbal structure, as the sole method of Gospel preaching.

It was no doubt fitting that in that day and circumstance the word of God should be so splendidly presented. And it is easy to see how such nobility of style and utterance caused these discourses to be taken as models, as the text books of pulpit oratory for the centuries

ix

that followed. But we have to recognize that they were the product of a particular time and a particular environment. Also that they were addressed mainly to a leisured and cultivated audience, and invariably lack a sense of urgency. Roundabout in manner, appealing as much to the refined intellect as to the will, they are without simplicity and directness. It has been evident for a long time that popular appreciation of this style has departed. Such sermons weary. There has been a sharpening of men's minds: so many things now claim their attention, the wisdom and distractions of the world coming in at every door. The abiding human need is for a message that is, like the Gospel itself, urgent, simple, direct.

Thus, many preachers who know no other style find themselves out of key with their hearers. To them it seems that the people are at fault. But such is not the case. The fault lies with themselves. True it is that many replace the exposition of the Gospel with systematic catechetical instructions on the truths of the Faith and on the formal doctrines of the Church. This, in itself, is indeed a most grave pastoral duty, and one which may in given circumstances become an even more pressing duty than the exposition of the Gospels. Yet, as St Jerome says: "Ignorance of the Scriptures leads to ignorance of Christ";[2] and many who may have mastered the full teaching of the Church, and indeed many who may be incapable of understanding it, will yet hunger for the food of the Word, and the tender divine wisdom of the parables, and thirst for *the living stream, that maketh joyful the city of God* (Ps. xlv, 5).

We must return to the preaching of the Gospel in its own simplicity; to the simplicity of those who first spread the Gospel message, and who received their rule of interpretation in direct line from the Apostles. From the beginning we have had our models, in the divine discourses themselves. They are simple, without loftiness. In them there is no vagueness, no elaboration. It is men who mystify, because of ignorance; and elaborate, because of vanity. Where Jesus is instructing the people there is no word or figure a child may not follow; words fitting thought as close as light lies to the earth. He is also brief: blessed brevity, that knows how to compassionate the weak and wandering minds of men.[3]

We must return to this simplicity that we may preach the Gospel in a manner that is acceptable to all men. But this will not be easy. The simplicity of the Gospel, if one may say so, is a deceiving simplicity; for it is the simplicity of pure divine wisdom, using simple human words. And the inner content of these words is not easy to grasp. In various ways it must be sought for, striven for. It is hidden from the proud, and from those whose hearts are held by this world. To those, however, who love and serve God the message of the Gospel will appear ever more deep and wide and inexhaustible. Yet this is the preachers' task: to make this message known. To do this they must seek to understand it, word for word. Each single word, whether noun or verb or preposition, and even the numbers spoken of, has its own deep and special significance, which may not be loosely or rashly interpreted. And how can they see this *unless someone shows it to them?* Here we have need of guides. And in a duty so sacred, so responsible, not everyone that presents himself is an acceptable guide. "Here *it is required among the dispensers of the mysteries of God,* that a man be found a faithful dispenser."[4] *Dearly beloved,* says St John, *believe not every spirit, but try the spirits if they be of God* (1 Jn. iv. 1, 6). Only such guides may be followed as the Church approves: for it is to the Church that the custody of the word of God has been confided.[5]

In the providence of God we have such guides: "Holy and illustrious men, whom we call the Fathers and Doctors of the Church those most shining lights whom God willed to shine in the firmament of His Church, so that by means of them the darknesses of the heretics might be dispelled. Men such as Irenaeus, Cyprian, Hilary, Athanasius, Basil, the two Gregorys, Ambrose, Jerome, Chrysostom, Augustine, Cyril. These are the Bishops and Shepherds, sober, learned, holy, who drank in the Catholic Faith with their mothers' milk, ate it with their food, who have ministered this food and this drink to great and simple. It was by means of such planters, cultivators, builders, shepherds, and teachers, that, since the Apostles, the Church has grown."[6]

Add to these great names that of Leo, Pope and Doctor, prince of the homilists, and most impressive of the Fathers, whose brief sermons affirm over and over again, in words of grave authority, simplicity, and earnestness, the need for the Christian formation of mens' lives, by the simple means of prayer, fasting, and almsdeeds. Add likewise Gregory, surnamed the Great, also Pope and Doctor, who joins to the same authority a most tender insight, as he brings the mysteries of God, and the new manner of the Gospel living, into the pattern of daily life. Add lastly, though first in time, the great Origen, "who, among the Easterns, holds chief place, in the liveliness of his mental powers, and the wondrous constancy of his labours, from whose manifold writings almost all have since drawn."[7]

These then are our guides; they who can say with the beloved Disciple: *We are of God, he that knoweth God heareth us.* These alone may we follow; and the reasons for this are of great moment.

Firstly, because, from the fruit of their lives, and by the attestation of the Church, we know that they were men of great holiness of life, and accordingly, ever responsive to the promptings of the Holy Spirit; not concerned with wordly wisdom. To such the word of God is made clear: to the pure of heart, who, loving God, would never depart from his inspirations, nor teach, or write, except in accordance with His holy truth.

Again, they are, apart from the teaching *magisterium* of the Church, our supreme witnesses as to the content of that sacred deposit of divine revelation which ended with the last of the Apostles; instructors who "acquired their understanding of the Holy Scriptures, not by their own lights and ideas, but from the writings and authority of the Ancients, who, in their turn, as we know, received their rule of interpretation in direct line from the Apostles."[8]

Besides their holiness and authority they were men who had devoted their great natural powers to the study of all Scripture. *Now, all Scripture inspired of God, is profitable to each* (2 Tim. iv. 16). But no explanation of the Gospels can be truly profitable which is not in harmony with the Scriptures of the Old Testament, "for the witness of both Old and New Testaments run together unto our instruction; for that which the trumpet of the prophet signalled, the deeds of the Gospel now make evident, even as it was written: *Deep calleth to deep, in the voice of thy floodgates* (Ps. xli. 8): and to show forth the glory of God, the deeps of either Testament call unto each other: and what was hidden beneath the cloak of figure, now in the unveiled Light shines clear."[9]

The final reason, which crowns all the rest, is that they are not alone witnesses of authority, sanctity, and learning, regarding the sacred mysteries of the Faith and the meaning of the holy Gospels, but also that they speak with harmonious voices, in a chorus that rises from every side, from age to age, proclaiming together what was made known from the beginning. In the progress of this holy revelation, by means of the teaching of the Church, the divine truth entered into certain minds of grace, power, and wisdom. Minds which saw deeply into its mystery, and unfolded what they saw, and taught it to others, and passed it on in their writings; not adding to it, not enlarging it, by the absorption of extraneous human wisdom, but solely making clear that which was uttered for our enlightenment by those who first revealed and taught it, namely: Christ the Lord, and after Him His holy Apostles.

Because of this last reason we have, in this work, immediately following the Gospel text, given its word for word exposition, taken from all the Fathers, and compiled at the command of supreme authority, by the purest and most powerful mind that has flowered in the bosom of the Church. In this compilation the commentary of the Holy Fathers and Doctors on each successive word of the Gospel, has been linked together in a golden chain of witness and sacred wisdom. The work to which I refer is the *Catena Aurea* of St Thomas Aquinas, the Angel of the Schools: a miracle of wisdom and knowledge, and possibly the least known of all the saint's works.

The purpose and method of this work is best explained in St Thomas' own words, in his dedicatory preface, which I here append. Regarding the method of abbreviation he uses, and of which he makes particular mention, it will be of interest to know that in verifying the quotations that make up the *Catena Aurea*, I found that the saint in citing, for example, St Augustine, would compend an entire homily of the latter into two or three modest paragraphs. Yet, with so much cut away, it was impossible to find an essential point of the homily omitted, or a word cited that was deprived of its relative significance within the homily.

At this point it is desired to affirm, that it is far from the author's mind to imply that we must return to the early ages to find again the true spirit of the Church, or to find there something that is missing from the life of the Church today. Than this, nothing could be further from the truth. For that which then enriched the Church, namely: the divinely promised assistance of the Holy Spirit, is the same which fructifies it today, and every day, until the end of time. Here in this work it is a question simply of the fuller use of the riches of Tradition, which, together with the Scriptures, form the sacred deposit of the Faith. And then as now there was one Voice, "one supreme teaching Authority, whose sacred task it was to guard, preserve, interpret, the whole deposit of faith, not only Sacred Scripture, but Tradition, which is no less divine in origin,"[10] namely the Church, so that nothing was innovated in practice, nothing explicitly taught, unless what was handed down from the beginning.

We may well indeed, oftentimes, turn our minds to those first ages of struggle and persecution, and draw encouragement from the manner in which the early Christians faced a darkness, a universal reign of evil, such as has never since existed, and which, by the power of the Christian spirit, they both overcame and transformed; fulfilling in this Christ's prophetic parable of the leaven, which transformed to its own virtue the mass in which it was buried. In this there is a divinely prophetical intimation of the efficacy and purpose of the Christian leaven, the Christian life, which is apt to be overlooked in the striving for formal achievement.

These then are the guides we have gathered into this first, and shall, we hope, gather into the three succeeding volumes of this work. The homilies presented, except in a few indicated instances, are given in their entirety, and they are translated from the best texts now available. They can be used either for direct preaching as they stand, or for reading to the faithful, as was an ancient and widespread custom, or they may be used as models for the preacher's personal exposition of the Gospels.

And they are, we venture to say, models and sermons to which the people will listen eagerly, as they listened to them long ago. And this because they proceed from minds filled with the love of God and His holy word, as well as by its knowledge and understanding. And they were written by men upon whom the Church has conferred the authority of Doctors, and of Teachers, of the Faith; holding their writings as channels, along which has come untarnished the pure stream of the saving divine Truth.

.   .   .

I desire here to pay a tribute of veneration and gratitude to the memory of a great patristic scholar, Father Francois Combefis, O.P. What is perhaps his greatest work, the *Bibliotheca Patrum Conciona-toria*, has been the guide in this present undertaking. This work, published in Paris in 1662, in eight tomes, is a vast compilation of patristic exposition and homilies, selected and arranged for the liturgical year. This plan, and in good part this selection, I have followed here, using, however, the later and more critical texts.

My attention was drawn to this treasure, and to the need to make something similar available to the English speaking world, by another member of the Order of Preachers, the Most Reverend Father Michael Browne, O.P., the present Master of the Sacred Apostolic Palace. I owe him, and here offer him, my warme thanks; for it is to his carefully deliberated suggestion, and to his encouragement and counsel, that this presentation of Patristic Homilies directly owes its existence. I desire also to thank him for his goodness in writing the Foreword to this first volume.

I wish also to thank the Reverend Father John Chrysostom Baur, O.S.B., at present of the Vatican Library, the contemporary authority on St John Chrysostom, for his much valued advice regarding the authenticity of many of the homilies of the saint which I have included here.

I desire also to express my deep thanks to the authorities of the Vatican Library. It is impossible to convey the value, even to the humblest searchers, of the great resources, and amenities, of the

Library: and in this latter I include the courtesy and helpfulness of its officials, including, particularly, the *bidelli*, who so cheerfully assist and guide all who come to use its treasures. To His Eminence, Cardinal Mercati, and to the Prefect, the Right Reverend Abbot Albareda, O.S.B., I offer my respectful homage and very sincere gratitude.

M. F. TOAL

Collegio Teutonico
Vatican
Easter Sunday, 1955

NOTES

[1] St Thomas Aquinas, Introduction to the *Catena Aurea*.
[2] Encyclical *Providentissimus Deus*, 1893: St Jerome in Isa. Prol. (PL 24, 17) EB, 86.
[3] "What is desired in the explanation of the Holy Scripture is, not elaborate discourses, adorned with oratorical flowers, but knowledge and the simplicity of truth." St Jerome; cf. Encyclical *Spiritus Paraclitus*, 1920, (PL, 24, 1058 C); EB, 487.
[4] Cf. *Spiritus Paraclitus*, EB, 487: 1 Cor. iv. 2.
[5] "Speaking in the Church there is grave danger, lest the Gospel of Christ become, through distorted interpretation, the Gospel of a man," *Spiritus Paraclitus*, citing St Jerome, in Comm. in Gal.; where he comments on Psalm xlix. 16, 17 (PL, 26, 322 D); EB, 487.
[6] St Robert Bellarmine, Sermon on the Doctors of the Church, Roman Breviary, Feast.
[7] Encyclical *Providentissimus Deus*.
[8] *Prov. Deus.* Rufinus PL 21, 518.
[9] St Leo M. PL 54, Sermo. 60.
[10] Cf. Encyclical *Humani Generis*, 1950.

REFERENCE LIST OF DOCTORS AND FATHERS IN THIS WORK

The Four Great Eastern Doctors of the Church

1. St Basil the Great, Confessor, Archbishop of Caesarea. A.D. 330–379.
2. St Gregory Nazianzen, Confessor, Patriarch of Constantinople. 329–390.
3. St John Chrysostom, Confessor, Archbishop of Constantinople. 354–407.
4. St Cyril of Alexandria, Confessor, Patriarch of Alexandria. Died 444.

The Four Great Western Doctors of the Church

1. St Ambrose, Confessor, Bishop of Milan. A.D. 339–397.
2. St Jerome, Priest and Confessor, Author of the Vulgate. 347–420.
3. St Confessor, Confessor, Bishop of Hippo. 354–430.
4. St Gregory the Great, Pope and Confessor. 540–603.

The supreme Doctor and Witness of Divine Tradition in all that relates to the Person of *Christ the Son of the living God* is St Leo the Great, Confessor, and Successor of St Peter. Died A.D. 461.

Alphabetical list of Doctors, Fathers of the Church, and Ecclesiastical Writers, Teachers and Preachers of the Gospel of Christ, and Witnesses of the Divine Tradition. The names occur principally in the Catena Aurea.

1. Ælred of York, Abbot, Homilist and Historian. A.D. 1109–1166.
2. Alcuin Albinus, Educator, Theologian. 735–804.
3. Amphilochius, St, Archbishop of Iconium, Greek Father. A.D. 339–400.
4. Anastasius, St, Abbot of Mt Sinai, Ecclesiastical Writer. Died 700.
5. Anselm, St, Archbishop of Canterbury, Doctor of the Church. 1033–1109.
6. Antipater, Bishop of Bostra (Syria), Ecclesiastical Writer. Died *c.* 460.
7. Anthony, St, Abbot, Founder of Christian Monasticism. 251–356.
8. Asterius, St, Bishop of Amasea, Pontus, Greek Father. Died *c.* 410.
9. Athanasius, St, Patriarch of Alexandria, Doctor of the Church. 296–373.
10. Bede, The Venerable, Priest and Confessor, Doctor of the Church. 672–735.

11. Bernard, St, Abbot of Clairvaux, Doctor of the Church. 1090–1153.
12. Caesarius, St, Bishop of Arles, Preacher. 470–543.
13. Clement, St, Martyr, Third Successor of St Peter, Apostolic Father.
    $+$ *c.* 90.
14. Clement of Alexandria, Ecclesiastical Writer. Died *c.* 215.
15. Cyprian, St, Martyr, Bishop of Carthage, Father of the Church.
    $+$258.
16. Cyril, St, Confessor, Bishop of Jerusalem, Doctor of the Church.
    318–386.
17. Didymus of Alexandria (*The Blind*), Great Teacher. 310–395.
18. Dionysius, St, The Great, Patriarch of Alexandria, Father of the
    Church. 190–264.
19. Ephraem, St, Confessor and Deacon, Doctor of the Church. $+$373.
20. Epiphanius, St, Metropolitan of Cyprus, Greek Father. 315–403.
21. Eucherius, St, Bishop of Lyons, Scriptural and Ascetic Writer. $+$450.
22. Eusebius, St, Bishop of Caesarea, Father of Church History. 260–341.
23. Fulgentius, St, Bishop of Ruspe (Africa), Theologian. 468–533.
24. Gaudentius, St, Bishop of Brescia, Father of the Church. $+$410.
25. Gregory, St, Confessor (The Miracle-Worker), Bishop of Neo-
    caesarea, Father of the Church. A.D. 213–270.
26. Gregory, St, Bishop of Nyssa, Confessor, Doctor of the Church.
    $+$394.
27. Haymo, Bishop of Halberstadt, Homilist. Died 858.
28. Hesychius, Priest of Jerusalem, Ecclesiastical Writer. Died 472.
29. Hilary, St, Confessor, Bishop of Poitiers, Doctor of the Church.
    $+$358.
30. Hilary, St, Bishop of Arles, Father of the Church. 401–409.
31. Ignatius, St, Martyr, Bishop of Antioch, Apostolic Father. 50–117.
32. Ildefonsus, St, Bishop of Toledo, Ecclesiastical Writer. $+$667.
33. Joannes (Geometra), Greek Ecclesiastical Writer. *c.* 600–700.
34. John Damascene, St, Priest, Greek Father, 676–754.
35. Josephus, Flavius, Jewish Historian. A.D. 37–101.
36. Irenaeus, St, Martyr, Bishop of Lyons, Father of the Church. $+$202.
37. Isidore, St, Abbot of Pelusium (Egypt), Ecclesiastical Writer, Disciple
    of Chrysostom. $+$450.
38. Ivo, St, Bishop of Chartres. 1040–1116.
39. Justin, St, Martyr, Apostolic Father. 100–165.
40. Maximus Confessor, St, Abbot, Greek Doctor. 580–662.
41. Maximus, St, Bishop of Turin, Homilist. 380–465.
42. Melito, Bishop of Sardis (Asia Minor), Father of the Church. $+$190.
43. Methodius, St, Martyr, Bishop of Tyre, Father of the Church. Died
    311.
44. Origenes, Priest and Confessor, Father of the Church. A.D. 185–253
45. Pacianus, St, Bishop of Barcelona, Ecclesiastical Writer. $+$390.
46. Patrick, St, Bishop, Confessor, Apostle of Ireland. $+$432.
47. Paulinus, Bishop of Nola, Ecclesiastical Writer. 353–431.
48. Peter Chrysologos, St, Bishop of Ravenna, Doctor of the Church.
    $+$450.

BIBLIOGRAPHY AND ABBREVIATIONS

Bibliotheca Patrum Concionatoria of P. Francois Combefis O.P. Paris 1681	BPC
Migne's Patrologiae Cursus Completus Series Graeca. Edition Paris 1886. Vols. 161	PG
Series Latina. Edition Paris 1844–66. Vols. 221	PL
Corpus Scriptorum Ecclesiasticorum Latinorum (*current*)	CSEL
Catena Aurea of St Thomas Aquinas	CA
Catena Sexaginta-quinque Graecorum Patrum in Lucam, Quae Quatuor simul Evangelistarum introduxit Explicationem. Luce ac latinitate donata a Balthasare Corderio Soc. Jesu. Antwerp 1628	Catena GP
Catena Patrum Graecorum in S. Joannem, ex antiquissimo Graeco codice MS nuncprimum in lucem edita, a Balthasare Corderio Soc. Jesu. Antwerp 1630	Catena GP
Graffin, Patrologia Syriaca	GPS
Sancti Epraem Syri. Hymni et Sermones, Lamy, Malines 1882	
Vossio, Sti Ephraèm Syri Opera Omnia, Cologne 1616	Vossio S. Eph.
Graffin, Patrologia Orientalis	GPO
Miscellanea Agostiniana (Sermones Reperti), by Dom G. Morin O.S.B. Rome 1930	MA
Denzinger, Enchiridion Symbolorum 1928	Denz.
Enchiridion Biblicum, 1954	EB
Dictionnaire de Theologie Catholique	DTC
Clavis Patrum Latinorum, Sacris Erudiri III, 1951	Clavis
Pour Revaloriser Migne, Tables Rectificatives, par Mgr. Glorieux, Lille 1952	PRM
A Glossary of Later Latin to A.D. 600, compiled by Alexander Souter, Oxford 1949	GLL
Altaner, Patrologie, 1951	
Septuagint	SEPT

CONTENTS

Following the Gospel of each Sunday and Feast, and, where they occur, the parallel Gospels, an Explanation of the Gospel, word for word, is also given, drawn from the writings of all the Fathers and Doctors, and translated from the *Catena Aurea* of St Thomas Aquinas. Then come the Sermons and Homilies for each Sunday and Feast in due order, as follows:

xx

INTRODUCTION TO THE
CATENA AUREA

Dedicatory Epistle of St Thomas Aquinas to Pope Urban the Fourth on the publication of the Catena on the Gospel of St Matthew.

The Fount of Wisdom, the Only Begotten Word of God, through Whom, ruling from on high, the Father hath wisely wrought and sweetly ordered all things, willed at the end of ages to take upon Himself our flesh, that human vision might look upon His Splendour, clothed in the garment of our corporal nature, Which it could not rise to contemplate upon the summits of the Divine Glory.

And as He had poured out His rays, that is, the tokens of His wisdom, upon all things which He made, He impressed, as a nobler endowment, His own image and likeness on the souls of men; and yet more lovingly formed it in the hearts of those who love Him, in a manner that corresponds to the generosity of His own Love.

But what is the soul of man in this so immense creation that it can comprehend the steps of the divine wisdom? And this when the light of that wisdom, poured out on man, has been dimmed by the shadow of sin, and the confusion of earthly cares; indeed so dark became the foolish heart of many, that they changed the glory of God into the likeness of dumb idols: and being brought low by their iniquities, they did what it is not fitting that men should do.

But the Divine Wisdom, Which hath made man for the enjoyment of Itself, not suffering that he remain in this ignorance, joined our human nature to the fulness of Its own perfection, uniting it to the Word in a wondrous manner, that He might restore unto Himself all erring humanity.

The Prince of the Apostles by his faith first merited to perceive the brightness of this Wisdom, Veiled in the cloud of our flesh, and to confess It steadfastly, fully, and without error, saying: *Thou art the Christ, the Son of the Living God* (Matt. xvi. 16). O Blessed Confession! which, not flesh and blood, but the Father Who is in heaven hath revealed. This Confession it is that makes firm the Church on earth, opens the way to heaven, merits pardon for sins; and against it the gates of hell shall not prevail.

Thy heart, Most Holy Father, who art lawful heir of this Faith and this Confession, gives watchful care that the light of this so wondrous Wisdom may fill the hearts of the faithful, and put to silence the dread folly of heretics, fittingly referred to as the gates of hell. If indeed, as Plato says, that people must be deemed fortunate whose rulers give themselves to wisdom: and to that wisdom which the infirmity of the human mind so often stains with error: how much more fortunate must we consider the Christian people under your rule, when with such zealous care you have given yourself to that most excelling wisdom which the Wisdom of God, Clothed in our earthly members, has both taught by word, and shown by example.

And because of this care, it has pleased Your Holiness to lay on me the task of explaining the Gospel, in doing which to the best of my ability I have carefully brought together, from the various works of the Commentators, a continuous exposition of the afore-mentioned Gospel: adding a few words to the quotations from certain authors, words taken for the most part from glosses, which, that they may be distinguished from their actual words, I have placed under the title of Gloss.

And I have taken care that the names of the Doctors should be set down, as well as the works from which their testimonies are taken; with this exception: that the writings and commentary which treat of those places in the Gospel that are being explained, did not need particular reference. For example: where the name of Jerome is found, but without reference to any work of his, it is to be understood that he is here speaking of Matthew; and similarly with regard to others: excepting however the quotations from the Commentary of Chrysostom upon Matthew, where it was necessary to add to the title the words *Super Matthaeum*, that in this way they might be distinguished from others taken from the Homiliarist himself.

In quoting the testimonies of the saints it was necessary many times to cut away some parts so as to avoid undue length: and, for greater clearness, and according to the purpose of the commentary, to change about the actual sequence of the parts quoted. Now and then I have given their meaning, and left out words, particularly in the case of the Homiliary of Chrysostom, because of the fact that the translation is defective.

It has also been my intention in this work, to seek, not alone the literal meaning, but also to set forth the mystical: on occasion to refute error, and proclaim truth; which appears to me an indispensable task, for it is principally in the Gospel that the form of the Catholic Faith and the rule of all Christian life is laid down.

I trust that this work will not seem to anyone too lengthy. For I could not achieve all these ends without abbreviating, nor yet, should I observe brevity in every way, set out the interpretations of so many of the saints. May Your Holiness then receive this work, as the fruit of your own solicitude, and of my obedience, to examine and to correct, as you shall decide; and as from you came the command, and to you is reserved the judgment, so *unto the place from whence the rivers come, they return, to flow again* (Eccles. i. 7).

FIRST SUNDAY OF ADVENT

I. St Ambrose: On the Gospel

II. St Ephraem: On Patience, the Second Coming, and the
Last Judgment

III. St Leo the Great: On the Fast of the Tenth
Month and Almsgiving

IV. St Gregory the Great: On the Gospel

V. St Bernard: The Advent of the Lord and its Six Circumstances

THE GOSPEL OF THE SUNDAY

Luke xxi. 25–33

At that time, Jesus said to His Disciples: There shall be signs in the sun, and in the moon, and in the stars; and upon the earth distress of nations, by reason of the confusion of the roaring of the sea and of the waves; men withering away for fear, and expectation of what shall come upon the whole world. For the powers of heaven shall be moved; and then they shall see the Son of man coming in a cloud, with great power and majesty. But when these things begin to come to pass, look up, and lift up your heads, because your redemption is at hand. And He spoke to them a similitude. See the fig tree, and all the trees: when they now shoot forth their fruit, you know that summer is nigh; so you also, when you shall see these things come to pass, know that the kingdom of God is at hand. Amen, I say to you, this generation shall not pass away, till all things be fulfilled. Heaven and earth shall pass away, but my words shall not pass away.

PARALLEL GOSPELS

Matthew xxiv. 29–35

And immediately after the tribulation of those days, the sun shall be darkened and the moon shall not give her light, and the stars shall fall from heaven, and the powers of heaven shall be moved: and then shall appear the sign of the Son of

Mark xiii. 24–31

But in those days, after that tribulation, the sun shall be darkened, and the moon shall not give her light. And the stars of heaven shall be falling down, and the powers that are in heaven, shall be moved. And then shall they see the Son of man

1

man in heaven: and then shall all tribes of the earth mourn: and they shall see the Son of man coming in the clouds of heaven with much power and majesty. And He shall send his angels with a trumpet, and a great voice: and they shall gather together his elect from the four winds, from the farthest parts of the heavens to the utmost bounds of them. And from the fig tree learn a parable: When the branch thereof is now tender, and the leaves come forth, you know that summer is nigh. So you also, when you shall see all these things, know ye that it is nigh, even at the doors. Amen I say to you, that this generation shall not pass away, till all these things be done. Heaven and earth shall pass away, but my words shall not pass.

coming in the clouds, with great power and glory. And then shall he send his angels, and shall gather together his elect from the four winds, from the uttermost part of the earth to the uttermost part of heaven. Now of the fig tree learn ye a parable. When the branch thereof is now tender, and the leaves are come forth, you know that summer is very near. So you also when you shall see these things come to pass, know ye that it is very nigh, even at the doors. Amen, I say to you, that this generation shall not pass, until all these things be done. Heaven and earth shall pass away, but my words shall not pass away.

EXPOSITION FROM THE CATENA AUREA

There will be signs in the sun, and in the moon . . . . BEDE, *in Luke Ch.* 88: Our Lord here foretells, and in their order, those things that will come to pass when the days of the nations shall have been fulfilled, saying: *there will be signs* . . . AMBROSE, 10 *Luke on the Second Coming*: Which signs are more clearly described in the gospel of Matthew. There, he relates that, *the sun shall be darkened, and the moon shall not give her light, and the stars shall fall from heaven.*

EUSEBIUS, from *Catena of Greek Fathers*: For now is the end of all perishable life, and, according to the Apostle, the outward appearances of this world will pass away and a new world will follow, in which, in place of the visible luminaries, Christ Himself will shine as the Sun and King of a new crea-

tion; and so great will be the power and splendour of this new Sun, that the sun which now shines, and the moon and the other stars, will grow dim before the face of this greater Light. CHRYSOSTOM. *Excerpta in secund. Advent. C.A.*: As swiftly as the moon and stars fade before the rising sun, so before the glorious appearance of Christ, the sun will be darkened, the moon will not give her light, and the stars will fall from heaven; stripped of their former splendour, that they may be clothed with the garment of a greater light.

EUSEBIUS, as above: What will happen to the world upon the darkening of its lights, from which will arise such dread anxiety amongst men, He then goes on to tell; saying: *and upon the earth distress of nations, by reason of the confusion of the roaring of the sea and of the waves.* Here He seems to teach that the starting point of the changing of the whole earth will be the drying up of its substantial moisture. For this first being consumed, or frozen, no longer will men hear the sound of the sea, nor will its waves again flood upon the seashore. And because of this universal dryness, the remaining parts of the world, not receiving their accustomed moisture from the falling rain, begin to suffer change. And since the coming of the Saviour must impose silence on these dread portents, wherein the work of God is undone, these events will precede His Coming, and the beginning of this *roaring* will be from this drying up, so that the voice of the storm, or the murmur of the sea, will never again be heard. Then will follow the *distress* of those who are left alive. Hence follows: *men withering away from fear, and expectation of what shall come upon the whole world.* What shall come upon the whole world He then declares: *for the powers of heaven shall be moved.*

THEOPHYLACTUS: Or, again: When the upper orb of creation will be changed, the lesser elements will also rightly suffer change. Hence follows: *and upon the earth distress of nations . . .* , as if He said: the sea will rage fearfully, and the sea coasts will be battered by the storm, so that terror will come upon all the people of the earth, that is, a common dread and anxiety, and they will be silent in fear and expectation of the evils now rushing upon the world. Hence *men withering away for fear, and expectation of what shall come upon the world.*

AUGUSTINE, *Ep. ad Hesych.*[1] But, you say, the miseries that afflict us compel you to say that the end is at hand, since there is now being fulfilled that which was foretold. For it is certain, you say, that there is no nation in these days that is not being assailed, or in actual torment. If then these miseries that now afflict mankind are true signs that the Lord is now about to appear, what does that mean which the Apostle says: *When they shall say: peace and security; then shall sudden destruction come upon them?* (I Thess. v. 3).

Let us see if perhaps it be not better to understand that the events which were foretold by these words shall not be fulfilled in this manner, but rather that they will come to pass when tribulations shall be so spread through the whole world that it will affect the Church, which will be persecuted in every place, and not those who will persecute her; for it is they who will say: *peace and security.*

Now as to those evils, which you believe to be the last and most dreadful, we note that they are common to both kingdoms, namely, to that of Christ and that of the devil; since the just and the wicked are equally afflicted by them: and also that in the midst of such great evils luxurious feasts and pleasure of every kind are being indulged in. Is this not rather a burning up with concupiscence, than a withering away from fear?

GREGORY, *Hom. I in Evang.*: Whom does He call the Powers of heaven unless the Angels, Dominations, Principalities and Powers, who at the coming of the dread Judge will then be visible to our eyes, as they sternly exact that which He, the Invisible Creator, now patiently requires of us.

THEOPHYLACTUS: Not alone shall men tremble when the world is being dissolved, but even the angels will be fearful in the presence of such terrifying destruction of the universe. Hence there follows: *For the powers of heaven shall be moved.*

EUSEBIUS: When the Son of God is about to appear in glory, to cast down the now ended tyranny of the son of sin, the gates of heaven, closed from all ages, will now by the hands of ministering angels be thrown wide open, so that the heavens shall stand revealed.

CHRYSOSTOM, *Ad Olympiam Ep.* 2: Whence in Job is it said (Job xxvi. 11): *The pillars of heaven tremble and dread at his beck.* What shall the little columns do when the pillars of the firmament tremble? What shall the reed in the desert endure when the cedar of paradise is stricken? EUSEBIUS: Or, again; the Powers of the heavens are they who rule over the visible parts of the universe, who shall now be changed that they may go on to a more perfect state. For in the new creation they will be freed from the tasks in which they now serve God in things which follow the course of change and decay.

AUGUSTINE, *Ad Hesych.* as above, par. 39 (in which letter Bishop Hesychius wrote asking St Augustine concerning the prophecies foretelling the end of the world and the signs preceding. Ed.): I consider that these things should be better understood in the Church, lest the Lord Jesus may appear to be foretelling, as extraordinary events which shall foretell His Coming, things which have happened in this world even before His First Coming, so that we may not be laughed at by those who have read of even more extraordinary events in the story of mankind. For the Church is the sun and the moon and the stars, to whom it was said: *Fair as the moon, bright as the sun* (Cant. vi. 9), and she then shall not be seen, as her persecutors rage against her without measure.

AMBROSE, 10 *in Luke*: Many apostatizing from Christianity, the brightness of the faith will be dimmed by this cloud of apostasy: since the heavenly Sun grows dim or shines in splendour according to my faith. And as in its monthly eclipse the moon, by reason of the earth coming between it and the sun, disappears from view, so likewise the holy Church, when the vices of the flesh stand in the way of the celestial light, can no longer borrow the splendour of His divine light from the Sun of Christ. And in the persecutions it was invariably the love of this life that stood in the path of the Divine Sun. Also *the stars*, that is, men surrounded by the praise of their fellow Christians, *shall fall*, as the bitterness of persecution mounts up; which must however come to pass, until the number of the faithful is made up; for so the good are proved and the weak made known.

AUGUSTINE, as above, par. 40: What is here said, *and upon the earth distress of nations*, is not to be understood as meaning the seed of Abraham, in whom all peoples shall be blessed (Gen. xxii. 18), but those who will stand upon the left hand side when all men are gathered together before the Judge of the living and the dead.

AMBROSE: So oppressive therefore will be the unrest of souls, that, unhappily conscious of the multitude of our offences, and fearful of the judgment to come, the very dew of baptism shall dry upon our brow. *For the powers of heaven shall be moved; and then they shall see the Son of man coming in a cloud.*

Again, His coming is also longed for, so that His Presence may work in the whole universe of angels as of men that which is wrought in single souls when with fitting dispositions we receive Christ. So the Powers of heaven at the Coming of the Lord of salvation will attain to an increase of grace, for He is the Lord of the Powers also, and they will tremble at this close manifestation of the fulness of His Divinity. Then too the powers who *proclaim the glory of God* (Ps. xviii) shall also be moved by this full revelation of the glory of Christ. AUGUSTINE, as above: Or, the powers of heaven shall be moved since, because of the persecutions of the godless, some even of the most steadfast among the faithful shall be filled with fear.

THEOPHYLACTUS: *And then they shall see the Son of man coming,* that is, faithful and unbelieving alike shall see Him. For both Cross and Redeemer shall shine more splendidly than the sun; hence they will be seen by all. AUGUSTINE, as above, par. 41: The saying: *coming in a cloud,* may be understood in either of two ways: either as com-

ing in the Church, as in a cloud, as even now He ceases not to come, but then it will be in great power and majesty, because more of His power and majesty will appear to the saints, to whom He will give strength, so that they shall not be overcome by such great tribulation; or, He will come in His own Body, in which He sits at the Right Hand of the Father. So, rightly must we believe that He will come, and not alone in His own Body, but also in a cloud, since as He departed from us so shall He come again; for *He was raised up: and a cloud received Him out of their sight* (Acts i. 9). And this because of what was then said by the angel: *He shall so come as you have seen Him going into heaven.*

CHRYSOSTOM, in *Catena G.F.*: For God always appears in a cloud, as according to Psalm 92, verse 2: *Clouds and darkness are round about him.* Hence also the Son of man will come in the clouds as both God and Lord, not humbly, but in the glory befitting the Godhead; accordingly he adds: *With great power and majesty.* CYRIL OF ALEXANDRIA, in *Catena G.F.*: Great events are to be understood in relation to each other. Just as His First Coming was in lowliness and humility, so His Second shall be in fitting majesty. GREGORY, *Hom. I in Evang.*: In power and majesty shall they behold Him, to whom when He came in lowliness they turned a deaf ear; so the more sharply will they now feel His power, the more they refused to humble their hard hearts to His clemency.

GREGORY, *Hom. I in Evang.*: Since that which He had just said had been directed against the reprobate,

He turns now to speak words of comfort to the Elect. For He adds: *When these things come to pass, look up, and lift up your heads*; as if to say: when the miseries of the world abound, *lift up your heads*, that is, rejoice in your hearts; for while the world to which you have not given your hearts is ending, the redemption you have eagerly sought is now at hand. In Sacred Scripture the head is often used to signify the mind, because as the members of the body are governed by the head, so are our thoughts governed by the mind. Therefore, to lift up the head is to raise the mind to the joys of the heavenly fatherland.

EUSEBIUS: Or, alternatively: Corporal things having passed away, there remain now only the intellectual and the heavenly, namely: the kingdom of a world that will never pass away, and the promised rewards that shall be given to the just. *But when these things begin to come to pass, look up, and lift up your heads, because your redemption is at hand.* Since we have received the promises of God, in which we place all our hope, we who before were bowed down shall now raise our heads, for the redemption we have longed for will then be at hand, that namely for which *every creature is waiting*.

THEOPHYLACTUS, on *Your Redemption is at hand*: That is, perfect freedom of body and soul. For as the Lord's First Coming was for the redemption of our souls, so the Second will bring about the redemption of our bodies. EUSEBIUS: He said this to His Disciples, not as if *they* were to continue on in this life till the end of the world, but He

so spoke as to one continuing Body, to them, to us, and to posterity, which will continue in belief in Christ until the end of the world.

GREGORY, as above: That the world is to be trodden on and despised He makes clear by a timely comparison when He goes on to say: *See the fig tree and all the trees: when they now shoot forth their fruit, you know that summer is nigh; so you also, when you shall see these things come to pass, know that the kingdom of God is at hand*; as if He said: as we know from the coming of the fruit on the trees that the summer is at hand, so from the ruin of the world it can be known that the kingdom of God is approaching. From this we may gather that the fruit of the world is ruin. To this end it germinates, that whatsoever blooms upon it, will be consumed in disaster. Happily however the kingdom of God is compared to summer, for when the clouds of winter pass, the days of our life will be resplendent in the glory of the eternal sun.

AMBROSE, in *Luke* xxi[2]: Matthew speaks of but a single tree, Luke of *all the trees* (Mt. xxiv. 31; Lk. xxi. 29). The fig tree has a twofold meaning; either as when the hard grows tender, or when sin abounds. Either therefore when the fruit is green on all the trees, and the fig tree branch blooms also; that is, when every tongue doth confess the Lord, confessing also the people of Israel, we must hope for the coming of the Lord, in which, as in the summer time, the fruits of the Resurrection shall be gathered in; or, when the son of iniquity shall have put on as a garland, vain and empty boast, the leaves of the synagogic branch, we must then see that the judgment approaches: for the Lord is hastening to reward faith, and to make an end of wrong doing.

AUGUSTINE, *Ad Hesych.* as above, 44 ,45: When He says, *when you shall see these things come to pass,* what must we understand unless the things already mentioned? Among these He said, *and then they shall see the Son of man coming.* So, when this is seen, the kingdom of heaven is not to come, it is close at hand. But are we to say that not all the things mentioned are implied in the words, *when you shall see these things come to pass,* but only some; this in particular being excluded, *and then they shall see the Son of man?* But Matthew clearly shows there is to be no exception, saying, *so you also, when you see all these things,* among which is that the Son of man will be seen coming, understood of the coming in which He now comes in His own members, as in clouds, or in the Church, as in a great cloud.

TITUS: Or, differently, He says *the Kingdom of God is at hand,* because when these things come to pass, the end of things has not yet come, but they now move towards their end; for the actual coming of the Lord, putting an end to the power of all other rulers, prepares the way for the kingdom of God. EUSEBIUS: Just as in this life, with winter going, and the spring time following, the sun pours out its warm rays and wakens to life seeds long buried in the earth, which then shedding their first covering come forth in new and varied forms, so the glorious coming of the Only Begotten of

God, pouring forth His life-giving rays upon a new world, brings to the light, seeds long buried throughout the whole earth, that is, those now sleeping in the dust of earth (Dan. xii. 2), and with bodies more perfect than before, and death being now overthrown the life of this new world will henceforth reign for ever.

GREGORY, as above: All that was foretold was confirmed with a great pledge, when He added: *Amen, I say to you.* BEDE: He confirms strongly what He thus foretells, and, if it is lawful to say so, His oath is, that He says: *Amen, I say to you,* amen meaning, that which is true. Therefore He who is Truth Itself, says to us: I tell you the truth. And even had He not confirmed His words in this manner, He still could not have spoken falsely. But *generation* may mean, either the whole human race, or the Jews of that day.

EUSEBIUS: Or, generation may mean, the new generation of His holy Church, thus showing that there would be an enduring body of believers until that time when it would witness all these things; and they would perceive with their own eyes the events which Our Lord here foretells.

THEOPHYLACTUS: For since He had foretold that there would be commotions, and wars, and changes in the elements, as well as in other things, lest some should fear that Christianity itself would be destroyed, He goes on to say: *Heaven and earth shall pass away, but my words shall not pass away,* as though saying: should all else be brought to nothing, my Faith shall not fail. In this He shows that He places the Church above every other creature; though all other creatures shall suffer change, the church of the faithful, and the promises of the Gospel, shall remain.

GREGORY, as above: or, alternatively: *Heaven and earth shall pass away, etc.*, as though He were to say: everything that seems to you enduring, shall not endure for eternity; and everything that with Me seems to pass away, will remain immovable and without change. For my speech, which passes away, utters that which shall abide without change. BEDE: The heaven that will pass away is not the ethereal, or sidereal, heaven, but the aerial, after which the birds of heaven are named. If, however, the earth shall pass away, how does Ecclesiastes say, *the earth standeth for ever* (Eccles. i. 4). But it is plain that He means, that the heavens and the earth shall pass away in their present form, but that in their essence they will endure for ever.

I. ST AMBROSE: ON THE GOSPEL[3]

And there shall be signs in the sun, and in the moon . . . Here is a linked chain of prophecy, and the reason of the mystery why the Jews, already twice led captive, to Babylon and to Syria, will again be captive in all the world: because they have denied Christ; and why Jerusalem, as was later seen, was to be laid waste by an invading host, and her people fall by the edge of the sword; and why all that was Judea was to be vanquished by the believing nations, by the sword of the spirit, which is the two-edged word of God.

There will be diverse signs in the sun, and in the moon, and in the stars, These signs are expressed more clearly in Matthew: *then*, says He, *the sun shall be darkened, and the moon shall not give her light, and the stars shall fall from heaven* (Mt. xxiv. 29). For, many falling away from Christianity, the brightness of faith will be dimmed by the cloud of apostasy; since the heavenly Sun grows dim, or shines in greater splendour, according to my faith. As when many together look at the rays of the earthly sun, it will seem dim or bright according to the eye of the beholder, so does the light of the spirit fill each one according to the measure of his faith. And as the moon in its monthly eclipse disappears from view, by reason of the earth coming between it and the sun, so likewise the Holy Church, when the vices of the flesh stand in the way of the celestial light, can no longer borrow the splendour of His divine light from the Sun of Christ. And in the persecutions it was invariably the love of this life that kept out the light of the Divine Sun.

The stars shall fall, that is, men now shining in the praise of their fellow Christians, even such as are lights to the rest of the world, who possess the word of life, and of whom it was said to Abraham that, *they shall shine as the brightness of the firmament* (Dan. xii. 3). Many esteemed as the Patriarchs shall fall, prophets shall fall, should the sharpness of the persecution mount up, which must come to pass, till the fulness of the merits of the

Church be made up in all her members, and in each one singly; for so the good are proved, and the weak made known. And so oppressive will be the unrest of souls, that upon the brow of many of us, unhappily aware of the multitude of our offences, the dew of the sacred baptism will dry up in fear of the judgment to come; for apostasy dries it, faith distills it.

For the powers of heaven shall be moved: and then they shall see the Son of man coming in a cloud. And in like manner the coming of the Son of man is longed for, so that by His presence there may be accomplished in the whole world of angels and of men, that which is wrought in single souls, who, with all fitting dispositions, receive Christ. So the Powers of heaven, at the Coming of the Lord of salvation, will also attain to an increase of grace; for He is the Lord of the Powers as well, and they will tremble at this appearance among them of the fulness of the glory of the divinity. Then too the Powers that *proclaim the glory of God* (Ps. xviii) shall also tremble before this fuller revealing of His glory, as they gaze on Christ.

David has told us in what manner these Powers are moved, saying: *Come ye to Him, and be enlightened* (Ps. xxxiii. 6); Paul also tells how we may see Christ: *for when they shall be converted to the Lord, a veil shall be taken away, and you will behold Christ* (II Cor. iii. 16). You will behold Him in the clouds. Not that I believe that Christ will come in lowering mist, or in the chill rain torrent, for when they appear, they cloak the sky in gloomy darkness. How then shall He set His Tabernacle in the sun

(Ps. xviii. 6), if His coming be in the rain clouds?

But there are clouds which serve, as is fitting, to veil the splendour of the divine mystery. There are clouds which moisten with the dew of spiritual refreshment. Consider the cloud in the Old Testament: *He spoke to them,* it says, *in the pillar of the cloud* (Ps. xcviii. 7). He spoke indeed through Moses, and by the mouth of Josue, who bade the sun stand still that he might have the light of the lengthened day. So Moses and Josue were clouds. And observe also that the Holy Ones are clouds, *who fly as clouds and as doves to their windows* (Is. lx. 8). Above me, like clouds, are Isaias and Ezechiel, of whom the former has shown me, through the Cherubim and Seraphim, the holiness of the Divine Trinity. The Prophets all are clouds; in these clouds Christ came. He came in a cloud in the Canticle, serene and lovely, refulgent with the joy of the Bridegroom (Cant. iii. 11). He came and *in a swift cloud,* becoming Incarnate through the Virgin, for the prophet saw Him come as a cloud from the east (Is. xix. 1). And rightly did he call Him a swift cloud Whom no stain of earth weighed down. Consider the cloud in which the Holy Spirit descended, and from wherein the power of the Most High shadowed forth (Lk. i. 35).

When therefore Christ shall appear in the clouds, the tribes of the earth shall mourn; for there is a certain number of offences, a certain series of sins against God, which will suddenly be interrupted by the advent of Christ.

Behold the fig tree, and all the trees: when they now shoot forth their fruit, you know that summer is nigh. The narratives of the Evangelists, each in his own manner, seem to run together into a single current of meaning. While Matthew has spoken of a single fig tree and of *when the* branch thereof is tender, Luke speaks of *all the trees.* When indeed the fruit is green on all the trees, and the fig tree branch is likewise in bloom, as when every tongue doth confess the Lord, and confessing also is the people of Israel, we are to hope for the Lord's Coming, in which as in summer time the fruits of the Resurrection shall be gathered in; or, when the son of iniquity, as a vain and empty boast, shall have put on as a garland the leaves of the Synagogic branch, we must then see that the judgment is approaching: for the Lord is hastening to reward faith, and to make an end of wrong doing.

The fig tree has therefore a two-fold meaning, either as meaning, when the hard fruit grows tender, or when sin abounds. For by the faith of those who believe, that which withered shall blossom; and on account of their offences, sinners shall grow boastful. In the one is the fruitfulness of faith, in the other the wantonness of apostasy. The husbandry of the dresser of the vineyard promises me fruit of the fig tree; nor must we lose hope if sinners clothe themselves with the leaves of the fig tree, as with a garment of deceit, that they may hide their conscience; mistrustful leaves therefore, without fruit. Such garments had they who were cast forth from paradise (Gen. iii. 7).

II. St Ephraem, Confessor and Doctor

On Patience, the Second Coming, and the Last Judgment[4]

Shining is the life of the Just, but in what does it shine if not in patience? Love this virtue, O Christian, as the mother of fortitude. For the psalmist admonishes us, saying: *Expect the Lord and keep his way* (Ps. xxxvi. 34). Paul also says, teaching us the way in which we must acquire virtue: *tribulation worketh patience* (Rom. v. 3). Exercising patience you will discover hope, the source of every good: *and hope confoundeth not.* Be subject therefore *to the Lord, and pray to him,* and you will then find that *he will give thee the requests of thy heart* (Ps. xxxvi. 7, 4). What more blessed than this, to obtain merciful hearing from such a King? Who does not eagerly wish that the ears of his judge shall be accessible and gracious? Thou art a worker of virtue, O Brother, and Christ has brought thee into His vineyard; therefore *while you have time, do good.*

Hear Paul saying: *For what things a man shall sow, those also shall he reap* (Gal. vi. 8); sow in the spirit, so that you *shall reap life everlasting. For he that soweth in his flesh,* he says, *of the flesh also shall reap corruption.* Hear the good exhorter reminding us: *sow for yourselves in justice, and reap in the mouth of mercy* (Osee x. 12). Be not then neglectful in striving, setting before your eyes the fruits of hope. Where there are contests, there are rewards. Where there are wars, there also are victories; and where there is war-fare, there is likewise a crown. Looking to this end, anoint thyself with patience. Say to thyself at all times the holy words: *Expect the Lord, do manfully, and let thy heart take courage, and wait thou for the Lord* (Ps. xxvi. 14).

Get ready to go forth to thy work, and gird thyself to cultivate thy field. The field is your present life, and for a hoe take with you the Old together with the New Testament. Put a hedge of thorns about your field and your soil, by prayer and fasting together with instruction. If you are protected by this enclosure, the wild beast shall not invade thee, by which I mean the devil. Tend thy soul after the manner of a beautiful vineyard. And as the guardians of the vineyard strike at the thieves with their fists, and call out to them with warnings, and keep them at a distance with stones, so you cry out in prayer, and shout with the song of psalmody, and put to flight the thieving fox, that is, the devil, of whom the Scripture says: *catch us the little foxes that destroy the vines* (Cant. ii. 15).

Be watchful of thy enemy, lest he pierce your heart with some obstinate and unfitting desire. If he seeks to possess your soul as a field, and places there his unclean thoughts, resist and oppose him with the shield of faith. Put on the helmet of hope. Draw the sword of the spirit, which is the word of God. And so armed against the enemy, stand fast, and be not unwatchful in the battle, but show yourself sober and vigilant in all things. For we are not ignorant of his designs. *Rejoice always in the Lord*, as it is written. *Let your modesty be known to all men* (Phil. iv. 4–5). Let the fear of the Lord have place in your heart. But be not a timid soldier, nor a slothful, lazy workman. Do not reject thy crown. Time is short, but judgment is long.

To what do you look back, O Monk; admonish thy heart, and speak to it with the Holy One and say: *Do manfully, and let thy heart take courage, and wait thou for the Lord*. Imitate David and with one stone prostrate thy adversary. The angels stand beside thee as spectators of thy courage; for *we are made a spectacle to the world, and to angels, and to men* (I Cor. iv. 9). Should they behold you victor in a good work, they will rejoice; and if they behold you overcome, since they cannot endure this, they depart unhappy; but the demons will rejoice over thee.

For thy sword and thy weapon, take hold of the fear of the Lord. For the fear of the Lord is like a two-edged sword, cutting off every wicked desire. Keep therefore ever in thy mind the fear of the Lord, being mindful at all times of that last and dreadful day, when the heavens shall be consumed by the heat of fire, and the earth and all that is upon it shall perish. When the stars shall fall like leaves, the sun and the moon shall be darkened, nor shall they give forth light. When the Son of man shall appear, and shall descend from heaven upon the earth, the Powers of heaven shall be troubled. When the appearance of the Angels, and the sound of their trumpets, shall prevail, then *fire shall burn before Him*, and hastening on, it will consume the earth.

Mighty tempests will rise about Him, and dreadful earthquakes and lightnings such as have never before been seen, nor will be, until that day; so that the very powers of heaven will be seized with a great trembling.

We, too, my Brothers, in what state shall we be then? What fear and dread shall fall upon us? Recall to mind, Brother, the Israelites in the desert, and how they were unable to endure the dark and obscurity, the sound of trumpets, and the voice of the Lord speaking from the midst of the flames (Ex. xx). And they pleaded that the Voice of the Lord should not come nigh to them. For they were unable to endure it, and what was being done there, though He had not descended in wrath, neither had He spoken directly to them, but rather as though comforting them, He had let them know that God was with them.

What then, dearest Brethren, if they could not even with this alleviation endure His descent amongst them, when the heavens were not consumed by fire, nor the earth, and all things upon the face of it? And there was no sound of trumpet, such as that future trumpet will make, to awaken all who *from the beginning have slept*. Nor had there then taken place any of these dreadful future events, and yet they could not endure it.

But what shall we do, I ask you, when God will come down in anger, and dread wrath, and sit on the Throne of His Glory, and summon to Him all the earth, *from the rising of the sun to the going down thereof*, and all the ends of the earth, so that He may judge His people, and render to each according to his works? Oh, Woe! Woe! What kind of people shall we be then? In what state of mind shall we be, when naked and fearful we shall appear there, delivered to that dread

tribunal? Woe! Woe! Woe is me! Where now is the pride of the flesh? Where now is vain and useless beauty? Where, all human delight? Where then, shameless and impudent boldness? Where the delight of sin, sordid and unclean? What then of those who wallow in the wickedness of lust, *of that which is filthy?* (Rom. i. 27.) Where then will they be who worship (Cybele) with drum and wine and dance, but the works of the Lord they have not considered? What then of those who have passed their lives in sloth and disorder? Where then will be the enticements of pleasure? All these things shall have passed away, and like a little cloud shall have been dissolved.

Where then shall avarice be, the desire of earthly possessions, from which rises up hardness of heart? Where the monstrous pride that disposes all things, and thinks to itself that it alone exists? Where now the vain and fleeting success and glory of men? Where then human might? Where now is the Tyrant? Where the King? Where the Prince? Where the Leader? Where the Magistrate? Where are they who revelled in luxury, who glorified in the multitude of their riches, and despised God? In that moment, look up; they shall be struck dumb, they shall be utterly confused and shaken. *Fear will seize them; their pains as of a woman in labour* (Osee xiii. 13; Ps. xlvii. 8). *With a vehement wind thou shalt break them in pieces.*

Where then will be the wisdom of the wise? Where all their vain cleverness? Woe! Woe! they are terrified; *and they were troubled and reeled like a drunken man; and all their wisdom was swallowed up* (Ps. cvi.

ϯ0?5:null`00!v?72—

93.74

27). Where now the learned? Where the scribe? Where the recruiting officer of this foolish world? My Brother, what shall we be then, and in what state of soul, as we render an account of all things, big and little, that we have done, even to the least; for even for an idle word we shall render account to the Just Judge? What must we do, that in that hour we may find mercy before Him?

And with what joy shall we be filled, if we are directed to the right hand of the King? What must we be like when the Just embrace us there? When, I repeat, they shall embrace thee there, Abraham, Isaac, Jacob, Moses, Noah, Job, Daniel, the Holy Prophets, the Apostles, the Martyrs, who all were pleasing to God in the days of the flesh? And whomsoever you have heard of, and whose life you have admired, and whom you now wish to look upon, they will come to thee, and embrace thee, rejoicing in thy salvation. What manner of men must we then be? Of what kind shall be that unspeakable delight which we are to receive, when the king shall with joyfulness say to those who will be on His right hand: *Come ye blessed of my father, possess the kingdom prepared for you from the foundation of the world* (Mt. xxiii).

Then, my Brother, then will you receive the kingdom of beauty, the crown of all your desires, from the Hand of the Lord, and reign with Christ for ever. Then you will receive for your inheritance the gifts, *which God has promised to those who love and serve him* (Jas. i. 2). From thenceforward you will be secure, . no longer filled with anxiety. Be mindful, my Brother,

of what kind of a person it must be, to whom it will be given to reign with Christ in heaven. Reflect upon what it means to dwell for ever in the light of His Countenance, to possess the source of all light. *For then you shall no more have the sun for thy light by day, neither shall the brightness of the moon enlighten thee* (Is. lx. 19), but Christ will be thy unfailing Light, and God thy glory. Behold, my Brother, what glory He has laid up for those who fear Him, observing His commandments.

Then think upon the end of sinners as they are led before that tremendous tribunal. What terror will lay hold of them in the presence of that just Judge, having now no way to escape His presence? What shame will seize them as they are turned towards the left hand of the King? What dread gloom shall fall upon them, *when in His anger He shall speak to them, and trouble them in His rage*, saying: *Depart from me, ye cursed, into everlasting fire, which was prepared for the devil and his angels?* (Mt. xxv. 41.)

Alas! Alas! with what torment and oppression of spirit shall they be afflicted, when that cry of woe shall rise up and all have heard it: *The wicked shall be turned into hell, all the nations that forget God* (Ps. ix. 18). Alas! Alas! what cries and groans they will give forth, as they are being led away to be tormented bitterly forever?

Alas! Of what kind is that place of wailing and of gnashing of teeth that is called Tartarus, at which even Satan shudders? O Woe! What kind of place is it, where the unsleeping worm dieth not? What dread misery to be sent into outer darkness? Of what kind are the angels placed over these torments, who, pitiless and frightful, punish by casting in there, while at the same time they reproach most grievously? Then shall those already in the midst of the torments cry out with pleading voices, and there will be no one to speak for them to the Lord, and they shall not be heard. Then they will learn that the things which happened to them in this life were as nothing; and those that here seemed sweet, were more bitter than gall and wormwood.

Where then shall be the pleasure falsely named of sin? Since there is no other joy than to fear the Lord and love Him, in this alone is there happiness. This indeed fills the soul *as with marrow and fatness.* Then they shall curse themselves and the evil they have done. Then they will confess that the judgment of God is just, and say: We used to hear of these things, but we would not cease from evil-doing. But then it will avail nothing thus to speak of the past.

Woe! Woe is me! Crush me with these unspeakable offences; for I have sinned above the number of the sands of the sea, and I am stooped with them as with many iron chains. I do not dare to raise my eyes to the glory of heaven. To whom then shall I turn but to Thee, Most Kind, Most Merciful? *Have mercy on me, O God, according to Thy great mercy; and according to the multitude of Thy tender mercies blot out my iniquities. Wash me yet more from my iniquity, and cleanse me from my sins. For I know my iniquity, and my sin is always before me. To Thee only have I sinned, and have done evil before Thee* (Ps. l).

Since therefore I have sinned, to Thee do I come because of Thy great mercy. I have provoked Thee to wrath, and because of Thy clemency to Thee do I fly. I have spurned Thee, yet because of Thy supreme goodness and kindness to Thee do I return; and beseeching Thee I cry: *Turn away Thy face from my sins, and blot out all my iniquities,* for Thy name's sake alone. I have nothing I may offer Thee; no good work, nor a clean heart. Relying solely on Thy mercies, I cast myself upon them, that Thou may *create a clean heart* in me, and *strengthen me with a perfect spirit* lest I speedily fall back into sin. From this day I shall serve Thee, *in holiness and justice all the days of my life.* Therefore, let all the Powers of heaven praise Thee. For Thine is the Kingdom, and the Majesty, for ever and ever. Amen.

III. St Leo, Pope and Doctor

On the Fast of the Tenth Month and on Almsgiving[5]

Synopsis:

    I. Abstinence prepares the way for the Lord, and raises the mind to heavenly things.

    II. Why the Ember Day Fasts were instituted; to which must be joined fast from the vices.

    III. On the worship of God and the use of temporal things. The twofold fast.

Chapter I. When the Saviour was instructing His Disciples concerning the coming of the Kingdom of God, and on the end of the world and of time, and in His Apostles He was teaching His whole church, He said: *Take heed to yourselves, lest perhaps your hearts be overcharged with surfeiting and drunkenness, and the cares of this life* (Lk. xxi. 34). And this command we know, dearest Brethren, is directed particularly to us to whom that day of warning, though hidden from us, is now without doubt near at hand.

For whose coming let every man make ready, lest it overtake him at a time when he is either given over to the flesh, or immersed in earthly cares. For it is made clear to us, my dearest Brethren, from the experience of our daily life, that by excess in drinking the vision of the mind is dimmed, and by excess in eating the vigour of the heart is brought down: so that the delights of appetite are hurtful to our bodily health, unless a rule of temperance offers resistance to temptation, and withdraws from our pleasure that which would afflict us.

Although it be true that the flesh without the spirit may desire nothing, and from it receives the power of feeling, whence in turn it derives the power of movement, yet is it the duty of the soul to deny certain things to the substance that is subject to it, and by its own inward decision, restrain the outward senses from the things that disagree with them, so that being frequently set free from bodily desires, it can give itself at leisure to divine wisdom, within the inner court of the mind, where, all sound of earthly strife being stilled, it may take its delight in holy meditation, and in joys that have no end.

And though it is difficult to remain continually in this manner of life, yet not infrequently may we take it unto us, that we may more and more become occupied with spiritual rather than carnal things, so that giving more and more time to the *better things*, even our earthly actions may be transformed into unfading riches.

Chapter II. The profitableness of this manner of living, dearest Brethren, is confirmed in the ecclesiastical fasts, which under the direction of the Holy Spirit are so distributed throughout the course of the year, that the law of abstinence is recalled to us in every season. Accordingly, we celebrate the fast of the season of spring during Lent, that of summer in Pentecost, that of autumn in the seventh month, and that of winter in this which is the tenth month; perceiving in this that nothing is exempt from the divine commandments, and that all the elements serve through the word of God for our instruction, so that by the very turns of the earth itself, as by the four Gospels, we learn both that which we are to proclaim and what we are to do.

For the prophet says: *The heavens show forth the glory of God, and the firmament declareth the work of his hands: day to day uttereth speech, and night to night sheweth knowledge* (Ps. xviii. 1–2). What is there through which Truth speaks not? His words are heard in the daytime, and the sounds of the Selfsame are listened to in the night, and the beauty of all that was made by the sole handicraft of the One God ceases not to make known its meaning to the ears of our heart, so that the invisible things of God are clearly seen by the things that are made (Rom. i. 20), to the end that we may serve, not creatures, but the Creator of all things.

Since, therefore, every vice is defeated by continence, and whatsoever avarice thirsts for, and whatsoever pride seeks in earthly honours, and whatsoever sensuality desires, is overcome by the power of this virtue, who is it that does not see what safeguards are given us by fasting, in which it is implicitly laid upon us that we abstain not alone from food, but from all carnal desires? Otherwise, it would be profitless to suffer hunger, and not to put away evil dispositions; to afflict ourselves by going without food, and at the same time not to turn away from evil desire. It is an unspiritual fast, not a spiritual one, where a man mortifies the body only, and remains fast in the delights that are more harmful to him than all delicacies.

What gain is it to the soul to act outwardly as mistress, and inwardly to be a captive; to command obedience of its members, and forfeit the right to its own freedom? And so for the most part she fittingly has to put up with a rebellious servant, who fails in due obedience to her Lord. While the body therefore goes without food, let the soul abstain from the vices; and let it measure the value of earthly desires and thoughts by the Law of its King.

Chapter III. Let it remember that it owes its first love to God, and the second to its neighbour, and all its affections must be governed by this rule, so that it departs neither from the service of the Lord, nor from what profits our fellow servant. But how is the Lord served unless that which pleases Him, is pleasing also to us; and that our affection be never withdrawn from His Will? For if we will that which He wills, our weakness draws strength from Him, from Whom we have received the power to will. *For it is God*, says the Apostle, *who worketh in you, both to will and to accomplish, according to His good will* (Phil. ii. 13).

Accordingly, a man will neither be puffed up through pride, nor cast down by despair, if he uses the good things divinely bestowed on him, to the glory of the Giver; withholding his desires from the things which he knows will hurt him. And so he that would preserve himself from the wickedness of envy, from the corruption of sensuality, from the unrest of anger, from the desire of revenge, will be purified by the sanctifying power of true abstinence, and will taste the joy of imperishable delights, so that by making spiritual use of them, he will learn to change earthly possessions into heavenly, not by storing what he has received, but by multiplying more and more that which he has given.

And so, from the affection of our paternal charity, we counsel Your Love,[6] that you make fruitful this fast of the tenth month by the generousness of your almsgiving, taking joy in this that the Lord through you doth clothe and feed His poor, to whom He could well have given that which He has bestowed on you; save that in His ineffable mercy He has willed that they shall be justified through patience in their tribulations, you by the works of charity.

Let us fast therefore on the fourth

and sixth day of the week; and on the sabbath we shall celebrate the vigils together with the Blessed Apostle Peter, who will graciously assist our prayers, our fasts, and our almsgiving, with his own prayers, by the favour of Our Lord Jesus Christ, Who with the Father and the Holy Spirit, liveth and reigneth, world without end. Amen.

IV. St Gregory: On the Gospel[7]

Given to the People in the Basilica of the Holy Apostle Peter (Homily 1)[7]

1. Our Lord and Redeemer, desiring to find us prepared, warns us of the evils that are to accompany the end of the world, so that He may keep us from the love of it. He makes known the disasters that will herald its approaching end, so that should we be unwilling to serve God in times of tranquillity, we may, made fearful by these happenings, at least be anxious concerning the judgment now at hand.

For a little prior to this passage of the holy Gospel which you, my Brethren, have just heard, the Lord forewarned us, saying: *Nation shall rise against nation, and kingdom against kingdom; and there shall be great earthquakes in divers places, and pestilences, and famines* (Lk. xxi. 10). Then having said certain other things in between, He adds this warning which you have just now heard: *There will be signs in the sun, and in the moon, and the stars, and upon the earth distress of nations, by reason of the confusion of the roaring of the sea and of the waves.* From among all these things we now see that some have already come to pass; the others that now fill us with dread are to come in the future.

For we behold nation rising against nation, and their distress prevails upon the earth, more now in these our times than we have read of in history. You are aware how frequently we have heard from other parts of the world that earthquakes have devastated innumerable cities. Pestilences we suffer without ceasing. Signs in the sun and moon and stars we have not yet clearly beheld: but that these are not far off we gather from the alteration of the heavens.

Just as before Italy was given over to be smitten by the heathen sword, we beheld fiery hosts in the sky, and saw him[8] glittering there who was afterwards to shed the blood of humanity. Extraordinary confusion of the waves has not yet risen. But since much that was foretold has happened, we cannot doubt that the events which remain shall come in time, for the witness of what has been fulfilled is the pledge of that which is to follow.

2. We tell you these things, dearest Brethren, in order that your souls may awaken to an eagerness for security, and lest you become torpid in a security that is false, and become lax through ignorance of Christian truth, but rather that you may become solicitous, and that anxiety may strengthen you in doing good, reflecting on this which the voice of the Redeemer added: *Men withering away for fear and expectation of what shall come upon the whole world. For the powers of the heavens shall be moved.*

Whom else does the Lord call by the name of Powers of heaven unless the Angels, the Archangels, the Thrones, Dominations, Principalities, and Powers, who at the Coming of the Just Judge will then appear visibly to our eyes, to the end that they may sternly exact an account of that which the Invisible Lawgiver now patiently suffers? Whereto is added: *And then they shall see the Son of man coming in a cloud, with great power and majesty*; as though He were openly to say: they shall see Him come in power and majesty to Whom, Present in lowliness, they turned a deaf ear, and so the more sharply will they then feel His severity, the more they now refuse to humble their hearts before His patience.

3. Since these words were directed at the reprobate, He then turns to speak words of comfort to the elect. For He says: *When these things come to pass, look up, and lift up your heads, because your redemption is at hand.* It is as if the Truth openly warns His Elect by saying: when the evils of this world mount up, when dread of the judgment is shown even by the trembling powers, lift up your heads, that is, be joyful in your hearts, because the world, of which you are not friends, is drawing to its end; the redemption you have been seeking is coming close. In Scripture the head is often used for the soul, because as the members are ruled by the head, so thoughts are governed by the soul. To lift up your heads therefore means to raise the heart to the joys of the heavenly fatherland.

They, therefore, who love God, are bidden to be glad, and to rejoice, because of the end of the world; since soon they will meet Him Whom they love, and that is passing away which they have never loved. Far be it then from any of the faithful who desire to see God that they should grieve over the stricken world, which we must know will end in these catastrophes. For it is written: *Whosoever therefore will be a friend of this world, becometh an enemy of God* (Jas. iv. 4). Who therefore does not rejoice at the approaching end of the world, testifies that he is its friend, and by this he is revealed as an enemy of God.

But let this be far from the faithful, far from the hearts of those who believe through their faith that there is another life, and who love it in very deed. Let them grieve over the ruin of the world who have planted the roots of their hearts deep in the love of it, who neither look for the life to come, nor are even aware that it is. But we who have learned of the joys of our heavenly home must hasten to it as speedily as we may. We should desire to go there with all haste, and to arrive by the shortest way. And with what miseries does not the world urge us forward? What sorrow, what misfortune is there, that does not press upon us? What is this mortal life but a way? And what folly would it be, let you carefully consider, to be weary with the fatigue of the way, and yet not eager to finish the journey!

That the world is to be trodden on, and despised, Our Redeemer then teaches us, by a timely similitude: *Behold the fig tree and all the trees: when they now shoot forth their fruit, you know that summer is nigh. So you also when you shall see these things come to pass, know that the kingdom of God is at hand.* This is as if he were openly to say: as from the fruit on the trees you know that summer is near, so from the ruin of the world you may know that the kingdom of God is likewise near. From which it may be truly gathered that the fruit of the world is ruin. To this end it arises, that it may fall. To this end it germinates, that whatever it has brought forth from seed will be consumed in disaster. But happily is the Kingdom of God compared to summer, because then the clouds of our sadness will pass away, and the days, of our life shall be resplendent in the glory of the eternal Sun.

4. All this is confirmed under a mighty pledge, when the sentence is added in which He says: *Amen, I say to you, this generation shall not pass away, till all things be fulfilled. Heaven and earth shall pass away, but my words shall not pass.* Nothing of this world is more durable than the heavens and the earth, and nothing in the order of nature passes away more quickly than speech. Words, as long as they are incomplete, are not yet words. Once completed, they cease utterly to be; because they cannot be perfected save in their own passing away. Therefore He says: *Heaven and earth shall pass away, but my words shall not pass.* As if he were openly to say: all that seems to you enduring and unchangeable, is not enduring and without change in eternity. And everything of mine that seems to pass away, is enduring and without change: because my speech, that passes away, utters thoughts (sententiae manentes) which endure for ever.

5. See, my Brethren, already we begin to perceive something of

that of which we have been hearing. The world is oppressed by new and ever-increasing miseries. How many survive of the innumerable multitude of men you may see, yet each day new scourges beset them, sudden disasters fall on them, new and unheard of disasters arise. Just as the body in youth is vigorous, the heart strong and steady, the shoulders upright, and the lungs vigorous, but in old age the figure is no longer upright, the shrunken neck is bowed, the chest labours with frequent sighs, strength fails us, and the speaker is impeded by a faltering breath. Although feebleness is yet absent, yet infirmity in our bodily senses is now our normal state of health. So in its early years, the world flourished as in its pristine strength, vigorous to propagate the offspring of mankind, blooming in the health of its bodies, fat with the richness of life. Now it is falling into its own old age, and, as if near to death, is oppressed with growing miseries.

Do not then, my Brethren, love that which you know cannot endure. Keep before your minds the apostolic counsels wherein we are admonished: *Love not the world, nor the things which are in the world. If any man love the world, the charity of the Father is not in him* (I Jn. ii. 15). The day before yesterday, Brethren, you heard that an ancient plantation was uprooted by a sudden storm, that houses were destroyed, churches razed to their foundations. How many were there, safe and well on the previous evening, who believed that in the morning they would fulfil some task, yet that very night were they of a sudden overtaken, caught in the trap of this disaster?

6. But we must carefully keep in mind that in the doing of these things it is the Invisible Judge that moves the breath of the faintest breeze, that awakens the storm from even one small cloud, or razes the foundations of so many buildings. But what shall happen when the Judge shall visibly appear, and when His anger burns against the wicked, if we cannot now endure His wrath when he inflicts upon us the least tempest? Before the face of His wrath what flesh shall stand, if He it is that moves the wind, and shakes the earth, incites the storms, and lays low so many buildings? Paul reflecting on this severity of the Judge to come, says to us: *It is a fearful thing to fall into the hands of the living God* (Heb. x. 31). The psalmist gives voice to the same reflection: *God shall come openly, Our God, He shall not be silent, and round about shall be a mighty tempest* (Ps. xlix. 3). Tempest and fire shall accompany the severity of this justice, because the tempest shall search out those whom the fire will burn.

Beloved Brethren, keep that day before your eyes, and then whatsoever may seem burthensome will become light in comparison. Of that day is it said by the mouth of the prophet: *The great day of the Lord is near, it is near and exceeding swift; the voice of the day of the Lord is bitter, the mighty man shall there meet with tribulation. That day is a day of wrath, a day of tribulation and distress, a day of calamity and misery, a day of darkness and obscurity, a day of clouds and whirlwinds, a day of trumpet and alarm* (Soph. i. 14–16). Of this day the Lord has spoken by the mouth of the prophet Aggeus (Ag. ii. 22): *Once again and I shall move not alone earth, but heaven.*

Behold, as we have said, He moves the tempest, and the earth cannot endure it. What will it do when He moves the heavens? What can we say of the terrors we now see, except that they are but heralds of the wrath to come? And let us keep in mind that these present afflictions are as far below the last tribulations, as is the person of the herald below the majesty of the judge he precedes. Reflect with all your mind upon this day, my dearest Brethren. Remedy what is now defective in your present life. Amend your ways. Conquer evil temptations by standing firm against them. Repent with tears of the sins you have committed. For the more you make ready against the severity of His justice by serving Him in fear, the more serenely shall you behold the Coming of that Eternal Judge, Who with the Father, and the Holy Spirit, liveth and reigneth, world without end. Amen.

V. St Bernard, Abbot and Doctor

The Advent of the Lord and Its Six Circumstances[9]

1. This day, Brethren, we celebrate the beginning of Advent; of which indeed the name, like those of the other solemnities, is truly honoured, and known to all the world, though the reason for the name is not. For the unhappy children of Adam, turning aside from serious and salutary reflections, give their minds only to that which is perishable and transitory. To whom shall we liken the people

of this generation? Or to whom shall we compare those whom we see cannot be torn from, separated from, earthly and bodily satisfaction? They are indeed like those in danger of death by drowning. For these as you may know cling fast and never let go their hold upon whatsoever may come into their grasp, whatever the thing may be, even if it is something that can be of no help to them, as the roots of grass, and such things. And if others should come to their assistance, seizing hold of them, they not infrequently involve these also in the same peril as themselves; so that aid can now come neither to themselves, not to these others.

And so they perish. In this wide and spacious sea so perish those unhappy ones, who, clutching hard at transitory things, lose what is enduring, of which had they taken fast hold they might have escaped and saved their immortal souls. For it was of Truth, not of wordly vanity it was said: *You shall know it, and it shall make you free* (Jn. viii. 32). You therefore, Brethren, to whom as to little children, God reveals what He has hidden from the wise and the prudent, dwell in earnest reflection upon the things that are truly salutary, and diligently seek out the reason of this season of Advent, asking namely: Who is it that is coming; whence He comes and how He comes; to what purpose; when, and where, does He come? Praiseworthy indeed is this curiosity, and most salutary: nor would the universal Church commemorate so devoutly this present time of Advent unless that there was contained within it some deep significance, some sacred mystery.

2. Before everything else, *consider* with the awed and wondering Apostle, *how great a man this is* (Heb. vii. 4) Who is coming: He is, according to the testimony of Gabriel (Lk. i. 32), *the Son of the Most High,* and, accordingly, co-equal with Him. Nor is it lawful to suppose that the Son of God is less than the Father: we must confess Him equal in majesty, wholly equal in dignity. For who does not know that the sons of princes are princes, and that the sons of kings are kings? Yet why is it that of the Three Persons Whom, in the Most Holy Trinity, we believe, confess and adore, it is not the Father Who comes, nor the Holy Spirit, but the Son? I cannot believe that this is without special cause. But *who hath known the mind of the Lord? Or who hath been His counsellor?* (Rom. xi. 34.) It was not without the most high deliberation of the Trinity that it was decreed that the Son should come. And if we reflect upon the reason of our own exile, we may perhaps discern, at least in part, how supremely fitting it was that we should be redeemed by the Son. For Lucifer, *who didst rise in the morning* (Is. xiv. 12) aspired in his mind *to be like the Most High,* and thought it to be but a matter of *violence to be equal to God,* which is the prerogative of the Son; but being cast headlong down he was ruined: for the Father hath a zeal for the Son, and here He appears to make known by deed, that *vengeance is Mine, I will repay* (Rom. xii. 19). Then suddenly, *I saw Satan like lightning falling from heaven* (Lk. x. 18).

In what then do you pride yourself, you who are but dust and ashes? If God spared not the prideful angels, how much the less shall He spare thee, who art but corruption and a worm? *He* did nothing, he wrought nothing. He but *said in his heart*, and, in a moment, in the twinkling of an eye, he was cast down for ever; because, according to the Evangelist, *he stood not in truth* (Jn. viii. 44).

3. Flee from pride, my Brethren: fly, I beseech you, from all pride. *Pride is the beginning of every sin* (Ecclus. x. 15); pride it was that so speedily thrust even Lucifer himself into eternal night, though he had shone more brightly than all the stars! Pride it was that transformed into a demon, not simply an angel, but the first of all the angels. And, forthwith, through jealous hate, he brought forth in man the iniquity he had conceived in his own heart, deluding him that tasting the forbidden tree he would become as God, knowing good and evil (Gen. iii. 5).

What is it that you promise, wretch: what is it that you offer, since it is only the Son of the Most High that has the Key of Wisdom; nay more, He is Himself *the Key of David; He that openeth and no man shutteth* (Apoc. iii. 7)? In Him *lie hid all the treasures of wisdom and knowledge* (Col. ii. 3). Will you then attempt to seize these by treachery, to keep yourself superior to man? You will see that He is in truth, as the Lord hath said, *a liar and the father thereof* (Jn. viii. 44). For he was a liar when he said: *I will be like the Most High* (Is. xiv. 14), and the father of liars, since he injected into man also the poisoned seeds of falsehood, saying: *You shall be as Gods, knowing good and evil* (Gen. iii. 5).

You also, O Man, *if thou didst see a thief thou didst run with him* (Ps. ilix. 18). You have heard what was read this night from the prophet Isaias; the Lord saying: *Thy princes are faithless*, or as another translation has it: *disobedient, companions of thieves* (Is. i. 23).

4. Our princes, Adam and Eve, the well spring of our race, were in truth disobedient, and the associates of thieves; who attempted through the seduction of the serpent, or rather, of the devil, using the instrument of a serpent, to take what belonged to the Son of God. Nor did the Father let pass unnoticed this injury to His Son, *for the Father loveth the Son* (Jn. v. 20), but forthwith visited on man due punishment, laying upon him the Hand of His Justice. And in Adam we have all sinned, and in him have received sentence of damnation.

What then does the Son do, beholding thus the zeal of the Father for Him, not sparing any one of His creatures? Behold, He says, through Me the Father has lost His creatures. The first of the angels hath desired My Throne; now he has power over those who trusted in him. But the zeal of My Father has punished him; he is stricken, together with all who belong to him, with a wound that heals not, with tormenting chastisements. Man too has sought to possess himself of the knowledge that is Mine only. Neither has the Father spared him, nor turned away His eye.

But *doth God care for oxen?* (I Cor. ix. 9.) Only two among His creatures has He ennobled by making them sharers of the light of His reason, capable of joy eternal, the angel, namely, and man. But behold! because of Me He has lost many angels, and all of mankind. Therefore, that they may know that I also love the Father, through Me shall He receive back what, through Me, He is seen to have lost. *Take me up and cast Me into the sea*, said Jonah, *for I know that for my sake this great tempest is upon you* (Jonah i. 12). All these now look upon Me with envy. *Behold I shall come*, and I shall so reveal Myself to them, that whosoever shall be envious of Me, whosoever shall eagerly desire to become like unto Me, his emulation shall be accounted to him unto justice.

5. I knew that the rebel angels were changed through malice and wickedness, that neither did they sin through ignorance or infirmity, and so, unwilling to repent, they must perish. For the love of the Father and *the honour of the King loveth judgment* (Ps. xciv. 4). Then did He create men, and, in the beginning, that they might take the place of those who were lost, and rebuild again the City of Jerusalem; for He knew that to the fallen angels there remained no way of return. Truly well He knew *the pride of Moab, that he is exceedingly proud* (Is. xvi. 6): and his pride did not admit of the remedy of repentance, nor, through it, of pardon. But in the place of sinful man He made no other creature, showing by this fact that man was yet to be restored; for he whom the malice of one had betrayed, the charity of Another would redeem. So, Lord, I beseech Thee: *be pleased to deliver me* (Ps. xxxix. 14) *for I am weak* (Ps. vi. 3): *for I was stolen away out of the land of the Hebrews and here without any fault*

was cast into the dungeon (Gen. xl. 15), Not that I am wholly innocent, but compared with him that seduced me, I am in a certain measure innocent. Falsehood persuaded me, Lord. Let Truth come that falsehood may be laid bare; that I may know the Truth; and the Truth will set me free; yet only if I renounce the uncovered falsehood and cling to the Truth I know. Otherwise the temptation will not be human, nor will the sin be human, but diabolical impenitence. For to continue in evil is in the character of the devil, and they deserve to perish with him who following his example, remain stubborn in iniquity.

6. Behold, Brethren, you have already heard Who it is that comes. Consider now whence He comes and whither He goes? He comes from the Heart of God the Father, and into the womb of the Virgin Mary; He comes from the sublimity of heaven to the lower parts of the earth. What then? Are we who are upon the earth not to be changed? Yes; if He abides here. For where is there good without Him? Or where is it evil, when He is there? *For what have I in heaven? And besides thee what do I desire upon earth? Thou art the God of my heart, and the God that is my portion forever* (Ps. lxxii. 25). *For though I should walk in the midst of the shadow of death, I will fear no evils, for thou art with me* (Ps. xxii. 4).

Now, as I behold, He has descended upon the earth, and descended also into hell itself; yet not as one bound there, but as one *free among the dead* (Ps. lxxxvii. 6), and *as a light which shineth in the darkness, and the darkness did not comprehend it*.

Hence thou wilt not leave His soul in hell, nor wilt Thou let His holy Body taste corruption upon the earth (Ps. xv. 10). For Christ *who has descended, is the same also that ascended above all the heaven, that He might fill all things* (Eph. iv. 9); of whom it was written: *who went about doing good, and healing all that were oppressed by the devil* (Acts x. 38). And elsewhere: *He hath rejoiced as a giant to run the way: His going out is from the end of Heaven, and his circuit even to the end thereof* (Ps. xviii. 6). Rightly then does the Apostle cry out, saying: *Seek the things that are above: where Christ is sitting at the Right Hand of the Father* (Col. iii. 1). In vain would He urge us to lift up our hearts, unless He could also teach us that the Author of our salvation was set on high.

But let us see what follows. For though the matter is abundant, and indeed abounding, the shortness of time does not permit of a lengthy sermon. To those who so meditate uponWho it is that comes, His great and ineffable Majesty becomes revealed. To those who look upwards to discern whence He comes, a great way is laid open to the eyes, according to the testimony of him on whom the spirit of prophecy descended: *Behold*, he says, *the name of the Lord cometh from afar* (Is. xxx. 27). And then to those who consider whither He goes, there is revealed an incomparable and wholly inconceivable dignity, which has deigned, from such great glory, to descend to the ignominy of this prison.

7. Who can still doubt that there is some great cause why such wondrous majesty has deigned to come down from such dignity, to an abode so unworthy of it? Plainly there is some great reason, because the mercy revealed is great, great the compassion, and great the charity. To what end then must we believe that He came? This reflexion, in accordance with the order we have proposed to ourselves, we shall now consider.

There is little need to dwell long upon it, since both His Words and His Works proclaim the reason of His Coming: to find the hundredth sheep, that had strayed, He has hastened down from the mountains; and that *the mercies of the Lord, might*, more clearly, *give glory to Him; and His wonderful works to the children of men* (Ps. cvi. 8), He came for our sakes. Wondrous dignity of the Lord, Who comes seeking; wonderful the dignity of men, so sought for! And in this if any man should wish to glory, he shall not be foolish; not because he appears to be something, as from himself, but because He that made Him is Mighty. For all riches, all the glory of this world, and all whatsoever in it that is desired, is less than this Might; neither is there anything with which to compare it. *Lord, what is man that thou shouldst magnify him? Or why dost thou set thy heart upon him?* (Ps. vii. 17).

8. But yet I would know what does it mean that He should come to us, and why rather have we not gone to Him. For it is we who were in need, and it is not usual for the rich to come seeking the poor, that is, if they still desire to retain their own superiority. And in truth, Brethren, it was more fitting that we should go to Him, but against this was a twofold barrier, our eyes were dim and groping, and

He *inhabiteth light inaccessable* (I Tim. vi. 16); and, lying paralysed upon our poor beds, we could not ascend to that divine sublimity. And so the Most Benign Saviour, the Physician of our souls, comes down from His Glory, tempering the brightness of His Splendour to our infirm sight. He veiled Himself as it were in a lantern, in that glorious, that most pure and stainless Body which He put on; this Body that is the swift and shining cloud upon which, as the Prophet had foretold, *the Lord would ascend* that He might *enter into Egypt* (Is. xix. 1).

9. We must now enquire as to the time in which the Saviour came. He came, and this we believe is not unknown to you, not in the beginning of time, nor yet in the centre, but at its end. Neither was this also without design, for Wisdom, in its order, had disposed that when we were most in need He would bring us aid; being mindful of the children of Adam, though they were prone to ingratitude.

Truly was it then towards the evening, and the day now far spent; the sun of justice was low, and its splendour and warmth had almost vanished from the earth. And the light of the knowledge of divine things was low, and, iniquity abounding, the fervour of charity had grown cold. No angel then appeared, no prophet spoke; they were silent, as though overcome by despondency, because of the hardness and obstinacy of men. *Then said I*, said the Son, *behold I come* (Ps. xxxix. 8).

And so *while all things were in silence, and the night was in the midst of her course, Thy Almighty Word, O Lord, leaped down from heaven* (Wisd, xviii. 14). Of the same mystery the Apostle speaks, saying: *but when the fulness of time was come, God sent His Son* (Gal. iv. 4). For the fulness and abundance of things temporal had induced forgetfulness and scarcity of things eternal. In fitting time did Eternity come, when the things of time had begun alone to prevail. For, passing over other proofs, so universal was peace among the nations that at the order of one man a census was taken of *the whole world.*

10. We have dwelt upon the Person of Him who comes, and on the two places, that is, whence He comes and whither He goes. The reason of His Coming, and the time of it, you are now also aware of. But one circumstance remains, namely; the way by which He comes, and this also we must earnestly seek to know, that we may, as is fitting, go out to meet Him. For though He came once visibly in the Flesh upon this earth, to work our redemption, He still comes daily, in the spirit, and *invisibly*, to redeem individual souls; as it is written: *The breath of Our mouth, Christ Lord, is taken in our sins.* And that you may know that this spiritual Coming is an invisible one, He goes on: *and under Thy shadow we shall live among the gentiles* (Lam.iv. 20).

Accordingly, it is but fitting that though the sick man may not travel far to meet this so great Physician, let him at least raise his head, and in some measure give greeting to Him who comes. There is no need for thee, O Man, to travel over the seas; it is not necessary to pierce the clouds, to cross the high Alps; no great way, I repeat, lies before thee

Hasten to meet Thy God within Thy very self: *The Word is nigh thee, even in thy mouth and in thy heart* (Rom. x. 8). Hasten to have compunction of soul, and confession from thy mouth, so that thou may at least go out from the dung-pit of a soiled conscience; for it is unfitting that the Author of all purity should enter such a place. And these things are said of that Advent whereby He deigns to illuminate with his invisible light the souls of individual men.

11. Let us now happily dwell upon the ways of His *Visible Coming: since his ways are beautiful ways, and all his paths are peaceful* (Prov. iii. 17). *Behold*, says the Bride, *He cometh leaping upon the mountains, skipping over the hills* (Cant. ii. 8). You see Him coming, O beautiful One, but you see not where he resteth in the midday. For she said: *shew me, O Thou whom my soul lovest, where thou liest in the midday* (Cant. i. 6). Resting He feeds the Angels for all eternity, nourishing them with the vision of His eternal and immortal Presence. But know you not, O beautiful One, that thy Vision *is become wonderful to thee: it is high, and you cannot reach to it* (Ps. cxxxviii. 6); but behold He has come forth from His holy place, and He Who, lying down, doth pasture the angels, has begun and will restore you to health, and in His Coming we shall see Him Who, while resting and feeding His angels, could not before be seen.

Behold He cometh, leaping upon the mountains, skipping over the hills. In place of mountains and hills understand patriarchs and prophets, and as He came leaping and skip-

ping, read in the book of the generation of Jesus: *Abraham begot Isaac: and Isaac begot Jacob* and so on. From these mountains came forth, as you will find, the Root of Jesse, whence, according to the prophet, *there came forth a Rod*, and thence *a flower shall rise up*, upon which the sevenfold Spirit of the Lord shall rest (Is. xi. 1).

And revealing this more plainly in another place, the same prophet says: *Behold a virgin shall conceive, and bear a Son, and His name shall be called Emmanuel, which being interpreted is, God with us* (Mt. i. 23). For He whom he first refers to as a flower, the same he here calls Emmanuel; and that which he before calls a rod, (virga) he here speaks of as the Virgin.[10]

From this I believe it to be evident who is the Rod coming forth from the Root of Jesse, and Who is the Flower upon which the Holy Spirit rests: that the Mother of God is this Rod, and her Son Jesus the Flower. A Flower accordingly is the Son of the Virgin; a flower *white and ruddy, chosen out of thousands* (Cant. v. 10); a flower *upon which the angels desire to look* (I Pet. i. 12); a Flower whose fragrance restores the dead to life; and as He himself has said, a *Flower of the field*, and not of the garden. For the field flowers without human help, it is by no man sown, unbroken to the spade, nor made rich with soil. So truly has flowered the Womb of the Virgin; so has the inviolate, the unstained, the pure flesh and blood of Mary, as a field, brought forth this flower of eternal beauty; Whose perfection shall see no corruption, Whose glory shall be forever unfading.

O Virgin, Sublime Rod, to what

holy eminence are you come on high? Even to the very Throne, even to the Lord of all Majesty? And what wonder, since to the very depths thou dost send down the roots of thy own humility. O Truly Celestial Blossoming Rod, more precious, more holy, than all the rest! O True Wood of Life, that alone was found worthy to bear the fruit of salvation!

Thou art caught, evil serpent, in the trap of thine own cunning, thy falsity is laid bare. Two things you had charged against your Creator: you had accused Him of falsehood, and of envy. But in either case it is you that is proved the liar. Because as to the first charge, he died to whom you said: *No, you shall not die the death* (Gen. iii. 4). And answer Him now if you can, of what tree, or, of the fruit of what tree, should He be envious, Who refused us not even this chosen branch, and its sublime Fruit? *For he that spared not even his own Son, and how hath He not also, with Him given us all things* (Rom. viii. 32).

You have already comprehended, if I am not mistaken, that the Royal Virgin is Herself the Way through which the Saviour comes, coming forth from her womb *as a bridegroom coming out of his bridechamber.*

Holding fast then to this way, let us strive, Beloved, to ascend through Her to Him, Who through Her has come down to us; to reach by Her aid to His divine forgiveness, Who came by way of Her to take away our woe.

Through thee have we access to Thy Son, O Blessed Discoverer of Grace, Mother of Life, Mother of Salvation! May He through Thee forgive us, Who by Thee was given unto us. May thy blameless integrity plead with Him, that He look not upon our corruption; and let thy humility that so pleases God, obtain the pardon of our pride.

Let thy boundless charity cover the multitude of our sins, and thy glorious fruitfulness bring us an abundance of mercies. Our Lady, Our Mediatrix, present us to Thy Son. Speak for us to Thy Son. Grant, O Most Blessed, through the graces thou hast earned, through the privileges thou hast merited, through the mercy thou hast received, that He Who deigned by means of Thee, to become a Sharer of our infirmity and sorrow, may through thy intercession make us sharers of His Glory and of His Joy, Jesus Christ Thy Son Our Lord, Who is above all God the Blessed for ever and ever. Amen.

NOTES

[1] Cf. CSEL, 57, Ep. 199, XI 36, 37.
[2] PL 15, 1814.   [3] PL 15, 1814.
[4] Vossio, St Ephraem I 161. This sermon, and others, edited by Vossio, Cologne 1616, is not given in the restricted edition of Lamy, Malines 1902. Vossio however makes substantial claims for its authenticity.
[5] PL 54, 185-188, Sermo 19 Sancti Leonis.

[6] Used in address, among Christians, from early iv cent. GLL 104.
[7] PL 76, 1077-1081 (Homily I).
[8] This reference is to the Lombards and their king, who later invaded Rome but withdrew at Gregory's persuasion.
[9] PL 183, 35-40 (Homily I).
[10] Continued from Sermo II, pars. 4 and 5, 42-43.

SECOND SUNDAY OF ADVENT

THE GOSPEL OF THE SUNDAY

Matthew xi 2–10

At that time: When John had heard in prison the works of Christ: sending two of his disciples he said to him: art thou he that art to come, or look we for another? And Jesus making answer said to them: Go and relate to John what you have heard and seen. The blind see, the lame walk, the lepers are cleansed, the deaf hear, the dead rise again, the poor have the gospel preached to them. And blessed is he that shall not be scandalised in me. And when they went their way, Jesus began to say to the multitudes concerning John: What went you out into the desert to see? A reed shaken with the wind? But what went you out to see? A man clothed in soft garments? Behold they that are clothed in soft garments, are in the houses of kings. But what went you out to see? A prophet? Yea, I tell you, and more than a prophet. For this is he of whom it is written: *Behold I send my angel before thy face, who shall prepare thy way before thee.*

PARALLEL GOSPEL

Luke vii. 18–27

And John's disciples told him of all these things. And John called to him two of his disciples, and sent them to Jesus, saying: Art thou he that art to come; or look we for another? And when the men were come unto him, they said: John the Baptist hath sent us to thee, saying: art thou he that art to come; or look we for another? And in that same hour, he cured many of their diseases, and hurts, and evil spirits: and to many that were blind he gave sight. And answering, he said to them: Go and relate to John what you have heard and seen: the blind see, the lame walk, the lepers are made clean, the deaf

28

hear, the dead rise again, to the poor the gospel is preached. And blessed is he whosoever shall not be scandalised in me. And when the messengers of John were departed, he began to speak to the multitudes concerning John. What went you out into the desert to see? A reed shaken with the wind? But what went you out to see? a man clothed in soft garments? Behold they that are in costly apparel and live delicately, are in the houses of kings. But what went you out to see? A prophet? Yea, I say to you, and more than a prophet. This is he of whom it is written: *Behold I send my angel before thy face, who shall prepare thy way before thee.*

EXPOSITION FROM THE CATENA AUREA

GLOSS: The Evangelist had previously told how through both signs and wonders, and by teaching, the Disciples as well as the people were being instructed by Christ. Now he goes on to tell in what manner this instruction came to be imparted to the disciples of John; who appeared to be governed by an attitude of rivalry towards Christ. Accordingly, he says: *Now when John heard in prison the works of Christ: sending two of his disciples he said to Him: art thou he that art to come, or look we for another?*

GREGORY, *Homily 6 in Evang*: Here we have to ask ourselves this question: John, a prophet, and more than a prophet, who had himself pointed out the Lord to his own disciples, as He came to John to be baptized, and the Baptist had said: *Behold the lamb of God, behold him who taketh away the sins of the world;* Why now from his prison does he send these two disciples to ask: *art thou he that art to come or look we for another?* As if he did not know Him Whom he had himself proclaimed by prophesying concerning Him, by baptizing Him, by pointing Him out to others?

AMBROSE, in *Luke Ch.* vii: Some however understand the passage in this way. John was truly so great a prophet that he could discern the Christ; that he could proclaim the future forgiveness of sins. But though he had acknowledged Him as the Holy Prophet Whom he had believed was to come, nevertheless he had not believed that He was to die. He doubted therefore, not through lack of faith, but through piety. He doubted as Peter doubted when he said: *Lord, be it far from thee, this shall not be unto thee* (Mt. xvi. 22).

CHRYSOSTOM, *Hom. 37 in Matth*: But this interpretation is not reasonable. John was not ignorant on this point. For he had testified from the beginning regarding it, saying: *Behold the Lamb of God, behold him who taketh away the sins of the world.* By calling Him lamb, he proclaimed the Cross. For it was only by the Cross that he took away the sins of the world. How is he greater than a prophet, if he knows not what the prophets knew? For Isaias says: *As a lamb he was led to the slaughter* (Is. liii. 7).

GREGORY, *Hom. 7 in Evang*: The question may be answered in another way, if the time of the action be considered. By the Jordan John had confessed Him to be the

Redeemer of the world. Now from his prison he sends to ask if He is to come. He doubts not that He is the Saviour of the world, but he seeks to know if He Who, of His own will, came into this world, will also of His own will descend into hell? JEROME: Hence he does not say: Art thou He Who hast come? But, *art thou he that art to come?* And the meaning is: send word to me, as I am about to descend into hell, whether I am to announce Thee there, or will you send another to fulfil this mission?

CHRYSOSTOM as above: but how can this interpretation be justified? John did not say: art thou the one that is about to descend into hell, but simply, *art thou he that art to come?* It is even more absurd that he should speak in this manner for the added reason, that descending into hell he might preach Him there. For the present life is the time of grace; after death there is but judgment and justice. Hence there was no need for a Precursor there. It would be different if the unbelieving could believe after death, and then be saved. Then no one at any time would be lost, for all would then do penance, and all would adore, *every knee shall bend.*

GLOSS: We must note that Jerome and Gregory did not say that John was so to announce the Coming of Christ in hell, that by his preaching some unbelievers might be converted; but that he might bring to the Just, who waited in expectation of the Coming of Christ, some consolation by the tidings of His near approach.

HILARY *Ch. XI in Matth:* It is nevertheless certain that, as Precursor,

he foretold that Christ was to come; as Prophet, he knew that He was already in the midst of men; as Confessor, he had venerated Him before men. Error did not shadow his perfect knowledge. Nor can we believe that the grace of the Holy Spirit was denied him in prison, when the light of that same Power was later to be given to the imprisoned Apostles.

JEROME: He asked, not as one who was ignorant, but as the Saviour asked where they had laid Lazarus: so that those who indicated the place of the sepulchre would be so much the better prepared to believe when they should see the dead rising. So John, soon to be put to death by Herod, sends his disciples to Christ, so that by seeing the signs and wonders wrought by the Master they would believe in Him, and by speaking with Him, would learn for themselves. That John's disciples had a certain feeling of bitterness towards the Lord, because of envy, is apparent from their question on a previous occasion, as when they said: *why do we and the Pharisees fast, and your disciples do not fast?*

CHRYSOSTOM: As long as John was with his disciples, he strove continually to convince them of the truth with regard to the Christ. Now, being about to be put to death, he strove even more earnestly. For he was fearful lest he leave his disciples in an unsettled state of mind, and that they might remain alienated from Christ, towards Whom, from the beginning, he had striven to lead them. If he were simply to say to them: go, *follow Him; for he is greater than me,* he would not at all have persuaded them. More, by speaking in this way, they would only think that he wished to humble himself, and thus they would have become even more attached to him. What therefore does he do? He waits till in due time he hears from them, that Christ is working miracles. Neither does he now send all of them, but only two, whom he perhaps knows to be more open to conviction than the rest, so that they themselves might make a straightforward enquiry, and, from what they saw, might learn for themselves how great was the distance between the Baptist and Christ.

HILARY, as above: John therefore was not studying his own ignorance, but that of his disciples. In order that they might learn that he had been preaching none other than this Christ, he sends his disciples that they might behold His works; so that what he had himself taught them, concerning Christ, might now be confirmed by Christ's own signs and wonders.

CHRYSOSTOM, as above: Christ, discerning the purpose of John, did not simply say in reply: *Yes, I am he.* Because by such a reply He would but revive their antipathy. For they would think, though they might not say, that which the Pharisees had already said to Him: *Thou givest testimony of thyself* (Jn. viii. 13). For this reason he made them learn the answer from His miracles, thus giving a reply that was simple and unanswerable. For the testimony of deeds is more credible than that of words. Accordingly, He there and

then cured the lame, the blind, and many others. He did this, not in order to teach John, who already knew, but these disciples, who were still doubtful. Hence the Gospel goes on: *and Jesus making answer said to them: go and relate to John what you have heard and seen. The blind see, the lame walk, the lepers are cleansed, the deaf hear, the dead rise again, the poor have the gospel preached to them.*

JEROME: What is last mentioned is not the least significant. For *the poor* understand either the poor in spirit, or, without doubt, the poor of this world. So that in the preaching of the gospel there is no distinction between high and low, rich and poor. This proves the impartiality of the Master, the truthfulness of the Instructor, since He seeks without preference the salvation of each one.

CHRYSOSTOM: Saying: *blessed is he that shall not be scandalised in Me,* He reproaches John's messengers. For they had been scandalised in Him. Without openly making known their doubt, leaving it within their own hearts, He secretly forgives their offence.

HILARY: He makes clear that of which John had already warned them, saying: blessed is he in whom there was nothing of scandal concerning Himself. For it was through fear of this, lest they be scandalised, that John had sent his disciples. So that they would learn from Christ Himself. GREGORY *Hom. 6 in Evang*: The minds of those who had not believed suffered grave scandal in regard to Christ, when after so many miracles they beheld Him dying. Hence

Paul has said: We *preach Christ cruci-fied a stumbling block to the Jews* (I Cor. i. 23). What then does He mean here: *Blessed is he that is not scandalised in me,* unless signifying in clear terms the abjection and lowliness of His own death? It is as if He openly said: "I perform wonders, but I do not refuse also to suffer humiliations. Because in my death I shall go the way of men, men must take care that they do not despise Me in death, though they now honour Me because of these wonders."

HILARY, as above: Mystically, an even fuller understanding is to be had of that which John did here. For as a prophet he prophesied even in the very circumstances of his imprisonment; because in him the Law became silent. The Law had been foretelling of Christ and the forgiveness of sins, and had promised likewise the kingdom of heaven. And John had brought to completion this work of the Law. The Law now silent, imprisoned by the wickedness of men, as it were held in bonds and shut away, so that Christ might not be made known, then sends to look upon the Gospel, so that doubt may be changed to belief in its doctrine, through seeing the works of the Gospel.[1]

AMBROSE, *on Luke Ch. 7:* Perhaps these two disciples whom he sent, signify the two peoples; the one believing for the Jews, the other for the Gentiles. CHRYSOSTOM, *in Matth, Hom. 36:* As to John's disciples, his purpose was accomplished. Now satisfied concerning Christ because of the wonders they had seen, they returned whence they came. But it was also neces-sary to correct the minds of the people who, from this interrogation by John's disciples, may have been led to erroneous conclusions, being unaware of John's purpose. They might have said among themselves that he who had testified so much concerning Christ, seems to believe differently now, and even doubts if He really is the Christ. Have they quarrelled, that he now speaks in this manner to Jesus? Or has prison changed his mind? Or was that which he proclaimed before but vain and foolish talk?

HILARY, *in Matth. 11:* Lest the words He had just spoken to the disciples be wrongly applied to the Baptist, as though it were he that were scandalised in Christ, Scripture adds: *And when they,* the disciples, *went their way, He began to speak to the multitudes concerning John.* CHRYSOSTOM: Only when they went their way did He speak, lest He might appear to flatter. Again, in correcting the people, He did not openly refer to their suspicions, but guided their minds towards an explanation of what had been troubling them, and had occasioned their doubts, thus show-ing them that He knew their hidden thoughts. For He did not say to them as He did to the Pharisees: *Why do you think evil in your hearts* (Mt. ix. 4). For though they had thought evil, it was through ignorance, not malice. And so He did not speak severely to them, but speaking on John's behalf He showed that the Baptist had not fallen away from his first belief. He proves this as well from their own testimony, as by His own words. He proved it, not alone by what they said, but by what they had done. And so He says: *What went you out into the desert to see?* As if He said: for what reason did you, abandoning the cities, gather together in the wilderness? So great a multitude would not have come and with such eagerness, into the desert, unless expecting to see something great, something wonderful, something more enduring than the arid desert.

GLOSS: They had not at this time gone out into the desert to see John, for he was not then in the desert, but in prison. But our Lord was speaking of the past. Because the people had gone out frequently to the desert to see John while he was in the desert.

CHRYSOSTOM, *Hom. 38 in Matth*: Passing over any other possible defect, He removes from their mind the suspicion of levity the crowd had inwardly entertained concerning John, saying: *a reed shaken by the wind?* GREGORY, *Hom. 6 in Evang*: Which suspicion He disposed of, not by alleging, but by denying. Scarcely does the breath of the breeze touch the reed than it bends the other way. In this the carnal soul is signified, which, as soon as it is touched by inclination or delight, inclines in that direction. *A reed shaken by the wind* John was not, but a man no allurement would turn from his path. As if the Lord should say: JEROME: was it for this you went out into the desert: that you might see a man like a reed in character turned about by every wind, of such changeable mind that he is uncertain now of what he before proclaimed? Or perhaps he is moved by jealousy against Me,

and his preaching was but a following after vain glory that from it he might make profit? But why should he seek wealth? That he might revel in feasting? But his food was locusts and wild honey. Was it that he might dress richly? But his clothing was of camel's hair. And so he adds: *but what went you out to see? A man clothed in soft garments?*

CHRYSOSTOM, *Hom. 38 in Matth*: That John is unlike a fickle reed you have proved by your own eagerness in going out to see him in the desert. No man either can say that John was first constant, then afterwards, giving himself to pleasure, became inconstant. For just as one is by nature irascible, and another becomes so by illness, some are fickle by nature, others become so by giving themselves to wantonness. John was not fickle by nature, for which it was He had said: *what went you out to see, a reed shaken by the wind?* Neither, giving himself to pleasure, had he lost the excellence of virtue which he possessed. That he was no servant of pleasure, his poverty alone, as well as his prison, confirms. Had he wished to be clothed in soft garments he would have dwelt, *not in the desert, but in the houses of kings.* Hence we have: *Behold they who are clothed in soft garments, are in the houses of kings.* JEROME: From this it is indicated to us that austere living and the preaching of the Gospel, must keep away from the palaces of kings, and the houses of luxury-living men.

GREGORY, *Hom. 6 in Evang*: Let no one think that sin can be absent from luxurious living and the love of precious garments. For if there were no fault in it Our Lord would not have praised John for his austerity, nor Peter have reproved women for their craving for precious adornment (I Pet. iii. 3).

AUGUSTINE, *De Doct. Christiana, 3*; 12: Yet in all these things the fault lies, not in the use of things, but in the disordered appetite of the user. Whosoever uses things more sparingly than those among whom he lives, is either temperate, or over-scrupulous. Whosoever uses them so as to exceed the measure of what is usual among goodliving people about him, either wishes to convey some meaning, or is a person without order in his life.

CHRYSOSTOM: Our Lord having vindicated the character of John, from the manner of his life and of his clothing, and from the thronging of people to him, shows also that he was a prophet, and more than a prophet, saying: *what went you out to see? A prophet? I say to you and more than a prophet.* GREGORY: it is the office of the prophet to foretell future events, not to point them out. John therefore is more than a prophet, because Him of whom He had prophesied, he had also pointed out, [indicating Him to his own disciples]. JEROME: in which he is greater than the other prophets; since to the office of prophet is added the dignity of Baptist, for he had baptised the Lord.

CHRYSOSTOM: Then he shows in what John is greater, saying: *This is he of whom it is written: behold I send my angel before thy face.* JEROME: That He might add to the merits of John, He recalls the testimony of

Malachy (Mal. iii. 1), in which he is foretold as an *angel.* Let us not however infer that John was called an angel by community of nature, but rather from the dignity of his office; he was a *messenger* who announced the Coming of the Lord. GREGORY: That which is called *angelus* in Greek is in Latin *nuntius* or *messenger.* Fittingly, therefore, is he called *angelus* who had come to announce the *Supernal Judge*; so that he may possess in his name the dignity of his office.

CHRYSOSTOM: He reveals, therefore, in what John is greater than the other prophets; in this, namely; that he is near to Christ. And so the Scripture says: *I send before thy face,* that is, before Thee. For those who precede the king's chariot are nobler than the others. In this way John is closer to the presence of Christ. GLOSS.: Other prophets were sent that they might announce the Coming of the Lord; he was sent to prepare His path. Hence it is said: *who shall prepare thy way before thee,* that is, by preaching penance, and by baptising, he prepared the hearts of Christ's hearers.

HILARY: Mystically, the *desert* must be considered as a place empty of the Holy Spirit, in which there is no dwelling place of God. In the *reed* we see a man who is absorbed in the vanity of the world, and in his own empty life. Within he is void of the fruit of truth, having a pleasing exterior, but an empty interior; responsive to the breath of every wind, that is, to every prompting of unclean spirits; never able to take a firm stand, and vain to the marrow of his bones.

By *garments* is mystically signified

the body which the soul as it were puts on, and which grows soft by luxury and wantonness. *Kings* is another name for the fallen angels. For these are the *Powers* of this world, not that they rule the world visibly, but rather the evil men in the world; hence they *lord it over men*. Accordingly, those dressed in luxurious garments are in the houses of kings, means, mystically:

those whose bodies are lax and dissolute, through wantonness, are plainly the habitations of demons. GREGORY: John was not clothed in soft garments, because he did not condone with flattery the lives of those who were living in sin, but rather upbraided them in bitter words, saying: *ye brood of vipers, who hath showed you to flee from the wrath to come?*

I. ST HILARY: ON THE GOSPEL[2]

1. *Now when John had heard in prison the works of Christ: sending two of his disciples, he said to Him. Art thou He that is to come or look we for another?* Did John in his prison not know the Lord? Did so great a prophet know not his God? But as Precursor he had foretold that He was to come; as Prophet he had recognised Him standing in their midst; as Confessor he had venerated Him before men. Did error creep into so profound and varied knowledge? The subsequent testimony of the Lord concerning John does not permit us to think so. Nor can we believe that the light of the Holy Spirit was denied him in prison, when the Light of that same Power was to be given to the imprisoned apostles.

Why John sent to Christ

2. But a clearer understanding is furnished from the things John did, and from the efficacy of the action the grace that was in him is evident. For as Prophet he prophesied by the very circumstances of his imprisonment; because in him the Law became silent. For the Law had foretold Christ, and the forgiveness of sin, and had promised men the kingdom of heaven. John

had continued and brought to a close this purpose of the Law. The Law was now silenced, imprisoned by the wickedness of men, and as it were held in bonds, lest Christ become known, because John has been fettered and imprisoned. The Law therefore sends messengers to behold the works of the Gospel, so that unbelief may contemplate the truth of the faith in the light of these wonders; so that whatever in it (the Law) is frustrated by the violence of sinful men, may be set free by an understanding of *the freedom wherewith Christ has made us free* (Gal. iv. 31).

In this manner John remedied not his own but his disciples' ignorance. For he had himself proclaimed that Christ was to come unto the forgiveness of sin. But that his disciples might learn that he had preached none other than Christ, he sends them to Him that they may behold His works, so that the works of Christ may confirm his own teaching, and, finally: so that they might look for no other Christ than He to whom the works gave testimony.

The Scandal of the Cross is Foretold

3. And when the Lord had re-

vealed Himself in wonders, namely: in the blind seeing, the lame walking, in lepers being cleansed, the deaf hearing, the dumb speaking, in the dead rising again, and in the preaching of the gospel to the poor, He says: *blessed is he that shall not be scandalised in Me.* Was there anything in what Christ had done which might scandalise John? Far from it. For in the whole course of his mission and teaching he had had nothing to say opposed to Him.

But the force and significance of the preceding sentence must be carefully dwelt on; on that, namely, which is preached to the poor; that is, they who have laid down their lives, who have taken up the cross and followed after, who have become humble in spirit, for these a kingdom is prepared in heaven. Therefore, because this universality of suffering was to be fulfilled in Christ Himself, and because His Cross would become a stumbling-block to many (I Cor. i. 23), He now declares that they are blessed to whom His Cross, His death, and Burial, will offer no trial of faith. So He makes clear that of which already, earlier, John has himself warned them, saying that blessed are they in whom there would be nothing of scandal concerning Himself. For it was through fear of this that John had sent his disciples, so that they might see and hear Christ.

Whom does the reed signify?

4. Lest however this saying should be referred to John, as if something in Christ had scandalised him, *the disciples going away,* Our Lord said to the crowd concerning John: *What went you out to the desert to see; a reed shaken by the wind?*

Mystically, the desert must be considered as a place empty of the Holy Spirit, in which there is no dwelling place of God. The *reed* must be taken as meaning a man such as is wholly absorbed in the glory of this world, and in the emptiness of his own life; within he is without fruit of truth, he has a pleasing exterior, but no interior; responsive to the breath of every wind, that is, to the suggestions of unclean spirits, unable ever to stand firm, and vain to the marrow of his bones. Therefore when He said, *what went you out into the desert to see? A reed shaken by the wind?* this is what He said. Did you go out to see a man who was empty of the knowledge of God, and responsive to the breath of every unclean spirit? For He spoke to them in a spirit of approval rather than reproach; wishing to affirm that they had not seen anything in John that was empty or fickle.

Bodies corrupted by lust are the dwelling places of devils

5. *But what went you out to see? A man clothed in soft garments: behold that they are clothed in soft garments are in the house of kings.* By *garments* are mystically signified the body which the soul as it were puts on, and which grows soft through luxury and wantonness. In *kings* we have a name for the fallen angels. For those are the powers of the world, lording it over men. Therefore, those dressed in luxurious garments are in the house of kings means that those whose bodies are lax and dissolute through wantonness are habitations of the demons, who choose such dwelling-places as being suited to their designs and evil works.

The glory of John

6. *But what went you out to see? A prophet? Yea, and more than a prophet.* The Lord makes plain to all the greatness of John, declaring him to be more than a prophet, because only to him was it given both to foretell the Coming of Christ and to behold Him. How then shall it be believed that he knew not Christ, who was sent with the power of an angel to make ready for His Coming, and than whom no greater prophet born of woman had arisen; excepting that he is less than Him Who was questioned by the disciples of John, Who was not believed, to Whom not even His works gave testimony. He is greater in the Kingdom of Heaven. Amen.

II. FROM ST JEROME'S EXPOSITION OF THE PROPHET ISAIAS

There shall come forth a Rod out of the Root of Jesse, and a flower shall rise up out of his Root. Isaias xi 1. Roman Breviary.[3]

A Rod shall rise out of Jesse. Up to the beginning of the vision, *which Isaias the son of Amos saw*, and which was *of the burden of Babylon*, all this prophecy relates to Christ; the which we propose to explain, part by part, so that the subject treated of, and the discussions upon them, may not confuse the mind of the reader. The Jews interpret the Shoot and the Flower of Jesse as the Lord Himself; namely, that by the Rod is signified His Royal Power, and by the Flower His Beauty.

We however believe that the Holy Virgin Mary is the Rod from the Root of Jesse, to which no enriching plant hath cleaved, and of whom we earlier read: *Behold a Virgin shall conceive, and bear a son.*

And the Flower is the Lord Our Saviour, Who says in the Canticle of Canticles: *I am the Flower of the field, and the lily of the valleys.*

Upon this Flower then which of a sudden will rise up from the stock and the root of Jesse, through the Virgin Mary, the Spirit of the Lord will rest: because in Him it hath pleased all the fulness of the Godhead to dwell corporeally: and not in part, as in others who were sanctified; but as the Nazarenes read in their Gospel, written in the Hebrew tongue: *The whole fountain of the Holy Spirit shall come down upon Him. Now the Lord is a spirit. And where the Spirit of the Lord is, there is liberty.*

III. ST JOHN CHRYSOSTOM: ON THE GOSPEL[4]

1. *Now when John had heard in prison the works of Christ . . .* Luke tells us that his own disciples came and told John of the miracles, and that he sent them (Lk. vii. 18, 19). This creates no contradiction, but it does provide us with a reflection, namely; that they seemed inflamed with envy against Jesus. What follows is to be carefully considered. What means this saying: *Art thou he that art to come, or look we for another?* For he who had known the Lord before these signs and wonders, who had been taught by the Holy Spirit, who had received knowledge of Him from the Voice of the Father, who had proclaimed Him

before all men, now sends to Him, that he may learn whether it is He or not?

And if you know not whether this is He, how can you deem yourself worthy of belief, giving testimony of things you know not? For he who gives testimony ought first be worthy of belief. Did you not say: The latchet of whose shoe I am not worthy to loose? (Lk. iii. 16) Did you not say: *And I knew him not, but He who sent me to baptize with water, said to me: He upon whom thou shalt see the Spirit descending He it is who baptizeth with the Holy Ghost* (Jn. i. 33). Have you not seen the Spirit in the form of a dove? Have you not heard the Voice? Did you not stay Him, saying: *I ought to be baptized by thee, and comest thou to me?* (Mt. iii. 14) Did you not say to your disciples: *He must increase, but I must decrease?* (Jn. iii. 30) Did you not teach all the people, that *He would baptize in water and the Holy Spirit* (Lk. iii. 16)? And that he was *the Lamb of God, who taketh away the sins of the world* (Jn. i. 29)? Did you not even before these signs and wonders preach Him to all men? How then, when He is known to all, when His fame flies in every direction, after He has raised the dead, put evil spirits to flight, and manifested such signs of power, do you send to ask this concerning Him? What then has happened? Were all these testimonies false, and but fables and old wives' tales?

Who of sound mind would utter such things? Not certainly of John, I say, *who leaped in the womb of his mother* (Lk. i. 41); who, unborn, had yet proclaimed Him; the dweller in the desert, of the angelic life. But even if he were one of the lowest of men, he could not be doubtful after such testimony, his own and that of others. And so it is plain that he did not send as one in doubt; nor inquire as one in ignorance. Neither may any one say that he did know, but that he had become timid through prison. For he did not expect to be freed from prison, nor if he did would he have betrayed the truth; prepared as he was again and again to die. For unless he were ready to die, he would not have shown such strength of soul before a people who were ever disposed to shed prophetic blood. Neither would he have rebuked the cruel tyrant with such courage, in the face of all the city and the people, if those who heard him could chide him as a coward.

If he had become timid, why was he not ashamed to send his own disciples, in whose presence he had borne testimony, to so many and to such tremendous things? Yet he inquired through them, when he ought rather to have put his question through others; especially since he knew well that they were envious of Christ, and were but seeking to find fault with Him. And how was it he was not also ashamed before the Jewish people; he who had prophesied to them so many things?

And whence could any help come to him, to free him from prison? For it was not on account of Christ that he was thrown there, or because he had proclaimed His Kingdom, but because he had condemned an unlawful union. Would it not rather be the conduct of a weak man, or of a worldly man, to win public favour for himself?

What then is in question here?

From what has been said there can be no question of doubt, as regards John, nor indeed of anybody, in like circumstances, even a weak minded person. We must then give an answer. Why did he send to ask? The disciples of John were moved by jealousy against Christ, as is seen from what they once said to their master: *He who was with thee across the Jordan, to whom you gave testimony, behold he baptizeth, and all men come to Him* (Jn. iii. 26). And again from the complaint made by the Jews, and by one of the disciples of John: *We and the Pharisees fast often, but your disciples do not fast.*

2. They did not yet know who Christ was; thinking that He was a mere man, but that John was more than a man, they were grieved at seeing Jesus now celebrated, and John's fame growing less; even as he had himself foretold. This attitude had kept them from drawing near to the Lord; envy holding them back. As long as John was among his disciples, he endeavoured to convince them of the truth regarding Christ. But now about to leave them, because of the death he expected at the hands of Herod, he was gravely concerned over them. He feared to leave them in an unsettled state of belief; and that they might remain thus separated from Christ towards Whom he had from the beginning striven to guide them. And since he had failed, now nearing his end, he tried again with great earnestness.

Had he said to them: "Go, follow Him, for He is greater than me," he would not have convinced them, and further, through speaking in this way, they would have believed that he spoke out of humility, and would only have become more attached to him. If he remains silent, the situation remains as it was.

What then does he do? He waits till he hears from them that Christ is working signs and wonders. Nor does he send all of them; just two, whom perhaps he believed more prejudiced than the rest; so that the questioning might be without suspicion, so that from what they saw, they might then learn how great was the distance between him and Christ. So he says: *Go ye and say: art thou he that is to come, or look we for another?*

Christ, understanding the mind of John, did not immediately reply: "Yes, I am He", for that would have offended His hearers; though it could well be answered. But he allowed them to learn the answer from the deeds they witnessed. For it is narrated, that then and there *He cured many from among those who came to Him.* Where would be the sequence of this action if, questioned as to whether He was the One, He makes no reply but immediately begins to cure the sick, unless that He wished to do as I say? He deemed testimony from deeds more credible than any words, and less liable to suspicion.

Since then as God He knew with what purpose John had sent those men, He forthwith heals the blind, the lame, and many others; not so as to instruct John; for why instruct one who already knew and believed: but that He might confirm the minds of John's doubting disciples. And then when He had cured many, He says: *Go and relate to John what you have seen and heard.*

The blind see, the lame walk, the lepers are cleansed, the deaf hear, the dead rise again, the poor have the Gospel preached to them. Then He adds: *And blessed is he that shall not be scandalised in Me*; showing that He knew the secret thoughts of their hearts.

If He had said, in answer to their direct question, *I am*, He would have offended them, as I have said before, and they would have thought, though they might not have said, that which the Jews had already said to Him: *Thou givest testimony of Thyself* (Jn. viii. 13). And so He did not say this, but so disposed that from His miracles they would learn that which they needed to know; giving them in this manner an answer that was simple and unanswerable.

In the same way He added the last sentence; secretly rebuking them. For they had been scandalised in Him. He had seen into their souls, and calling no one to witness their inward railing against Himself, He left this to their own consciences, and so drew them the more to Him by saying simply: *Blessed is he that is not scandalised in Me.* He said this, revealing themselves to themselves.

Lest however we appear to be giving only our own opinion in this question, we think it desirable to present to you that also which has been said by others, so that from a comparison of opinions, the truth may be evident. Now what do others say about John sending his disciples? That the explanation which we give is not the true one; that John did not really know; that he did not know fully; that he knew indeed that this was truly the Christ, but that He was to die for men John did not know, and so for this

reason he asks: *art thou he that art to come*, that is, *who is about to descend into hell?*

This conflicts with right reason. John was not ignorant of this truth. For he had proclaimed it from the first, when he said to his disciples: *Behold the lamb of God who taketh away the sins of the world.* He here truly calls Him lamb, thus foretelling the Cross, as when he says: *Who taketh away the sins of the world*, he signifies the same thing. For in no other way than that of the Cross was this accomplished. This Paul has also declared: *He cancelled the deed which excluded us, the decree made to our prejudice, swept it out of the way by nailing it to the Cross* (Col. ii. 14).

Again, when he said: *He shall baptise with the Holy Ghost* (Lk. iii. 16), he foretold that which was to happen after the Resurrection. But, they say; that He was to rise again from the dead John knew, and also that He would bestow the Holy Spirit; but he did not know that Christ was to be nailed to a cross. But how was He to rise again, Who would neither have suffered, nor have been crucified? How was he greater than the prophets, if he knew not the things the prophets knew?

3. That John was more than a prophet Christ has testified (Lk. vii. 28). That the prophets foreknew the passion of Christ, there is no one who does not know. Isaias says (Is. liii. 7): *He was led as a lamb to the slaughter, He stood before the shearer and without voice.* Even before this testimony he had said: *And a root shall be in Jesse, and He who shall rise up will rule the nations and in Him the gentiles shall hope* (Is. x. 11).

Not alone does he foretell that He will be fastened to the Cross, but with whom He will suffer: *and He shall be refuted among thieves.* Not alone does he foretell this, but also that He shall offer no defence of Himself: *And He opened not His mouth*; again, that He would be unjustly condemned: *and He was taken away from distress, and from judgment* (Is. liii. 8).

Before Isaias David also had spoken, and described the judgment: *Why did the Gentiles rage, and the people meditate vain things? . . . against the Lord and against His Christ* (Acts iv. 25)? Elsewhere he speaks of the manner of the crucifixion: *They have pierced my hands and my feet* (Ps. xxi. 17). Again he accurately describes what the soldiers had dared to do: *They parted my garments among them, and upon my vestures they cast lots* (Ps. xxi. 19). Elsewhere he speaks of the proffered vinegar; *and they gave me gall for my food and in my thirst they gave me vinegar to drink* (Ps. lxviii. 22).

The prophets therefore, so many years before, spoke of the judgment, the condemnation, the companions of the Cross, the division of the garments, the casting of lots, and so many other events. It is unnecessary to relate them all lest our sermon run too long. He then who is greater than all the prophets, did not know these things? How can this be sustained? Why then did he not say: *art thou he who is to descend into hell,* and not simply: *art thou He that is to come?*

What is more ridiculous is that they say that John said this so that going down to hell he might preach Him there. To those who propound such notions is it aptly said: *brethren, do not become children in understanding, but in malice be as children* (I Cor. xiv. 20). For the present life is the time for doing good; after death there is but judgment and justice; for it is written: *in hell who shall confess thee* (Ps. vi. 6)?

But how hath he broken the *gates of brass, and brought down the iron bars?* (Ps. cvi. 16) Through His Body. For then for the first time hath appeared a Body, that was immortal, and ending the tyranny of death; as it made plain to all that the dominion of death was overcome, but not that the sins of those who died before His Coming were cancelled.

For if this were not so, but all who were from the beginning in hell were pardoned, how could the Lord Himself declare: *It shall be more tolerable for the land of Sodom and Gomorrha in the day of Judgment?* (Lk. x. 12.) Which certainly shows that these will also be punished, though not as severely. And though they have suffered punishment in this life also, not for that reason will they escape retribution in the next. And if they who have here been so gravely punished, shall also be punished there, how much more severely shall they be punished, who have suffered nothing in this life?

But you may say that this is a great injustice to those who died before Christ came? By no means. For men could then be saved, even though they knew not Christ. It was not required of them that they worship Him, Who had not yet come. But that setting aside false Gods they should adore the One God alone, the Creator of all things: *The Lord thy God, He says, is One*

God (Deut. vi. 4). So the Macchabees are honoured in that they preferred to die rather than betray the Law. We honour the Three Youths of the Fiery Furnace, and many others among the Jews, who lived good, even perfect lives, and preserved inviolate that measure of the Law that was required of them. Then it sufficed to salvation to know God alone. Now it is no longer so; the knowledge of Christ is necessary to salvation, according to His own words: *If I had not come and spoken to them, they would not have sin; but now they have no excuse for their sin* (Jn. xv. 22).

Greater things are also required of us, in the discipline of our lives. For then homicide was deemed worthy of death; now for anger a man may perish. Then to sin with another's wife, to commit adultery, was deemed worthy of grievous punishment; so now are unchaste looks. For as knowledge leads to a better life, so does discipline. Therefore there was no need of a Precursor in hell.

Again, if after death the wicked could be converted, then no one at any time would be lost. All will do penance, and all will adore. And that this last is true, hear the testimony of Paul: *That in the name of Jesus every knee shall bow, of those that are in heaven, on earth, and under the earth* (Phil. ii. 10); and again: *And death the enemy shall be destroyed last* (I Cor. xv. 26). But this conversion would not be the effect of a good and loving will, but merely the result, if I may say so, of the pressure of the dread evils in which they find themselves.

4. But let us put such notions far from us; as old wives' tales and

entirely foolish. Let us listen to Paul, so positively differing from any such ideas: *For whosoever have sinned without the Law, shall perish without the Law* (Rom. ii. 12); which was said by him concerning those who were before the Law; *and whosoever have sinned in the Law, shall be judged by the law*; that is those who came after Moses. And again: *The wrath of God is revealed from heaven against all ungodliness* (Rom. i. 18). And again: *wrath and indignation, tribulation and anguish upon every soul of man that worketh evil, the Jew first, and also the Greek* (Rom. ii, 8, 9).

And truly did the heathen suffer much tribulation on this account, from the vengeance of God, as the Scriptures, as well as the histories of other peoples reveal. Who can ever describe what the Babylonians have endured? Miseries that equal anything in tragedy. And who shall accurately recount the plagues and sufferings of Egypt?

That they who died before Christ, and accordingly knew Him not, could attain to happiness and eternal joys, if, abandoning the worship of idols, they adored the true God and tried to live justly, again hear Paul: *glory, and honour, and peace to every one that worketh good, to the Jew first, and also to the Greek.* Behold here, openly laid up for them, are the rewards of all who have done good; as against the torments and punishments that await those who have done all things contrarily.

Where are they, where, I ask, who believe there is no hell? For if they who lived before the advent of Christ, who had never heard the name of hell, or heard of the resurrection, and who having endured punishment in this life, are also to be punished in the next, what then of us brought up on the highest teaching of wisdom? But on what ground should they go to hell who have never heard of hell? They would say to us: if you had threatened us with hell, if we had known, we would have lived better lives? Perhaps. But perhaps also they might have lived, as we are living, who daily hear sermons about hell, and live as if we had not?

Besides, this also may be said: whoever is not restrained by the punishments of this present life, will be less likely to overcome through fear of future punishment. For the general run of men are made fearful by present, rather than by future evils. But again, a man may say: why torment ourselves with the fear of a greater punishment to come, since men are still punished in hell who were never tormented by this greater fear? It is not so. For first we have to remember that the same demands are not made of them, and of us. Much more is required of us. And he from whom more is required has need of more help. And this added fear of hell is no slight help and safeguard. And if we thus are stronger, knowing the wrath to come, they had another advantage, in that they were punished more speedily and more vehemently.

But some will say to me: how is God just; since if a man sins, he will be punished both here and there? Do you wish me to recall to you your own words, so that without labour of mine you may have the answer from yourselves? I have myself heard some among you say, when they learned that some

thief or murderer was condemned to death, What! for the thirty murders or more that thief and murderer has committed, he dies but one death? Where is there justice here? You say yourself that he does not satisfy justice, who expiates his crimes with one sole death. Why now do you profess a different opinion? Shall I tell you why? Because you are judging others, and not yourselves. But in what concerns ourselves we are hindered by our too great love of self from seeing what is just, for then we are involved in shadows and understand but little. But if we examined our own case, with the sharp scrutiny we give the affairs of others, we should give a sincere and honest opinion. Our sins deserve, not one, but many deaths.

Let us recall here, omitting other offences, how often have we received the body of Christ unworthily. We are not ignorant that they who so receive, are *guilty of the body and blood of Christ*. When, therefore, you speak of a homicide, think to yourself whether you have not the same guilt upon you? Recollect that that man killed someone who was but a mere man; but that you are guilty of the blood of the Lord. He was not a sharer in the divine mysteries; we are nourished from the sacred table. What shall I say of those who eat, who devour their neighbours, with their cruel speech; pouring poison into them? What of those who take away the bread of the poor? If he who never gives an alms in charity does this, how much more evil he, who deliberately steals what is anothers? And the mean and covetous are they not worse than many thieves? How many great thieves and despoilers are there, who are worse than murderers and the defilers of tombs? Have we not heard often of those who not content to rob, hunger also for the blood of their victims? No, no, you will say, But I would wish that you could say, no, no, when assailed by an enemy.

I ask that you keep all that I say before your memory; that living according to what is worthy, you may escape the punishment of Sodom. Let not the dread evils of Sodom draw near to you, lest you suffer the visitations of Tyre, and the punishments of Sodom, and lest, above all, you offend Christ; which to me appears as the evil to be feared above all others. For though to others hell is the last and supreme punishment, this I believe, this I shall without ceasing proclaim: it is more dreadful to offend Christ, than to be tormented in hell. I pray and exhort you, that in this you be of one mind with me. So shall we both escape hell, and enjoy the glory of Christ, to whom be honour and praise for ever and ever, Amen.

IV. St Patrick, Bishop and Confessor

Sermon for Advent

(From the Book of the Three Habitations)[5]

Three are the abodes subject to the Almighty Hand of God; that on high, that in the depths, and that which is between; of which the first is named the Kingdom of God, or the Kingdom of heaven, the lowest is called hell, and the middle abode is the present world, or this earth. Of these abodes the two extremes are wholly opposed, the one against the other; and between them is no bond of any kind. And indeed what fellowship hath light with darkness, or Christ with Belial? (II Cor. vi. 14) But the middle abode has many resemblances to the two extremes.

Whence it has light and darkness, cold and heat, it has pain and it has sound health, sadness and joy, love and hate, good as well as bad, just and unjust, servants and masters, servitude and dominion, hunger and satiety, life and death, and endless such similiarities. Of all which the one half has likeness unto heaven, the other unto hell. For the commingling together of good and evil belongs to this world; but in the Kingdom of God there are none evil, but all are good; in hell none are good, but all are evil. And either place is filled from the middle abode.

For of the people of this middle world, some are raised to heaven; others are borne down into hell. Like are joined to like, that is, the good are joined to the good, the evil to the evil; just men are joined to the just angels, and sinful men to the angels that have sinned; the servants of God are united to God; the servants of the devil are united with the devil; the Blessed are invited to possess *the kingdom prepared for them from the foundation o, the world;* and the Accursed are cast down into *the everlasting fire which was prepared for the devil and his angels* (Mt. xxv. 34, 41).

The Joys of the Kingdom of God

no man can tell, nor even conceive or understand, while he is yet clothed in the flesh; for they are greater and more wondrous than they are imagined or conceived to be. Whence it is written: *that eye hath not seen, nor ear heard, neither hath it entered into the heart of man, what things God hath prepared for them that love Him* (I Cor. ii. 9). For the Kingdom of God is greater than all report, better than all praise of it, more manifold than all knowledge, more perfect than every conceivable glory. The miseries of hell, as they truly are, no tongue can tell; no mind conceive; for in their reality they are far more dreadful than they are thought to be.

And likewise the Kingdom of God is so full of light, and peace, and charity, and wisdom, and glory, and honesty, and sweetness, and loving kindness, and every unspeakable and unutterable good, that it can neither be described nor envisioned by the mind. But the abode of hell is so full of darkness, of discord, of hate, of folly, of unhappiness, of pain, of burning heat, of thirst, of inextinguishable fire, of sadness, of unending punishment, and of every indescribable evil that neither can it be told nor yet conceived by man.

The citizens of heaven are the just and the angels, whose King is Almighty God; the people of hell are evil men and the demons, whose prince is the Devil. The Just are filled with the vision of the holy people of God and of the angels, and, above all, by the Vision of God Himself. The evil and the impious are tormented by the sight of the damned, and the demons, and, above all, by the sight of the Devil himself.

In the Kingdom of God nothing is desired that may not be found: but in hell, nothing is found that is desired. In the Kingdom of God is nothing that does not delight and satisfy; while in that deep lake of unending misery nothing is seen, nothing is felt, which does not displease, which does not torment

In the Kingdom of God every good abounds and there is nothing of evil; in the prison of hell every evil abounds and there is nothing of good. In the kingdom of heaven no one who is unworthy is received; but no one worthy, no just one, is brought down to hell. In the eternal Kingdom there shall be life without death, truth without any falsehood, and happiness without shadow of unrest or change, in Christ Jesus Our Lord, Who liveth and reigneth world without end, Amen.

V. St Gregory: On the Gospel

Sermon given to the people in the Basilica of SS. Marcellinus and Peter[6]

1. We have here to ask, dearest brethren, why John a prophet, and now more than a prophet, who had testified to the Lord as He came to the baptism of the Jordan, saying: *Behold the lamb of God, behold Him who taketh away the sins of the world* (Jn. i. 29); and who regarding both His humility and the power of His divinity, declared: *He that is of the earth, of the earth he speaketh. He that cometh from Heaven, is above all* (Jn. iii. 31), now in prison, sending his disciples, enquired: *Art thou he that art to come, or look we for another?*

As if he knew not Him whom he himself had pointed out; as if he now were ignorant of Him Whom he had himself proclaimed by prophesying concerning Him, by baptizing Him, by pointing Him out to others. But this question is quickly solved if both the time and the order of the event be considered. By the waters of the Jordan he had asserted that He was the Redeemer of the world; now, thrown into prison, he enquires if He is to come, not because he doubts that He is the Redeemer of the world, but he seeks to learn whether He Who, of His own will, came into the world, will also, of His own will, descend into hell? He who, by going before Him, had announced Him to the world, the same, now dying, goes down before Him into hell.

He says therefore: *Art thou he that art to come, or look we for another?* As if to say: since for men Thou hast deigned to be born, will You also deign for men to undergo death so that I who have been the Precursor of Thy Birth, may also become the Precursor of Thy Death: to announce Thee as about to descend into hell, as already I have announced Thee as come into this world?[7] And the Lord being thus asked, having first given manifest proofs of His power forthwith answers in words that foreshadow also the abjection of His own death; saying: *The blind see, the lame walk, the lepers are cleansed, the deaf hear, the dead rise again, the poor have the gospel preached to them. And blessed is he that shall not be scandalised in me.*

Who could not be astonished rather than scandalised at the sight of so many signs and wonders? But the mind of the unbelieving suffered grievous scandal in Him, when after so many miracles they saw Him dying. Whence Paul has said: *We preach Christ Crucified, unto the Jews indeed a stumbling block, and unto the Gentiles foolishness* (I Cor. i. 23). For to men it did indeed seem foolish, that the Author of life should die for men: and so man has taken scandal at Him, whence he ought rather to become yet more His debtor. For the more He has borne indignities for men, the more fittingly is God to be honoured of men.

What then does He mean by the words: *Blessed is he that shall not be scandalised in me*, if not to signify clearly the abjection and lowliness of His own death? As if He were openly to say: I indeed work wonders, but I disdain not to endure humiliations. Because, however, I shall go thy way to death, men must take care not to despise Me in death, who now honour Me because of these wonders.

2. The disciples of John going their way, let us hear what He says to the multitude concerning the same John. *What went you out into the desert to see? A reed shaken by the wind?* Here He reproves them, not by asserting, but by denying something. Scarcely does the breath of a breeze touch a reed, when it bends the other way. And what is here meant by a reed unless a worldly human soul? Which, as soon as it is touched either by praise, or by detraction, is immediately inclined whatsoever way you will.

For if the wind of acclaim from a human mouth should caress it, it rejoices, it is lifted up, and bends itself over in gratitude. But should the wind of detraction blow from whence has already come the breath of praise, it immediately bends again the other way, yielding to the force of the storm. But John was no reed shaken by the wind, for he was neither flattered by praise, nor angered by detraction. Neither did prosperity uplift him, nor adversity cast him down. A reed shaken by the wind John was not, but a man whom no change of circumstances would turn aside from his path. Let us also learn, my dearest Brethren, not to be as reeds, shaken by the winds. Let us keep firm of soul amid the varying winds of mens' tongues; let our minds be steadfast. Neither let detraction provoke us to anger; and let no favour move us to bestow some harmful gift. Let good fortune not exalt us, nor adversity cause us unrest of soul, so that anchored to the security of faith, we may in no way be moved by the insecurity of temporal things.

3. Our Saviour continues to praise John's austerity: *But what went you out to see? A man clothed in soft garments? Behold they that are clothed in soft garments, are in the houses of kings.* John is described as being clothed in a *garment of camel hair.* And what means, *behold they that are clothed in soft garments are in the houses of kings*, unless that he openly makes it plain that they fight not for a heavenly but for an earthly kingdom, who in God's service ever shun what is painful, give themselves over solely to outward things, and seek the soft things and the delights of this life.

Let no one believe that sin can ever be absent from soft living, and from the love of precious clothing. Because if there were no fault in it, Our Lord would scarcely have praised John for the austerity of his clothing. If there were no fault, neither would the Apostle Peter have reproved women in his Epistle for this very desire for precious garments, saying: *not in costly attire* (I Pet. iii. 2; I Tim. ii. 9). Consider then, what fault there may be should men also seek for the things from which the Pastor of the church has said that even women should abstain.

4. That John is said not to be clothed in soft garments can be interpreted in yet another way. He was not clothed in soft garments, because he did not condone with flattery the conduct of those who lived in sin, but rather upbraided them in bitter words, saying: *Ye brood of vipers who hath showed you to flee from the wrath to come?* (Lk. iii. 7.) Whence Solomon also has said: *The words of the wise are as goads, and as nails deeply fastened in* (Eccles. xii. 11). The words of the wise are compared to nails, and likewise to goads, because they do not caress, but pierce the follies of sinners.

5. *But what went you out to see? A prophet? Yea, I tell you and more than a prophet.* It is the prophet's office to foretell future events, not also to point them out. For this reason John was more than a prophet, because Him, of Whom he had prophesied, going before Him, he also pointed out, showing Him to his own disciples. Since it is denied that he is a reed shaken by the wind, since he is said not to be clothed in soft garments, since the name of prophet is inadequate to him, let us hear what then may fittingly be affirmed of him.

6. It follows on: *This is he of whom it is written: Behold I send my Angel before thy face, who shall prepare thy way before thee* (Mal. iii. 1). That which is called *angelus* in Greek, is in Latin messenger (*nuntius*). Fittingly therefore is he called Angel, who is sent to announce the Heavenly Judge; so that he may be in name that which he fulfils in his office. Exalted indeed is his name; but his life was no less exalted than his name.

7. Would, my dear Brethren, that we say not this to our own condemnation, namely: that all who are called by the name of priest, are also named as angels, as the prophet testifies; saying: *For the lips of the priest shall keep knowledge, and they shall seek the law at his mouth: because he is the angel of the Lord of hosts* (Mal. ii. 7).

You likewise can reach to the sublimity of this name, if you so wish. For each one among you, in as far as he is able, in as far as he responds to the grace of the heavenly invitation, should he recall his neighbour from evil-doing; should he seek to encourage him in doing what is good; when he reminds him of the eternal kingdom, or of the punishment of wrong-doers; whenever he employs words of holy import, he is indeed an angel. And let no one say: I am not capable of giving warning; I am not a fit person to exhort others. Do what you can, lest your single talent, unprofitably employed, be required of you with punishment. For he that had received no more than one talent was careful to bury it in the earth, rather than put it to profit. (Mt. xxv.)

We read that in the Tabernacle of God there were not alone golden drinking goblets but, at the command of the Lord, there also were made ladles, or spoons, for filling the drinking vessels. For the goblets here understand fulness of holy doctrine, for the ladles a small and restricted acquaintance with doctrine. One person being filled with the doctrine of sacred truth, inebriates the minds of those that hear him. Through what he says he perfectly fills the cup. Another knows that he cannot give fulness, but because he gives warnings as best he can, he truly offers a taste from his ladle!

You, therefore, who live in the Tabernacle of the Lord, that is, in the Holy Church, if you cannot fill up the goblets with the teachings of holy wisdom, as well then as you can, as far as the divine bounty has endowed you, give to your neighbours spoonfuls of the good word!

And when you consider that you have yourself made some little progress, draw others along with you; seek to make comrades on the road to God. Should one among you, Brethren, stroll out towards the forum or the baths, he will invite a friend whom he thinks is not busy to keep him company. This simple action of our ordinary life is pleasant to you, and if it be that you are going towards God, give a thought not to journey alone. Hence it is written: *He that heareth, let him say: come* (Apoc. xxii. 17); so let him who has heard in his heart the invitation of divine love, pass on to his neighbours around about him, the message of the invitation. And though a man may not have even bread wherewith to give an alms to the hungry; yet, what is still more precious, he is able to give who possesses but a tongue. For it is a greater thing to strengthen with the nourishment of a word that will feed the mind for ever, than to fill with earthly bread a stomach of perishable flesh.

Do not, my dearest Brethren, withhold from your brother the charity of a word. I admonish myself with you, that we abstain from every idle word, that we turn away from useless chatter. In as far as you are able to overcome the tongue, scatter not your words to the wind, since our Judge has said: *Every idle word that men shall speak,* *they shall render an account for it in the day of judgment.* (Mt. xii. 36.)

An idle word is one that is spoken without any profit in uprightness, or that is uttered without grounds of sufficient need. Direct your idle conversation towards a fondness for what will edify; think how quickly the days of your life are passing; recall how stern is the Judge Who is coming. Keep this counsel before the eyes of your soul; bring it to mind of your neighbour, so that, as far as in you lies, you may not fail to warn him, and so you also may with John, merit to be called angels, by Him Who liveth and reigneth world without end, Amen.

NOTES

[1] "We cannot doubt that whatsoever is spoken of in the psalms is to be considered as Evangelical prophecy: so that whoever it is speaks, a prophet speaks. And it is all to be referred towards the understanding of Our Lord Jesus Christ, to the knowledge of His Incarnation, Passion, and Kingdom, and to the power and glory of our own resurrection. But prophecies are closed and sealed to worldly wisdom, and to the prudence of this world." St Hilary, Introduction to the Psalms.

[2] PL 9, 978.

[3] This brief homily forms the three lessons of the second nocturn of this Sunday, in the Roman Breviary, and is translated from there. The reading, and exposition, of this prophecy of Isaias, in the first and second nocturns of the Second Sunday of Advent recall the prophetical, and mystical, preparation for the Coming of the Saviour; of which the third nocturn (the Gospel lesson, and homily) sets out the immediate and historical preparation.

[4] PG 57: hom. 36, 37. col. 413.

[5] PL vol. 53. Not challenged in PRM. Given also, as doubtful, under the name of St Augustine, 40, Appendix.

[6] PL. 76, 1095–1099.

[7] This interpretation St John Chrysostom vigorously refutes. See Homily Three for this Sunday.

THIRD SUNDAY OF ADVENT

THE GOSPEL OF THE SUNDAY

John i. 19–28

At that time: the Jews sent from Jerusalem priests and Levites to John, to ask him: Who art thou? And he confessed. and did not deny: and he confessed. I am not the Christ. And they asked him: What then? Art thou Elias? And he said: I am not. Art thou The Prophet? And he answered: No. They said therefore unto him: Who art thou, that we may give an answer to them that sent us? What sayest thou of thyself? He said: I am the voice of one crying in the wilderness, make straight the way of the Lord, as said the prophet Isaias. And they that were sent, were of the Pharisees. And they asked him, and said to him: Why then dost thou baptize, if thou be not Christ, nor Elias, nor The Prophet? John answered them, saying: I baptize with water; but there hath stood one in the midst of you, whom you know not. The same is he that shall come after me, who is preferred before me: the latchet of whose shoe I am not worthy to loose. These things were done in Bethania, beyond the Jordan, where John was baptizing.

Exposition from the Catena Aurea

Origen, *Tom. 6 in John*: The testimony which follows, spoken by John the Baptist concerning Christ, is read from the words beginning, *This was He of whom I spoke*, and ends with the words, *he hath declared himself*. Theophylactus: Or, differently: After the Evangelist narrated that which John was testifying concerning Christ: *He is preferred before me*, he now adds *when* John gave this testimony to Christ: hence he says: *and this is the testimony of John, when the Jews sent from Jerusalem priests and Levites to him*.

ORIGEN: The Jews of Jerusalem, being cousins of John the Baptist, who was of the priestly tribe, send priests and Levites in order to find out who John was; that is, they sent persons of importance, and from Jerusalem. So they treat him with a certain deference. We read of no similar approach by the Jews to Christ. But what the Jews sought of John, John sought from Christ, asking Him, by the mouth of his own disciples: *Art thou he that is to come, or expect we another* (Lk. vii. 19).

CHRYSOSTOM, *Homily 15 in John*: They regarded John as being of such upright character that they were prepared to accept his own testimony concerning himself. Hence is said: *to ask him: Who art thou?* AUGUSTINE, *Tr. 4 in John*: They would not have sent unless they had been impressed by the strength of his confidence; shown in this that he had taken it upon himself to give baptism.

ORIGEN: John, as it appears, saw from their question, that the priests and Levites were in doubt, thinking that perhaps it might be the Christ who was baptizing; but they took care not to confess this openly, lest they be thought indiscreet. Whereupon, so that straightaway this erroneous notion might be removed, and also that he might make clear the truth, he declares before all present that he is not the Christ. Hence there follows: *And he confessed, and did not deny: I am not the Christ*. Here we may add, that the time of the Coming of the Christ began to occupy the minds of the people, as being possibly now here; for those who were learned in the Law had ascertained that it was the time when He was to be looked for. For which reason Theodas had risen up, many joining him, and after him Judas of Galilee, *in the days of the enrolling* (Acts v. 36, 37). Since then they were eagerly awaiting the Coming of Christ, the Jews send to John, to ask, *Who art thou?* trying to find out if he would declare himself to be the Christ. But not because he said: *I am not the Christ*, did he deny the truth; for in this he confessed it.

GREGORY, *Homily 7*: He denied only that which he was not, not that which he was; so that, speaking the truth, he became His member, whose name he would not falsely usurp. CHRYSOSTOM: *Homily 15 in John, sparsim*: Or, differently; The Jews had a certain human attachment to John. They deemed it unfitting that he be held as less than Christ, because of the many proofs of John's excellence, chief of which was his illustrious origin, for he was a son of a Prince of the priests. Then there was his austere youth, and his renouncing of all human ties. In Christ was seen the opposite: His lowly birth, with which they reproached Him, saying, *is this not the son of the carpenter?* Then His poor food; the poverty of His clothing (Mt. xiii. 55). Since, therefore, John was continually sending them to Christ, they, preferring to have John as Teacher, send to him: thinking to draw him by flattery, so that he would declare himself the Christ.

They send to him, therefore, not such persons as they sent to Christ, obscure messengers, servants and partisans of Herod, but priests and Levites; and not those from anywhere, but from Jerusalem, that is, the most honoured among them. And they came that they might ask him, *Who art thou?* They came too, not as men, who were ignorant, and desirous of learning, but, as I have said, to lead him on. But John answered them, not in accordance with their questions, but according to their own hidden purpose. *And he confessed and he did not deny: and he confessed: I am not the Christ.*

Note here the wisdom of the Evangelist; for the third time saying almost the same thing, and revealing both the virtue of the Baptist, and the malice and foolishness of the Jews. No true servant will seize on the dignity of his master; and will reject it though profferred to him by many. The multitude, because of ignorance, had come to think that they should regard John as the Christ; but these others were aiming, from the perverse mind with which they questioned him, to entice him by flattery to do what they wished. For unless this was their aim, they would not have immediately put the other questions, and would have answered his words, *I am not the Christ*, by saying: "we had not thought that you were; did you think we came to ask you that"? But being caught as it were and shown up, they go on to another question. Hence follows: *And they asked him: What then: Art thou Elias?*

AUGUSTINE, *Tr. 4 in John*: They knew that Elias was to precede the Christ: for there were none among the Jews to whom the name of the Christ was unknown. They did not believe that this was the Christ: nor did they wholly believe that Christ was not to come. While they were hoping that He would, in the future, they stumbled on Him, as upon a stone, and already in their midst.

The Gospel continues: *and he said: I am not.* GREGORY: From these words a complicated question arises. On a certain occasion Our Lord, being questioned by His Disciples concerning the Coming of Elias, said to them: *If you will receive it, John is Elias* (Mt. xi. 14). John however, being also questioned, makes answer: *I am not Elias.* How can he be the prophet of the Truth, if his words agree not with the words of the same Truth?

ORIGEN: Someone may say, that John did not know that he was himself Elias; and they who believe in the theory of repeated incarnation, as of the soul putting on successively other bodies, use him as proof. The Jews inquire through the priests and Levites if he were Elias, since they regarded him as a living proof of re-incarnation; he being also of their own kindred, and not a stranger to their secret doctrines. On this account John replied: *I am not Elias.* For he knew of no earlier personal life. How otherwise does it seem reasonable, if, as a prophet enlightened by the Spirit, and as one who has spoken such things of God and the Only-Begotten, such a man did not know if his soul was ever in Elias[1]?

GREGORY: But if the truth is carefully sought for, that which appears contradictory will be found not to be so. For the angel said to Zachary concerning John: *and he shall go before him in the spirit and power of Elias* (Lk. i. 17); because as Elias will precede the Second Coming,

John precedes the First. As Elias is the Precursor of the Judge Who is to come, John is the Precursor of the Redeemer now present. John was therefore Elias in spirit, but not in person. That which the Lord said concerning his spirit, John denies of his person; for it was fitting that the Lord should speak to His Disciples regarding the spiritual character of John; but that John should make answer to a carnal minded people, not with reference to his soul, but to his body.

ORIGEN: He therefore replies to the priests and Levites, *I am not*; divining the purport of their question. For this last question put by the priests and Levites to John did not seek to find out if the same spirit were in both, but if John were Elias, who was taken up into heaven, now, without birth, appearing again, according to the expectation of the Jews. Apart from the question touching on transmigration, of souls . . . someone may say, that it is illogical that the son of Zachary the High Priest, born to him in his old age, and beyond human expectation, should be unknown to the priests and Levites; especially as Luke testifies (Lk. i. 65), that *at his birth fear came upon all their neighbours.* But perhaps since they expected Elias to come before the end of the world, they appear to be questioning him metaphorically: are you the one who will announce Christ at the end of the world? and he guardedly replies: *I am not.*

But as to the other question, that the birth of John could not be unknown to the priests, this is not surprising; for many were in similar error regarding the Saviour.

There were many who knew of His Birth from Mary, yet some were in doubt, believing He was John the Baptist, or Elias, or one of the prophets. So likewise in regard to John. Some did not know of his birth from Zachary. Some were doubtful, and believed indeed that Elias, whom they were expecting, had now appeared in John.

But though many prophets had come forth from Israel, one was especially awaited; he of whom Moses had foretold: *The Lord will raise a prophet out of the midst of their brethren like to thee: and I will put my words in his mouth.* (Deut. xviii. 18.) In the third place they then ask him, not if he was simply a prophet, but a prophet with the definite article. Hence follows: *Art Thou the Prophet?* The people of Israel knew that among all the prophets there had been, none among them was this one of whom Moses had spoken, who would stand as Mediator between God and men; and Who, having received from God a New Covenant, would bequeath it to His Disciples. Though they did not give this name to Christ, deciding that He was someone other than the Christ, John knew that Christ was the Prophet. Hence he answers: *No.* AUGUSTINE: or, because John was more than a prophet; since prophets foretell from afar; John showed Who was present in their midst.

The Scripture continues: They said therefore unto him: *Who art thou, that we may give an answer to them that sent us? What sayest thou of thyself?* CHRYSOSTOM: Note how insistent they are in their questioning, and how John, while dissipating with mildness those notions that were not true, puts forward that which was. Hence follows: *I am the voice of one crying in the wilderness.* AUGUSTINE: Elias had spoken those words; in John the prophecy is fulfilled.

GREGORY: From our own speech we know that the voice must first sound, that the word be heard. So John declares that he is a voice, because he precedes the Word; that by his ministry, the Word of God is heard.

ORIGEN, on the words *who art thou, that we may give an answer*: HERACLION, reflecting on John and the prophets, says, not very elegantly, that since the Saviour is the Word, we may think of John as the Voice; for the prophetic voice, of every degree, is but sound alone. To whom we must answer that unless the trumpet gives forth a certain sound, no one will prepare himself for the battle. If then the prophetic voice is but sound, how is it that the Saviour bids us to hear it? *Search*, He says, *the Scriptures.* John says of himself, not that he is a voice crying in the wilderness, but that he is the voice *of one crying* in the wilderness; the voice, namely, of Him Who stood and cried, saying: *if any man thirst, let him come to me, and drink* (Jn. vii. 37). He cries out, so that they who are far off may hear, and that those who are dull of hearing may understand, the greatness of the things that are proclaimed[2].

THEOPHYLACTUS: Or, because he now openly makes known the truth; for all who were of the Law spoke obscurely. GREGORY: Or, John cried out in the desert, because

he was announcing to the forlorn and unhappy Judea the consolation of a Redeemer.

ORIGEN: The purpose of the voice crying out in the wilderness is that the soul which has abandoned God may be recalled to the straight way of the Lord, not following the wickedness of the serpent path. The way of the Lord is made straight through contemplation; revealing itself in truth, and without mingling of error, and in deeds that conform with right reason, and which, after due reflection, are seen to be lawful. Hence follows: *make straight the way of the Lord, as said the prophet Isaias.* GREGORY: The way of the Lord to the heart is made straight, when the word of truth is received with humility; and life is guided by precept.

And they that were sent . . . ORIGEN: Having given a reply to the priests and Levites, they send to him again, from the Pharisees. Hence is written: *and they that were sent, were of the Pharisees.* As far as can be conjectured from the words themselves, I would say that this is a third testimony. Observe how, according to the sacerdotal or levitical character of the person who is questioning, the words *who art thou* are pronounced with fitting courtesy. There is nothing arrogant or bold in their manner, but all is as befits true ministers of God. But the Pharisees, true to their name, divided and quarrelling among themselves, thrust their overbearing voices at the Baptist. Hence follows: *And they asked him, and said to him: why then dost thou baptize, if thou be not Christ, nor Elias, nor The Prophet?*

Their manner was not of persons who desired to learn, but of such as would wish to prevent him from baptizing. As to this, I do not understand why they came to John, and even disposed for baptism. A possible answer is that the Pharisees came seeking baptism, not because they believed, but because they were afraid of the people. CHRYSOSTOM: Or, the priests and Levites were themselves Pharisees, and seeing they were unable to trip him by flattery, they now strive to work up an indictment against him, and make him declare himself what he was not. Hence follows: *And they asked him, and said to him: why then dost thou baptize etc.*, as though it seemed audacity to baptize if he was not the Christ, nor his precursor, nor the herald, that is the Prophet.

GREGORY: But a sanctified person, even when confronted with someone of perverse mind, is not turned from his zeal for good. So here also John answers the words of deceit with the words of life. Hence the Gospel continues: *John answered them, saying: I baptize with water,* ORIGEN: To this question what answer was there except to make it clear, that his was a corporal baptism?

GREGORY: John baptizes, not *with the Holy Ghost,* but with *water,* because, unable to forgive sins, he washes the bodies of those baptized by him with water; but their souls he cannot wash with pardon. Why therefore does he baptize who cannot, by his baptism, forgive sins? Unless that preserving the order of his Office of Precursor, he, who in his birth preceded Him that

was to be born, preceded also the Lord Who was to baptize. So he who was the Precursor of Christ in his preaching, became also His Precursor in baptizing; in imitation of the sacrament. He likewise declares, while he is announcing in their midst the Mystery of our redemption, that This was standing in the midst of men, and they knew it not. Hence follows: *There hath stood one in the midst of you, whom you knew not.* For the Lord, while appearing in the flesh, was visible indeed in the body, but invisible in majesty.

CHRYSOSTOM: He said this since it was fitting that Christ should mingle with the people, as one among many, everywhere teaching men to be humble. When however, he says, *whom you know not,* he means knowledge in the truest sense, that is, as to Who He is, and whence He comes. AUGUSTINE: The Lowly One could not be seen, and so *a shining light was lit.* THEOPHYLACTUS: Or, the Lord stood in the midst of the Pharisees, yet they knew Him not, though they considered themselves versed in the Scriptures. In so far as the Lord is there foretold, He was in their midst, that is, in their souls. But they knew him not because they did not know the Scriptures. Or, in another way. He was in their midst, because as Mediator between God and men, Christ Jesus stood in the midst of the Pharisees, desiring to unite them with God; but they knew Him not.

ORIGEN: Or again; To their first question, *why do you baptize,* he answered, *I baptize in water.* To their second, *if thou be not Christ,* he brings forward a public commendation of the super-excelling perfection of the nature of Christ; that such was His power that His Godhead, though veiled, is yet present in each one, and present everywhere throughout the world; which is thus briefly pointed out in the sentence, *there hath stood one, etc.*

This power is so diffused throughout the whole fabric of creation, that whatever is therein created, is by It created: *all things were made by him;* hence it is clear that He was in the midst of those who were inquiring from John the Baptist, why do you baptize? Likewise, that he said, *there hath stood one in the midst of you,* must be understood of us men. For since we are rational creatures, He stands in the midst of us; for this reason, that the soul, the principal part of man, is seated in the midst of his body. They therefore who so bear the Word in the midst of them, but do not know His nature, nor from what source He comes, nor in what manner He abides within them, these, therefore, though having the Word in their midst, know Him not, as John perceived. Hence, reproaching them, he says to the Pharisees, *Whom you know not.* Because the Pharisees, looking for the coming of Christ, had not reflected profoundly concerning Him, believing that He would be only a man, though a holy one.

But he says *there hath stood*: for the Father stands, being invariable and unalterable; His Word also stands, ever ready to save, even if He takes flesh, even though He is in the midst of men, uncomprehended and invisible. Lest however anyone may think, that He Who is

invisible, and Who penetrates every man, and the whole world, is other than He Who has assumed human flesh *and was seen upon earth and conversed with men* (Bar. iii. 38), he adds these words: *the same is he that shall come after me,* that is, Who after me will become visible. The word *after* here does not mean the same as when Jesus invites us to *follow after* Him. For in this latter case we are bidden to follow in His footsteps, so that we came to the Father. Here John means, as is plain from his teaching. He comes following upon John, so *that all may believe through Him,* being prepared by John's humbler doctrines, to receive the Perfect Word[3].

CHRYSOSTOM: As if to say: Believe not that my baptism suffices; for if my baptism were perfect, another would not come after me to give another baptism. This is but a preparation for His, and will be absorbed into that which is nigh, as a shadow and image. But after me He must come. Who will declare the reality. For if the first were perfect, place for a second would not be required. And so he adds: *Who is preferred before me.* He is nobler, more glorious. GREGORY: For, *who is preferred before me* is so said, as if to say *who was before me.* He comes after me, because born after me; He is preferred before me, because *He was before me.*

CHRYSOSTOM: Lest you think this excellence to be something comparative, and desiring to make plain His Incomparability, he proceeds: *the latchet of whose shoe I am not worthy to loose.* As much as to say: He is so far above me, that I am not worthy to rank among the least of

His servants: for to unlace shoes was the task of the most menial. AUGUSTINE: Even had he said that he was worthy only to untie His shoes, he would still have shown great humility. GREGORY: Or, in a different sense; it was a custom of the ancients that if a man were unwilling further to retain the woman who was his wife, he should untie the sandals of the one who came, by right of kinship, to claim her as a bride. How has Christ appeared among men, save as the Bridegroom of Holy Church? John has said: *he that hath the Bride is the Bridegroom* (Jn. iii. 29). Rightly therefore does John declare that he is unworthy to untie His shoes; as though he were openly to say: I am unworthy to uncover the feet of the Redeemer; and the title of bridegroom, which belongs not to me, I shall not usurp.

This can be interpreted in yet another way. Who does not know that sandals are made from the skins of dead animals? The Lord, becoming Incarnate, has appeared among us, as it were shod, because, over His Divinity, He has put on the mortality of our corruptibility. The shoe strings are the seals of a mystery. John therefore was unable to untie the strings of His shoes, because he was unable to unveil the mystery of the Incarnation. It is as if he were openly to say: is it to be wondered at, that He is preferred before me, Whose birth I see is after mine, but the *mystery* of Whose birth I cannot comprehend? ORIGEN: Some one not very elegantly has said that this is so to be understood: that I am not worthy that, because of me, He should come down from above and put on, as a shoe, our flesh.

CHRYSOSTOM: And because John, with befitting courage, preached to the multitude all that concerned Christ, the Evangelist also commemorates the place, saying: *These things were done in Bethania beyond the Jordan.* For John preached, not in a house, not *in a corner*, but across the Jordan, in the midst of a great multitude, all they being present who were baptized by him. Certain codices have, more correctly, Bethabora; for Bethania is not across the Jordan, nor in the desert, but close to Jerusalem.

GLOSS: There are two Bethanias, one across the Jordan, the other this side of it, and not far from Jerusalem; where Lazarus was raised from the dead.

CHRYSOSTOM: The Evangelist names the place, and for another reason. Since he is not telling of remote events, but of happenings in the recent past, he makes of those who were present and saw these things, witnesses of that of which he speaks; confirming his proof with the name of the place. ALCUIN: Bethania is interpreted as meaning the House of Obedience, through which it is implied that, in obedience to faith, all ought to come to baptism.

ORIGEN, *Tom. 6 in John.*: Bethabora is interpreted to mean the House of Preparation, and this agrees with the baptism of one who was preparing to the Lord a perfect people; Jordan, however is interpreted as *their descent.* What is this river unless Our Saviour, through Whom, entering into this world, it behoves us to be made clean; meaning however, not His Descent, but that of men? He it is Who separates those who receive their inheritance from Moses from those who receive their portion through Jesus; *whose streams maketh the city of God joyful* (Ps. xlv. 5).

As the great Dragon is said to dwell in the river of Egypt (Ezech. xxix. 3), so God dwells in this, rejoicing the City of God; for the Father is in the Son. And they who go down to it where they may wash themselves, put away the stains of Egypt, and are made ready to receive an inheritance; they are cleansed from leprosy, and made capable of receiving a duplication of grace. They also are made ready for the reception of the Holy Spirit; for that Spiritual Dove descends upon no other stream. John baptizes across the Jordan, as Precursor of the One who came to call, not the just, but sinners, to repentance.[4]

I. St Augustine: On the Gospel[5]

From Tract 4 in St John's Gospel

1. Your Sanctity[6] has often times heard, and it is something that is well known to you, that John the Baptist, as there was none greater born of woman, and none more humble in the knowledge of God, so in like manner none more merited to be the Bridegroom's friend: being zealous, not for himself, but for the Bridegroom; seeking not his own honour, but that of the Judge Whom he preceded as Herald. And as to the prophets who went before it was given to foretell what was to be fulfilled in Christ, so to John it was given to point Him out, as with the finger. For as Christ was not known by those who, before He came, believed not in the prophets, so was He unknown to them, though in their midst. For he first came in a lowly manner, and unperceived; and the more lowly, the more hiddenly; but the people through pride despised the lowliness of God, crucified their Saviour, and made Him their Condemner.

2. But He Who first came hiddenly, because He came in lowliness, shall He not in due time come manifestly, because He shall come in glory? You have heard the psalmist say: *God shall come manifestly: Our God shall come, and shall not keep silence* (Ps. xlix. 3). He kept silence that He might receive judgment; He shall not keep silence, when He shall begin to give judgment. It would not have been said that He *shall come manifestly*, unless before He had come hiddenly. Nor that He *shall not keep silence*, unless before He had been silent. In what manner did He keep silence? Ask of Isaias: *He shall be led as a sheep to the slaughter, and shall be dumb as a lamb before its shearer, and he shall not open his mouth* (Is. liii. 7).

But He *shall come manifestly, and shall not keep silence*. How shall He be manifest? *A fire shall burn before Him: and a mighty tempest shall be round about him* (Ps. xlix. 3). This tempest has the power to sweep all chaff from the threshing floor, where it is now being treaded out; and the fire power to burn what the tempest has scattered. Now he keeps silence; silent in judgment, but not silent in precept. For if Christ keeps silence, what do these

Gospels mean? And what the Apostolic teachings? What the song of the psalms, and the voices of the prophets? For in all these Christ keeps not silence. He keeps silence that He may not now give judgment; He is not silent in the Voice of His Teaching.

To give judgment He shall come in glory, and will appear to all, even to those who now believe not. But, among men, and Lowly, it must be that He was despised. For unless He were despised, He would not be crucified. Unless He were crucified, He would not shed His Blood; by which as with a price He redeemed us. He was crucified, that He might pay the price for us. He was despised, that He might be crucified. He came in lowliness, that He might be despised.

3. And because He appeared as it were in the night, in this mortal body, He lit for Himself *a shining light,* that He might be seen, This light was John (Jn. v. 35), of whom you have already heard many things: and the present passage of the Gospel contains the words of John, wherein He confesses from the beginning, what is most noteworthy: that he was not the Christ. For there was in John such virtue, that he would have been accepted as the Christ: and here his humility was tested: because he said that he was not, when it would have been believed of him that he was. Therefore *this is the testimony of John, when the Jews sent from Jerusalem priests and Levites to him, to ask him: who art thou?* They would not send, unless shaken by the power within him whereby he dared to give baptism. *And he confessed and did not deny.* What did

he confess? And he confessed that: *I am not the Christ.*

4. *And they asked him: What then? Art thou Elias!* For they knew that Elias was to precede Christ. To no one among the Jews was the name of the Christ unknown. They did not believe this man was the Christ; nor did they entirely believe that Christ was not to come, since they were hoping He would come. And so they stumbled on Him, present among them; they stumbled as upon an unnoticed stone. That stone till now was small, though already cut out, without labour of hands, from the mountain: as the prophet Daniel says that he is a stone *cut out of the mountain without hands.* Then what followed? *And it grew and became a great mountain and filled the whole earth* (Dan. ii. 35).

Let your Charity reflect upon what I say. Christ, before the Jews were, was already cut out from the mountain. The kingdom of the Jews is the mountain. But the kingdom of the Jews did not fill the whole earth. From there was this stone cut, because from there was the Lord born into this world. But wherefore without hands? Because without the work of man the Virgin brought forth Christ. And now this stone, but without work of hands, was present before the eyes of the Jews. But it was unnoticed. And understandably, for this stone had not yet grown and filled the whole earth; as He made clear in His Kingdom, which is the Church, by which He has filled the whole earth.

Because it had not yet grown they stumbled on it, as upon a stone: and there happened to them as was written: *Whosoever shall fall*

upon that stone, shall be bruised and
upon whomsoever it shall fall, it will
grind him to powder (Lk. xx. 18).
They first stumbled on the Lowly
One; He being raised on high will
come down upon them; but that
He Who is to come in glory may
crush them, first as a humble stone
He bruised them. They stumbled
at Him (Rom. ix. 32), and they
were bruised; not crushed, but
bruised. Coming in glory, He will
crush them.

But if the Jews are to be forgiven,
because they stumbled at the stone
that had not yet grown, what of
those who stumbled even at the
mountain? You know of whom I
am speaking. They who deny the
Church that is spread through the
whole earth stumble, not at a
humble stone, but at the mountain
which this stone became when it
grew. The Jews being blinded saw
not the humble stone: what blindness not to see the mountain?[7]

5. Accordingly they saw the
Lowly One, and they did not know
Him. He was revealed to them by
a shining light. For from the very
first he, than whom a greater
among them born of woman had
not arisen, declared: *I am not the
Christ.* Then was it said to him:
*art thou then Elias? He answered:
I am not.* For Christ will send
Elias to prepare the way before
Him: and he said: *I am not*; pre-
senting to us a difficulty.

For men must beware, lest understanding but little in this matter,
they may think that Christ has said
that which is contrary to what John
said. For in a certain place in the
gospel, when Our Lord Jesus Christ
had told them many things concerning Himself, His Disciples

asked Him: *why then do the scribes,*
that is, those skilled in the Law, *say
that Elias must come first?* And the
Lord answering, said, *Elias is
already come, and they have done unto
him whatsoever they had a mind; and
if you will receive it, he is John the
Baptist* (Mt. xvii. 10–13; x. 11–14).

The Lord Jesus Christ said: *Elias
is come and he is John the Baptist.*
But John, when asked, declared
that he was not Elias, as he was not
the Christ. And as he spoke truly
in saying that he was not the Christ,
so likewise did he speak the truth
when he declared he was not Elias.
How then reconcile the words of
the Herald with the words of the
Judge? It is not to be thought of
that the Herald spoke what was
false! For he spoke that which he
had heard from the Judge. How
then is it John says: *I am not Elias,*
and the Lord says: *he is Elias.*

On this occasion the Lord Jesus
Christ desired to prefigure His
own second coming, and to affirm
this: namely that John came in the
spirit of Elias. For what John was
in relation to the first coming,
Elias will be to the second. Since
there are two Advents of the Judge
so are there two Heralds of His
Coming. He Himself is the Judge;
the Heralds are two, but there are
not two Judges. For the Judge
must first come, that He may receive judgement. He sends before
Him the first Herald, and He calls
him Elias; because what John is
in the first coming, Elias will be in
the second.

6. And now let Your Charity
apply your mind to the truth of
what I am saying. When John was
conceived, or rather when he was
born, the Holy Spirit foretold that

which was to be fulfilled concerning this man: *and he shall*, He says, *go before Him in the Spirit and power of Elias* (Lk. i. 17). Not Elias, but in the spirit and power of Elias. What means, *in the spirit and power of Elias*? In the same Holy Spirit as in the case of Elias. Wherefore as in the case of Elias? Because what Elias will be to the second coming, this same John was to the first coming.

John therefore answered rightly. For the Lord said in figure, *John is Elias*; but John spoke literally when he answered, *I am not Elias*. If you consider the allegorical meaning of the office of Precursor, John is Elias; for what the one is to the first coming, the other is to the second. If you consider the distinct being of each person, John is John, and Elias is Elias. Having regard to prefiguration, the Lord rightly said, *He is Elias*; having regard to his own distinct being, John rightly answered, *I am not Elias*. Neither John spoke falsely, nor Christ; neither the Herald, nor the Judge, declared what was not true; provided you understand. Who shall understand? He that will imitate the humility of the Herald, and discern the majesty of the Judge. None was there more humble than this Herald. My Brethren, John had no greater merit than that which came from this humility; for when he could have deceived men, and could have been believed to be the Christ, and could have been accepted as the Christ, as he was of such excellence and virtue, yet he confessed to all men, and said, *I am not the Christ*.

Art thou Elias? Had he said, I am Elias, then Christ, already appearing in His second coming, would have given judgement; nor would He, even now, in His first coming, be judged. As though answering: Elias is yet to come, he says: *I am not Elias*. Have regard for the Lowly One, Whom John preceded, lest you feel the might of the Exalted One, before Whom Elias will come. For the Lord so ended His words: *he is John the Baptist that will come*. Here Elias came in figure; in his own person he is yet to come. Then Elias shall be Elias in person, whom John is now in figure. Now John is John in his true person, who is Elias in figure. Both Heralds portray each other in figure, yet each retains his separate being. But the Lord Judge is One, whether this Herald or that shall go before Him.

7. *And they ask him: what then? art thou Elias? And he said: I am not. Art thou the prophet? And he answered: No. They said to him: who art thou that we may give an answer to them that sent us? What sayest thou of thyself? He said: I am the voice of one crying in the wilderness.* Isaias said this last. In John is the prophecy fulfilled. *I am the voice of one crying in the wilderness.* What does the voice cry out? *Prepare ye the way of the Lord, make straight his paths.* Does it not seem to you that it is the office of the Herald to cry out: stand aside, make way? Unless it be that where a Herald says, *make way*, John says, *come*. A Herald sweeps men from before the path of the Judge; but John calls us to the Judge. Nay, John calls us nigh to the Lowly One, lest we feel the power of the Mighty Judge. *I am the voice of one crying in the wilderness.* He did not say: I am John, I am Elias, I am the Prophet. But what

did he say? I am called *the voice of one crying in the wilderness, prepare ye the way of the Lord*: I am prophecy itself.

8. *And they that were sent were of the Pharisees, that is,* from the princes of the Jews. *And they asked him and said to him: why dost thou baptize, if thou art not Christ, nor Elias, nor the Prophet?* As if it seemed temerity on his part to baptize; as if they asked, by what authority? We asked you whether you are the Christ. You say you are not. We ask whether perhaps you are not His precursor, for we know that Elias will come before the advent of the Christ. You say you are not. We ask if perhaps you are a certain surpassing Herald, that is, The Prophet, and have received this power? And you say that neither are you The Prophet. And John was not a prophet. He was greater than a prophet. The Lord has given this testimony of him: *what went you out into the desert to see? A reed shaken by the wind?* Not indeed one shaken by the wind, as you will agree; for such John was not, as one moved about by the wind: for one that is moved by the wind, means one who is blown about by every seductive spirit.

But what went you out to see? One clothed in soft garments? For John was clothed in rough garments, in a tunic made from camel's hair. *Behold they who dress in soft garments are in the houses of kings.* You did not therefore go out to see a man clothed in soft garments. *But what*

went you forth to see? A prophet? Yea, I tell you and more than a prophet (Mt. xi. 8, 9). Because prophets announced Him long before hand; John proclaimed Him here present.

9. *Why dost thou baptize, if you are not Christ, nor Elias nor the Prophet? John answered them saying: I baptize with water, but there hath stood one in the midst of you whom you know not.* The Humble One was not seen, and accordingly *a shining light* was lit. See how he stands aside, who could have been taken for the Other. *The same is He that shall come after me.* As we have said before, this means, Who was before me. *The latchet of whose shoe I am not worthy to loose.* How greatly he humbles himself? And for this was he the more exalted, since *he that humbleth himself shall be exalted* (Lk. xiv. 11).

John is not worthy to untie the laces of His shoe; and were he to say that he was, how humble would he yet be? Were he to say he was worthy, and had so spoken: "He comes after me, who was preferred before me, whose shoes I am barely worthy to loose"; he would yet have greatly humbled himself. But when he says that he is not even worthy of this, then was he truly filled with the Holy Spirit, who thus, as a servant acknowledged his Lord, and from a servant merited to become a friend, Through Jesus Christ Our Lord, Who with the Father and the Holy Ghost liveth and reigneth world without end, Amen.

II. St Leo: On Fasting and Almsgiving

On the Fast of the Tenth Month and on Offerings[8]

That of which the season of the year and our customary devotion reminds us, we, Dearly Beloved, in our paternal duty, now preach to you, namely; that you must observe the fast of the tenth month, whereby, for the complete harvest of all fruits, there is most fittingly offered to God, the Giver of them, an offering of self mortification. For what can be more salutary for us than fasting, by the practice of which we draw nigh to God, and, standing fast against the devil, defeat the vices that lead us astray.

For fasting was ever the food of virtue. From abstinence there arise chaste thoughts, just decisions, salutary counsels. And through voluntary suffering the flesh dies to the concupiscences, and the spirit waxes strong in virtue. But as the salvation of our souls is not gained solely by fasting, let us fill up what is wanting in our fasting with alms-giving to the poor. Let us give to virtue what we take from pleasure. Let the abstinence of the man who fasts be the dinner of a poor man.

Let us have thought for the protection of the widow, for the welfare of the orphan, for the comforting of those that mourn, for the peace of those who live in discord. Let the stranger be given shelter. Let the oppressed be aided, the naked be clothed, the sick cherished; so that whosoever has offered from his own works of justice a sacrifice of righteousness to God, the Author of all good things, may merit to receive from the Selfsame the reward of a heavenly kingdom.

Let us then fast on the fourth and sixth day of the week. On the sabbath let us likewise keep watch, together with the Blessed Apostle Peter, by the help of whose merits we may obtain that for which we pray, through the mercy of Jesus Christ Our Lord, Who with the Father and the Holy Spirit, liveth and reigneth, world without end, Amen.

III. St Maximus: On the Preparation for the Lord's Coming[9]

1. Last Sunday I spoke, I trust fully and sufficiently, of how, prepared and becomingly adorned, we should greet the Natal Day of the Lord, and observe in a worthy manner the coming festival. To observe the festival I repeat, so that though the day's solemnity may pass, the joy of its sanctifying grace may abide. For this is the special grace of the Lord's Birth Day, that while it goes on to all who in the future will receive it, it still remains with the devout souls to whom it was already given. Let us then be made clean in holiness, clothed in modesty, worthy in heart; and the nearer we approach the festival, the more circumspectly let us walk.

2. If women who have the care of a home will on certain days wash with water the garments that are soiled, should we not also make ready our souls for the Birth Day of the Lord, cleansing with our tears the stains of our conscience.

And they, should they find the garments so soiled and stained, that they cannot be made clean with water alone, add to the water the softening of oil and the acrimony of soap. We likewise, should we have committed sins that are not washed away by repentance alone, let us add the oil of almsgiving and the bitterness of fasting.

There is no sin so grave that abstinence will not cleanse, that almsgiving will not blot out. For, as the Holy Prophet says: *as water puts out fire, so the giving of alms extinguishes sin* (Ecclus. iii. 33). Great then is the power of almsgiving, which cools the glowing mass of our burning sins as from the fountain of its own good will, and puts out the fires of evil as with the waters of its own generosity; so that God, though offended by us, though provoked by our iniquities, is compelled to free him, because of alms, whom He had decreed to punish because of sin.

For in a manner we do violence to Him, when He is forced by our actions to change His own decree, and against the one and the same person to be moved first by the sternness of a judge, and then by the tender affection of a father. For God is the Father of the Just. He is the Judge of sinners. The Lord is therefore compelled by our good works to bestow His mercy on us, as He has Himself declared in the Holy Gospel; *From the days of John the Baptist until now, the kingdom of heaven suffereth violence, and the violent bear it away* (Mt. xi. 12). Let us examine the meaning of these words.

3. The kingdom of heaven is none other than Christ the Lord Who reigns on high. The phrase, to suffer violence, originally meant the action whereby something vague and indefinite was made more concrete by constant action. From the time therefore that John the Baptist announced the coming of the Saviour, from there the kingdom of heaven, which had for so long been fluid and undefined in the mind of the Jewish people, began, from the steadfast faith of those who believed, to become more definite, and all that former insubstantiality of the kingdom began, by reason of the frequency of his preaching, to take concrete form. So undefined was this kingdom to the Jews, that it passed over to the Gentiles; so fluid was it, that it flowed out among all peoples.

Now however it is compacted together, by the mass of those who believe, so that it remains firm and defined for ever, as the Scripture says: *and of His Kingdom there shall be no end* (Lk. i. 33). We are therefore, in a manner, making this kingdom defined, and we do violence against it, as the Gospel lesson says: *and the violent bear it away.* We do violence, I say, against the Lord, not by compelling, but by weeping; not provoking Him by insults, but by pleading with tears of repentance; not by blaspheming in pride, but by grieving in humility, O Blessed violence! Which is not repelled with indignation, but forgiven in mercy. Blessed violence, I repeat, which stirs up goodness in the one who suffers this violence, and brings reward to the one who inflicts it. An assault is made, and no one complains of injury; violence is suffered, and respect for order is increased. He that used most violence against Christ, is by Christ esteemed the most devoted.

Let us attack the Lord on the way, because He is the Way (Jn. xiv. 6), and after the manner of robbers let us despoil Him of His goods; let us take from Him His kingdom, His treasures and His life. But He is so rich and so generous that He will not resist us, and when He has given us all that is His, He still possesses all things. Let us assault Him, I say, not with sword, or staff, or stone, but with mildness, with good works, with chastity.

4. These are the weapons of our Faith, by means of which we wage war. That we may use these weapons we must however do violence to ourselves. We must drive out vice from our own members, that we may attain to the rewards of virtue. For we must first rule in our own hearts, before we can seize the kingdom of heaven. The Gospel says: *and the violent bear it away.* We are therefore thieves; thieves seize that which belongs to others. I can see that this is truly so. The Church has stolen Christ from the Synagogue; and, by doing violence, has seized the kingdom for another people. For the Saviour, sent under the Law, born under the Law, reared according to the Law, being neglected by the Jews, was seized by the Gentiles. He was lost by the Priests, and was found by sinners; as He Himself has said: *Publicans and sinners shall go into the Kingdom of Heaven before you* (Mt. xxi. 32). We are therefore thieves.

5. Nor is this to be wondered at, seeing from what source we descend. For it is written of our patriarch Benjamin: *a ravenous wolf* (Gen. xlix. 27). For he seized what was not his. So likewise we, as children of a ravenous wolf, have by our own effort carried off the Shepherd of another flock, as He Himself has said: *I was not sent but to the sheep that are lost of the house of Israel* (Mt. xi. 14). Christ then is carried off, when, rejected by the Jews, He is praised by the Gentiles. He is carried off, when, slain by the Jews, He was buried by us. He was carried off by the watching Apostles, and lost by the sleeping Pharisees; for even in their lying they confessed Him, when after His Resurrection they placed guards at His sepulchre, saying: *His Disciples came by night, and stole him away when we were asleep* (Mt. xxviii. 13).

Whence, mystically, we are to understand, that all who sleep lose Christ, and the vigilant find Him; and so the Apostle says: *Rise thou that sleepest, and rise from the dead; and Christ will enlighten thee* (Eph. v. 14). You see then that he is as one dead, who so sleeps that he does not guard the Saviour: so too the Pharisees being as it were dead could not keep watch over the Living. So, Brethren, let us not sleep, but keep watch about Our Lord and Saviour, to make sure with unceasing vigil that no one shall steal Him from the sepulchre of our hearts, lest we may have to say at some time: they came while we were sleeping and stole Him away. For we have enemies who will try to steal Christ from our hearts, should we lapse into sleep. So with unceasing watch let us keep Him within the sepulchre of our souls; there let Him rest; there let Him sleep; there when He wills, let Him rise again.

6. Therefore, Brethren, let us who are about to greet the Birth Day of the Lord clean our consciences from all defilement; and let us prepare for ourselves, not silken garments, but precious works. Elegant garments may adorn the body, but they do not adorn the conscience; unless you consider it more decorous, to go about elegant in dress and defiled in mind. That the clothing of the outward man may in all ways be becoming, let us first make worthy the dispositions of the interior man; that our bodily adornment may be the more perfect, let us wash away all spiritual stain.

It is of little profit to be well clothed, and stained with crime. Where the conscience is darkened, the whole person is under shadow. But we have the means whereby we may wash the stains of our consciences; as it is written: *give alms, and behold all things are clean unto you* (Lk. xi. 41). Good is the precept of almsgiving, whereby *we work with our own hands* (I Thess. iv. 11), and are made clean in heart, by the mercy of Our Lord Jesus Christ, Who with the Father and the Holy Spirit, liveth and reigneth world without end, Amen.

IV. St Gregory: On the Gospel

Given to the People in the Basilica of St Peter the Apostle [10]

1. In the words of this lesson the humility of John is commended to us, who, though he was of such virtue, that he could have been accepted as the Christ, chose steadfastly to remain as himself, so that he was not foolishly raised above himself by human esteem. For he confessed and did not deny, and he confessed: *I am not the Christ.* But by saying *I am not* he clearly denied that he was that which he was not, but did not deny that which he was; so that speaking the truth, he became His member Whose name he would not falsely usurp. For since he sought not the name of the Christ, he was made a member of Christ; because while he humbly sought to make clear his own lowliness, he thereby truly merited to share in His glory.

But from this portion of the Gospel that was read to us, some other words of Christ are brought to our memory, which give rise to an in-

volved question. In another place, Our Saviour, being questioned by His Disciples concerning the coming of Elias, replied: *Elias is already come, and they knew not, but they have done unto him whatsoever they had a mind and if you will receive it, John himself is Elias* (Mt. xvii. 12; xi. 14).

John, however, being questioned, says: *I am not Elias.* What is this, Brethren, that what Truth affirms, the prophet of Truth denies? There is a wide difference between, *He is* and, *I am not.* How then can he be the prophet of Truth, if, in his words, he is not in agreement with this same Truth?

But if the truth itself is carefully looked into, that which sounds contradictory, will be found not to be contradictory. For the Angel said to Zachary concerning John: *and he shall go before Him in the spirit and power of Elias* (Lk. i. 17). He is here said to come in the spirit and power of Elias, because, as Elias will precede the Second Coming of the Lord, so John precedes His First Coming. As the former is the Precursor of the Judge to come, the latter was made the Precursor of the Redeemer. John therefore in spirit was Elias, he was not Elias in person. What the Lord therefore declares as to the spirit, John denies of the person; as was fitting, as the Lord was giving utterance to a spiritual reflection regarding the character of John to His Disciples, while John was answering a carnal people, not concerning his spirit, but concerning his body; what John uttered seems contrary to truth, yet in no way does it depart from the path of truth.

2. But since he also denies that he was the Prophet, because not alone was he to foretell the Redeemer, but also to point Him out, he goes on to say who he is, when he continues: *I am the voice of one crying in the wilderness.* You know, Dearest Brethren, that the Only-Begotten Son is called the Word of the Father, as John testifies when he says: *In the beginning was the Word, and the Word was with God, and the Word was God.*

From your own speech you are aware that the voice first sounds, that the word may then be heard. John accordingly declares that he is a Voice, because he precedes the Word. Going before the Lord, Who is coming, he is called a voice, because through his ministry the Word of the Lord is heard by men. He also cries out in the desert, because he is announcing to the lost and unhappy Judea the consolation of her Redeemer.

What it is that he cries out, he goes on to say: *Make straight the way of the Lord, as saith the prophet Isaias.* The way of the Lord to the heart is made straight, when His words of truth are received with humility. The way of the Lord to the heart is made straight, when our life is lived in harmony with His precepts. Hence was it written: *if any one love Me, he will keep my word, and My Father will love him, and We will come to him, and make our abode with him* (Jn. xiv. 23). Whosoever therefore lifts up his heart in pride, whosoever burns with the fever of avarice, whosoever soils himself with the defilement of lust, closes the gate of his heart against the entrance of Truth, and, lest the Lord gain entrance, he fastens the gates with the locks of evil habits.

3. But they that were sent were insistent in their questioning: *why then dost thou baptize, if thou be not Christ, nor Elias, nor the Prophet?* This was said, not out of desire to learn the truth, but from an evil desire to foment discord; as the Evangelist implies when he says: *and they that were sent, were of the Pharisees*; as if he were openly to say: these people question John about his actions, because they know not how to inquire as to doctrine, only to be envious regarding it. But no devout person is ever turned aside from his zeal for what is good, even when confronted with a person of perverse mind. So likewise John, who answers the words of envy with the words of eternal life. For forthwith he replies: *I baptize with water; but there hath stood one in the midst of you, whom you know not.*

John baptizes, not *with the Holy Ghost*, but *with water*, because, being unable to forgive sins, he washes with water the bodies of those whom he baptizes; but their souls he cannot wash in pardon. Why then does he baptize, who cannot by his baptism, forgive sins, unless that, maintaining the order of his office of Precursor, he who in his birth preceded Him that was to be born, likewise, by baptizing, preceded the Lord Who was to baptize; and he who in preaching became the Precursor of Christ, became likewise His Precursor in baptizing, in imitation of the sacrament?

Who likewise while he was in this way, announcing the Mystery of our redemption, declares that This is already in the midst of men, and unknown to them; because the Lord, appearing in the flesh, was visible in His Body, but invisible in Majesty. Of Whom he also says: *He that comes after me, is preferred before me*. For, *is preferred before me* is so said, as if to say, Who Was before me. He comes after me therefore, because He was born after me; He is preferred before me, because He was before me. Speaking a little later, he adds this very reason, why He was preferred, when he says: *because He was before me*; as if to say: though born after me, He is far above me, because with Him the times of His Nativity impose no straitening. For He that in time was born of a mother, was Begotten of the Father before all time.

What reverence is due to Him he then teaches us by his own humility; going on to say: *the latchet of whose shoe I am not worthy to loose*. It was a custom of the ancients, that if a man were not willing to retain the woman who was his wife, that he should untie

the shoes of the one who came by right of kinship to claim her as bride. How has Christ appeared among men, except as the Bridegroom of the Church? Of Whom also the same John says: *He that has the Bride is the Bridegroom* (Jn. iii. 29). But as men believed that John was the Christ, which he denied, he rightly makes it plain, that he is unworthy to untie His shoes. As if he were openly to say: I am not worthy to uncover the feet of the Redeemer, and the title of Bridegroom, which is not mine, I shall not usurp.

This may be understood in yet another way. Who does not know that sandals are made from the skins of dead animals? The Lord, in becoming Incarnate, appears among men, as though shod; because over His Divinity, he has put on as it were the mortal covering of our corruptibility. Hence also the prophet says: *Into Edom will I stretch out my shoe* (Ps. xv. 10). The Gentiles are signified by Edom; His assumed mortality by the shoe. The Lord therefore declares that He extends His shoe into Edom, because through the flesh He became known to the Gentiles; as if the Divinity had come to us with feet shod.

But the human eye does not suffice to penetrate the mystery of this incarnation. For in no way may we search out how the Word became embodied; how the Supreme Life-Giving Spirit, was quickened within the womb of a mother; how That Which has no beginning was both conceived and came into existence.

The latchets of His shoe are therefore the seals of a mystery. John was not worthy to loose His shoe, because he was unable to search into the mystery of His Incarnation. What then does he mean when he says, *the latchet of whose shoe I am not worthy to loose,* except openly and humbly to confess his ignorance? It is as though he were to say: what wonder that He is preferred before me, Whom I know to be born after me, but the Mystery of Whose Birth I am unable to comprehend. Behold John, filled with the Spirit of prophecy, shining with knowledge, yet he plainly declares that as to this mystery he knows nothing.

4. In this connection, Dearest Brethren, we should note and ponder with careful thought, how holy men of God, in order to safeguard themselves in humility, when they know many things well, endeavour to keep before their minds that which they do not know, so that on the one hand, they remind themselves of their own limitations, and on the other, they are not raised above themselves because of those things in which their mind is accomplished. Knowledge indeed is virtue, but humility is the guardian of virtue. For the future then, let you be humble in your minds with regard to whatever you may know, lest what the virtue of knowledge has stored, the wind of vanity may carry off.

When therefore, Dearest Brethren, you do any good, ever recall to memory the sins you may have committed, so that while you are discreetly mindful of the evil you may have done, your mind will never indiscreetly rejoice over the good you do. Let each esteem his neighbour as better than himself,

especially those who are strange to you, even those whom you see do that which is wrong, because you know not the good that may be hidden in them. Let each one seek to be worthy of esteem, yet let him be as if he knew not that he was, lest haughtily claiming esteem, he lose it.

Hence was it also said by the prophet: *Woe to you that are wise in your own eyes, and prudent in your own conceits* (Is. v. 21). Hence likewise Paul says: *be not wise in your own conceits* (Rom. xii. 16). Against Saul who had grown proud, was it said; *when thou wast a little one in thine own eyes, wast thou not made the head of the tribes of Israel* (I Kgs. xv. 17); as if it were openly said: when you looked upon yourself as but a youth, I raised you above others, but because you now look upon yourself as a great man, by Me you are regarded as a child.

David on the contrary, holding as nothing the dignity of his kingship, danced before the ark of the covenant, saying: *I will both play and make myself meaner than I have done: and I will be little in my own eyes* (II Kgs. vi. 22). Whom it hath not exalted to break the jaws of lions, to overcome the strength of bears, to be chosen while his elder brothers are set aside, to be anointed in the place of the rejected king, to lay low with one stone the warrior dreaded by all, to bring back the number of foreskins desired by the king, having avenged the kings enemies, to receive a kingdom by promise, to possess the whole Israelitish people without challenge (I Kgs. xvii. 37; II Kgs. xii. 7; I Kgs. xvii. 25, 28, 49; II Kgs. vii. 12, 16); yet with all this he despised himself, and confessed that he was but little in his own eyes.

If therefore holy men, even when they do mighty things, think themselves worthless, what must be said of those who, without fruit of virtue, are yet swollen with pride? But any works, although they be good, are as nothing unless seasoned with humility. A great deed done boastfully, lowers rather than uplifts a man. He who would gather virtue without humility, carries dust in the wind; and where he seems to possess something, from the same is he blinded and made worse.

In all things whatsoever, Dearest Brethren, that you do, hold fast to humility, as to the root of every good work. Pay not heed to the things in which you are better than others, but to those in which you are worse; so that while you keep before you the example of those that are better than yourself, you may, through humility, be enabled to ascend to greater things, by the bountiful mercy of Our Lord Jesus Christ, to whom be honour and glory for ever and ever, Amen.

NOTES

[1] Cf. PG 14, 222.

[2] Cf. PG 14, 231.

[3] PG 14, 251, *et seq.*, *sparsim*.

[4] Cf. PG 14: cols. 270, 283, 293.

[5] PL. 35, 1406–1410.

[6] Title used from the iv cent. on; also used, Your Charity, Your Holiness, et sim.; addressed to Emperor, clergy, nuns, congregations. GLL.

[7] The reference here is to the schismatic Donetists.

[8] This brief homily provides the lessons of the second nocturn of the Third Sunday of Advent, and is translated from the Roman Breviary.

[9] Variously attributed to St Augustine and to St Ambrose, PL 17, 608, now in Bruni's edition of St Maximus.

[10] PL 74. 1099–1103 (Homily 7).

FOURTH SUNDAY OF ADVENT

I. Origen: On the Gospel

II. St Leo the Great: On Fasting and Offerings

III. St John Chrysostom: On the Gospel

IV. St Gregory the Great: The Mystical Church

THE GOSPEL OF THE SUNDAY

Luke iii. 1–6

Now in the fifteenth year of the reign of Tiberius Caesar, Pontius Pilate being governor of Judea, and Herod being tetrarch of Galilee, and Philip being tetrarch of Iturea, and the country of Trachonitis, and Lysanias tetrarch of Abilina; under the high priests Annas and Caiphas; the word of the Lord was made unto John, the son of Zachary, in the desert. And he came into all the country about the Jordan, preaching the baptism of penance for the remission of sins; as it was written in the book of the sayings of Isaias the prophet: *a voice of one crying in the wilderness: prepare ye the way of the Lord, make straight his paths. Every valley shall be filled: and every mountain and hill shall be brought low; and the crooked shall be made straight; and the rough ways plain; and all flesh shall see the salvation of God.*

PARALLEL GOSPELS

Matthew iii. 1–6

And in those days cometh John the Baptist preaching in the desert of Judea. And saying: do penance: for the kingdom of heaven is at hand. For this is he that was spoken of by Isaias the prophet, saying: *A voice of one crying in the desert, prepare ye the way of the Lord, make straight his paths.* And the same John had his garment of camel's hair, and a leathern girdle about his loins: and his meat was locusts and wild

Mark i. 4–8

John was in the desert baptizing, and preaching the baptism of penance unto remission of sins. And there went out to him all the country of Judea, and all they of Jerusalem, and were baptized by him in the river of Jordan, confessing their sins. And John was clothed with camels' hair, and a leathern girdle about his loins; and he ate locusts and wild honey. And he preached, saying: There cometh after me one mightier than

71

honey. Then went out to him
Jerusalem and all Judea, and all the
country about Jordan: And were
baptized by him in the Jordan,
confessing their sins.

I, the latchet of whose shoes I am
not worthy to stoop down and
loose. I have baptized you with
water; but he shall baptize you with
the Holy Ghost.

EXPOSITION FROM THE CATENA AUREA

1. *Now in the fifteenth year of the
reign* . . . GREGORY, *Hom.* 20 *in Ev:*
The time in which the Precursor of
the Redeemer received the word of
his mission is marked by the commemoration of the names of the
rulers both of the Roman Republic
and of the Kingdoms of Israel,
where it is said: *In the fifteenth year
of the reign of Tiberius Caesar,
Pontius Pilate being governor of Judea*
. . . Because he was come to announce Him that would redeem
some in Israel, and many from the
Gentiles, the time of this announcing is signified as well through the
King of the Gentiles as by the
Princes of the Jews. Because the
Gentiles were to be brought together, but one person is recorded
as ruling the Roman Republic, in
the words: *The reign of Tiberius
Caesar.*

METAPHRASTES, *Catena of G.F.*;
Augustus, from whom the Roman
rulers adopted the name of Augustus, being now dead, and following him Tiberius, having succeeded
to the Imperial power, was now
in the fifteenth year of his reign.
ORIGEN, *Hom.* 21 *in Luke:* In
Prophesying to the Jews alone, only
the kingdom of the Jews is referred
to, as: *The vision of Isaias in the days
of Izias, Joachim, and Ezechias, kings
of Israel* (Is. i. 1). But in the gospel,
which was preached to the whole
world, the empire of Tiberius is
spoken of; he who now seemed

master of the world. If only those
from the Gentiles were to be saved,
it would have sufficed to mention
Tiberius Caesar; but since it was
also necessary for the Jews to
believe, the kingdoms of the Jews,
or the tetrarchies, are also recorded
in the words: *Herod being* . . .

GREGORY, as above: Since because
of their perfidy the Jews were to
be dispersed, their kingdom was
divided among many, according to
the words: *Every kingdom divided
against itself shall be brought to
desolation.* BEDE, *in Luke* 3, 19:
During the twelfth year of Tiberius
Caesar, Pilate was sent into Judea as
Procurator of the Gentiles and remained there for ten continuous
years, almost till the end of the
reign of Tiberius. Herod and Philip
and Lysanias were the sons of that
Herod under whom the Lord was
born, among whom was also Herod
Archelaus their brother, who
reigned for ten years, and who being denounced to Caesar by the
Jews, died in exile at Vienne. That
the kingdom of the Jews might be
made weak, the same Augustus
commanded it to be divided into
tetrarchies.

GREGORY: Because John preached
Him Who was both King and
Priest, Luke the Evangelist designates the time of his preaching,
not alone through kings, but also
through priests. Hence: *Under the*

High Priests Annas and Caiphas.
BEDE: Both, that is, Annas and Caiphas, were High Priests when John began his preaching. But Annas governed that year, Caiphas the year Our Lord ascended the Cross, three others having fulfilled the office of Pontiff in the meanwhile; but those who had especially to do with the Passion are commemorated by the Evangelists. For by this time all legalities had been set aside, and because of violence and ambition the honour of the Pontificate was given to no one by reason of merit or descent; the dignity of the office being now allotted by the supreme power of Rome. Josephus relates that Valerius Graccius, Annas being deposed from the Pontificate, named Ismael son of Baphos as Pontiff. A little later, setting him aside, he put in his place Elazar, the son of the Pontiff Ananias. After a year he excluded him from the office, and gave the Pontificate to a certain Simon, son of Caiphas, who, barely filling it for the space of a year, was succeeded by Josephus, to whom the name Caiphas also belonged. So that all this time in which it is written that our Lord was teaching, is contained within the space of four years.

AMBROSE. *Book II in Luke:* The Son of God, being about to bring together His Church, first works through his young servant: and so it is well said: *the word of the Lord was made unto John,* etc., so that the church has its beginning not from man, but from the Word. Fittingly does Luke use brevity in declaring John a prophet, saying: *The word of the Lord was made unto John.* He does not add more. He needs no confirmation who abounds in the word of the Lord. He therefore speaks but one word, and in that says all. But Matthew and Mark wished also to show him a Prophet, in his clothing, in his cincture, and in his food.

CHRYSOSTOM, *Homily 10 in Matth:* The *word* of God is here said to have been *sent*; because not of himself went forth the son of Zachary, but moved by God. THEOPHYLACTUS: All the time previous to this, until his manifestation, he was hidden in the desert, and this is why there is here added: *in the desert,* so that no suspicion would arise among men, that he undertook this task by reason of kinship with Christ, or because of their association in childhood; hence he himself giving testimony says: *and I knew Him not* (Jn. i, 33).

GREGORY NYSSA, *De Virginitate:* Entering this life as he did, in the spirit and power of Elias, he also removed himself from all human concourse, giving himself to the consideration of things invisible, lest, habituated to the kinds of deceptions that enter through the senses, he might fall into confusion or error in the discernment of the true good. Because of this he was raised to such a degree of divine favour, that even more than the prophets was he enriched with divine grace; because, being free of the world, and of every natural passion, he made to the divine Presence the offering, from the beginning unto the end, of all his desire. AMBROSE: The desert is also the church; for *many are the children of the desolate, more than of her that hath a husband* (Is. liv. 1).

The word of the Lord came therefore, so that she who before was desolate, might from the earth bring forth fruit in us.

2. *And he came into all the country about the Jordan,* etc., AMBROSE: The word being made, the voice follows; the word being formed interiorly, then follows the service of the voice; hence is said: *and he came into all the country about the Jordan.* ORIGEN *Luke 2, Homily 2*: Jordan means a *descent.* The river of God descends, a stream of wholesome water. What place more fitting to go to give baptism than the neighbourhood of the Jordan? So that should it happen that a man is moved to repentance, the contrite soul could quickly run to the nearby stream, to receive the baptism of penance. The Evangelist continues: *preaching the baptism of penance unto the remission of sins.*

GREGORY, *Homily 20*: It is plain to all who read, that John not merely preached the baptism of penance, but also bestowed it on many; yet he could not give his baptism in forgiveness of sins.

CHRYSOSTOM, *Homily 10, 2, in Matthew*: Since the Victim had not been offered, nor had the Holy Spirit yet descended, of what kind was this remission of sins? What does Luke mean by this: *for the remission of sins?* Because the Jews were ignorant and unreflecting, and had not weighed carefully the evil of their own sins. And since this was the reason of their tribulations, that they might acknowledge their sins, and make ready for the Redeemer, John came, exhorting them to penance, so that being thus disposed and truly contrite, they may be ready to receive forgiveness. Fittingly therefore, when he had said he came *preaching the baptism of penance,* he adds: *for the remission of sins;* as if to say: he persuaded them to repent of their sins, so that later they might the more easily receive pardon through believing in Christ. For unless brought to it by repentance, they would not seek for pardon. His baptism therefore served no other end than as a preparation for belief in Christ.

GREGORY: Of John it is written, *preaching the baptism of penance for the remission of sins;* since he preached the baptism which could wipe out sins, but which he was unable to bestow. As he preceded the Incarnate Word of the Father by the word of preaching, so did he precede the baptism of penance, by which sins are forgiven, by his own baptism, by which sins could not be forgiven. AMBROSE: And for this reason many regard John as a Type of the Law, in this, that he could reprove sin, but could not pardon it.

GREGORY NAZIANZEN, Oratio 39: Let us here treat briefly of the different kinds of baptism. Moses baptized, but in water, *in the cloud and in the sea;* but this he did figuratively. John also baptized, not indeed in the rite of the Jews, not solely in water, but also unto the remission of sins; yet not in an entirely spiritual manner, for he had not added: *in the spirit.* Jesus baptized, but *in the Spirit;* and this is perfection. There is also a fourth baptism, which is wrought by martyrdom and blood, in which Christ Himself was also baptized, which is far more venerable than the others, in as much as it is not soiled by repeated contagion. There is yet a fifth, but more laborious, by tears; with which David each night bedewed his bed, washing his couch with tears (Ps. vi. 7).

3. The Gospel continues: *as it was written in the book of Isaias*, etc.

AMBROSE: John, as harbinger of the Word, is fittingly called a Voice; the voice, as the inferior, goes before; the Word, which excels, follows after. GREGORY, *Homs. 7 and 20 in Evang*:Which cried out in the wilderness, that it may also announce to the lost and unhappy Israel the consolation of its Redeemer. That which he cries is told to us, when it is announced: *prepare ye the way of the Lord*. Everyone who preaches true faith and good works, what else does he do but prepare the way of the Lord to the hearts of his hearers; so that he may make straight the path for God, when he forms worthy desires within their soul by the influence of his own good words.

ORIGEN, *Hom.* 21: The way of the Lord must be prepared within our heart; for great and spacious is the heart of man, as if it were a world. But see its greatness, not in bodily quantity, but in that power of the mind which enables it to encompass so great a knowledge of the truth, Prepare therefore in your heart the way of the Lord, by a worthy manner of life; and by good and perfect works keep straight this path of your life, so that the words of the Lord may enter in without hindrance.

BASIL, *in Catena G.F.*: Because the path is a way along which those who have gone before have walked,and which earlier men have neglected, these words command those who have fallen from the zeal of those who went before, to remake it. CHRYSOSTOM: To cry out, *prepare the way of the Lord*, was not the office of the King, but of the Precursor; and so Scripture calls him a Voice, because he was a precursor of the Word.

CYRIL, *Book 3 in Isaias*, 40: But if one should answer to this and say: which way of the Lord shall we prepare, or, what paths shall we make straight, since many are the obstacles to those that desire to lead a virtuous life? To this the prophetic words make answer. There are certain ways and paths, which are by no means suitable to this end; since some lead over hills and mountains, and others lead down the slope. To meet this he says: *Every valley shall be filled: and every mountain shall be brought low*. Certain also of the paths are unevenly laid down, here they rise up, there again they drop down; and they also are dangerous in regard to this same purpose. As to this he adds: *And the crooked shall be made straight and the rough ways plain*. This is accomplished, spiritually, however, through the power of the Saviour. Before, the way of evangelical belief and living was difficult for men, because worldly pleasures bore heavily on the minds of all men. But God, made man, *has condemned sin in the flesh* (Rom. viii. 3), and all things have become straight and unimpeded, and easy, to this end; nor will hill or valley now stand in the way of those who wish to go forward.

ORIGEN, *Hom.* 22: For when Jesus came, and sent forth His Spirit, every valley was filled with good works and the fruits of the Holy Spirit; which, if any one possesses, not alone does he cease to be a valley, but he begins to be a mountain of God. GREGORY NYSSA, *in Catena of G.F*: By enclosed valleys is signified a peaceful manner of living, and one filled with good works; as in Psalm 64: *and the vales shall abound with corn.* CHRYSOSTOM, *in cat. G.F.*: Scripture gives to the vain and the proud the name *mountain,* and these the Lord has humbled; *hills* it applies to those who are without hope; not alone because of the pride of their own minds, but because of the sterility of despair; for the high hills bring forth no fruit. ORIGEN, *Hom.* 22 *in Luke*: Or, you can understand by hills and mountains the inimical powers which were thrown down by the coming of Christ. BASIL: As hills and mountains differ, in respect of size, in other things they are the same; so the powers of evil, are alike in their evil purpose, but differ from each other in the intensity of their malice.

GREGORY, *Homily* 20: Or, the valley that is filled will grow, the mountain and the hill that is brought low will dwindle away; because in faith in Christ, the Gentiles will receive the fulness of grace, and Judea, through the error of her pride which hath caused her to swell up, has been brought down. For the humble have received the gift which the proud in heart rejected.

CHRYSOSTOM, *Hom. in Matth*: Or, by this he declares that the harshness of the Law has been changed into the simplicity of faith, as if he says: no more do toil and grief oppress us, for grace and the pardon of sin make easy the way of salvation. GREGORY NYSSA: Or, He orders the valleys to be filled, and the hills and mountains laid low; desiring to show that the straight path of virtue is neither made void by sin, nor disturbed by any excess. GREGORY: Crooked ways are made straight, when the hearts of men, distorted by evildoing, are made straight by the rule of justice. Rough ways are made smooth, when cruel and angry men are led by the infusion of heavenly grace to the mildness of gentle conduct.

CHRYSOSTOM, as above: Then Scripture adds the reason of all these things: *and all flesh shall see the salvation of God*; showing that the power and the knowledge of the Gospel will be spread to the ends of the world, converting the human race from their animal life, and stubborn will, to clemency and gentleness. Not alone, therefore, the proselyte Jews, but the whole human race, will see the salvation of God. CYRIL, *Book* 3 *in Isaias* 40: That is, of the Father, who has sent His Son as our Saviour. Flesh in this context is to be taken for all humanity. GREGORY, *in Homily* 20: Or again; all flesh, that is, every man, cannot see the salvation of God, that is Christ, in this life. The Prophet therefore directs his eye to the last day of the Judgment, when all, the elect equally with the reprobate, shall behold Him.

I. ORIGEN: ON THE GOSPEL[1]

When a prophetic message was intended for the Jews alone the names of the Jewish Kings were placed at the beginning. For example: *The vision of Isaias . . . in the days of Ozias, Joachim, Achaz, and Ezechias, Kings of Israel:* (Is. i, 1) nor other names do I see designated in the time of Isaias, except the kings of Judah. In certain prophets we can read narratives of the Israelite kings, as in Osee (Osee i, 1), where he says: *In the days of Jeroboam, the son of Joas, a king of Israel.* When however the mystery of the Gospel was to be proclaimed, and its word spread abroad through the whole world, in which John in the desert was the leader, and the world lay under the Roman Empire of Tiberius, it is recorded, that in the fifteenth year, *the word of the Lord was made unto John.* If salvation was to be announced alone to the nations that were to believe, and Israel was to be entirely excluded, it would have sufficed to say: *in the fifteenth year of Tiberius and under the governorship of Pilate.* But, because many were to believe both from Judea and from Galilee, these kingdoms are also recorded in the inscription; and so it is written: *and Herod being Tetrarch of Galilee, etc.*

Of old the word of the Lord was made unto Jeremiah, the son of Elchias in Anatoth, in the days of Josia King of Judea. Now a message of God is made unto John the son of Zachary, which never was given to the prophets in the desert; but since *more are the children of the desolate, than of her that hath a husband,* accordingly, the word of

God is made unto John the son of Zachary in the desert. Note, that this has more meaning if the desert is considered mystically, and not according to its literal sense. For he who preaches in the desert it is needless to cry out aloud, since there is no one to hear him speaking. Therefore the Precursor of Christ, and the voice of one crying in the wilderness, preach in the desert of the soul that has known no peace. Not alone then, but even now a bright and burning lamp first comes and preaches the baptism of repentance unto the forgiveness of sins. Then follows the True Light, as itself has said: *He must increase, but I must decrease* (Jn. iii. 30).

The word was made in the desert, and came forth to all the country about the Jordan. For around what other places should the Baptist journey unless those close to the Jordan, so that whosoever had the will to repent, would there be near the water of purification? The name of Jordan is interpreted as *descent,* or *coming down.* Coming down and running in a bounteous flood is the River of God, the Lord our Saviour, in which we were baptized. This true and life-giving water is, he proclaims in his baptism, unto the forgiveness of sins. Come then, Catechumens, do penance that you may receive in baptism the forgiveness of your sins. He that ceases to commit sin, will, in his baptism, be forgiven his former sins. But if he remain in his sins, and so approaches the baptismal font, his sins will not be forgiven him.

Therefore I beseech you, that

you approach not to receive baptism without due caution and careful reflection. Strive first for *fruits worthy of penance.* Remain for some time in a becoming manner of living. Cleanse yourself of uncleanness. Keep yourself free from the vices; then when you have begun to stamp out your offences, remission of your sins will be given unto you. And that you may be forgiven, forgive those that offend you.

This same message we find in the Old Testament, in the prophet Isaias: *A voice of one crying in the wilderness* . . . For the Lord wishes to find in you a way prepared before Him, where He may enter in, and have there a right of way. Prepare for Him this path, of which is written: *Make straight his path.*

The voice cries: *Prepare ye the way of the Lord.* First the voice strikes upon the ear, then after the voice, indeed together with the voice, the word penetrates the mind. In this way was Christ announced by John. Let us then hear what the Voice announces concerning the Word. *Prepare ye,* it says, *the way of the Lord.* Which way shall we prepare for the Lord? A way on the earth? Can the Word of God travel such a road? Or rather must we not prepare the way within us, setting up in our hearts a straight and true way?

This is the way through which the Word of God enters, and comes to rest within the bounds of the human body. And great indeed is the heart of man, wide and spacious as if it were a world in itself. Do you wish to know how great and how profound it is? Behold what a sweep of divine knowledge it can embrace: *For he hath given me true knowledge of the things that are: to know the disposition of the whole world, and the virtues of the elements, the beginnings and the endings and midst of the times, the alterations of their courses, and the changes of the seasons, the revolutions of the year, and the dispositions of the stars, the natures of living creatures, and the reasonings of men* (Wisd. vii. 17).

See then that no small thing is the heart of man which can contain so much. And see also that its greatness is not in bodily quantity, but in the power by which it can receive such knowledge of the truth. Let me recall to you a simple example from our daily life, so that you may see how great is this power. Let us consider this. Through whatever cities we may have passed, we have still within our minds the style and the shape of their squares and houses and walls and buildings, stored in our memory. We keep within us, as in a picture, the roads, we have travelled. The sea we have voyaged over we can recall in moments of quiet recollection. No small thing, as I have said, is the heart of man.

If then it can contain so much, and is not something small and narrow, then let a way for the Lord be prepared in it, and let His path be made straight, so that the Word of God and His Wisdom may enter there. Prepare this way by a worthy manner of living. and with good works make straight the path, so that without hindrance the Word of God may tread this way to you, and give you understanding, both of His Coming and of His Mysteries, to Whom be glory and empire for ever and ever, Amen.

II. ST LEO, POPE AND DOCTOR

On the Fast of the Tenth Month and on Offerings[2]

Synopis:

    I. Man is so created that he imitates His Author; and this is a gift of God.

    II. The wideness of Christian love requires of us, that our charity embraces, not alone God and our neighbour, but also our enemies.

    III. That we be submissive to every judgment of God, and render thanks, no less for scarcity than for abundance.

    IV. All the virtues are comprised in prayer, fast, and almsdeeds.

Chapter I. If we, most dearly Beloved, judiciously and with reliance on God, seek to understand the beginnings of our own creation, we shall find that man was made to the image of God, in order that he might be an imitator of his own Creator; that it is but the natural dignity of our origin, if there should shine forth in us, as in a kind of mirror, the beauty of the divine goodness. To which dignity the grace of the Saviour does indeed daily restore us, in that what was overthrown in the first Adam, is raised up in the Second.

The reason of our restoration is none other than the mercy of God, we would not love Him unless He first loved us, and scattered the darkness of our ignorance, with the Light of His Own Truth; as the Lord, speaking through the holy Isaias, says: *I will lead the blind into the way which they know not: and in the paths which they were ignorant of I will make them walk: I will make darkness light before them, and crooked things straight: these things have I done to them, and have not forsaken them* (Is. xlii. 16). And again: *They have found me*, He says, *that sought me not, and I have appeared openly to those who did not call upon me* (Is. lxv. 1).

And in what manner this was fulfilled, the Apostle John teaches, saying: *We know that the son of God is come: and he has given us understanding that we may know the true God, and may be in His True Son* (I Jn. v. 20; iv. 19). And again: *Let us therefore love God, because God hath first loved us.* Accordingly, by loving us He restores us to His own Image: and that He may find in us the likeness of His own Goodness, He gives to us that whereby we also may do that which He worketh in us; lighting the lanterns of our minds, and kindling in us the fire of His own love, so that we may not alone love Him, but whatsoever He loveth.

For if among men that and that alone is true friendship which rests on resemblance of character, yet since equality of will at times tends towards unsound affections, how much must we strive and desire that we may not in any least way be in disagreement with those things which are pleasing to God! Concerning which the prophet says: *For wrath is in His indignation, and life in His good will* (Ps. xxix. 6); because in no other way does the dignity of the divine majesty appear in us, except in the imitation of His will.

Chapter II. Accordingly, the Lord says to us: *Thou shalt love the Lord thy God with thy whole heart, and with thy whole soul, and with thy whole mind.* Let the christian soul receive within it the unfading love of its Maker and its Guide, and let it submit its entire self to His Will, in Whose works and in Whose judgments nothing is wanting of the perfection of justice, nothing of the tenderness of mercy. Even though a man should suffer, in toils and in manifold afflictions, he has a good motive to sustain him who understands that he is being either proved, or corrected, by these misfortunes.

But the filial devotion of this love cannot be perfect, unless our neighbour is likewise loved. By which name not they alone are to be understood who are joined to us by friendship or by relationship, but all men whatsoever with whom we share our common nature, whether they be enemies or friends, freemen or slaves. For One Sole Maker has formed us, One Sole Creator has given us life; we all alike enjoy the same sky, the same air, the same days and nights; although some are good, some are evil; some are righteous, some unrighteous; yet to all God is the Provider, His bounty is for every man, as was said by the Apostles Paul and Barnabas to the people of Lycaonia, concerning the Providence of God: *Who in times past suffered all nations to walk in their own ways. Nevertheless he left not himself without testimony, doing good from heaven, giving rains and fruitful seasons, filling our hearts with food and gladness* (Acts xiv. 15–16).

But we have greater reasons for the love of our neighbour, given

to us in the widespread diffusion of Christian grace, which now, extending itself over every portion of the earth, teaches us, that while no one is to be despised, neither is any one to be neglected. And rightly does He bid us love our enemies, and pray for them that persecute us, Who daily from among all peoples, by inserting in the wild olive a graft from the holy branches of His own Tree, makes friends out of enemies, adopted children of strangers, and righteous men from evil-doers; *so that in the name of Jesus every knee should bow, of those that are in heaven, on earth, and under the earth, and that every tongue should confess that the Lord Jesus Christ is in the glory of God the Father* (Philip ii. 10).

Chapter III. Since God, because He is Good, wishes us to be good, nothing in His judgment should displease us. And not to give thanks to Him for all things, what is this other than to reproach Him for some part of them? And at times human folly presumes to murmur against the Creator, not alone because of want, but even because of abundance; so that when something is not supplied in abundance, it is querulous; and when certain other things abound, it is thankless.

The owner of that bountiful harvest who was annoyed at the overflowingness of his barns (Lk. xii. 16), and aggrieved at the richness of the yield, gave no thanks for the abundance of his crop, but complained at its cheapness. If the yield of the earth from the seed received is poor, and if the wine and the olives have failed because the crop was damaged, the years are blamed, the elements reproached, nor is the air itself spared, nor the sky; while on the other hand, nothing more sustains and strengthens Christian souls, the devout disciples of peace and truth, than persevering and unwearied praise of God, saying with the Apostle: *Always rejoice, pray without ceasing. In all things give thanks; for this is the will of God in Christ Jesus concerning you all* (I Thess. v. 16–18).

But how can we be partakers of this spirit of submission, unless that the very inconstancy of things exercises us in steadfastness of mind, so that the love that leads us to God does not grow into pride in prosperity, nor fall away in adversity? May what is pleasing to God, be pleasing also to us! Let us rejoice in their measure in every gift of God. He that has used great things well, let him use well the simple things also. Let him take equal care of scarcity as of abundance. If the fruitfulness of our own souls does not displease us, neither should we be grieved over the poverty of the fruits in the spiritual harvest. Let that which the earth fails to bring forth, rise up in the field of our own heart.

He to whom a generous will is not wanting, shall ever have that which he may bestow. Towards all the works of piety, the quality of the years will help us; nor does temporal difficulty ever stand in the way of Christian benevolence. The Lord knew how to fill up the vessels of the hospitable widow, made empty by her own works of mercy (4 Kgs. iv. 5); He knew when to change water into wine (Jn. ii. 9); He knew how, from a few loaves, to feed a multitude of five thousand hungry people (Jn. vi. 9). He Who in that with which He fed His poor, could increase by giving, can also multiply by taking away.

Chapter IV. There are three things that especially pertain to the practise of religion, namely: prayer, fast, and almsgiving, in the practise of which every moment is an acceptable time; but that time should be more devoutly observed which we have received as consecrated by apostolic traditions; as also does this tenth month record for us a custom of ancient institution: that we should now more fervently observe these three practises I have mentioned. For by prayer we obtain the divine favour, by fasting we extinguish the concupiscences of the flesh, by almsgiving sins are redeemed (Dan. iv. 24); and by all three together, the image of God is renewed in us, provided that we are ever ready in His praise, eager without ceasing for our own purification, and disposed at all times to assist our neighbour.

This threefold observance, most dearly Beloved, embraces the ends of all the virtues. It leads us to the image and likeness of God, and makes of us inseparable companions of the Holy Spirit, because faith endures steadfast by prayer, purity of life by fasting, and the heart ever merciful through almsdeeds.

Let us then fast on the fourth and sixth day of the week; and on the sabbath we shall celebrate the vigils together with the most blessed Apostle Peter; who will deign to assist our prayers, our fasts, and our almsdeeds, with his own prayers, through Our Lord Jesus Christ, Who with the Father and the Holy Spirit, liveth and reigneth world without end. Amen.

III. St John Chrysostom: On the Gospel[3]

1. *In those days.* What do these words mean: *in those days?* For John came, not when Jesus was a child, and had come to Nazareth, but after thirty years, as Luke testifies. Why therefore does the Evangelist say: *in those days?* It is a custom of Sacred Scripture to use this figure of speech, not alone in referring to events that are close to that time in which the writer speaks, but even when it speaks of those that are to happen after many years. So when His disciples came to Our Lord as He sat on Mount Olivet, and questioned Him as to His Second Coming, and about the fall of Jerusalem,—you know how great is the interval between both events—and when He had spoken of the siege, and had finished speaking concerning it, and was about to speak of the end of the world, He inserted the words: *then will these things be.*

By saying *then* He did not join together the two times, but only indicated the times in which the events would take place. Scripture does the same when it now says: *in those days.* It does not signify the days immediately following, but those in which will happen the events it goes on to narrate.

But why, you will ask, did Jesus come to be baptized at the age of thirty years? Because after this baptism the Law would come to an end. Accordingly, He continues to fulfil the precepts of the Law—lest it be said that since He could not fulfil the Law He dissolved it—and waits till an age which is capable of every sin. For not all temptations, nor all the vices, press on us at the same time; in the early years there

is much folly and inconstancy; in the years that follow the passions are stronger; later, comes the desire of wealth. Accordingly, awaiting the fulness of life, and having in all this time fulfilled the Law, so, when He had fulfilled the other precepts, He came for baptism, which He added as the last. That He regarded this as the last of the works of the Law, He implies, saying: *for so it becometh us to fulfill all justice* (Mt. iii. 15). What is here meant is this: all things that are of the Law We have fulfilled, none have We passed over. Because this work is over and above, it is fitting that we add it also, so that we shall *fulfil all justice.* For here He calls justice the fulfilling of the precepts. It was therefore for this cause that Christ, manifestly to all, came to be baptized.

But for what reason did he devise this baptism? Not of himself, but under the inspiration of God, did the son of Zachary come to this work, as Luke tells us, saying: *the word of the Lord was made unto John in the desert,* that is, a command. He himself tells us: *but He who sent me to baptize with water, said to me: He upon whom thou shall see the Spirit descending, and remaining upon Him, He it is that baptizeth with the Holy Ghost* (Jn. I, 33). Why was he sent to baptize? This also the Baptist declares: *and I knew Him not, but that He may be made manifest in Israel, therefore am I come baptizing with water* (Jn. I. 31).

And if this be the only reason, how does Luke say: *and He came into all the country about the Jordan, preaching the baptism of penance for the remission of sins* (Lk. iii. 4)? Never–

theless this baptism had not the power to forgive; this being the gift of the baptism that was given later; for it was in this later baptism that we *were buried together with Christ*, and *our old man was* at the same time *crucified with Him*; and before the Cross no where hath forgiveness appeared, for this everywhere is attributed to His Blood. Paul also says: *But you are washed, you are sanctified*, not through the baptism of John, but in the Name of *Our Lord Jesus Christ, and the spirit of our God* (I Cor. vi. 11). And elsewhere he says: *John baptized the people with the baptism of penance*, but does not say of forgiveness, so that *they should believe in Him that was to come after Him* (Act. xix. 4). Since the Sacrifice was not yet offered, nor had the Spirit descended, nor had the sin been wiped out, nor the enmity taken away, nor the curse removed, how could pardon for sin be given?

2. What does the phrase *unto the forgiveness of sin* mean? The Jews were ignorant and unreflecting, nor had they a real sense of their sins; and while guilty of great wickedness, they spoke everywhere of themselves as just; which more than any other fault had brought about their ruin, and led them from truth. Paul reproved them for this, saying: *For they, not knowing the justice of God and seeking to establish their own, have not submitted themselves to the justice of God* (Rom. x. 3). And again: *What then shall we say? That the Gentiles, who followed not after justice, have attained to justice, even the justice that is of faith. But Israel, by following after the law of justice, is not come unto the law of justice.*

Why so? Because they sought it not by faith, but as it were of work (Rom. ix. 30, 32).

Because their ignorance was the cause of their afflictions John came, and for no other end than that he might awaken them to the knowledge of their sins. Even his clothing revealed this purpose, for it signified confession and repentance. His preaching too showed this purpose. For nothing else did he proclaim than that they should *bring forth fruits worthy of penance*. And because they would not turn from their sins, they turned their backs to Christ, as Paul has declared. For to reflect on their sins would awaken a desire for forgiveness, and the Redeemer would be sought for. John came to bring this about, to exhort them to penance, not that they might be punished, but that they might, becoming humbler through repentance, and by accusing themselves, hasten to seek pardon.

See how accurately he has expressed these things. For when he had said that he came preaching *the baptism of penance* in the desert of Judea, he added, *unto remission of sins* (Mk. i. 4); as if he said: he so exhorted them that they might confess their sins and do penance, not because of punishment, but that they might readily receive forgiveness later. For unless they accused themselves, they would not seek pardon, and unless they seek pardon they will not be forgiven. So this baptism prepares the way for the other to come; and so he says that *they should believe in Him that was to come after him* (Act. xix. 4), adding this reason also for this other baptism to those we have already mentioned.

Nor could he have done more had he gone from house to house, even leading Christ by the hand, and said to all: "Believe in this man," than he did now, in the midst of all who were present and beheld him, lifting up that blessed voice, and fulfilling all the other things. And so he came to baptize. The great fame of the Baptist, and the circumstances of his appearance, had attracted the whole city and brought them to the Jordan, and the multitude was very great. And for this purpose he strives to make humble those who had come, and shows them that they had no cause for this self pride, and that unless they did penance they were in danger of grievous afflictions, and that forgetting about their forefathers, and putting away their boasting because of them, they should receive Him Who had already come. For their earlier expectations concerning the Christ had by now become vague, and many believed they were now ended, because of the slaughter committed at Bethlehem. And though He had revealed Himself, when He was twelve years old, sitting in the midst of the doctors, hearing them and asking them questions, and speaking such words of wisdom that all were astonished: yet He had as quickly hidden Himself again. Accordingly, there was need of this striking introduction, and of a more exalted beginning. And so for the first time he announces, and with resounding voice, that which the Jews had never before heard, neither from the prophets, nor from any others, and he spoke only of the kingdom of heaven, saying nothing of the things of earth. And the kingdom here means His Coming, both His first and His last.

But why do you so speak to the Jews, you will say? For they understand not what you say? He answers: I so speak to them so that they being awakened by the strikingness of what I tell them, may seek Him Whom I preach. And he did in fact awaken good desires among those that came close to him, so that even many from among the publicans and soldiers asked him what they should do, and how they might begin to put their lives in order; which was an indication that they, putting away worldly desires, were now looking towards other and better things, and beginning to have a vision of the future. Indeed for all who were present, everything, whether things heard or things seen, lifted up their minds to an understanding of the sublimer things.

3. Consider what is meant to see this man coming forth from the desert after thirty years there; the son of a High Priest; one who had ever been above the needs of ordinary men; and for every reason venerable, because with him was the spirit of Isaias. For he was present with him, proclaiming him, and saying: This is he of whom I foretold you, that he will come and crying out in the wilderness with a mighty voice, declaring to you all things. So great was the zeal of the prophets concerning these things that, long before, they had foretold not alone the coming of the Lord, but his coming also who was to minister unto Him. And not alone did they foretell him, but they foretold also where he would dwell, the manner of speaking he would

employ in teaching them, and what great good was thence to follow.

Note how the Prophet and the Precursor convey the same message, though they use not the same words. The Prophet foretells that He is to come, saying: *prepare ye the way of the Lord, make straight his path.* The other when he came, began to say: *Bring forth fruit worthy of penance*, which has the same meaning as: *Prepare ye the way of the Lord.* Yet see that whatever be said, whether by the Prophet or by the Baptist, one thing alone is meant, namely: that he came that he might prepare the way; that he came not that he himself might bring the gift, namely, of forgiveness, but that he might prepare the souls of those who were to receive this gift of all gifts.

But Luke adds something more: for he did not think it sufficient to give the beginning, but gave the whole prophecy. For he says: *Every valley shall be filled; and every mountain and hill shall be brought low; and the crooked shall be made straight; and the rough ways plain; and all flesh shall see the salvation of God* (Lk. iii. 5, 6; Is. xl. 4, 5). See how long ago the prophet has foretold everything: the gathering together of the people, the changing of things for the better, the simplicity of what was made known, and the reason why all this was done; even though he has spoken in figure? For he was a prophet of the things to come. For when he said: *every valley shall be filled, and every mountain and hill brought low, and the rough ways plain*, he was foretelling that the humble shall be exalted, and the proud brought low, and that the harshness of the Law shall be changed into the mildness of the Gospel. No

more, he says, the *sweat* and *pain*; but grace and forgiveness for sin, thus opening wide the way of salvation. Then he sets forth the reason for all this, saying: *that all flesh shall see the salvation of God*; not, as before, the Jews and the Proselytes alone, but all flesh, the sea, and the whole race of men, By the rough ways and the crooked ways he means, whatever manner of life that is corrupted: publicans, fornicators, thieves, dealers in magic: who before were perverse in their ways and then entered the straight way, as the Lord Himself has said: *Amen I say to you that the publicans and the harlots shall go into the kingdom of heaven before you* (Mt. xxi. 31), because of this, that they have believed in Him.

The Prophet says the same thing in other words: *the wolf and the lamb shall feed together* (Is. lxv. 25). For as before this he spoke of mountains and valleys, meaning that diversities of nature are blended into one through the knowledge of wisdom, so here likewise, by the differing natures of the brute beasts he means the diverse dispositions of men, and foretells that they shall all be brought to one harmony of just living. And here again, as before, he gives the reason for this: saying, *And he that shall rise up to rule the gentiles, in him the gentiles shall hope* (Is.xi. 10; Mt. xii. 21). Which means the same as when he says: *and all flesh shall see the salvation of God*; showing by this that the power and the knowledge of the Gospel must be proclaimed to the ends of the earth, which will change the race of men from animal ways and ferocity of soul to mildness and gentleness of character.

And the same John had his garments of camels' hair, and a leathern girdle about his loins. Note how some things are mentioned by the Prophet, others are left to the personal narration of the Evangelist. Accordingly, Matthew relates the prophecies, and then adds his own details, and he does not think it out of place to speak of the clothing of the Baptist.

4. It was a wonderful and astonishing thing to see such endurance in a human body. It was this in great measure that drew the attention of the Jews, who beheld in this man the great Elias, and from what they saw in him the memory of that great and holy man was recalled to their minds. Indeed they were filled with an even greater admiration of John. The Prophet had been reared in cities, and in the midst of peoples; the Baptist had dwelt from his childhood alone in the desert.

And it was necessary that the Precursor of Him Who was to undo the age-long burthens of men[4], as toil, malediction, pain, and sweat, should in his own person give some token of the gifts to come, and stand himself above all these tribulations. And so it was that he neither tilled the earth, nor ploughed the furrow, nor did he eat bread of his own sweat, for his table was easily prepared, and his clothing more easily than his table, and his dwelling more easily than his clothing. For he had need, neither of roof, nor bed, nor table, nor any such like; but even while still within this flesh of ours lived an almost angelic life. His clothing was put together from the hair of camels, so that even from his garments he might teach us that we free ourselves of human needs, and be not bound to this earth, but that we must return to the pristine dignity in which Adam first lived, before he had need of garments or of clothing. So his manner of dress was in itself a symbol, as well of our dignity as of our need of repentance.

Do not say to me: where did this desert dweller procure his garment of hair, and his girdle of leather? For if you ask me that question, you raise many more; how did he fare in the winter, and how in the summer, and alone, especially while still tender of body and young in years? How could the constitution of a young boy endure such extremes of nature, upon such food, and in face of all the other hardships of that vast solitude?

What have the philosophers to say to this, especially those who follow the impudent school of the Cynics—of what profit was it for them to sit themselves in a wine tub, if afterwards they behaved licentiously—who indulge themselves with rings, and goblets, with manservants and maidservants, and all the other signs of luxury, and despite their philosophy give themselves over to every excess? Truly great was this man, who dwelt in the desert as though in heaven, showing himself a model of true wisdom. From there he came to the city, as an angel from heaven; an athlete of every virtue, crowned before the world; a philosopher of the philosophy that is worthy of heaven.

And these things were when sin had not yet been overcome, while the Law yet ruled, before death had been defeated, before the brazen gates had yet been broken, and while the former state in which men lived still endured. Such indeed is the character of the strong and watchful soul, for everywhere it leaps forward and strains beyond the border of the limits set, as Paul says in the New Testament (II Cor. x. 14).

You may ask, *why* did he wear a leathern girdle? That was a custom among the ancients, before this present soft and flowing style of clothing came to prevail. Similarly Peter and Paul are mentioned as wearing a girdle; for it is said: *the man whose girdle this is* (Acts xxi. 11). Elias also was so clothed, and likewise many others of the holy men, either because they were engaged in heavy labour, or were upon a journey, or in any other necessity that involved labour, and because they despised ornament, and followed an austere way of life; which won praise from our Saviour, as we learn from his words: *But what went you out to see? A man clothed in soft garments? Behold they that are in soft garments are in the houses of kings* (Lk. vii. 25).

5. If he who was so pure, and brighter than the heavens, who was above all the prophets, than whom none greater was born among men; who had such faith, if he lived so austerely, wholly rejecting every delight, what excuse have we, who after so many favours, though laden with countless bundles of sin, can show not the least part of his penance, but give ourselves to drinking and gluttony, softening ourselves by every means, and making ourselves an easy prey for the devil? Let us, putting away all excess, and drinking the healthy cup of moderation, live in a manner that is becoming and temperate; and let us give ourselves in earnest to prayer. And if we do not receive that for which we pray, let us persevere that we may receive it. And if we do receive it, let us persevere the more, because we have received. For it is not His Will to withhold the gift we ask for, but, in His wisdom, to encourage our perseverance by delaying it. So He delays the answer to our prayers, and even permits us to fall into temptation, so that we may then turn to Him, and there remain with Him. Thus do loving fathers and mothers of children act; when they see their little ones go from them to play with others of their years, they cause their servants to pretend to frighten them, so that the children may fly back to the maternal-arms.

So oftentimes does God threaten us, not that He may inflict evils upon us, but to draw us to Himself. And when we return to Him, immediately He banishes our fear; for were we to feel the same security in temptations as when at peace, then there would be no need for us to be tempted. But why do I speak of us? For even holy men for this purpose were grievously tried: *It is good for me that thou hast humbled me* (Ps. cxviii. 71). And He Himself has said to the Apostles: *In the world you shall have distress* (Jn. xvi. 33). And Paul implies the same thing, when he says: *There was given me a sting of my flesh, an angel of Satan to buffet me* (II. Cor. xii. 7); who though he had prayed to be delivered from temptation, yet was his prayer not answered, because from his very temptation he drew great profit.

And if we consider the whole life of David we shall find, that in the midst of dangers he was still greater; and not he alone, but all like unto him. Job also for this same cause shines forth; so likewise Joseph shone out yet more. Jacob too, and his father, and his father's father, and all who have been great, and have been crowned; only by trials and tribulation have they been proved and received their crowns.

Since we know all these things, *Let us,* in the words of Wisdom, *make not haste in the time of clouds* (Ecclus. ii. 2), but let us school ourselves to one thing only, that we may bear all things with courage, and neither inquire too curiously, nor search too sharply, into that which may befall us. For to know at what time our hardships will come to an end belongs only to God, Who permits them to happen. It is for us to bear our afflictions and give thanks that is the duty of trustfulness. And if we do this, every good thing will follow. That they may follow, that we may become more trusting, that we may come to shine above, let us accept whatever be laid upon us; giving thanks always to Him Who knows better than we know, what is good for us, and Who loves us more than our own parents love us.

And let these thoughts be at all times as it were a melody in our hearts, in whatsoever tribulations, so that we may rise above grieving, and give praise unto God, Who arranges all things within all things for our benefit. Thus shall we overcome all dangers and come to our imperishable crown, to which may we all alike attain, by the grace and mercy of Our Lord Jesus Christ, to Whom, with the Father and the Holy Spirit, be glory and empire and honour, now and for ever and ever, Amen.

IV. St Gregory, Pope and Doctor: On the Mystical Church[5]

Given to the People in the Basilica of St John the Baptist on the vigil of the Fourth Sunday of Advent[5]

1. The time in which the Precursor of the Redeemer received word to preach is commemorated by the names, both of the Ruler of the Roman Republic and of the Kings of Judea, as it is written: *In the fifteenth year of the reign of Tiberius Caesar, Herod being tetrarch of Galilee,* etc. Because he came to preach His Kingdom who would redeem some from Israel, and many from the Gentiles, the times of his public appearance are indicated both through the King of the Gentiles and the Princes of the Jews. This recording of earthly rule also reveals that the Gentiles were to be gathered together, and Judea, by reason of its perfidy, to be dispersed; since in the Roman Republic one only is said to rule, while the kingdom of Judea is divided between several, each having a fourth part of its divided rule. By the voice of the Redeemer it is said: *every kingdom divided against itself shall be brought to desolation* (Lk. xi. 17).

It is clear then that Israel had reached the end of its kingdom, which was now divided, and sub-jected to the rule of many. And fittingly was it commemorated, not alone under what kings, but under what priests, had this come to pass; for since John the Baptist had come to proclaim Him Who was both King and Priest, Luke the Evan-gelist makes known the time of this proclamation by mention of both kingdom and priesthood.

2. *And he came into all the country about the Jordan*, etc. It is plain to all who read, that not alone did John preach the baptism of penance, but likewise that he gave it to many; yet he could not give his baptism unto the remission of sins. Forgive-ness of sin is bestowed upon us only by the baptism of Christ. We must note therefore what is said: *preaching the baptism of penance for the remission of sins*; since he was preaching a baptism by which sins could be forgiven, but which he could not confer. As he preceded the IncarnateWord of the Father by the word of his own preaching, so he preceded the baptism of penance, by which sins are forgiven, by his own baptism, by which sins could not be forgiven. And as in his preaching he went before the Liv-ing Presence of the Redeemer, so going before Him also in baptizing, he became as it were the very shadow of Truth.

3. The Scripture continues: *As it was written in the book of the sayings of*, etc. John the Baptist, being asked who he was, replied, saying: *I am a voice of one crying in the wilderness*; who, as we have shown elsewhere, is called a *voice* by the prophet, because he preceeded the *Word*. What the voice was to cry is

made plain, when he adds: *prepare ye the way of the Lord, make straight his paths*. Everyone that preaches true faith and good works, what does he do but prepare the way of the Lord so that He may come into the hearts of his hearers, and may make straight the path for God, forming right dispositions within them by the words of his exhorta-tions, so that this power of pardon may enter in there, and the light of truth shine there?

Every valley shall ' be filled and every mountain and hill brought low. What is here meant by valleys unless the humble, and by the hills and mountains but the proud? At the Coming of the Redeemer there-fore, the valleys shall be filled, the mountains and hills brought low, according to His Word: *Every one that exalteth himself shall be humbled: and he that humbleth himself shall be exalted*. The valley that is filled in grows, the mountain and hill that is brought low grows less, because in the faith of the Mediator of God and of men, the Man Jesus Christ, the Gentiles shall receive the fulness of grace, and Judea through the error of her pride which has caused her to swell, shall be brought low. Every valley shall be filled, because the hearts of the humble will be replenished, by the teachings of sacred truth, with the gift of the virtues, according to that which was written: *Thou sendest forth springs in the vales* (Ps. ciii. 10). And whence again was it said also: *And the val shall abound with corn* (Ps. lxiv. 14)

But as water falls away from the mountain, so the words of truth forsake the mind of the proud. But springs well up in the vales. because the minds of the humble accept the words of prophecy.

We already behold, we already look upon the valleys abounding in corn, because the mouths of those who are mild and gentle and who seem to the world contemptible, are now filled with the food of truth.

4. Because they had seen that he was endowed with rare holiness, the people began to believe that John the Baptist was that high and solid mountain of which it had been written: *And it came to pass in the last days, that the mountain of the house of the Lord, shall be prepared in the top of the mountains* (Mich. iv. 1). For they began to think he was the Christ, as the Gospel relates. *The people were of opinion, and all were thinking in their hearts of John, that perhaps he might be the Christ, whom they questioned, saying: Art thou the Christ?* (Lk. iii. 15) But unless that the same John was a valley in himself, he would not have been filled with the Holy spirit; who, that he might show who he truly was, said: *There cometh after me one mightier than I, the latchet of whose shoes I am not worthy to stoop down and loose* (Mk. i. 7), And again he says: *He that hath the Bride, is the Bridegroom? but the friend of the Bridegroom, who standeth and heareth him, rejoiceth with joy because of the Bridegroom's voice. This my joy therefore is fulfilled. He must increase, but I must decrease* (Jn. iii. 29, 30).

Behold how, by reason of his wondrous virtue, he was such that he could be believed to be the Christ, he answers that not alone is he not the Christ, but that he does not hold himself as worthy to stoop and undo His shoes, that is, to search into the mystery of His Incarnation. Because they believed

that he was the Christ, they believed that the Church was his spouse. But he said: *He that hath the Bride is the Bridegroom.* It is as if he said: I am not the Bridegroom, but the friend of the Bridegroom. And he said that he rejoiced, not in his own voice, but because of the voice of the Bridegroom; for he did not therefore rejoice in his heart because he was heard by the people speaking humbly of himself, but because he himself had been hearing the voice of truth within him, that he may declare it abroad. Well does he say that his joy is fulfilled; because whosoever rejoices in his own voice, his joy will not be fulfilled . . . At which point he adds:

5. *He must increase, but I must decrease.* Here we must ask in what manner Christ increased, and in what manner John decreased, unless it be that the people, seeing John's austerity, and his remoteness from men, believed him to be the Christ, while seeing Christ eating with the publicans, walking among sinners, they believe, not that he is the Christ, but that he is a prophet. But as, with time, Christ, whom they believed to be a prophet, is acknowledged as the Christ, while John whom they had believed to be the Christ is known as but a prophet, there has in this way been fulfilled that which the Precursor spoke concerning Christ: *He must increase, but I must decrease.* In the minds of the people Christ increased, because He came to be acknowledged for that which He was; and John decreased, because he ceased to be thought that which he was not. But John did not change, but remained steadfast in

holiness, because he remained humble in his heart, while many in like circumstances have fallen away, because in their vanity they had become blown up through some vain notion. So it is rightly said: *Every valley shall be filled, and every mountain and hill shall be brought low;* because the humble accept the gift which the proud of heart reject.

6. Then there follows: *The crooked ways shall be made straight; and the rough ways plain.* Crooked ways become straight when the hearts of sinners, twisted by evil, conform to the way of righteousness. And rough ways are changed to smooth when cruel and wrathful men turn to the mildness of clemency, through the infusion of heavenly grace. When the word of one who preaches is rejected by an angry mind, it is as if the roughness of the path turns back the footsteps of the traveller. But when the angry mind through the grace of meekness, to which it has responded, receives within it the word of exhortation and correction, the preacher finds smoothness where before, because of the roughness of the way, he could make no advance.

7. *And all flesh shall see the salvation of God.* Since all flesh means every man, and in this life every man cannot see the salvation of God, which is Christ, where then does the prophet in this sentence turn his prophetic vision unless towards the day of the last judgement? Then, with opened eyes, in presence of the adoring angels and of the Apostles seated there, Christ will appear upon His Throne of majesty, and all, the elect and the reprobate, shall behold Him; the Elect that they may without end enjoy the possession of their reward, the reprobate to grieve for ever in the torment of retribution. Because such is the meaning of this sentence: that all flesh shall see Him at the final judgement, there is here fittingly added:

He said to the multitudes that went forth to be baptized by him: ye off-spring of vipers, who hath showed you to flee from the wrath to come? The wrath to come is the chastisement of the last judgment, which the sinner may not escape who now turns away from repentance. Observe that when wicked children imitate the actions of evil parents, they are called the *offspring of vipers,* because they envy the good and persecute them, because they render evil to many and torment their neighbours; because in all this they are following in the footsteps of their fathers in the flesh, they are called the poisonous offspring of poisonous parents.

8. But since we also have sinned, who are held fast in the bonds of evil habits, tell us what we must do, that we may escape the wrath to come? The answer follows on: *Bring forth therefore fruits worthy of penance.* Let us note in these words that the friend of the Bridegroom here admonishes them that they must not alone bring forth fruits of penance, but fruits worthy of penance. It is one thing to bring forth fruits of penance, another to produce fruit worthy of penance.

Regarding the question of fruits worthy of penance, it must be known to you that to a man who commits no crimes, the use of lawful things rightly belongs. Again, a man may give himself to works of piety, but should he not wish to do so, he may not yet neglect the tasks of daily life. But should a man commit fornication, or what is worse fall into adultery, he should deny himself lawful pleasures in the measure that he recalls having indulged in unlawful. Nor are equal fruits of good works looked for in one who has offended but little, as from one who has sinned greatly; or from one who has committed no crimes, as from the man who has committed some, or has fallen into many.

By this therefore which is here spoken of: *Bring forth therefore fruits worthy of penance*, the conscience of each man is taken into account; so the more ought he to strive for a greater profit of good works through penance, who has the more grievously injured his own soul through the guilt of sin. But the Jews, glorying in the greatness of their descent, were unwilling to regard themselves as sinners, because they were descended from Abraham. To whom it was therefore rightly said: *Do not begin to say, we have Abraham for our father. For I say unto you, that God is able of these stones to raise up children to Abraham* (Lk. iii. 8).

9. What do stones here mean but the hearts of Gentiles, as yet insensible to the understanding of the Omnipotent God? As also was said of some of the Jews: *I will take away the stony heart out of their flesh* (Ezech. xi. 19). Nor undeservedly are the Gentiles signified by the name of stones, since they worshipped stones. Hence was it written: *Let them that make them, become like unto them; and all such as*

trust in them (Ps. cxiii. 8). And from these stones children have been raised to Abraham, for when the hard hearts of the Gentiles believed in the Seed of Abraham, that is, in Christ, they became his children, to whose Seed they have been united.

Accordingly, to the same Gentiles was it said by the great Preacher: *And if you be Christ's then are you the seed of Abraham* (Gal. iii. 29). If we therefore because of our faith in Christ are deemed children of Abraham, the Jews therefore because of their perfidy have ceased to be his seed. In that fearful day when men shall be judged, good parents shall avail nothing to wicked children, as the prophet Ezechial says: *And if these three men, Noe, Daniel, and Job, shall be in it, they shall deliver neither sons nor daughters; they shall deliver their own souls by their justice* (Ezech. xiv. 14): Again, good children will avail nothing to evil parents, rather will the goodness of their children increase the guilt of the parents, as the Truth Himself said to the unbelieving Jews: *Now if I cast out devils by Beelzebub; by whom do your children cast them out? They therefore shall be your judges* (Lk. xi. 19).

10. Then there follows: *For now the axe is laid to the root of the trees. Every tree therefore that bringeth forth not good fruit, shall be cut down and cast into the fire.* The trees of this world are the race of mankind. Our Redeemer is as it were an axe, made from haft of wood and steel, which is wielded by His humanity, but cuts by the power of His divinity. Which *axe is now laid to the root of the trees*, because though He delays through patience, yet already He has declared that which the axe shall

do: *Every tree therefore that bringeth not forth good fruit, shall be cut down and cast into the fire*; for every one who has scorned to lay by the fruits of good works, has speedily found prepared for him the fiery consumation of Gehenna.

And note that the axe is laid, not to the branches, but to the root. For when the children of the wicked are destroyed, what is this except the cutting off of the unfruitful branches of the tree? When however the whole offspring, together with the parent, are destroyed, then the unfruitful tree is cut down from the root, and nothing remains from which an evil shoot may arise. In these words of John the Baptist it is evident that he had shaken the hearts of his hearers, for immediately there follows: *and the people asked him, saying: what then shall we do?* For they were stricken with terror, and sought his counsel.

11. *And he answering said to them: he that hath two coats let him give to him that hath none; and he that hath meat let him do in like manner*, verse 11. Because the tunic is more necessary for our use than the overmantle, it pertains to the fruit worthy of penance, that we ought to share with our neighbours not alone the exterior things that are less necessary, but also those which it pains us to go without, such as the food by which we live, and the essential garments by which we are covered. For since it is written in the Law: *thou shalt love thy neighbour as thyself* (Mt. xxii. 39), a man is proved to love his neighbour less, who, in his neighbour's necessity, does not share with him the things that are necessary, even for his own

life. Likewise the precept here given, is of sharing *two* tunics between a man and his neighbour, because this cannot be said where there is but *one* tunic, since if one tunic is divided, neither will be covered. With half a tunic he remains unclad, both he who gave, and he who receives.[6]

From this one learns how greatly the works of mercy profit us, since they, before others, are counselled us as fruit worthy of penance. Hence Truth Itself said the same: *give alms; and behold, all things are clean unto you* (Lk. xi. 41). And again He says: *give and it shall be given to you* (Lk. vi. 38). Hence also was it written: *water quencheth a flaming fire, and alms resisteth sin* (Ecclus. iii. 33). Hence again was it written; *shut up alms in the heart of the poor, and it shall obtain help for thee against evil* (Ecclus. xxix. 4). Hence, finally, the good father admonishes his blameless son, saying: *if thou have much, give abundantly; if thou have little, take care even so to bestow willingly a little* (Tob. iv. 9).

12. That Our Saviour might show how much virtue there is in continence, and in succouring the needy, He says: *he that receiveth a prophet in the name of a prophet, shall receive the reward of a prophet: and he that receiveth a just man, in the name of a just man, shall receive the reward of a just man* (Mt. x. 41). In which words we must note that that he does not say: a reward *from* a prophet, or a reward *from* a just man, but: *the reward of a prophet, and the reward of a just man will he receive.* One thing is a reward *from* a prophet, another the reward *of* a prophet; and likewise it is one

thing to receive reward from a just man, and another to receive the reward of a just man.

What does it mean to say: *he shall receive the reward of a prophet*, unless that he who helps a prophet by his bountifulness, though he himself have not the gift of prophecy, will have from the Omnipotent God the rewards of prophecy? He, the prophet, is, no doubt, a just man, and although possessing little in this world, has, for his office of speaking in behalf of justice, greater confidence. This other, who aids him, while he may possess somewhat of this world's goods, and though perhaps he may not presume to speak freely on behalf of justice, yet he makes himself a participator in the defense of justice by the other, and equally is rewarded with him, whom, by sustaining in his need, he aided so that he was able freely to speak in defence of justice.[7]

Now the prophet is filled with the Holy Spirit, but for his body he needs food. And if his body is not fed, it is certain that his voice will fail. He who therefore gives food to a prophet, because he is a prophet, gives to the prophet his strength so that he may speak. When therefore the prophet will receive the reward of his prophecy, his helper, although he was not filled with the spirit, has this to show to the Lord: that he helped. Hence we have that which John said to Caius concerning certain of the Brethren who went forth for Christ: *Because, for his name they went out, taking nothing of the Gentiles. We therefore ought to receive such, that we may be fellow-helpers of the truth* (III Jn. vii. 8).

He who therefore gives temporal aid to those who have spiritual gifts

to bestow, is a co-operator in this spiritual giving. For since they are few who possess spiritual gifts, and many abound in temporal things, through this means they who have possessions, partake in the virtues of those who are needy, by relieving, from their own abundance, the wants of these sanctified poor. Whence the Lord, by the voice of Isaias, promised to the forsaken people that is, to the Holy Church, the reward of spiritual powers, that will be as an oasis in the desert, and he promised also the elm: *I will open rivers in the high hills: and fountains in the midst of the plains: I will turn the desert into pools of waters, and the impassable land into streams of waters. I will plant in the wilderness the cedar, and the thorn, and the myrtle and the olive tree: I will set in the desert the fir tree, the elm and the box tree together: that they may see and know, and consider, and understand together* (Isa. xli. 18–20).

The mystical figures explained

13. The Lord has in truth turned the *desert into pools of water*, and *opened fountains in the midst of the plains*, because to the Gentiles he has given waters of knowledge who before, because of the aridity of their souls, brought forth no fruits of good works; and the land, to which, because of the severity of its dryness, no way lay open to preachers, later sent forth rivers of doctrine; To which, for the purpose of this great office, there is promised: *I will plant in the wilderness the cedar and the thorn.* The cedar, because of its strong perfume, and incorruptible nature, we have inherited from the promise. As to the thorn, since it was said to man: *thorns and thistles shall it bring forth*

thee (Gen. iii. 18), is it to be wondered at, that that is promised to the church, which is multiplied to sinful man as punishment?

By cedars are meant those who show forth virtues and wonders in their ministry, who say with Paul: *For we are the good odour of Christ unto God* (II Cor. ii. 15). They whose hearts are so made fast to love eternal, that no taint of earthly love corrupts them. By thorns are signified men of spiritual teaching, who, while they discourse on sins and virtues, and now threaten with eternal punishments, and again promise the joys of the eternal kingdom, pierce the hearts of their listeners. And they so transfix them with the pain of repentance, that from their eyes tears flow, as though the blood of the soul ran out in tears.

The myrtle possesses the power of soothing so that it binds loosened members together by its own restraint. What is meant then by myrtle, but they who know how to comfort their neighbour in affliction, and temper sorrow by their own compassion? Of these is it written: *Blessed be the Lord who comforteth us in all tribulations; that we may be able to comfort them who are in all distress* (II Cor. I. 4). They also who, while they bring the word of consolation to their afflicted neighbour, restrain them within the bounds of what is becoming; lest through immoderate grief they fall into despair.

Whom do we understand by the olive, if not the merciful? Because the word in the Greek means mercy, and the fruit of mercy shines, like the oil of the olive, before the eyes of the Omnipotent God. To the Gentile there was also

added, in the promise: *I will set in the desert the fir tree, the elm, and the box tree.* Who is signified by the fir tree, which, growing strongly, soars into the air above, but those, who while dwelling in their earthly bodies within the Church, already contemplate heavenly things? And although in their growing they come out from the earth, yet the summits of their souls they raise close to the heavens by contemplation.

And what is signified by the elm, unless that here are described the minds of those living in the world? They who, since they are planted amid earthly concerns, yield no fruit of the spiritual virtues. But though the elm has no fruit of its own, it is wont to carry the grape-laden vine; so also, secular men within the church, who although they have no gifts of spiritual powers, yet sustain by their goodness the holy men who are endowed with these spiritual gifts, what are they doing, but supporting the vine and its fruit?

The evergreen box tree, though it grows not high, nor bears fruit, stands for certain others who within Holy Church, by reason of the infirmity of their age, are unable to produce good works, yet following the belief of believing parents, cherish a faith of unfading freshness.

After all these there is fittingly added: *that they may see and know and consider and understand together, that the hand of the Lord hath done this.* For this is the cedar planted within the Church, that whoever from close at hand breathes in the perfume of her spiritual virtues, may not grow dull in his love of life eternal, but that it may enkindle in him the longing for celestial joys. For this was planted the thorn, so that he who was pierced by the word of the gospel, may learn from this to pierce the hearts of those who follow him, by the same word of preaching. For this was the myrtle planted, that he who in the sharpness of sorrow has received the comfort of consolation, either from the word or by the deed of his compassionate neighbour, may himself learn in what manner he may bring to his afflicted neighbour the balm of his own consolations.

For this was the olive planted, that he who has seen the working of another's mercy, may learn in what manner he ought to show pity to his neighbour in need. For this was the fir tree planted, that he who has come to perceive its power of contemplation, may also be moved to make contemplation of the rewards of eternity. For this was the elm tree planted, that whosoever looks carefully upon those who though unable to yield fruit of spiritual gifts, yet sustain those who are endowed with them, may also unite himself, in as far as he may, to the works of the spiritually endowed, and so may bear, by supporting them, the grapes of heaven which he should not himself bring forth. For this was the box tree planted, that those who observe the great numbers who lie stricken by infirmity, yet keeping fresh the green of faith, may be ashamed to be themselves without faith.

Having described the trees, there was well added: *that they may see and know, and consider, and understand together.* Aptly was the word *together* added; since within the Church diverse are the customs, and diverse the kinds of men, it is then necessary that all shall learn together. And within it also are to be seen many spiritual men, of diverse quality, and age, and kind, that we are to imitate.

But look! While we have been striving to come to the elm tree, we have been tediously wandering through many plantations. So let us then return to that of which we have been speaking; because of the testimony of the prophet: *He that receiveth a prophet, in the name of a prophet, shall receive the reward of the prophet* (Mt. x. 41); although the elm tree has no fruit, yet because it supports the vine with its fruit, he who thus supports others makes their fruits his fruits.

14. Because John exhorts us to do great things, saying: *Bring therefore fruit worthy of penance* (Mt. iii. 8; Lk. iii. 8); And again: *He that hath two coats, let him give to him that hath none* (Lk. iii. 11); there is here clearly indicated to us what the Truth has said: *From the days of John the Baptist until now, the kingdom of heaven suffereth violence, and the violent bear it away* (Mt. xi. 12). The words of this divine reflection should be most carefully considered by us. For we must find out how the kingdom of heaven suffers violence. Who dares to counsel violence against heaven? And again we must ask, if the kingdom of heaven suffereth violence, why has it suffered this violence from the days of John the Baptist, and not also before? But when the Law said: If any man has done this or that, let him die, it is plain to all who read, that it punished sinners of all kinds with the penalties of its own sternness, but it did not return

them to life, through repentance. But when John the Baptist, preceding the forgiveness of the Redeemer, preached repentance, so that the sinner who was dead through sin might live through being converted, truly has the kingdom of heaven suffered violence since the days of John the Baptist.

For what is the Kingdom of Heaven unless the dwelling place of the Just? For to the Just alone are due the rewards of the heavenly city, so that only the humble, the chaste, the gentle, and the merciful may come to heavenly joys. When any one therefore, either swollen with pride, or soiled by the evil deeds of the flesh, or inflamed with anger, or undutiful through inhumanity, has returned to penance after these offences, and receives life eternal, this sinner makes entry into another's kingdom. And so from the days of John the Baptist the kingdom of heaven suffers violence, and the violent take posession of it; for he who has imposed repentance upon sinners, what has he done but taught them to do violence to the kingdom of heaven?

15. Let us then, Dearest Brethren, recall the evil we have done, and humble our souls in continuing repentance. Let us seize by this repentance the inheritance of the just; which till now has been slipping from us because of the manner of our lives. The Omnipotent has willed to submit Himself to this violence. For He wills that the Kingdom of heaven, unearned by our merits, may be seized by our tears. Therefore, let not the kind or

the multitude of our iniquities weaken the certitude of our hope. A strong confidence in forgiveness was shown by the venerable Thief, who however not for this was venerable, that he was a thief; for he was a thief through impiety; but he is venerable in that he confessed Christ.

Reflect, therefore, reflect, how incomprehensible is this innermost mercy of the Omnipotent God. This thief, snatched with blood-stained hands from the wayside ambush, was hanged upon the gallows; there he confesses; there he is healed of his sins; there he merited to hear: *this day thou shalt be with me in paradise* (Lk. xxiii. 43). What are we to think of this? Who can describe this so great goodness of God? Who can measure it? In the very expiation of crime, he reaches the reward of virtue. So likewise does the Omnipotent God sometimes permit his elect to fall into offences, that he may give hope of pardon to others who lie down despairing in their guilt, if they will but turn to Him with their whole hearts; to such as these He opens the way of justice, because of their tears of repentance.

Let us then be earnest in our repentance. Let us wash away with tears, and with fruits worthy of repentance, the evil we have committed. Let not that time be lost that is in mercy given to us, for we who see so many already healed from their sins, what have we here but a pledge of heavenly mercy, in Jesus Christ Our Lord who with the Father and the Holy Spirit, liveth and reigneth world without end. Amen.

NOTES

[1] PG 12 homily 21 col. 1854–1856.

[2] PL 54 col. 169. Serm. 12 of St Leo.

[3] Homily in St Matthew. -Migne PG 57 col. 183–192.

[4] Τὰ παλαιὰ λύειν ἄπαντα.

[5] Migne PL 76 cols. 1159–1170.

[6] The word *tunica* (coat) in the Gospel refers to the inner essential garment, then worn by all, and without which a man was not clothed. All had this, but not all had the pallium or outer garment, or mantle. The Holy Pontiff's exception would not apply to St Martin of Tours, who divided this latter garment between himself and the divine Mendicant.

[7] Prophet is used here throughout in the Pauline sense of one who reveals things unknown and of which the knowledge comes from God. So it is applied, apparently, by the Holy Pontiff to the preachers of the Gospel and to those who assist materially in its diffusion.

CHRISTMAS DAY

MASS OF MIDNIGHT

MASS OF THE AURORA

I. St John Chrysostom: Christmas Morning

II. St Ambrose: The Beginning of the Church

III. St Leo the Great: The Mystery of the Nativity

IV. St Gregory the Great: On the Feast

V. Bishop Paul of Emesa: The Divinity of Christ

THE GOSPEL OF THE MASS OF MIDNIGHT

Luke ii. 1–14

And it came to pass that in those days there went out a decree from Caesar Augustus, that the whole world should be enrolled. This enrolling was first made by Cyrinus, the governor of Syria. And all went to be enrolled, every one into his own city. And Joseph also went up from Galilee, out of the city of Nazareth into Judea, to the city of David, which is called Bethlehem: because he was of the house and family of David, to be enrolled with Mary his espoused wife, who was with child. And it came to pass, that when they were there, her days were accomplished, that she should be delivered. And she brought forth her first-born son, and wrapped him up in swaddling clothes, and laid him in a manger, because there was no room for them in the inn. And there were in the same country shepherds watching, and keeping the night-watches over their flock. And behold an angel of the Lord stood by them, and the brightness of God shone round about them, and they feared with a great fear. And the angel said to them: Fear not, for, behold, I bring you good tidings of great joy, that shall be to all the people. For this day is born to you a Saviour, who is Christ the Lord, in the city of David. And this shall be a sign unto you: You shall find the infant wrapped in swaddling clothes, and laid in a manger. And suddenly there was with the angel a multitude of the heavenly army, praising God, and saying: Glory to God in the highest, and on earth peace to men of good will.

EXPOSITION FROM THE CATENA AUREA

V. 1. *And it came to pass, that in those days there went out a decree from Caesar Augustus, that the whole world should be enrolled.*

BEDE, in Luke 2: As the Son of God by being born of a Virgin showed that the dignity of virginity was pleasing to Him, so also being now about to take flesh He chose to be born during the most peaceful period of time, teaching us also to seek after peace, and deigning to visit those who loved peace. There could be no greater sign of the peace of this time than this, that the whole world could be enrolled under one census; the world, whose ruler Augustus had now, about the time of the birth of Christ, reigned for twelve years amid such peace that the words of the prophet seemed (Is. ii. 4) literally fulfilled. Hence is said: *There went out a decree from Caesar Augustus, that the whole world should be enrolled.*

V. 2. *This enrolling was first made by Cyrinus, the governor of Syria.*

GREEK COMMENTATOR: Then was Christ born, when the Princes of the Jews had fallen from their authority, and their rule had passed to the Romans, to whom the Jews now paid tribute. Thus is the prophecy fulfilled which had foretold: *That the sceptre shall not be taken away from Judah, nor a ruler from his thigh, till He come that is to be sent* (Gen. xlix. 10). Caesar Augustus, now in the forty-second year of his reign, sends forth a decree, *that the whole world should be enrolled* for the purposes of paying tribute, and this task he gives to a

certain Cyrinus whom he had made governor of Judea and Syria. Hence: *This enrolling was first made by Cyrinus.*

V. 3. *And all went to be enrolled, every one into his own city.*

BEDE: The gospel notes that this enrolment was either the first which included the whole world, because there many places of which it is recorded that a census had been made of them, or that it was first begun when Cyrinus was sent to Syria. AMBROSE, in Luke 3: The name of the governor is aptly recorded so as to indicate the precise time. For if the names of the Consuls then governing are attached to the deeds of purchase, how much more should their names be attached to the deeds of the redemption of mankind? BEDE: A census in the ancient practice was so arranged that everyone was required to go to his own native city, according to what follows: *And all went to be enrolled, every one into his own city*; which came to pass so that the Lord, conceived in one place and born in another, might the more easily escape the fury of the treacherous Herod. Hence there follows: *Joseph also went up from Nazareth into Judea.*

V. 4. *And Joseph also went up from Galilee, out of the city of Nazareth into Judea, to the city of David, which is called Bethlehem, etc.*

CHRYSOSTOM, *In diem Nat. Christi:* Augustus decreed this edict, the Lord directing, so that it might help His Only-Begotten, now among men. For this decree drew the

Mother to the city of which the prophets had spoken, namely, *to the city of David which is called Bethlehem.* GREEK COMMENTATOR: So the gospel therefore adds *the city of David,* that it may announce that the promise made to David had been fulfilled: that from him would come a King Who would reign forever (Cf. II Kgs. vii. 12, 13). Hence follows: *Because he was of the house and family of David.* The Evangelist considers the fact that Joseph was of the house of David sufficient to make known that the Virgin was also of the house of David, since divine law prescribed that marriages took place only within the same family or lineage; hence, *with Mary his espoused wife, who was with child.*

V. 5. *To be enrolled with Mary his espoused wife, who was with child.*

CYRIL: in Catena of Greek Fathers: Scripture speaks of her as *espoused wife,* implying that only subsequent to the espousals did the Conception take place; nor did the Holy Virgin conceive of the seed of man. GREGORY, *Hom. 8 in Evang.*: That the world was enrolled at the coming of Our Lord has a mystical significance: because He then appeared in the flesh, Who would enrol His Elect for eternity.

AMBROSE, *in Luke* 2: While the secular census is referred to, the spiritual is implied; to be made known, not to the king of the earth, but to the king of heaven. It is a profession of faith, an enrolment of souls. The ancient enrolment of the synagogue is ended, while the new one of the church has begun. Lastly, that you may know that this census is of Christ, not of Augustus, *the whole world* is ordered

to be enrolled. Who could decree the enrolment of the whole world, unless He Who had dominion over the whole world? Not of Augustus, but of the Lord, was it said: *The earth is the Lord's and the fulness thereof* (Ps. xxiii. 1). BEDE: Who perfectly fulfills the meaning of the name *Augustus,* that is, He who desires, and has the power, to increase His own.

THEOPHYLACTUS: It was fitting that through Christ the worship of many Gods should come to an end, and that the One God be alone adored. So one king orders the whole world to be enrolled. ORIGEN, *Hom. 2 in Luke:* To one who considers this closely a certain mystery seems here to be prefigured: that Christ was enrolled in the census of the whole world, so that He might sanctify all men; and He was recorded with the whole world, that He might unite all men in Himself. BEDE: As during the reign of Caesar, and under the governorship of Cyrinus, *each one went to his own city that he might be enrolled,* so now in the reign of Christ, and under the governorship of the rulers of the Church, we must enroll ourselves unto justice.

AMBROSE, as above: This is the first enrolment of souls to the Lord, to whom all make profession; not at the proclamation of a herald, but of a prophet who says: *O clap your hands, all ye nations* (Ps. xlvi. 2). And now, that men may truly know that this is an enrolment unto justice, there come to it Joseph and Mary, that is, the Just Man and the Virgin; he that would defend the Word, She that would bring it forth, BEDE: Our true home and fatherland is that country towards which we daily must travel, ever growing in virtue. For daily the holy church, in the company of her Teacher, going up by the chariot of earthly conversation, in which Galilee is implied, to the city of Juda, that is, of worship and praise, pays the tribute of her devotion to the eternal King. Who, likewise, after the example of the Blessed Virgin Mary, as a virgin has conceived us of the Holy Spirit; while espoused to One, is made fruitful by Another; visibly joined to Himself by the Chief Priest, She is filled with the power of the Invisible Spirit. Whence is Joseph well interpreted as, strengthened in authority, showing by the name that the presence of the master speaking avails little, unless he has received an increase of heavenly aid, so that he may be obeyed.[1]

V. 6. *And it came to pass, that when they were there, her days were accomplished, that she would be delivered.*

AMBROSE: St Luke briefly relates how, and at what time and place, Christ was born according to the flesh, saying: *and it came to pass . . .* In what manner, because though a spouse conceived, a Virgin brought forth. GREGORY NYSS. *Cat. of G.F:* For though He appeared as man yet He was not in all things subject to the laws of humanity; that He was born of woman, savoured of lowliness; the virginity however that attended His birth shows that He transcended mankind. His carrying in the womb was joyful. His birth immaculate, His coming forth without pain, His nativity free of blemish, neither taking rise *from the will of the flesh,* nor *brought forth*

in sorrow; for since she who by her fault had brought death to our nature was condemned to bring forth in sorrow, it was fitting that the Mother of Life should bring forth in joy. And in that hour, in which *the shadows began to retire,* and the immense gloom of night was forced back by the splendour of this Light, Christ, through this virginal incorruption, comes to share the life of mortal men. For death had reached the boundary of the domination of sin, and now it moves towards nothingness, because of the presence of the True Light, which by its evangelical rays has given light to the whole world.

BEDE: He deigned to become incarnate in that time when, Newborn, He would be enrolled in the census of Caesar, and for our freedom would submit Himself to servitude. Hence, not alone in consideration of His royal lineage was the Lord born in Bethlehem, but also because of the mystery of the name. GREGORY, *Hom. 8 in Evang.:* Bethlehem is interpreted as the House of Bread. For it is He Who says: *I am the Living Bread that came down from Heaven.* The place where Our Lord was born was therefore formerly called the House of Bread, because it was there He was to appear in the nature of our flesh, Who would fill the hearts of the faithful with inward satiety. BEDE: And even to the end of the world the Lord would not cease to be conceived in Nazareth and born in Bethlehem, as often as any one of those who hear Him, taking the flour of His Word, make unto themselves a House of Eternal Bread. Daily in the virginal womb, that is, in the souls of the faithful, is He conceived by faith, and brought forth by baptism.

V. 7. *And she brought forth her firstborn son, and wrapped him up in swaddling clothes, and laid him in a manger; because there was no room for them in the inn.*

And she brought forth her firstborn son. JEROME, contra Helvetius: From this Helvetius endeavours to prove, that he cannot be called firstborn unless he has brothers, as he only is called only-begotten, who is alone born to his parents. This is how we decide the matter. Every only-begotten child is also a firstborn; but not every firstborn is only-begotten. We do not call him firstborn only, whom others follow, but him before whom there was no other child born. For if he alone is firstborn whom brothers follow, then firstfruit offerings would not be due to the priests as long as others were not yet born, lest, no other birth following, this might be an only-begotten child, and not a firstborn.

BEDE: He is the Only-Begotten of the substance of the divinity, Firstborn in the assuming of humanity; Firstborn in grace, Only-Begotten in nature. JEROME, as above: Here was no midwife, no tender care of female friends. She wrapped her own Child in swaddling clothes; she was both midwife and mother. Hence: *And wrapped Him up in swaddling clothes.* BEDE: He who was clothed with varied ornament the world, is folded in poor swaddling clothes that we may receive *the first robe.* He *through whom all things were made* is bound both hand and foot, that our hands may be employed in

every good work, and our feet directed in the way of peace.

METAPHRASTES, *in the Catena G.F.:* O wondrous bondage and sojourn which He endured, Who holds the world in His hand! From His first day He seeks only poverty, and honours it in His own Person. Had He wished He might have appeared moving the heavens, shaking the earth, hurling down the lightnings. But not in this way did He come. He wished to save, not to cast down, and from the beginning to tread under foot the foolish pride of man. So He not alone became man, He became a poor man; and choose a poor mother, who had not even a cradle wherein her new born Babe might lie. For there follows: *And she laid Him in a manger.*

BEDE: Straightly is He, Whose Throne is in the heavens, confined in the narrowness of a crib, so that He might open wide to us the joys of His eternal kingdom. He that is the Bread of Angels reclines in a manger, that we as sanctified beasts might be fed with the corn of His flesh. CYRIL, *Cat. of G.F.:* He found that man had become a beast in his soul, and so He is placed in the manger, in the place of fodder, that we, changing our animal way of living, may be led back to the wisdom that becomes humanity: stretching out, not towards animal fodder, but to the heavenly Bread for the life of this body.

BEDE: He Who sits at the right hand of the Father goes without shelter from the inn, that He may for us get ready *many mansions* in the house of His heavenly Father.

Hence we have: *Because there was no room for Him in the inn.* He was born, not in the house of His parents, but at the inn, by the wayside, because through the mystery of the Incarnation He is become the Way by which He guides us to our home, where we shall also enjoy the Truth and the Life. GREGORY, as above: That He might also show us, that in the humanity He had assumed, He was as it were born in a strange place; strange, not to His power, but to His nature.

AMBROSE: Because of thee, weakness: within Himself, Power; because of thee, poor; within Himself, all riches. Do not measure by what thy eye sees, but acknowledge this: that you are redeemed. More, Lord Jesus, do I owe to Thy sufferings, whereby I was redeemed, than to Thy works, wherein I was made. Unless man were redeemed, it would avail him nothing to be born.[2]

V. 8. *And there were in the same country shepherds watching and keeping the night watches over their flocks.*

AMBROSE: See in what manner the divine solicitude prepares the way of faith. An angel teaches Mary, an angel teaches Joseph, an angel guides the shepherds, of whom it is recorded: *And there were in the same country . . .*

CHRYSOSTOM *in Cat. G.F.:* An angel appeared in his sleep to Joseph, as to a man who was readily disposed to believe; to the shepherds he appears visibly, as to ruder men. But an angel did not go to Jerusalem, nor seek out the Scribes and Pharisees; for they were corrupted, and tormented with

envy. But the shepherds were sincere of heart, observing the ancient teaching of the patriarchs and of Moses. For blamelessness is one of the paths that lead to wisdom.

V. 9. *And behold an angel of the Lord stood by them, and the brightness of God shone round about them; and they feared with a great fear.*

BEDE: Nowhere in the whole course of the Old Testament do we find that the angels, who so dutifully ministered to the holy men of old, had ever appeared in light. This privilege was rightly reserved to the days when *to the righteous a light is risen up in darkness* (Ps. cxi. 4). Hence follows: *And the brightness of God shone round about them.*
AMBROSE: He comes forth from the womb, yet shines resplendent in heaven; He lies in an earthly resting place, but abounds in light celestial.
GEOMETER, in *Cat. G.F.:* They were fearful in the presence of this wonder; hence is said: *And they feared with a great fear.* But when fear came upon them, the angel banished it. Hence:

V. 10. *And the angel said: Fear not, for, behold, I bring you good tidings of great joy, that shall be to all the people:*

Not alone does he banish fear, but he fills them with joy of spirit. For there follows: *Behold, I bring you good tidings of great joy.* And not to Israel alone, but to all men. The cause of this joy is declared; a new and wondrous Birth is revealed by the names of the Newborn Child: *For this day is born to you a Saviour, Who is Christ the Lord, in the city of David.* Of which names, the first is a name of accomplishment: *Saviour*; the third of Majesty, *Lord.* CYRIL, in *Cat. G.F.*: But that which is placed between is a name of unction, and signifies, not a nature, but an hypostatic union (*hypostasim compositam.*) For we confess that in Christ Our Saviour the anointing was glorious; not figurative alone, as with the kings, pouring oil upon their heads, as it were a prophetic instrument of the divine favour; nor in dedication to some task, as: *Thus sayeth the Lord to Cyrus, my anointed* (Is. xlv. 1), who though an idolator, was yet called anointed, because as a visitation sent from above, he would occupy the land of the Babylonians. But the Saviour, becoming Man in the form of a servant, was anointed with the Holy Spirit; God also anointing with the Holy Spirit all those who believe in Him.

V. 11. *For, this day is born to you a Saviour, who is Christ the Lord, in the city of David.*

GREEK COMMENTATOR: The angel also tells the time of this birth: *This day is born to you a Saviour*; and the place: *In the city of David*; and the signs: *And this shall be a sign unto you, you shall find.* See in what manner the angels announce to the shepherds the Prince of Shepherds: as a new-born Lamb, seen in a cave. BEDE: With frequent heralding of angels, and with manifold testimonies of the Gospels, the Infancy of the Saviour is impressed on our hearts, so that deep within may be implanted the remembrance of what He has done for us. And let us note that the sign given to us of the Saviour is not that of a Child reclining in Tyrrhennian purple, but of one wrapped in poor swaddling clothes; not of One resting on a gilded bed, but lying in a manger.

V. 12. *And this shall be a sign unto you. You shall find the infant wrapped in swaddling clothes and laid in a manger.*

MAXIMUS, *sermon for the Nat.*: But if these swaddling clothes seem to you unbecoming, look up and hear the heavenly choir. Should you deplore the manger, raise your eyes a little and see the new star in the sky, proclaiming to the world the Birth of the Lord. If you believe these unworthy, believe that these are wondrous. If you do not hold with the things that savour of lowliness, worship those that are sublime and heavenly.

GREGORY, *Hom. 8 in Evang.*: That an angel appears to the watching shepherds, and that the Brightness of God shone round about them, may also be understood in a mystical sense; and this is: that they above others merit to behold the sublime mysteries, who know how to guard carefully their believing flocks. While they dutifully keep guard over their flocks, the divine grace will shine abundantly on them. BEDE: For these shepherds of the flocks mystically signify the Teachers and Rulers of the faithful. The night, in which they keep watch over their flocks, stands for the danger of the temptations against which they must without ceasing defend both themselves and the flocks committed to them. And well indeed, since the Lord is born, do the shepherds keep watch over their flocks, since He is born who has said: *I am the Good Shepherd.* The time was now drawing near when this Shepherd would recall to His own living pastures, those of His sheep who had strayed.

ORIGEN, *Hom.* 12 *in Luke:* And if one should seek a still higher meaning, I affirm that there were certain angelic shepherds who ruled over human affairs, and while each stood guard over his flock, upon the birth of the Lord, an angel came and announced to them that the True Shepherd was born. For before the Advent of the Lord these angels could bring little help to their flocks. For scarce any one from among the Gentiles believed in God. But now the people are drawing to faith in Jesus.

V. 13. *And suddenly there was with the angel a multitude of the heavenly army, praising God, and saying:*

BEDE: So that the authority of one angel might not seem insufficient, when one from among them had announced the mystery of the nativity: *suddenly there was with the angel a multitude of the heavenly army.* Fittingly does the approaching choir of angels receive the name of *heavenly army,* which now humbly comes to adore that *Leader who is mighty in battle*; Who has appeared to break down the infernal gates; Who alone, in Power and with heavenly might, has cast down those inimical powers whom man himself was powerless to overcome, however much he strove or desired. Since both God and man is truly born, then rightly is peace proclaimed to men, and glory to God. Hence there follows:

V. 14. *Glory to God in the highest; and on earth peace to men of good will.*

Upon one angel, one messenger, announcing that God was born in the flesh, of a sudden the multitude of the heavenly host break forth in praise of their Creator. That their example may inspire us, that devotion to Christ may ever increase, as often as one of the brethren shall give forth a word of the sacred praise, or should we in our hearts recall the things of holy love, let us immediately give praise to God, with voice, with deed, and in our hearts.

CHRYSOSTOM, *in Cat. of G.F.:* Where before angels were sent to punish, as to the Israelites, to David, to the Sodomites, and to the valley of tears (Jdg. ii. 5), now they sing on earth, giving thanks to God because He had revealed to them His coming down amongst men. GREGORY, 28 *Moral.* 7. All together they give praise, blending in harmony the sounds of their exultation because of our redemption; all together they rejoice, since seeing us brought back amongst them, they give praise that their number is made full.

BEDE: They wish also peace to men, adding: *And on earth peace to men of good will*; because they whom before they had seen as weak and lowly, now that the Lord is born in human flesh they honour as equals. CYRIL: This peace was made through Christ. For by himself He reconciled us to the Father, and to God (II Cor. v. 16, 19), taking from our midst the inimical guilt, reconciling two peoples through one Man (Eph. ii. 16), and joining together into one Flock both those in heaven and those on earth (Col. i. 20).

BEDE: Towards which men do they wish peace is also revealed as they exclaim: *To men of good will*; to those, namely, who shall receive the New-Born Christ. For *there is no peace for the wicked* (Is. lvii. 21), but there is peace in abundance to those who love the name of God (Ps. cxviii. 21). ORIGEN in Luke, hom. 13: But the diligent reader will ask, how is it that the Saviour says: *Think ye that I have come to give peace on earth?* And now the angels of the nativity sing: *On earth peace to men of good will*. That peace is said to be given to men of good will itself answers the question; for the peace which God gives not, is not the peace of good will. AUGUSTINE, *De Trin.* 13: For justice pertains to good will. CHRYSOSTOM,: Behold this wondrous progress.

He first sends angels to men, then leads men to heavenly things. A heaven is made on earth, since heaven must take to itself the things of earth.

ORIGEN, *Hom.* 13 *in Luke:* Mystically, the angels began to see that the task that had been given them they could not fulfil, without His aid Who alone can truly save, and that their own remedies were inadequate to the needs of men. And as when someone appears who possesses the highest medical skill, they who till now could effect no cure, beholding the touch of a master, are not envious at the sight of the healing wounds, but loud in praise of the physician and of God, Who had sent both to themselves and the sick a man of such eminence, so too the multitude of the angels praise God for the Coming of Christ.

THE GOSPEL OF THE MASS OF THE AURORA

LUKE ii. 15–20

At that time, the shepherds said one to another: Let us go over to Bethlehem, and let us see this word that is come to pass, which the Lord hath showed to us. And they came with haste; and they found Mary and Joseph, and the infant lying in the manger. And seeing, they understood of the words that had been spoken to them concern-ing this child. And all that heard, wondered; and at those things that were told them by the shepherds. But Mary kept all these words, pondering them in her heart. And the shepherds returned, glorifying and praising God, for all the things they had heard and seen, as it was told unto them.

EXPOSITION FROM THE CATENA AUREA

V. 15. *The shepherds said one to another: let us go over to Bethlehem. . .* GEOMETER, *from Cat. of G.F.:* What they had seen and heard so astonished the shepherds that they, forgetful of their flocks, set off in the night for Bethlehem, to find out concerning the meaning of this light of the Saviour. Hence is said *one to another . . . and let us see this word.* BEDE: As being truly vigilant they did not say: *let us see this child*, but, *this word that is come to pass;* that is, let us see how the Word, Which always was, has become flesh; since this *word* is the Lord, for there follows on: *Which the Lord has made and showed to us;* that is, let us see how the Word has made Himself, and has shown to us His flesh.

V. 16. *And they came with haste; and they found Mary and Joseph, and the infant lying in a manger.*

AMBROSE, *in Luke Ch.* 2: See how the Scriptures weigh carefully the meaning of each word. For when the Flesh of the Lord is seen, the Word is seen, which is the Son. Do not let it seem to you but an indifferent proof of your faith, this that the persons of the shepherds are lowly. Simplicity is aimed at here, grandeur is not desired. Hence follows *And they came with haste;* no one comes seeking Christ in sloth. ORIGEN, *Hom.* 13 *in Luke:* Because they came in haste, not leisuredly, it then follows that: *they found Mary,* who, without pain, had brought forth Jesus, *and Joseph,* that is, the Protector of the Divine Infancy; *and the infant laid in a manger,* namely the Saviour Himself.

V. 17 and 18. *And seeing, they understood of the word . . . And all that heard, wondered.*

BEDE: Right order demands that having fittingly commemorated the Incarnation of the Word, we raise our minds to the Glory of the Word; hence: *And seeing, they understood of the word that had been spoken to them concerning this child.* PHOTIUS, *in Cat. G.F.:* The joyful things that had been seen and heard they tell, not alone to Mary and Joseph, but to others, and what is more, they

impressed them deeply, for, *all that heard, wondered.* How could it be other than wondrous to see a Heavenly Being among men, and earth at peace with heaven, and that Ineffable Child uniting celestial Majesty and earthly humanity, and in His own Person sustaining this wondrous harmony.

GLOSS: Nor did they wonder only at the mystery of the Incarnation, but at such testimony from the shepherds, who would not know how to invent such unheard of things, but would only proclaim in simple language what was true.

V. 19. *But Mary kept all these words, pondering them in her heart.*

AMBROSE, *Bk.* 2 *in Luke:* Do not despise the words of the shepherds; for from the Shepherds Mary enriched her faith.   Hence there follows: *But Mary kept all these words, pondering them in her heart.* Let us learn from the Holy Virgin to be chaste in all respects; who no less modest in speech as in person, quietly gathered to her heart all the proofs of her faith. BEDE, in Mass of Aurora: Observing all the restraints of virginal modesty, she desired not to make known the secrets she had learned from Christ, but places the things she had read were yet to be accomplished with those she knew were now fulfilled; not breaking forth in speech, but keeping these things enclosed within her heart.

METAPHRASTES, *in Cat. G.F.:* Whatsoever the Angel had told her, whatsoever she had learned from Zachary, and from Elizabeth, and from the shepherds, all these she stored in her mind, and, comparing them one with another, the Mother of Wisdom discerns one harmony of truth in all: that He was truly God that was born of her.

V. 20. And the shepherds returned, glorifying and praising God . . .

ATHANASIUS, *in Cat. G.F.:* One by one they exult in the Birth of Christ, not however after the manner of men, as men rejoice at the birth of a child; but as in the presence of Christ, and in the glory of divine light; hence follows: *And the shepherds returned, glorifying and praising God, for all the things they had heard.* BEDE: Namely, from the angels; *and seen,* namely, in Bethlehem, *as it was told unto them*; that is, they glorify God that, having come there, they found all that had been told to them; or *as it was told unto them,* they glorify and praise God. For this they were bidden to do by the angels, not commanding them in words, but by giving them the example of their own devotion, when they praised and gave glory to God in the highest.

BEDE, *in Nat. Dom.:* Mystically, let the shepherds of the flocks that reason, and indeed let all the faithful, following the example of the shepherds, go over in spirit to Bethlehem, and there fittingly celebrate the Incarnation of Christ. Let us with all the desire of our souls, and casting aside all carnal desires, cross over to that heavenly Bethlehem which is the House of the Living Bread, so that Him Whom we now behold lying feeble in the manger, we may merit to look upon seated on the Throne of His Father. So great a joy is not to be sought for in sloth and ease;

only with eagerness may the footsteps of Christ be followed. *And seeing, they understood.* Let us likewise hasten to take unto ourselves, with all the joy of our hearts, what has been said of the Saviour, that we may be able to understand in that future vision of perfect knowledge.

BEDE: The shepherds of the Lord's Flock follow after the life of the Fathers that have gone before us, by as it were contemplating the gates of Bethlehem, in which the Bread of life abides, and there find nothing save the virginal beauty of the Catholic Church, as it were Mary; the steadfast company of Her spiritual guides, as though Joseph; and the humble advent of Christ, inserted between the pages of Sacred Scripture, as it were *the Infant lying in a manger.*[3]

ORIGEN, as above: It was of this manger the prophet spoke, saying: *The ox knoweth his owner, and the ass his master's crib* (Is. i. 3). BEDE: hom. in *Nat.*: The shepherds did not conceal in silence that they which had learned, so also for this are the shepherds of the Church ordained, that what they have learned from the Scriptures, they may make known to those who listen. BEDE, as above, in Luke 2: The pastors of the spiritual flocks, while others sleep, seek heavenly things in contemplation; now they go about among the churches of the faithful, seeking to form models of virtue; now they return to the public task of the pastoral office of teaching.

BEDE, *in Hom. Auroris:* Each one though he seems to live simply as a private person, holds the office of shepherd, if gathering together a flock of good deeds and chaste thoughts, he endeavours to guide it with fitting rule, nourishing it on the pastures of the Scripture, and defending it against the snares of the demons.

I. St John Chrysostom, Bishop and Doctor[4]

Christmas Morning

I behold a new and wondrous mystery. My ears resound to the Shepherd's song, piping no soft melody, but chanting full forth a heavenly hymn. The Angels sing. The Archangels blend their voice in harmony. The Cherubim hymn their joyful praise. The Seraphim exalt His glory. All join to praise this holy feast, beholding the Godhead here on earth, and man in heaven. He Who is above, now for our redemption dwells here below; and he that was lowly is by divine mercy raised.

Bethlehem this day resembles heaven; hearing from the stars the singing of angelic voices; and in place of the sun, enfolds within itself on every side, the Sun of Justice. And ask not how: for where God wills, the order of nature yields. For He willed, He had the power, He descended, He redeemed; all things move in obedience to God. This day He Who is, is Born; and He Who is, becomes what He was not. For when He was God, He became man; yet not departing from the Godhead that is His. Nor yet by any loss of divinity became He man, nor through increase[5] became He God from man; but being the Word He became flesh, His nature, because of impassibility, remaining unchanged.[6]

When He was born the Jews denied His extraordinary birth; the Pharisees began to interpret falsely the Sacred Writings; the Scribes spoke in contradiction of that which they read. Herod sought Him out Who was born, not that he might adore, but to put Him to death. Today all things proclaim the opposite. *For they have not been, that I may speak with the psalmist, hidden from their children, in another generation* (Ps. lxxvii. 4). And so the kings have come, and they have seen the heavenly King that has come upon the earth, not bringing with Him Angels, nor Archangels, nor Thrones, nor Dominations, nor Powers, nor Principalities, but, treading a new and solitary path, He has come forth from a spotless womb.

Yet He has not forsaken His angels, nor left them deprived of His care, nor because of His Incarnation has he departed from the Godhead. And behold kings have come, that they might adore the heavenly King of glory; soldiers, that they might serve the Leader of the Hosts of Heaven; women, that they might adore Him Who was born of a woman so that He might change the pains of childbirth into joy; virgins, to the Son of the Virgin, beholding with joy, that He Who is the Giver of milk, Who has decreed that the fountains of the breast pour forth in ready streams, receives from a Virgin Mother the food of infancy; infants, that they may adore Him Who became a little child, so that *out of the mouth of infants and of sucklings*, He might perfect praise;

children, to the Child Who raised up martyrs through the rage of Herod; men, to Him Who became man, that He might heal the miseries of His servants; shepherds, to the Good Shepherd Who has laid down His life for His sheep; priests, to Him Who has become a High Priest according to the order of Melchisedech; servants, to Him Who *took upon Himself the form of a servant* that He might bless our servitude with the reward of freedom (Phil. ii. 7); fishermen, to Him Who from amongst fishermen chose catchers of men; publicans, to Him Who from amongst then named a chosen Evangelist; sinful women, to Him Who exposed His Feet to the tears of the repentant; and that I may embrace them all together, all sinners have come, that they may look upon the Lamb of God who taketh away the sins of the world.

Since therefore all rejoice, I too desire to rejoice. I too wish to share the choral dance, to celebrate the festival. But I take my part, not plucking the harp, not shaking the Thyrsian staff, not with the music of the pipes, nor holding a torch, but holding in my arms the cradle of Christ. For this is all my hope, this my life, this my salvation, this my pipe, my harp. And bearing it I come, and having from its power received the gift of speech, I too, with the angels, sing: *Glory to God in the Highest*; and with the shepherds, *and on earth peace to men of good will.*

This day He Who was ineffably begotten of the Father, was for me born of the Virgin, in a way no tongue can tell. Begotten according to His nature before all ages from the Father: in what

manner He knows Who has begotten Him; born again this day from the Virgin, above the order of nature, in what manner knoweth the power of the Holy Spirit. And His heavenly generation is true, and His generation here on earth is true. As God He is truly begotten of God; so also as man is He truly born from the Virgin. In heaven He alone is the Only-Begotten of the One God; on earth He alone is the Only-Begotten of the unique Virgin.

And as in the heavenly generation, to imply a mother is heretical, so in this earthly generation, to speak of a father is blasphemy. The Father begot in the spirit (*Pater absque defluxu genuit*), and the Virgin brought forth without defilement. The Father begot without the limitations of flesh, since He begot as became the Godhead; so neither did the Virgin endure corruption in her childbearing, since she brought forth miraculously. Hence, since this heavenly birth cannot be described, neither does His coming amongst us in these days permit of too curious scrutiny. Though I know that a Virgin this day gave birth, and I believe that God was begotten before all time, yet the manner of this generation I have learned to venerate in silence, and I accept that this is not to be probed too curiously with wordy speech. For with God we look not for the order of nature, but rest our faith in the power of Him who works.

It is indeed the way of nature that a woman in wedlock brings forth; when an unwed virgin, after she has born a child, is still a virgin, then nature is here surpassed. Of that which happens in accord with nature we may enquire; what passes above it we honour in silence; not as something to be avoided, passed over, but as that which we venerate in silence, as something sublime, beyond all telling.

But give me now your indulgence, I beg you, that I may bring this exordium to a close. But since I fear to pursue the scrutiny of this sublime theme, I know not on what ground, at what part of this discourse, to make the separation.

What shall I say to you; what shall I tell you? I behold a Mother who has brought forth; I see a Child come to this light by birth. The manner of His conception I cannot comprehend. Nature here is overcome, the boundaries of the established order set aside, where God so wills. For not according to nature has this thing come to pass. Nature here rested, while the Will of God laboured. O ineffable grace! The Only Begotten, Who is before all ages, Who cannot be touched or be perceived, Who is simple, without body, has now put on my body, that is visible and liable to corruption. For what reason? That coming amongst us he may teach us, and teaching, lead us by the hand to the things that men cannot see. For since men believe that the eyes are more trustworthy than the ears, they doubt of that which they do not see, and so He has deigned to show Himself in bodily presence, that He may remove all doubt.

And He was born from a Virgin, who knew not His purpose; neither had she laboured with Him to bring it to pass, nor contributed to that which He had done, but was the simple instrument of His Hidden Power. That alone she knew which she had learned by her question to Gabriel: *How shall this be done, because I know not man?* Then said he; do you wish to hear his words? *The Holy Spirit shall come upon thee, and the power of the Most High shall overshadow thee.*

And in what manner was the Almighty with her, Who in a little while came forth from her? He was as the craftsman, who coming on some suitable material, fashions to himself a beautiful vessel; so Christ, finding the holy body and soul of the Virgin, builds for Himself a living temple, and as He had willed, formed there a man from the Virgin; and, putting Him on, this day came forth[7]; unashamed of the lowliness of our nature. For it was to Him no lowering to put on what He Himself had made. Let that handiwork be forever glorified, which became the cloak of its own Creator. For as in the first creation of flesh, man could not be made before the clay had come into His hand, so neither could this corruptible body be glorified, until it had first become the garment of its Maker.

What shall I say! And how shall I describe this Birth to you? For this wonder fills me with astonishment. The Ancient of days has become an infant. He Who sits upon the sublime and heavenly Throne, now lies in a manger. And He Who cannot be touched, Who is simple, without complexity, and incorporeal, now lies subject to the hands of men. He Who has broken the bonds of sinners, is now bound by an infants' bands. (These last three sentences are an insert from St Cyril of Alexandria.) But He has decreed that ignominy shall become honour, infamy be clothed with glory, and total humiliation the measure of His Goodness. For this He assumed my body, that I may become capable of His Word; taking my flesh, He gives me His Spirit; and so He bestowing and I receiving, He prepares for me the treasure of Life. He takes my flesh, to sanctify me; He gives me His Spirit, that He may save me.

But what can I say? And of what shall my feeble tongue speak? *Behold a Virgin shall conceive* (Is. vii. 14). This is no longer said of something that is to be, but received as something fulfilled. And it was fulfilled among the Jews, to whom it was foretold; it is believed by us, to whom it was not at any time announced. *Behold a Virgin shall conceive.* The Deed was given to the Synagogue, but to the Church was given possession. The one found a document, the other a pearl of great price. The one was clothed in wool, the other in a royal robe. Judah brings Him forth, the whole world acclaims Him. The Synagogue nourished and instructed Him, the Church seized Him and holds Him fast. The Synagogue has the vinebranch, I have the Fruit of Truth. Israel garnered the grapes, the Gentiles drink the mystical wine. The one sowed the seed wheat in Judea, and the Gentiles have reaped the harvest with the sickle of faith. The Gentiles have reverently plucked the rose, and to the Jews remain the thorn of hard-heartedness. The nestling has taken wing, but the foolish still wait by the empty nest. Israel still ponders the leaves of the Book, while the Gentiles enjoy the fruit of the Spirit.

Behold a virgin shall conceive. Tell, O Judea, Whom has she brought forth? Confide it to me as you did to Herod. But you confide not in men. I know the reason. Because of treachery. You spoke to Herod, but that Herod might destroy Him. To me you are silent, lest I adore Him.

Whom has she brought forth? Whom? The Lord of nature For though thou art silent, nature cries out. For She has brought forth as He Who was born decreed to be born. Not as nature decreed, but He as nature's Lord has made for Himself a new and unheard of birth, that He may show Himself as man; but not brought forth as men are born, but born as God. For from a Virgin He came forth this day, He Who hath set nature aside, and risen above the ways of nuptials.[8]

It was fitting that the Giver of all holiness should enter this world by a pure and holy birth. For He it is that of old formed Adam from the virgin earth, and from Adam without help of woman formed woman. For us without woman Adam produced woman, so did the Virgin without man this day bring forth a man. *For it is a man,* saith the Lord, *and who shall know him* (Jer. xvii. 9. (LXX). For since the race of women owed to men a debt, as from Adam without woman woman came, therefore without man the Virgin this day brought forth, and on behalf of Eve repaid the debt to man.

That Adam might not take pride, that he without woman had engendered woman, a Woman without man has begotten man; so that by the similarity of the mystery is proved the similarity in nature. For as before the Almighty took a rib from Adam, and by that

Adam was not made less; so in the Virgin He formed a living temple, and the holy virginity remained unchanged. Sound and unharmed Adam remained even after the deprivation of a rib; unstained the Virgin though a Child was born of her.

Not elsewhere did He form for Himself a living temple; nor other body did He take than this, so that men should not remain branded with dishonour. For man being deceived became the devil's slave. So him that was thus supplanted, He took as His own living temple, that being joined to his Maker, man might then be wrested from this bond, and from subjection to the devil.

Yet in becoming man He was born, not as man is born, but as God. If He had been born from an ordinary union, as I was, He would have been reckoned a fraud. And for this cause He is now born of a Virgin, but in being being born He preserves undefiled this womb, and protects that spotless virginity; so that this unheard of manner of bringing forth is for me a pledge of its sublime truthfulness.

So should Gentile or Jew ask me, did Christ Who is God by nature, become man in a manner above nature, I answer: "that is so," and call as witness the unstained seal of virginity. It is God alone Who can so rise above nature; for He is the Maker of the womb, the Author of virginity, Who has thus without stain preserved the manner of His own Birth, and in a mysterious way has formed there, according to His will, a temple unto Himself.

Tell me, O Judea, Has a virgin brought forth, or has she not? If she has, then acknowledge this wondrous birth. If she has not, why did you lead Herod astray? Why didst thou, to his urgent inquiry as to where the Christ is to be born, make answer: *In Bethlehem of Juda*. Did I know the village, or the place? How have I learned of the dignity of His lineage? Was it not Isaias that spake of it, as being of God Himself? *Behold a Virgin shall conceive, and bear a son, and His name shall be called Emmanuel* (Is. vii. 14).

Is it not you, O wicked enemies, that have brought forth the truth? Have you not, Scribes and Pharisees, diligent custodians of the Law, taught us these things? Did we know the Hebrew tongue?

Was it not you who interpreted the Scriptures? After the Virgin brought forth, and before She brought forth, lest these words be interpreted in praise of God, did you not, when questioned by Herod, bring forward the witness of the prophet Micheas, that he might confirm your words? *And thou Bethlehem the land of Juda, are not the least among the princes of Juda: for out of thee shall come forth the captain that shall rule my people Israel* (Mt. ii. 6; Micheas. v. 2).

Rightly did the prophet say, *out of thee*. He has gone out from thee, and gone into the whole world. He Who is, has gone forth. He who is not, is created, or becomes. And of Himself He was, and before was, and always was: but always as God, governing the world. This day He comes forth; as Man He rules the people, as God He saves all men.

O Kindly Enemies! O Modest and Gentle Accusers! Who, without knowing it, proclaimed that God was born in Bethlehem; who made known that He was laid in a manger; who, unwittingly, pointed out the cave where He lay hidden, and, against their own will, laid on us a debt of gratitude. For they made known that which they strove to keep hidden. Behold them! The Foolish Teachers! That which they teach, they themselves know not; consumed with hunger, they feed others; thirsting, they give to drink; needy, they yet enrich.

Come, then, let us observe the Feast. Come, and we shall commemorate the solemn festival. It is a strange manner of celebrating a festival; but truly wondrous is the whole chronicle of the Nativity. For this day the ancient slavery is ended, the devil confounded, the demons take to flight, the power of death is broken, paradise is unlocked, the curse is taken away, sin is removed from us, error driven out, truth has been brought back, the speech of kindliness diffused, and spreads on every side, a heavenly way of life has been implanted on the earth, angels communicate with men without fear, and men now hold speech with angels.

Why is this? Because God is now on earth, and man in heaven; on every side all things commingle. He has come on earth, while being Whole in heaven; and while complete in heaven, He is without diminution on earth. Though He was God, He became Man; not denying Himself to be God. Though being the impassable Word, He became flesh; that He might dwell amongst us, He became Flesh. He did not become God. He was God. Wherefore He became flesh, so that He Whom heaven did not contain, a manger would this day receive. He was placed in a manger, so that He, by whom all things are nourished, may receive an infant's food from His Virgin Mother. So, the Father of all ages, as an infant at the breast, nestles in the virginal arms, that the Magi may more easily see Him. Since this day the Magi too have come, and made a beginning of withstanding tyranny; and the heavens give glory, as the Lord is revealed by a star.

And sitting upon the swift cloud of His Body the Lord flies into Egypt; to escape the treachery of Herod without doubt, but also that the words of Isaias may be fulfilled (Is. xix. 24, 25): *In that day shall Israel be third to the Egyptian and the Assyrian, and blessed be my people of Egypt, and the work of my hands to the Assyrian.* What dost thou say, O Juda, who was first and has become third? The Egyptians and Assyrians are placed before thee, and Israel, the first born, is last?

Rightly shall the Assyrians be first, since they through the Magi first adored Him. The Egyptians after the Assyrians, since it was they received Him flying from the treachery of Herod. Israel is numbered in the third place, as only after His ascent from the Jordan was He acknowledged by His Apostles. He entered Egypt, deliberately causing the idols of Egypt to tremble, and after He had closed the porches of Egypt by the destruction of her firstborn (Is. xix. i).

And so as Firstborn He enters Egypt this day, that He may end the mourning over her ancient grief. Luke has testified that Christ shall be called a firstborn: *And she brought forth her firstborn son.* He enters therefore that He may dissolve the ancient sorrow, and instead of plagues bring joy. In place of night and darkness, He brings the Light of salvation. The stream of young life was stained by the slaughter of the Innocents. He has therefore entered the land of Egypt, Who of old made her rivers red. Now He grants the flowing river the power to give salvation; and cleanses their stains and afflictions with the power of His Holy Spirit. The Egyptians had been punished, and turning with fury they had denied God. He went therefore into Egypt, and filled religious souls with the knowledge of God, and disposed that the river should nourish martyrs more numerous than its reeds.

But because of shortness of time I must make an end of speaking. What remains I shall keep till the following day. I shall end today when I have explained how it is, since the Word is impassible, that the Word became flesh, Its nature remaining unchanged.

But what shall I say? What shall I utter? *Behold an infant wrapped in swaddling clothes and lying in a manger.* Mary is present, who is both Virgin and Mother. Joseph is present, who is called father. He is called husband, she is called wife. The names indeed are lawful, but there is no other bond. We speak here of words, not of things. He was espoused to her, but the Most High overshadowed her. Hence, Joseph, doubting, knew not what to call the Infant. He would not dare to say that It was conceived in adultery; he could not speak harshly against the Virgin; he shrank from calling the Child his own. He

knew well that here was something unknown to him; how or whence was this Child born? And being anxious because of this, there came to him a message, by the voice of an angel, which said: *Fear not to take unto thee Mary thy wife, for that which is conceived in her, is of the Holy Ghost.*

The Holy Ghost overshadowed the Virgin. Wherefore was He born of a virgin, and wherefore was her virginity preserved? Because the devil had deceived the virgin Eve; accordingly, to Mary, who was a virgin, Gabriel bore a message of joy. As Eve, being deceived, uttered a word that was the cause of death, so Mary, receiving good tidings, brought forth in the flesh a Word that gave us eternal Life. The word of Eve led to the tree, because of which Adam was driven from Paradise; the Word which the Virgin brought forth, led to the Cross, because of which the Thief, standing in the place of Adam, was led into Paradise.

As neither the Gentiles, nor the Jews, nor heretics, believed that God begot as men, accordingly, coming forth this day from a passible body, the Impassible preserved inviolate the passible body, that He might show, that just as He was born of a virgin, while She remained a virgin, so likewise God, His Sacred Substance remaining unchanged, as God, and, as befitted God, begot God.

Seeing that men, abandoning Him, fashioned for themselves statues, to which, offending God, they gave adoration, for which cause, on this day, the Word of God, being truly God, appeared in the form of man, that He might set aright this falsehood; and in a veiled manner, has turned all adoration unto Himself. To Him, then, Who out of confusion has wrought a clear path, to Christ, to the Father, and to the Holy Ghost, we offer all praise, now and for ever. Amen.

II. St Ambrose, Bishop and Doctor

The Beginning of the Church[9]

Behold the beginning of the Church now appearing. Christ is born, and the Shepherds begin their watch: they who will gather the flocks of the Gentiles, before living as untended beasts, into the Fold of the Lord, lest through the thick dark of the night they remain exposed to the ravages of reasoning wild beasts.

And well do those Shepherds watch, whom the Good Shepherd teaches. The people then are the flock, the world is the night, and the priests are the Shepherds. Perhaps he also is a Shepherd to whom it was said: *Be watchful and strengthen* (Apoc. iii. 2); because for the defence of His flock the Lord has not alone ordained Bishops, but also appointed angels to this office.

And behold an angel of the Lord stood by them. See in what manner the divine solicitude prepares the way of faith. An angel teaches Mary, an angel teaches Joseph, and an angel guides the shepherds; it is not enough that one be sent, for in the mouth of two or three witnesses every word shall stand.

And suddenly there was with the angel a multitude of the heavenly army, praising God, and saying: Glory to God in the highest; and on earth peace to men of good will. Well is that army of the angels named who followed the Lord of Hosts. To whom do they give praise save to their Lord, as it is written: *Praise ye the Lord from the heavens: praise ye Him in the high places; praise ye Him all His angels* (Ps. cxlviii. 1).

Fulfilled now is the prophecy. The Lord is praised from the heavens; and He is seen on earth. Of Him the Holy Mark says: *And He was with beasts, and the angels ministered to Him* (Mk. i. 13). As in one is a sign of mercy, in the other you behold a witness of divine power. It was because of men He suffered the beasts; it was because of Himself He is proclaimed by the angels.

Let us go over to Bethlehem, and let us see this word that is come to pass, which the Lord hath showed to us. And they came with haste. See the Shepherds come with haste; none come seeking Christ in sloth. See how the Shepherds believe the angels; so must thou believe the Father, Son and Holy Spirit, and in the angels, prophets, and apostles. See how carefully the Scripture weighs the meaning of each single word: *They hasten*, it says, *to see this word.* For the Word, that is, the Son is seen, when the Body of the Lord is seen.

Because the shepherds are persons of humble state, do not esteem lightly the testimony of their faith. For the more humble the testimony appears to human wisdom, the more precious is it to the eyes of faith. For the Lord did not seek out the schools of learning, filled with the wise, but the simple people, who would not know how to twist, to colour, what they learned; for he sought not ambition, it was simplicity He looked for.

Neither must you lightly regard the words of the shepherds, as being those of ignorant men. For from the shepherds also Mary added to her faith: by the shepherds were the people joined together unto the praise of God; *for they wondered at those things that were taught them by the shepherds.*

But Mary kept all these words, pondering them in her heart. Let us learn from this of the chaste manner in all things of the Holy Virgin, who no less guarded in word, than modest in person, pondered in her heart upon these proofs of her faith.

If Mary learns from the shepherds, why do you turn from the teaching of the priests? If Mary was silent before the Apostles had taught, why do you wish, now that the Apostles have spoken, to teach rather than learn? And learn that sinfulness belongs to the person, not to the sex; for sex is sacred. Lastly, Mary received no precept, but she has given an example to the world. Amen.

III. St Leo, Pope and Doctor

The Mystery of the Nativity[10]

Synopsis:
> I. That no one is shut out from the joy of the Lord's Nativity; which alone had place without stain of sin.
> II. Wondrous is the ordering of this Mystery.
> III. Whosoever wishes to put on the New Man, must put off the Old.

1. Our Saviour, dearly Beloved, was born this day. Let us rejoice. Sadness is not becoming upon the Birth Day of Life Itself, which, now that the fear of death is ended, fills us with gladness, because of our own promised immortality. No one is excluded from sharing in this cheerfulness for the reason of our joy is common to all men. Our Lord, the Conqueror of sin and death, since there was no one free from servitude, came that He might bring deliverance to all.

Let him who is sanctified rejoice, for he draws nigh to the palm. Let the sinner rejoice, since he is invited to grace. Let the Gentiles exult, for they are called to life. For the Son of God, in the fulness of time, has taken upon Himself the nature of our humanity, as the unsearchable depths of the divine counsel hath decreed, in order that the inventor of death, the devil, by that very nature which he defeated, would be himself overcome.

And in this contest that was undertaken for us, the battle was waged in accordance with a great and wondrous law of justice. For the Omnipotent God engaged in combat with His most bitter enemy, not in the strength of His own Majesty, but in our human infirmity; confronting him with our very form and nature, and sharing likewise in our mortality; but free of all stain.

Unlike this Holy Nativity, is that of which we read of all men: *No one is there free from sin, not even the infant whose life upon the earth is but a day* (Job xiv. 4 (LXX). But of the concupiscence of the flesh, nothing has been transmitted in this unique generation; nothing of the law of sin has descended. A royal virgin of the house of David is chosen as the bearer of the Sacred Fruit, who had conceived her divine and human Offspring in her soul, before she conceived Him in her body.

And knowing not the divine purpose, and lest she be fearful at such unheard of tidings, she learns from the angelic colloquy of that which was to be wrought in her by the Holy Spirit; nor did she, who was about to become the Mother of God, believe that this betokened the loss of her virginity.

Why should she be fearful, to whom fruitfulness is promised through the power of the Most High? The faith of the believer is confirmed by the witness of the miracle that went before, when to Elizabeth was given unlooked for fruitfulness; that it might not be doubted, that He Who had given to the barren to conceive, would give it likewise to the Virgin.

2. The Word of God, therefore, God, the Son of God, Who in the beginning was with God, by Whom all things were made, and without Whom was made nothing that was made, became Man, that He might free man from eternal death; bending down to the taking of our lowliness, without diminution of His own Majesty, so that remaining what He was, and taking upon Himself what He was not, He might join the form of a true servant to that form in which He is equal to God the Father (Phil. ii. 6); and by such a bond so link both

natures, that this exaltation might not swallow up the lesser, nor adoption lessen the Higher.

Preserving therefore, the substance of both natures, and uniting them in One Person, lowliness is assumed by Majesty; infirmity, by Power; mortality, by Immortality. And to pay the debt of our present state, an inviolable Nature is united to our suffering one; and true God and true man are welded into the unity of One Lord, so that, as was needed for our healing, one and the same Mediator of God and men, might, by the one, suffer death, and by the Other, rise again from the dead. Rightly then, did this Birth of our salvation bring no taint of corruption to the Virginal integrity; for the birth of Truth, was the defence of virginity.

Such a birth, dearly Beloved, befitted Christ, the Power of God, and the Wisdom of God; whereby He would be both joined to our lowliness, yet remain far above us in His divinity. For unless He were true God, He could bring us no aid; and were He not true man, He could offer us no example. The exulting angels, therefore, sing to the new born Lord, *Glory to God in the Highest*, and they announce unto me, *peace on earth to men of good will*. For they see the heavenly Jerusalem made up from all peoples of the earth. With what joy may not the lowliness of mankind rejoice in this unspeakable work of the divine compassion, when the angels in their glory so greatly rejoice.

3. Let us, therefore, give thanks, dearly Beloved, to God the Father, through the Son, in the Holy Spirit; Who, because of the exceeding great love, wherein He

has loved us, has had compassion on us. And *even when we were dead in sins, hath quickened us together in Christ* (Eph. ii. 5), that in Him we might be a new creature, and a new clay. *Let us strip ourselves of the old man with his deeds;* for being made partakers of the Birth of Christ, let us renounce the deeds of the flesh (Col. iii. 9).

Acknowledge, O Christian, the dignity that is yours! Being made a partaker of the divine nature, do not by an unworthy manner of living fall back into your former abjectness of life. Be mindful of Whose Head, and of Whose Body, you are a member. Remember, that wrested from the powers of darkness, thou art now translated into the Light and the Kingdom of God. By the sacrament of baptism you have become the temple of the Holy Spirit. Do not, by evil deeds, drive out from you such a One dwelling with thee, and submit yourself again to the bondage of the devil. Because your price was the Blood of Christ; because in strickness He shall judge you Who in mercy has redeemed you, Who with the Father and the Holy Spirit, liveth and reigneth, world without end. Amen.

IV. St Gregory, Pope and Doctor

On the Feast[11]

Given to the People in the Basilica of the Blessed Virgin Mary on the day of the Nativity of Our Lord.

1. Because by the Divine Bounty we are on this day thrice to celebrate the sacred mysteries of the Mass, we cannot therefore speak at length on the Gospel lesson. But the Birth of Our Redeemer Himself demands of us that we say something for the occasion, however briefly.

Why was it that at the time when the Lord was to be born, the whole world was enrolled, unless that it so might openly be declared, that He had appeared in the flesh Who would enrol His elect for all eternity? Against which is the sentence spoken by the prophet concerning the wicked: *Let them be blotted out of the book of the living; and with the just let them not be written* (Ps. lxviii. 29).

Also was he, fittingly, born in Bethlehem: since Bethlehem is interpreted as the House of Bread. For this is He Who says: *I am the Living Bread, which came down from Heaven.* The place therefore in which the Lord was born was formerly called the House of Bread, because there it was to be that He would appear in future times, in the substance of our flesh, Who would fill the hearts of the faithful with inward abundance.

And He was born, not in the house of His parents, but upon a journey that He might truly show, that because of the humanity He had taken to Himself, He was born as it were among strangers. Strange I say, not to His power, but to His Nature. For of His Power it is written: *He came into His own.* In His own Nature He was born before all time; in ours He came to us in time. To Him therefore Who while remaining Eternal hath appeared in time, strange must the place be where He has descended.

And because the prophet says: *All flesh is grass* (Is. xl. 6), becoming man He has changed this our grass into wheat Who has declared of Himself: *Unless the grain of wheat falling into the ground die, itself remaineth alone* (Jn. xii. 24). Hence when he was born He was laid in a manger so that He might nourish with the Wheat of His flesh the beasts that He sanctifies, that is, all the faithful; so that they may not be left hungry for the food of eternal knowledge.

And what does it mean that an angel appears to the watching shepherds, and that the Brightness of God shone round about them, if not mystically signifying that they, more than others, shall merit the vision of heavenly things, who have learned to rule carefully over their faithful flocks? For while they are devoutly keeping watch over them, the divine favour shines abundantly upon them.

2. The Angel announces that a King is born, amd the choirs of angels unite their voice with his, and rejoicing all together they sing: *Glory be to God in the highest, and on earth peace to men of good will.* Before the Redeemer was born in the flesh, there was discord between us and the angels, from whose brightness and holy perfection we stood afar, in punishment first of original sin, and then because of our daily offences. Because through sin we had become strangers to God, the angels as God's subjects cut us off from their fellowship. But since we have now acknowledged our King, the angels receive us as fellow citizens. Because the King of heaven has taken unto Himself the flesh of our earth, the angels from their heavenly heights no longer look down upon our infirmity. Now they are at peace with us, putting away the remembrance of the ancient discord; now they honour us as friends, whom before they beheld weak and despised below them.

Hence was it that both Lot and. Josue adored the angels (Gen. xix 1; Jos. v. 15), and 'were not forbidden to adore. But when John, in his Apocalypse, wished to adore the angel, this same angel forbade him to adore, saying: *See thou do it not, for I am thy fellow servant, and of thy brethren* (Apoc. xxii. 9). What is the significance of this, that before the coming of the Redeemer angels were adored by men, and the angels were silent; and after, they turned away from being adored; unless that our nature which they before despised, they see now is raised above themselves, and fear exceedingly to see it prostrated before them? Nor dared they now look down on that as beneath them, which they venerate as far above them, in the King of Heaven. Nor do they refuse to accept us as equals, who now adore God made man.

Let us then be careful, dearest Brethren, that no uncleanness shall defile us, who, in the divine foreknowledge, are destined to be the subjects of God's heavenly Kingdom, and the equal of His angels. Let us prove our worthiness by the manner of our lives. Let no sensuality soil us, no evil purpose come to accuse us; let malice not devour your hearts, nor pride exalt it, nor the desire of worldly gain blow it about in every direction, nor anger inflame it. For men are called to be as Gods. Defend then the honour of God within you, O Man, against these vices, since it was because of you that God became man, who liveth and reigneth for ever. Amen.

V. BISHOP PAUL OF EMESIA[12]

The Divinity of Christ

Given on the 29th day of the month of Chaeac, i.e., the 25th of December, in the great church of Alexandria, in the presence of the blessed Cyril, on the Nativity of Our Lord Jesus Christ; and that the Blessed Virgin Mary is the Mother of God; and that we declare that there are not two Sons, but One Son, Who is the Lord Christ; and in praise of the arch-bishop Cyril.

It is fitting that on this day we should exhort your pious devotion, that you form together with us a holy choir, and with the blessed angels sing: *Glory to God in the highest: and on earth peace to men of good will.* For this day a Child is born to us, through Whom all things, visible and invisible, have obtained steadfast hope of salvation.

This day a wondrous Child is born; and the delivery of the Virgin that *knew not man* has come to pass. O most wondrous happening! A virgin brings forth, and remains a virgin; she becomes a mother, yet scarce suffers aught that mothers all must suffer: for the Virgin brings forth, as is the way of women, but remains a virgin, against that which must happen to women who give birth.

Isaias of old foreseeing this wonder, exclaimed: *Behold a Virgin shall conceive, and bear a son, and his name shall be called Emmanuel* (Is. vii. 14). And making this known to us, the Evangelist interprets His name to mean: *God with us.* Mary therefore the Mother of God brought forth Emmanuel (Matt. i. 23).[13]

The people here cried out: This is our belief; this is the gift of God; O worthy teacher of the faith, Cyril. This we have waited to hear. Who denies this let him be anathema. Bishop Paul continues.[14]

Whosoever does not profess this, understand this, mean this, let him be shut out from the Church. Mary, therefore, the Mother of God has borne unto us Emmanuel: Emmanuel, Who is God made man. For God the Word, Who in a mysterious and unspeakable manner was begotten by the Father before all ages, in these days was born of a woman (Gal. iv. 4).

For having perfectly assumed our nature, and uniting mankind to Himself from the moment of His conception, and making our body a temple for Himself, He came forth from the Virgin fully God, and the Same is fully man. For the meeting of two perfect natures, the divine namely, and the human, has given to us One Son, One Christ, One Lord.

The people cried out: Welcome, right-teaching Bishop. He is worthy of honour and praise. The Christians exclaim: This is the gift of God, O True-teaching (*Orthodoxe*) Cyril. The Bishop Paul goes on.

And I also knew that I had come

to a Father who teaches true doctrine. For neither do we adore a Quaternity, but a Trinity; Father, Son, and Holy Ghost. We anathematise those that say there are two Sons and we banish them from the sacred enclosure of the Church.

We accordingly proclaim that there are not two Sons, that Emmanuel is not a mere man, who was born of the Virgin Mother of God, and who became worthy of grace, as a prophet or any just man, but more worthy than others. *For in him dwelleth all the fulness of the Godhead corporeally* (Col. ii. 9), that is, in his Body, for He made our body His own.

Upon this faith the Church has been founded, upon this true doctrine, upon this rock the Lord God has set the foundation of the Church, for when Christ the Lord had set out for Jerusalem, He questioned His Disciples, saying: *Whom do men say that the Son of man is?* The Apostles answered: Some say Elias, others Jeremias, or one of the prophets. And He said to them: And *you*: that is you who were chosen by Me, do you also affirm these erroneous notions, as those who say I am Elias, and the others who say Jeremias, or one of the prophets? You who have now followed Me for three years, and who have witnessed My power and miracles, who have seen Me walk upon the water, and have eaten with Me at the same table, *whom do you say that I am?*

And straightaway Peter, the leader of the Apostles, the voice of the Disciples, answered: *Thou art Christ the Son of the Living God* (Matt. xvi. 13-16). Thou art Christ, the twofold nature that has become man. *Thou art Christ.* But he said not Sons, but the Son of the Living God. He recognised the oneness of the Person.

This Father therefore do we pray, that He prepare for us His wonted banquet, His precious and varied dishes, and that He place in the centre the bowl of His holy teaching; and that He may give us to drink of that strong drink which is the mother of sobriety. Let us then cry out to Him: Arise, O My Father, *arise O my Glory, arise psaltery*, and the harp of the Holy Spirit (Ps. lvi. 9), and the harp of glory and empire for ever.

Amen.

NOTES

[1] vide PL 92, col. 330.

[2] Vide St Ambrose in Luke PL 15 col. 1368; 42, 41.

[3] cf. PL 92 col. 334.

[4] PG 56 col. 385. The authenticity of this homily has been questioned; but expert opinion accepts it as the work of St John Chrysostom; it contains however two significant inserts from Cyril of Alexandria, here noted.

[5] Κατὰ προκοπήν.

[6] This paragraph, from: *and in place of the sun*, is an addition from St Cyril, who used those words speaking of the Blessed Virgin.

[7] Καὶ ἐνδυσαμενος αὐτὸν.

[8] ὑπερβάσης γάμον.

[9] CSEL, Ambr. iv, pp. 69-71.

[10] PL 54 col. 190.

[11] PL 76 col. 1103 (Homily 8).

[12] Paul, Bishop of Emesia, now Homs, near Damascus, a friend of St Cyril. Vide PG 77, 1413.

¹³ ἡ Θεοτόκος Μαρία.

¹⁴ Witness of the spontaneous manner in which the Greek churches were wont to express their appreciation of the living force of the divine truths of the Gospel, and of the grasp, even by simple people, of the significance of the manner in which they were taught, and also of their love and venera-tion for the Holy Mother of the Word Incarnate, and their zeal and concern for Her dignity. For them the central point of this sacred festivity was their fervent pro-fession of the Divinity of the New-born Child, in Whom all creation hopes, and Which alone makes efficacious His redeeming passion, and His teaching.

CHRISTMAS DAY

THE THIRD MASS

I. St Augustine: On the Gospel

II. St Leo the Great: For the Nativity of Our Lord Jesus Christ

III. St Leo the Great: On the Lord's Nativity (III)

THE GOSPEL OF THE THIRD MASS

John i. 1–14

In the beginning was the Word, and the Word was with God, and the Word was God. The same was in the beginning with God. All things were made by him: and without him was made nothing that was made. In him was life, and the life was the light of men. And the light shineth in darkness, and the darkness did not comprehend it. There was a man sent from God, whose name was John. This man came for a witness, to give testimony of the light, that all men might believe through him. He was not the light, but was to give testimony of the light. That was the true light, which enlighteneth every man that cometh into this world. He was in the world, and the world was made by him, and the world knew him not. He came unto his own, and his own received him not. But as many as received him, he gave them power to be made the sons of God, to them that believe in his name. Who are born, not of blood, nor of the will of the flesh, nor of the will of man, but of God. And the Word was made flesh, and dwelt among us, and we saw his glory, the glory as it were of the only begotten of the Father, full of grace and truth.

Exposition from the Catena Aurea

John i. 1–14. V. 1. *In the beginning was the Word, and the Word was with God, and the Word was God.*

I. *In the beginning was the Word.* Chrysostom, *Hom.* 3 *in John*: All other evangelists begin from the Incarnation, John, passing over the conception, birth, childhood, and growing years, begins immediately to speak of His Eternal Generation, saying: *In the beginning,* etc., Augustine, *Lib* 83 *quaes.* 63: That which in the Greek is called *logos,* in Latin means, both reason and word. Here it is more fittingly called Word, so that not alone His relationship to the Father may be signified, but also to those things made, through the power of creation, by the Word. Reason, although nothing may be wrought by it, is rightly called reason. AUGUSTINE, *Tr.* 1 *in John:* Daily in our speech words dissolve and vanish, because in giving them sound and utterance they disappear. But there is a word within the speaker, which remains with him, for only sound goes forth from the mouth. That which you have understood from the sound is truly and properly called the word.

AUGUSTINE, *De Trin.,* 15, 10: Whosoever can form an idea of a word, not alone before it is uttered, but even before the images of its sounds are being considered by the action of the mind, can already perceive, through this image, in this obscure way, a certain figure of the Word of which it was said: *In the beginning was the Word.* For it is necessary, when we wish to utter that which we know, that, from the knowledge we already hold in memory, the word is born, and more, that it be such as conforms exactly to the knowledge from whence it arises. The thought thus formed from that which we know, is the word, which we utter in the heart; and it is neither Greek, not Latin, nor any tongue. But when there is need to utter knowledge, of the things of which we are speaking, a certain sign is employed, by which it is conveyed. So the word that sounds outwardly, is but a sign of the word that remains concealed within, and to which the name more properly belongs. For that which is uttered by the mouth of the flesh, is the voice of the word; and it too is called word, because of that which

employed it, that it might itself appear forth.

BASIL, *Hom.* on these words: But this Word is not a human word. For how *in the beginning* was there any human word, since last of all did man receive the power of generation? Not therefore in the beginning was there any word of man, nor yet of angels; for every creature is within the bounds of the ages, receiving from the Creator the beginning of existence. But hearken with reverence to the Evangelist: This, he said, is the Only-Begotten Word.

CHRYSOSTOM, *Hom.* 1 *in John:* One may ask why the Evangelist begins to speak of the Son, unmindful of the Father? Because He was already manifest to all, although not as Father, yet as God; but the Only-Begotten was unknown. So fittingly he hastens to instill at the beginning that knowledge in those who knew Him not; but neither was he silent regarding the Father, in the things which he spoke of the Son. For it is for this that he calls Him the Word. As he was about to teach us that this Word was the Only-Begotten Son of God, lest anyone should think that this was a begetting subject to suffering, he anticipates this by calling Him the Word, and removes all dangerous notions; declaring that, without suffering, the Son was begotten of the Father. A second reason was, that it was He who would announce to us the things of His Heavenly Father.

He did not call him Word simply, but, with the addition of the article, he separates Him from all other words. For it is a custom of Holy Scripture to give the name *words* to the Laws and Commandments of God. But this Word is a substance, existing hypostatically, proceeding in an impassible manner from the Father.

BASIL: But why is He called Word? Because He was begotten impassibly. Because He is the Image of the Father, wholly showing His Begetter in Himself, not separating from Him, yet existing complete within Himself. AUGUSTINE, *De Trin.* 15; 13: As our knowledge is unlike to the knowledge of God, so is our word, that arises from our knowledge, unlike to the Word of God, Who is born of the Essence of the Father. It is the same as if I were to say, from the Knowledge of the Father, or from the Wisdom of the Father, or, more concisely, the Paternal Knowledge, or the Paternal Wisdom

Ch. 14: The Word therefore, is the Only-Begotten Son of God the Father, similar and equal to the Father in all things. It is wholly what the Father is, yet not the Father. For this is the Son; this is the Father; and through this He knows all that the Father knows. But in Him to know, as to be, is from the Father. But to know and to be there are one. But as to be in the Father is not from the Son, so neither is to know.

Accordingly, the Father, as it were uttering Himself, begot the Son equal to Himself in all things; He would not wholly and perfectly have uttered Himself, if anything less or more were in His Word than in Himself. Our own word that is within us, we find is in some way like this, but how much unlike it is, let it not shame us to consider.

Ch. 15: For that is a true word of the mind, formable, but not yet formed, a something of the mind, which we turn this way and that with a sort of revolving motion, while we reflect now on this, now on that, as we light on it, or as it happens. And then a true word is fashioned, when that which we said we turn over as it were, reaches in to that which we know, and from there is given form, taking on its total likeness, so that, as a thing is which is known, so also is it put together in the mind.

Who does not see how great is the unlikeness there is here to the Word of God, which is so of the Essence of God, that it was not before formable, and then formed, and could not at any time have been formless, but is a Perfect Image, Equal in Itself to Him from Whom It is? For which reason It is therefore called the Word of God, that It may not be called the Thought of God, lest anyone say that there is something unresolved in God, which now may have, and now receives, a form that it may be a word, and may lose it, and then as it were be again formlessly turned ever in the mind.

AUGUSTINE, serm. on the Word of God, 117: The Word of God is a certain Form, not Itself Formed, but the Form of all forms, Form Unchangeable, without falling away, without defect, outside of time, without extension, surpassing all things, within all things, a foundation as it were, on which all things rest, a summit beneath which all things are.

BASIL: Our word has, exteriorly, a certain resemblance to the Divine

Word. For our Word brings forth the whole conception of our mind; for what we conceive in the mind we bring forth by a word. Our heart is as it were a fountain; the word that is uttered a stream flowing out from it.

CHRYSOSTOM, *Hom.* 1 *in John:* Consider also the spiritual wisdom of the Evangelist. He knew that men honour, and place above all things, that which is before all and above all, God. From here he makes his beginning. *In the beginning*, he says, *was the Word.*

ORIGEN, *in John* 1: Many things are signified by this word *beginning.* It is a commencement, as of a journey, or a period of time for example as: *the beginning of a good way is to do justice* (Prov. xvi. 5). It is also the beginning of a generation, as: *He is the beginning of the ways of God* (Job xl. 14). And not incorrectly does anyone declare that God is the beginning of all things. Again, that from which, as from pre-existing matter, other things are made, is the *beginning*, in the opinion of those who believe that it is uncreated. There is also a beginning according to kind; as Christ is the beginning of all who are made in the image and likeness of God (Col. i, 18). There is also a beginning of discipline, as the Apostle says: *you have need to be taught again what are the first elements of the words of God* (Heb. v. 12).

Twofold is the beginning of proof; where it begins in reality, and where it begins for us; as if it were said that the beginning of wisdom, in its nature, is Christ, in that He is the Wisdom and the Word of God; for us it began when *the Word was made flesh.*

From the many meanings o *beginning* that occur to us, that can be taken in which beginning is a principle of action.[1] Christ as Creator is a beginning, in that He is Wisdom; so the Word was in the beginning, that is in Wisdom. Many properties are attributed to the Saviour. As in the Word was life, so the Word was in the beginning, that is, in Wisdom. Consider if it be not possible for us to take beginning according to this meaning, that all things are made according to Wisdom, and according to the image in it[2]; or, that the Father is the beginning of the Son, and the beginning of creatures, and of every being. Through this *in the beginning was the Word*, you may understand that the Son, the Word, was said to be in *the Beginning*, that is, in *the Father.*

AUGUSTINE, *De Trin.* 6, 2: Or, *In the beginning* was said, as if were said: before all things. BASIL: The holy Spirit had foreseen that there would be certain men, jealous of the glory of the Only-Begotten, who would put forth subtleties for the undoing of their hearers, saying: if He was begotten, He was not; and before He was begotten He was not. Lest they presume to utter such folly, the Holy Spirit says: *In the beginning was the Word.* HILARY, *De Trin.* 1, 2: The years are put aside, the centuries passed over, the ages rolled back. Place where you will that which is the *beginning.* You reach it not in time. He was there, whence He was drawn forth.

CHRYSOSTOM, *Hom.* 2 *in John:* Why then does he lift us up to this height? It is as when a man stands on a ship close to the shore, and sees cities and ports. Then someone brings him far out to sea, and removes his gaze from the objects that held it before, yet imposes no limit to his view, rather gives him now a vision without limit. So the Evangelist, lifting us above every created thing, towards that which is beyond, leaves the eye as it were suspended, not limiting it to any point away above it, for indeed there is none. The mind seeks here this beginning, and finds it always *was*, and straining ever upwards, grows weary, and turns back to lower things, for this *In the beginning*, signifies but unending and infinite Being.

AUGUSTINE, *serm.* 117: They (the Arians) dispute in this manner: If He is the Son of God, He was born. This we confess. They then go on: If the Son is born to the Father, the Father was before the Son was born to Him. This faith spurns. Then, they say: explain to me, how the Son can be born of the Father, yet coeval with Him of whom He was born? A son is born after his father, and succeeds him at his death. This we find in men, in animals. They thus seek to transfer carnal ways of life to spiritual things. What must we do? We too must seek comparisons and examples for the truths we profess. But where is there an example like unto Him? I cannot find in time similitudes that I can compare with eternity. Where can we find in creatures one that is coeternal, when in no creature do we find anything that is eternal. If I find not a father that is coeternal, it suffices if I find one that is coeval; that is, one that has the same measure of time. If I can find two coevals, one begetting, the other begot, then we

may understand the eternal generations.

We read in Sacred Scripture that Wisdom is called *the brightness of eternal light* (Wis. vii. 26); it is called the Image of the Father. Here we have a similitude that may lead us to things that are coeval, and from which in turn, to those that are coeternal. Fire gives forth light; light flows out from fire. No one doubts that the splendour derives from the fire; not the fire from the splendour. Let us consider the fire as the Father, whence proceeds this splendour. If there be no fire there is no splendour. As soon as I shall light the fire, fire and light leap up together. Give me fire without light, and I shall believe the Father *was* without the Son.

The Son is called the Image of the Father. Here we have another similitude for things so widely differing. The image exists in the mirror, of a man looking at himself in the mirror. As soon as he looks, the image is there. But he who looks *was* before the mirror. How then shall we make the comparison effective, as in the case of fire and light. Let us begin a little lower. You readily know in what manner water gives back the images of objects. Let us consider something born by the water, a young tree, or grass. Is it not born together with its image? The tree and the image both begin together. If the shoot were there always, so also would be its image. That which arises from another, is indeed born. There can therefore be that which forever begets, and that which is forever born of it.

These pictures give a likeness, but in no way do they reflect the true reality. What are we to say if someone says: Now I have grasped the Eternal Father, I understand the coeternal Son; yet, as the light given forth is less than the fire, or as the image is less than the standing tree? But equality in all respects, I do not believe, because you have not found a similitude. Perhaps from these two kinds of examples we may yet find in creatures a similitude whereby we may understand in what manner the Son is coeternal with the Father, yet in no way less. But this we shall not find in one single similitude. Let us join them both. One from whence they give similitudes; the other from whence we have given them.

They have given an example from things that are born in time, and which are preceded in time by those from whom they are born, as man from man. Yet both are of the same substance. What do we praise here? Equality of nature. What is wanting? Equality of time. Let us retain here the equality of nature. In the other kind of example, which we gave from the brightness of fire, and from the image of the tree in water, you do not derive equality of nature, but you find coevity. What is wanting? Equality of nature. Join together the two that you praise. Must we not render to God that which you praise? Let all the works of God praise their creator. I find in one coevity; I learn of coeternity from the other. In one I find equality of nature, in the other equality of substance. The Totality is there, which here is found in each separate single thing. And it is wholly there, not as I find it in creatures, but as it is in their Creator.

From the Acts of the Council of Ephesus: In one place therefore He is named Son of the Father; elsewhere He is called the Word; the divine Scripture again calls Him the Brightness of Eternal Light; each name speaking of the same Person, from which you may learn that the things spoken against Christ are blasphemy. Because your son is made from the same nature as yours, human speech, seeking to make plain the unicity of the substance of the Father and the Son, calls him the Son of the Father Who alone was begotten from Him. Again, since with man nativity and a son bespeak a nature subject to suffering, He is therefore called *Son and Word*, manifesting through this name the impassibility of His birth. But a man becoming a father is thereby revealed as older than his son; lest you should think the same of Him that is born of the divine essence, Scripture names Him the Only-Begotten Brightness of the Father. Brightness is indeed born from the sun, yet it is not regarded as later in time than the sun. Brightness therefore speaks to you of the coeternity of the Son and the Father; Word shows forth the impassibility of His Begetting; the name Son conveys to us His Consubstantiality with the Father.

CHRYSOSTOM, *Homily* 3 *in John:* What then do they say: "that the phrase, *in the beginning was the word*, does not completely imply eternity. For that same word was used of the heavens and the earth: *in the beginning God made heaven and earth*"? But what has *was* in common with *made*? For the word *is* when spoken of man refers only to the present time, but spoken of

God it means eternity. So also *was* when used concerning our nature, signifies time past; used regarding God, it speaks of eternity.

ORIGEN, *Hom. 2 in Div. Locis:* The word *I am* has a twofold meaning; sometimes it means bodily movements, according to its relation with other words; sometimes the substance of any given thing of which it is predicated, without reference to movement. In this sense it is called substantive. HILARY II, The Trinity: Look at the world. Read what is written of it: *In the beginning God made heaven and earth.* That therefore was made *in the beginning* which was created, and which the ages contain, and which in the beginning was encompassed, that it might be made. An illiterate untaught fisherman, unhampered by time, freed from the ages, soars above every beginning: there *was* that which is, nor was it at any time contained, that it might begin; because in the beginning it *was,* rather than *was made.* ALCUIN: Against those who say, that because of His Birth in time, Christ was not always, the Evangelist begins with the eternity of the Word, saying: *In the beginning was the Word.*

II. *And the Word was with God.* CHRYSOSTOM, *Homily 4:* Because it is the supreme attribute of God that He is eternal, and without beginning, the Evangelist places this first. Then, lest anyone, hearing the words: *In the beginning was the Word,* might say, an unborn Word, he immediately removes this possible doubt, saying: *And the Word was with God.* HILARY, II The Trinity: For, without beginning is He with the Father. He Who is

apart from time, is not apart from His Author. BASIL, in Homily on these words: He says this because of those who blaspheme, saying: that at one time *He was not.* Where therefore *was* the Word? The unconfinable are not contained in place. But *where* was He? *With God.* Neither is the Father contained in place; nor the Son by any circumscription.

ORIGEN: It is fitting to note that word is said to have been *made* to certain persons; as to Osee, to Isaias, to Jeremiah. To God it was not made, as there was no being before Him. But from this that He is inseparably in Him is it said: *And the Word was with God,* because not from *the beginning* was the Son separated from the Father.

CHRYSOSTOM, *Homily 3 in John:* For the Evangelist has not said: the Word was *in* God, but *the Word was with God*; showing us His co-eternity, in His own Person, with the Person of the Father.

THEOPHYLACTUS: It seems to me that Sabellius is overthrown by these words; for he taught that the Father, Son, and Holy Ghost, are one Person, which now appears as Father, now as Son, and again as the Holy Spirit. This is plainly confuted by the sentence: *and the Word was with God.* For here the Evangelist declares that the one is the Son, the other is God; that is, the Father.

III. *And the Word was God.* HILARY, II *The Trinity, Ch. 15,* 2: You will say: a word is the sound of a voice, a proposal as to affairs, the expression of thought. This Word was *in the beginning with God*, because the expression of His Thought is eternal, since He Who is thinking is eternal. But how was that *in the beginning* which is neither before time nor after time? Nor do I know that He can have existence in time. For the discourse of those who speak does not exist before they begin to speak, and when they have spoken, it will no more be. From the very fact that they speak, when they finish, there is then no longer where they began. But if you, listener, set aside the force of the first sentence of the unlettered Evangelist, *In the beginning was the Word*, what have you to say of the one that follows: *and the Word was with God?* Have you had speech with God that you have grasped the expression of His hidden thought? Or has John fallen into error as to the difference between *to be in*, and *to be with?* That which *was* in the beginning is declared to be, not *in* another, but *with* another.

Await next the name and the dignity of the Word. For he says: *And the Word was God.* The sound of a voice ceases, and the expression of thought: this Word is a Being, not a sound; a Nature, not an utterance. It is God, not emptyness. HILARY continuing, VII. *The Trinity*, 9, 10: *And the Word was God*. It is a simple naming, unconfused by any additional word. Consider other names, given or assumed. To Moses it was said: *Behold I have appointed thee the god of Pharo* (Exod. vii. 1). But is not the reason of the name added when it says: *of Pharo*. For Moses is given as god to Pharo, while he is feared and entreated, while he was castigating and while he was healing. It is one thing to *to be*

given as god, another *to be God*. Recall also another naming, when in the psalm (Ps. lxxxi. 6) it is said: *I have said, you are Gods*. But in this the significance is simply of a name bestowed. And where it is recorded: *I have said*, we have here speech of someone, rather than the name of a being. But when I hear: *and the Word was God*, I believe that the Word is not alone called God, but I understand that it is signified that He *is* God.

BASIL: And so meeting the accusation of blasphemers, and of those who question what is the Word, he replies: *And the Word was God*. THEOPHYLACTUS: Or, continue in another way: After the sentence, *and the Word was with God*, it is manifest that there are two Persons, though the one nature exists in both; whence is it said: *And the Word was God*; since the Godhead is one, so the one nature belongs to both Father and Son. ORIGEN: We must also add that the word which *was made to* the prophets, illumined them with the light of wisdom. But the Word is *with* God, having from this the Godhead. And so he places the words, *the word was with God*, before those that say, *and the Word was God*.

CHRYSOSTOM, *Hom*. 3 *in John:* And not as Plato, saying that the Word was a kind of intellect, or the soul of the world. For these things are remote from the divine nature. But they (the Arians) say, "the Father is called God with the addition of the definite article, the Son without it." What of it? The Apostle says, *the glory of the great God and Our Saviour Jesus Christ* (Tit. ii. 13); and again, *Who is over*

all things, *God blessed for ever* (Rom.
ix. 5; i. 7). But writing to the
Romans he says: *Grace to you and
peace from God Our Father*, without
the addition of the article. It was
superfluous here, since just above it
was continually attached to the
Word. Not therefore because the
article is not added to the Son, is the
Son less God.

V. 2. *The same was in the
beginning with God.* HILARY 2 *De
Trin.:* I tremble in my speech because he has said, *and the Word was
God*, and the unheard of speech
troubles me, since the prophets
announced but one God. But lest
my trepidation should increase, the
fisherman gives me the plan of this
so great mystery, and refers all
things to the One, without irreverence, without diminution, without
time, saying: *the same was in the
beginning with God.* He is declared
to be with the One Unbegotten
God, from Whom is the Only-
Begotten of the One God.

THEOPHYLACTUS: And again, lest
the diabolic notion should confound some, that, since the Word is
God, He has risen against the
Father, as some of the fables of the
Gentiles have it, and, separated
from the Father, is now opposed to
Him, he says: *The same was in the
beginning with God*; as if to say: this
Word of God *never* existed
separate from the Father.

CHRYSOSTOM, *Hom.* 3 *in John:* Lest
you may think that He is not
eternal, when you hear, *In the
beginning was the Word*, and that the
life of the Father is greater by a
certain interval, he adds: *The Same
was in the beginning with God.* For

He was never separate from Him,
but was always God with God, yet
each in His own Person. Or, again,
because he said, *and the Word was
God*, that no one might be led to
believe that the divinity of the Son
was less, he immediately sets forth
the things that proclaimed His
Deity, stating His eternity when he
says, *and the same was in the beginning
with God*; and adding what was
done by Him, saying: *All things
were made by Him.*

ORIGEN: Or, in another way; After
the Evangelist has stated the first
three propositions, he repeats them
again in one phrase, saying: *The
same was in the beginning with God.*
In the first of the three we learned
when the Word was, that it was *in
the beginning*; in the second, with
Whom it was, that it was *with God*;
in the third, what was the Word,
that *It was God.* As it were pointing
out the Word, already declared to
be God, by calling Him The Same,
and bringing together into a fourth
proposition that which he had
already declared, namely: *In the
beginning was the Word, and the Word
was with God, and the Word was God*,
he says: *The Same was in the
beginning with God.*

Someone may ask, why did he
not say: In the beginning was the
Word of God, and the Word of
God was with God, and the Word
of God was God? Whosoever confesses that truth is one, it is plain
that its manifestation, which is
wisdom, is also one. But if truth is
one, and wisdom is one, one also
is the Word that announces truth,
and explains wisdom, in those
things which are capable of receiving explanation. We state this, not
denying in any way that the Word

is *of God*, but showing the usefulness of the omission of the words *of God*. John himself writes in his Apocalypse: *and His Name* is called *The Word Of God* (Apoc. ix. 13 Cf. PG 14 col. 115). ALCUIN: What was the reason of employing the substantive word *was*? That you may understand that the Word, coeternal with God the Father, preceded all time.

V. 3. *All things were made by Him: and without Him was made nothing that was made.*

I. *All things were made by Him.* ALCUIN: After he had spoken of the nature of the Son of God, he goes on to speak of His work, saying: *All things were made by Him*; that is, whatever is, either in its substance or in any property of the substance. HILARY, *De Trin.* 2: Or, differently, The Word was in the beginning. But could He not have been before the beginning? What *was*, cannot not be. But what says the Evangelist? *All things were made by Him.* He is Infinite by whom all things are made that are made; and since by Him all things are made, by Him therefore was time made.

CHRYSOSTOM, *Hom.* 4 *in John:* Moses opening the Writings of the Old Testament, speaks to us of visible things, and tells us much concerning them. *In the beginning*, he says, *God made heaven and earth.* Then He caused that light be made, and the firmament, and the birth of the stars, and the varieties of the animals. But the Evangelist soaring above all these things, embraces all, as known already to his hearers, in one phrase, and presses on to a sublimer theme: his whole book

discoursing, not of the created, but of the Creator.

AUGUSTINE, *in Genesis* 1 *Ch.* 2: For since it is said that *All things were made by him*, then is it clearly shown that light also was made by Him, since God said: *Let there be light*; and similarly with regard to other things which if it be so, eternal is the saying of God, *let there be light*, because the Word of God, God with God, is coeternal with the Father, although it is a temporal creature that was made. Though words are of time, since we say, *when*, and *sometimes*, yet is it eternal in the Word of God that something is to be made; and it then shall be, when it was decreed that it shall be in the Word, in which there is no *when* and *sometime*; since the Word is wholly eternal.

AUGUSTINE, *Tr.* 1 *in John par II:* How therefore can it be that the Word of God was made, when God, by the Word, made all things? And if the Word was made, by what other Word was it made? If you say this, that there is a Word of the Word by which that other was made; the same I declare is the only Son of God. If you do not say it is the Word of God, then you must grant that the Word was not made, by which all things were made. AUGUSTINE, *De Trin.*, I, 6: And if it was not made, it is no creature. If it is not a creature, it is of one substance with the Father. For every substance that is not God is a creature; what is not a creature, is God.

THEOPHYLACTUS: The Arians say that just as we say that a door is made by a saw, as by an instrument, so were all things made by the Son; that He is not Himself the Maker, but only the Instrument. So they say the Son is a creation, made to this end, that by Him all things might be made. To the inventors of this kind of falsehood we simply say: If, as you say, the Father has created the Son, to the end that He might use Him as an instrument, it would then seem that the Son is less honourable than the things that were made by Him, as those things made by the saw are more precious than the tool that wrought them. For the saw is only for their making, so likewise only because of the things that are made did God make the Son. What could be more foolish than such speech? But, they say: wherefore did he not say that the Word made all things? Why, rather, did he use the preposition *by?* Lest you might think that the Son was Unbegotten, and without source, and a rival of God. *Chrysostom, Homily* 4 *in John* (near the middle): But if the preposition *by* causes you concern, and you seek in Scripture that the Word Itself made all things, hear David: *In the beginning, O Lord, thou foundest the earth: and the heavens are the works of Thy Hands* (Ps. ci. 26). That he spoke here of the Only-Begotten you may learn from the Apostle, using this saying concerning the Son, in his epistle to the Hebrews: *Thou in the beginning, O Lord, didst found the earth: and the works of thy hands are the heavens* (Heb. i. 10). If however you say that the Prophet said this of the Father, which Paul applied to the Son, the conclusion is the same. For the Apostle would not have applied the term to the Son, unless he profoundly believed

Them to be equal in dignity. If, again, it seems to you that a certain notion of inferiority is implied in the use of the preposition *by,* why does Paul use if of the Father? *God is faithful,* he says, *by Whom you are called unto the fellowship of His Son* (I Cor. i. 9). And again: *Paul, an apostle by the will of God* (I Cor. i. 1).

ORIGEN, as above: Valentinus erred also in this, saying: that the Word exists so that It might serve the Creator as an instrument for the creation of the world. But if this were the truth as he understood it, then it should have been written, that the universe was made by the Word, through the Creator, not contrarily, by the Creator, through the Word.

II. *And without Him was made nothing that was made.* CHRYSOSTOM, *Hom.* 4 *in John:* So that you may not believe, when he says, *All things were made by Him,* that he speaks only of those things that were spoken of by Moses, he fittingly adds: *And without Him was made nothing that was made,* either in the visible, or invisible, world. Or, again, lest from this that he said: *All things were made by Him,* you think that this was said only of the signs and wonders, concerning which the remaining Evangelists have spoken, he adds: *And without Him was made nothing that was made.*

HILARY, *The Trinity, Book* 2: Or, differently: That which is here said: *All things were made by Him,* has no limitation. There is the Unbegotten Who was made by no one. There is the Begotten Himself, from the Unbegotten. The Evangelist acknowledged Him as

Creator, when he proclaimed Him Co-operator, saying: *Without Him was made nothing that was made.* Since nothing was made without Him I here understand that He was not alone; for it is one thing to say *by whom,* and another *without whom.*

ORIGEN, *Hom. 3 in div. locis:* Or, another interpretation: Lest you think that of the things which are, some were made by the Word, some pre-existed of themselves, and were not contained in the Word, he says: *And without Him was made nothing that was made,* that is, nothing was made outside of Him. He enfolds all things, preserving them. AUGUSTINE, Quest. de N. & V. Test. 97: Saying that without Him was made nothing, he in no way taught that the Word itself is to be considered as a creation. For how can it be said "He is the divine handiwork", if it is declared that *without Him* God made nothing.[3]

ORIGEN *in John, II:* Or, differently again: If by the Word all things were made, malice is included in the number of all things, and the whole tide of sin. Then these too were made by the Word? Which is false. For as to their meaning, nothing and *non-ens* are one. The Apostle seems to call evil things non-beings: *God calleth those things that are not, as those that are* (Rom. iv. 17). All depravity is called nothing, since without the Word was it made.

AUGUSTINE, *Tr. 1 in John,* (near the middle): Sin was not made by Him; and this is evident, for sin is nothing; and when men sin, they make nothing. And the idol by the Word was not made. It has

indeed a certain human form, and man was himself made by Him. But the form of man in an idol, was not made by the Word, for it is written: *We know that an idol is nothing in the world* (I, Cor. viii. 4). Therefore these were not made by the Word; but whatever was naturally made, the whole order of nature, and each single creature, from an angel to the smallest worm.

ORIGEN as above: Valentinus excluded from *all that was made* by the Word, the things made in the present world; which he believed existed before the Word, speaking without proof. If indeed the works which by him are considered as divine, are excluded from *the all that was made,* which, in his opinion, are corruptible, then that which he calls corruptible are *all things.*[4]. Some say, falsely, that the devil is not a creature of God. In that he is a devil, he is not God's creature; but he to whom it has come to pass that he is a devil, is the creature of God. As if we were to say, a murderer is not a creature of God, who as a man is still God's creature.

AUGUSTINE, *De Nat. Bon.* 25: Nor must we heed the ravings of those who declare, that in this sentence *nothing* is to be understood as something, because it is placed at the end of the sentence. They do not understand that it is a matter of indifference whether one says, that *without him was made nothing,* or, *without Him nothing was made.*

ORIGEN, as above: If we take the Word for that *logos* or *word* that is in every man, placed in each one by the Word that was in the beginning, here also, without this word we can do nothing, accepting simply what is called *nothing*, For the Apostle says: *for without the law sin was dead, but when the commandment came, sin revived* (Rom. vii, 7, 9). For sin is not imputed where the Law does not exist, neither did sin exist where the Word was not, for the Lord says: *If I had not come they would not have sin* (Jn. xv. 22). Every pretext therefore is taken from him who wishes to defend himself from crime, since he has not obeyed the Word, both present in him, and showing him that which he should do.

But not for this is the Word to be blamed, as neither is the master to be blamed, because of whose diligence there remains no ground of excuse to the pupil for ignorance or idleness. All things therefore were made by the Word, not alone natural things, but all the things done by irrational creatures.[5]

III. BEDE, *in John* 1: Because the Evangelist said that every creature was made by the Word, let none believe because of this that His Will is mutable, as if He should now wish to make a creature which from eternity He had not before made. So he is solicitous to instruct us, that the creature was indeed made in time, but that when, and whom, He would create was ordered from the beginning in the eternal wisdom of the Maker. Hence he says: *that was made, in Him was life.*

AUGUSTINE, *Tr.* 1 *in John:* It could be thus punctuated: *that was made in him*, then let there be added, *was life.* If we so declaim it, it means that all that was made was life. And what is there that was not made in Him? For he is the Wisdom of God, and it is said: *thou hast made all things in wisdom* (Ps. ciii. 24). All things therefore, as they were made by Him, were made in Him. If therefore what is made in Him is life, therefore the earth is life, a stone is life. But it is improper so to interpret, lest the sect of the Manichees artfully intrude among us, and say, that a stone has life, and therefore having life it will bring forth. For they are wont in their ravings to say such things; and when they are checked and answered, they come forth with, as from the Scriptures, a phrase such as: as was said, *what was made in Him was life.*

But declaim it thus: *that was made*, here put a comma, and then add: *In Him was life.* The earth was made. But the earth that was made is not life. There was in the Wisdom Itself of God, spiritually, *the plan* from which the earth was made; *this* is life. As the execution in every work has not life; only the idea in the work lives, because it lives in the mind of the artist. Because therefore the divine Wisdom, by which all things are made, contains all things in idea which are made according to the divine plan, these are not necessarily living; but whatever is made, there is *life* in it.

ORIGEN, *Hom.* 2 *in div. locis:* It can also be punctuated in this manner, and without error. *That was made in Him*; then let there be added: *was life*; in such manner that the meaning is: *all things which by him and in him were made, in Him have life, and are one.* For they were, that is, they had existence in Him as cause, before being actually fulfilled in themselves. But if you seek to find out how, and in what form all things that were made by the Word subsist in Him, vitally, uniformly, and causally, you must seek examples from the order of nature.

Note how the clauses of all the things that the sphere of this visible world contains, dwell together in harmony in the sun, which is the supreme luminary of the world; how the multitude of all the herbs and fruits are contained together in their single seeds; how the multiple rules of any art, are but one in the art of the artificer, and have life in the mind that disposes of them; how an infinity of life becomes one, at a given point. Consider these various natural examples by which as on wings of natural reflection, we rise by the power of our mind to a clearer view of the hidden things of the Word, and, as far as it is given to human intelligence, discern how all things that were made by the Word, were made in Him, and in Him live.

CHRYSOSTOM, *Hom.* 4 *in John:* Or, differently: Let us not, as the heretics, place a full stop where it is said: *without him was made nothing.* They, wishing to say that the Holy Spirit was created, say: *what was made in Him, was life.* But read in this way it is unintelligible. In the first place it was not the time to speak here of the Holy Spirit. But if it were said of the Holy Spirit, then let us read it for a moment in their way, for in that way its incongruity will be evident to us. When you read: *what was made in Him, was life*, the Holy Spirit they say is here called Life. But this Life is also called Light, for he adds: *and the Life was the Light of men.*

Therefore, according to them, the Evangelist calls the Holy Spirit *the Light of men.* That which he previously calls Word, he here, successively calls God, and Life, and Light. But *the Word was made flesh*; it must then be the Spirit that was made flesh, not the Son.

Let us then, rejecting this manner of reading, come to the proper reading and exposition. It is this. When we read: *all things were made by him, and without him was made nothing that was made.* Here pause. Then begin from the sentence which opens: *In him was life.*

What he says is this: *without him was made nothing that was made*, that is, of the things that are makeable. Note how by this brief final phrase he has resolved all discordances. For by first writing *without him was made nothing*, and adding, *that was made*, he includes all things knowable by the mind, but excludes the Holy Spirit; for the Holy Spirit is not of the things that are makeable.

V. 4. *In Him was life, and the life was the light of men.*

That which is here spoken of, John related of the order of nature. He then goes on to treat of the divine Providence, saying: *In him was life.* As a fountain which rushes forth in great torrents, however much is drawn from it, the source remains undiminished, so in the operation of the Only-Begotten One, whatsoever you may believe was done by him, not by this is His Power become lessened. For the word *life* here relates not alone to His state of being, but also to His care of all things as to their continuance and preservation. When you hear that *in Him was life* do not consider Him as something composite; *For as the Father has life in Himself, so He hath given to the Son also to have life in Himself* (Jn. v. 26). As the Father is not composite, so neither is the Son.

ORIGEN, *in John, tom. II*, 12, 13: Again, differently: we must recall that the Saviour said that some things were not His, but another's; some belonged both to Himself and to others. In this therefore that is said: *What was made in the Word, was life*, we must investigate whether this life belongs both to Him and to others, or to others only; and if to others, to what others? Life is the same as light. He is the Light of men. He becomes then the life of men of whom He is the Light. And so in this that the Saviour is called life, He can be called the Life not of Himself, but of others, of whom He is the Light.

This life is inseparable from the Word, and together with Him came forth. This life shall be a support to the already existing reason in the soul, to the end that once purified of sin it may be become tranquil, and so that life may be implanted in him who renders himself capable of the Word of God. Hence he did not say that in the beginning the word was made; for there was not when *the beginning* was without the Word. But this life of men was made, since the Life was the Light of men; for when man was not, neither was there the Light of men, light being understandable only in relation to men; and so he says; *What was made in the Word, was life*. We find another reading also, not altogether

inept: *What was made in Him, was life*. But if we understand that the life of men which is made in the Word is He Who said: *I am the Life* (Jn. xiv. 6), we shall then confess that none of the unbelieving have life in Christ, but that they are all dead who live not in God.[6]

THEOPHYLACTUS: He said *In Him was life* so that you might not think that the Word was without life. Now he shows that it is a spirit life, and the light of all beings endowed with reason. Hence is said: *And the life was the light of men*; as if he says: this light is not a bodily light, but of the mind, illumining the soul. AUGUSTINE, Tr. 1 *in John*: By this light men are enlightened, sheep are not, because they have not minds whereby they may know wisdom; but man who is made in the image of God has a rational soul, through which he can come to wisdom. Therefore that life by which all things are made, is light, and the light, not of any animals whatsoever, but of men. THEOPHYLACTUS: He did not say, the light is for the Jews alone, but for all men. For all men, in the measure that we receive intellect and reason from Him who created us by The Word, in the same measure we are said to be enlightened by Him. For the reason that is given to us, and whereby we are called rational, is a light, directing us as to what we must do and what we must not do.

ORIGEN, (Cf. PG 14 col. 151): We must not forget that life came to men before light; for it was incongruous that a non-living being receive light, and for life to follow illumination. If it be the same to say, *the life was the light of men*, as the light of men only, Christ will then be the light of men alone, and this is heretical. That which is said of certain persons of former days, was not said of them alone. For it is written concerning God, that He is the God of Abraham, of Isaac and of Jacob. Yet He is not the God of these alone. Not therefore from this that He is called *the light of men* is it thereby excluded that He is also the light of other beings. Someone else using that testimony of Scripture: *let us make man to our own image*, might likewise contend, that whatever is made in the image of God is therefore a man. Hence the light of men is also the light of every rational creature.

V. 5. *And the light shineth in darkness and the darkness did not comprehend it.*

9. AUGUSTINE, *Tr.* 1, *in John:* Although this life is the light of men, yet the foolish of heart cannot comprehend that light, because they have grown blind through sin, so that they cannot perceive it. Lest therefore they should think that there is no light, because they do not see it, there follows: *and the light shineth in the darkness, and the darkness did not comprehend it.* For though to a blind man standing in the sun, the sun is indeed present, but he is absent to the sun; so the foolish heart is truly blind to wisdom, though it is beside him. But while thus present to the blinded, it is absent to his eyes; not because it is absent to him, but because he is absent to it.

ORIGEN, (PG 14 col. 150): Darkness of this kind is not of the nature of man as Paul says:

For you were heretofore darkness, but now light in the Lord (Eph. v. 8). ORIGEN, *Hom.* 2 *in div. locis:* Or, differently; The Light shines in the darkness of believing souls, beginning from faith, and approaching to hope. The deceit and ignorance of wordly hearts cannot perceive the Light of God, shining in their flesh. But this is spoken in a moral sense. The physical explanation of these words is this.

Human nature, even if it had not sinned, could not shine by its own powers, for it is not naturally light, but a partaker of light. It is capable of wisdom, but not wisdom. As the air itself does not give light, but is named from the word of darkness, so our nature, considered in itself, is a dark substance, but capable of and a partaker of the light of wisdom. And as the air, while it is partaking of the sun's rays, is not said of itself to give light, but to share in the light of the sun, so the rational part of our nature, while it possesses the presence of the Word of God, knows things that are intelligible, and its own God, but not through itself, but through the implanted divine light.

The light, therefore, *shineth in darkness,* because the Word of God, the life and the light of men, ceases not to shine in our nature, which looked at and considered in itself is found to be a sort of unformed darkness. And since this light is incomprehensible to every creature, *the darkness did not comprehend it.*

CHRYSOSTOM, *Hom.* 5: First the Evangelist taught us of creation, then he tells us of the spiritual gifts the Word bestowed in coming to us. Hence he said: *and the life was the light of men.* He did not say the light of the Jews; the Gentiles also came to the light of this knowledge. He did not say *of angels,* since his words were only concerned with the race of men, to whom the Word came announcing good tidings.

ORIGEN, *II in John:* They ask why the light of men is not called the Word, but the life which comes forth from the Word. To this we answer. Because the life of which we here speak, is not that common to rational and irrational creatures, but is united to the word which is formed in us through partaking of the Primary Word, so that we may discern the seeming and not true life, and desire the true life. First then we partake of that life, which with some indeed is but a disposition to, not actually, the light; those namely, who are not eager to seek after that which pertains to knowledge. With others this becomes truly the light, those who, according to the Apostles, *are zealous for the better gifts* (I Cor. xii. 31), namely, the Word of Wisdom.

CHRYSOSTOM, *Hom.* 5 *in John:* Life having come to us, the dominion of death is ended; and the Light shining in our midst there is no darkness. That Life will remain for ever which death cannot overcome, nor darkness this Light. Hence follows, and *the light shineth in the darkness.* He calls death and error, *darkness;* for visible light does not shine in darkness, but apart from it. The preaching of Christ has shone out in the midst of the error that rules the world, and caused it to disappear; and Christ dying has changed death into life, so triumphing over it that He has led back those who had been held in bondage. Since neither death has overcome this Life, nor error this Light, for its splendid proclaiming is everywhere on the earth, he therefore adds: *And the darkness did not comprehend it.*

ORIGEN, *in John, tom.* 2: We must also know that as the light of men means two different spiritual things, so also in regard to darkness. For we say that a man that possesses light, does the works that are of the Light; and that to know means to be as it were illuminated by the light of knowledge. Contrarily, we call evil actions darkness; and likewise that which appears as knowledge but is not.

As the Father is Light, and *in Him is nothing of darkness* (I Jn. i, 5) so also is the Saviour. But because He took upon Himself *the likeness of sinful flesh* (Rom. viii. 3), not incorrectly is it said of Him that in Him is a certain darkness; He having taken our darkness upon Him that He might dispel it. This Light therefore which has become the light of men, shines in the darkness of our souls, and enters in where *the ruler of this darkness* wars with the human race (Eph. vi. 12). The darkness persecutes this light, which is plain from the things which the Saviour and His children sustain; the darkness contending against the children of light. But since the Father is their defender, the darkness will not prevail.

The darkness does not comprehend the light, either because it cannot through its own sloth overtake the swift course of the light, or because should it lie in wait for it approaching, it is put to flight by the oncoming light.

We must note that darkness is not always taken in an evil sense, but also sometimes in a good sense, as: *He made the darkness his hiding place* (Ps. xvii. 12); in that the things that pertain to God are unknown and unknowable. Of this excellent obscurity I may say, that it moves towards the light, and lays hold of it: because what was darkness, because unknown, is changed into the light of knowledge for him who has learned.

AUGUSTINE, *City of God* 10, 29: A certain Platonist said that the commencement of this holy gospel should be written in letters of gold and set up in the most conspicuous place in all the churches. BEDE: For the other evangelists describe the birth of the Lord in time, but John has given testimony that the Same was in the beginning, saying: *in the beginning was the Word.* Others record that of a sudden He appeared among men; John that He was forever with God, saying: *And the Word was with God.* Others show that He was a man; John that He was True God, saying: *And the Word was God.* Others show that as man He walked for a time among men; John that as God He was with God, and from the beginning, saying: *The same was in the beginning with God.* Others make known the wonders He wrought in man; John teaches that by Him God the Father made every creature, saying: *all things were made by Him: and without Him was made nothing that was made.*

V. 6. *There was a man sent from God, and his name was John.*

AUGUSTINE, *Tr. 3 in John, sparsim:*

Those things said above, were said of the divinity of Christ; after He had appeared as man. Because He was so truly man that the Godhead was concealed in Him, a great man was sent before Him, by whose testimony He was revealed as more than man. And who was this? He *was a man.* THEOPHYLACTUS: Not an angel; so that he might break down the mistrust of many. AUGUSTINE, *Tr. 2 in John:* And how could this man speak what was true of God, unless he were sent by God. CHRYSOSTOM, *Homily 6 in John:* I do not however regard as purely human any of the things spoken by him. All that he tells us is not his own, but His Who sent him. Accordingly, he is also called *angel* by the prophet Malachy, saying: *behold I send my angel before thy face* (Mal. iii. 1). It is the office of an angel to announce, and not something of his own. This that he said, *there was a man sent,* is indicative, not of his own simple coming into the world, but of his mission.

V. 7. *This man came for a witness, to give testimony of the light, that all men might believe through him.*

AUGUSTINE, as above: What is he called? *Whose name was John.* ALCUIN: That is, grace of God, or, he in whom there is grace; or, he who first makes known to the world the grace of the new testament, which is Christ. Or again, John may be interpreted as, to whom it is given; because through the grace of God it was given to him, not alone to herald the King, but also to baptize Him. AUGUSTINE: Wherefore did he come? *He came for a witness, to give testimony of the light.*

ORIGEN: Some have tried to disprove the published testimonies of the prophets concerning Christ, saying: the Son of God has no need of witnesses, possessing in Himself sufficient of credibility, both in the things He spoke in His saving words, and in His wondrous works: since even Moses merited to be believed by reason of his speech, and by the wonders he wrought, not requiring the testimony of witnesses who would speak of him beforehand. To this we reply, that while there are no doubt many present reasons that move us to belief, yet there are generally some who can be moved to faith by one proof, and not by another. And God can give men manifold proofs, that they may believe that He is God, Who for all men became man. It is evident therefore, that many will be stirred by the prophetic utterances, to the praise of Christ; awed at so many voices proclaiming, even before His Coming, the place of His birth, and other such things.

This also we must note, that the wonders He wrought could in the days of His life among men cause many to believe in Him, but not after much time has elapsed; rather would they then come to be regarded as fabled events. More than the wonders wrought does prophesy, which is looked for together with the wonders, move men to belief. There is this also to be added: that some among them are honoured, because they give testimony to God. He will therefore deprive the prophets of great praise, who say that there is no need for their testimony to Christ. To their number is now added John, who came *to give testimony of the light.*

CHRYSOSTOM, *Hom. 6 in John:* Not that he needed witnesses. John himself tells us why he came, saying: *That all men might believe through him.* As He clothed Himself in our flesh, that all men might not perish, so he sent a man as a herald, that hearing a voice like their own, they would more readily draw near. BEDE: He did not however say: that all men might believe in him: for *accursed is the man who puts his trust wholly in man* (Jer. xvii. 5).

V. 8. *He was not the light, but he was to give testimony of the light.*

THEOPHYLACTUS: If however anyone should not believe, John will not be to blame. For it is as if one should shut himself up in a darkened house, he must blame himself, not the sun, if its rays do not give him light. So John was sent that all might believe; but should this not come to pass, the fault is not John's. CHRYSOSTOM, *Hom. 6 in med:* Among us the person giving testimony is more esteemed than the one to whom testimony is given, and also greater; so, lest anyone should think thus of John, he destroys this suspicion, saying: *He was not the light, but was to give testimony of the light.* If he did not repeat the words: *to give testimony of the light,* against this possible suspicion, it would have been mere repetition rather than an unfolding of his teaching.

THEOPHYLACTUS: But someone will say: then we are not to say that John or any of the saints is, or was, light. If we wish to attribute light to any of the saints, let us use the word light without the article; so that were you asked if John is light, without the article, you may agree. He is not The Light, above all lights, but he shares in the light of the True Light, and is called light.

V. 9. *That was the true light, which enlighteneth every man that cometh into this world.*

AUGUSTINE, *Tr. 2 in John:* Of what light he gives testimony, the Evangelist clearly states, saying: *That was the True light.* CHRYSOSTOM, *Hom. 7 in John,* (near beginning): Because above he had said of John that he came, and that he was sent, that he might give testimony of the light, lest any one hearing of this, because of the recent presence of the witness, have a similar suspicion concerning Him of Whom testimony was given, he raises up our mind, and directs it to that existence which is above all beginning, saying: *He was the True Light.*

AUGUSTINE, *in John 6, 2:* Why is *true* added? Because a man who is enlightened is also called light, but it is the True Light that gives this light. For our eyes also are called lights, yet unless by night a lamp be lit, or by day the sun shines forth, it avail not that they be open. Hence he goes on: *that was the true light, which enlighteneth every man.* If every man, then also John. He enlightened him therefore, by whom He willed to become known. It often happens that from seeing some object bathed in light we know that the sun is now risen, though with our eyes we cannot see the sunrise. For even those who have weak eyes are able to see the sunlight on a wall, or something of that sort. Likewise all to whom

Christ had come were not all able to see Him. But His light shone on John, and through him, confessing himself enlightened, He becomes known Who gives light.

THEOPHYLACTUS: Let the Manichaean blush who said that we are the creatures of Evil and Darkness. For we would not be enlightened, unless that we were created by the True Light. CHRYSOSTOM, *Hom. 8 (in princip.):* Where are they who say that He is not the True God? Here He is called the True Light. But if He enlightens every man that comes into this world, why have so many remained without light? For not all have learned the religion of Jesus Christ. It enlightens every man to whom it reaches. If however some, shutting up the eyes of the mind, do not wish to receive the beams of this Light, then their darkness comes not from the nature of the light, but from the folly of those who freely cut themselves off from the gifts of His grace. For grace is poured out upon all. Who wishes not to enjoy it, let him blame himself if he is blind.

AUGUSTINE, *Enchiridon 103:* Thus do we understand that what is written in the Scriptures, namely: *which enlighteneth every man,* means not that there is no man who is not enlightened, but that save by Him no man is enlightened. BEDE: Either by natural endowment, or by divine wisdom; for as no one receives existence from himself, so no one can from himself be wise. ORIGEN: Or again in another sense: We are not to understand that the words: *Which enlighteneth every man that cometh into this world,* are said of those who from the hidden seeds of life come forth in bodily forms, but of those who, through re-birth in grace, which is bestowed in baptism, come spiritually into the world invisible. Those so entering the world of virtue, the True Light enlightens; not those rushing down into the world of sin. THEOPHY-LACTUS: Or differently: The intellect given to us, and guiding us, and which is called natural reason, is the light given to us by God. But some, using reason evilly, debase themselves by means of it.

V. 10. *He was in the world, and the world was made by Him, and the world knew Him not.*

AUGUSTINE, *Tr. 2 in John, circa med:* The light which enlighteneth every man coming into this world, came through the flesh; because while present in His Divinity He could not be seen by the foolish, the blind, the wicked, of whom it was said above: *The darkness did not comprehend it.* Accordingly is it said, *He was in the world.*

ORIGEN, *Hom. 2 in div:* For as when one speaks: when he ceases to speak, his voice dies, and fades away; so the Heavenly Father, if His Word should cease to speak, the effect of His Word, that is, all things made by His Word, would cease to be. AUGUSTINE, as above: Do not imagine that He was in the world, as are the earth, and sheep, and men, upon the earth, or as the sun and moon and stars are in the heavens, but rather as the Artificer, directing that which He has made. Hence follows: *And the world was made by him.* For He made, not as a carpenter makes. He who so fashions

something, is outside of that which he makes. But God is diffused throughout the world, and wherever He is, He makes, and from no place does He depart. *He was* therefore *in the world* as the One through Whom the world was made.

CHRYSOSTOM, *Hom. 8 in John:* He *was in the world,* but not as contemporaneous with the world, on account of which the Evangelist continues: *and the world was made by him,* by this again leading the mind upwards to the eternal existence of the Only-Begotten. For he who has heard that the universe is His work, even though he be very dull, is yet forced to agree, that the Maker exists before that which He makes. THEOPHYLACTUS: Here, at the same time, he refutes the folly of the Manichaeans, who declared that an Evil Creator made everything; and that also of Arius, who said that the Son of God was a creature.

AUGUSTINE, *Tr. 2, in media:* What means, *the world was made by him?* The heavens, the earth, the sea and all that is in it, are called the world. Again, the lovers of the world are also called the world, but with another meaning. Concerning this latter world he goes on: *and the world knew him not.* For did the heavens, or the angels, or the stars, know not their Creator, Whom the demons confess, and to Whom all things bear witness? Who then knew Him not? They who loving the world, are called the world. For by loving the world, we abide in our hearts in the world. They who love not the world, in the flesh are in the world, but in their hearts they abide in heaven, as the Apostle said to the Phillipians: *our conversation is in heaven.* Loving the world they therefore merit to be called by that wherein they dwell. For as we say that a house is bad or good, not blaming or praising the walls, but the inhabitants, so do we call those the world, who dwell in the world, loving it.

CHRYSOSTOM, *Hom. 8 in John, circ. med:* They who were the friends of God knew Him even before He appeared bodily among them. So, in this regard, Christ also said: *Abraham your father rejoiced that he might see my day* (Jn. viii. 56). When the Gentiles therefore question us, saying: why is it at this late hour He comes to work our salvation, neglecting us for so long a time? Let us answer that even before this He was already in the world, His Providence governed it, and He was known to all who were worthy of Him. Although the world knew Him not, yet those of whom the world was not worthy had known Him. Saying: *the world knew him not*, he shows briefly the cause of their ignorance, for he calls those the world who are attached to the world alone, and relish only the things of the world. Nothing so darkens the mind as being made soft by earthly things.

V. 11. *He came unto his own, and his own received him not.*

CHRYSOSTOM, *Hom. 9 in John:* The Evangelist has said: *The world knew him not*, speaking of the former times. Then he moves on to the times of His Manifestation and says: *He came into his own.* AUGUSTINE: since *all things were made by Him.* THEOPHYLACTUS: Or, by *His own* we may understand Judea

which He had *chosen for his inheritance* (Ps. xxxii. 12). CHRYSOSTOM, *Hom. 9 in John:* He came into His own, not because of need, but for our benefit who were His own. But whence came He, Who fills all things, and Who is everywhere present? He left no place, for how could He? He wrought these things, coming down amongst us, which pertain to our salvation. For though in the world, He seemed not to be there, because He was not yet known; then He showed Himself, putting on our flesh. This manifestation and Descent amongst us the Evangelist calls His Coming.

God, being full of mercy, does all things that we may shine in holiness. And for this cause He draws no one to Himself by compulsion, but by persuasion and by gifts He draws unto Him those who are willing; and accordingly, when He came these last received Him, the others did not receive Him. But He desires not service that is unwilling, or forced. For one drawn unwilling to His service is as one who serves not at all; hence follows, *and his own received him not.* Here the Evangelist calls the Jews His own, as they were His own race; but all men are His, as being made by Him; and as a little previously the Evangelist, being shamed for our common nature, declared that the world made by Him knew not its Maker, so here likewise, indignant at the ingratitude of the Jews, he pronounces a graver reproach, *and His own received him not.*

V. 12. *But as many as received him, he gave them power to be made the Sons of God, to them that believe in his name.*

AUGUSTINE, *Tr.* 1 *in John:* If none had received Him, none would have been saved. For no one will be saved unless he receives Christ coming to him. And so the Evangelist says: *but as many as received him, etc.* CHRYSOSTOM, *Hom.* 9 *in John:* Whether slaves or free, Greek or barbarian, either foolish or wise, either women or men, children or aged, all are worthy of the same dignity, of which he then speaks: *He gave power to be made the sons of God.* AUGUSTINE, as above: Wondrous benevolence. Born the Only Begotten, He chose not to remain alone. He feared not to have co-heirs; for His inheritance is not diminished if they too should possess it.

CHRYSOSTOM, *Hom.* 9 *in John:* He did not say however that He *made them sons of God*, but that *He gave them power to be made the sons of God*, showing that there is need of great zeal, that the image that is impressed and formed in us at our baptism, may be preserved in us undefiled. Showing at the same time that no one can deprive us of this power, unless we first deprive ourselves. For if those who receive power from men over certain things, have the same power as they who conferred it, how much more we who partake of this honour from God. He wishes also to make clear, that this grace comes to the willing and the diligent. For it is within the power of the free will of man, and by the operation of grace, *to become sons of God.*

THEOPHYLACTUS: Or again, because by the resurrection we shall attain to the most perfect filiation, as the Apostle says: *waiting for the adoption of the sons of God, the redemption of our body* (Rom. viii. 23). *He gave us* therefore *power to be made the sons of God*, that is, of attaining to this grace in the future. CHRYSOSTOM, as above: and because in these ineffable gifts it is God's part to give grace: that of man to offer faith, he adds: *To those who believe in his name.* But why do you not tell us, O John, what their punishment shall be who receive Him not? Indeed, what greater punishment can there be, than that being endowed with the power to become the sons of God, they become not sons; of their own will depriving themselves of this honour? But the inextinguishable fire will also receive them, as He will later more clearly reveal.

V. 13. *Who are born, not of blood, nor of the will of the flesh, nor of the will of man, but of God.*

AUGUSTINE, as above: Believers therefore, as they become sons of God and brothers of Christ, are indeed born; for if they are not born, how can they become sons? But the sons of men are born of flesh and blood, and of the will of man, and from the embrace of spouses. How the former are born he tells us, *who are born of blood*, as from the male and female. For from the blood of male and female are men born. BEDE: We must know that in the Scriptures the word *blood*, when written in the plural, is wont to signify sin; hence *Deliver me from blood, O God* (Ps. l. 16).

AUGUSTINE, *Tr.* 2 *in John:* In the words that follow: *Nor of the will of the flesh, nor of the will of man,* the

Evangelist places the word *flesh* to stand for the female, because Adam said of the rib, when Eve was made: *This now is bone of my bones, and flesh of my flesh* (Gen. ii. 23). Flesh therefore stands for the wife, as sometimes spirit stands for the husband; because it is his part to command, hers to obey. What is worse than a house where the woman has dominion over the man? These therefore *are born*, not of the will of the flesh, nor of the will of man, *but of God*. BEDE: The carnal birth of every single man arises from the embrace of spouses; the spiritual, from the grace of the Holy Spirit.

CHRYSOSTOM, as above: The Evangelist records this, so that contemplating the humility and baseness of the first birth, which is by blood, and the will of the flesh, and coming to see the greatness of the second birth, which is by grace, and in honour, we may thus receive a deep enlightenment, and one worthy of His gift Who has begotten us, and henceforth manifest an earnest zeal.

V. 14. *And the Word was made flesh, and dwelt among us, and we saw his glory, the glory as it were of the only begotten of the Father, full of grace and truth.*

I.—*And the Word was made flesh.* AUGUSTINE, *Tr.* 2 in John: When he had said, *Who are born of God*, lest we be overcome, and fearful, at so tremendous a favour, and lest it seem a thing incredible to us that men should be born of God; and as it were reassuring us, he says: *And the Word was made Flesh.* Why then be astonished that men are born of God? See here how God Himself is born of man.

CHRYSOSTOM, *Hom.* 10 *in John:* Or again: When he had declared that they who received Him *were born of God*, he gives the reason of this honour, namely, that *the Word was made Flesh.* For God's own Son became the Son of man that He might make the sons of men children of God. But when you hear that the Word was made Flesh, be not troubled. For He changed not His own Substance into flesh: to think so would be a grave irreverence; but, remaining what He was, *He took upon Himself the form of a servant.*

There are those who say that all that had to do with the Incarnation is but a seeming, and without reality. To meet this blasphemy he uses the words, *was made*; desiring by this to express, not a change of substance, but the taking to himself of true flesh. If they should then say: since God is Omnipotent, why could He not change Himself into flesh? Let us reply that change of any sort is far from His perfect simplicity; for in Him change would be towards what is less, and He would not then be God.

AUGUSTINE, *De Trin.* 15, 11: As our word becomes in a manner the voice of the body, assuming that by which it is made manifest to mens' ears, so the Word of God becomes flesh, taking that form in which It likewise is made visible to mens' eyes. And as our word becomes a voice, yet is not changed into a voice, so the Word of God is indeed made flesh: but let no one say that It is changed into flesh: by taking on that form, not by being changed into it, does our word become a voice, and the Word of God become flesh.

From the Acts of the Council of Ephesus: Even the discourse we utter, in which we use varying tongues, is an incorporeal discourse; not visible to the eye, or palpable by the hand. But when the discourse has clothed itself in words and literary form, it is visible; it may be comprehended by the eye, and touched by the hand. So likewise does the Son of God become visible, Who, by His Nature, is Invisible; and what by nature is incorporeal, is now found palpable.

ALCUIN: Since we also believe that an incorporeal soul is joined to a body, so that from the two one man is made, we may readily believe, that the divine incorporeal substance is joined to a soul in a body, in the Oneness of a Person; so the Word is not changed into flesh, nor flesh into the Word; since body is not changed into soul, nor soul into body. THEOPHYLACTUS: Apollinaris of Laodicea stated a heresy regarding this passage. For he said that Christ did not possess a rational soul, but only flesh, having in the place of the soul His Own Divinity, Which directed and governed the body.

AUGUSTINE, *contra Arianos* 9: If they attack on this ground, that it is written, that *the Word was made flesh*, but that there is no mention of a soul, let them understand that *flesh* stands for *man*; as in figurative language the whole is represented by the part; just as it is said: *all flesh shall come to thee* (Ps. lxiv. 2); again that: *by the works of the law no flesh shall be justified* (Rom. iii. 20), which was more clearly said in another place: *Man is not justified by the works of the Law* (Gal. ii. 16).

Accordingly, it was said: *The Word was made Flesh*, as if he had said: The Word was made man.

THEOPHYLACTUS: The Evangelist, wishing to make clear the ineffable condescension of God, here speaks of the *flesh*, that we may praise His mercy; since, for our salvation, He took upon Himself that which is so unlike, and so remote, from His own Nature; namely, *flesh*; for *soul* has some relationship with God. But if the Word had become Incarnate, yet did not assume a human soul, it would follow that our souls would not yet be healed; for what He did not assume, He did not sanctify.

And what mockery would this then be, that though it was the soul that first sinned, He should sanctify the flesh by assuming it; and take no thought for that which was chiefly wounded? Nestorius perverted the meaning of these words by saying, that God the Word did not Himself become man from the sanctified blood of the Virgin, but that the Virgin brought forth a man who was endowed with the beauty of every virtue, and to him the Word of God was united. And from this he declared there were two sons: one born of the Virgin, namely, a man; the Other of God, namely, the Son of God, joined to the former by the relationship of grace, and of love. Against whom the Evangelist has said, that the Word Itself was made man: not, that the Word, finding so virtuous a man, has united Himself to him.

CYRIL TO NESTORIUS, ep. 8: The Word, substantially uniting Himself to flesh made living by a rational soul, in an ineffable and incomprehensible manner became man, and is called the Son of man,[7] not in a simple union of will, nor of love, nor yet only by the assumption of a person. Diverse indeed are the natures brought into union; but one the Christ and the Son from the union of both; yet not as if the difference of the natures was ended because of the union.

THEOPHYLACTUS: We learn therefore from what is here said, that *the Word was made flesh*, that the Word Himself is a man, and while being the Son of God, has become the son of a woman, who, from the beginning, is called the Mother of God, as having given birth to God in the flesh.

HILARY, *De Trin.* 10: Certain persons, holding to the opinion that the Only Begotten God, Who, in the beginning was God the Word, with God, was not of the substance of God, but only the utterance of His Voice: as is their own word to those who are speaking, this the Son is to God the Father; astutely seeking to evade the truth that Christ, while being God the Word, and remaining in the Form of God, was born as man; that, since it was an instrument of human origin rather than a mystery of spiritual conception that gave life to this man, not God the Word has come forth, becoming man as born of the Virgin, but that as the spirit of prophecy was in the prophets, so was the Word of God in Jesus.

And they are accustomed to argue with us that we should not say that Christ was born a man, of our body and soul; since we proclaim that the Word made flesh

was born a man like unto us, so that He was born True Son of God and True Son of man: but that as He took for Himself a body from the Virgin, so likewise He took from Himself, unto Himself, a soul; which certainly is not provided by man from the elements of human generation. And since He is the Son of man, and the Son of God, how ridiculous that, besides the Son of God, Who is the Word of God made flesh, we preach some other being, whom I know not, who, as though he were a prophet, is animated by the Word of God, when the Lord Jesus Christ is both Son of God and Son of man?[8]

CHRYSOSTOM, as above: Lest, because it was said that *the Word was made flesh*, you might incorrectly be led to conceive of change in that incorruptible nature, he adds: *and dwelt among us.* That which inhabits is not the same as the habitation, but diverse. Diverse, I repeat, according to nature; for by union and conjunction, One is God the Word and the Flesh; made without commingling of substances. ALCUIN: It dwelt among us, that is, sojourned among men.

II. *And we saw his glory.*
CHRYSOSTOM, *Hom.* 11 *in John:* When the Evangelist had said that *we are made the sons of God*, and solely through this, that *the Word was made flesh*, he goes on to speak of another gain through Him: *and we saw His glory*; which in very deed we could not have seen unless it was shown to us through the sharing of our humanity. For if men could not endure to look upon the shining countenance of Moses, if that needed to be veiled, how

could we poor creatures of clay, earthy as we are, have endured the Unveiled Divinity; dwelling Inaccessible, even to the Powers of heaven?

AUGUSTINE, *Tr.* 2 *in John:* Or, differently; *Because the Word was made flesh, and dwelt amongst us,* He made from this Nativity an eyesalve, with which the eyes of our heart were anointed, so that by means of His humanity we might be enabled to look upon His Divinity. Accordingly it is written: *And we saw His glory.* His glory no man could see unless he were first healed of the infirmity of his flesh. For this hath afflicted man, as dust in the eyes from the earth. This eye had been wounded, and earth was put into it to heal it; it was wounded by the earth, and by the earth it was healed; for all medicaments what are they but of the earth? Flesh blinded thee; Flesh now heals thee. Carnal was the soul, consenting to carnal delights; thence was blinded the eye of the soul. Thy Physician made thee an eye-salve; since for this did He come, that He might extinguish in the flesh the vices of the flesh. For the Word was made flesh, so that you could say: *we saw His glory.*[9]

III. *The glory as it were of the only begotten of the Father.*

CHRYSOSTOM, *Hom.* 11 *in John:* To this he adds: *The glory as it were of the Only Begotten of the Father.* Because many of the prophets were made glorious, such as Moses, Elias, Eliseus, and many others who worked wonders. And angels have appeared among men, manifesting the shining splendour of their natures. The Cherubim and Sera-

phim also were seen in great glory by the prophet. The Evangelist withdrawing our gaze from all, these, and raising our minds above all creatures, even above the splendour of these our fellow servants, leads us to the supreme glory, as if saying; the glory that *we saw* is not the glory of a prophet, or of any other man; or of an angel, or of any of the heavenly powers, but of the Lord of all; of the Only-Begotten Son of the King Himself.

GREGORY, *Book* 18 *Morals* 6: In sacred speech *as* and *as it were* are sometimes used, not to convey similitude, but the exact truth. Hence the glory *as it were* of the Father. CHRYSOSTOM: We have beheld glory such as became Him, the True and Only-Begotten of God the Father. It is the way of people often, seeing the king wondrously adorned, and not being able to describe all about him in detail, to add: "but what can I say except that he was as a king should be". So John says: *We saw his glory, as it were,* etc.

Even the angels do all things as servants, and as having the Lord as Master. The Lord Himself appeared in the form of a servant; yet creation knew its Lord. The stars summon the Wise Men, the Angels call the Shepherds, the infant exults in its mother's womb. Likewise from the heavens the Father proclaims His Son, and the Paraclete descends upon Him. The very voice of nature itself, proclaims more loudly than any trumpet, that the King of heaven had come. For the spirits of evil fled, infirmity of every kind was healed, the graves gave back their dead, and from wickedness He led souls upwards to the heights of virtue. Who can describe the wisdom of His precepts, the virtue of His commandments, the perfect order of His Heavenly City?

IV. *Full of grace and truth.*
Origen, *Hom. 3 in div. locis:* Of that which follows: *full of grace and truth,* the meaning is twofold. It can be understood both of the humanity, and of the divinity of the Word Incarnate, so that the fullness of grace may refer to the Humanity, whereby Christ is Head of the Church and First-Born of every creature; since the first and supreme example of sanctification, in which, without preceeding merits, man becomes God, was first shown forth in Him. The plentitude of the grace of Christ

could be understood as the Holy Spirit, Whose sevenfold operation fills the Humanity of Christ, as Isaias foretold. The fulness of truth again may be referred to His Divinity.

Origen *in John* II: If however you prefer to understand *the fulness of grace and truth* as being the New Testament, you will not incorrectly declare that the fulness of grace of the New Testament is given through Christ, and the truth of the figures of the Law have in Him been fulfilled. Theophylactus: Or *full of grace,* as was His gracious speech, David declaring of Him: *grace is poured abroad in thy lips* (Ps. xliv. 3); *and truth:* as Moses and the prophets spoke and wrought in figures, so Christ spoke and wrought *in truth.*

I. St Augustine: On the Gospel[10]

1. *The world was made by him, and the world knew him not.*
The world was made by the Lord, and the world knew Him not. Which world was made by Him? Which world was it that knew Him not? For it was not the world which was made by Him, which knew Him not. Which world was made by Him? The heavens and the earth. How could the heavens not know Him, when the sun grew dark during His passion? How can it be that the earth knew Him not, since it trembled when He hung upon the Cross? But *the world knew Him not,* the world of which he is prince of whom it was written: *For the prince of evil of this world cometh, and in Me he hath not anything* (Jn. xiv. 30). Men who are evil are called the world, men without faith are called the world. From what

they love they receive the name. Loving God, we become as gods: loving the world, we are spoken of as the world. But *God was in Christ, reconciling the world to Himself* (II Cor. v. 19), the *world* therefore, *knew Him not;* but did all not know Him?

2. He came into His own, and His own received Him not. All men are His, but they are peculiarly His own from whence came His Mother, from among whom He Himself took flesh; they to whom He had sent Heralds before His Coming, to whom He gave the Law, whom He delivered from the bondage of Egypt, for whom He chose Abraham as father according to the flesh. For he declared the truth. *Before Abraham was made, I am* (Jn. v. 58). He did not say that He was

made before Abraham, or, before Abraham was made I was made. For *in the beginning* the Word *was*, not *was made*. Therefore *He came into His own*, He came to the Jews. *And His own received Him not.*

3. *But as many as received Him . . .* For there were indeed the Apostles, who received Him. There were those who bore palms before His donkey. They went before Him, and followed after Him, and spread their garments in His way; and they cried aloud: *Hosanna to the Son of David; Blessed is he that cometh in the name of the Lord.* Then the Pharisees said to Him: *Rebuke thy disciples.* And He answered: *if these hold their peace, the stones will cry out* (Mt. xxi. 9–16; Lk. xix. 39–40). He was looking at us, when He said these words: *if these hold their peace, the stones will cry out.*

Who are the stones, but they who worship stones? If the children of the Jews be silent, both the young and old of the Gentiles shall cry out. Who are the stones, but they of whom the same John speaks, who came *that he might give testimony of the light* (Jn. i. 8). For when he saw these same Jews pride themselves on being children of Abraham, he said to them: *Ye brood of vipers* (Lk. iii. 7). They spoke of themselves as the children of Abraham; he called them *a brood of vipers.* Did He affront the name of Abraham? Far from it. He gave them this name from their own dispositions. For if they were truly children of Abraham, they would follow Abraham's example:

As he told them, who had said to Him: *We have never been slaves of any man, we have Abraham for our father*; and He said, *if you are the*

children of Abraham, do the works of Abraham. You seek now to kill me, because I speak the truth to you; this Abraham did not (Jn. viii. 33, 39, 40). From him have you been begotten, but you have become degenerate children.

What then did John say? *Ye offspring of vipers, who hath showed you to flee from the wrath to come* (Mt. iii. 7, 9)? Because they came to be baptised by the baptism of John unto penance. *Who hath showed you to flee from the wrath to come? Bring forth therefore the fruit worthy of penance. And think not to say within yourself, We have Abraham for our Father. For I tell you that God is able of these stones to rise up children to Abraham* (Lk. iii. 7, 8). God is able of these stones, whom He foresaw in the Spirit; He was speaking to them, but His eyes were on us. God is able of these stones to raise up children to Abraham. Of what stones? *If these shall hold their peace the stones will cry out.* You have heard, and you have cried out. It is fulfilled, *the stones will cry out.*

For from the Gentiles we have come, and in our forefathers we worshipped idols of stone. So we also have been called dogs. Recall to mind what the woman heard, she who cried out after the Lord, who was a Chananean, a worshipper of idols, a servant of devils. What did Jesus say to her? *It is not good to take the bread of the children, and to cast it to dogs* (Mt. xv. 26). Have you not seen how dogs will lick greasy stones? Such are all who worship idols. But to you grace, has come. *As many as received Him, He gave them power to be made the sons of God.* See! You have some here newly-born (by baptism): *he gave them power to be made the sons of*

God. To whom did he give it? To them that believe in His Name.

4. And how do they become the children of God? *Who are born, not of blood, nor of the will of the flesh, nor of the will of man, but of God.* They are born of God, when they have received the power to become the sons of God. Note carefully; they are born of God; *not of blood,* as was their first birth; as was that unhappy birth, springing from unhappiness. But they who are born of God, what were they? Whence were they first born? From blood. From the commingling blood of male and female, by the commingling of male and female flesh; thence were they born. From whence are they now born? *They are born of God.* The first birth is from a male and a female; the second from God and from the Church.

5. Behold they are born of God. How does it arise that they are born of God, who first were born of men? How has this come to be? How? *And the word was made flesh, and dwelt amongst us.* Wondrous exchange! He is made flesh; they become spirit. What is this? What honour is this, my brethren? Lift up your heart to the possession and the enjoyment of higher things. Do not stick fast in earthly cravings. You have been purchased at a price: for your sake the Word was made flesh. He Who was the Son of God, for you has become the Son of man, so that you who were children of men, might become the children of God. What was He; what became He? What were you; what have you become? He was the Son of God. What did He become? The Son of man. You were the sons of men. What have you become? Children of God. That He might give us of His good things, He shared with us our infirmities.

But He, even by that through which He became the Son of man, is still far removed from us. We are children of men, by means of the concupiscence of the flesh. He is the Son of man, because of the faith of a virgin. The mother of every man commingles and conceives; each one of us is born of a father from men, and of a mother from men. Christ is born from the Holy Ghost, and from the Virgin Mary. He came unto us, departing but little from Himself; nay, from Himself as God He never departed: but joined that which He was, to our nature. He drew close to that which He was not; he surrendered not that which He was. He became the Son of man, without ceasing to be the Son of God.

Through this He is Mediator between both. Between both, what means this? Neither above, nor below. How neither above, nor below? Neither above, being flesh; nor below, being sinless. Yet above always, since He is God. For not so came He amongst us, as to leave the Father. He went from us, yet He leaves us not. He will come again to us, and will not depart from Him, Who liveth and reigneth, world without end, Amen.

II. St Leo, Pope and Doctor

For the Nativity of Our Lord Jesus Christ[11]

1. Dearly Beloved, a true worshipper, and devout observer of this day's Festival, is one whose mind has not been defiled with any false belief regarding the Incarnation of the Lord, nor with anything unbecoming concerning the Godhead. The sin is of equal gravity, whether it be denied, that He truly possesses our nature, or, that He is equal to the Father in glory. Coming together, therefore, to raise our minds to the mystery of the Birth of Christ, this day born of a Virgin Mother, let us put aside all shadow of earthly reasoning, and let the smoke of earthly wisdom move away from eyes that are lit by faith; for divine is the authority in which we believe, divine the faith we profess.

Since, whether we incline the ears of our soul to the witness of the Law, or to the sayings of the Prophets, or to the sound of the evangelical trumpet, this is the truth, which John, being filled with the Holy Ghost, intoned: *In the beginning was the Word, and the Word was with God, and the Word was God. The same was in the beginning with God. All things were made by Him: and without Him was made nothing.* And true also is that which the same preacher has added: *And the Word was made Flesh, and dwelt among us, and we saw his glory, the glory as it were of the Only-Begotten of the Father.*

In each nature is the same Son of God, taking ours, yet not giving up His Own; restoring man, in Man; continuing Himself without change. For the Godhead, which is common to Him with the Father, undergoes no diminution of Its Omnipotence; nor has *the form of a servant* profaned the Image of God; because the Supreme and Eternal Nature, which has lowered Itself for mens' salvation, has lifted us to Its own glory. Yet what It was, It ceaseth not to be. When therefore the Only-Begotten Son of God confesses that He is less than the Father (Jn. xiv. 28), to Whom He has said that He is equal (Jn. x. 30), He is pointing to the reality of both natures in Himself; that He may show that subordination relates to His human nature, equality to the Divine.

2. Corporal birth, therefore, has subtracted nothing from the majesty of the Son of God, and bestows nothing; because that unchangeable substance can neither be lessened, nor increased. That *the Word was made flesh* does not mean this, that the nature of God was changed into flesh, but that flesh was received by the Word into the oneness of His Person; in Whose Name the whole man is received, with whom the Word of God was so inseparably united within the womb of the Virgin, made fruitful by the Holy Ghost, without loss of her virginity, that He who was, before time, Begotten of the Essence of the Father, the Same, in time, is born from the womb of the Virgin. For in no other way could we be freed from the chains of eternal death, save through His becoming lowly in our nature, Who abides Omnipotent in His own.

Being then born truly man, Our Lord Jesus Christ, Who never ceases to be True God, made in Himself the beginning of a new creature, and in the manner of His Birth has given man a spiritual foundation, so that to wipe out the infection of his carnal birth, the birth of the regenerated might be without the seed of sin, and of these is it said: *Who are born, not of blood, nor of the will of the flesh, nor of the will of man, but of God.*

What mind can comprehend this mystery? What tongue describe this wondrous grace? Iniquity returns to the ways of innocence, old age to newness of life. Strangers are received into adoption as sons, and they without claim enter upon an inheritance. The evil-living begin to live as righteous, the parsimonious become bountiful, the incontinent chaste, and the earthly heaven minded. What is this transformation unless the witness of the Hand of God? Since the Son of man came that He might destroy the works of the devil, and has so joined Himself to us and us to Him, that the descent of God to what was human, has brought about the raising of man to what is divine (I Jn. iii. 8).

3. But, most dearly Beloved, in this mercy of God, Whose munificence towards us we cannot declare, Christians must remain ever watchful, so that they fall not into the snares of the devil, and become again entangled in errors they have renounced. For the ancient enemy, *transforming himself into an angel of light* (II Cor. xi. 14), ceases not to lay about us the snares of his deceptions, striving to corrupt in whatever way is open to him the faith of those who believe. He well knows to whom he may apply the fever of greed, to whom suggest the pleasures of gluttony; whom he may seduce by the allurements of sensuality, in whom to pour the poison of envy. He knows how to unsettle us by grief, and whom he may deceive by pleasure; whom he can overcome through fear, or deceive by flattery.

He unsettles the minds of all men, preying upon our anxieties, searching into our dispositions; seeking opportunities of causing evil, where he sees each one to be most vulnerable. He has among those who are his slaves many who are skilled in various wiles, whose talents and tongues he uses to undo others. By means of these he will promise remedies for illness, and knowledge of future events, and how to propitiate evil spirits, and to banish the spectres of darkness.

Add to these the persons who lyingly declare that every circumstance of human life depends on the influence of the stars, and that which in truth is but the consequence of the divine will, or of our own, they say is the act of unalterable fate. And that they may further injure us they promise that these things can be altered, if we pay worship to those stars that are contrary. An impious fabrication, which is destroyed by its own reasoning; for if the decrees of fate do not endure, then they are not to be feared; if they endure, then it is idle to worship the stars.

4. From inspirations such as these that form of impiousness arises, in which, from some eminence, the sun is worshipped at day break; so that even Christians believe that they are acting religiously, when, just before they arrive at the doors of the basilica of the Blessed Apostle Peter, which is dedicated to the One, Living and True God, and after they have ascended the steps by which one reaches the level of the upper open place, turning round, they face towards the rising sun, then bending their heads they bow down in honour of the shining orb. We have long grieved and deplored this practise, which is due partly to ignorance, and partly to the influence of paganism. For even if these latter venerate the Creator of this beauteous light, more than the light itself, which is but a creature, yet we must abstain from even the appearance of this rite; which, should any one who has abandoned the worship of idols find

among us, will he too not hold on to this part of his former belief, as credible, which he observes to be common to Christians as well as to the unbelieving?

5. Let this reprehensible pagan practise be rejected from among the customs of the faithful, and let not the honour due to the One God be mingled with the rites of those who worship creatures. For the Divine Scripture says: *The Lord thy God thou shalt adore—and Him only shalt thou serve* (Mt. iv. 10). And the Blessed Job, *a man without blame and avoiding evil,* as sayeth the Lord, declares: *If I have beheld the sun when it shined, and the moon going in brightness, and my heart in secret hath rejoiced, and I have kissed my hand with my mouth: which is a very great iniquity, and a denial of the most High God* (Job xxxi. 26, 28).

What is the sun, or what is the moon, but elements of the visible creation, and of material light? Of whom one is of greater splendour, and the other a means of lesser light. For as one is the time of day, and another that of the night, so has the Creator established a diversity in the quality of their light; for before He had done this, the days went by without the presence of the sun, and the nights without the service of the moon. But these things were established for man's convenience, so that the rational being might not be led astray in the reckoning of the months, or in the recurring of the years, or in the numbering of the seasons; since it is by the varying periods of the changing hours, and through the clear indications of each succeeding moonrise, that the sun rounds off the years, and the moon the months. For on the fourth day, as we read, *the Lord said: Let there be lights made in the firmament of heaven, to divide the day and the night, and let them be for signs and for seasons, and for days and years: to shine in the firmament of heaven, and to give light upon the earth* (Gen. i, xiv. 15–16).

6. Awake, O Man, from sleep, and recognise the dignity of your own nature! Remember that thou art made in the image and likeness of God; which, though corrupted in Adam, was made new in Christ. Use visible things as they must be used, as you use the earth, the sky, the sea, the air, springs and rivers; and whatever there is in them that is beautiful and wondrous, offer to the praise and glory of the Creator. Give not worship to that light in which winged things and creeping things, beasts and herds, flies and worms, also take delight. Partake of this material light with thy bodily sense, but with the whole desire of thy soul, embrace that true light *which enlighteneth every man that cometh into this world*, and of which the prophets says: *Come ye to him and be enlightened, and your faces shall not be confounded* (Ps. xxxiii. 6).

For if we are the temple of God, and if the Spirit of God doth dwell in us (I Cor. iii. 16), greater far is that which each faithful has in his own soul, than he beholds in the heavens. Most dearly beloved Brethren, we are not therefore declaring to you, or advising you, that you look down upon the works of God, or that you should see something contrary to your faith in those things which the Good God has made good; but only that you use every kind of creature, and all the visible beauty of this world, with reason, and with moderation; *for the things that are seen are temporal; but things that are not seen, are eternal* (II Cor. iv. 18).

Therefore, though we are born into the things of the present, yet are we reborn to the things that are to come. Let us therefore be not given over to temporal things, but rather let us be eager for the things of eternity. And that we may behold our hope yet nearer us, let us in this mystery of the Birth of Our Lord dwell upon that which the divine favour has conferred upon our own nature. Let us listen to the Apostle speaking: *For you are dead; and your life is hid with Christ in God. When Christ shall appear, Who is your life, then you also shall appear with Him in glory* (Col. iii. 3, 4), Who livest and reignest world without end. Amen.

III. St Leo, Pope and Doctor

On the Lord's Nativity (Homily 3)[12]

Synopsis:

    I. That both the origins of Christ are unutterable, and that both natures were born of Mary.

    II. Whence arose the Arian error? The mystery of the Incarnation explained.

    III. The necessity of the Incarnation, that the sins and errors of men be taken away.

    IV. That the faith and the power of the Incarnation was ever one and the same as it is today.

    V. That the Lord's Nativity is to be celebrated with pure Christian joy and not in carnal pleasure. That as Christ by being born became our flesh, we by being reborn become His.

1. The truths that belong to this day's solemnity are truly well known to you,. Dearly Beloved, and you have frequently been instructed in them; but just as this visible light delights the healthy eye, so to the heart that is healed there comes joy without end from the Birth of the Saviour; which we must not pass over in silence, though it can never be spoken of in a manner that is worthy of it. For the words of the prophet: *Who shall declare this generation?* (Is. liii. 8) refer not alone to that mystery wherein the Son of God is coeternal with the Father, but also to this Birth in which *The Word was made flesh.*

God therefore, the Son of God, equal to, and of the same nature, as the Father, and together with the Father the Creator and Lord of all things, present in His Entirety everywhere, and exceeding all things in the order of time, which moves as He has disposed, chose upon this day to be born of the Virgin Mary, for the salvation of the world; preserving in all things the purity of her who bore Him. Whose Virginity as it was not profaned by birth, so neither was it defiled at conception. *That it might be fulfilled which the Lord spoke by the prophet, saying: Behold a Virgin shall be with child, and bring forth a son, and they shall call his name Emmanuel, which being interpreted is, God with us.*

This wondrous delivery of the Holy Virgin brought forth as offspring One Person, Who was both truly human and truly divine, since either nature did not so retain its separate being that there is in Him a distinction of persons; neither was the created being so joined with its Creator, that the creature became a dwelling, and He the dweller there. And though one is the nature that is received, and another that which receives, yet the diversity of each is united in such unity, that one and the same is the Son Who declares, that as true man, He is less than the Father (Jn. xiv. 28), and as true God, He is equal to the Father (Jn. x. 30).

2. This unity, Dearly Beloved, in which the creature is united to the Creator, the Arian blindness could not discern with the eyes of the mind, not believing that the Only Begotten is of the same nature and substance as the Father, basing their argument on that which was said regarding *the form of a servant*, but which the same Son of God, to show that in Him (the Divinity) is not separate, nor of another person, in relation to the same says: *I and the Father are one* (Jn. x. 30).

In the form of a servant, which for the purpose of our redemption He assumed till the end of ages, He is less than the Father; in the Form of God, which He was before all ages, He is equal to the Father. In His Human lowliness He was *made of a woman*, and *made under the law* (Gal. iv, 4); in the Majesty of His Divinity He is the Word of God, through Whom *all things were made*. In like manner He Who in the Form of God has made man, in the form of a servant was made man; but both one and the other are God, in the might of Him Who assumes, and man in the lowliness of that assumed. Each nature retains without diminution its separate substance, and as the Form of God does not take from the form of a servant, so the form of a servant does not take from the Form of God (Phil. ii. 6).

The mystery then of power joined to our infirmity, does not, because of this same human nature, permit that the Son be said to be less than the Father. For the Godhead, which is One and the Same in the Trinity of Father, Son, and Holy Spirit, excludes all notion of inequality. For eternity has no part with time, and nature with that which is outside it. For there is but One Will, the same Substance, equal power, and not three Gods, but One God; because Oneness is true and indivisible, where there can be no diversity.

God therefore was born into the whole and perfect nature of a true man, whole and entire in all His parts, whole and entire in ours. We call these ours which God in the beginning created in us, and which He took upon Himself that He might restore. For of that which the deceiver corrupted, and which was lost to us by deceit, there is no part whatsoever in the Saviour; for though He shared in our infirmities, He was not a partaker of our sins. He took the form of a servant, without the baseness of sin; raising up what was human, not lessening what was divine. That emptying of Himself whereby the Invisible made Himself Visible, was a bending down of mercy, not a fall from power.

3. He came down to us, to Whom we could not ascend, that we might be brought back from our former bondage and from mundane errors to His eternal blessedness, because though many possessed the love of truth, yet the wavering of unformed minds was beguiled by the craft of deceiving demons; and human ignorance was drawn into diverse and conflicting errors by a learning so-called. To remove this mockery, by which minds made captive served the pride of the evil one, the teaching of the Law was not enough, neither could our nature be healed by the exhortations of the prophets; to these mortal means there had to be

joined the truth of the redemption, and our nature, corrupted in its very well-spring, must be born again.

A Victim must be offered as a sacrifice for our reconcilement, Who would be one from amongst us, yet free from our contamination: that this purpose of God, by which it pleased Him to wipe out the sins of the world by the Birth and Passion of Christ would extend to the times of all generations; neither should these mysteries make us confused, by reason of changing times, rather they would strengthen us, since the faith by which we live shall never vary in any age.

4. Let there be an end therefore to their complaining who speak with impious murmurings against the divine decrees, and bring forward the delayed coming of the Lord's Nativity, as if that was not expended for former ages, which has been accomplished in this last age of the world. For the Incarnation of the Word has brought it about that what needed to be done, is done; and the mystery of human redemption did not lie idle at any time in the remote past. That which the Apostles preached, the same the prophets have proclaimed; nor was that late in fulfilment, which was at all times believed.

The wisdom and mercy of God, by this delay of the lifebringing event, has made us the more ready for His call; so that what was foretold throughout so many ages by manifold signs, by many voices, by many mysteries, would not be obscure in these days of the Gospel. And the Birth of the Saviour, which is above all wonder and above all human understanding, has begotten in us a faith which is the more enduring, the more ancient and the more frequent was its foretelling.

Not then because of some new purpose, or because of a late rising feeling of compassion, did God provide for human needs; but from the beginning of the world He ordained for every man one and the same means of salvation. For the grace of God, by which all the saints have been sanctified, was increased, not begun, when Christ was born. And this mystery of so great tenderness with which the whole world has been filled, was so potent, even in its figures, that they have not received less who believed in the promise, than they who received the gift.

5. And so, Dearly Beloved, since such great gifts of the Divine Goodness have been, and with such manifest kindness, poured out upon us, the usefulness of the ancient figures has not alone been our aid, who have been called to an eternal inheritance, but Truth Itself, Visible and in bodily form, hath appeared; we must therefore celebrate, not with dull, carnal joy, this day of the Lord's Nativity. And this will be worthily and lovingly fulfilled, if each one recalls of Whose Body he is a member, and to what Head he is united; so that there may be no deformity within the holy Edifice.

Reflect then, Dearly Beloved, and in the light of the Holy Spirit carefully turn your mind to perceive, Who it is that has received us into Himself, and Whom have we received within us; for since the Lord Jesus Christ by being born has become our flesh, we also, by being reborn, have become His Body.

Therefore are we both members of the Body of Christ, and the temple of the Holy Spirit: and for this cause the Blessed Apostle says: *Glorify and bear God in your body* (I Cor. vi. 20): Who, placing within us the nature of His own gentleness and humility, begins in us that power whereby He has redeemed us, as the Lord Himself promises: *Come to me, all you that labour, and are burthened, and I will refresh you. Take up my yoke upon you, and learn of me, because I am meek, and humble of heart; and you shall find rest to your souls* (Mt. xi. 28–29).

Let us therefore take upon us His not heavy or bitter yoke of truth, and let us be like unto Him in simplicity of heart, in Whose Glory we desire to share, He also helping us and guiding us towards the fulfilment of His own promises, Who, according to His great mercy, is powerful to wipe out our sins, and bring to perfection in each of us His own gifts, Jesus Christ our Lord, Who liveth and reigneth world without end. Amen.

NOTES

[1] ἀρχή καὶ τῆς πράξεώς

[2] νομινάτα, exemplars, images or ideas, which pre-exist in the divine mind and, according to which, He has decreed all things shall be made. Cf. PG, 14, C. 55, 21.

[3] PL 35 col. 2213–2415—Inauthen. Ambrosius? ou auteurs divers. cf. PRM 35.

[4] PG 14. 138.

[5] PG 14 col. 139.

[6] cf. also, Migne PG 14 147.

[7] cf. also Denzinger 114.

[8] cf. PL 10, Bk. 10: 21, 22.

[9] cf. PL 35 col. 1395, 16.

[10] PL 38, col. 678, Serm. 121 De Script.

[11] PL 54, col. 216, Sermon 7.

[12] PL 54, col. 199 (Homily 3).

SUNDAY WITHIN THE OCTAVE
OF CHRISTMAS

I. ORIGEN: ON THE GOSPEL

II. ST AMPHILOCHIUS: IN PRAISE OF VIRGINITY, MARRIAGE AND WIDOW-
HOOD, AND ON THE MEETING OF OUR LORD JESUS CHRIST, THE MOTHER OF
GOD, ANNA AND SIMEON

III. ST AMBROSE: ON THE GOSPEL

IV. ST JOHN CHRYSOSTOM: ON THE GOSPEL

V. ALBINUS ALCUIN: ON THE THREE SILENCES

THE GOSPEL OF THE SUNDAY

LUKE ii. 33–40

At that time: Joseph, and Mary the Mother of Jesus, were wondering at those things which were spoken concerning him. And Simeon blessed them, and said to Mary his mother: Behold this child is set for the fall, and for the resurrection of many in Israel, and for a sign which shall be contradicted; and thy own soul a sword shall pierce, that, out of many hearts, thoughts may be revealed. And there was one Anna, a prophetess, the daughter of Phanuel, of the tribe of Aser; she was far advanced in years, and had lived with her husband seven years from her virginity. And she was a widow until four score and four years; who departed not from the temple, by fastings and prayers serving night and day. Now she, at the same hour, coming in, confessed to the Lord, and spoke of him to all that looked for the redemption of Israel. And, after they had performed all things according to the law of the Lord they returned into Galilee, to their city Nazareth. And the child grew, and waxed strong, full of wisdom; and the grace of God was in him.

EXPOSITION FROM THE CATENA AUREA

LUKE ii. 33, 40

V. 33. *And his father and mother were wondering at these things.*

PHOTIUS from the Catena of Greek Fathers: As often as the memory of wondrous things returns to the mind, so often does the mind renew its wonder; hence is it said: *And His father and mother were wondering at these things which were spoken concerning him.* ORIGEN, *Hom.* 17 *in*

Luke: both by the message of an angel and by the multitude of the heavenly host; by the shepherds and then by Simeon. BEDE, *in Luke Bk. I:* Joseph is called the father of the Saviour, though he was not His father; but that the good name of Mary might be protected, he is regarded by all as His father.

AUGUSTINE, *de Consens. Ev. II* 1: Although he may be called father in the same way that he is called the husband of Mary, but rightly understood without intercourse of the flesh, but in union of marriage. And thus was he closer in relationship to Him than if He had been adopted from without. Neither must Joseph be denied the title of father because he had not begotten Him carnally, seeing that he could be truly father to one not begotten by his own spouse, but adopted from elsewhere.

ORIGEN: Whoever is content with a simple exposition will say: the Holy Spirit honoured him with the title of father because he nurtured the Saviour. He however who inquires more deeply will say: since the order of the generation is brought from David down to Joseph; and, lest Joseph may not seem to be named to no purpose, since he did not beget the Saviour, that this order may have fitting reason, he is called the father of the Lord.

V. 34. *And Simeon blessed them, and said to Mary his mother . . .*

PHOTIUS: Having offered up praise to God, Simeon turns to bless those who bring the Child. Hence follows: *and Simeon blessed them.* He

bestowed a blessing on both of them; the intimation of things hidden he directs to the Mother only. In that he bestowed upon them a common blessing, Joseph is not deprived of the appearance of fatherhood; but by that which he said to Mary, separately from Joseph, he proclaims that she is the true parent; hence follows: *and said to Mary his mother.*

AMBROSE, *in Luke* 2: Observe the bountiful diffusion of grace among all at the birth of the Lord, and that prophecy is denied to the unbelieving, but not to the just. See also that Simeon prophesies that Christ has come for the fall and the resurrection of many. ORIGEN: He who interprets the words in a simple manner, may say that He came for the ruin of the unbelieving, and the resurrection of those who believe. CHRYSOSTOM, in Catena of Greek Fathers: For as light, though it may afflict the weak-sighted, is still light; so the Saviour goes on with His appointed work, though many perish. For their destruction is not His aim, but the consequence of their own unwisdom. Wherefore His power is made manifest, not alone in the salvation of the just, but also in the scattering of the wicked. So the sun, because it shines strongly, troubles those whose eyes are weak.

GREGORY NYSSA, *Oratio in Occursu Domini*: Observe the careful setting forth of the distinction. He is called the salvation that is prepared before the face of all peoples; but likewise the fall and the resurrection of many. The divine wish is the salvation and the sanctification of each person. Their fall or resurrection is within the will of the many; of those who believe and of those not believing. It is reasonable to believe that those who now lie prone, and unbelieving, will be raised up.

ORIGEN: A careful interpreter will not say that he falls who before did not stand upright. Give me then the one who stands upright for whose fall the Saviour came. GREGORY NYSS: By this the Evangelist means a fall to the lower world; because not in the same way, or equally, are those punished who are prior to the mystery of the Incarnation, and those coming after the Dispensation bestowed, and its public announcement. And of these last those especially who are of the Jewish people, shall be deprived of their former privileges, and made to suffer more grievously than all other peoples, for the reason that they refused to receive Him, Who of old was prophesied and adored among them, and from whom He came forth. Therefore are they in particular threatened with ruin, not alone by spiritual disaster, but also by the destruction of their city, and of those who dwell there. But resurrection is promised to those who believe, of whom some are still under the Law, and are now to be delivered from its servitude, and others have been buried with Christ and are risen with Him.

This child is set for the fall. Understand by these words that, in harmony of meaning with regard to prophetic utterances, the One and the Same God speaks both in the prophets and in the New Testament. For the prophetic speech declared, so that those who believe would not be confounded, that He would be *a stone of stumbling*, and *a rock of scandal* (Is. viii. 14; I Pet. ii. 6). *Ruin* is meant therefore for those who falter at the lowliness of His Humanity; *resurrection* for those who bow to the enduring of the divine decrees.

ORIGEN: We have to search deeper to oppose those who bark against the Creator, saying: behold the God of the Law and of the Prophets. See what kind He is. For He says: *I will kill, and I will make to live* (Deut. xxxii. 39). If therefore He is a bloody Judge and a cruel Creator, it is indeed evident that Jesus is His Son; since the same is written of Him: that He came for the fall and for the resurrection of many. AMBROSE: That He may judge between the merits of the just and the unjust, and that this just and stern judge may decree punishment or reward, according to the quality of our deeds.

ORIGEN: Let us consider whether or not the Saviour has come for the ruin of some, and the resurrection of certain others. For when I was standing in sin, it was at first profitable to me that I fall down, and die to sin. So also the holy Prophets, when they looked upon that which was sacred, they were wont to fall upon their faces, so that their sins might be more efficaciously wiped out by their fall. This the Saviour has conceded to you also, that you may fall to the ground. For you were a sinner; let the sinner in you perish, that you from there may rise up, and declare: *For if we be dead with him, we shall live also with him* (II Tim. ii. 11). CHRYSOSTOM: A new manner of living is truly a resurrection. For when the lascivious becomes chaste, the avaricious merciful, and the fierce gentle, then we have here a resurrection; since sin being dead, justice is now risen. *And for a sign that shall be contradicted.* BASIL: The cross in Scripture is called a sign of contradiction. *For Moses,* it says, *made a brazen serpent and set it up for a sign* (Num. xxi. 19). GREGORY NY.: Shame commingles with glory. And of this, to us who worship Christ, this sign is an indication; for while by some it is regarded as a thing to be despised, and fearful, to yet others is it a sign to be venerated. Or perhaps he is speaking of Christ himself, the Author of signs, as a sign, being above nature. BASIL: For it is a sign of a wondrous, yet hidden thing; seen by the simple, but understood only by those whose minds are prepared.

V. 35. *And thy own soul a sword shall pierce.*

ORIGEN, *Hom.* 17 *in Luke:* All that history tells of Christ is contradicted; not that they contradict who believe in Him; for we believe as true all that is written concerning Him; but because among those who do not believe, all that is written of him is a sign to be contradicted. GREGORY NY.: These things are said of the Son; but they also apply to the Mother, in that she takes unto herself each single happening, the sufferings as well as the glories; for he tells her not alone of the propitious events, but of the sorrowful; for there follows: *And thy own soul a sword shall pierce.* BEDE: History does not in any place tell us that the Blessed Mary departed

this life by the death of the sword, especially since the sword is wont to pierce, not the soul, but the body. So here we must understand as the sword that of which it is said: *and a sword is in their lips* (Ps. lviii. 8); that is, that it was the pain of the Lord's passion that pierced her soul, who, though she did not doubt that Christ, as Son of God, died of His own will, and also that He would overcome death, yet she could not without deepest sorrow behold Him crucified, who was born of her flesh.

AMBROSE, as above, *in Luke Bk.* 2: Or the words may show that the wisdom of Mary was not unacquainted with heavenly mystery; *for the word of God is living and effectual, and more piercing than any two-edged sword* (Heb. iv. 12). AUGUSTINE, Quaest. de N. & V. Test. 73: Or by this he signifies that Mary, through whom was wrought the mystery of the Incarnation, at the death of the Lord doubted in stupefaction, at seeing the Son of God humiliated unto death. As a sword passing close to a man causes fear, though it touches not, so doubt causes grief, though it slays not; since it does not lie upon the soul, but passes as a shadow.[1]

GREGORY NYSSA: Nor does it mean that she alone would be caught up in this passion, when it adds: *that, out of many hearts, thoughts may be revealed.* For by saying *that* he points to a consequence; it is not placed causally. For when all these things had come to pass there took place in many a laying bare of soul. For as some confessed God upon the Cross, so others ceased not from revilings and recriminations. Or this was said in that at the time of the passion the thoughts in the hearts of many persons were revealed, and they were purified in His resurrection. For sudden certitude followed on their state of doubt; unless one wishes to understand illumination as revelation, as Scripture sometimes does.

BEDE: But even to the end of this present world, the sword of most dire tribulation will not cease to pierce the soul of the Church, when the sign of faith is contradicted by the wicked; when, the word of God being received, many will rise with Christ, but it will lead many to ruin through deplorable apostasy; when the thoughts of many hearts being revealed, where She has sown the perfect seed of the Gospel, there will she see, either that the seeds of the vices have overcome the just, or that they alone have germinated.

ORIGEN: There were also evil thoughts in men, that were revealed for this purpose, that He might destroy them Who dies for us. As long as they were hidden it was impossible wholly to destroy them. Hence, we also, if we have sinned, must say: *My injustice I have not concealed* (Ps. xxxi. 5). For if we have made known our sins, not alone to God, but to those who can heal our wounds and sins, our sins shall be wiped out.[2]

V. 36. *And there was one Anna, a prophetess, the daughter of Phanuel, of the tribe of Aser.*

AMBROSE, *in Luke* 2: The holy Simeon had prophesied, and she who was joined in marriage had prophesied, the Virgin had pro-

phesied, and now the widow needs must prophesy, so that no state or sex should be wanting. And so it is written: *And there was . . .*
THEOPHYLACTUS: The Evangelist pauses in his account of Anna, recording her father's name, and her tribe; as though to bring forward many witnesses, who had known her father and her tribe. GREGORY NYSSA: and this perhaps because there were at that time many others who were known by the same name; so that he might therefore make clear who she was, he tells her father's name, and speaks of her own condition. AMBROSE: Anna was so dedicated to the duties of her widowhood, and such was her virtue, that she is deemed worthy to announce to others that the Redeemer of all men had come. Hence Scripture relates: *She was far advanced . . .*

V. 37. *And she was a widow fourscore and four years.*

ORIGEN, *Hom.* 17 *in Luke:* Nor is it by chance that the holy Scripture dwells on her. It is good if, from the first, a woman lay hold of the grace of virginity. But if she cannot do this, and it happens to her that she loses her husband, let her remain a widow. And on this she should resolve, not alone after the death of her husband, but while he lives; so that if this should not happen, her will and her purpose will be yet crowned by God. And so let her say: This I vow; this I promise: Should anything human befall me, which I desire not, I shall do no other thing than keep myself a widow, and unspotted. Justly therefore did the holy woman merit to receive the spirit of prophecy, since by steadfast chastity, and by long fastings, had she reached to this eminence. Hence follows: *who departed not from the temple, by fastings and prayers.*

V. 38. *Now she, at the same hour, coming in, confessed to the Lord.*

GREGORY NYSSA: From which it is evident that she possessed many other virtues; and see likewise how she conformed in virtue to Simeon. They were together in the temple, and together they were found worthy of the prophetic office; hence, *she at the same hour, confessed to the Lord.* That is, she gave thanks because of seeing in Israel the Salvation of the world, and she began to give witness unto Jesus, that He was the Saviour and the Redeemer. Hence there follows: *And spoke of Him to all that looked for the redemption of Israel.* Because Anna the prophetess spoke but little regarding Jesus, and that with no clear meaning, the Gospel does not recount in detail what was said by her. Perhaps someone will say that it was for this reason that Simeon came before her: because he stood for the Law; for his name means obedience; but that she stands for the Dispensation of grace, which is the meaning of her name. Between them stood Christ. Accordingly He dismisses the former, now dying with the Law, and cherishes the latter, living on through grace.

BEDE, *in Luke* 2: In a mystical sense Anna stands for the Church, which in this present world is as it were widowed by the death of her Spouse. Even the number of the years of her widowhood designates the time in which the Church, continuing on in the body, sojourns afar from her Lord. Seven times twelve make fourscore and four. And seven relates to the full course of this world, which was wrought in seven days. But twelve belongs to the completeness of the apostolic teachings. Whosoever therefore, whether the universal church, or anyone of the faithful, devotes the whole course of life to apostolic labours, is praised as serving the Lord for fourscore and four years.

The period of seven years during which she lived with her husband is in accord with the time of the Lord's Incarnation. For as I have said the completeness of time is wont to be expressed by the number seven. Here because of the special quality of the Lord's majesty, the simple number of seven years expresses, in sign of its perfection, the time in which He taught while clothed in the flesh. It also favours the mysteries of the Church that Anna is interpreted as the Lord's grace, that she is the daughter of Phanuel, who is called the face of the Lord, and descended from the tribe of Aser, that is, *blessed with children* (Deut. xxxiii. 24).[3]

V. 39. *And after they had performed all things according to the Law.*

BEDE: Luke here omits that which he knew was already sufficiently recorded by Matthew: that after this the Lord, lest He be discovered and slaughtered by Herod, was taken into Egypt by His parents, and that when Herod was dead He returned finally to Galilee, and began to live in His own village of Nazareth. Individual Evangelists are wont to omit certain things, which they see were recorded by others, or which they foresee in the Spirit will be recorded by others, so that in the continuous thread of their narration nothing seems omitted. What has thus been passed over by the diligent reader will discover by carefully going through each of the Gospels in turn. Accordingly, having omitted many things, Luke says: *And after they had performed* . . . THEOPHYLACTUS: Their city, meaning their city of origin, was Bethlehem; Nazareth was their dwelling place.

AUGUSTINE, *Harmony of Gospels II*, 9: Perhaps some one will raise the question; How does Matthew say that His parents went with the Child to Galilee because, through fear of Archilaus, they were unwilling to go into Judea, whereas it appears they went into Galilee because Nazareth of Galilee was their city, as Luke does not fail to say? But we must keep in mind where the angel, in Egypt, spoke to Joseph as he slept, saying: *Arise and take the boy and his mother and go into the land of Israel* (Mt. ii. 19,20), which was at first understood by Joseph as meaning that he was bidden to go into Judea; for that was the first interpretation of *the land of Israel*. But, hearing that Archelaus the son of Herod was reigning there, Joseph was unwilling to expose Him to that peril, especially since the words *land of Israel* could also be interpreted to include Galilee, because there also dwelt people of Israel.[4]

GREEK COMMENTATOR *in Catena G.F.*: Or, Luke here treats of the time before the descent into Egypt. For Joseph would not have taken

him there before the slaughter. Before they descended into Egypt he had not yet received the message that they should go to Nazareth; rather he had gone there of his own accord as one dwelling freely in his own land. Since his journey to Bethlehem was only for the purpose of the census, that for which they had come being accomplished, they went down again into Nazareth.

V. 40. *And the child grew, and waxed strong, full of wisdom; and the grace of God was in him.*

THEOPHYLACTUS: He could have come forth from the womb in the fulness of adult life, but this would have seemed fantastic. So He grew up naturally; hence, *the child grew and waxed strong*. BEDE: Observe the choice of words: that the Lord Jesus Christ, in that He was a Child, that is, that He had put on the garment of our humanity, had thus need to grow, and to become strong. ATHANASIUS, *Contra Arianos*, IV: If according to some, flesh was changed into the divine substance, how did it receive an increase? To attribute growth to the Uncreated is an abomination. CYRIL, *in Catena G.F.*: The increase in wisdom is fittingly joined with the increase in years, where the Evangelists says, *and waxed strong*, that is, in the spirit. Proportionate to the increase of the body's age, the divine nature shows forth the wisdom that belonged to It.

THEOPHYLACTUS: for if while yet a Child He had revealed all His wisdom, He would be looked upon as something strange. So He revealed Himself with the growth of the years, that He might fill the whole earth. Not as one who receives wisdom is He said to grow in wisdom. How can that be perfected which was from the beginning perfect? Hence, *full of wisdom; and the grace of God was in Him.*

BEDE: *Wisdom* in very truth, *for in Him dwelleth all the fulness of the Godhead corporeally* (Col. ii. 9); *grace,* because the Man Jesus Christ was endowed with great grace, so that from the time He began to become a man, He might be perfect as He was as God; much more since He was the Word of God, and God, He had not any need to wax strong, or to grow. Though yet an infant He possessed the grace of God; and as in Him all was wondrous, that His Childhood might also be wondrous, He was filled with the wisdom of God.

I. ORIGEN: ON THE GOSPEL

Luke who wrote: *The Holy Ghost shall come upon thee, and the power of the most high shall overshadow thee. And therefore also the Holy which shall be born of thee shall be called the Son of God:* and who has openly made known to us that Jesus is the Son of the Virgin, conceived without human seed; the same has testified that Joseph was His father, when he says: *And his father and mother were wondering at these things which were said concerning him.* For what reason is he, who was not His father, here spoken of as His father?

He that is content with a simple explanation will say: the Holy Spirit honoured him with the title of father, because he nurtured the Saviour. But he who inquires more deeply may say: because the line of descent leads from David down to Joseph (Mt. i), and so that Joseph who was not the father of the Saviour might not be named without purpose, and that the genealogy may be justified, he is called the father of the Lord.

They were wondering therefore, his father and mother, at those things that were said about Him, as well by the angel as by the multitude of the heavenly army, and also by the shepherds. Hearing all these things they wondered exceedingly. Thereupon the Scripture says: *And Simeon* blessed them, and said to Mary his mother: *Behold this child is set for the fall, and for the resurrection of many in Israel, and for a sign which shall be contradicted; and thy own soul a sword shall pierce, that, out of many hearts, thoughts may be revealed.* We must consider in what way the Saviour has come for the fall, and for the resurrection of many.

A simple explanation is that He came for the ruin of the unbelieving, and for the resurrection of the believing. But a more attentive interpreter will say, that no one falls down unless someone who before was standing upright. Tell me, then, he will say, who were they who before were standing up, for whose fall Christ came, and who were they that were to rise. For only they rise who before were prone. We must see then whether it was not for the fall of these here and those there, and for the resurrection of many, that He came, but to the same people, either for their fall or for their resurrection.

For judgement I am come into this world; He says, *that they who see not may see; and they who see, may become blind* (Jn. ix. 39). There is in us that which before used to see, and afterwards ceased to see; and yet another thing which saw not, and afterwards began to see. For example. I wish to see with those eyes with which before I saw not, and which afterwards were opened to me; as after their disobedience the eyes of Adam and Eve were opened, of which we have spoken in a previous sermon.

But now we must inquire what do the words mean: *Behold this child is set for the fall, and for the resurrection of many in Israel.* I must first fall down, and, when I shall have fallen, rise again in justice, so that the Saviour shall not be the cause of my fall into wickedness; but he causes me to fall, that I may rise again, and more profitable to me was the fall, than that time in which I seemed to stand. For I was standing in sin in that time in which I was living in sin. And because I was standing in sin, my first need was that I should fall, and that I should die to sin. Even the holy prophets, when they looked upon that which was sacred, fell upon their face upon the earth. And for this reason did they fall prostrate, that their sins might be the more fully purified by their fall.

This also the Saviour first gives to you, that you fall down. You were a heathen; then let the heathen in thee fall down. Didst thou love fornication, let the fornicator in thee perish. You were a sinner, then let the sinner that is in thee fall, that from thence you may rise and say, *if we have been planted together in the likeness of his death, we*

shall be also in the likeness of his resurrection* (Rom. vi. 5); and again, *if we be dead with Him, we shall also live with Him* (II Tim. ii. 11). He is therefore set for the fall and the resurrection of many in Israel, that is, among those who can look before them with clear vision and understanding.

And for a sign which shall be contradicted. All that has been recorded of the Saviour has been contradicted. That His Mother was a virgin is contradicted. The Marcionites contradict this sign, and they declare that in no way was He born of woman. The Ebionites also contradict this sign, and they say that He was born of a man and a woman, even as we are born. He had a human body; and this is a sign to be contradicted. For some say that He came down from heaven; others that He had a body such as ours, so that in the likeness of the body He might redeem our bodies from sin, and bestow on us the hope of resurrection. He rose from the dead; and this is a sign to be contradicted; how He has risen, and whether it is truly He Who died, or whether indeed He may not have risen in a body of more glorious substance. And the contention is without end. Again, some say that He showed Thomas the place of the nails in His hands; others following this logically inquire, if this then be the same body, how then did he enter in, *the doors being closed*?

You see then by what manner of objections even His Resurrection is questioned, and becomes a sign to be contradicted. I believe that this also, that He was foretold by the mouth of the prophets, is also a sign to be contradicted. For there are many heretics who declare that He was in no way foretold by the prophets. What need is there for me to continue? All that history has spoken of Him is a sign to be contradicted. Not that they who believe in Him contradict; for we believe that all that is written concerning Him is true. But among the doubting Christians everything that is written of Him is a sign to be contradicted.

Then Simeon continues: *and thy own soul a sword shall pierce.* What is this sword which pierces, not alone the souls of others, but even the heart of Mary? It is written plainly that at the time of the passion all the Apostles were scandalised, even as Our Lord has said: *all you shall be scandalised this night* (Mt. xxvi. 31). Therefore were they all scandalised, so that even Peter, the Prince of the Apostles, three times denied Him. What then? Shall we think that when the Apostles were scandalised that the mother of the Lord was immune? If she suffered not scandal in the passion of Our Lord, then Christ did not die for her sins. If however *all have sinned, and do need the glory of God, being justified by His grace,* and redeemed, then indeed Mary in that hour was also scandalised.

And this is what Simeon now prophesies, saying: *and thy own soul,* which knows that thou, the Virgin, brought forth without knowledge of man, and which has heard from Gabriel the words: *the Holy Spirit shall come upon thee, and the power of the Most High shall overshadow thee,* the *sword* of unfaith *shall pierce,* and the sharp edge of doubt shall wound, and thy thoughts shall tear thee asunder, when thou shalt look upon Him, Whom you have be-

lieved to be the Son of God, and Whom you have known was conceived without seed of man, crucified and put to death, and subjected to human torments, and, at the end, sorrowfully complaining and calling out, *Father, if it be possible, let this chalice pass from me.* (Mt. xxvi. 39.)[6]

And thy own soul a sword shall pierce, that, out of many hearts, thoughts may be revealed. Evil thoughts there were in man, and therefore were they revealed, that being brought to light, they might be destroyed, and that being slain and destroyed, they might cease utterly to be, and that He might kill them Who for us has died. For as long as they were hidden, and not brought forth, it was impossible wholly to destroy them. So we also, if we have sinned, we ought to proclaim: *I have acknowledged my sin to thee, and my injustice I have not concealed. I said I will confess against myself my injustice to the Lord* (Ps. xxxi. 5, 6). For if we have done this, and if we have made known our sins, not alone to the Lord, but to those also who can heal our sins and our wounds, our sins shall be blotted out by Him Who says: *I have blotted out thy iniquities as a cloud, and thy sins as a mist* (Is. xliv. 22).

Since women also are to be saved, after the prophecy of Simeon there comes a woman prophet, of whom it is written: *And here was one Anna, a prophetess, the daughter of Phanuel, of the tribe of Aser.* What admirable sequence! Not before the man came the woman, but first came Simeon, who took the Child and held Him in his arms, then came the woman, whose words are not set down in any given order;

we are but told that she confessed the Lord, and spoke of Him to all who looked for the redemption of Israel. And fittingly did this holy woman merit to receive the spirit of prophecy, because it was in steadfast chastity and with much fasting that she had ascended to this eminence. Behold, women, the example of Anna, and imitate it, should it happen to you that you lose your husbands. For consider what is written of her: *she had lived with her husband seven years from her virginity*, and so on, and it was for this reason she was a prophetess. For it was not because it pleased her, or by accident, that the Holy Spirit dwelt in her.

It is a great good if from the beginning a woman can lay hold of the grace of virginity. But if she cannot do this, and it happens to her that she lose her husband, let her remain a widow. And on this she ought to resolve, not alone upon the death of her husband, but while he lives, so that if this should not come to pass, her will and her purpose will yet be crowned by God. And so let her say: This I vow: this I promise: should anything human befall me; which yet I desire not, I shall do no other thing than keep myself a widow, and unspotted. But now we hear of second, and third, and even of fourth marriages, not to speak of others, and we are not unaware that such marriages exclude from the kingdom of God.[7]

For as well as fornication, all such marriages exclude from ecclesiastical dignities, for neither a bishop nor a priest nor a deacon, nor a deaconess (*vidua*) can marry a second time: accordingly, if anyone pass to second nuptials, let him be excluded from the company of the firstborn and the unstained of the Church, which is *without spot or wrinkle*: not to the extent that he is given up to hell fire, but that he have no part in the kingdom of God (Eph. v. 27).

You will remember that when I interpreted for you that which was written to the Corinthians: *To the Church of God that is at Corinth, with all that invoke the name of Our Lord Jesus Christ* (I Cor. i. 2), I spoke of the diversity of the Church, and of those that invoke the name of the Lord. I believe that the monogamist, and the virgin, and he that perseveres in chastity, are of the Church of God. But he that is twice wed, though he be of good life, and possess other virtues, is yet not of the Church, and of the number *not having spot or wrinkle, or any such thing*; but is of the second grade, and of those who invoke the name of the Lord, and who are truly saved in the name of Jesus Christ, yet are they in no wise crowned by Him. To Whom be honour and glory for ever and ever. Amen.

II. St Amphilochius, Bishop of Iconium

In praise of Virginity, Marriage and Widowhood, and on the Meeting of Our Lord Jesus Christ, the Mother of God, Anna and Simeon[8]

1. Many among the greatest of men have praised virginity; and it is truly worthy of praise, in its nature angelic, akin to the heavenly powers, belonging to the company of incorporeal natures, as the shining glory of Holy Church, as that which overcomes the world, that which

rises above earthly affections, which restrains desires, without relationship to Eve, as free of pain, immune from anguish, that need not hearken to that dread decree in which it is said: *I will multiply thy sorrows, and thy conceptions: in sorrow shalt thou bring forth children, and shalt be under thy husband's power, and he shall have dominion over thee* (Gen. iii. 16).

Venerable in truth is virginity, as an unconquered possession, a fruit tree that withers not, a dwelling of freedom, as the glory of the ascetic life, as something above the power of man, as being free of the compulsion of the appetites, as that which enters with Christ the Bridegroom into the bridal chamber of the kingdom of heaven.

And these are the glories of virginity, and of those who draw near to it: but *marriage is honourable in all* (Heb. xiii. 4), and above every gift of earth, as a fruit-bearing branch, as a flowering tree, as the root whence comes virginity, the husbandman of the living and reasoning shoots, as the gift bestowed for the increase of the world, as the comfort of the race of men, as the creator of humanity, as the painter of the image and likeness of God, as blessed of the Lord, as chosen to bring forth the whole world, as governing the same, and which He also honoured that He might become man, as being able freely to declare: *Behold I and my children, whom the Lord hath given me* (Is. viii. 18).

Take away honourable marriage and where will you find the flower of virginity? For from nowhere else is this flower gathered. In saying this to you, Beloved, we in no way desire to place conflict between marriage and virginity, for both we admire, as one completing the other, since the Lord, Who in His Providence has ordained both has not set one against the other; for the true service of God embraces both the one and the other. For without the holy and precious love of God, neither is virginity to be revered, nor is marriage honourable.

2. I have said these things in this present discourse, because of that which is written in the Law, and confirmed in the Dispensation of grace; which is proclaimed of all, but fulfilled in the Lord alone. I speak of the first-born fruits of marriage. And to what end? You have heard the Evangelist speaking: *And after eight days were accomplished, that the Child should be circumcised, His name was called Jesus, which was called by the angel, before He was conceived in the womb. And after the days of purification, according to the law of Moses, were accomplished, they carried Him to Jerusalem, to present Him to the Lord: as it is written in the law of the Lord: every male opening the womb shall be called holy to the Lord.*

See you not here the blessing of marriage, and that which is said of all, is found only in the Lord? That, namely: *every male opening the womb shall be called holy to the Lord.* To the Lord alone does this refer, though spoken of all who are firstborn, and not to any other. For to her that is a virgin it is the way of nature that the womb be opened by concourse with man, and from thence will she bring forth. It was not thus with Our Saviour, but He Himself, opening without intercourse the womb of the Virgin, came forth in an ineffable manner.

Wherefore the words, *every male opening the womb shall be called holy to the Lord*, refer to the Lord alone.

For was Cain holy, who laid violent hands on life, and who was the first of all that came from the maternal womb? Was Esau holy, *the wild man*, whose inheritance was the sword, since he also came first from the womb of his mother? Was Ruben holy, who violated his father's bed, and provoked the curse, since he too came forth first from the fertile womb of Lia? Of these not one was holy, and all were given to chastisement. By which it is shown that only to the Lord has this saying reference, *every male opening the womb shall be called holy to the Lord*, in accordance with that which Gabriel said to the Virgin: *The Holy Ghost shall come upon thee, and the power of the most High shall overshadow thee. And therefore the Holy that shall be born of thee shall be called the Son of God* (Lk. i. 35).

3. And he is of those who are contradictory who says, that if this has reference to the Lord, namely, what was written in the Law: *every male opening the womb shall be called holy to the Lord*, then the Virgin has not remained a virgin. For the Scripture says clearly: *every male opening the womb*, and the Virgin's womb was then truly opened, if this has reference to the Lord. But listen intelligently: in the Virgin Birth, the virginal gates were in no way opened, as He fittingly hath willed, Who was conceived there, according to the words that were spoken concerning Him: *This gate shall be shut, it shall not be opened, and no man shall pass through it: because the Lord the God of Israel hath*

entered in by it, and it shall be shut (Ezech. xliv. 2).

As to what pertains to the Virginal nature, in no manner were the virginal gates opened, but as to what relates to the power of the Master Who was born, nothing is shut to the Lord, but all things are open unto Him. Nothing stands in His way, nothing impedes Him. For all things are open to the Lord. Wherefore do the powers of heaven command the powers beneath: *Lift up your gates, O ye Princes, and be ye lifted up, O eternal gates: and the King of Glory shall enter in* (Ps. xxiii. 7, 9).

Venerable truly is virginity, and by this I mean true virginity, since in virginity there are degrees of excellence. For some virgins fell asleep, but others kept watch. And honourable indeed is marriage, that, I say, which is true marriage is honourable. Many there are who keep it in honour, and there are many that have brought it down. Honourable likewise is widowhood; it is but fitting that I speak of all three orders.

4. And as I have just been saying, honourable too is widowhood, and by this I mean true widowhood, which has triumphed, *winning the reward of undefiled conflicts* (Wisd. iv. 2); that is honourable and pure and not feigned, which though deprived of its yoke-fellow, yet turns from what is stained. And such is she who just now has been made known to us, Anna the prophetess, grown to a good old age, but who has renewed her youth like the eagle (Ps. cii. 5). You have heard what the Evangelist Luke has recorded of her. You have learned how she had spent the days of her widowhood. *There was one Anna a*

prophetess, the daughter of Phanuel, of the tribe of Aser, she was far advanced in years, and had lived with her husband seven years from her virginity. And she was a widow until four score years and four years, who departed not from the temple, by fastings and prayers serving night and day.

See you not how the sacred Gospel adorns her name with praise? Anna, truly Anna, that is, grace. The meaning of her name becoming the holiness of her life. Let women hearken, and let them imitate this venerable woman, that they may bring their life to an equal end, and merit a similar crown. Let not infirmity be offered in excuse for throwing away the chastity of the single marriage.

5. Anna is the glory of widowed women; a woman truly in sex and state, but in the order of the prophets. Her life was passed in widowhood, her conversation was in heaven. Frail in body and bowed with age, strong and upright of soul. Wrinkles lined her face, but prudence showed itself there. Brought to time's infirmity by years, but vigorous in the knowledge of God. Given to fasting, and averse to all greediness. Devoted to prayer, not empty of mind. She departed not from the temple, not going from house to house. Her delight was in singing the praises of God, not in idle nonsense. Prophesying, not recounting fables. Meditating on divine things, not preoccupied with the things that are not becoming.

Anna excelled even that widow whom the Apostle called blessed, in her years and in the manner of her life. Let a widow be chosen of no less than three score years, who hath been the wife of one husband; if she have brought up children, if she have washed the saints' feet; if she have ministered to them that suffer tribulation; if she have diligently followed every good work (I Tim. v. 10). Who indeed is to be esteemed above others, but she who has attained to the gift of prophecy, who was a vessel of the Holy Ghost, and pointed out the signs of His Coming to all who awaited the advent of Christ in the flesh? Of which the Evangelist has indeed spoken, as you have just now heard: Now she, at the same hour, coming in, confessed to the Lord; and spoke of Him to all that looked for the redemption of Israel.

See you not that Anna is worthy of praise? She acted as a protectress of the Lord, and in his presence spoke in His behalf. O new and unheard of thing! She was but a poor widow, and she makes plain that over which the Priests and Scribes had long pondered, uplifting the hearts of those who heard her with fervent hope. She made manifest to Israel the salvation of its Lord, which she declared by arguments and by signs was now about to be delivered. Anna discerned the Infant Lord. She perceived too the gifts and little offerings which were borne with Him, and for Him. Not on that account was she confused, nor by His helpless and tender age. She confessed that this Child was both the Lord, and the Destroyer of sin.

6. Do not, Beloved, pass lightly over the testimony of Anna, in which she described the power of the Lord to all who were present. See you not, she says to those who stood about her, this little Child, nursed at the breast, resting in the

bosom of His mother, unable as yet through infancy to press the soles of His feet to the earth, circumcised on the eighth day after the manner of other infants? This Child whom you see before you has laid the foundations of the world (Heb. i. 2), He has perfected the heavens (Is. xl. 22); It is He who has shut up the sea with doors when it broke forth (Job. xxxviii. 8); this Child has brought the winds from out His stores (Ps. cxxxiv. 7); in the days of Noah He opened the cataract of heaven (Gen. vii. 11); this Child covereth the earth with clouds, and prepareth rain for the earth; He giveth snow like wool (Ps. cxlvii. 8, 16); by the rod of Moses he freed our forefathers from the land of Egypt (Ex. vii. 17); He dried up the Red Sea, and led forth the people who trusted in Him, and led them with dry feet as through a smiling field (Ex. xiv.); This Child rained manna upon them in the desert (Ex. xvi); He gave our fathers a land flowing with milk and honey as their inheritance (Jos. v. 6); This Child decreed that this temple be dug and raised on high (Esd. iii); it was this Child that made the compact with Abraham, confirmed on oath (Gen. xxii. 17): *I will bless thee, and I will multiply thy seed as the stars of Heaven.*

Esteem not lightly this Child, because He is a child. He Who is a child, is coeternal with the Father. His age is measured within a month, yet there were none who went before Him. This is but a babbling Infant, but the Mouth whence wisdom is imparted to others; the one because of birth from the Virgin, the other because of the incomprehensible nature of His substance. This too is He of whom Isaias has

told us, saying: *for a Child is born to us, and a Son is given to us* (Is. ix. 5). He says the one is born, the other is given. What is born is seen with the eyes; what is given is known by the mind and the thought alone.

7. Such were the words of Anna, such was her wondrous testimony. So was the mission of her widowhood happily fulfilled. Truly a widow, who faithfully pursued the way of her state. A widow who had lost her husband, and had received the Lord in his place. Seven years from her virginity had she lived with her spouse. She had filled out the week of years. In the seventh year she had been bereaved of the company of her spouse. Happily the seventh, aptly had she celebrated the sabbath; fittingly had she taken hold of the gift of the Lord's Day. Anna, lamenting as the mournful dove, forgot not her first faith; her abode invited no scandal; the bond of marriage she sought to impose on none other, for though her first pledge was dead, she sought him in the spirit; her wedding garment she stained not, nor incurred she the reproof of the Apostle. *For when they have grown wanton in Christ they will marry. Having damnation, because they have made void their first faith* (I Tim. v. 11).

Worthy indeed of reproach is she who buries, together with him, the memory of her husband, and covers it over with the earth, especially if she has borne him children, for which marriage was made. If however the widow is still young and has not children, she cannot be blamed if moved by the desire of offspring she enters again into nuptials. For this also was the wish of Paul, as he said: *I will therefore that the younger should marry;* and then showing what the addition of a second marriage is meant to secure, he added: *bear children, be mistresses of families* (I Tim. v. 14). It is the aim then of the second marriage to have children. When however she who enters into a second marriage already has children, this latter offspring seem unnecessary, the reasoning young shoots warring with each other.

8. Let us in our discourse return again to our first reflections. What does the Evangelist then say? It is best to continue with our present detailed exposition. You have just now heard Luke the Evangelist telling us how Simeon said to the Virgin: *Behold this Child is set for the fall, and for the resurrection of many in Israel, and for a sign which shall be contradicted; and thy own soul a sword shall pierce.* What does this mean: *and thy own soul a sword shall pierce?* Listen with attention. Hearing as it were from afar off the voice of Simeon speaking to the listening ears of the Virgin concerning the Lord, and when he had said that that He was set for the fall and the resurrection of many in Israel, and for a sign that would be contradicted, was the Virgin, as Mother of the Lord, displeased with Simeon, saying to him: "you know not, O man, what you are saying. Is it of the Christ you are foretelling these sorrows? You know not of the wondrous conception of this Child, and as though He were of common birth you make it known that He is a sign that shall be contradicted? In Him there is no fall, but a great raising upwards, and great condescension to those who labour well.

Why, instead of rendering praise to God, do you say: *Behold the Child is set for the fall, and for the resurrection of many in Israel, and for a sign which shall be contradicted?"*

And then did Simeon reply to the Virgin: 'It is enough for thee, O Virgin, that you are called Mother. It is more than enough that you have attained to be the nurse of Him Who nurses the world. Great indeed is thy dignity, that thou hast borne in the flesh Him Who bears all things. Christ, Who found in thee a dwelling is the self Same, if I may so speak of Him, Who hath Himself decreed: *Behold this Child is set for the fall, and for the resurrection of many in Israel.* For the fall of the unbelieving Jews, but for the resurrection of the believing Gentiles.' *And for a sign that shall be contradicted:* calling the Cross a sign that shall be contradicted. And why? Because many who believed not gainsaid Him on the Cross, making ridicule of it both by deeds and words, giving Him vinegar to drink, offering Him gall for His thirst, binding a wreath of thorns on His brow, piercing His side with a spear, striking Him with their hands, and shouting at Him with offensive clamour: *He saved others; Himself He cannot save* (Mt. xxvii. 42).

And setting this forth Simeon said: *and for a sign that shall be contradicted.* For many have contradicted Him; When Peter denied Him; when the Apostles, like sheep without a shepherd, were all scattered. Therefore also was the heart of Mary filled with sorrow by the sign of the Cross. Wherefore did she say (within herself) Why have I not died ere this? Wherefore have I come to this day? A Virgin I have remained, and yet greater is my suffering than the heart of a mother. To these crowding thoughts of the Virgin the holy Simeon gives the name of a sword, which would pierce her heart, as would the scandals yet to come, as the Lord Himself foretold: *All shall be scandalised in me this night* (Mt. xxvi. 31). Whence also Simeon added these words: *and thy own soul a sword shall pierce, that out of many hearts, thoughts may be revealed.*

See how Simeon calls innumerable thoughts a sword, since they would pierce her heart, and enter its inmost recesses. Into the midst of these afflictions has fallen the Virgin Mary, because she did not yet know the might of the resurrection, neither had she known that the resurrection was near. Whence, after the resurrection no more the two-edged sword; only joy and exaltation. A sign therefore of contradiction, Simeon calls the sign of the Cross, when it shall be that the sword of her thoughts shall transfix her virginal heart.

But to all this someone may say: from whence have we proof of all this? From the Lord's own teaching. Listen to Him speaking: *This*

generation is a wicked generation: it asketh a sign, and a sign shall not be given it, but the sign of Jonas the prophet. For as Jonas was in the whale's belly, so shall the Son of man be in the heart of the earth three days and three nights (Lk. xi. 29, 30; Mt. xii. 39, 40). See how the tribulation of the cross is called a sign, not alone in the New Testament, but also in the Old? For the things of the Old Testament are wholly in harmony with the New. And why? For the same God Who decreed them has so ordained it.

And who is it that bears witness to this? The Lord Himself. For hear Him as He speaks, in the prophet Ezechiel, to the angel reapers as He announces the final consummation: *Let not your eyes spare, nor be ye moved with pity. Utterly destroy old and young maidens, children, and women. But upon whomsoever thou shalt see Thau, kill him not* (Ezech. ix. 6).[9] Behold here the same sign of the New and the Old Testament, the Cross that saves the world, through Jesus Christ Our Lord, to Whom be glory and empire, now and for ever and ever, Amen.

III. St Ambrose: On the Gospel[10]

And behold there was a man in Jerusalem named Simeon, and this man was just and devout, waiting for the consolation of Israel. Not alone from angels and prophets, from shepherds and parents, do the Children of the Lord receive testimony, but also from elders and from the just. Every age and either sex, and the wondrous things that happened to them, add to our faith: a Virgin has a Child, she that was sterile brings forth, the dumb speak,

Elizabeth prophesies, the Magi adore, he that was enclosed in the womb exults, the Widow confesses to the Lord, the Just Man awaits Him; and he is truly a just man, who was seeking, not his own, but the consolation of his people; for himself desiring only that he be freed from the bonds of earthly infirmity, waiting however to look upon the One that was promised; for he knew that blessed are the eyes that would see Him. Now, he says, Thou mayest dismiss thy servant!

Behold the Just Man, who is as it were shut up in the prison of this earthly body, desires to be set free, that he may begin to be with Christ; for to be dissolved and to be with Christ is far more perfect. He then that desires to be free, let him come to Jerusalem, let him look for the Anointed of the Lord, let him receive in his hands the Word of God, and let him embrace It with the arms of his faith. Then let him be dismissed; as he sees not death who has looked upon the Life.

See how at the Birth of the Lord His grace is poured out on all men; and prophecy, denied to the unbelieving, is given to the just. Thus Simeon prophesies that the Lord Jesus Christ is come, and for the fall and for the resurrection of many, that He may disclose the payment of just and unjust; that He the true and just Judge may decree reward or punishment, according to the quality of our deeds.

And thy own soul a sword shall pierce. Neither Scripture nor history tell us that Mary departed this life by a violent death. For it is not the soul but the body that can be pierced by a material sword.

This therefore proves that Mary was not unaware of the heavenly mystery: for the word of God is living and effectual, and more piercing than any two-edged sword; and reaching unto the division of the soul and the spirit, of the joints also and the marrow, and is a discerner of the thoughts and intents of the heart, because all things are open and naked to the eyes of Her Son (Heb. iv. 12), to Whom the secrets of our conscience are visible.

Simeon then prophesies, the Virgin had prophesied, she that was joined to her husband prophesied; a widow then must prophesy, so that no state or sex might be excluded. And so Anna, who, by reason of her years of widowhood and her virtues, is set before us as wholly worthy of belief, announces that the Redeemer of all men has come. But since we do not believe that that which we said in praise of her merits, in our Exhortation to Widows, we should here repeat, let us go on to other things. Not however without purpose does he make mention of the eighty-four years of her widowhood, because both the seven twelves and the two forties seemed to imply a number that is sacred. Amen.

IV. St John Chrysostom: On the Gospel[11]

And Simeon blessed them, and said . . . For whose fall? Without doubt those who believe not, and they who placed the Innocent upon the Cross. For whose resurrection? They who give thanks; they who turn to him with a grateful heart. *And for a sign which shall be contradicted.* Of what nature is the sign that is here spoken of? None other

than the torment of the Cross: the Sign that the Church proclaims as the salvation of the world, which Judea has wholly rejected, which the heavens themselves more than once have openly proclaimed. It is exposed to contradiction, that truth may triumph. For complete victory is not won by numbers alone, without the contest. It must then meet contradiction, whereby in every age the Judge may triumph, through gentleness and patience.

And accordingly he says: *and for a sign which shall be contradicted*; that is, by the unbelieving and by the impious. And Thou, he adds, who art His Mother, shall you also not suffer? Is it perhaps because you avow yourself the Mother of this Child, because you have brought Him forth to the light, because you have sheltered Him in your womb, for thy womb was the vessel in which was wrought this wondrous work, that you shall be free from all trial? Is it because you are called the God-Bearer, and the Mother of God, and because thou hast conceived without nuptials, and become the Mother of thy Creator, that you shall be free from every temptation? Far from it: for even *thy own soul a sword shall pierce.*

And wherefore, O Lord? Is it that I have sinned? Thou hast not sinned; yet when you shall behold Him raised on high upon the Cross, when you behold Him suffering for the sins of the world, when His hands are extended upon the Cross, and you look upon them fastened to the wood, then at last you will begin to hesitate, and to say: He has come to this of Whom the angel spoke such wondrous things? Was it for this was accomplished the glorious mystery of His conception? I was a Virgin; I brought forth, for what cause is He fastened to the wood? *And thy own soul a sword shall pierce.*[12]

And so, according to the prophecy of the just Simeon, there shall be no one left free of temptation. Peter, who was the Prince of the Apostles, a third time denied; the other Apostles, deserted by him, all

fled; for it is not the shepherd that must be defended by the sheep: and the pugilist does not require the protection of the guard. Only Christ, as the ram caught among the briars, remained steadfast. Then temptation as a sword pierced her heart, that is, a certain hesitation of the soul. *And thy own soul a sword shall pierce, that, out of many hearts, thoughts may be revealed.* Jesus suffered and to this end, that the apostasy of those who believed not might be revealed, and openly convicted; and likewise, that the love and the gratitude of those who have believed in Him might be shown forth and confirmed.

This sign shall be exposed to contradictions, that they may be refuted and confounded, who, incited solely by malice and evil, stand up against it. For if the truth be not exposed to contradiction among men, virtue would receive no fitting confirmation. But the contest that is permitted, makes clear the light of truth, to the soul that perseveres.

This sign is assailed, but not without profit. For how else were the martyrs proved during the persecutions? Was it not when they manfully withstood evil, and through courage and patience of soul triumphed over it? For not alone does contradiction bring forth believers, but the martyrs likewise, as they went to torment, and even unto death, openly gave testimony to all the world, of how great is the power of the grace of Christ.

Therefore when holy Simeon says, *behold this Child is set for the fall, and for the resurrection of many in Israel, and for a sign which shall be contradicted*, his words are not to be understood to mean that Christ was the fall of such men, or that by force He has brought about their resurrection, but that *He is set for the fall* of those who strike against Him, as against *a stone of stumbling*; and *for the resurrection* of those who believed in Him, or who now believe in Him, and of their own free will. He *is set* as though one should say, the sun is risen, so that the sound of eye may see, but those whose eyes are diseased are hurt by the splendour of its light. And unless the Sign be contradicted, how shall some fall, those namely that merit condemnation, and others rise, those namely who live in hope that is freely believed?

And for this likewise does Simeon say, *and for a sign which shall be contradicted.* So that the faithful might not be troubled, or turned from faith, because of the persecutions that were to come, and that they might learn that it is God Himself that permits that even His own divine faith shall be from time to time attacked. For who could contradict it, or how would they dare to contradict it, unless God so permits? His permission therefore is necessary.

But there shall come a time when there shall be no more contradiction. For once this Sign has begun to disappear then *every tongue, of those that are in heaven, and under the earth, will confess that the Lord Jesus is in the glory of God the Father* (Phil. 2. 10, 11). For only as long as the Sign shall be seen, that for which it stands not yet being visible, so long shall this Sign be contradicted. But when He Whom the Sign foreshadows, shall, at His Second Coming, appear to all the world, then no longer shall any one dare to contradict the Sign.

When then, I repeat, He that was presignified shall openly appear in His Glory, against those who have contradicted Him, then they who have embraced the Sign shall be raised to His Glory Whom the Sign prefigured. But they who withstood the Sign shall be condemned by Him for Whom it stood. Then shall there be an end to contradiction, an end to doubt, an end to infidelity, an end to error. But there shall be a beginning of rewards, and of crowns, in which may we all take part, through Jesus Christ Our Lord, to Whom be Glory and Empire, now and for ever and ever, Amen.

V. Albinus Alcuin: The Three Silences[13]

For while all things were in quiet silence, and the night was in the midst of her course, thy almighty word leaped down from heaven from thy Royal thrones. (Wisd. xviii. 14, 15)

There are three silences. The first silence, the unawareness of infirmity; the second silence, the despair of healing; the third silence, the attainment of complete health. The first silence was before the Law, the second between the Law and Grace, the third will be after this life.

The first silence was when man knew not his own infirmity, and so was silent and sought no remedy. But afterwards the Law came, and showed to the sick their own wounds, and then immediately the silence was broken, and soon the sick began to look for healing. But because they sought to be healed by the works of the Law, in which there was no salvation, they could not find what they were seeking. But man at length, having come to learn that by the works of the Law no man could be made just, and as though weakened by the prolonged clamour, and now despairing, ceases again from speaking, and there follows the second silence.

Then the Omnipotent Word of God the Father, coming in the flesh, again broke the silence, and spoke of peace and gave grace, taught us mercy, and promised forgiveness; and the infirm began to run to their Physician, and as it were with a great outcry, and with the pure faith of the heart, and sincere confession of the tongue, began to implore the grace of healing. And this is accomplished in this present life, so that man through the grace of God receives restoration to health.

But when man will have received full health, and shall have arrived to that happiness which is life eternal, there will be no more that he can ask. And then will follow the third silence, which shall have no end.

Between the first and second silence many words resounded. Between the middle and last One Word alone is heard. Many were the words, multiple the precepts, of the Law which was given by Moses. But the Grace of Christ is One Word, which was made by Jesus Christ, or rather is Jesus Christ. Moses the servant of God spoke many words, many were his utterances: God the Father sends forth but One Word, One Utterance.

But the words of Moses were not omnipotent, for what they said they could not do. Then at length came the Omnipotent Word, the Word of God, Who not alone speaks, but whatsoever He has said, nay, whatsoever He has wished, He does. This Word yet speaks, when it fulfils the promises given to those that believe. And when the promises are fulfilled, then He will as it were cease to speak; for when the promises are fulfilled, since there is nothing more that we may ask, then shall there be eternal silence.

While therefore all things were in quiet silence. It is well said: *all things*; that is, not alone those who were without hope of that which they desired, but those too who had lost heart in the promises. *And the night was in the midst of her course.* Night in Holy Scripture is sometimes employed to represent the spirit of darkness, and sometimes his members, that is sinners and evil doers, sometimes sin itself, and sometimes it stands for this present life. Here, by *night* is meant the passing of this mortal life; as elsewhere the word *day* signifies the brightness of eternal life. This present life therefore is the *night*, the *day* is the life that is to come. This *night* has its ending, that *day* its dawn. The ending of this night, is the approach of that day; and the aurora of that day, is the approaching end of this present world.

Likewise, the evening of this night was from that moment when Adam sinned until the hour when, having received the sentence of death, he was driven from paradise and went out into the darkness of this world. The aurora of the day that is coming, is from the resurrection of Christ unto the end of the world. Therefore this present life is night.

But what is the course of this life? Let us see whither it is hastening. Through this mortal life it runs on to death, and through death to condemnation. Therefore mortal life runs downward, as life eternal leads ever upwards. The upward road leads to heaven, the downward into hell. The middle road is the stage of this present life, which we enter at birth, follow by living, and leave by dying. When therefore does *night in its course* follow the middle way, unless when death draws with it down to hell, all whom it finds at the stage of this present life, and while none of mortal man can ascend to life immortal?

Or, by *night* we may understand sin, and which night began from original sin, and continues on through actual sins. When therefore after the first disobedience, first by the violation of the natural law, then following on that by the violation of the written Law, sin came to its fullest growth, as if night was in the *midst of its course*. But the True Light appearing, this night began soon to come to an end, and by a sort of reciprocal change, decreasing, began gradually to fade, while the Light steadily growing, moves towards the fullness of day.

Behold the supremely ordered sequence of the divine plan of our redemption. When every hope of recovering health had gone, and death had taken all downwards to itself, and sin had come to the full, then the Omnipotent Word is sent down to those that are to be delivered, that the gift of the divine grace may be the more efficaciously defended. *He came*, it is said. Who came? And whence came He? And wherefore? The Word of the Most High, the Word of God, the Only Son of the Father, the King and the Son of the King. He came, by agreement with the Father, to the endurance of His passion. From the equality of the Divine Majesty, to the place of execution. From the Throne of heaven, to the workshop of sin. From the Light of heaven, to the darkness of hell.

Did He therefore lose His throne? Rather, freeing those who were the slaves of sin, he raised them up to reign with Him. He came likewise from royal thrones, for in His Father's house are many mansions (Jn. xiv. 2), and they shall reign with Him for ever, when they have received the kingdom that was prepared for them from the beginning of the world. He was the Only One of the King, His alone was the Kingdom. But since He came to adopt brethren unto Himself, to reign there with Him, He needs therefore to come, not from a royal throne, but from royal thrones; just as the kingdom to which the Elect of God are called, was prepared already from the beginning of the world. Amen (Mt. xxv. 34).

NOTES

[1] This work is now considered unauthentic; possibly Ambrosiaster, or various authors. Clavis 185. PRM 35.

[2] Cf. PG, 13, 1846, translation of St Jerome. An early witness to private confession.

[3] Cf. also PL, 92: 347.

[4] Cf. CSEL, 43, p. 118.

[5] PG 13, 1842.

[6] An opinion unsupported by the Fathers of the Church, and which arose from the total acceptance of the universality of the redeeming sacrifice of Christ's passion and death, without as yet discerning the special graces and privileges of Mary. Though thus piously rooted, it is wholly against the belief of the Church, which was set out formally by the declaration, of the Council of Trent, of Mary's freedom, *by a special privilege*, from all, even venial, sin. Cf. Denz. 833.

[7] An opinion that rested on no authority within the Church. It was disapproved by the Church at the Council of Lyons in A.D. 1274., in *the Profession of Faith of Michael Palaeologus*, viz.: *a lawful marriage being dissolved by the death of one or other of the spouses, second and third marriages thereafter are lawful.* Cf. Denz. 465.

[8] PG 39. 44.

[9] St Jerome and other interpreters believe that this is the form of the letter *Thau*, which in the ancient Hebrew characters had the form of a cross.

[10] CSEL, 32, p. 73.

[11] Combefis BPC, Ex S. Joannis Chrysostomi, Theodori Peltani Interpretatione. This may be unauthentic, but, as with many works attributed to Chrysostom, the question of its authenticity has not yet been decided.

[12] This suggestion of hesitance in the soul of Mary is opposed to Christian belief and piety, and theological reasoning, and to the words of Scripture regarding her fullness of grace. Here however it seems to be put forward as a devout exhortation; and while speaking of trial and temptation, there is no question of consent. Our Saviour also was subjected to temptation in the desert.

[13] This homily is listed in Migne, PL, CI, under Alcuin's name, but given in full in the Homiliary of Paul the Deacon, PL 45, 1177, under the title: 'Sermon on Silence', or, 'The Three Silences'.

SUNDAY OUTSIDE THE OCTAVE OF CHRISTMAS, AND FEAST OF THE HOLY NAME

I. St Ambrose: On the Gospel

II. St John Chrysostom: On the Holy Name

III. St Bernard: The Name of Jesus a Medicine in all Afflictions

THE GOSPEL OF THE SUNDAY

Luke ii. 21

And after eight days were accomplished, that the child should be circumcised, his name was called Jesus, which was called by the angel before he was conceived in the womb.

Exposition from the Catena Aurea

Bede, in *Hom. de Circum. Domini*: Having told of the Lord's birth, the Evangelist continues, and says: *And after eight days were accomplished, that the child should be circumcised.* Ambrose, *Bk. 2 in Luke, de Cir.*: What Child, save He, of Whom Isaias has said, *a Child is born to us, a Son is given to us* (Is. ix. 6). He was *made under the Law, that He might redeem those who were under the Law* (Gal. iv. 4, 5). Epiphanius, *Adv. Heresa.* 30: The followers of Ebion and Cerinthius say, *it is enough for a disciple if he is as his master* (Mt. x. 25). But Christ circumcised Himself, therefore you ought to be circumcised. But they are mistaken, and their arguments fall to the ground. For if Ebion had professed that Christ as God, descending from heaven, was circumcised on the eighth day, then he would provide some ground for his argument. But since he asserts that He was simply a man, the child was not then the cause of His own circumcision, since children are never the cause of their own circumcision. We however profess that He, coming down from heaven, lingered for the due time within that virginal sanctuary, so that in her virginal womb He might form to Himself the flesh of our humanity, in which He was truly, not figuratively, circumcised on the eighth day. And since the figures have now come to their spiritual fulfillment, both He as well as His Disciples no longer proclaim figures, but the truth alone.

Origen, *Hom. 14 in Luke*: For as we have died with Him dying, and

186

have risen with Him in His Rising, so likewise in Him we were circumcised, so that we do not now need the circumcision of the flesh. EPIPHANIUS, as above: For many reasons was Christ circumcised. In the first place to prove the reality of His flesh against the Manichees and those according to whom He was only apparently born. Then to make plain that His body was not consubstantial with the Deity, as Appollinarius has taught, and that He did not bring it down from heaven, as Valentinus asserts; and also that He might confirm circumcision, which of old He had instituted, and which served until He should come, and also that no pretext might be offered to the Jews; for if He were not circumcised, they could have objected that they could not receive an uncircumcised Christ.

BEDE, as above: That He might commend to us by example the virtue of obedience, and also that those who were subject to the Law, yet were unable to sustain its burdens, might be helped by His suffering with them. Also, that He Who came in the likeness of *sinful flesh*, might not despise the remedy whereby sinful flesh was wont to be cleansed. In the Old Law circumcision achieved the same relief of salutary healing against the wound of original sin (Cf. Rom. viii. 3), as Baptism now achieves in this time of revealed grace, except that they, in the former time, could not yet enter the gates of the heavenly kingdom, but after death, solaced in blessed repose in the bosom of Abraham, they awaited in serene hope their entry to eternal peace.

ATHANASIUS, in sermon *Omnia mihi*

tradita sunt: Circumcision expressed nothing more than the despoiling of *the old man*, by this, that that part of the body was circumcised which serves as the instrument of corporal generation. This was then done in sign of the future baptism in Christ. And so when that which was prefigured had come, the figure became void; for where all that was *the old man* is taken away by baptism, that is now superfluous which prefigured it, through the cutting away of a part.

CYRIL, *ex Hom.* 17 *in Catena G.F.*: It was customary on the eighth day to celebrate the carnal circumcision. On the eighth day Christ rose from the dead, and wrought in us a spiritual circumcision, saying: Go, *teach all nations, baptizing them* . . . (Mt. xxviii. 19). BEDE, as above: In His resurrection is prefigured our own twofold resurrection, of the body and of the spirit. For Christ circumcised teaches our nature, that now through the resurrection we are to be cleansed from the blemish of sin, and that on the last day we shall be delivered from the pestilence of death. And as the Lord rose from the dead on the eighth day, that is after the seventh, which is the sabbath, so also shall we, after the six ages of this world, and after the seventh of the sabbath of our souls, which is in the meanwhile passed in another life, shall rise again as it were on the eighth day.

CYRIL, as above: According to the precept of the Law, on the same day He also received the imposition of His Name; hence follows, *His name was called Jesus*, which is interpreted Saviour. He was brought forth for the salvation of the world, which He prefigured in His circumcision, according to that which the Apostle said: *in whom also you are circumcised with circumcision not made by hand, in despoiling the body of the flesh, but in the circumcision of Christ* (Col. ii. 11).

BEDE: And this that in the same day of His circumcision He received His name, He did also in imitation of the former observance. For Abraham, who first received the sacrament of circumcision, merited in the day of his circumcision to be blessed in the enlargement of his name (Gen. xvii. 5). ORIGEN, *Hom.* 14 *in Luke*: It was not becoming that

the glorious Name of Jesus, worthy of all veneration, the name that is above every name, should have been before this borne by other men, or borne about the world by them. Hence significantly the Evangelist goes on: *which was called by the angel, before he was conceived in the womb.*

BEDE: The Elect, in their spiritual circumcision, rejoice to stand forth as sharers of that Holy Name, so that as they are called Christians from Christ, so from the Saviour they are called the Saved, which name was given them by God, not alone before they were in the womb of the Church, but before all ages.

ADDITIONS TO THE CATENA AUREA FOR THE FEAST OF THE HOLY NAME[1]

ORIGEN, *Preface in John*: Jesus is not alone One and Good, He is every good. Life is good, Jesus is Life. Resurrection is good, Jesus is the Resurrection. The light of the world is good; Jesus is the Light of the World. *Ex Contra Celsus, Book I*: Christians are seen to draw their courage, not from incantations, but from the Name of Jesus, and from the commemoration of what He has done. For by His Names it has often happened that demons are put to flight from man, especially as often as they who invoke them, pronounce them with the right disposition, and with all trust. So great indeed is the power of the name of Jesus, that sometimes it is efficacious even when spoken by the wicked. The name of Jesus heals the afflicted in mind, puts to flight the spirits of darkness, and to the sick is an ever present remedy.

ARNOBIUS, *Book I, contra Gentes*: The sound of the Name of Jesus

drives away evil spirits, puts the oracles to silence, leaves the soothsayers unheard, and undoes the spells of presumptious magicians. GREGORY NAZIAN, *Ep. ad Nemes*: I myself have called upon the name of Christ at times, and scarcely have I uttered that august name, when the demors scatter in clamorous and headlong flight, shouting aloud the power and the might of the Immortal God. CHRYSOSTOM, *Hom.* 8 *im Ch.* 4 *ad Romans*: We too, I repeat, have our spiritual incantations, the Name of Our Lord Jesus Christ, and the power of His Cross. This spell not alone drives the dragon from his lair, and casts him back to the fire, but also heals our wounds. This Name is terrible to demons, and salutary to the troubled and the sick. Let us honour His Name, and rest secure in Its power to defend us.

AUGUSTINE, *de contritionε Cordis V*: Hope again, O sinner; hope and despair not. Hope in Him Whom you fear; fly to Him from Whom you fled; beseech Him with violence Whom you have offended. Jesus, for Thy Name's sake, do that for me which Thy Name proclaims. Jesus pardon the pride that offended Thee. Look upon the unhappy one that invokes Thy sweet Name; Name of delight, Name of comfort to sinners, Name of blessed hope. For what does Thy Name mean

Jesus, but Saviour. Therefore, for Thy Name's sake be to me Jesus, be to me, a Merciful Saviour.[2] CHRYSOSTOM, *Catech. II pr. finem*: I beseech you hold the Name as a staff. If none of you would go abroad unclad or unshod, so neither go forth without this Name, but speak it as you cross the threshold. Never go forth without it. It will be to you as staff, armour, and tower of defence.

I. ST AMBROSE: ON THE GOSPEL[3]

[*Introduction:* In the exposition of the preceding verse 19, the holy bishop speaks of the Blessed Virgin, in words which form a suitable prelude to his exposition of today's gospel. In this verse the Evangelist says of her: *But Mary kept all these words, pondering them in her heart.* The sermon begins from his comment upon verse 19.]

Let us learn chastity in all things from the Holy Virgin, who no less contained in word as in person, reflected in the quiet of her heart upon the proofs of her faith. If Mary learns from the Shepherds, why will you not learn from the priests? If Mary kept silence before the Apostles had taught, why, now that they have spoken, do you wish to teach rather than learn? Learn also, that vice belongs to the person, not to the sex; for sex is holy. Mary received no command to teach, yet she has left us an example.

And so the Child was circumcised. Who is this Child, unless He of Whom it was said: *a Child is born to us, a son is given to us?* (Is. ix. 6). *He was made under the Law, that He might redeem those Who were under the Law* (Gal. iv. 4, 5). *To present Him to the Lord.* What it

means to be presented to the Lord in Jerusalem I would explain but that I have already spoken of it in the commentary on Isaias. For He was circumcised *with the vices* (Gal. v. 24), and is judged worthy to be looked upon by the Lord: *the eyes of the Lord are upon the just* (Ps. 33. 16). You see how every practice of the Old Law was a figure of that to come; for circumcision was a sign of the forgiveness of our sins.

But since by reason of a certain base inclination to sin, the fragility of the human body and soul is enfolded in a never ending maze of evil, the cleansing from all guilt, that shall be at the time of the resurrection, was prefigured by the circumcision on the eighth day. This was because of the saying: *Every male opening the womb shall be called holy to the Lord.* By the words of the Law the Child of a Virgin was promised. And He was holy, because immaculate. Then, that it was He that was signified in the Law, the words that were spoken by the Angel make clear: *The Holy which shall be born of thee shall be called the Son of God.*

He alone of all that are born of woman is Holy: the Lord Jesus.

Who, in the immaculate newness of His Birth, has received no contagion of our earthly corruption; nor has He put off his celestial might. For if we adhere to the letter: how would every male be holy, since it is plain that there have been many who were very wicked? Was Achab holy? Were the false prophets holy whom, at the prayer of Elias, the Avenger of offence against heaven consumed by fire? But He is Holy Whom the sacred precepts of the divine law presignified in the figure of the Mystery that was to come; in that He alone would open the hidden womb, of unblemished fruitfulness, of the Holy Virgin Church, so as to bring to life the people of God.

He alone therefore opened the womb, for Himself. Nor is that a wonder in Him Who had said to the prophet: *Before I formed thee in the bowels of thy mother, I knew thee: and before thou comest forth out of the womb, I sanctified thee* (Jer. i. 6). He who sanctified another's womb, that a prophet might be born, He it is Who opened the womb of His own Mother, that He might come forth Immaculate. Amen.

II. St John Chrysostom: On the Holy Name[4]

All whatsoever you do in word or in work, do all in the name of the Lord Jesus Christ, giving thanks to God and the Father by him. (Col. iii, 17.)

If we do this, there will indeed be nothing of evil, nothing impure, in our invoking of the Sacred Name. If you eat, if you drink, should you marry, if you set out on a journey, do all in the Name of Jesus; that is, calling upon Him to help you. And having in all that you do invoked Him, then apply yourself to the thing in hand. Should you wish to speak concerning any business, do this beforehand. For this reason do we also place the name of the Lord at the head of all our epistles. Wherever there is the Lord's name, everything will be well. For if the names of the consuls are affixed to documents, to insure that they are authentic, how much more the name of Jesus.

Again, the Apostle likewise means: say and do everything as is right and fitting in relation to God. But do not bring in the angels. Do you eat? Offer thanks to God, both before you eat, and afterwards. Do you sleep? Give thanks to God, both before and after. Are you going out among people? Do the same; not some worldly thing. Do everything in the name of the Lord, and all that you do will bring you happiness. Wherever the Name of the Lord is set up, all things prosper. If it has power to drive away demons, if it can banish illness, much more will it aid your own actions.

And what does he mean when he says: *whatever you do in word or in deed.* Whether you pray, or whether you do anything else whatever. Recall how Abraham sent his servant in the Name of God. And David in the Name of the Lord slew Goliath; great and wonderful is His Name. Again Jacob sends to his sons, saying: *and may my Almighty God make him favourable to you* (Gen. xliii. 14).

He who does this has God for his helper: without Whom he can do nothing. And the Lord, accepting the honour of being called upon, returns the honour by making possible what we strive to do. Invoke the Son, give thanks to the Father. For invoking the Son, we invoke the Father; and giving thanks to the Father, we give thanks also to the Son. Let us learn these things, but not restricting ourselves merely to the words, but fulfilling them in our deeds. Nothing is so great as this Name, that in every place is wondrous. *Thy name is oil poured out* (Cant. i. 3). He who speaks it is filled with its fragrance. *And no man can say the Lord Jesus Christ, but by the Holy Ghost* (I Cor. xii. 4).

So many are the wonders wrought by this Name! If you say with faith: in the Name of the Father, and of the Son, and of the Holy Ghost, you have done what is asked. See what great things you *have* done; for you have created within you a man, a new man, as well as the other effects that also follow from baptism. So likewise in commanding the sick this is a name of power. For this reason the devil, envying the honour given to us, has brought in the use of the name of angels. These are incantations of the demons. Even if it should be an angel, even an archangel, or even the very Cherubim, do not suffer it. For these very Powers will not hearken, but turn away, when they have seen that it is but an affront to the Lord.

I have honoured thee, He says, and I have said, *Call upon Me*; and dost thou offend Him with dishonour? If you chant this hymn with praise, you will put to flight both demons and infirmities: and if you banish not sickness, this happens, not from want of power, but because it is not expedient for you.

According to Thy Name, so also is Thy praise (Ps. xlvii. 11). By this Name was the whole world changed, tyranny laid low, the devil trodden under foot, the heavens thrown open. What do I say: the heavens? We by this Name are born again. If this has happened to us, we are already glorified! This name makes both Martyrs and Confessors; let us hold fast to it, as to a great gift, that we may live in glory, and that we may be pleasing to God, and be held worthy of the good things that are promised to those who love Him in grace and generosity of heart, through Jesus Christ Our Lord, to Whom be honour and glory, now and for ever. Amen.

III. ST BERNARD ON THE CANTICLES[5]

How the Name of Jesus is to faithful Christians a healthful Medicine in all Afflictions

The Spirit of Wisdom is benevolent (Wisd. i. 6), and not wont to be ungracious to those who invoke Him, Who often, and even before He is called upon, will say: *I will hear* (Is. lxv. 24). Listen, and I shall show thee a Name that is fittingly compared with oil, and for what reward I speak. Many names of the Bridegroom have you read, scattered across every divine page, but I shall embrace them all for you in two. There is none of them, as I think you will find, but gives an echo of the grace of His Compassion, or the power of His Majesty. The Spirit tells us so Himself, and by that instrument which is most familiar to Him: *These two things have I heard, that power belongeth to God, and mercy to Thee, O Lord* (Ps. lxi. 12, 13). Therefore as to His Majesty, *holy and terrible is His Name* (Ps. cx. 9), and as to His Compassion, *there is no other name under heaven given to men, whereby we must be saved* (Acts iv. 12).

But this will become clearer by examples. *This*, He says, *is the name they shall call Him, the Lord our Just One* (Jer. xxiii. 6). This is a name of power. Again: *And His Name shall be called Emmanuel* (Is. vii. 14). This is a name of compassion. Again He says of Himself: *You call Me Master and Lord; and you say well, for so I am* (Jn. xiii. 13). The first is a name of grace, the second of majesty. For it is not less kind to nourish the soul with wisdom, than to provide food for the body. Again the prophet: *And His Name shall be called wonderful, counsellor, God the Mighty, the Father of the world to come, the Prince of peace* (Is. ix. 6). The first, third, and fourth are names of majesty; the rest of compassion. Which of them is *poured out*? Clearly the name of majesty and power is in a certain manner poured out into that which is of kindness and compassion, and this is poured out abundantly through Jesus Christ Our Saviour.

For example, the name God, does it not in God-with-us, which is Emmanuel, liquefy and flow forth? So does the name Wonderful flow into that of Counsellor; so likewise *God* and *mighty* flow into *Father of the world to come*, and *Prince of peace*; and the names: *Lord our Just One* into *Merciful and gracious Lord* (Ps. cx. 4). In this I speak no new thing: for of old Abram was softened into Abraham, and Sarai into Sara (Gen.

xvii. 5, 15); here we have mention of the mystery of this life-giving pouring out; commemorated and prefigured.

Nor is it to be wondered at that, when the fullness of time was come, there was a pouring out of the Name: Almighty God fulfilling that which He had before promised by the word of Joel, pouring out His Spirit on all flesh. (Joel ii. 28). Hasten then, all ye peoples! Thy Salvation is now here! The Name is poured out, and whosoever shall call upon it shall be saved. He that was the God of angels, now proclaims Himself the God of men. He poured out oil upon Jacob, and it overflowed upon Israel. Say to your own brethren: *Give us of your oil* (Mt. xxv. 8). If they will not give, turn to the Lord of oil, and ask that He gives it also to you. Say to Him: *Take away our reproach* (Is. iv. 1). Let not the Evil One insult thy beloved, I beseech Thee, whom it has pleased to call from the end of the earth; and the less I was worthy of Thy call, the more kindly hast Thou called me. Is it fitting, I pray Thee, that a wicked servant should close the door on those who were invited by the Kind Master of the house?

I am, you say, the God of Abraham, of Isaac, of Jacob. And of none others? Pour out, pour out! Open still more Thy Hand, and fill every creature with blessing! Let them come from the east and the west, and let them sit down with Abraham and Isaac and Jacob in the kingdom of heaven (Mt. viii. 11). Let them come and sit down, let them eat and take their fill in joy, *with the voice of joy and praise, and the sound of one eating* (Ps. xli. 5).

Thy Name is as oil poured out. Of

one thing I am sure. If Andrew and Philip are the doorkeepers, we shall not be refused when we come seeking oil, we who would *see Jesus.* For Philip will go and tell Andrew, and Andrew and Philip will tell Jesus. And what will Jesus say? Jesus will of a certainty say: *Unless the grain of wheat falling into the ground die, itself remaineth alone; but if it die, it bringeth forth much fruit* (Jn. xii. 21). Let the Grain die, and the harvest of men arise. It must be that Christ shall die, and rise again from the dead, and that repentance and forgiveness of sin be preached in His Name, not, alone in Judea, but in every nation. Since then from this one Name which is Christ, thousands of thousands are named Christians, let them say: *Thy name is as oil poured out.*

I recognise the name which I have in Isaias: *He will call His servants by another name, in which he that is blessed upon earth, shall be blessed in God* (Is. lxv. 16). O Blessed Name! O Oil everywhere poured out! How far? From heaven down to Judea, and from thence it flowed into every country, and every place cries out: *Thy Name is as oil poured out.* Poured out in abundance, and flowing, not alone over heaven and earth, but upon those in hell; so that in the name of Jesus every knee is bowed, *of those in heaven, on earth, and under the earth* (Phil. ii. 10); and every tongue shall confess and proclaim: *Thy Name is as oil poured out.*

Behold Christ, behold the name of Jesus; both have been poured out on the angels, both have been poured out on men, and even upon men who had become soiled like beasts of burthen, by their own filth, healing both men and beasts, since *Thou, O Lord, hast multiplied Thy mercies* (Ps. xxxv. 8). How precious, yet how cheap! Cheap, but health-giving! If it were not cheap, it could not be everywhere poured out. If it were not wholesome, it would not have won me. I am a partaker of the Name, I am a sharer of the inheritance. I am a Christian; I am a brother of Christ. If I am what I am called, I am the heir of God, and co-heir with Christ (Rom. viii. 17).

And what wonder that the name of the Spouse is everywhere poured out, since He Himself is also poured out. For, *He emptied Himself, taking the form of a servant* (Phil. ii. 7). He said also: *I am poured out like water* (Ps. xxi. 15). The fullness of the divinity is poured out dwelling bodily upon the earth, so that of His fullness all we who wear *this body of death* may share, and, saturated with that living fragrance, may exclaim: *Thy Name is as oil poured out.* Behold the Name that is poured out, and in what manner, and how far. But why oil? There is no doubt a resemblance between oil and the name of the Bridegroom.

Not without reason does the Holy Spirit compare the name of the Bridegroom to oil, when He teaches that in this manner does the Spouse greet the Bridegroom: *Thy Name is as oil poured out.* For oil gives light, nourishes, and anoints. It feeds the flame, sustains the body, eases pain. It is light, food, medicine. Notice how the same may be said of the Name of the Bridegroom: for it throws light upon what is preached, it nourishes our thoughts, it soothes and anoints those that are called. Let us briefly consider each one of these. Whence came, do you think, so great and so swift a light of faith upon the whole earth, unless by the preaching of the Name of Jesus? Is it not in the light of this Name that God has called you into *His own marvellous light*? And we being by this enlightened, and in that light beholding the True Light, with truth does Paul declare: *You were heretofore darkness, but now light in the Lord.*

This then is the Name that the Apostle was commanded to bring to the children of Israel, before peoples, and kings; and he bore the Name as a shining light, and illuminated the race of men, and he cried everywhere: *The night is passed, and the day is at hand. Let us therefore cast off the works of darkness, and put on the armour of light. Let us walk honestly as in the day* (Rom. xiii. 12). And he pointed out to all the Light upon his candlestick, proclaiming in every place Jesus, *and Him crucified* (I Cor. ii. 2). How that light has shone forth, and seized the vision of all who beheld it; when from the mouth of Peter, as lightning going forth, it strengthened the soles of the feet of *a certain man who was lame* (Acts iii. 7), and gave light to multitudes who were spiritually blind? Did he not cast fire on the earth when he said: *In the Name of Jesus Christ of Nazareth, arise, and walk.*

The Name of Jesus is not light alone, it is also food. Are you not strengthened as often as you recall it? What so fills the heart of him who meditates upon it? What so refreshes the tired senses, strengthens virtue, nourishes good and worthy habits, fosters pure affections? Dry indeed is all food of the soul, if it be not dipped in this oil; tasteless, if unseasoned by this salt. If you write anything, that which you write has for me no flavour unless I perceive

there the Name of Jesus. Should there be discussion, or if we converse together, for me it is again without flavour, unless I hear there the Name of Jesus. Jesus is sweet upon the tongue, melody to the ear, and joy in the heart. But it is also a healing medicine. Is one among us sorrowful? Let Jesus come into his heart, and rise thence to his lips. And behold, at the risen light of Thy Name, every cloud is scattered, and calm returns. Has anyone fallen into sin? More, does anyone run despairing into a noose of death? If he calls upon the Name of Jesus, shall he not breathe again in life?

Call upon me in the day of trouble: I will deliver thee, and thou shalt glorify me (Ps. xlix. 15). Nothing so restrains the violence of anger, eases the swellings of pride, heals the wounds of spite, checks the flow of sensuality, extinguishes the flame of lust, restricts the thirst of greed, and puts to flight the craving for whatever is unbecoming. Since when I name the Name of Jesus, I place before my mind a Man, who is meek and humble of heart, kindly, calm, chaste, merciful, and conspicuous in every virtue and grace, and the Same is the Omnipotent God, Who heals me by His example, and strengthens me by His aid. All this speaks to me, when I speak the Name of Jesus.

Keep then as a medicinal lozenge, O my Soul, that which is hidden in the tiny capsule of this word that is Jesus, which is truly salutary; nor is there any infirmity against which it has been known to fail. Let it be ever in your bosom, ever in your mind; and by means of it all your thoughts and actions will be directed unto Jesus.

You have here truly the means whereby you are helped in heart and hand. You have, I say, in the Name of Jesus, that by which you can correct your evil ways, or improve those that are less perfect. You have that whereby you may defend your heart, lest it be corrupted; and should it be corrupted, that whereby you may restore it, through Jesus Christ Our Lord. Amen.

NOTES

1 Combefis BPC tome 2.
2 PL 40, 941–951. Considered inauthentic; possibly Alcher de Clairvaux. PRM 40.
3 PL 60, 1572.
4 PG 62, 363, ex hom. 9.
5 PL 183, 843.

FEAST OF THE EPIPHANY

THE GOSPEL FOR THE MASS OF THE EPIPHANY

Matthew ii. 1–12

When Jesus therefore was born in Bethlehem of Juda, in the days of king Herod, behold, there came wise men from the East to Jerusalem, saying, Where is he that is born king of the Jews? For we have seen his star in the East, and are come to adore him. And king Herod hearing this, was troubled, and all Jerusalem with him. And assembling together all the chief priests and the scribes of the people, he inquired of them where Christ should be born. But they said to him: In Bethlehem of Juda. For so it was written by the prophet: And thou Bethlehem the land of Juda are not the least among the princes of Juda: for out of thee shall come forth the captain that shall rule my people Israel.

Then Herod, privately calling the wise men, learned diligently of them the time of the star which appeared to them; and sending them into Bethlehem, said: go, and diligently inquire after the child, and when you have found him, bring me word again, that I also may come and adore him. Who having heard the king, went their way; and behold the star which they had seen in the East, went before them, until it came and stood over where the child was.

And seeing the star they rejoiced with exceeding great joy. And entering into the house, they found the child with Mary his mother, and falling down they adored him; and opening their treasures, they offered him gifts; gold, frankincense, and myrrh. And having received an answer in sleep that they should not return to Herod, they went back another way into their country.

Exposition from the Catena Aurea

Matthew ii. 1–12

V. 1. *When Jesus therefore was born in Bethlehem of Juda, in the days* *of King Herod, behold, there came wise men from the East to Jerusalem,*

AUGUSTINE, *Sermon 5 on Nativity*: After the miracle of the Virgin Birth, in which, from the womb that was filled with the divinity, from a Maiden undefiled, God and Man came forth into the dim obscurity of a stable, and to the narrowness of a manger, in which the Divine Majesty with limbs close bound began to dwell; and while God is nursed at the breast, and submits to the bonds of the humble swaddling clothes, suddenly, a new star shines from heaven upon the earth, banishing the dark from all the world, and changing night to day, lest the Day be hidden by the night. So the Evangelist begins: *When Jesus therefore . . .*

REMIGIUS: In the beginning of this gospel reading three things are stated: the Person, since it begins, *When Jesus*; the Place, when it says, *in Bethlehem of Juda*; the Time, as when it records, *in the days of King Herod*. And these three things are set down in confirmation of that which is now to be told. *Jerome, in Matth.* 2: We think that it was first written *Juda* by the Evangelist, as in the Hebrew, not Judaea. For where is there another Bethlehem, so that to distinguish it is called *of Juda*? It is described as Bethlehem of Juda, because in the Book of Josue, son of Nave, we read of another Bethlehem of Judaea (Jos. xix. 15). GLOSS: There are two Bethlehems, one which is in the land of Zabulon, the other in the land of Juda, and which was first called Ephrata.

AUGUSTINE, *Harmony of the Gospels*, 2, 15: As to the city of Bethlehem, Matthew and Luke are in agreement. But Luke explains how, and for what reason, Joseph and Mary came to it, which Matthew omits. On the other hand while Luke says nothing of the journey of the Magi from the East, Matthew records it. CHRYSOSTOM, *Hom. 2 ex Op. Imp.*: Let us see in what way it serves that the Evangelist indicates the time in which Christ was born, saying, *in the days of King Herod*. This he says so that he may show that the prophecy of Daniel was fulfilled, in which it was foretold that Christ would be born after seventy weeks of years. From that time until the reign of Herod seventy years of weeks had passed. And also because while the Jewish people were under the rule of the Judaic kings, even though these were sinners, prophets were sent for their correction: now however that the Law of God is subject to the power of an evil king, and that the Justice of God is swamped under the Roman domination, Christ the Saviour is born. For a great and desperate infirmity needs a great physician.

RABANUS MAURUS: Or it may be that he makes mention of an alien king so that the prophecy might be fulfilled which says: *The sceptre shall not be taken away from Juda, nor a ruler from his thigh, till He come that is to be sent* (Gen. xlix, 10).

AMBROSE, *Lib. III in Luc.*: It is related that Idumaean robbers having entered Ascalon, among others took Antipater captive. He having acquired the lore of the Idumaeans, became joined in friendship with Hircanus King of Judea, whom Hircanus later sent on his behalf to Pompey; and because he succeeded in his embassy bestowed on him part of his own kingdom. Antipater being killed, his son Herod was appointed by the Senate, under Anthony, to rule the Jews. From this it is clear that Herod had obtained the kingdom without any racial affinity to the Jewish people.

RABANUS MAURUS: The Magi were of those who had made study of all things, but the common speech represent them as magicians, evildoers; but they were esteemed otherwise by their own people; for they were the philosophers of the Chaldees, and it is according to the philosophical knowledge of their arts that the Kings and rulers of that people do all things. Whence it is that they first came to know of the birth of the Lord.

AUGUSTINE, *in Sermon 4 on the Epiph.* (*De Temp.* 42): These Wise Men, what were they but the first fruits of the Gentiles? The shepherds were Israelites, the Magi Gentiles. The former from close by, the latter from far away; both hasten to the Corner Stone. (*Again, from Sermon 2.*) Jesus is made manifest neither to the learned nor to the just. For ignorance dominated the rusticity of the shepherds, impiety the practices of the Magi. But that Corner Stone joins them both to Himself, Who came to select the foolish that He might confound the wise, and to call not the just but the sinners to repentance; so that no great one might take pride in himself, and no lowly one despair.

GLOSS: These Magi were kings, who, if they are recorded as having presented three gifts, they are not accordingly proved to have been not more than three, but through them the peoples who were born of

the three sons of Noah are prefigured as destined to come to belief; or there was such a number of kings, who had many others in their train. They came however, not after a year, for then He would be found in Egypt, not in the manger, but on the thirteenth day. To show whence they came the Evangelist says: *From the East.*

V. 2. *Saying, Where is he that is born king of the Jews? For we have seen his star.*

REMIGIUS: We must keep in mind that there is a variety of opinions regarding the Magi. Some say they were Chaldeans. The Chaldeans worshipped a star for God, and accordingly they said that their so-called God had declared that the true God was born. Others say they were Persians. Some say that they came from the farthest parts of the earth. Others again that they were descendants of Balaam, which is more credible. For Balaam among the things which he prophesied said also: *A star shall rise out of Jacob* (Num. xxiv. 17). They possessing this prophecy, as soon as they had seen the star, understood that the king was born, and they therefore came.

JEROME: And so they learned of this star that was to come, from the prophecy of Balaam whose descendants they were. But what we wish answered is, if they were Chaldeans or Persians, how could they have come to Jerusalem in such a short space of time? REMIGIUS: But we must know what some say, that the Child who was born then could have brought them from the ends of the earth in a brief space of time. GLOSS: It was not such a remarkable thing that they should have come to Bethlehem in thirteen days, since they had Arab horses and dromedaries which are swift to travel.

CHRYSOSTOM, *Ex Op. Imp.*: Or, they could have set out two years before His birth, the Star travelling before them, and neither food nor drink being wanting on the way. REMIGIUS: Or, if they were the descendants of Balaam, they were not far distant from the Land of Promise, and so could have come to Bethlehem in a short while. Then we have to ask why does the Evangelist say they came from the East? This was because they came from that region which lies generally to the east of the Jews. Rightly are they also said to come from the East, because all who come to the Lord, come from Him and through Him. He is the Orient, according to the words: *Behold a Man, the Orient is his name* (Zach. vi. 12).

CHRYSOSTOM, *Ex Op. Imp.*: He came from the East: whence the day is born, thence faith had its beginning: because faith is the light of the soul. From the East therefore they came, but to Jerusalem. REMIGIUS: Although the Lord was not born there: because, although they knew the time of his birth, they did not know the place. Jerusalem was a royal city, and they believed that only in a royal city would the Child be born. Or it may be that they came there so that the Scripture might be fulfilled: *For the law shall go forth out of Sion, and the word of the Lord out of Jerusalem* (Mich. iv. 2); because there

Christ was first announced. Or, that the indifference of the Jews might be reproved by the zeal of the Magi. They come therefore to Jerusalem, saying: *Where is he that is born king of the Jews?*

AUGUSTINE, *Sermon 2, et 7, de Epiph.*: Since many kings of Juda were born and died, would it be one of those the Magi were seeking? No. Because of none of these had they heard a voice speaking from heaven. And they did not think that to a king of Juda such as these were wont to be was due such a great honour from them, strangers and wholly remote from the kingdom. But they had learned that one was born, in adoring Whom they firmly believed they would attain to the salvation that is according to God; for He was scarcely yet at an age in which human flattery could avail. He was not clad in the purple, nor did a diadem shine upon His brow. Neither did the splendour of a court, nor the fear of a great army, nor the renown of victories, bring these men from remote lands in such fervour of supplication. He lay in a manger, a child newly born: tiny in body, abject in poverty. But in this Child something great lay hidden, of which these, the first-fruits of the Gentiles, had learned, not from earthly rumour, but from heavenly revelation. Hence we have: *We have seen His Star in the East.* They announce, yet they ask; they believe, and yet they seek to know: as though prefiguring those who walk by faith, yet still desire to see.

GREGORY, *in Hom. 10*: You must know that the Priscillian heretics who believe that the birth of every man is determined by the stars, take this as a confirmation of their error, that a new star came forth when the Lord appeared in the flesh, Whose fate, they hold, was linked with this star. But far be it from the minds of the faithful to believe that there is such a thing as fate.

AUGUSTINE, *De Civ. Dei. V,* 1: For men when they hear of fate, understand it according to the common meaning of the word, that is, the significance of the position of the stars, such as it is at the conception or birth of someone: which some presume to exclude from dependence on the will of God, and these should be avoided by the ears of all, not alone of those who cultivate true religion, but all who desire to be worshippers of any gods whatsoever. Some however claim that this power was given to the stars from the supreme majesty of God. Such a notion offers offence to God, in whose most glorious counsel, they would have it believed, are decreed the most horrid crimes, which if any earthly power had decreed them, it would have been destroyed by the common consent of men.

CHRYSOSTOM, *Hom. 2 in Op. Imp.*: If therefore any one should commit a murder, or an adultery, through the direction of the stars, great indeed is the evil of the stars, but greater would be His who made the stars. For since God can foresee all future events, if such great evil was to be wrought through the stars, it must be that if He did not amend them, He is not good; if He wished to amend them, but could not, He is not omnipotent. If it depends on the stars, whether we be

good or bad, then the good we do must not be praised, nor the evil blamed; since neither act depends on our will. Why should I be blamed for my evil acts, since I committed them not of my own will, but from necessity? The very commandments of God, that men shall not sin, or His exhortations to do good, come to nothing in this foolishness. For who would command or exhort another that he do not evil from which he cannot turn aside? Or that he seek after some good to which he can never attain?

GREGORY NYSSA, *Phil. Bk.* 6, 1: All talk is foolish, according to which all things that are, are determined by fate. It makes an end of Providence and the divine goodness, since, to such people, man is but the instrument alone of heavenly rotation. By this they say man is moved to action, not alone in his members, but even in the thoughts of his soul. And those who say this destroy both the nature that is ours, and the order of Providence; and this is nothing else than to overthrow everything. Where then is our free will? That which is in us must be free.

AUGUSTINE, *City of God, Bk.* 5, 6: But it is not wholly incorrect to say that the influence of the stars has power to bring about certain effects, but in bodies only, as we see the seasons varied by the solar risings and settings, and that certain kinds of things, as shell-fish, and the wondrous tides of the ocean, change with the waxing and waning of the moon; but not that the wills of men are subject to the stars. *Bk. 5 Ch. I:* But if the stars are said to portend rather than cause things, why is it that there is such diversity in the life of twins, in their actions, fortunes, deeds, callings, honours, and all such things pertaining to human life, so that strangers are often more like them in these things than the twins are to each other, separated though they be from each other by but a tiny interval of time, and conceived in the same moment?

Bk. 5 Ch. 2: What do they attempt to make of this small interval of time between the birth of twins? Is it in proportion to the diversity that is found in their wills, in their actions, their characters and circumstances? Some however call by the name of *fate*, not the constitution of the stars, but the series and the connection of all causes, which they attribute to the will power of God. If anyone therefore attributes human events to fate, because he calls by the name of fate the will and power of God, let him withdraw from this opinion, let him correct his tongue, since the word fate is employed by those who use it, to mean the position of the stars. *Ch. 9:* Hence we do not give the name of fate to the will of God, unless we understand fate to be derived from *fari* to speak, for it was written: *God hath spoken once, these two things have I heard, that power belongeth to God, and mercy to thee, O Lord* (Ps. lxi. 12). So we should not strive and contend with them as to the meaning of the word.

AUGUSTINE, *Contra Faust. II,* 5: If we however do not subject the beginnings of even one man to the fate of the stars, so that we may vindicate the freedom of the will from all compulsion, how much the less are we likely to believe that His

earthly Birth was subject to the disposition of the stars, Who is the eternal Creator and Lord of the whole universe? Accordingly, that star which the Magi saw did not have dominion over Christ, New-Born according to the Flesh, but rather obeyed Him in witness. Neither was it of those stars which, from the beginning of creation, followed the order of their motion in accordance with the law of their Creator; but a new star that appeared at this wondrous birth from a Virgin, which rendered the service of its function to the Magi who were seeking Christ; since it went before them, lighting them on their way until it led them to the place where the Word of the Lord lay, an infant.

But what astrologers so subject the fate of men new born to the stars as to declare, that at the birth of any given man a certain star forsakes its appointed course and continues onward towards the one just born? For they are rather of opinion that the lot of those who are born is bound to the course of the stars, not that the order of the stars can be changed upon the birth day of a man. And so if that star were one of those that pursue their allotted course in the heavens, how could it decree what Christ when born shall do, which, at the birth of Christ, is itself bidden to depart from its accustomed course? If, however, as is more likely, a star which before was not, now arose to point the way to Christ, then Christ was not born because it was there, but it came forth because Christ was born. If we must speak of fate, then rather let us say, not that the star was Christ's destiny, but that Christ was the destiny of the star.

Since He was to it, not it to Him, the cause of its rising.[1]

CHRYSOSTOM, *Hom. 6 in Matt.*: It is not the function of astronomy to know from the stars who are born, but rather, as some of them tell us, to foretell, from the hour at which they were born, that which will happen to them. But these men did not know the time of His birth, so that they could from that point foretell His future from the movement of the stars; rather the contrary. They say therefore: *We have seen His star.* GLOSS: That is, His personal star; for He created this star for the purpose of His own manifestation.

AUGUSTINE, *Serm. 6 de Epiph.*: The Angels show Christ to the Shepherds: the Star reveals Him to the Magi; and to both the voice of heaven speaks, since now the prophet's voice is silent. The Angels dwell in the heavens: the stars adorn it. Through both the heavens *proclaim the glory of God* (Ps. xviii). GREGORY, *Hom.* 10, *in Matt.*: And it was fitting that a rational being, that is, an angel, should tell the Jews, as beings of reason. The Gentiles however, because they knew not how to use their reason to learn of God are guided, not by the voice, but by signs. For to the former, as believers, prophets had been sent; to the latter, as unbelievers, signs were given. To these same Gentiles the Apostles preach Christ, but now of the full age of man; but while He was yet an infant, nor yet capable of human speech, a star reveals Him to the Gentiles: for reason required that He be proclaimed by word of mouth, the Lord Himself having

spoken: and by the mute element while He spoke not.

LEO, *Serm.* 3 *De Epiph.* II: For Christ *was the expectation of the Gentiles*, from whom there was promised to the holy patriarch of old an innumerable posterity, to be born, not from the seed of the flesh, but from the fruitfulness of faith; and which was compared in multitude to the stars, so that a heavenly, not an earthly, offspring was to be looked for, from the Father of all men. The heirs of this promised heredity, that were likened to the stars, are called to belief by the rising of this new star, so that the ministry of the heavens may be used in the service of Him by Whom the heavens were used in witness.

CHRYSOSTOM, *Hom. 6 in Matt*: That this was not one of the heavenly bodies seems manifest. For no other star moves in this way. For this moved from the east to the south, for so Palestine lies in relation to Persia. In the second place, this is evident also from the time of its appearance; for it seems to have been visible, not only in the night, but in the full light of day, which is not within the nature of any star, nor even of the moon. Thirdly, from this, that now it appears, now it hides itself. For after they had entered Jerusalem it hid itself; and when they had left Herod it showed itself once more. Neither had it any course of its own, but when the Magi travelled, it travelled with them. When they halted, it likewise halted, as the pillar of cloud in the desert (Exod. xiv. 9). Fourthly, it pointed out the Offspring of the Virgin, but it accomplished this, not by remaining on high, but coming low, which indicates, not the action of a star, but of some rational power. So this star was but the sign of invisible power, revealing itself in this form.[2]

GLOSS: The Gospel narrative says: *in the East.* Whether this star rose in the East, or whether they, being there, beheld it already born, and moving to the West, is doubtful. For it could have been born in the East, and thence led them to Jerusalem. REMIGIUS: Some have thought that this star was the Holy Spirit, Who afterwards descended above the Lord at His baptism, and appeared to the Magi under the form of a star. Some have said it was an angel; as that which appeared to the Shepherds, may also have appeared to the Magi.

AUGUSTINE, *in Serm. de Epiph.*: But you will say: from whom did they learn that such a star signified that Christ was born? Truly from the angels, through some revelation. You ask perhaps: from good angels or bad? For even the bad angels, that is, the demons, confessed that Christ was the Son of God. But why did they not hear it from good angels, since, in adoring Christ, they were seeking salvation, not serving iniquity? The angels therefore could have said to them: the star which you see is Christ. Go, adore Him where He is born, and see at the same time of what kind He is, and how great He is that is born.[3]

LEO, *Serm.* 4 *in Epiph.*: Besides the image of the star, which strikes upon the bodily eye, more brilliantly had the light of truth illuminated their hearts, leading them, even before they had set out, to

prepare gifts that were befitting to His dignity; and this pertains to the illumination of faith. AUGUSTINE, *Quest. of N. and O. Test.* 63: Or, they understood that the King of the Jews was born; because oftentimes an earthly king is designated by the symbol of a star. For these Magi did not speculate upon the course of the stars out of evil purpose, but from the desire of learning. For we know that they followed the tradition of Balaam who had said: *A Star shall rise out of Jacob and a sceptre shall spring up from Israel.* Hence, seeing a star that appeared outside the accustomed order of the world, they believed that it was this that Balaam had foretold was the future token of the King of the Jews (Num. xxiv. 17).[4]

LEO M, *Serm.* 4 *in Epiph.*: And these things, inasmuch as they pertain to the illumination of faith, being understood and believed, could have sufficed for them, so that they needed not, with the eye of the body, to look upon that which they already beheld with the fullest vision of the mind. But persevering in the ardour of their discerning allegiance, until they beheld the Child, they did a service to the peoples of future times, to the men of our own day. For just as it has been a gain to all of us, that after the resurrection of the Lord, the hand of the Apostle Thomas explored the places of His wounds, so also to our gain has it been, that the eyes of the Magi have looked upon His Infancy; hence, *we have come to adore Him.*

CHRYSOSTOM, *Homily 2 ex Op. Imperfect:* Did they not know that

Herod reigned in Jerusalem, and did they not understand that whosoever, while a king is yet living, proclaims another king, or does honour to him, is punished in blood? But with their minds on their future King, they feared not this present one. They had not yet seen Christ, and already they were prepared to die for Him. O Blessed Magi! Who, before they had known Christ, confessed Him in the presence of a most cruel king.

V. 3. *And King Herod hearing this, was troubled, and all Jerusalem with him . . .*

AUGUSTINE, *Serm. 2 in Epiph.*: As the Magi desired a Redeemer, so Herod feared a successor; hence follows, *hearing this he was troubled.* GLOSS: He is called King Herod, in contrast to Him they are seeking, so that the former may appear as an alien. CHRYSOSTOM, *Hom. 2 ex Op. Imp.*: And so, since he was himself an Idumean, he was troubled for fear that his kingdom might return to a Jew, and lest he himself be driven out by the Jews and his posterity cut off from the kingship. For great power is always subject to great fear. As the topmost branches of a tree are moved in the slightest wind, so men in high places are sensitive to every rumour. The lowly however, like trees in the valley, are generally left undisturbed.

AUGUSTINE, *Serm. 2 in Epiph.*: What shall the tribunal of the Judge be like, when the Nativity of an Infant, makes proud kings tremble? Let kings fear Him, now sitting at the Right Hand of the Father, Whom the impious king feared, while yet at His Mother's breast. LEO, *in Serm. 4 in Epiph.*: Herod, you are troubled with idle fear. Your kingdom would not contain Christ; nor is the Lord of the world to be confined within the narrow limits of the power of your sceptre. He Whom you wish not to reign in Juda, already reigns everywhere.

GLOSS: Or, it may be that he feared, not alone on his own account, but also because of the anger of the Romans. For the Romans had decreed that no one be called king, or god, without their consent. GREGORY: The King of heaven being born, an earthly king is troubled; for an earthly supremacy is threatened when a heavenly one appears.

LEO M, *Serm. 4 in Epiph.*: Herod here stands for the devil, who then was his inciter; as he is now his unwearied imitator. For he is troubled by the calling of the Gentiles; he is tormented by the daily breaking down of his kingdom. CHRYSOSTOM, *in Hom. 2 ex Op. Imp.*: Each is troubled by his own greed, and fears a succession to his kingdom: Herod an earthly successor, the devil a heavenly one. See too how the Jewish people are troubled, though they should rejoice that it was a Jewish king was born. But they were troubled because the wicked can never rejoice at the coming of the just; hence we have: *And all Jerusalem with him.*

GLOSS: Wishing to favour him whom they yet feared. The ordinary people, however, favoured the just rather than the one whom, though he was a cruel tyrant, they must obey.

V. 4. *And assembling together all the chief priests and the scribes of the people, he inquired of them where Christ should be born.*

REMIGIUS: Scribes are so called not so much because of their office of writing as from their office of interpreting that which was written. They were the doctors of the Law. Note here that Scripture says, not "when He was born", but *where Christ should be born.* Cleverly he interrogates them so as to find out if they would rejoice over the New King. He calls Him the Christ, because he had known that the kings of Juda were anointed.

CHRYSOSTOM, *Serm. 2 ex Op. Imp.*: To what end did Herod, who did not believe in the Scriptures, question them? Or, if he believed, how did he hope to kill Him Whom they said was to be the future King? But he was urged on by the devil, who did not believe that the Scriptures lied; like all sinners who believe, they are not permitted to believe fully that which they believe. For what they believe in is the power of truth, which cannot be hidden. What they do not believe in is the blinding of themselves by the enemy. For if they believed perfectly, they would so live as if in a little while they were to pass from this world; not as though they were to live here for ever.

V. 5. *But they said to him: In Bethlehem of Juda. For so it is written by the prophet.*

In Bethlehem of Juda. LEO M, *Serm. I in Epiph.*: The Magi believed that the King Whose birth had been revealed to them should be looked for, humanly, in the royal city. But He that had taken upon Himself *the form of a servant*, Who came not to judge, but to be judged, chose Jerusalem for His Passion, but Bethlehem for His Birth.

THEODORETUS, *in Sermon before the Council of Ephesus*: If he had chosen the great city of Rome, men would have said that the transformation of the world had been accomplished by the might of that people. Had he come as the son of the Emperor, they would attribute that gained to military power. But what did He? He chose only what was poor and humble, so that it would be seen that divinity had changed the world. And so He chose a poor woman as His Mother, a poorer fatherland. He had no money, and this the crib makes plain to you.[5]

GREGORY, *in Hom. 8 on the Gospels*: Fitting was it that He was born in Bethlehem. For Bethlehem is interpreted as the House of Bread, and He it is Who says of Himself, *I am the living bread that came down from heaven.* CHRYSOSTOM, *Hom. 2 ex Op. Imp.*: Since the Scribes should have tried to conceal the mystery of the King predestined by God, especially from the sight of an alien king, they became, not preachers of the works of God, but betrayers of His mysteries; and not alone do they divulge His mysteries, but they also cite prophetic testimony. Hence they say: *It is written by the prophet,* that is, by Micheas. GLOSS: He gives this as said by them, who however, if not the words, give in a measure the truth of the sense.

V. 6. *And thou Bethlehem the land of Juda are not the least among the princes of Juda: for out of thee shall Come the captain that shall rule my people Israel.*

JEROME: Here the Jews are to be reproved for ignorance, since the prophet says: *And thou Bethlehem Ephrata.* But they say: *Bethlehem the land of Juda.*

CHRYSOSTOM, *Ex. Op. Imp.*: Mutilating the prophecy in this manner, they have become the cause of the slaughter of the infants. For it was so written: *Out of thee shall he come forth unto me that is to be the ruler in Israel; and his going forth is from the beginning, from the days of eternity* (Mich. v. 2). If therefore they had quoted the entire prophecy, Herod, reflecting that this could not be an earthly king whose days were *from the days of eternity,* would not have raged so furiously.

JEROME, *in. Matth.* 2; *in Michaeam* 5: This is the sense of the prophecy: *Thou Bethlehem land of Juda,* or *Ephrata* (which is so said, because there is another Bethlehem situated in Galgal), although thou art but a little hamlet among the thousands of cities of Juda, yet from thee will come the Christ that will be the Ruler of Israel; Who is of the tribe of David according to the flesh, but born from Me before time was. And accordingly is it said: *and his going forth is from the beginning,* because, as John was to declare: *In the beginning the Word was with God.*

GLOSS: But this last part the Jews suppressed, as has been said, other parts they changed, either through ignorance, as has been said, or for greater clearness, so that they might open out the prophecy to the alien

Herod. So, where the prophet had said *Ephrata,* whiah was the ancient name, and perhaps unknown to Herod, they said: *The land of Juda* In the place where the prophet had said: *Thou art least among the thousands of Juda,* wishing to show its insignificance in relation to the multitude of the people, *they* said: *Thou art not the least among the princes of Juda,* wishing to show the greatness of its dignity, arising from the dignity of the Prince that was to be born there; as though they said: Thou art great among the cities from which princes have come forth.

REMIGIUS: Or, this is the sense: Although you seem the least among the cities that have princes, yet thou art not the least, for out of thee shall He come forth, the Captain, Who shall rule my people Israel. This leader is Christ, Who leads and governs the people of Israel.

CHRYSOSTOM, *Hom.* 7 *in Matth.*: Note the precision of the prophecy, For it does not say that He will live in Bethlehem, but that He will come out of Bethlehem; showing that He will be born there. How can it be that these things were said of Zorobabel, as some have said? For his going forth was not from *the days of eternity.* Neither did he come forth from Bethlehem. He was born, not in Jerusalem, but in Babylon. And to this also bears witness the testimony that says: *Thou art not the least, for from thee shall come forth.* For none other except Christ made famous this village in which He was born. For after His Birth they came from the ends of the earth to see the manger, and the place of the Stable where He was born.

Neither did the prophet say: from thee will go forth the Son of God, but: *From thee will go forth He Who will rule my people Israel.* For, at the beginning, it was necessary to come down to their level so that they might not suffer scandal. And so the Wise Men did not say: where is the Son of God, but: *Where is He that is born King of the Jews?* That was first said which related to their personal security, so that they might then be won over.

Mystically, however, did He say: *That shall rule my people Israel.* By Israel He means those who have believed from among the Jews. If however Christ does not rule all of them, the fault is theirs. Of the Gentiles He is silent for the present, lest the Jews be scandalised. Behold this wondrous dispensation: the Jews and the Magi mutually teach each other. The Jews learn from the Magi that a star in the East has proclaimed the Christ, and the Magi learned from the Jews that of old the prophecies had foretold Him; so that strengthened by this twofold testimony they might desire Him with more ardent faith, Whose Coming both the brightness of the star, and the authority of the prophets, had revealed.

AUGUSTINE, *Serm. 2 in Epiph.*: The star that led the Magi to the place where the God-Child was with His Mother, could have led them also to the city where He was born; but it withdrew, nor did it appear to them again until the Jews themselves had said of the city in which Christ would be born: *In Bethlehem of Juda.* And so they have become like the carpenters who made the Ark for Noah: who made for others a way of escape, but themselves perished in the Flood. Or they are like the milestones that show the way, but cannot walk themselves. The inquirers learn, and go on their way; the teachers speak, and remain behind. Even now the Jews cease not to afford us a similar illustration. For some from among the pagans, after we have put forward clear proofs from Scripture, so that they may know that Christ was formerly spoken of by the prophets, suspecting that these proofs may have been fabricated by the Christians, they prefer to use only the codices of the Jews. And, as the Magi did then, they leave the Jews, still vainly reciting, while they press on in ardent faith to adore.

V. 7. *Then Herod, privately calling the wise men, learned diligently of them.*

CHRYSOSTOM, *Hom. 2 ex Op. Imp.*: After Herod had received an answer, that was credible for two reasons: first, because it was spoken by the priests; second, because it was confirmed by prophetic testimony, he was not inclined towards reverence for the King that was to be born, but rather to the dread evil of the slaughter, and that by treachery. For he saw that he could not beguile the Magi by flattery, nor frighten them by threats, nor corrupt them by gold, so as to force them to consent to the death of the future King. Accordingly he planned to deceive them. Hence: *Then Herod, privately calling the wise men . . .* He calls them secretly, so that the Jews might not see that he suspected them; lest also, perhaps, they, preferring a king of their own race, might betray his purpose: *He learned diligently of them the time of the star.*

REMIGIUS: *Diligently*, because he was clever, and feared they might not return to him, so that he might then know what to do to kill the Child.

AUGUSTINE, *Serm. 7 on the Epiph.*: For about two years before, the star was seen: to the astonishment of those who saw it. It was then revealed to them Whose star it was they had so long been seeing, when He was born Who was signified by it. For when Christ was born, it was revealed to the Magi, who then travelled from the East, and, on the thirteenth day, they adored Him Whom but a few days before they had learned was born.[6]

CHRYSOSTOM, *Hom. 7 in Matt.*: Or, this star appeared much earlier, since the Magi were to consume time in travelling; so that as soon as He was born they might be near Him. For they must adore Him in swaddling clothes, that the event might seem more wondrous. GLOSS: According to others, the star is believed to have appeared only from the day of the birth of Our Saviour, and having fulfilled its purpose, and while still new, ceased to be. For, as Fulgentius says in his homily on the Epiphany, this star, the Lord's announcer of the Nativity, had never before appeared, but the Child then created it. The place and time being now known, he wishes to learn concerning the person of the Child; hence we have:

V. 8. *And sending them into Bethlehem, said: Go and diligently inquire*

after the child, and when you have found him, bring me word again, that I also may come and adore him. He tells them to do that which they were about to do without his command. CHRYSOSTOM, *Hom. 7 in Matt.*: He did not say, inquire about the king. For he envied Him the name of power.

CHRYSOSTOM, *Ex Op. Imperf. Hom. 2*: And that he might induce them to do so, he pretends devotion, and through this hides the sword, and paints with the colours of simplicity the malice of his own heart. Such is the way of all who do evil. When they plot in secret to wound another, they feign both simplicity and friendship. Hence he says: *and when you have found him, bring me word again, that I may come and adore Him.* GREGORY, *in Hom. 10*: He pretends a wish to adore Him, so that he may destroy Him should he find Him.

V. 9. *Who having heard the king, went their way; and behold the star which . . .*

REMIGIUS: The Magi listened to Herod telling them that they should go and seek the Lord, but without intending to return to him. They symbolise good hearers of the word, who practise the good they hear of from unworthy preachers, while not imitating their actions.

CHRYSOSTOM, *Op. Imp.*: In this place it is shown, that when the star had brought the Magi near to Jerusalem, it hid from them, so that, being abandoned by the star, they were compelled to make inquiry in Jerusalem concerning Christ, and at the same time to make Him known;

and this for two reasons. First, for the confounding of the Jews; for the Magi, encouraged only by the rising of a star, have been seeking Christ, and in strange lands, while the Jews, who have been reading from their childhood the prophecies that spoke of Christ, and though He was born in their midst, have not received Him. Secondly, so that the priests, being questioned as to where Christ was born, would make answer to their own condemnation: "from Bethlehem"; because they who had instructed Herod concerning Christ, were themselves without knowledge of Him. And accordingly after their inquiry, and after receiving an answer, there is added: *and behold the star which they had seen in the East, went before them*; so that observing the obedience of the star, they might understand the dignity of the King.

AUGUSTINE, *Serm. de Epiph.*: And that it might render full homage to Christ it went before them, until it led the Magi to the Child. It tendered obedience, it did not exact it; it revealed the suppliants, it bathed the lodging with its splendid light, it poured down upon the roof of the Child, and so departed.[7]

Until it came and stood over where the Child was.

The Mystical significance of the Star. CHRYSOSTOM, *Op. Imp.*: Is it to be wondered at that a divine Star ministers to the Rising Sun of Justice? It halts above the head of the Child as if saying: *This is He*: as though being unable to proclaim Him in words it proclaims Him by standing above Him. GLOSS: From

this it appears that the Star was in the lower atmosphere and very close to the house in which the Child lay, otherwise it would not have pointed out the house.

AMBROSE, *in Luke Book* 2, 2: This star is the way and the Way is Christ; because in the mystery of the Incarnation, Christ is a Star, *the bright and morning Star*. Where Herod is, it is not seen; where Christ is, it is seen again, and points the way. REMIGIUS: Or, the star signifies the grace of God, and Herod the devil. He who by sin subjects himself to the devil, immediately loses grace; but should he return through penance, he will immediately refind grace, which does not leave him until it guides him to the house of the Child, which is the Church. GLOSS: Or, the star is the illumination of faith, which leads to Christ; which the Magi lost when they turned aside to the Jews. For while they are seeking counsel of the wicked they lose the true light.

V. 10. *And seeing the star they rejoiced with exceeding great joy.*

GLOSS: After he had recounted the help of the star, the Evangelist then speaks of the great joy of the Magi, saying: *They rejoiced with exceeding great joy.* REMIGIUS: Let us note that it did not seem sufficient to the mind of the Evangelist to say: *they rejoiced*, but he also adds: *with great joy*, and, *exceeding*.

CHRYSOSTOM, *ex Op. Imp.*: They rejoiced because their hope, far from being in vain, was yet further confirmed, that they had not undertaken the toil of so great a journey without good reason. GLOSS: He rejoices with joy who rejoices in God, Who is the True Joy. He adds: *with great joy*; because they rejoiced over a great happening. CHRYSOSTOM, *as above*: For by the mystery of the star they had come to understand that the dignity of the New Born King exceeded the measure of all earthly kings; and so he says: *exceeding*. REMIGIUS: because he wishes to show that men rejoice more over things that were lost than over those they always had.

V. 11. *And entering into the house, they found the Child with Mary His Mother, and falling down they adored Him; and opening their treasures, they offered Him gifts; gold, frankincense, and myrrh.*

And entering in . . . the Child. LEO M., *Serm. 4 in Epiph.*: Small in size, depending on others, powerless to act, differing in no way from any other human infant; because as the testimonies were true which showed in Him the Majesty of the Unseen Divinity, so must it be also completely manifest that the sempiternal essence of the Son of God has assumed the true nature of man.

With Mary His Mother . . . CHRYSOSTOM, *ex Op. Imp.*: He was not crowned with a diadem, nor resting on a gilded bed; but scarcely possessed a single tunic, and that served, not for the adorning of His Body, but to clothe His nakedness, and was such as the wife of a poor man, far from her home, could provide. If therefore they had come seeking an earthly king, they would have been mortified rather than filled with exceeding joy, for they would have undertaken the toil of such a journey without reward. But now because they seek a heavenly king, though they saw in Him nothing regal; yet satisfied by the testimony of a single star, their eyes were glad as they looked upon a poor little Child; for the Spirit within them showed that He was a Being of Awe. Hence: *falling down they adored Him.* They see man, but adore God.

RABANUS: By divine arrangement it happened that Joseph was absent, lest occasion of evil suspicion be given to the Gentiles. GLOSS: *and opening their treasures*; who, though they followed the custom of their people in offering gifts, and the Arabs are rich in gold, incense, and different kinds of spices, sought also to manifest by their gifts something of the Mystery. Hence follows: *they offered him gifts; gold, frankincense, and myrrh.*

GREGORY, *Hom. 10 in Matth.*: Gold befits a king; frankincense is offered in sacrifice to God; with myrrh the bodies of the dead are embalmed. AUGUSTINE, *Serm. de Epiph.*: Gold is offered as to a great King, incense is immolated before God, myrrh is given to Him Who is to die for all men.[8] CHRYSOSTOM, *Op. Imp.*: Although the Magi understood not then according to what mystery they tendered the gifts, or what each single gift might signify, yet there is nothing out of place in their offerings; for the grace that had stirred them to do all these things, is the same which orders the universe.

REMIGIUS: We must know that it was not that each singly offered a gift, but that each singly offered the three; and each singly, by his gifts, gave testimony to the King, to

God, to Man. CHRYSOSTOM, *Hom. 7 in Matth.*: Let therefore Marcion and Paul Samosatenus be ashamed, who will not see what the Magi saw; they who are the forefathers of the Church, and who adored God in our flesh. That He is truly present in the flesh the swaddling clothes bear witness, and the crib. That they adore, not a simple man, but God, the gifts bear witness; which are such as belong to God. And let the Jews be ashamed, to see themselves forestalled as it were by the Magi, yet not eager to follow after them.

GREGORY, *Hom.* 10: Another thing may be understood by these signs. By gold wisdom is also symbolised, as Solomon testifies, saying: *There is desirable treasure in the mouth of the just* (Prov. xxi. 20 (Sept.)); by frankincense, which is burnt before God, the power of prayer is symbolised, according to the psalm: *let my prayer be directed as incense in thy sight* (Ps. cxl. 2); by myrrh is typified the mortification of the flesh. To the New Born King we offer gold, if in His sight we shine with the light of wisdom. We offer incense when by the fervour of our prayer we offer up that which is agreeable to Him. We offer myrrh when by abstinence we mortify the vices of the flesh.

GLOSS: *They offered him gifts.* The three men who offer, signify the people coming from the three parts of the world. They *open their treasures*, when by confession they make manifest the faith of their heart. Rightly also, *into the house*, teaching us not to throw away the treasure of a good conscience by idle chatter in the streets. They offer three gifts, that is, the faith of the Holy Trinity; or, opening the treasures of Scripture, they offer historical, moral, and allegorical meanings; or, even logic, the physical sciences, and ethics; as long as they do this in the service of the faith.

V. 12. *And having received an answer in sleep that they should not return to Herod, they went back another way into their country.*

AUGUSTINE, *in Sermon on the Epiphany*: The perverted Herod, made cruel through fear, now seeks to glut his cruelty. But how can he lay hold of Him Who has foiled his snares? For that his snare may be evaded there then follows: *And having received an answer in sleep.*[9] JEROME: For they who had offered their gifts to God received in due time an acknowledgement. The reply is made, not by the angel, but by the Lord Himself, so that the special quality of the dignity of Joseph might be shown.[10]

GLOSS: This reply was given by the Lord Himself; for no one else laid down the way of their return save He Who has said: *I am the Way* (Jn. xiv. 6). For the Child did not speak to them, lest before due time His Divinity be revealed, and so that His humanity be received as true. It says: *and having received an answer*; for as Moses cried out within himself, so these with holy desire seek to know what the divine will commands. For it says: *They went back another way into their country*; because they must not commingle with the unbelief of the Jews.

CHRYSOSTOM, *in Hom.* 8 *in Matt.*: Behold the faith of the Magi. See how they are not scandalised, saying to themselves: If this Child is mighty, where is the need of flight, and of remaining hidden? It is ever the way of true faith that it seeks not to know the reasons of the things that are commanded, but is persuaded to obey simply by the command. CHRYSOSTOM, *Ex Op. Imp.*: Had the Magi been seeking Christ as an earthly king, having found Him they would have remained with Him. Instead, they adore Him, and then return to their own home. And when they had returned they continued to worship Him, more than before. And they preached Him, and instructed many. Finally, when Thomas came to that region they joined themselves to Him, and were baptised, and they became his helpers in the work of preaching the Gospel.

GREGORY, *Hom.* 10 *in Evang.*: In returning to their own land by another way, the Magi intimate to us something of great import. Our true country is Paradise, to which, having now come to the knowledge of Jesus, we are forbidden to return

by the path we left it. For we left our land by the path of pride, of disobedience, by following after wealth, by eating forbidden food. And so we must return another way: by the way of tears, by the way of obedience, by contempt of the world, by restraining the desires of the flesh.

CHRYSOSTOM, *Op. Imp.*: It was not possible that having come from Herod to Christ, they would return again to Herod. They, however, who leave Christ and go over to the devil by sin, frequently return to Christ, through repentance. For he that was inexperienced, and knew not what evil is, may easily be deceived. But having made trial of the evil he encounters, and recalling the good he has lost, now, moved by repentance, he turns back to God. But he that has rejected the devil, and returned to Christ, with difficulty does he return to the devil; for he now rejoices in the good he has found, and remembers the evil from which he has been delivered, and will not readily return to it.

I. ST AMBROSE: ON THE GOSPEL[11]

Here is the Lord, in this manger, in Whom is made known to us the divine secret: that the peoples of the pagan world, now living after the manner of beasts in their stalls, are to be nourished from the abundance of the sacred Food. *The ox knoweth his master, and the ass his master's crib* (Is. i. 3). The ass therefore, which is the figure and type of the heathen peoples, knoweth the manger of his Lord. And he says accordingly: *The Lord ruleth me: and I shall want nothing* (Ps. xxii).

Can anyone say that the Lord is made known to us by signs of little import, when the Magi come and adore Him, the angels serve Him, and the martyrs confess Him? He comes forth from a womb, but He shines like lightning from above; He lies in an earthly resting place, but round about Him is the brightness of heaven. The espoused has brought forth; but a Virgin hath conceived. A wife hath conceived; but a Virgin hath given birth. There is here another mystery of no small significance, which the holy Matthew makes known, and which the holy Luke believed he might omit, as it was already fully related, believing he had recorded sufficient when he had given testimony of the manger of the Lord. Now to this little Child, Whom you, if you believe not, will consider as an ordinary child, the Wise men from the East, following on so long a journey, now come, *and falling down they adored Him*, and call Him King, and profess that He shall rise from the dead; and this they do by offering Him from their treasures, gold, frankincense, and myrrh.

What are these gifts, offered in true faith? Gold, as to a King; incense, as to God; myrrh, for the dead. For one is the token of the dignity of a king; the other the symbol of the divine majesty; the third is a service of honour to a Body that is to be buried, which does not destroy the body of the dead, but preserves it. We also who read and hear these things, let us, Brethren, offer similar gifts, from our treasures. For we have treasures, *in earthen vessels* (II Cor. iv. 7). If you consider that which you are as being, not from thee, but from Christ: how much more ought you not to consider that which you own as being, not yours, but Christ's?

The Magi therefore offer Him gifts from their treasures. Do you desire to know how precious was their reward? The Star is seen by them; where Herod is it is not seen; it is seen again where Christ is, and shows them the way. Therefore this Star is the way, and the way is Christ: for in the mystery of the Incarnation Christ is a star. *A Star*

shall rise out of Jacob, and a man shall rise up from Israel (Num. xxiv. 17). Where then Christ is, the star is. For He Himself is *the bright and morning star*. He shows us Himself therefore, by His own light.

Here is yet another proof. The Magi come by one way, and return by another. For they who had seen Christ, had come to know Christ; and they returned more truly believing than they came. The way is twofold: one that leads to destruction, and the other that leads to the Kingdom. There is the way of sinners, that leads to Herod: this way is Christ by which we return to our country. For here we have no lasting dwelling, as it is written: *My soul hath long been a sojourner* (Ps. cxix. 6). Let us turn away from Herod, ruler for a while of an earthly power, that we may come to the everlasting dwelling of our heavenly country.

And not to the Elect alone are these rewards promised, but likewise to all men: *for Christ is all, and in all* (Col. iii. 11). For you observe that it was not by chance, or because of the Chaldees, who were reputed to be skilled in numbers, that Abraham believed in God; it was not by chance that the Magi believed in the birth of the Lord on earth, although they devoted much time to the appeasing of the divine powers by means of magical arts. As I say, not by chance, but that a witness to the true and holy religion, and a model of true fear of the Lord, might be chosen from among hostile peoples.

And who are these Magi if not they who, as history tells us, descend from that Balaam by whom it was foretold that, *A Star shall rise out of Jacob*; so that they are no less the heirs of his faith than heirs of his blood. He beheld the Star in spirit; they saw it with their eyes, and believed. They beheld a new star, which had not been seen by a creature of this world. They beheld a new creation, and they sought, not alone on earth, but in heaven, for the friendship of the New Man, according to that which Moses had prophetically declared, for *a Star shall rise out of Jacob and a man shall spring up from Israel* (Exod. xxiv. 17).[12]

And they understood that this was the Star, which meant both God and man; and they adored a Child: nor would they have adored, had they believed He was but a Child. The Magician here saw that his arts were no more; do you not see that your gifts have come? He confesses Someone that is strange to him; do you not recognise the Promised One? He believed against himself; do you not see that you must believe for your own sake?

The Magi come speaking of a King that is born. Herod is troubled and assembles the chief priests and the Scribes, and asks them where Christ should be born. The Magi speak only of a King: Herod inquires for Christ. He confesses therefore that He is a King for Whom he inquires. Then he inquires when it is that Christ should be born, showing that He is foretold: for he cannot be inquired for who was not already foretold. O foolish Jews! Will you not believe that He is now come Whom you see has come? Will you not believe that He is come, Whom you declared was to come?

Bring me word, he says, that I too may come and adore the Child. Herod plots evil, but he does not deny the God Whom he remembers must be adored. Then he orders the Infants to be put to death. To whom but to God is such a sacrifice offered? The Infants, though they understand not, confess the Lord, for Whom they are slaughtered.

These few reflections I have drawn from the Gospel of Matthew, that I may make plain to you, that not even the times of His Infancy were wanting in the signs and wonders of His Divinity, Who with the Father and the Holy Ghost liveth and reigneth world without end. Amen.

II. St John Chrysostom

The Epiphany and the Flight into Egypt [13]

And entering into the house, they found the Child with Mary His Mother, and falling down they adored Him; and opening their treasures, they offered Him gifts; gold, frankincense, and myrrh. How is it then that Luke says He was *laid in a manger?* Because, as soon as He was born, she had laid Him there; since so many people having come for the enrolment they could not find a house, as Luke likewise tells: *because there was no room for them in the inn.* Later, she took Him up and placed Him on her knee. As soon as she had reached Bethlehem she had brought forth her Son, and so from all this you may discern a general purpose; that it was not by chance, and without plan, that all these things took place, but in accordance with a certain order of providence, and the order foretold by the prophets.

But what was it that moved the Magi to adore Him? For the Virgin bore upon her no distinguishing mark, and the abode was not one of splendour; neither was there any other material circumstance which would either compel them or induce them to do this. Yet not alone do they adore Him, but opening their treasures they offer Him gifts; and such gifts as are offered, not to man, but to God. For gold and incense especially were a symbol of the divinity. What then was it that moved them? It was that which had before moved them, so that leaving their own country they had begun this so weary journey, namely: the Star, and together with the Star the light that God had placed in their hearts, which was to lead them step by step to more perfect knowledge.

For unless it were so they would not have shown Him such great honour, since all that they see here is but poor and lowly. For of the things that fell upon their outward senses there was nothing striking: there was only a manger, a mud hut, a poor mother. Thus you may comprehend the pure wisdom of these Wise Men, and by it you may learn that they came to Him, not as to a simple man, but as to God and to their source of blessing. And so they were not offended by the outward things they saw, but adoring Him they offered their gifts: gifts which differed so greatly from the gross offerings of the Jews. They sacrificed no sheep or calves, but rather those things which bring them near to the heart of the Church; for they make a beginning of offering to Him: knowledge, wisdom, and love.

And having received an answer in sleep that they should not return to Herod, they went back another way into their own country. Observe their simple faith, and how they are not resentful, but peaceful and restrained. Neither are they put out, nor do they say to each other: if this Child is so great what need have we for flight or secret departure? And why since we came here openly and trustfully to this great people, and dared the anger of their king, does an angel now send us from the city like fugitives? But they neither thought nor said such things. For it is the special character of true faith, that it asks for no reasons for the precepts laid upon it, but simply obeys what is commanded.

And after they were departed, behold an angel of the Lord appeared in sleep to Joseph, saying: Arise, and take the child with his mother, and fly into Egypt: and be there until I shall tell thee. There is something here which we should inquire into, touching the Magi and touching the Child. For even if they were not troubled, but received all things in submission, why is it that both they and the Child are not preserved from danger where they are: and why must they seek flight towards Persia, and He with His Mother go down to Egypt? But why not? Must He be allowed to fall into the hands of Herod; and being taken would He not be slain? Then it might not have been believed that He had ever taken flesh, and the greatness of the divine plan of our redemption would not have been believed. For although these things happened, and many other things took place afterwards in a merely human manner, yet there are some who have dared to say that His taking of our flesh was but a myth; into what blasphemy would they not have fallen had He done all things in a divine manner and of His own power?

The Wise Men He sends away quickly, sending them likewise as teachers into the land of Persia; frustrating the evil rage of the tyrant, so that he would learn that he had attempted that which was beyond his power, and so put away his rage and cease from his futile efforts. For it is the way of the divine power not alone to scatter openly those that oppose it, but also simply to allow them to be deceived. So did He allow the Egyptians to be deceived in favour of the Jews, and though He had the power, to transfer their wealth openly into the hands of the Hebrews, yet He bids them do this in secrecy, and with craft: which no less than His signs and wonders renders Him fearful to those that withstand Him.

For the people of Ascalon, and the others, after they had seized the Ark and had been struck by Him, exhorted their people not to fight, nor to stand against Him, and brought this proof forward with the rest, saying: *Why do you harden your hearts, as Egypt and Pharo hardened their hearts? Did not he after he was struck, then let them go, and they departed?* (I Kgs. vi. 6). They said this as though they believed this latter sign was no less striking than those He had openly performed when He showed His power and majesty.

That which here took place could also strike terror in the heart of the tyrant. For consider to yourself how Herod felt, how he must have been choked with rage, at being so fooled and made to look ridiculous by the Magi. And what if he did not learn to be better? That cannot be imputed to Him who has ordered those things, but to the unmeasured fury of this person who would not take notice of things which ought to have brought him to his senses, and turn from evil-doing: but he rushes on the more, so that he earns a more grievous chastisement for his enormous folly.

But why, you will say, is the Child sent into Egypt? The Evangelist himself tells us the reason: *That it might be fulfilled which the Lord spoke by the prophet, saying: Out of Egypt have I called my son* (Mt. ii. 15); and so that at the same time the beginning of bright hopes might be made known to the whole world. For since Babylon and Egypt, more than the rest of the world, burnt with the fire of iniquity, the Lord, manifesting even from the beginning that He desires to restore both these regions to Himself, and bring them to worthier things, and by this at the same time intimating to the whole earth that His gifts were now to be looked for, to the one sends the Magi, and to the other goes Himself, together with His Mother.

These things also teach us something else, which in no little way encourages us to seek true wisdom. What is this? That from the very beginning we must look for temptations and dangers? See how this happened to Him, even in His swaddling clothes. For as soon as He was born the tyrant rages; then comes flight, and a journey into exile; and without cause His Mother is forced to fly into a land of strangers: so that you hearing of these things and being yourself thought worthy to serve God in a spiritual manner, should you see yourself suffering grievous afflictions, and placed in the midst of tribulations without end, might not be troubled, and might not murmur: Why is this? Should I not rather be honoured and praised, and considered as worthy, and to be esteemed, since I have fulfilled the commandments of the Lord? But supported by His example, endure with courage; knowing that this is the lot of all spiritual men, that they are everywhere tried by afflictions.

And note accordingly that this happens not alone to the Mother and Child, but also to these strangers. They also had to fly, secretly and as fugitives: and She, who scarcely ever went outside her home, is bidden to set out on a long and wearisome journey, because of this wondrous new-born Child and His miraculous birth.

And behold yet another wondrous thing. Palestine lies in wait for Him, Egypt receives Him, and delivers Him from treachery. For types and figures have place not alone in the sons of the Patriarch, but even in the Lord Himself. For through the things which He then did, many events were foreshadowed, which afterwards would take place: as happened in the case of the ass and the colt. The angel therefore who appeared spoke not to Mary but to Joseph: and what did he say: *Arise, and take the child, and his mother.* Here he no longer says: *Thy wife,* but *His Mother.* For since the Birth had taken place, and the suspicion dissipated, and the man reassured, the angel now says openly, speaking neither of wife nor son: *Take the child and his mother,*

and fly into Egypt; and he gives also the reason for the flight: *For it will come to pass that Herod will seek the child to destroy him.*

In praise of Joseph

And Joseph is not offended at hearing this, nor did he say: this is hard to understand. Did you not but lately say: He shall save His people: now He cannot save Himself, and we must take flight, and go a long journey, and dwell at length in another land? These things are contrary to what you promised. But he said nothing of this sort, for he was a man of faith; nor does he make inquiry as to when they shall return, although the angel had spoken in an indefinite manner, saying: *Be there until I shall tell thee.* Neither was he regretful at this command, but submissive and obedient, bearing these trials with cheerfulness.

For the loving God mingled joy with his labours: as He does with all who are devoted to Him; not permitting their tribulations or their peace to be continuous, but ordering the life of the just by commingling the one with the other. This He did here also: and it is this on which I wish you to reflect. For Joseph saw that the Virgin was with child: and he was troubled by this, and in great anxiety: for he began to suspect the maiden of adultery; but immediately an angel stood by him, who undid his suspicion and banished his fear. And when he beheld the Child born he was filled with great joy: and then to this joy there succeeds this great peril, for the city was troubled, and the king was raging with anger, and seeking the Child.

But to this anxiety another joy

succeeded, namely: the Star, and the adoration of the Wise Men. Again, following on this joy, there is danger and fear: for Herod, he says, seeks the life of the Child, and so He must fly, and go into another country after the manner of men: for the time for miracles had not yet come. For if from His Infancy He had begun to perform signs and wonders it would not have been believed that He was a man. And for this reason a temple was not at once prepared for Him, but there is first a conception, then the space of nine months, and child-bearing, and birth, and nursing at the breast, then silence for a long space of time; the full years of manhood are awaited, so that the mystery of the plan of our redemption might be made credible to all.

But then, you may ask, why were there signs wrought from the beginning? Because of His Mother, because of Joseph, because of Simeon now ready to depart this life, because of the shepherds, because of the Magi, because of the Jews. For if they had paid close attention to the things which were then taking place, they would have gained no small profit from what was later to come. That the prophets do not speak of the Magi do not concern yourselves; for they neither foretold all things, nor were they silent as to all. For as to behold such great things without having been previously told of them would cause consternation, and grave unrest; so, if men had learned all that was to be known, the hearers would then have become indifferent: nor would anything be left to the Evangelist.

And should the Jews, questioning the prophecy, say that the words,

Out of Egypt have I called my son, was spoken of themselves we shall answer them, that this is the way of prophecy: that many things are often said concerning some persons and fulfilled concerning others, as that which was said of Simeon and Levi: *I will divide them in Jacob, and will scatter them in Israel* (Gen. xlix. 7), was not fulfilled in them, but in their posterity. And that which was spoken by Noah concerning Chanaan, came to pass in the Gibeonites, who were from the stock of Chanaan (Gen. ix. 25; Jos. ix. 27). And this is seen to have happened also to Jacob: for those blessings, *be thou lord of thy brethren, and let thy mother's children bow down before thee*, were not received in him (for how could they relate to him who was in fear and trembling before his brother, and adored him repeatedly), but was spoken of his Offspring (Gen. xxvii. 29; xxxiii. 3). Which may be said also in this connection. For who more truly can be called the Son of God: he that adored a calf, and worshipped Baal, or He that was His Son by nature, and hath honoured His Father? And so had He not come, the prophecy would not have received a worthy fulfilment.

See therefore how the Evangelist hints at this, saying, *that it might be fulfilled*, showing that unless He had come, it could not be fulfilled. And this too to no small degree makes the Virgin also more honoured and worthy of honour. For that which a whole people held as their pride, she now could hold as hers. For that they gloried in, and made a boast of their return from Egypt (to which the prophet refers when he said *Did not I bring up Israel, out of the land of Egypt?*

(Amos ix. 7), this he now makes the prerogative of the Virgin. More than that, for both people and patriarch going down there and returning again, gave significance to the figure of that ascent and descent. For they went down to escape death from imminent famine; He that He might escape the death prepared for him by treachery. And they on coming there out of famine, were delivered; He in going there sanctified a whole country by His coming.

I would that you would reflect with me how in the midst of this lowliness the marks of His divinity are revealed. For when the angel said, *fly into Egypt*, he did not promise to journey with them, either in going there or returning, letting them see in a veiled manner that they would have a mighty Fellow-traveller, the new born Child, Who, as soon as He appeared, changed all things, so that His enemies in a manner should serve His design for man's redemption. For the Magi and the Gentiles, putting away the superstitions of their fathers, come to adore Him; Augustus rendered service to Him at His birth in Bethlehem, when he commanded that a census be made; Egypt receives Him and preserves Him, when a fugitive, and sought for by treachery, and through this achieves a certain bond of friendship with Him, so that afterwards when she would hear Him preached by the Apostles, she would glory in this that she had been the first to receive Him.

The Monks and the companies of Virgins in Egypt

And this was the privilege of Palestine alone; yet was Egypt more

fervent. For now should you enter the desert land of Egypt, you will find the solitudes more wonderful than any paradise, thousands of choirs of angels in human form, nations of martyrs, hosts of virgins, the whole evil dominion of the demon cast down, the kingdom of Christ resplendent. She that was the mother of poets, of philosophers, of wise men (magicians); she who had discovered every form of sorcery, and had given them to others, she, I say, you now will see glorying in the fishermen, and treating with contempt all those ancient arts: giving honour to the Publican, and the tentmaker, and invoking the protection of the Cross, and this not alone in the cities, but even more in the desert than in the cities. For everywhere throughout that land may be seen the army of Christ, and the flocks of the King, and the way of life of the heavenly kingdom, and this not alone among men, but also you will find it among the women. Not less than the men do they follow after wisdom, not taking up the shield, not taking to horse, as certain grave and worthy guides of the Greeks lay down, but they take on a warfare that is more serious. For common to both men and women is the war against the devil and the powers of darkness. In that warfare never does the delicacy of their sex stand in the way. For not by the powers of the body, but that of the soul is battle won. And so not rarely has it happened that women have fought more courageously than men, and given more proofs of victory. Heaven itself with all the splendour of the stars is not as splendid as the solitudes of Egypt, which spread out before us in every direction the dwelling places of her contemplatives.[14]

If anyone has known of ancient Egypt, the enemy of God, and raging against Him, the worshipper of cats, she who feared and trembled at omens, such a one will learn perfectly of the power of Christ. Indeed one needs no ancient histories: for even today there are still surviving memorials of that foolish people, bearing witness to their former madness. Yet all they who at one time fell into such absurdities, now seek after the knowledge of heaven and of heavenly things, and laugh at their ancient customs, belittle their forefathers, and regard as worthless the doctrines of their philosophers. For they have learned from reality that these *foolish old wives' fables* were but the inventions of those who were drunk with wine, and that true wisdom and that which is worthy of heaven is this which was made known to them by the fishermen.

And so together with great purity of doctrine, they manifest a great earnestness of life. For having freed themselves from all things, and being crucified to the world, they have gone yet further, using the labour of their own bodies to give aid to those in need. For not because they fast and keep watch are they for this reason idle by day; for they give the night to hymns and watchings, and the day to prayer, and to the labour of their hands, imitating the zeal of the Apostle.

For, they say, if he upon whom the eyes of the world were turned, kept a workshop that he might help the needy, and followed his craft, going without sleep at night, how much the more should we who live in the desert, and have nothing to do with the tumult of the cities, use as is but fitting the peace of our retirement for the works of the spirit:

Let us therefore, both rich and poor, all of us, be ashamed, when they who have nothing but their hands and bodies, yet strive to procure by means of them wherewith to feed the poor, while we who have endless things stored in our homes do not make over to them even what is superfluous. What excuse, I ask you, have we to offer? How shall we be forgiven.

And I would that you would also consider with me, how these people were lovers of money, and how much they were given to gluttony, and to the other vices. For it was there were *the flesh pots* which the Jews recalled (Exod. xvi. 3): there was the great dominion of the stomach. Yet because they willed it, they are changed; and having taken fire from Christ, they of a sudden took wing towards heaven; and though a more fiery people than others, more prone to anger, and to the pleasures of the body, they imitate the spiritual powers in mildness and in the other restraints of their holy wisdom.

Whosoever has been in that country will know of what I am speaking. If however he has never visited these dwelling places, let him reflect upon the life of the man whose name is now in the mouths of all men, whom Egypt places after the Apostles, the great and blessed Anthony, and let him remind himself that this man was born in the same country as Pharo. But he suffered nothing by this, but was even esteemed worthy of the divine vision, and practised such a way of life as the teaching of Christ demanded. And this any man may learn who carefully reads the book in which is written the story of his life,[15] in which also there is much prophecy. For he foretold of what related to those caught in the Arian evil, and declared beforehand the harm that would arise from it, according as God revealed it to him, and placed before his eyes all future events, which, especially considering the other circumstances of his life, is the greatest proof of the truth, that none among the heresies can possess such a man.

But so that you may not learn this alone from us, you may accurately learn all that regards him should you read the book in which these things are written, besides deriving from it much true wisdom. This I ask you however that you do not merely peruse the book, for we are to imitate what is written there, making no excuses because of where we are, or our occupation, or because of the depravity of our forefathers. For if we wish to learn, none of these things will be a hindrance. For Abraham had an impious father, but he did not inherit his wickedness; Ezechias was the son of Achaz, and yet became a friend of God. And Joseph in the midst of the Egyptians, was adorned with the crown of chastity; and the three youths in Babylon, and in the royal house, when a Sybaritic table was set before them, showed supreme self-denial; and Moses also in Egypt; and Paul throughout the world: to all these nothing was a hindrance along the course of true virtue.

Let us then bearing all these things in mind, put away from us all needless excuses and pretences, and let us devote ourselves to the labour of seeking after holiness. So shall we draw down upon us greater divine approval, and we shall thus implore of Him that He aid us in our struggles, and so we shall come to the enjoyment of an eternal reward, to which may we all attain by the grace and mercy of Our Lord Jesus Christ, to Whom be honour and glory for ever and ever. Amen.

III. St John Chrysostom: Sermon for the Epiphany

When Jesus therefore was born in Bethlehem of Juda, there came wise men from the east to Jerusalem saying: Where is that is born king of the Jews. For we have seen his star in the east, and are come to adore him.[16]

Isaias had foretold that this would come to pass, saying: *The multitude of camels shall cover thee, the dromedaries of Madian and Apha: all they from Saba shall come, bringing gold and frankincense: and showing forth praise to the Lord* (Is. lx. 6). This is He, Christ the Lord, Whom the Magi, having seen the sign of the star, announce as the King of the Jews.

Things unheard of, and exceeding the measure of human astonishment, all took place together at the Birth of Our Lord. An angel appears and speaks to Zachary, promising that to Elizabeth, his wife, a son will be born, and he, not believing the angel, is stricken dumb: she that was sterile conceives: in the womb of a Virgin a Child takes life. John, inspired in his mother's womb, leaps for joy: Christ the Lord New-Born is announced by an angel. He is proclaimed by the shepherds as the salvation of the world. Angels exult, the shepherds rejoice. Upon this glorious nativity joy and gladness rise up both in heaven and on earth.

The new sign of a star in the heavens is pointed out to the Magi; through this sign it is made known to them that the Lord of the heavens is born King of the Jews; He of Whom it was written: *A star shall rise out of Jacob and a sceptre shall spring up from Israel* (Numb. xxiv. 17), so that from the symbol of a star the union of man with the Son of God, of human nature with the divine, might become known.

Thus it was the Lord spoke of Himself in the Apocalypse: *I am the root and stock of David, the bright and morning star* (Apoc. xxii. 16) for in the rising of His own Nativity, the night of ignorance being scattered, He shines forth, *the bright and morning star*, unto the salvation of the world; the splendour of Whose light reaching also to the hearts of the Magi, filled them with spiritual light, so that by the sign of the new-risen star they know the Creator of heaven as the King of the Jews.

The Magi, teachers of a false faith, could never have come to know Christ Our Lord, had they not been illumined by the grace of this divine condescension. Indeed the grace of God overflowed at the Birth of Christ, so that each single soul might be enlightened by His Truth. The Magi are enlightened so that the goodness of God may be made manifest: so that no one need despair, doubting that salvation through faith will be given to him, seeing He bestowed it on the Magi. The Magi therefore were the first from the Gentiles chosen for salvation, so that through them

a door might be opened to all the Gentiles.

But perhaps someone will wonder how it was that the Magi knew of the Lord's Nativity from the sign of a star? In the first place we say that this was a gift of the divine goodness. Then we read in the books of Moses that there was a certain prophet of the Gentiles, Balaam, who foretold in definite words the coming of Christ and His incarnation from a virgin. For among other things he said: *A star shall rise out of Jacob, and a sceptre shall spring up from Israel.* The Wise men, who saw the new star in the East, are said to be descendants of this Balaam, a prophet from the Gentiles. And seeing the sign of the new star they accordingly believed, knowing that the prophecy of their ancestor was fulfilled: in this showing themselves to be not alone his descendants in the flesh, but the heirs also to his faith. Balaam their prophet beheld the Star in spirit; with their eyes they saw It, and believed. He by prophecy foretold that Christ would come, they with the vision of faith knew that He had come.

Then they came straightaway to Herod, saying: *Where is He that is born King of the Jews? For we have seen His star in the east and have come to adore Him.* They sought the Lord Christ, born King of the Jews, among those from whose race they knew that Balaam had prophesied He would come. But the faith of the Magi is the condemnation of the Jews. They believed on the authority of their one prophet, these others refused to believe many prophets. The former knew that through the Coming of Christ their magic arts were ended, the latter refused to accept the mysteries of the divine dispensation. They confessed a Stranger; the Jews rejected their own. *He came unto His own, and his own received Him not.* And this same star was seen by all, but not by all understood. As Our Lord and Saviour was truly born for all, as Man He was born for all men, not by all was He received, nor understood by all. He was understood by the Gentiles, He was not understood by the Jews; acknowledged by the Church, He was denied by the Synagogue.

When therefore the Magi, after the splendid toil of their long journey, had come to Jerusalem seeking the King of the Jews, immediately, says the Evangelist, King Herod, and with him all Jerusalem, was disturbed by the fervent faith of the Magi. The Chiefs of the Priests and the Scribes of the people are gathered together. They are asked: *where Christ should be born.* They answer: in Bethlehem of Juda, for *so it is written by the prophet: And thou Bethlehem the land of Juda are not the least among the princes of Juda. For out of thee shall come forth etc.* Herod therefore, and the men of Jerusalem, knowingly, they were not ignorant, reject Christ the Lord. For they sought the testimony of the prophets, when they searched out where Christ would be born.

This place, Bethlehem, where the Lord was born, had received a name of prophecy. For Bethlehem is interpreted: *House of Bread*; because the Son of God Who was to be born here is the Bread of Life, as He himself said in His Gospel: *I am the Living Bread that came down from heaven.* This too is the place that is spoken of elsewhere by the prophet: *God will come from the south, and the Holy One from Mount Pharan* (Hab. iii. 3). These words describe the site and aspect of the place. The words of this prophet agree with the previous prophecy for, after the words of Micheas saying: *Out of thee He shall go forth the ruler in Israel,* there is added: *And his going forth is from the beginning, from the days of eternity* (Mich. v. 2); so that, contrary to Photinus, it is not to be supposed that the Lord had a beginning only from the moment in which He was born of the Virgin. For it is clearly shown that He *is* from *the beginning of days,* and that He is the Lord, Who was born in Bethlehem.

Then the Evangelist continues: *Herod calling etc.*

Herod the evil king, while he feared for the kingdom which he unjustly held, became the betrayer of the eternal King. For this Herod was neither of the Tribe of Juda, nor the House of David, and occupied the kingdom of the Jews by guile; and, by favour of the Romans, ruled it as tyrant. Accordingly he began to lie in wait for the Lord, Whom he now learns from the Jews is born King of the Jews. He inquires of them the time of the star's appearance, then sends them on their way to Bethlehem, as if he too desired to come and adore. He pretends solicitude to conceal his treachery. For he had in mind, not to adore, but to slay the Lord.

The Magi meanwhile, guided by the star, arrive at the place *where the Child was,* and there they knew the Creator of heaven. They sought not the guidance of a man because they had received from heaven the guidance of a star. Neither could they go astray, who were inquiring for the True Way, which is Christ the Lord Who has said: *I am the way, the truth, the life.* With every new wonder the star travels in the sky above them, and for the whole journey does not leave them, and at an equal pace they come together to Bethlehem, and there the star, standing still points out the Lord Our Saviour, the Only Son of God.

The Evangelist relates: *And seeing the star they rejoiced with exceeding great joy. And entering in to the house . . .*

Let us now see, after the star had come to rest, after the journey of the Magi, what wondrous dignity accompanies the Newborn King. For immediately the Magi, falling down before the Lord, adore Him Newlyborn, and lying in a Manger, and offering gifts they venerate the Infancy of a weeping Babe. With the eyes of their body they saw one thing, another with the eyes of the mind. The lowliness of the assumed Body is before their eyes, yet the glory of the Divinity is not concealed. It is a Child that is adored. And together with it the unspeakable mystery of the divine condescension! That invisible and eternal nature has not disdained, for our sakes, to take to Itself the infirmities of our flesh.

The Son of God, Who is the God of all things, is born a Man in body. He permits Himself to be placed in a crib, Who holds the heavens in His Hand. He is confined in a Manger whom the world cannot contain; He is heard in the voice of a wailing Infant, at Whose voice in the hour of His passion the whole earth trembled. The Magi, beholding a Child, profess that this is the Lord of Glory, the Lord of Majesty, Whom Isaias has shown was both Child and God, and King Eternal, saying: *for a CHILD is born to us, and a son is given to us, and the government is upon his shoulder: and his name shall be called Wonderful, Counsellor, God the Mighty, the Father of the World to come, the Prince of Peace* (Is. ix. 6).

To Him the Magi offer gifts, that is: gold, frankincense and myrrh; as the Holy Spirit had in time past testified concerning them: *All they from Saba shall come, bringing gold and frankincense: and showing forth praise to the Lord.* This prophecy is manifestly fulfilled by the Magi, who both announce the salvation of the Lord, born Christ the Son of God, and by their gifts proclaim Him Christ and God, and King of Man. For by gold the power of a king is signified, by frankincense the honour of God, by myrrh the burial of the body; and accordingly they offer Him gold as King, frankincense as God, myrrh as Man.

David also has testified concerning these things, in this way: *The Kings of Tharsis and the islands shall offer presents: the kings of the Arabians and of Saba shall bring gifts. And all kings of the earth shall adore Him: all nations shall serve Him* (Ps. lxxi. 10). And that he might show especially to whom these gifts would be offered, he adds: *And to him shall be given of the gold of Arabia.* The same David in another psalm is not silent regarding myrrh, as when speaking of the passion of the Lord, he says: *Myrrh and stacte and cassia perfume thy garments* (Ps. xliv. 9). Of myrrh Solomon, in the person of Christ, also speaks: *I yielded a sweet odour like the best myrrh* (Ecclus. xxiv. 20), in which he evidently testifies concerning the sepulture of

His Body, which by its most sweet and divine odour has made the whole earth fragrant. Lastly David also is seen to have foretold the Magi in figure, when he said: *Ambassadors shall come out of Egypt, Ethiopa shall soon stretch out her hand to God* (Ps. lxvii. 32). For since holy Scripture often speaks of this world as Egypt, rightly may we regard the Magi as the *ambassadors from Egypt*, who being chosen as legates for the whole world, dedicate, in the gifts they offer, the will to believe of all mankind, and the beginnings of the faith.

And after they had offered their gifts the Magi were warned that *they should not return to Herod*, and *they went back another way into their country*. In this they give us an example of virtue and faith, so that we too, having once known and adored Christ our King, and having forsaken the road that we formerly travelled, that is the way of our past errors, and travelling now another road with Christ as Guide, may return to our true country, which is Paradise, from which Adam was driven forth. Of this country the psalmist says: *I will please the Lord in the land of the living* (Ps. cxiv. 9).

The Magi being warned return home another way, frustrating the cruelty of the tyrant; and thus the Child born King is, by the Magi, made known to men, and the treachery of the tyrant Herod is brought to nothing. That Our Lord and Saviour as a Child would thus triumph, and in the very beginning of His Infancy, Isaias had of old made prophecy: *For before the Child know to call his father and mother, the strength of Damascus, and the spoils of Samaria shall be taken away before the king of the Assyrians* (Is. viii. 4). The gold that was offered by the Magi, and which the Son of God Born a Child has received, is interpreted as *the strength of Damascus*; *the spoils of Samaria* are the Magi themselves, whom He has drawn out of the error of the superstitions of Samaria, that is, the worship of idols; and who formerly because of their false religion were the spoil of the devil, now through the knowledge of Christ have become the spoil of God. The kings of the Assyrians means Herod, or at all events the devil, against whom the Magi stood forth as adversaries, namely, by adoring the Son of God, Our Lord and Saviour, Who is blessed for ever and ever. Amen.

IV. St Leo, Pope and Doctor

On the Solemnity of the Epiphany of Our Lord Jesus Christ.[17]

Synopsis:

I. Christ being born wills to be known by all men. He gives us the sign of the Star, and with it the grace of understanding and inquiry.

II. In vain does Herod rage against Christ. The Magi declare their faith by gifts.

III. Christ turns the wickedness of Herod to the good of the Infants. What virtues in the Infant God ought we to imitate.

I. Having celebrated in the recent festival the day in which the most pure Virgin gave birth to the Saviour of Mankind, the venerable feast of the Epiphany, Dearly Beloved, brings to us a continuation of joy, so that between the kindred mysteries of these linked solemnities, the liveliness of our rejoicing and the fervour of our faith, may not grow cool. For it was in view of the salvation of all men that the infancy of the Mediator between God and Man was revealed to the world while He was detained in the little village. For even though He had chosen the people of Israel, and one family among that people, from which to assume the nature of humanity; yet it was not His will that His Birth be concealed within the obscurity of His Mother's dwelling; He wished rather to become known at once to all men, since He had deigned to be born for all.

And so there appeared in the East, to the three Magi, a star of new splendour, which, being brighter and more beautiful than the other stars, would readily draw to itself the eyes and minds of all beholders, so that it would immediately be seen that a sight so strange had a special meaning. Then He Who set up the sign gave to those who beheld it an understanding of its meaning; and what He gave them to see, He led them to seek, and being sought for He let Himself be found. The three men follow the guide of this heavenly light, and journeying together, with eyes fixed upon the light going before them, they are led by the brightness of His grace to the knowledge of the Truth; they who believed, from human reasoning, that they must seek the newborn King, Whose sign they had seen, in the royal city. But He Who had taken the form of a servant, and had come not to judge but to be judged, chose Bethlehem for His birth, but Jerusalem for His passion.

II. Herod learning that a King was born to the Jews, and suspecting a successor, is in great fear; and while he is planning death for the Author of our salvation, he makes false promises of coming to pay homage to Him. How happy would he be had he imitated the faith of the Magi, and bestowed on religion what he gave to treachery. O blind impiety of senseless envy! Do you propose in your madness to defeat the divine will? The Lord of the world seeks no earthly kingdom, but bestows an eternal one. To what end do you strive to overthrow the unchangeable order of what has been decreed, or take upon yourself beforehand another's crime?

The death of Christ is not for your time. For before that the Gospel must be established, before that the kingdom of heaven has to be preached, the sick must be healed, miracles must be wrought. And why do you wish that to be your crime which is to be the work of another? And why, since your attempt must fail, do you bring upon yourself the guilt of an evil will? You will gain nothing by this contriving, you accomplish nothing. He that of His own will was born, will die at a time that He shall decide.

The Magi then fulfil their desire, and following this very star, they come at length to the Child, the Lord Jesus Christ. They adore the Word in our flesh, Wisdom in infancy, Power in weakness, and in true man the Lord of Majesty. And that they may make clear the mystery of their faith and understanding, that which they believe in their heart, they proclaim by their gifts. They offer incense to God, myrrh to man, and gold to a King, with knowledge adoring in unity the human nature and the divine: for what was proper to the persons is not separated from the Godhead.

III. The Magi return to their own country, and Jesus by divine warning is taken into Egypt, and the madness of Herod, foiled in its evil purpose, now flames up. He gives order that the little children of Bethlehem be put to death, and since he knows not who the infant may be Whom he fears, he extends the sentence to that age which is suspect to him. But that which the impious king cuts down in this world, Christ replants in heaven: and they for whom He has not yet given the ransom of His Blood, now receive the glory of martyrdom.

Therefore, Dearly Beloved, lift up your hearts to the shining grace of the sempiternal Light, and adoring the precious mysteries of man's redemption, give earnest thought to what has been done for you. Love the purity of chastity, because Christ is the Son of virginity. Refrain from carnal desires which war against the soul, as the Blessed Apostle presiding over us has, as we read, exhorted us in his own words (I Pet. ii. 11). In malice be children (I Cor. xiv. 20), the Lord of glory has subjected Himself to the childhood of mortal men.

Follow in the way of humility, which the Son of God deigned to show His Disciples (Mt. xi. 29). Clothe yourself with the strength of patience, in which you shall have the power to possess your souls; since He Who is the Redemption of all men, is also the strength of all men (Lk. xxi. 19). Mind the things that are above, not the things that are on the earth (Col. iii. 2). Walk in steadfastness along the way of truth and of life, and neither let things of earth ensnare you, for whom the things of heaven are prepared, through Jesus Christ Our Lord, Who with the Father and the Holy Spirit liveth and reigneth world without end. Amen.

V. St Leo, Pope and Doctor
For the Solemnity of the Epiphany II[18]

Synopsis:

I. Herod proclaims to the world that Christ is born when He attempts to remove Him from the world. Christ, flying into Egypt, prepares the way for the salvation of the Egyptians.

II. How much we are indebted to God is seen from the blindness of the Jews, who know Him not that they might slay Him.

III. More blessed the ignorance of the Children than the learning of the Jewish Priests. In His own Infancy Christ sanctifies the infancy of all children.

IV. The calling of the Magi is the beginning of our calling. Each should seek to offer like gifts, that we may unite with Christ working our salvation.

I. Rejoice in the Lord, Dearly Beloved, again I say rejoice (Phil. iv. 4): since in a brief while after Christ's birth, the solemn event of His manifestation to the world takes place: and He Whom the Virgin on that day brought forth, on this the world acknowledged Him. For the Word that was made flesh, has so ordered the beginnings of His life as man, that the newborn Jesus is made visible to those who believe in Him, and remains hidden from those seeking to destroy him.

Then indeed did the heavens proclaim the glory of God (Ps. xviii), and the sound of His truth went forth into all the earth (Rom. x, 18), when to the shepherds appeared the hosts of heaven, announcing the birth of the Saviour, and a star that went before them, led the Magi to adore Him; so that from the East unto the West, the birth of our true King might shine forth; since through the Magi the kingdoms of the East would learn the truths of faith, nor were they to be hidden from the empire of Rome.

Even the cruelty of Herod, seeking to destroy at birth Him Whom he feared might be king, ministers unawares to the purposes of God: so that while intent upon his horrid crime, and pursuing in the indiscriminate slaughter of the infants the Child that is unknown to him, he everywhere makes known, by a more extraordinary fame, the birth of the Ruler that was announced from the heavens: and both the strangeness of the heavenly sign, and the impiety of this most cruel tyrant, caused it to be more speedily and more precisely spoken of among men.

Then also the Saviour was carried into Egypt, so that a people given over to longstanding errors, would now be called, by this secret grace, to share the salvation that was nigh; and that they who had not yet rejected their ancient superstitions, might now receive the Truth as guest.

II. Fittingly, Dearly Beloved, is that day made sacred by the Epiphany of the Lord, held in special honour throughout the world; and it should also shine with becoming brightness in our hearts, so that not alone by faith but also by our understanding, we may show reverence to the course of these divine events. The blindness of the Jews proves to us what thanks we owe to God for the enlightenment of the Gentiles. Who so blind, who so inimical to the light, as these Priests and Scribes of Israel? They who to the inquiries of the Magi, and to the questioning of Herod as to where, according to the Scriptures, the Lord would be born, gave the same answer from the testimony of the prophet, as the Star proclaimed from heaven.

Which star could well, passing by Jerusalem, have brought them to the cradle of the Child, as it later did, were it not intended to trouble this obduracy of the Jews, by making the birth of the Saviour known, not alone by the guidance of a star, but also through their confession. Already therefore the prophetic voice had gone over to teaching the Gentiles, and the hearts of strangers begin to learn of the Christ Who was foretold by the ancient prophecies; since the infidelity of the Jews spoke truth with their mouth, while they kept falsehood in their heart. For they wished not to see Him with their eyes, of whom they gave evidence from the Scriptures: so that Him Whom they would not adore, lowly in the helplessness of infancy, they might afterwards crucify, shining in the fullness of manhood.

III. Whence in you, O Priests of Juda, this so faulty knowledge, this so unlearned learning? Asked where Christ was to be born you answer truthfully and from memory what you had read: In Bethlehem of Juda. For so it was written by the prophet: *And thou Bethlehem the land of Juda are not the least among the princes of Juda: for out of thee shall come the captain that shall rule my people Israel.* This prince that was born the angels announced to the shepherds, and the shepherds announced to you. Of this prince that was born the far distant peoples of the Eastern kingdoms have learned, through the strange splendour of a star. And lest they err as to the place where lay the newborn King, your learning betrayed what the star did not tell.

Why do you close to yourselves the way you open to others? Why does the doubt remain in your infidelity, which was made clear in your answer? The place of the nativity you point out from the testimony of Scripture, the time you learned from the testimony of both heaven and earth: yet when the mind of Herod flamed to destroy, your mind hardened in unbelief. Happier then the ignorance of the children whom the tyrant slew, than your learning to which in his disquiet he turned. You refused to accept His kingdom, Whose city you were able to proclaim. But they died for Him, who were as yet unable to confess Him.

And so Christ in silence used the power of the power of the Word, so that no years of His would be without their miracle; and as if already saying: *Suffer the little children to come to me, for the kingdom of heaven is for such* (Mt. xix. 14). He crowns children with a new glory, and in His own made sacred the infancy of all little ones: that we might learn that each age of man is capable of the divine mystery, since even this age was found ready for the glory of martyrdom.

IV. Let us then, Dearly Beloved, acknowledge in the Magi adoring

Christ, the first-fruits of our calling and of our faith, and with souls rejoicing, let us celebrate this beginning of our blessed hope. For from that time we began to enter into our eternal inheritance; from that time the words of Scripture that were obscure have revealed Christ to us; and the truth which the blindness of the Jews rejected, has shed its light upon all nations.

May this sacred day be therefore honoured among us, in which the Author of salvation revealed Himself to all men: and let us adore Omnipotent in heaven, Him Whom the Magi adored an Infant in His cradle. And as they from their treasures offered to the Lord mystic kinds of gifts, so let us bring forth from our hearts gifts that are worthy of Him. For though He is the Giver of all gifts, yet He also looks for the fruits of our diligence: for the kingdom of heaven is not given to those who sleep, but to those who labour and watch in the commandments of God; so that if we have not wasted His gift, through that which He gave us, let us merit to receive that which He promised.

Therefore we exhort your Charity, that you refrain yourselves from every evil work, and follow after those that are chaste and just (Rom. xiii. 12). For the children of light should cast from them the works of darkness. Accordingly, turn away from hatreds, put away lying, overcome pride with humility, cast out avarice, love bountifulness: for it is fitting that the members are in harmony with their Head, that we may merit to be sharers of His promised joys: through Jesus Christ Our Lord, Who with the Father and the Holy Spirit liveth and reigneth world without end. Amen.

VI. St Gregory: The Gifts of the Magi

Given to the People in the Basilica of the holy Apostle Peter on the day of the Epiphany[19]

1. As you have heard in the reading of the Gospel, Dearly Beloved, an earthly king was troubled when the King of heaven was born: for earthly supremacy is troubled when heavenly greatness appeared. But we must ask why it was that at the birth of the Redeemer an angel appeared to the shepherds of Judea, and a star not an angel, led the Magi from the East to adore Him? Because it was fitting that an angel, that is, a being of reason, should announce Him to the Jews, who used their reason to know God; while the Gentiles who knew not **how** to use their reason are led to **the** knowledge of God, not by a voice, but by signs. For this reason Paul also said: *Prophecies not to unbelievers, but to believers; a sign is not for believers, but for unbelievers* (I Cor. xiv. 22); because to the former prophecies were given, as to believers, not unbelievers; and to the latter signs were given, not as believers, but as unbelievers.

And we must note that the Apostles preached our Redeemer, come to man's age, to the Gentiles; and when He was a Child, and not yet able to use the organs of speech, a star proclaims Him to these same Gentiles: for the order of reason required that men, preachers, should make known the Lord, Who had spoken, and the mute elements Him that had not begun to speak.

2. But amid all the signs that appeared at the birth or death of the Lord, we must here consider the hardness of heart of the Jews, who would acknowledge Him neither through prophecies nor through miracles. Yet all elements bore witness that their Author had come. For if I may speak of them as if they were human, the heavens recognised Him as God, since forthwith they send a star. The sea knew Him as God, for it stood firm beneath His steps. The earth knew Him, for it trembled at His death. The sun knew Him, for it hid the light of its beams. The walls and rocks knew, for at His death they rent themselves asunder. Hell knew, for it gave up the dead it held. Yet He Whom all dumb elements proclaimed as Lord, the hearts of the unbelieving Jews will not accept as God, and, harder than the rocks, they will not dissolve in penance, refusing to accept Him Whom nature with signs and rendings of itself proclaim as God.

And to the increase of their condemnation, He Whom they despised in His birth, they long foreknew that He would be born. And not alone did they know that He was to be born, but they also foreknew where He was to be born. For when questioned by Herod they described the place of His birth, learned from the authority of the Scriptures. And they offer proof that Bethlehem will be honoured by the birth of the new Ruler, so that their very knowledge is at once a help to our faith, and a witness to their condemnation. It was indeed these whom the patriarch

Isaac signified when blessing his son Jacob; for being blind he saw not the son that stood before him, yet prophesying he beheld the greatness of his posterity: and so the Jews, blind, yet filled with the spirit of prophecy, Him for Whom they foretold great things to come, they now deny present in their midst (Gen. xxvii. 28).

3. But when Herod had learned that Our King was born, so that he shall not lose his kingdom, he turns his thoughts to treachery. He asks the Magi to return, to tell him where they find the Child, pretending that he too desires to come and adore Him, but so that he may destroy Him should he find Him. But what avails human cunning against the wisdom of God? For it is written: *There is no wisdom, there is no prudence, there is no counsel against the Lord* (Prov. xxii. 30). For the star, which had reappeared, guides the Magi: they find the newborn King: they offer Him their gifts, and in sleep they are warned that they must not return to Herod. And so it comes about that Herod cannot find Jesus Whom he is seeking. Who but hypocrites are here symbolised, who as long as they falsely seek, shall never merit to find the Lord?

4. But meanwhile you must know that the Priscillian heretics believe that every man is born subject to the rule of the stars, and they assume this to support their error, that a new star came out when the Lord appeared in the flesh, and they hold that this same star was His destiny. But if we reflect upon the words of the Gospel which speak of this very star: *Until it came and*

stood over the house where the child was, we see that it is not the Child that hastens to the star, but the star that hastens to the Child, and so, if I may say this, it is not the star that is the Child's fate, but rather it is the Child Who is the destiny of the star.

But far be it from the heart of the faithful to speak of anything as fate. For it is the Creator Who has made the lives of all men Who alone governs them. Man was not made for the stars, but rather the stars were made for man; and if a star can be called the ruler of man, then must man be considered the subject of his own servants. Now when Jacob was emerging from his mother's womb, he seized with his hand his brother's foot, and the first child could not come forth till he began to come who was following him; and though their mother brought them both into the world at one and the same time and moment, yet not one and the same was the lot of each one's life.

5. But to this the astrologers are wont to reply, that the influence of a particular star begins at a given point of time. To which we reply that there is usually a great slowness in birth. If therefore the star is assigned at a single point of time, it seems that when we must say that all who are born have as many fates as they have limbs.

And the astrologers also tell us, that whoever is born under the sign of Aquarius will follow in life the trade of a fisherman. Getulia (in the Libyan desert), I am told, has no fishermen. Who will say that no one in Getulia is born under the sign of Aquarius, although it has no fishermen? Again, they say that those born under Libra will all be moneylenders: yet the provinces of many nations know nothing of moneylenders. They must therefore admit, either that this sign does not appear there, or that if it does it has no significance as fate.

In the land of the Franks, and also among the Persians, kings come to the throne by way of descent. While such a person is being born, who can estimate how many others of servile condition are being born in these same moments? And yet the sons of kings, born in the same hour as the slaves, go on to a kingdom, while slaves born together with them die in slavery. We have spoken thus briefly concerning this star, so as not to seem to let pass the groundless nonsense of the astrologers.

6. The Magi come bearing gold, incense and myrrh. Gold is offered in tribute to a king, incense is offered in sacrifice to God, with myrrh the bodies of the dead are embalmed. The Magi therefore proclaim also by their mystic gifts, Who it is they adore; with gold they proclaim Him King, with incense that He is God, by myrrh that He is mortal.

There are heretics who believe that He is God, but they do not believe that He reigns everywhere. These indeed offer incense, but refuse to offer Him gold. There are others who believe He is a King, but deny He is God. These offer gold, but deny Him incense. And there are others who confess He is both God and King, but deny that He assumed a mortal body. Such as these offer Him gold and incense, but refuse the myrrh of His assumed mortality.

Let us then offer gold to the new-born Lord, that we may confess He reigns everywhere; let us offer incense, inasmuch as we believe that He Who appeared in time, was God before all time; let us offer myrrh, that as we believe He was impassible in His divinity, let us also believe that in our flesh He was mortal.

The gold, incense and myrrh we may interpret in yet another way. For by gold wisdom is also symbolised, as Solomon testifies: *Desirable treasure lies in the mouth of wisdom* (Prov. xxi. 10 (LXX)). By incense, which is burnt in honour of God, we signify the power of prayer, as the psalmist testifies who says: *Let my prayer be directed as incense in thy sight* (Ps. cxl. 2). By myrrh is symbolized the mortification of our flesh; whence it is that Holy Church says of her workers who have laboured for God until death: *My hands dropped with myrrh* (Cant. v. 5).

To the newborn King we offer Gold, if we shine before Him in the brightness of heavenly wisdom. We offer Him incense, if we consume the thoughts of the flesh upon the altar of our heart, so that in our heavenly desires we send up to God an odour of sweetness. We offer Him myrrh, when we mortify through abstinence the vices of our flesh. For by myrrh, as we have said, we preserve dead flesh from corruption. And we say that flesh is corrupt when this mortal body is given over to wantonness, as was said of certain people by the prophet: *The beasts have rotted in their dung* (Joel i. 17). For beasts to rot in their dung means, that carnal men will end their lives amid the foulness of their lust. Therefore do we offer myrrh to God, when we safeguard this mortal body of ours from the corruption of wantonness by the preservatives of chastity.

7. In that they return to their own land by another way, the Magi intimate to us something of great importance. In doing that which they were bidden to do, they convey to us what we must do. It is paradise that is our true country, to which, having come to know Jesus, we are forbidden to return by the way we came. For we left our land by the way of pride and disobedience, by following after the things of this world, by tasting forbidden food; and so we must return to it by the way of tears, by obedience, by contempt of the world, and by restraining the desires of the flesh.

Let us return then to our own country by another way, and since we cut ourselves off from the joys of heaven because of earthly delights, let us recover them again through penance. So, Dearly Beloved, we must in fear and watchfulness ever keep before our eyes, both the guilt of our offences and the sentence of the last judgement. Let us remember how strict is He Who comes as Judge; Who now is hidden, though He warns us of judgement; Who threatens sinners with chastisements, yet still suffers them; Who delays His judgement, that He may find fewer to condemn.

Let us punish our offences with tears, and, with the voice of the psalmist, let us come before His presence with thanksgiving (Ps. xciv. 2). Let therefore no enticement of sensual pleasure deceive us, and no vain delight seduce us. For the Judge is close at hand Who said: *Woe to you that now laugh: for you shall mourn and weep* (Lk. v. 5). For Solomon too says of these things: *Laughter shall be mingled with sorrow, and mourning taketh hold of the end of joy* (Prov. xiv. 13). And again he says: *Laughter I counted error: and of mirth I said: why art thou vainly deceived* (Eccles. ii. 2). And of this again he says: *The heart of the wise is where there is mourning, and the heart of fools where there is mirth* (Eccles vii. 5).

If we are truly celebrating a solemnity of God, let us fear exceedingly the commandments of God. And a sacrifice that is pleasing to God, is sorrow because of sin, as the psalmist bears witness: *A sacri-* *fice to God is an afflicted spirit* (Ps. l. 19). When we received baptism our past sins were wiped away; we have committed many since then, but we cannot again be washed in the waters of baptism. Since, therefore, after our baptism we have again stained our soul, let us cleanse our conscience with tears, thus returning to our own land by another way; we who, delighting in the good things of the world, have departed from it, let us, embittered of its evils, hasten to return to it, by the help and grace of Our Lord Jesus Christ, Who with the Father and the Holy Spirit, liveth and reigneth world without end. Amen.

NOTES

[1] Cf. Contra Faust. II, 5 (CSEL 26, 259).

[2] Cf. PG 57. 64.

[3] This passage is from sermo 374, De Epiph. PL 39, 1666, Sermones Dubii; listed as doubtful also in PRM 39.

[4] This work Qu. Vet N. Test., is now considered inauthentic.

[5] Sermon on the Nativity of the Lord Jesus.

[6] Sermo 131, Epiph I, PL 39, 2006, now attributed to St Optatus.

[7] This passage is not verifiable in any of the known sermons of the saint on this feast; it may be a summary of sermon 199, 2, PL 38.

[8] This homily (vide PL 39, Appendix, serm. 131, 6) now attributed to St Optatus. PRM 39.

[9] Possibly sermo 373; doubtful, PRM 39.

[10] As compared with the Magi, of whom it is simply said that, *they received an answer in sleep*, while to Joseph *an angel of the Lord appeared*.

[11] PL 15, 1568, 2 in Luc.

[12] From Vetus Itala (based on Septuagint).

[13] PG 57, 81, sermo 8.

[14] This sermon speaks of the great flowering of the Christian life, of almost the whole Egyptian nation seeking perfection, and of St Anthony of the Desert.

[15] Life of St Anthony, by St Athanasius of Alexandria.

[16] Cf. Combefis BPC tom. 2, 56 seq. Hom. I ex variis in Matth; edited Basle 1525, tom. 5. Codices Florence, Laur. 17 (saec 11) in. 37, 0.85, lists it as of St Ambrose; Laur. 17, 42 (saec 11), n. 31, p. 74, attributes it to Johnn. *Osaurei*. This pious and instructive homily cannot be regarded as of St John Chrysostom, but is included because of its venerable antiquity, and simple authority and dignity, as a testimony to the early existing devotion to this great Feast.

[17] PL 54, 234.   [18] Pl 54, 237.

[19] PL 74, 1110, hom. 10 on the Gospels.

SUNDAY WITHIN THE OCTAVE OF THE EPIPHANY, AND FEAST OF THE HOLY FAMILY

I. Origen The Child Jesus in the Temple

II. Origen: The Wisdom of the Child Jesus

III. St Ambrose: On the Gospel

IV. St Bernard: The Feast of the Holy Family

V. St Ælred: Jesus Twelve Years Old

THE GOSPEL OF THE SUNDAY

Luke ii. 42–52

And when Jesus was twelve years old, they going up into Jerusalem, according to the custom of the feast, and having fulfilled the days, when they returned, the child Jesus remained in Jerusalem; and His parents knew it not. And thinking that He was in the company, they came a day's journey, and sought Him among their kinsfolk and acquaintances.

And not finding Him, they returned into Jerusalem, seeking Him. And it came to pass, that, after three days, they found Him in the temple, sitting in the midst of the doctors, hearing them, and asking them questions. And all that heard Him were astonished at His wisdom and His answers. And seeing Him, they wondered.

And His mother said to Him: Son, why hast thou done so to us? behold Thy father and I have sought Thee sorrowing. And He said to them: How is it that you sought me? Did you not know, that I must be about my father's business? And they understood not the word that He spoke unto them. And He went down with them, and came to Nazareth, and was subject to them. And His mother kept all these words in her heart. And Jesus advanced in wisdom, and age, and grace with God and men.

Exposition from the Catena Aurea

Cyril, *Catena G.F.*: Since the Evangelist had said that the Child grew and waxed strong, he thereupon verifies his words, and shows Jesus going up to Jerusalem together with the sacred Virgin. Hence he says: *And when He was twelve years old, they going into Jerusalem.*

GEOMETER, *Catena G.F.*: Not that the unveiling of His wisdom exceeded the measure of His years; but when as with us the age of discretion is usually attained, that is, in the twelfth year, the wisdom of Christ was made known.

AMBROSE, *in Luke* ii. 32: Or, the beginning of the Lord's Disputation is reckoned from His twelfth year. For here the number of those announcing the faith that was to be made known ought to be commemorated. BEDE *in Luke*: This we may here affirm: that because by the septenary number, as by the duodenary (which is made up from the parts of the · septenary number multiplied by each other) the whole universe of things and events and their perfection is signified; and accordingly that He may teach in what manner all places and times are to be employed, the divine Light of Christ rightly makes a beginning from the number twelve.

BEDE, *in Hom. Dom. infra oct. Epiph.*: That Our Lord went each year with His parents to Jerusalem for the Pasch is an indication of His humility as man. For it is in the nature of men to come together to offer sacrifice to God, and to join in prayer to Him. The Lord, therefore, born a man among men, did that which God commanded by His angels.[1] Hence it is said: *According to the custom of the feast.* Let us then imitate the way of His earthly converse among men if we desire to rejoice in the vision of His glory.

GEOMETER: The feast being over and the others having departed, Jesus secretly remains behind. Hence

there follows: *And having fulfilled the days, when they returned, the child Jesus remained in Jerusalem; and his parents knew it not.* He says: *Having fulfilled the days*; for the solemnity continued for seven days. He then remains, secretly, lest His parents be a hindrance to the disputations He was about to hold with the Doctors of the Law. Or perhaps, putting this reason aside, that He might not appear to despise them if He did not obey their commands. He therefore remains secretly lest He be either brought back, or become disobedient.

ORIGEN, *Hom.* 19 *in Luke*: We need not wonder they are called parents, since one, by giving Him birth, the other through obedience, merited the names of mother and father. BEDE *in Luke*: But someone may ask how could the Son of God, cherished with such care by His parents, be forgotten and left behind? To which we answer, that it was the custom of the children of Israel that when they were either going or returning from Jerusalem at the time of the festival that men and women journeyed separately: infants and children could go with one or other parent as they pleased; hence we have: *Thinking he was in the company.*

ORIGEN: As when the Jews rose up against Him and He passed through the midst of them (Lk. iv. 29; also Jn. viii. 59; x. 39), so now I believe did the Child Jesus remain, and His parents did not know that He had remained; for there follows: *And not finding him, they returned into Jerusalem, seeking Him.* GLOSS: On one day they travel home from Jerusalem. On the next they search among their kindred and friends, and not finding Him with them they return on the third day to Jerusalem and there they find Him. Hence: *And it came to pass that after three days they found him in the temple.*

ORIGEN: He is not found immediately He is looked for; nor is He found among cousins and kindred of the flesh; no mere human tie could stand in the way of the Son of God. He is not found among the famous of the world, because He is above all fame. He is not found *in the company* of those travelling; they find him nowhere but in the Temple. And you must therefore seek Him there in the Temple, seek Him in the Church, where you will find the Word and the Wisdom of Christ, that is, of the Son of God.

AMBROSE: After three days He is found in the Temple for, a sign that after the three days of His triumphal passion, He rising up that was believed dead, would reveal Himself to our faith in the heavenly Seat, surrounded with divine honour. GLOSS: Or, because, the Coming of Christ was sought first by the Patriarchs, before the Law, and was not found; secondly, it was sought by the prophets and by the just, under the Law, and not found; it was then sought for by the Gentiles, under the dispensation of grace, and found.

ORIGEN, as above: Because He was the Son of God He was found in the midst of the Doctors, giving them wisdom, and instructing them; because He was a little boy He is found in their midst, not teaching, but asking them questions; hence: *they found Him, sitting*

in the midst of the doctors, hearing them and asking them questions; and this was a task of piety, that He might teach us what is becoming to the young, although they be wise and learned, that they should rather desire to hear their Masters than wish to teach them, and not leave themselves open to idle boasting. He questioned, not that He might learn, but that by questioning He might instruct. For to question and to answer wisely flows from the same source of knowledge. Hence: *and all that heard were astonished.*

BEDE: To show He was a Man He humbly listened to men as to teachers: to show that He was God He answers these same with Wisdom from on high. GEOMETER: He questions reasonably, He listens prudently, and replies yet more prudently; at which *they were astonished.* CHRYSOSTOM, *Hom.* 20 *in John*: The Lord performed no miracles in His Childhood. Luke however discloses this single event, through which He is seen to be astonishing. BEDE: The divine tongue showed forth the divine wisdom, but the tender years give the semblance of human frailty. Hence the Jews, between the sublimity of what they hear, and the lowliness of what they see, are troubled with doubting wonder. We however do not wonder, knowing from the Prophet Isaias that the Child that is thus born to us remains still *God the Mighty* (Is. ix. 6).

GEOMETER: The most admirable Mother of God, sorrowing in her Maternal heart makes anguished inquiries, as if with tears, and as a

mother puts all into words, truthfully, humbly, and lovingly. Hence:
*And His mother said to Him: Son,
why hast thou done so to us? Behold
thy father and I have sought thee sorrowing.* ORIGEN, *Homily* 19: The
sacred Virgin knew that He was not
the son of Joseph, and yet calls her
spouse His father, because of the
Jews, who commonly regarded
Him as conceived. *Homily* 17: It
may perhaps be said simply that the
Spirit honoured him with the name
of father because he had nurtured
the Child Jesus; but legally, because
the genealogy of Joseph descended
from David, and lest the genealogy
be considered superfluous, he is
called father. *Homily* 19: Why did
they seek Him sorrowing? Was it
that He had perished or strayed?
Far from it. Was it possible they
feared that the Child could be lost
Whom they knew to be the Lord?
But it was as when you are reading
Scripture, and you seek with pain
to find the meaning within it, not
that you think that the Scripture
has erred, or narrated something
wrongly, but you strive to find the
truth that is hidden there. So they
sought for Jesus, lest perhaps leaving
them He might have returned to
heaven, whence He would again
descend when it pleased Him.
Whoever therefore seeks Jesus must
not seek Him carelessly, or disconnectedly, as many seek but do not
find Him; but with toil and anxiety.

GLOSS: Or they were fearful lest
what Herod had sought to accomplish when Jesus was an Infant,
now, grown into boyhood, others,
finding an opportunity, might
achieve. GEOMETER: But the Lord
Himself replied to all their anxieties,
and correcting in a certain measure

her saying regarding him who was
reputed His father, revealed His
true Father; teaching that here He
walked not with weak footsteps,
but that He was raised on high.
Hence follows: *and he said to them:
how is it that you sought Me?* BEDE
Not that He chides them for seeking Him as a son, but rather He
compels them to raise the eyes of
their mind to what is due to Him
of Whom He is the Eternal Son.
Hence: *Did you not know, that I must
be about my Father's business?*

AMBROSE: There are two generations in Christ, one paternal the
other maternal; the Paternal is the
more (*divinior*), the maternal is that
in which He has descended for our
need and benefit. CYRIL, *in the
Catena of G.F.*: He said this showing
that He passed above the measure
of men; and intimating that the
sacred Virgin had been made the
Handmaid of a purpose when she
brought forth a man. He Himself
was naturally and truly God and
Son of the Heavenly Father. Hence
let the followers of Valentinus,
reading that it was the Temple of
God, be ashamed to say that the
Creator, and the God of the
Temple, and of the Law, was not
the Father of Christ.

EPIPHANIUS, *contra Haer. I* 32: Let
Ebion note carefully that it was
after twelve years, and not after His
thirtieth year, that Christ is found
to be astonishing in utterances of
power. Accordingly, it may not
be said that after the Spirit descended
upon Him in baptism He became
the Christ, that is, *was anointed with
divinity*, but that from His very
Childhood He acknowledged both
Temple and Father. GEOMETER:

This was the first showing of the wisdom and power of the Child Jesus. To speak, here of boyish actions (*puerilia*) we believe to be the conception of a diabolic mind, and of a perverse intention, and of one striving to calumniate that which is contained in the Gospel, and in Sacred discourses; unless one wishes to take them in the sense in which they are received by many, and as not opposed to anything we believe, yet more in accord with prophetic phrases; for he was *beautiful above the sons of men*, obedient to His mother, calm and pleasing in countenance, eloquent, graceful, and prudent in speech, learning with alacrity, as one replete with wisdom. And as in other things, though above man, He was also the perfection and model of human behaviour and discourse; gentleness seeming to have in Him its special abode. Besides all this, nothing, no human hand, save His Mother's, ever touched the crown of His head.

From this we may draw a lesson. For while the Lord chides Mary for seeking Him among their kinsfolk, He aptly suggests the giving up of the ties of blood; showing that he does not reach the goal of perfection who is still preoccupied with those things that pertain to the body; and that through attachment to kindred a man falls short of perfection.

And they understood not the word that He spoke to them. BEDE: Because namely, He spoke to them of His divinity. ORIGEN, *Homily* 20: Or they did not know whether in saying: *that I must be about my father's business*, He signifies *in the temple*, or something higher, and which edified yet more: for each one of us, if he be good, is an abode of God the Father. If God the Father dwell with us, there in the midst of us is Jesus.

And he went down with them, and came to Nazareth, and was subject . . . GEOMETER: The whole intermediate life of Christ, which lay between His manifestation to the Gentiles and His baptism, being without any famous and public miracle or teaching, is recorded by the Evangelist under one phrase: *And He went down*.

ORIGEN: Not always does He dwell on the mountain tops: frequently He descends with His Disciples. For they who are afflicted with various miseries are unable to ascend the mountain. And so He now comes down to those that are below.

And was subject to them. GEOMETER: Sometimes instituting a law by word, He then fulfils it in Person, by some accompanying work, as that recorded by John (x. 11): *The Good Shepherd lays down his life for his sheep.* For He a little later lays down His life for our salvation. Sometimes having given an example of how we should live, afterwards by word of mouth He lays down an obligation, as here. But three things He especially taught us by example: to love God, to honour our parents, but to place God before our parents. When however He was reproved by His parents, He considers other things as of lesser concern than those of God: then in due order He renders obedience to His parents.

BEDE: What does the Teacher of virtue do here but fulfil the duties of virtue? What does He ever do in our midst but that which He wishes that we should do? ORIGEN:

Let us therefore who are children learn from Him to be subject to our parents, and if we no longer have our parents, then, be subject to those that are of the age of our parents. Jesus the Son of God is subject to Joseph and Mary. I am subject to the bishop, who is to me as a father. I believe that Joseph knew that Jesus was greater than he, and so with trepidation ruled Him. Let each one remember that oftentimes he that is the subject is the greater: which if he understands he will not swell with pride who is higher in dignity, being aware that his subject is more worthy.

GREGORY NYSSA, *in Catena G.P.*: Moreover, since children have not yet full discretion, and require to be guided by their elders to a more formed state of mind, so, when He was in His twelfth year He obeyed His parents, that He might show that whatever is accomplished by degrees, before the goal is reached, obedience, as leading to that good, is profitably embraced.

BASIL, *Monastic Institutions*: Obedient to His parents from His earliest years, He humbly and reverently undertook any corporal labour. For when just and worthy men are poor and in want of what is necessary, as witness the use of a manger at the sacred Childbirth, they will be familiar with the bodily toil of those that must strive for the necessities of life. Jesus being obedient to His parents, as the Scripture testifies, was fully obedient to them likewise in sharing such labours.

AMBROSE, *in Luke Bk.* 2, 65: Do you wonder He obeyed the Father

that was subject to His Mother? This is the submission of filial piety, not of weakness. Though the heretical serpent raises his head to say, that he who is sent stands in need of the help of others. Did He need human help that He might obey His Mother? He obeyed the Handmaid, He obeyed His reputed father; need you wonder if He obeyed God? Or is it a virtue to obey man, but a sign of infirmity to obey God?

BEDE: The Blessed Virgin, either because she understood, or because she could not yet understand, in either case kept all these words in her heart, as though to turn them over in her mind and more closely examine them; hence we have: *And His Mother kept* . . . GEOMETER: Consider the most prudent woman Mary, Mother of true wisdom, as the pupil of her Son. For she learned from Him, not as from a Child, or man, but as from God. More she dwelt in meditation on His words and actions; therefore nothing of what was said or done by Him fell idly on her mind; but as before, when she conceived the Word Itself in her womb, so now does she hold within her His ways and words, cherishing them as it were in her heart; and that which she now beholds in the present, she waits to have revealed with greater clarity in the future. And this practice she followed as a rule and law through all her life.

And Jesus advanced in wisdom, and age, and grace with God and man.

THEOPHYLACTUS: Nor that as He grew He became more wise, but that He unveiled His Wisdom gradually. He did this in speaking with the Scribes, asking them questions with regard to the Law; to the astonishment of all who heard Him. You see how it was that He advanced in wisdom, in that His wisdom began to be known by many, and *they wondered at Him.* The progress then of His wisdom consists in the manner of its being shown. Note how the Evangelist interprets what is meant here by advancing in wisdom: for he adds immediately: *and age*; for the increase in age is, he says, itself the growth of wisdom.

CYRIL, *in Thesaurus of the Trinity, Ass.* 28: But they (the Eunonian heretics) say: "How can He be equal to the Father in His substance, Who, as though He were imperfect, is said to grow?" But not in that He is the Word is He said to grow; but in that He has become man, and bearing a nature that is capable of growth. As the Word He does not grow. He is perfect as is the Father. That which is said of Him by the Evangelist is because of the manner of human growth. If the Word had grown when it was made man, and bore our flesh, then the Incarnation would have been no gain to us, but rather the flesh would have brought gain to It. For if the Word advanced when It was made flesh, then It was imperfect before the Incarnation and now becomes perfect: (according to the Eunonian heretics).

How then if He is the true wisdom can He be increased in it? How does He Who gives grace to others receive an increase in it Himself? How do we render Him thanks, as made flesh for us, when He ought rather attribute His perfection to the flesh He has received?

But this is absurd. He had not therefore, as the Word, advanced in wisdom. This is said only because of the regulation of the growth of the flesh.

Paul elsewhere says of the Son, that He humbled Himself, taking the form of a servant. If then no one is offended by this saying, nor when anyone hears that He humbled himself, do they think lowly of the Word of God, but rather wonder at His condescension. Is it not then absurd to stumble when we read that He advanced in wisdom, and age, and grace? And since it was for us He humbled Himself, so also was it for us He wished to advance, that we in turn, in Him, may advance in wisdom, who before were in the darkness of sin? All our disabilities Christ took upon Himself, for our sakes, that He might bring us to a better state, and that in man He might make a beginning of every good.

A certain natural law forbids that a man be not endowed with more wisdom than the age of the body sustains, but that wisdom grow in us at equal pace with the body's growth. The Word had become man in flesh, as it is written. He was perfect. He was the Wisdom and Knowledge of the Father. Since however as man He had to endure the manner of growth of His nature (lest He seem strange and diverse from it) so, with His body's growth, He revealed Himself to those who saw and heard Him as growing in wisdom from day to day.

AMPHILOCHIUS, *in Catena G.P.*: He advanced therefore *in age*, His body advancing towards manhood; *in wisdom*, by means of those who, by Him, were instructed in divine things; *in grace*, by which we go forward in joy, believing that we shall in the end obtain the things He has promised; and this *with God*, because having taken flesh He was doing the work His Father gave Him to do; *and men*, through their conversion from the worship of idols to the knowledge of the Supreme Trinity. THEOPHYLACTUS: The Evangelist says: *with God and men*, because it behoves us first to please God, and afterwards to please men. GREGORY NYSSA, *Homily 3 in Cant.*: Diversely does the Word advance in those who receive it. According to each one's measure does he appear as an infant, an adult, or as perfected.

I. ORIGEN, PRIEST AND CONFESSOR
The Child Jesus in the Temple[2]

When He was twelve years old He remained in Jerusalem. His parents not knowing where He was seek earnestly everywhere for Him, but do not find Him. They seek Him among their friends, they seek Him in the company travelling, they seek Him among the people they know, and among all these they do not find Him. Jesus is therefore sought for by His parents, by the father who is his guardian, and was the companion of His flight into Egypt; and yet when He is looked for He is not found. Jesus is not found among His kindred and blood relations; not among those who have bodily ties with Him. In the company of the throng my Jesus cannot be found. Learn where those who seek Him will find Him; that you, seeking with Mary and Joseph may find Him.

And *seeking Him*, says the Evangelist, *they found Him in the Temple*. Not anywhere, but in the temple. And not simply in the temple, but sitting in the midst of the doctors, hearing them and asking them questions. Do you therefore seek Him in the temple of God: seek Him in the Church: seek Him among the teachers who are in the temple, and who depart not from it. If you so seek Him you will find Him. Further, if anyone calls himself a teacher, and has not Jesus with Him, he is a teacher only in name, and with such a one Jesus the Word of God, and His Wisdom, cannot be found.

They find Him, says the Evangelist, *sitting in the midst of the doctors*. As it was written in another place, regarding the prophets, so here understand with regard to sitting in the midst of the doctors. *If* says the Apostle, *anything be revealed to another sitting, let the first hold his peace* (I Cor. xiv. 30). They find Him sitting in the midst of the doctors, and not alone sitting there, but questioning them, and listening to their answers. Even now Jesus is in our midst; He questions us, and listens to our answers.

And all that heard Him were astonished. For what reason were they astonished? Not because of His questions, which also were admirable but *at His answers*. It is one thing to put questions, another to answer them. He questions the teachers, and because they could not reply, He Himself answers the questions which He had asked. That His replies were not merely an exchange of speech, but that they spoke of the wisdom contained in the sacred Scriptures, the divine law teaches thee. *Moses spoke, and God answered him* (Ex. xix. 19). That answer was upon those things which Moses knew not, and in which the Lord instructed him. Sometimes Jesus questions, sometimes He replies, as we said above: and truly astonishing are His questions, yet more wondrous are His replies.

That we may therefore hear His words, that He may put questions to us, which He Himself will answer, let us beseech Him, let us seek Him in much labouring, and with sorrow of spirit, and then we shall be able to find Him Whom we seek. For not idly was it written: *Thy father and I have sought Thee sorrowing.* He who seeks Jesus, let him not seek carelessly, or casually, or for the passing moment; as many

seek Him, and so cannot find Him. Let us however say to Him: We have sought thee sorrowing. And when we have said this, He will make answer to our labouring soul that has sought Him with anguish and He will say: *Did you not know, that I must be about my father's business?*

Where are the insane and impious heretics who say that the Law and the Prophets of the Father do not belong also to Jesus Christ? Jesus was indeed in the Temple, which had been built by Solomon, and He confesses that this is the Temple of His Father, Whom He has revealed to us, Whose Son He declared Himself to be. Let them explain how the one God is just, the other good. Since therefore the Saviour is the Son of the Creator, we praise in One the Father and Son, of Whom is both the Law and the Temple. To Whom be glory and empire for ever and ever, Amen.

II. Origen, Priest and Confessor
The Wisdom of the Child Jesus[3]

Although there are men who appear to believe that the Sacred Scriptures, in order to safeguard the glory of the Omnipotent God, deny the divinity of the Saviour, to me it seems well founded that they are taught that the divinity has come to us in a human body: and not alone in a human body, but also in a human soul. Although if we look carefully to the content of the Sacred Writings we find that this soul had something more than the souls of other men. For the soul of every man until he reaches virtue is stained with many sins. But the soul of Jesus was never stained with the blemish of sin. For even before He had come to His twelfth year, the

Holy Spirit writes of Him in the Gospel of Luke: *The Child grew, and waxed strong, full of wisdom.*

It is not in the nature of men to be full of wisdom before they have reached their twelfth year. It is one thing to partake of wisdom, another to be filled with wisdom. We have then no doubt that something divine appeared in the flesh of Jesus: not alone exceeding man, but every other rational creature also. *The Child grew*, he says. For He had humbled Himself, taking upon Himself the form of a servant; and by that same power whereby He humbled Himself He also grew. He had appeared as something imperfect, because He had assumed an imperfect body, and for this reason also He grew strong.

The Son of God had emptied Himself (Phil. ii. 7), and wherefore was He then filled with wisdom. *And the grace of God was in Him.* Not alone when He came to young manhood, and when He taught openly; but while He was yet a Child the grace of God was in Him: and as in Him all things were wonderful, so also was His Childhood wondrous, because He was full of the wisdom of God.

And so His parents went up according to custom for the solemnities of the Pasch: *And when he was twelve years old.* Carefully observe that before He was twelve years old He was filled with the wisdom of God and the other virtues which are written of concerning Him. When therefore, as we have said, He was twelve years old, and when the days of the Feast were completed according to the custom, and when His parents and the little Boy would likewise have returned, the Boy remained in Jerusalem and His parents were not aware of it.

And here we are to understand something that far surpassed mere human nature. For He did not simply remain behind, and His parents were merely ignorant of His whereabouts. It was rather as we read in the Gospel of John (Jn. viii. 59), where the Jews rose up against Him, but He *passing through the midst of them went His way.* So now I believe did He remain in Jerusalem, and His parents did not know He remained.

Neither should we wonder that they are called His parents, since one of them, in giving Him birth, and the other through obedience, merited the names of mother and father. And so there follows: *Thy father and I have sought thee sorrowing.* I do not think that they grieved through thinking that the Boy had lost His way or disappeared; for it could not happen, that Mary, who knew she had conceived of the Holy Spirit, and who had heard the angel announcing, and had seen the shepherds come in haste, and had heard Simeon speaking in prophecy, would fear that the Child be lost through wandering. Put away this notion, especially with regard to Joseph whom an angel had commanded to take the Child and fly into Egypt (Mt. ii. 13) and who had heard the words: *Fear not to take unto thee Mary thy wife, for that which is conceived in her, is of the Holy Ghost.* It would never happen he should be in fear that this Child Whom he knew was divine should be lost. Far other is the grief and anxiety of the parents than a simple reader might think.

It is as when you, if you are reading the Scriptures, seek to find the sense that is hidden there, and this with a certain pain and grief of mind; not that you believe the Scriptures have erred, but because you cannot yourself reach the true and mystic sense within. So do they seek, grieving lest He has gone from them, and leaving them has passed on to other things, or lest, and this I find myself disposed to think, He may have returned to heaven, whence He would return when it pleased Him.

Because He was a Child they find Him in the midst of teachers, sanctifying them, and instructing them. Because He was a Child He is found in their midst, not teaching them, but asking them questions;

this was in accordance with what was becoming to His age: that He might teach us what is becoming to the young, even though they are intelligent and well instructed: that they should rather listen to their instructors than seek to teach others, and not lay themselves open to empty boasting.

He was questioning the teachers of the Law, not, I say, that He may learn something from them, but that asking He may instruct them. For from the one Fount of wisdom does it come to ask questions and to answer wisely; and to the same wisdom does it belong to know what to ask and what to answer. It was necessary to become a master of wise questioning that afterwards He might answer according to the word and the wisdom of God, to Whom be glory and honour for ever and ever. Amen.

III. St Ambrose: On the Gospel[4]

And when he was twelve years old. The public teaching of the Lord had, as we read, its beginning from His twelfth year, for herein should be foreshadowed the number of those announcing the faith that was to be preached. Nor was it that He was heedlessly unmindful of His parents according to the flesh, Who in the flesh was filled with grace and wisdom, that He was found in the Temple after three days, but for a sign that He that was believed dead would present Himself to our faith, risen in heavenly glory and divine honour after the three days of that triumphal passion.

How is it that you sought me? Did you not know that I must be about my Father's business? There are two generations in Christ: the one is Paternal, the other maternal; that which is Paternal is more divine (*divinior*), the maternal that whereby He has stooped to our need and benefit. And therefore what was accomplished in a manner above nature, above age, above what was usual, must not be ascribed to His human excellence, but must be referred to the power of His divinity.

Elsewhere His mother pleads with Him for a miracle: here she requires of Him a reason, since she still looks to the things that are human. But while here He is described as being but twelve years old, there He is spoken of as having disciples. See how the mother has learned to know her Son, so that she seeks a miracle from Him now in His full strength, who was astonished at this wonder in His boyhood.

He came to Nazareth, and was subject to them. What is the Master of virtue doing here but fulfilling the duties of filial piety? Are we to be astonished that He obeys His Father Who was obedient to His mother? A subjection this, not of dependence, but of filial love; and let the snake, emerged from his evil lair, uplift his head of heresy to jet forth poison from his abject breast.[5] When the Son says that He *is sent* (Jn. viii. 29), the heretic then declares that the Father must be the greater, and this that he may prove that the Son is imperfect, since He acknowledges that there is a greater than Himself; and that he may assert that he that *is sent* is dependent on the help of others.

Did He require human help that He might obey the will of His Mother? He was obedient to man,

He was obedient to His Handmaid (for she said, *Behold the handmaid of the Lord*), He was obedient to His reputed father, and you are surprised that He should be obedient to God? Or is it a virtue to obey man, but a sign of imperfection to obey God? Learn even from human things to weigh carefully what is divine, and acknowledge what is due to the Father of love. The Father *glorifieth the Son* (Jn. viii. 43, 59); and would you not have the Son glorify the Father? The Father by a voice from heaven proclaims that in His Son He is well pleased; would you not have the Son, clothed in the garment of our humanity, declare with human voice and human affection that the Father is greater than He? (Jn. xiv. 28). For if *great is the Lord, and greatly to be praised, and of his greatness there is no end* (Ps. cxlvi. 5), it is a greatness which truly has no end, and receives no increase. Why do I not accept with devout mind that the Son, in the taking on of flesh, is obedient to the Will of the Father, when I piously accept that the Father pays honour to the Son?

Learn rather the precepts that are profitable; and acknowledge what are true examples of filial piety.

Learn what you owe to your own parents as often as you read that the Son departed not from His Father, either in will, or in work, or in time; for though they are two in Person, in Power they are One. Yet this heavenly Father has endured nothing of the labours of generation. To your mother you owe the invasion of her modesty, the loss of virginity, the peril of childbearing. For you she suffered wearisome illness, prolonged anxiety: her pangs in the very fruition of her vows were a still greater trial. And when she has brought forth that which she desired, she is delivered of childbirth, but not of care. And what shall I say of the father's anxieties, for the future life of his children, their number added to for others' gain: seeds scattered as by a farmer, for the benefit of future generations?

Ought you not for all these things pay them back at least with filial reverence? Why should the life of a father seem too prolonged to an unfilial son, or the common inheritance too straitened, when Christ Himself sought co-heirs of His own inheritance: Who liveth and reigneth world without end, Amen.

IV. St Bernard, Abbot and Doctor

The Feast of the Holy Family[6]

In Mary we praise that which places her above all others, that is, fruitfulness of offspring together with virginity. For never has it been known in this world that anyone was at the same time mother and virgin. And see of Whom she is mother. Where does your astonishment at this so wondrous dignity lead you? Is it not to this, that

you may gaze in wonder yet never sufficiently revere? Is she not in your veneration, nay, in the esteem of Truth itself, raised above choirs of angels? Does not Mary address the Lord and God of all the angels as Son, saying: *Son, why hast thou done so to us?*

Who among the angels may thus presume? It is enough for them, and for them their greatest honour, that while they are spirits by nature they have become and are called *angels*, as David testifies: *Who makest thy angels spirits* (Ps. ciii. 4). Mary, knowing herself a mother, with confidence calls that Majesty Son Whom the angels in reverence serve. Nor does God disdain to be called that which He disdained not to be. For the Evangelist adds a little later: *He was subject to them.*

Who was subject to whom? A God to men. God, I repeat, to Whom the angels are subject: Whom principalities and powers obey: was subject to Mary; and not alone to Mary, but to Joseph also, because of Mary. Admire and revere both the one and the other, and choose which you admire the more: the most sweet condescension of the Son or the sublime dignity of the Mother. For either am I at a loss for words: for both are wondrous. For that God should obey a woman is humility without compare; and that a woman should have rule over God dignity without equal. In praise of virgins is it joyfully proclaimed: *that they follow the lamb whithersoever he goeth* (Apoc. xiv. 4). Of what praise shall you esteem her worthy who also goeth before Him?

Learn, O Man, to obey. Learn, O Earth, to be subject. Learn, O Dust, to submit. The Evangelist in speaking of thy Maker says: *He was subject to them*; that is, without doubt, to Mary and to Joseph. Be you ashamed, vain ashes that you are. God humbles Himself, and do you exalt yourself? God becomes subject to men, and will you, eager to lord it over men, place yourself above your Maker? O

would that God might deign to make me, thinking such thoughts at times in my own mind, such answer as He made, reproving him, to His apostle: *Go behind Me, Satan: because thou savourest not the things that are of God* (Mk. viii. 33).

For as often as I desire to be foremost among men, so often do I seek to take precedence of God; and so do I not truly savour the things that are of God. For of Him was it said: *And he was subject to them.* If you disdain, O Man, to follow the example of a Man, at least it will not lower thee to imitate thy Maker. If perhaps you cannot follow Him wheresoever He goeth, at least follow in that wherein He has come down to you.

If you are unable to follow Him on the sublime way of virginity, then follow God by that most sure way of humility; from whose straitness should some even from among the virgins go aside, then must I say what is true, that neither do they *follow the Lamb withersoever he goeth.* He that is humble, even though he be stained, he follows the Lamb; so too does the proud virgin; but neither of the two whithersoever He goeth: because the one cannot ascend to the purity of the Lamb that is without stain, nor will the other deign to come down to the meekness of the Lamb, Who stood silent, not merely before the shearer, but before the one that put Him to death. Yet the sinner who makes after Him in humility, has chosen a wholesomer part than the one that is proud in his virtue; since the humble repentance of the one washes away uncleanness, but the pride of the other contaminates his own virtue.

Truly blessed was Mary who

possessed both humility and virginity. And truly wondrous the virginity whose fruitfulness stained not, but adorned her; and truly singular the humility, which this fruitful virginity has not troubled, but rather exalted; and wholly incomparable the fruitfulness which goes hand in hand with her humility and her virginity. Which of these things is not wondrous? Which is not beyond all comparison? Which that is not wholly singular? It would be strange if you did not hesitate to decide which you regard as most worthy of praise: whether the wonder of fruitfulness of offspring in virginity, or of virginal integrity in a mother: sublimity of Offspring, or humility joined to such dignity: unless it be that we place both together above each one singly: and it is truly beyond any doubt more excellent and more joyful to have beheld these perfections united in her, than to see but one part of them.

And can we wonder that God, of Whom it is written that *He is wonderful in his saints* (Ps. lxvii. 36), shows Himself in His own Mother yet more wondrous still? Venerate them, Ye spouses, this integrity of flesh in our corruptible flesh. Revere likewise, Ye virgins, fruitfulness in virginity. Let all men imitate the humility of God's Mother. Honour, Ye angels, the Mother of your King, you who adore the Offspring of our Virgin; Who is your King and our King, the Healer of our race, the Restorer of our fatherland: Who among you is so sublime, yet among us was so lowly: to Whose Majesty as well from you as from us let there be adoration and reverence: to whose Perfection be there honour and glory and empire for ever and ever. Amen.

V. St Ælred, Abbot of Rievaulx
Jesus Twelve Years Old[7]

You ask me, Beloved Son, that I send you some seeds of pious meditation and holy love on the portion of the gospel that tells of the doings of Jesus as a Boy of twelve. And while yet the messenger was speaking to me of your request, already I felt within my heart, how great, of what kind, how ardent and how sweet the affection from which this request of the Brethren proceeds, since there comes at once to my own mind what I have felt, what was in my heart, at hearing the divine praises, either when they were read or when they were sung. I have looked back, unhappy that I am, I have looked back, and I see how far behind me are those sweet-

nesses, and how far the cords of duty and of care have drawn me from these delights, for that which once my soul wished not to touch is now my daily bread. *These I have recalled, and I have poured out my soul* (Ps. xli. 5), when your letter reached me, and the Hand of the Lord touched my heart, and anointed it with the unction of His mercy.

You see what light, what clarity, the affection that is revealed in the very manner of your request awakens in my soul, when you desire so earnestly to know where the Boy Jesus was in those three days when He was sought for by His Mother; in what home was He received, with what food was He nourished, with what company refreshed, and with what was He occupied? I feel, my son, I too feel within me these same things with which you, so confidently, so affectionately, with what holy tears in prayer are wont to question Jesus, when that sweet image of the Beloved Boy comes before the eyes of your heart, when you picture in spiritual reflection that most beautiful of countenances, when you feel those most gentle and most kind eyes smiling tenderly upon thee. Then, as it seems to me, you cry out in tender affection: O sweet Child, where wert Thou? Where were you hidden? Where did you receive hospitality? Who enjoyed Thy company? Were you in heaven, or upon the earth? Did you abide in some home, or perhaps you have been with boys of Your own age, hiding with them in some secret place, unfolding to them the secrets of Your mysteries, according to Your own words in the Gospel: *Suffer the little children to come unto me and forbid them not?* Happy they, if there were such children, upon whom for so many days You bestowed the sweetness of your Presence!

But what means this, My sweet Lord, that Thou hast not shown sympathy to Thy grieving anxious holy Mother seeking Thee? And also Thy father, who with her has sought Thee sorrowing? And Thou, My Most Sweet Lady, why wert thou seeking thy Son, Whom thou knowest was God? Was it lest He be tormented by hunger or troubled by the cold, or did'st thou fear He would be molested by some boy of His own age? Is it not He Who gives to eat to every living

thing, Who nourishes every thing? Is it not He that clothes and adorns more gloriously than Solomon, *the grass of the field, which is today, and tomorrow is cast into the oven* (Mt. vi. 29)? Rather, My Lady, with your kind leave I say it, why hast thou so easily lost thy most precious Child: so negligently guarded Him: noticed so late that He was no longer with Thee?

Would that Jesus might deign to inspire me with what interior and spiritual speech He would answer one so loving, so beseeching, one so earnestly seeking Him, that knowing I might write to thee, and having tasted I might give forth of my delight.

And when He was twelve years old, they going up to Jerusalem, according to the custom of the Feast, and having fulfilled the days, when they returned, *the Child Jesus remained in Jerusalem.* First, lest the wondrous sweetness of this holy narrative escape us, you must know, that it was the custom of the Jews, that when going up to the festival, the men and women travelled apart, lest they experience defilement, the divine law prescribing that they should celebrate the feast clean from all defilement. Whence it is believable that the Boy Jesus bestowed the delight of His Presence, now on Joseph and the men with him, now on His Mother and the women who travelled with her. Let us think of what happiness was theirs during these days, to whom it was given to see His Face, to hear the sound of His Voice; to behold shining out in man, and in a boy, the marks of celestial power, and to commingle the mystery of the Saving Wisdom with their mutual converse.

Elders wonder in astonishment,

the young men admire, boys of His own age hold back in fear, because of the gravity of His ways, and the authority of His speech. I believe that in that most beautiful countenance there shone such beauty of heavenly grace as to draw the eyes of all, incline their ears, and awaken their love. See, I ask you, in what manner each one seeks Him, each one draws Him to himself. The old caress Him, the young men gather round Him, the boys obey Him. What tearfulness among the boys when He is held too long among the men? What complaints among the holy women, when He delays a little longer with His father and those with him? I believe that each one cried with the most tender affection: *Let Him kiss me with the kiss of his mouth* (Cant. i. 1). And the boys, longing for His Presence, but not presuming to intrude on the company of their elders, used language such as this: *Who shall give thee to me for my brother, sucking the breasts of my mother, that I may find thee without, and kiss thee?* (Cant. viii. 1).

Thus as they travel all together in this cheerfulness towards the holy city, reflect, I pray you, upon the pious holy contention between the separate families, each desiring to enjoy to itself His most sweet Presence. Happy was the one that succeeded. Perhaps this was the reason that when they returned, having fulfilled the days, *the Child Jesus remained unnoticed in Jerusalem*, each one thinking He was with some other family, being sought for by all; His parents not knowing that He was missing, until the day's journey ended. And then they sought Him among the families that had gone up to Jerusalem together,

among their cousins and acquaintances. Not finding Him, they return to Jerusalem: and after three days they find Him in the Temple.

Where wert Thou, O Good Jesus, during those three days? Who was it gave Thee to eat and to drink? Who prepared Thee a bed? Who took off Thy sandals? Who bathed and anointed Thy young limbs? I know that as Thou didst voluntarily assume our infirmity, so also when Thou wilt Thou showest Thy Power: and so when Thou wilt Thou needest not man's ministrations. Where then wert Thou, O Lord Jesus? Upon these things it is lawful to dwell, to meditate; but not to rashly affirm.

What shall I say, O My God? Is it that you conformed in all things to our poverty, and took upon yourself all the misfortunes of human nature, and, as one of the crowd of beggars, sought an alms by the gates? Who will grant me to be a sharer of these begged mouthfuls, or that I might even feast on the remains of that divine meal?

But that we may turn to an understanding of the higher meaning of this event, perhaps, on the first day, He presented Himself before the Face of His Father; not that He might rest there, but that He might take counsel with the Paternal Will upon the order of the Dispensation He had undertaken. Nor does such a notion appear improbable if it is considered that He is Co-equal, Co-substantial, with the Father and the Holy Spirit in the Divine Nature; but in the form of a servant, which He has taken on, man takes counsel with God; the lowly with the great. But not that He may learn that which He has known from eternity in the

Form of God, but that He might show humility, proffer obedience, and defer in all things to the Father. There He treated in the secret council of the Father: of receiving baptism, of making known the Gospel, of performing miracles; and, at the end, of undergoing His passion, and of rising from the dead.

All things being determined, on the next day He bestowed on the choirs of angels and archangels the vision of His Holy Countenance, and being now engaged in undoing the ancient loss of its heavenly citizens, He makes joyful the whole city of God, soon to be fully restored. On the third, resting with the Patriarchs and Prophets, that which they had heard already from the recital of holy Simeon, He now confirms by the sight of His own Face. And consoling them for the long delay in His Dispensation, by the promise of the Redemption now at hand, He brings them all to cheerfulness and to peace of soul.

With reason therefore was He found after three days in the Temple, in the midst of the Elders and Doctors, where He began gradually to make known the design of the Paternal Mercy for the salvation of men, as He had revealed it, it would seem, to the angels, and to the holy ones who had died; beginning with those who had protected the most precious treasure of His Promise, in the Sacred Promise, in the Sacred Writings; at first listening, and asking questions, then making known the mysteries. And *all that heard him were astonished at his wisdom and his answers.* There was here given to boys and growing young men an example of reverence, so that they might be silent in the midst of their elders: that they should listen and ask questions, and learn.

Say to me, O My Most Sweet Lady, Mother of My Lord, what then was your state of soul, what wonder, what joy was yours, when you found this most sweet Son, the Lord Jesus, not among other boys, but in the midst of the Doctors: when you observed the eyes of all upon Him, and their ears attentive to Him: when great and small, learned alike and unlearned, were astonished at His wisdom and His answers.

I found Him, She says, *Whom my soul loveth: I held Him: and I will not let Him go* (Cant. iii. 4). Hold Him fast, O Sweet Lady: hold Whom thou lovest, and with multiplied delights make up the three days that were lost.

Son, why hast thou done so to us? Behold thy father and I have sought thee sorrowing. Again I ask you, O Lady, why were you grieving? I believe that you feared not hunger, nor thirst, nor want, for the Boy Whom you knew was God; but that you sought only the ineffable, but now withdrawn, delights of His Presence. For so sweet is the Lord to those Who taste Him, so beauteous to those who see Him, so gentle to those who embrace Him, that even His brief absence is a source of deepest pain.

How is it that you sought me? Did you not know that I must be about my Father's business? Now he begins to unlock the secret of the heavenly mystery in which He had hidden those three days. That He may however give an example of humility and obedience, together with renunciation of one's own will, and of obeying the will of superiors, even to the abandoning of what is useful: and of obeying promptly and worthily: putting aside these most sublime, these most worthy and even necessary undertakings, He submits Himself to the will of His elders as the Evangelist tells us: *And He went down with them, and was subject to them.*

But what is the meaning of that which the Evangelist then says: *And they understood not the word that He spoke unto them.* I do not think that this was spoken of Mary, who from the time when the Holy Spirit descended upon her, and the power of the Most High had overshadowed her, could not be unaware of the purposes of her Son; but of the others, either not knowing, or not understanding, what He said. Mary *kept all these words in her heart.* She kept them in her memory, turning them over in quiet meditation, comparing them with other things she had seen and heard regarding Him. And so the most Blessed Virgin even then mercifully provided for us that these so precious, so sweet, so necessary words, should not through any negligence be lost, and never come to be written down, or made known; and so those that came after would have been deprived of the delight of this spiritual manna. *All these things* therefore this most Prudent Virgin faithfully preserved, and modestly keeping silent, opportunely revealed and committed to the Holy Apostles and Disciples that they might make them known.

Of that which follows: *And Jesus advanced in wisdom, and age, and grace with God and men,* many minds have said many things; and different people feel differently regarding it; of whose opinions it is not for us to judge. Some think that the Soul of

Christ, from this that it was created and assumed by God, had equal wisdom with God. Others, fearful of making a creature seem equal with God, say that since He grew in age, so He also grew in wisdom, relying on the authority of the Evangelist who says: *Jesus advanced in wisdom, and age, and grace.* Nor is it surprising that if He is said to have been a child in wisdom, that, since He was mortal and passible, He may also have been most truly called a child in happiness. But of these opinions let each one judge as he wills. For me it suffices to know and believe that the Lord Jesus, from this that He was assumed with God into the unity of One Person, was perfect God: and through this perfect wisdom, perfect righteousness, perfect happiness, and was and is perfect in power: and whatsoever can be said of God, as to His nature, I doubt not that the same can be said of Christ, even within the womb of His Mother.

Nor do we by this deny Him, prior to His resurrection, either mortality, or the power to suffer: since we confess that He was not a seeming man, but truly man; and that He possessed the true nature of a man, in which He could increase in age. Whether He could grow in wisdom let them decide who know how to treat of such things.

But you, my son, you seek not disputation, but devotion: whence the tongue is not sharpened, and the soul is left undisturbed. Leaving then the things that belong to history, let it pass on to purifying our spiritual understanding, according as He of Whom we speak shall deign to inspire us.

The Lord Our God is One God,

nor can He change, or be changed, as David declares: *Thou art always the self same, and thy years shall not fail* (Ps. ci. 28). This therefore Our God, Eternal, Timeless, Unchangeable, became in our nature both changeable and a subject of time, so that for changeable men He might prepare that way to His own Eternity, and give us steadfastness, for which He took on our frailty so that in one and the same Saviour might be *the way* by which we would ascend, *the life* to which we would come, and *the truth* we would enjoy, as He Himself says: *I am the way, the truth, the life* (Jn. xiv. 6).

The great God abiding in His own nature is born a Child according to the flesh, and grows for a certain space of time, and after the manner of the flesh, so that we who are children in mind, and almost without mind, may be spiritually reborn, and that we may grow up according to the grades of the spiritual ages, and advance in wisdom and grace. So His bodily growth is our spiritual growth, and the things that are recorded as done by Him in the successive ages are seen as done in us, as we advance through the diverse stages of spiritual growth.

So let His corporal birth be our spiritual birth, that is, the beginning of our conversion. Let His persecution, that which He suffered from Herod, be to us a sign of the temptation we suffer from the devil in the beginning of our conversion. Let His growing up in Nazareth express our advancement in perfection. Earlier, the prodigal son, perishing with hunger, was invited to the house of bread (Lk. xv. 16, 17), where there is bread baked in ashes, not fine wheaten bread; so that he *may eat bread like ashes,* and *mingle drink with weeping* (Ps. ci. 10). But He is the pure wheaten bread, clean, without ashes, without ferment, without chaff, which we must seek.

He went down with them, and was subject to them. Tranquilly He goes down with such a guardian, with such a Mother. Happily does he go down, who moved by the Spirit of God lovingly helps those weaker than himself. Willingly would I go, even into Egypt (Hell) with such guides, if only, leading me there, they lead me back again; should they bring me there, that they enable me to return. Joyfully would I submit myself to such teachers: with pleasure would I bow my shoulders to the burthen they impose: willingly would I take upon me the yoke they would place on me, knowing that their *yoke is sweet,* their *burthen light*: aided by His grace of Whose Boyhood we have been speaking, Who was filled with power, and grace, and wisdom, Jesus Christ Our Lord Who with the Father and the Holy Ghost liveth and reigneth world without end, Amen.

NOTES

1 Possibly referring to *ordained by angels,* Gal. iii. 14; or to the sacrifices of Gedeon, or Manue, Judges vi. 21; xiii. 16.
2 PG 14, Homily 18 in Luke.
3 PG 14, 10 in Luke.
4 PL 15 in Luke, 63.
5 The reference is to the Arians.
6 PL 183, 55. Pars. 7, 8, 9.
7 PL 184, 849. Ex. Tr. de Jesu Puero Duoden.

SECOND SUNDAY AFTER THE EPIPHANY

THE GOSPEL OF THE SUNDAY

John ii. 1-11

At that time: there was a marriage in Cana of Galilee; and the mother of Jesus was there. And Jesus also was invited, and his disciples, to the marriage. And the wine failing, the mother of Jesus saith to him: They have no wine.

And Jesus saith to her: Woman, what is that to me and to thee? My hour is not yet come. His mother said to the waiters: Whatsoever he shall say to you, do ye.

Now there were set there six water pots of stone, according to the manner of the purifying of the Jews, containing two or three measures apiece. Jesus saith to them: Fill the water pots with water. And they filled them up to the brim. And Jesus saith to them: Draw out now, and carry to the chief steward of the feast. And they carried it.

And when the chief steward had tasted the water made wine, and knew not whence it was, but the waiters knew who had drawn the water; the chief steward calleth the bridegroom, and saith to him: every man at first setteth forth good wine, and when men have well drunk, then that which is worse. But thou hast kept the good wine until now.

This beginning of miracles did Jesus in Cana of Galilee; and manifested his glory, and his disciples believed in him.

EXPOSITION FROM THE CATENA AUREA

CHRYSOSTOM, *from Homily 20 in John*: Since the Lord was known in Galilee, they invite Him to the wedding. Hence there follows *And the third day there was a marriage in Cana.* ALCUIN: Galilee is a province, in which Cana is a village. CHRYSOSTOM: They invite the Lord to the wedding, not as someone famous, but as one known to them, and as one of many. Hence the Evangelist stating this, says: *And the mother of Jesus was there*: for as they invite the Mother, so do they invite the Son; hence, *And Jesus also was invited, and His disciples*: and He came; for He was not considering His own dignity, but our benefit. For He Who disdained not to take *the form of a servant*, did not disdain to come to the nuptials of simple people. AUGUSTINE, *De Verb Dom. Serm.* 41: Let every man therefore take shame to imagine himself superior, since God Himself became humble. For, with others, the Son of the Virgin came to the wedding, Who, with the Father, had instituted nuptials.

BEDE, *Hom. Dom. I post Epiph.*: That He condescended, according to the Gospels, to come to the wedding feast, truly confirms the faith of those who believe. Furthermore it shows how reprehensible is the false teaching of Tation, and of Marcion, and the others, who slander marriage. For if there were evil in the unstained bridal bed, and in nuptials chastely celebrated, the Lord would not have come to them. But because conjugal chastity is good, and better still the continence of the bereaved spouse, and virginal perfection best of all, and so that He may approve the choosing of all three grades of life, and in order to distinguish the merit of each, He deigned to be born from the immaculate womb of the Virgin Mary; Newborn, to be blessed by the prophetic mouth of the Widow Anna; and now a young man, He is invited to the celebration of a wedding, and honours it by the presence of His holiness.

AUGUSTINE, *Tr.* 8, 4 *in John*: Why should we wonder if He comes to that house to a wedding feast, Who came into this world for His own nuptials? For He has here a Bride, whom He purchased with His Blood, to whom He has given the Holy Spirit as the pledge of His love; whom He joined to Himself in the womb of the Virgin Mary. For the Word is a Bridegroom, and our flesh is the Bride, and both together are the Only Son of God, and the Same is the Son of man. The womb of the virgin is the bridal chamber, whence He comes forth *as a bridegroom coming out of his nuptial chamber* (Ps. xviii. 6).

BEDE: Nor is it lacking in mystical significance, that the nuptials are recorded as celebrated *on the third day*. For, first, previous to the Law, He came to us through the patriarchs; second, under the Law, in the writings of the prophets; third, under the Dispensation of grace, in the announcements of the Evangelists, when He shone forth as it were in the light of the third day, in which the Lord appeared, born in the flesh. But in this that these nuptials are declared to have been celebrated in Cana of Galilee, that is, in the zeal of transmigration (Cana signifies zeal, Galilee transmigration), He mystically conveys that they are especially worthy of the grace of Christ who burn with the fervour of religious dedication; and who learn to cross over from vice to the virtues, from earthly things to heavenly. The Lord however, sitting down to the feast, the wine runs short, so that by means of a better wine, made by Him, the hidden glory of God might be manifested. Hence: *And the wine failing, the mother of Jesus saith to Him: They have no wine.*

CHRYSOSTOM, as above: But it is fitting to inquire: whence came it to the mind of His Mother to expect something striking from her Son; for He had not previous to this performed wonders; for later it is said: *This beginning of miracles did Jesus in Cana of Galilee.* But He had begun to reveal Himself, through John, and likewise by other things He had said to His Disciples. But before all this there was the Conception, and the events that followed the Nativity, which had engraven in her heart a profound veneration for her Child. For which reason it was that Luke said: *Mary kept all those words in her heart.* Why then had she not before this time asked Him to perform a miracle? Before this time He lived as but one among many, so that His Mother did not presume to say such a thing. But now because she had heard that John had given testimony to Him, and that He had begun to have His own Disciples, she began from then to have confidence.

ALCUIN: Here she symbolizes the Synagogue, which challenged Christ to work a miracle: for it is characteristic of the Jews to seek signs.

And Jesus saith to her: Woman what is that to me and to thee? AUGUSTINE, *Tr. 8 in Joannem:* Some, contradicting the Gospels, and saying that Jesus was not borne of the Virgin Mary, have put forward from this text an argument for their error, saying: How could she be His Mother to whom He said: *Woman, what is it to thee and to me?* But who

is it that tells us this, that we should believe that the Lord said it? John the Evangelist. For he said: *And the mother of Jesus was there.* Why did he say this unless that both incidents are true? Did He then come to the wedding feast to teach that mothers are to be despised?

CHRYSOSTOM, as above: That He greatly venerated His Mother hear Luke relating how *He was subject to His parents.* For where parents do not stand in the way of the things of God it is their due that we be subject to them; but when they ask anything at an undue time, and keep us from spiritual things, be not by this led astray.

AUGUSTINE, *On the Creed*, 2: 4: That He might distinguish between God and man; because as man He was the inferior and subject, as God He was above everyone, He said: *Woman, what is that to me and to thee?*[1]

CHRYSOSTOM, *Homs.* 21, 22: He so answered for yet another reason: that the miracles He did might not be suspect (for they who were in need ought to have asked, not His Mother). He wished to show that all things have a due time, that all are not done at the same time, which would be confusion; so there follows: *My hour is not yet come,* that is: I am not yet known to those present: nor do they yet know the wine is failing. Let them first know this: for he that has not yet felt the sense of need, will neither have much sense of the benefit received.

AUGUSTINE, *Tr. 8 in Joannem,* o, 10: Our Lord, as God, had not a mother. As man He had a Mother, the miracle He was about to perform, He would perform through His divinity, not through His human infirmity. His Mother sought a miracle, but He, not acknowledging human feelings, being about to do a divine work, said: *Woman, what is that to me, and to thee?* As if to say: That which in Me works wonders, My divinity, you have not brought forth. She is called *Woman* simply, according to the feminine sex, not according to the corruption of integrity. But because you have borne my humanity then shall I know thee, when this same humanity will be hanging from the Cross. Hence He adds: *My hour is not yet come*, as though to say: when this weak body, which thou hast brought forth, has begun to hang upon the Cross, there shall I acknowledge Thee. For when He was about to die, before she died, and rise again, before her death, He commended His Mother to His Disciple.

See how just as the Manichaeans sought to find justification for their false doctrines from the fact that the Lord said, *Woman what is it to thee and to me*, so the astrologers find a pretext for their fallacies in His saying that *My hour is not yet come*. For they say: See how Christ was subject to the fates, since He said: *My hour is not yet come.*

But let them rather believe the Lord when He says: *I have the power to lay down my life, and I have power to take it up again* (Jn. x. 18), and let them seek to learn why it was that He said *My hour is not yet come*. Neither let them presume to subject the Creator of heaven under the rule of the stars as though His fate depended on them: for the Creator of the stars cannot be de-

pendent upon the stars He has made. Furthermore, not alone has Christ no such destiny, but neither have you or any man. Why then does He say, *My hour is not yet come?* Because He had it within His power when He would die, but it did not yet seem opportune that He should use this power: The Disciples were to be called, the kingdom of heaven to be announced, miracles were yet to be wrought, the lowliness of the Lord was yet to be shown in the very suffering of this mortality. But as He wrought only what He judged expedient, His hour was to come, not of necessity, but of His own will; not because of circumstances, but through His power.

His mother saith to the waiters . . . CHRYSOSTOM, *Hom.* 21: Although He had said *My hour is not yet come*, afterwards He did as she had asked, so that from this also He might show that He was not subject to the hour. For if He were, how could He do this when the hour had not yet come? Then also for the honour of His Mother, that He might not appear to deny her request and put her to shame in the presence of so many. For she had brought the waiters to Him, so that the request might be made by many. For there follows: *Whatsoever He shall say to you, do ye.*

BEDE: As though she said: although He seems to refuse, yet He will do this. For His Mother knew that He was kind and merciful.

Now there were six water pots of stone. ALCUIN: The vases for water were got ready according to the custom of purification of the Jews; for among other traditions they also observed this, that they frequently performed ablutions. CHRYSOSTOM, *Hom.* 22: Palestine is not plentiful in water, and there are not many wells or springs to be found in these places, and so that they will not have to run to the stream if they become soiled, and have not at hand the means of purification, they fill up jars with water. But lest someone, unbelieving, might think that the lees of wine remaining in the jars, and then water being poured in, a light wine would thus be made, the Evangelist for this reason records: *Water pots of stone, according to the manner of purification of the Jews*, showing that these vessels had never been the receptacles of wine.

Containing two or three measures apiece. AUGUSTINE, *in Joan., Tr.* 9, 7: That he says two or three does not mean that some held two measures, some three; but that the same would hold two, which held three. *Jesus saith to them: Draw out now, and carry to the chief steward of the feast.* But why was the miracle not wrought before the filling of the jars with water? This would have been more wonderful. For indeed it is one thing to give an actual substance another quality, and another to make a new substance out of nothing. This is indeed the more wonderful, but to many it will not seem so credible. It is for this reason that many times He seems to diminish the impressiveness of His miracles, wishing to make more credible that which He does.

In this way He has also overthrown certain perverted teachings. For since there are those (the Manichaeans) who say that the Maker of the world is another being (and that visible things are not His work, but those of a rival creator), He accordingly performs His miracles from the materials at hand. For if He were indeed contrary to the Being Who is the Creator of the world, He would not thus use the creations of His enemy to make known His own power. He did not Himself draw the water, and then reveal the wine: but ordered the servants to do this, so that they might be witnesses of what He had done. Then follows: *And Jesus saith to them: draw out now, and carry to the chief steward of the feast.*

ALCUIN: The chief steward was the chief among the guests, who in the manner of the ancients reclined on couches. Some think that the chief steward was one of the Jewish priests who was present at the feast, so as to instruct them as to how the nuptials were to be conducted. CHRYSOS., *Hom.* 21: Or, lest some one might say that the guests were drunk and their judgement unreliable so that they would not know whether it was wine or water. But those to whom the entertainment of the guests was confided were extremely vigilant, this being their especial duty: that they conduct everything in an orderly and worthy manner. Accordingly, in view of their testimony who fulfilled this office He said: *Carry to the chief steward*; because of his necessary watchfulness; He did *not* say: *pour out now to the guests.*

HILARY, *De Trin.* 3: 5, *prope prin.*: Water accordingly is poured into the jars; wine is drawn out in the drinking vessels; the mind of the one drawing forth is different from the mind of the one pouring in.

They who poured in thought to draw forth water: those drawing forth, believed that wine had been poured in. Hence: *and when the chief steward had tasted the water made wine, and knew not whence it was, but the waiters knew who had drawn the water; the chief steward calleth the bridegroom.* This was not a mixing, but a new creation. The simplicity of water disappeared, and the taste of wine was born. Not by the pouring in of what is the stronger element, is there obtained what was diluted; but what was ceased to be, and what was not began to be.

CHRYSOSTOM, *Hom.* 22: Jesus wished the power of His miracles to be known gradually, and so He did not reveal what had been done; nor did the chief steward call the servants. For they would not have been believed, saying such a thing about One who was regarded as an ordinary man; but he called the bridegroom, who especially could inquire into what had happened. For Christ had not simply made wine, He had made the best wine. Hence: *and saith to him: every man at first set forth good wine etc.*

Such are the wonders of Christ; which are more beautiful and more advantageous than those done by nature. That water was changed into wine the waiters bear witness; that it was the best wine the chief steward and the bridegroom testify. It is likely that the bridegroom also made some comment, but the Evangelist passes over this, touching only on that which it was necessary to know, namely: that He changed water into wine. Then immediately he continues: *This beginning of miracles did Jesus in Cana of Galilee.*

CHRYSOSTOM, *Hom.* 22: It was necessary then to work miracles, since disciples were already gathered about Him, and there were devout persons present and such as gave attention to the things which were done. And (Hom. 21) if anyones say it is not sufficient proof that this was the beginning of miracles, because there is added: *in Cana of Galilee,* as if it had happened that there had been signs already elsewhere, we shall say, as we said before, what John says: *I knew Him not, but that He may be made manifest in Israel, therefore am I come baptizing in water* (Jn. i. 31). Now if he had wrought miracles at an early age, the Israelites would not have needed another to go before Him to announce Him. For He who in a brief time became renowned by His miracles, so that His name was made known to all men, would much the more have become known, had He wrought wonders while yet a child. But what He would have done then would have seemed fantastic, being done by a child. Fittingly, therefore, He did not begin as a Child to perform wonders. For then men might have regarded the Incarnation as but a semblance of humanity and His enemies, carried away by malice, would have hastened Him before due time to the cross.

AUGUSTINE, *Tr.* 9, 1, *in John*: This miracle of the Lord, in which He made wine from water, does not astonish those who know that God wrought it. For on that day He made wine in the water jars, Who each succeeding year makes it in the vines. But this latter through familiarity loses its wonder. So God made use of unaccustomed means to rouse men, who were now as sleepers, to the worship of Himself; for which reason the Evangelist says: *and manifested His glory.* ALCUIN: Because He Himself is the King of glory, Who disposes of all creatures. CHRYSOSTOM, *from Hom.* 22: He manifested His glory, in so far as this depended from His own act. For if all did not hear of it then, yet they would afterwards come to hear of it. Then follows: *and His disciples believed in Him.* For they were obliged to believe in Him, and also, more readily and with more diligence pay attention to the things that were being done.

AUGUSTINE, *Harmony of the Gospels,* 2: 17: Now if it was on this account that they believed in Him, they were not yet His disciples when they were invited to the marriage, but this was said of them in that manner of speech used when we say that the Apostle Paul was born in Tarsus of Cilicia: for he was not then an apostle. So when we read that the disciples were invited to the wedding feast, we are not to understand that they were already His disciples, but they were to become disciples.

AUGUSTINE, 9: 5, *in John*: Consider the mysteries that are concealed within this miracle of Our Lord. That must be fulfilled in Christ which was written concerning Him in the Scriptures. There was water. From the water He made wine, when He opened their powers of perceiving, and expounded the Scriptures to them (Lk. xxiv. 13–47), so they tasted what they had not yet tasted, and drank of what they had never drunk. BEDE: The Lord appearing in the flesh, the

sweetness of the wine of the former dispensation began, because of the worldly outlook of the Pharisees, to lose its pristine flavour.

AUGUSTINE, *Tr.* 9, *in John,* 5, 6, 7: If He had ordered that the water be poured out, and He had poured in wine from the hidden boundaries of His creation, it would seem as if He rejected the Scriptures. When however He changed the water into wine, He showed us that the Old Testament was also from Him; for it was at His order the water jars were filled.

But Scripture is without meaning if Christ be not there understood. Listen to what He Himself says: *All things which are written in the Law, and in the prophets, and in the psalms, concerning me* (Lk. xxiv. 44). We know from what times the Law begins to speak, that is, from the beginning of the world. Thence to this period in which we now are, which is the sixth age. For the first age is computed from Adam to Noah; the second from Noah to Abraham; the third from Abraham to David; the fourth from David to the transmigration into Babylon; the fifth from then until John the Baptist; the sixth from then till the end of the world. The six water jars therefore signify the six ages of the world, in each of which prophecy was not wanting. The prophecies have been filled; the water jars are *filled to the brim.*

What significance is there in saying, *they contained two or three measures apiece?* If he had said three only, would not our minds have run immediately to the mystery of the Trinity? But not thus must we do violence to the sense, because He said, *two or three.* For if the

Father and Son are meant, the Holy Spirit must also be understood; as we must know that the Love of the Father and the Son, which is the Holy Spirit, is indivisible. But there is another meaning that is not to be overlooked: the *two measures* are understood as meaning the two kinds of men, that is, the Jews and Greeks; the *three measures* stand for the three sons of Noah.

ALCUIN: The waiters are to be interpreted as the Teachers of the New Law, who spiritually interpret the sacred Scriptures to others; the chief steward is one skilled in the law, as Nicodemus, Gamaliel, or Saul. When therefore the word of the Gospel, which is concealed in the letter of the Law, is committed to such as these, it is as though the water made wine is brought to the chief steward of the feast. And in the house of the wedding three orders of guests are aptly noted: for the Church is composed of three classes of the faithful: of the espoused, those called to continence, and those who teach. Christ has kept the good wine until the last, that is, the Gospel, which He reserves till the sixth age of the world.

I. ST JOHN CHRYSOSTOM, BISHOP AND DOCTOR

My Hour is not yet Come[2]

Woman, what is it to me, and to thee? My Hour is not yet come.

1. There is toil in preaching, as Paul testifies: *Let the priests that rule well, be esteemed worthy of double honour: especially they who labour in word and doctrine* (I Tim. v. 17). And it is for you to make this toil either light or heavy. Should you reject what we say to you, or, not rejecting it, yet bring forth no fruit, our labour is heavy, because we have laboured in vain. But should you hearken, and do that which you have heard, we shall not feel the labour, for the fruit born of our toil makes labour seem light. So then should you wish to help our zeal, not to extinguish or lessen it, show proof, I pray you; so that seeing the fields fruitful, and joyful in the hope of an abundant yield, and counting our riches, we shall not weary in this honoured calling.

It is no light subject that we must speak of today. For when the Mother of Jesus said, *they have no wine*, Christ answered: *Woman, what is that to me, and to thee? My Hour is not yet come.* When He had thus answered her, He did that which His mother wished. This, no less than what was said previously, is something we must consider. Therefore calling on His name Who wrought the miracle, let us seek to understand it.

Not here alone do we find this saying: *My hour is not yet come*; for the Evangelist says in a subsequent chapter, that they could not lay hands on Him, *because his hour was not yet come*. And again, *and no man laid hands on him, because his hour was not yet come*; and again: *Father, the hour is come, glorify thy son* (Jn. viii. 20; vii. 30; xvii. 1). I have gathered these sayings from the whole Gospel, that I may give a common explanation to all of them. What is this explanation? Not because He was subject to the need of the times, or because He was governed by the hour, did

Christ say: *My hour is not yet come*: must the Maker observe the times, and the Creator the years and the ages He has made?

By these words He desires to make plain that He does all things at a fitting time; not doing all things at once, lest the order of things might appear confused if He did not bring forth each single happening at its due moment, but should as it were commingle all things: such as, His Birth, His Resurrection, the Judgement. But observe carefully. Creation was to be made, but not all at once: man and woman, but not even these at the same hour. The rest of men were to be condemned to death, and judgement was to follow; but long ages were to pass between. He must decree the Law; but the Dispensation of grace was not given with it, but each was given at its proper time.

Christ therefore was not subjected to the necessity of the times and hours, since it was He, as their Creator, Who laid down their order. But John here speaks of Christ as saying, *my hour is not yet come*, meaning that He was not yet known to the many; neither had He yet the full company of His Disciples: Andrew had followed Him, together with Philip: but no one else. Nor did these all truly know Him, not even His Mother, or His Disciples. For even after He had wrought many miracles, the Evangelist could still say of His brethren: *For neither did His brethren believe in him* (Jn. vii. 5).

Neither did they know Him who were present at the wedding feast: or they would have come to Him, and petitioned Him in their need. So He says: *My hour is not yet come.* I am not yet known to those who are present, neither do they know that the wine is failing. Leave it till they learn this. Neither should I learn of this from Thee. Thou art my Mother, and this will render the Miracle suspect. They should have come to Me, they who were in need, and asked: not that I have need of them, but that they might with full accord accept the miracle when it is performed. For he that knows his own need, when his prayer is answered, is very grateful; but he that has not adverted to his need, will have no clear sense of a favour received.

And why, you will ask, after He had said, *My hour is not yet come*, and had seemed to refuse her, did He then do what His mother said? So that those who withstood Him, and believed that He also was subject to the hour, might be shown that He was subject neither to time nor the hour. For if He were subject to the hour, how could He do this; seeing that the fitting hour had not yet come? He did it also to honour His Mother, lest He seem to contradict her, and shame before all present the Mother who had borne Him. For she had brought the waiters to Him.

For as He said to the woman of Canaan: *It is not good to take the bread of children, and cast it to the dogs.* Yet he gave it to her, after saying this. And He had also said: *I was not sent but to the sheep that are lost* (Mt. xv. 26, 24). And after this He delivered the woman's daughter. By this we learn that though we be unworthy, yet by persevering we often render ourselves worthy of being heard. Because of this His Mother waited, and wisely brought forward the waiters, that He might be requested by many. And therefore she added: *Whatsoever He shall say to you, do ye.* For she knew that He did not refuse from want of power, but because He was retiring, and neither did He wish to appear to hasten to perform this miracle, and therefore she led forward the waiters.

2. *There were set there six water pots of stone, according to the manner of the purifying of the Jews, containing two or three measures apiece. Jesus saith to them: Fill the water pots with Water. And they filled them up to the brim.* Not without purpose does he write, *according to the manner of the purifying of the Jews:* but so that no one of those who believed not might suspect that the lees being left within, then water being poured in, He would thus have made a very diluted wine. Therefore he says: *According to the manner of the purifying of the Jews;* showing that there never had been wine in these vessels. For Palestine is a land not plentiful in water, and many wells and springs are not to be found there. So they were wont to fill jars with water, so that if they were soiled they would not have to run to the stream, but would have the means of purifying themselves near at hand.

But why did He not work this wonder before filling the pots with water? This would have been more wonderful. It is one thing to give an actual substance another quality, and yet another to make a new substance out of nothing, this indeed is the more wonderful. Yet to many it would appear less credible. And accordingly He often abstains from impressiveness in performing His wonders, desiring to make more easily credible that which He did.

And why, you may say, did He not himself produce the water, that He might then change it into wine, instead of ordering the servants to do this? For the same reason; and that those who drew it might be witness of what happened, and of the fact that there had been no illusion. For should there be anyone who would imprudently dare to deny that it happened, the waiters could contradict them and say: we ourselves drew the water.

By this He also defeats the doctrine that rose up against the Church. For there are some (the Manicheans) who say that the creator of the world is another being, and that what is visible is not His, but the work of another deity opposed to Him; and so that He may reprove this foolishness, He works many of His miracles from the material present to His Hands. For if the Creator were a being contrary to Him, He would not thus use the creation of an enemy to show forth His own power.

And now showing that it is He Who changes water within the vine, and sends the rain upwards through the roots into the grape, He does that in a moment at the wedding feast which He accomplishes within the vine itself over a longer period of time. And when they had filled the water jars, He said: *Draw out now, and carry to the chief steward of the feast. And they carried it. And when the chief steward had tasted the water made wine, and knew not whence it was, but the waiters knew who had drawn the water; the chief steward calleth the bridegroom, and saith to him: every man at first setteth forth good wine, and when men have well drunk, then that which is worse. But thou hast kept the good wine until now.*

Here again some ridicule this happening, saying: this was a gathering where the people were drunk, their taste was dulled, and they could not reason well, nor give a true judgement; since they would not know whether they drank wine or water: for that they were drunk the chief steward has himself said. That this is absurd is easily evident: yet even against this suspicion the Evangelist has provided. For it was not the guests who gave their opinion, but the chief steward: who was sober, and had yet tasted nothing. For you know well that they to whom the care of the guests is committed are the soberest of all, having this especial obligation, that they should conduct everything in an appropriate manner. And accordingly He appeals to such a person, as being sober and watchful, in witness of what had taken place. For He did not say: "Pour out the wine now to the guests", but: *Carry to the chief steward of the feast; the chief steward calleth the bridegroom.*

Why did he not call the waiters? For the miracle then would have been revealed. Because Jesus Himself had not made known that He had wrought a miracle, desiring that the power of His miracles come slowly and gradually to be known. If He had then made it known, the waiters telling of it would not have been believed, but would be thought to have gone mad, should they ascribe such a thing to one who in the common belief was but an ordinary person. They indeed knew what had taken place, from personal experience; for they could not deny the evidence of their own hands; yet they were not persons suited to make others believe.

So He did not make it known to all; but to the person who could best discern what had been done, reserving a fuller knowledge of the event till later: after other remarkable happenings had taken place, this also would, later, become credible. For when He healed the Ruler's son, the Evangelist implies by what he then says, that by that time this miracle had become known. It was especially because of this that the Ruler had appealed to Him, because he was aware of this miracle, as I have said; and as John shows when he says: *He came again therefore unto Cana of Galilee, where he had made the water wine* (Jn. v. 46), and not alone made wine, but He made the best wine.

3. Such are the wonders of Christ; more beautiful and more advantageous than those done by nature; and so also the other happenings, as when He healed an afflicted limb, He made it better than the sound one. That it was wine, and the best wine, not alone the waiters, but the chief steward and the bridegroom bear witness; and that it was made from water, they testify who drew the water. And so, though the miracle was not yet revealed, it could not in the end remain in silence, so many and so close linked were the testimonies provided for future times.

That He had made water into wine, He had the waiters as witnesses; that the wine was good, He had as witnesses the chief steward and the bridegroom. It is likely that the bridegroom made some answer but the Evangelist, having recorded this wonder, goes on; pressing on to what was more necessary. For what was strictly necessary was, that it be truly known that He changed water into wine; what the bridegroom said to the chief steward he did not think needed to be recorded.

And many of the miracles at first obscure have become clearer in the course of time: Then those who saw the event from the very beginning narrated what had taken place. Jesus then made wine from water: and now as well as then He ceases not to change our weak and unstable wills into that which is better. For there are, I affirm, men who differ in nothing from water; they are cold, weak, and never stand firm. Let us bring those who are so afflicted to the Lord, that He may change their will to the quality of wine: that they no longer flow away, but be steadfast; and become to themselves and to others a source of comfort.

Who are those cold ones but they who cling to the passing things of this life? They who scorn not the delights of the world: who love pomp and power. For all these things flow away: they never stand firm, but rush ever precipitously downwards. Today such a one is rich, tomorrow a pauper; one day he appears in a carriage, with a girdle around him, a herald, and many attendants; often on the morrow he is in prison, unwillingly leaving his pomp for the next.

And the glutton after he is filled to bursting, cannot retain what fills him for longer than a day; when that has disappeared he is forced to heap up more for himself, and in nothing differs from the running torrent. For as there when the first water has run on, yet ever more takes its place, so we also after one meal need another. Such is the nature of the things of this life;

never at rest: ever flowing: ever drawn hither and thither.

But the delights of gluttony not alone flow away and pass, but they bring with them many afflictions. For when they flow with violence, they carry away the strength of both mind and body; and the violence of the torrent does less damage to the river bank, than the delights of the table in carrying away the very foundations of our strength. And if you approach a physician and ask: you will learn that it is from this that every cause of our bodily infirmities rises. For a simple plain table is the mother of health. Thus the physicians describe it. For they call it health not to be sated.

And if you would wish to know the diseases of the soul it causes men, you will find that from here arises covetousness, sloth, melancholy, dullness of mind, impurity, and every incontinence. For after the excessive delights of the table, their souls are like asses that are being torn asunder by suchlike wild beasts. Nor shall I speak of the loathings to which they are a prey who are slaves to this evil, because one cannot enumerate them: but I shall refer to one which is the worst of them all. At such tables as we speak of men never eat with pleasure. For since frugality is the mother of health, so likewise is it the mother of pleasure; but satiety, as it is the source and root of disease, so is it also of disgust. For where there is satiety there can be no desire, and where there is no desire, where can there be any pleasure? Therefore is it that we see the poor more alert and more vigorous in body than the rich, and also much more cheerful in heart.

Reflecting on all these things let us fly from drunkenness and from every excess; not alone from the excessive delights of the table, but from all others that are to be had in worldly things; and in their place let us take our pleasure in the delights of the soul, and as the prophet says let us take our delight in the Lord: *Delight in the Lord*, he says, *and he will give thee the requests of thy heart* (Ps. xxxvi. 4). In this way we shall have joy in what is good, both now and in the life to come, by the grace and favour of Our Lord Jesus Christ, by Whom and with Whom be there glory to the Father together with the holy Spirit for ever and ever. Amen.

II. St John Chrysostom, Bishop and Doctor

The First Miracle[3]

This beginning of miracles did Jesus in Cana of Galilee.

Unremitting and fierce is the devil in his attacks on us, and on all sides he lies in wait against our salvation. We must therefore be very vigilant, and cut off from every side his approach to us. For if he find but the least opening, he will soon make for himself a broad way, and then gradually enter in with all his forces. If we have any real care for our salvation, let him not come near us, even in small matters, so that we may be free to meet him more vigorously in greater things. For it would be very grievous foolishness indeed, that while he employs such zeal to destroy our soul, we show no equal anxiety for its salvation.

Not without reason do I say this to you, because I fear lest that wolf even now, unseen by us, may be standing in the midst of this sacred enclosure, and because of their own folly, and his guile, may have seized on one of the flock from among those now listening to me. If we could see the wounds he inflicts, or if his blows were felt by the body, it would not be difficult to guard against his plotting. But because the soul is invisible, and the wounds it receives are invisible, we have need of the greatest watchfulness, so that every man may prove himself. For: *what man knoweth the things of a man, but the spirit of a man that is in him?* (I Cor. ii. 11).

This exhortation is offered to you all, and to all a common remedy is offered. But it is for every man to take the remedies that are required for his own infirmity. I know not who is ill of soul, or who is well, and for this reason I speak of every illness, so that from what I preach each one may find a remedy for himself. Sometimes in my discourse I attack avarice, now sensuality, now the excessive delights of the table. Again I preach almsgiving, and I exhort you to give, and so in turn each of the other virtues. For I fear lest in seeking to heal you of one sickness, unknowing, I offer you a remedy for another, which you have not.

If this congregation were but one person I would not need to vary my sermons. But because amongst so many people it is likely that there are very many different maladies of soul, so it is not without reason that I vary my discourses. And they being spread so as to apply to all, each will hear for himself the remedy he needs. For this same reason Scripture also varies, and speaks of a hundred themes, because it speaks to the nature that all men have in common. In such a multitude it is inevitable that every kind of infirmity will be found, though they will not all be found singly in each person. So cleansing ourselves from all such things, let us listen with eager hearts to the divine words of the Gospel of today.

This beginning of miracles did Jesus in Cana of Galilee.

I have said earlier that there are some who say that this was not the beginning of miracles. Why, they argue, was this beginning linked with Cana of Galilee? For *this beginning*, he says, *He did in Cana of Galilee.* But upon this point I offer no opinion. But this I affirm, that after His baptism Christ began to perform miracles, and before that He wrought none; but whether this or another was the first performed after the baptism it is not necessary to discuss.

And he manifested his glory. In what manner? For not many beheld what He had done, only the waiters, the chief steward, and the bridegroom. How then did He manifest His glory? In what way? He manifested it so far as His own action was concerned; and if others who were present did not then hear of it, they would soon hear of it: for it is spoken of even to this day, and it is not forgotten.

That all did not know it on that day is evident from what follows; for after He had written, that *He manifested his glory*, the Evangelist goes on: *And his disciples believed in him*: they who already regarded Him with awe. Do you not see

that signs and wonders were necessary at this time, when honest and impartial men were present who would give close attention to what was being done? For these men would be more readily disposed to believe, as well as accurately to observe, what was done.

And how could He have become known to all without miracles? Because His doctrine and the prophecies sufficed abundantly to inspire wonder in the minds of those who heard Him, so that they who were well disposed would have paid attention to what was done. It was because of this that in many other places the Evangelists tell us He would not work a miracle, because of the antagonism of the men living there (Mt. xiii. 58; xii. 38).

Again, no one could help believing what is made known by manifest signs; although they might disbelieve what was revealed to them by words alone. Therefore, at first, the Lord allowed the meaning of His words to be veiled. But after the prophecies had been fulfilled He gave the disciples an understanding of His words, and likewise such grace of the Spirit that they took in the whole of His truth: *He will*, He says, *teach you all things and bring all things to your mind.* For they who in one night forgot Him, flying from Him, and denying even that they knew Him, would scarcely have remembered all that He had said over a long period of time unless they had received special assistance from the Holy Spirit.

But if they were to learn from the Holy Spirit, you will say, what need was there to be in the company of Christ, since they would not understand what Christ said? But the Holy Spirit did not teach them, but only recalled to their minds what Christ had said. And it is no small glory to Christ that the memory of His words was thus to be recalled to them. In the beginning it was only from the benign will of God that the grace of the Holy Spirit was so copious and great a gift; then later it was due to their own virtue that they retained so great a gift. For they lived lives of shining virtue, and manifested great wisdom, and suffered great toils: they set little value on this present life, and regarded lightly the things of this world, rising above them, like eagles soaring on swift wings in the sky, and by their works they obtained great illumination of the Holy Spirit, and by these same good works reached to heaven itself.

Let us imitate them, and not put out our own lights, but keep them bright with oil: for so is the splendour of this light kept bright. Let us gather oil for our vessels while yet we live, for leaving this life we can no longer buy it, nor procure it elsewhere, save at the hands of the poor. Let us while we are here gather it abundantly, if we wish to enter in with the bridegroom; if we do not we must remain outside the Bridegroom's chamber. For I tell you that though we have done a thousand other good works, it is impossible to enter there without almsdeeds. Let us then pour our charity in abundance, that we may receive those rewards of which no tongue can speak: to which may we all attain through the mercy and grace of Our Lord Jesus Christ, to Whom be honour and glory for ever and ever. Amen.

III. St Gaudentius, Bishop of Brescia

Christian Life[4]

Since we have completed our series of discourses given to Your Charity on the Book of Exodus, where the law of the celebration of the Pasch is described, let us now with God's help speak of that portion of the Gospel which has just been read to you, that we may show from the testimony of this event that the same God is the author of both the Old and the New Testament.

We have heard that Jesus the Saviour of men being invited went to a wedding feast, and that there He changed water into the nature and taste of wine. This narration has plainly the character of truthfulness; for He Who blessed the nuptials at Cana is the same Who in the beginning instituted them: and the creature that He made He can by that same power change to what He wills. As to the power of the Omnipotent God, no doubt can enter the mind of anyone who believes; yet one might wonder, and not without reason, why He should go to a wedding feast, that is, to a house of rejoicing? For almost every line of the Gospels tells us that the Lord Jesus Christ while He dwelt among men brought help to all who were in trouble, but especially to the afflicted, while He reproached the blaspheming Jews, and accused the Scribes and Pharisees of deceit and treachery and greed, and reproached the unbelieving cities; tormented the evil spirits that He might succour the captive spirit, and having driven out the demons

He restored to their right minds those who had been obsessed; that He healed the lepers who implored Him; restored with a word the paralysed; that He came walking upon the water in the midst of the tempest to succour those in fear, calming them; that He restored sight to eyes that were blinded or poured the new light into the eyes of those born blind; that He stood as a physician amid those who mourned, and took away grief and sorrow at the prayer of different parents, restoring their dear ones to health, or their dead to life.

To these ends the Son of God, God from the beginning, in the end of ages took a beginning of Flesh from the Virgin, and deigned to live among men, that He might succour a perishing world; since as He said those need the physician who are ill, not those that are healthy. And so this Physician was wont rather to enter the house of grief, than that of rejoicing. For He was the dear Friend of those tormented by the pain of wounds, or afflicted with some sickness, or given over to some wasting away of the flesh; for those who are well do not seek out the Physician.

What then is the meaning of this lesson of the Gospel, which has to-day been read to you, that the Lord being invited went to a marriage feast, if not that there one thing was wanting, and the lips of the thirsty guests thirsted for the wine that cheers the heart of man? But before we make known to you the knowledge of mystical things, let us re-call first the simple history of the event.

Christ did not turn away from the celebration of nuptials, so that He might give testimony that He was the same God Who in the beginning formed man and woman from the slime of the earth, and bestowed on them their conjugal authority, saying: *increase and multiply and fill the earth.* This displeases the Manichaeans, whose real displeasure however arises, not against marriage, but against the law which unites, not many women to one man, nor one woman to many men, but one woman to one man. For these same execrable Manichaeans are unwilling to live according to the doctrine of the Apostle Paul, *that every man have his own wife, and let every woman have her own husband* (I Cor. vii. 2).

Christ therefore blessed what He had instituted from the beginning, lawful espousals, when, being invited, He refused not to come to the wedding. And yet He taught that virginity was the better part, when He deigned through it to be born. God chose as His abode a holy Virgin, where, having entered in, He preserved the undimmed glory of her modesty, as without loss of integrity to His mother He was born, and without corruption conceived. And so that vessel of election, Paul, invited others to that good after which he himself followed, saying to the unwed: *It is good for them if they so continue even as I* (I Cor. vii. 8). He encourages them to this by the example of his own happiness; not compelling them by the power of his authority.

Speaking of virtue, he goes on: *I have no commandment of the Lord, but I give counsel, as having obtained mercy of the Lord, to be faithful. I think that it is good for a man to be so.* And after a long admonition, in which he extols the blessedness of chastity above the married state, he concludes with the following words: *therefore, both he that giveth his virgin in marrige, doth well: and he that giveth her not, doth better.* This I believe was not said to parents of virgins by the Blessed Apostle: since it is evident that they cannot be governed by the choice of another's will: but to each one, both man and woman, the choice is set before them, that he conserve the integrity of his own virgin, that is, his own flesh, born virginal, choosing the better, and the free part; or, that understanding the marriage state, let him enter it, if he is unable to be continent.

As to parents, or any relatives whatsoever of virgins, be they boys or girls, let them not delude themselves as to the above-mentioned power of choice; because we have set out that those concerned cannot be over-ruled by the desires of others. They cannot impose perpetual continence on those subject to them, because be it known to all that this is a matter of individual choice. They may guide their minds in this direction, and this they ought to do, that they may be eager to dedicate themselves to God, rather than to the world, so that from among their own kindred they may offer up, in the order of the priesthood, servants who will be worthy to serve the Divine Altar, or nurture maidens dedicated to chastity in the ranks of the consecrated women, so that providing the church of God with such helpers, they may themselves attain to blessedness in return; for it is written: *Blessed is he that has seed in Sion, and kindred in Jerusalem* (Is. xxxi. 9 (Sept.)).

There is in this sublime prophetic saying a higher meaning, which we shall explain in its proper time. But as we have taken it upon us to engage in this treatise out of zeal for chastity, we shall make it clear that it was on account of this virtue that the Saviour came to the wedding feast; meanwhile we shall suggest a brief consideration, for the instruction of our neophytes, and will then show the spiritual content of this lesson which we shall explain figuratively in the subsequent discourse.

You must direct your mind to a realisation of this: that through baptism you have been reborn, and regenerated, and because of this you are called infants. If there be any among you who are joined in wedlock, and are yet desirous of keeping themselves as virgins rather than give themselves in marriage, let them possess their spouses as though they possessed them not; and great will be their reward with the Lord Our God, because they have preserved their own flesh, as it was re-born in the sacrament of Baptism. But *I say this for your profit; not to cast a snare upon you* (I Cor. vii. 35). For should you after baptism still observe your lawful wedlock, *thou hast not sinned* (I Cor. vii. 28).

Take care in another direction, so that you lose not your faith: namely; that, being now a believer, you fly from fornication. You can safeguard yourself against this if you avoid drunkenness, and that unworthy conviviality where the seductive gestures of evil-living women awaken unlawful desires, where the harp and the trumpet sound, and every kind of music mingles with the dancers' cymbals.

Unhappy those houses which are but little removed from resorts of pleasure. Let all such things, I beseech you, be removed from among you. Let the houses of the Christian, and of the baptised, be free from the devil's chorus: let it be refined, hospitable, and sanctified by earnest prayer: let you come together for psalms and hymns and spiritual singing. Let the word of God, and the sign of Christ, be in your heart, and on your lips and brow, in your eating and in your drinking, in your conversations, at the baths, in your chambers, in your coming and in your going, in joy and in sadness; so that according to the teaching of the most blessed Paul: *whether you eat or drink, or whatever else you do, do all in the Name of Our Lord Jesus Christ* (I Cor. x. 31; Col. iii. 17), Who has called you to His grace. For it is He that has given you pardon for your past offences, and promises you reward for your amended lives.

Having explained these things for the common moral instruction. I come to the promised spiritual explanation of this Gospel reading: though I do not consider myself fitted to explain the mysteries of Christ; neither do I presume to take upon myself the authority of the most blessed Paul in so speaking: but since *we speak, not in the learned words of human wisdom; but in the doctrine of the spirit, comparing spiritual things with spiritual* (I Cor. ii. xiii), I desire, as God will deign to help me, to make known to you the hidden celestial meaning contained within this reading of the Gospel.

A little earlier, at the beginning of my sermon, explaining the reason why the Saviour came to the wedding feast, I spoke for a while on the preserving of virginity, and seem to have dwelt a little upon the subject. Now I shall resume the

narrative of the Evangelist, so that we may inquire further into its spiritual meaning. *And on the third day, there was a marriage in Cana of Galilee: and the mother of Jesus was there. And Jesus also was invited, and his disciples, to the marriage. And the wine failing . . .*

That we may understand, as we ought, the true history of this event we should first expound to you, spiritually, what is this *third day*, on which the nuptials were celebrated? It is the day of light, dearly Beloved; and so it was most fittingly prepared for the teaching of the Lord, Who is the True Light, as the Prophet testifies: *The commandment of the Lord is lightsome, enlightening the eyes* (Ps. xviii. 9). And again elsewhere: *Because the commandment is a lamp, and the law a light* (Prov. vi. 23). Hence well does the Saviour admonish us that we must walk in the light: *If a man walketh in the day, he stumbleth not, because he seeth the light of the world* (Jn. xi. 9). And in truth if a man walks by the light of the commandments of God, he will not stumble.

The first day was from Adam unto Moses: the second was the time subject to the law of Moses: the third is the time in which the Grace of the Redeemer prevails. In this day the heavenly Bridegroom, Jesus Christ, the Lover of all who believe, joined unto Himself the Church as a Spouse from among the Gentiles, to whom He gave a ring in pledge of their union, and the precious earrings of faith, *for faith cometh by hearing, and hearing by the word of God* (Rom. x. 17), that is, by the Son of God. To which Spouse the same God the Word, the Son of God, gave also golden bracelets, in sign of the good works that she would do with her right hand, and one by one each single jewel by which her virtues are symbolised.

And that you may understand that these spiritual nuptials were celebrated with the people of the Gentiles, they took place, not in Judea, but in Cana of Galilee, which is clearly shown by the interpretation of the names, as well as by the testimony of Isaias, who spoke of *Galilee of the Gentiles.* For Cana means possession: and Galilee a wheel, or that which revolves, in the Hebrew speech. For it has appeared that the people of Galilee have turned from the error of idolatry, in which they formerly were involved, to the height of Christian truth, hastened by the speed of a running wheel. Hence figuratively also David has said: *The voice of thy thunder in a wheel* (Ps. lxxvi. 19). For the Lord spoke from the heavens, and the Most High declared: *This is my Beloved Son, in whom I am well pleased: hear ye him* (Mt. xvii. 5). The voice of whose thunder is rooted in the hearts of His people, which hastens, as speedily as a running wheel, from the gentile superstition to the faith of the Lord Jesus.

Jesus also was invited, and His disciples. A great mystery of piety. He that is the Bridegroom is invited: He is invited by the voices of the Prophets who so beseech Him: *Lord, bow down thy heavens and descend* (Ps. cxliii. 5). And again: *Stir up thy might, and come to save us* (Ps. lxxix. 3). And with these are many other voices, like to those of the beseeching prophets. Together with Christ His holy disciples are invited, as the near friends of the heavenly Bridegroom, since it was said by the Prophet: *There are no speeches, nor languages where there voices are not heard:* for filled with the Holy Spirit they will soon speak in the tongues of all races of the Gentiles. Hence the spirit of prophecy, speaking as though that was now fulfilled which was yet to come, adds: *Their sound hath gone forth into all the earth: and their words unto the end of the world* (Ps. xviii. 4, 5).

Then the narrative continues: *And they had no wine.* Because the wedding wine was consumed, which means that the Gentiles had not the wine of the Holy Spirit. So what is here referred to is not the wine of these nuptials, but the wine of the preceding nuptials; for the nuptial wine of the Holy Spirit had ceased, since the prophets had ceased to speak, who before had ministered unto the people of Israel. For all the prophets and the Law had prophesied until the coming of John; nor was there anyone to give spiritual drink to the Gentiles who thirsted; but the Lord Jesus was awaited, who would fill the new bottles with new wine, by His baptism: *For the old things have passed away: behold all things are made new* (II Cor. v. 17).

All things are made new, but so that their origin from the old remains, since wine is produced, not from nothingness, but from the ancient element of water. Neither think ye that the letter of the Law is to be despised, whence the Holy Spirit, by the operation of Jesus, is drawn forth by faithful servitors; and for that reason, men perished in the ancient flood, and are now in Baptism reborn; *for the letter killeth, but the spirit quickeneth* (II Cor. iii. 6). The letter alone killeth, but tempered by the Holy Spirit it regenerates.

It is known that all men of that time perished, save those who had merited to be in the Ark, which was a figure of the Church to come. Likewise even now they cannot be saved who will have turned away from the Apostolic Faith and the Catholic Church. Let each one of you, therefore, strive most earnestly to remain within the house of the Lord, doing the things that are becoming to the grace that is within you, that you have received.

Let those reborn into *the new man* be on guard against your former sins. Safeguard, I beseech you, the new bottles, O Neophytes; lest returning to your old way of life, and breaking the bottles, you spill the new wine: *for the new wine will break the bottles, and the wine will be spilt* (Lk. v. 37). Safeguard therefore the whole newness of the reborn man, and preserve the heavenly wine of grace in your vessels, so that your faith, being defended, will defend you, through the Saviour of all men, Jesus Christ Our Lord, reigning with the Father and the Holy Spirit before all things were, and now, and for ever and ever, Amen.

IV. St Augustine, Bishop and Doctor

Christ in His Mystical Body [5]

1. *Christ's humility is the remedy of man's pride.* You know, Brethren, for as believers in Christ you have learned this, and we in our preaching have continually reminded you of it, that the remedy of man's pride is the humility of Christ. For man would not have fallen, had he not fallen through pride. *For pride*, as Scripture says, *is the beginning of all sin* (Ecclus. x. 15). To undo the beginning of sin, there had to be a beginning of grace. So if pride is the beginning of sin, whence could pride's swelling be healed, had God not deigned to become lowly? Let man be ashamed to be proud; since God Himself has become humble.

For when it is said to a man that he be humble, he becomes scornful; and when he is injured, he is urged by pride to seek vengeance. For scorning submissiveness, men only desire revenge: as if another's punishment could bring anyone profit. Being offended then, and having suffered injury, he seeks to be revenged; he seeks ease for his own hurt in another's pain, and acquires only a greater affliction. And therefore has the Lord Christ deigned to become lowly, showing us the way, if we but deign to walk by it.

2. *Why Christ being hungry, made not bread from stone, as He made wine from water at the wedding feast.* See how among other things the Son of the Virgin came to a wedding: He that with the Father made marriage. As the first woman, through whom sin came, was made without woman from man, so the Man, through whom sin was destroyed, was made without man from a woman. We fell because of the first; through the second we rise again. And what did He do at the marriage feast? He made wine from water. What power could be greater? Yet He Who did this suffered hunger. He Who made wine from

water could have made bread from stones. The power was the same.

But then it was the devil tempted Him, and so Christ did not make it. For as you know that when the Lord was tempted, this the devil suggested to Him. For He was hungry: for to this also had he lowered Himself, because this too was part of His humiliation. For the Bread has hungered, the Way was lost, Our Healing was wounded, and Life died. When therefore He was hungry the tempter, as you know, said to Him: *If thou be the Son of God, command that these stones be made bread* (Mt. iv. 3). And He answered the tempter, to teach you how to answer the tempter. For so the leader fights, that he may give an example to the soldiers. What did He answer? *Not in bread alone doth man live, but in every word that proceedeth from the mouth of God.* And He did not make bread from stones, as He well could Who made wine from water.

For by the same power could He make bread from stone, but He did not, that He might spurn the solicitation of the tempter. For the tempter is not overcome unless he be despised. And when the tempter, the devil, was defeated, the angels came and ministered to Him (Mt. iv). He therefore Who could do so much, why has He done this but not that? Read, recall rather, what you have just heard, when He wrought this sign, that is, made water into wine: what did the Evangelist also say? *And His Disciples believed in Him.* Was the devil then ready to believe?

3. *Christ in Hi humility is the way to heaven.* He then Who could do such things was hungry, He thirsted, He was weary, He slept;

He was seized, beaten, and put to death. This is His way: walk by humility, that you may come to life eternal. Christ as God is the land towards which we are going: Christ as man is the way by which we go. To Him we go: by Him we go. Should we be afraid that we shall go astray? He departed not from the Father: He came to us. Nursed at the breast, He holds the world in His hand. He lay in the manger, yet He had care for His angels. God and Man: the same is God Who is Man; the same is Man Who is God. But He is not God in that whereby He is Man. He is God because He is the Word: Man, because the Word was made flesh. He is God, in remaining God: He is Man, by assuming the flesh of man; by taking on Himself what He was not, not by losing what He was.

And so having suffered in His lowliness, having died, and been buried, He has risen again, and ascended into Heaven, and there He abides; sitting at the Right Hand of the Father: but here on earth He is destitute, in His poor. Yesterday also I placed this reflection before Your Charity, in the previous sermon, because of that which He said to Nathaniel: *Greater things than these shalt thou see. I say to you that you shall see the heaven opened, and the angels of God ascending and descending upon the Son of Man* (Jn. i. 51). And we examined the meaning of these words, and spoke to you at some length. Do we need to repeat the same today? Those of you who were present will remember: nevertheless I shall recall it briefly to your minds.

4. *Christ is above and below. Christ is rich and poor.* He would not

have said: *Ascending to the Son of Man,* unless He were above: nor would He say: *Descending to the Son of Man,* unless He were below. He is above, and He is below. Above in Himself: below in His members. Whence also that voice that spoke to Saul: *Saul, Saul, why persecutest Me?* He would not have said, *Saul, Saul,* unless that He were above. But Saul was not persecuting Him above. He that was above would not have said: *Why persecutest thou Me,* unless He were also below.

Fear Christ above: acknowledge Him here below. Possess Christ the bountiful Giver above: acknowledge Him here below, among the needy. There He is Rich: here He is poor. That He is poor here below He has left us word: *I was hungry, I was thirsty, naked, a stranger, I was in prison.* To some He said: *You ministered to me.* To some He said: *You ministered not to me* (Mt. xxiv. 35, 45). See, we have shown you that Christ is poor: that Christ is rich, is there anyone who does not know? And this is part of His richness: that He changed water into wine. As God He is rich: as Man He is poor. As a rich man He has already ascended into Heaven: yet here a poor man He hungers, He is thirsty, He is naked.

5. *Every man is poor, and a beggar of God.* You, what are you? Rich or poor? Many say to me: I am poor, and they speak the truth. But I distinguish a poverty that possesses something, and a poverty that has nothing. Someone has much, both of silver and gold. Oh would that he might believe himself poor! He proclaims that he is poor, if he acknowledges the poor around him. Who so? Because however much you, whosoever you are, possess, you are a beggar of God. I shall prove it to you, from the hour of prayer.

You pray for something. How are you not poor who beg? And more, you ask for bread. For do you not say: *Give us our daily bread?* You who beg for daily bread, are you rich or poor? Yet Christ says to you: Give Me of that which I gave to you. For when you came hither, what did you bring with you? You brought nothing here; you take nothing thence. Wherefore then do you not give Me of what is Mine? For you have abundance, but the poor man is in need. Recall your birth: you were both born naked. So you also were born naked. Here you have found many things: did you bring anything with you? I ask for what is Mine. Give, and I will repay. I have been a bountiful Giver; make me quickly your Debtor. I said: I have been to you a bountiful Giver, make me your Debtor; I say more: Let you be my moneylender. Give me but a little, and I shall return thee much. Give me things of the earth, I will repay in heavenly things. Give me the things of the present, I will return thee eternal. I shall return thee to thyself, when I shall return thee to Me. Amen.

V. ST CYRIL: ON THE GOSPEL[6]

JOHN ii. 1–11

ii. 1. At an opportune time does Christ go there to perform a miracle; though it seems as though He were invited by chance. Since the festivities would be celebrated modestly and becomingly, the Mother of the Saviour is present; He also, being invited, came, and with Him His Disciples. He came, not so much to partake of the wedding feast, as to perform His miracle; and furthermore, that He might sanctify the beginning of human generation in that which pertains to the flesh. It was but fitting that He Who was about to restore the nature itself of man, and bring it wholly to a better state, should give His blessing, not alone to those already born, but also prepare a blessing for those who were afterwards to be born, sanctifying their coming into this world.

And there is yet a third reason. It had elsewhere been said by God to man: *In sorrow shalt thou bring forth children* (Gen. iii. 16). How is this curse to be lifted, or for what reason was it to be lawful to avoid the nuptials that were thus condemned? The Saviour, most Beloved of men, has solved our difficulty. By His Presence He sanctified marriage, and He Who is the Joy and the Delight of all men, has taken away the ancient sadness of childbearing. *If there be in Christ a new creature, the old things are passed away, as Paul says, and behold all things are made new* (II Cor. v. 17).

ii. 4. He comes therefore to the wedding feast, and His Disciples with Him. It was fitting that they should be present while He performed these wonders, who were to keep in their minds the significance of these wonders, gathering up as food for their faith that which was now about to be done. The wine for the guests giving out, His Mother asks, desiring Him, that

He use His wonted goodness and kindness, saying: *They have no wine.* For since it was in His power to do all things whatsoever He wished, she urges Him to perform a miracle.

And Jesus saith to her: Woman, what is that to me, and to thee? My hour is not yet come. His answer the Saviour has also admirably disposed. For it was not becoming to Him that He should hasten, or freely offer, to perform miracles: but, being invited to come there, that He should grant this favour rather for the purpose of supplying a need than to astonish the beholders. Things asked for are more gratefully received, if they are not too readily bestowed on those who ask, but with a little delay are offered as an object of earnest hope. Here too Christ gives us example, that the greatest honour is due to parents, since it is out of reverence for His Mother that He now undertakes to do that which He had not yet desired to do.

ii. 5–6. *His Mother said to the waiters . . .* The Woman, having, as was fitting, great authority over the Lord, Her Son, persuades Him to work a miracle. She also prepares the way for it, bidding the waiters of the feast to be at hand, and to have prepared that which the Lord will presently command.

ii. 7–10. *Jesus saith to them . . .* The waiters fulfil His requests. With ineffable power He changes the water into wine. For what is there difficult to the Omnipotent? He Who calls things from nothingness into being, how could it be difficult to change what was made into what He willed? They wonder, as at something extraordinary. But not otherwise could that be which was done by Christ. And the Chief steward chides the bridegroom, not ungracefully, I think, if the order of what has taken place be considered:- because he gives out the better wine as the supper comes to an end.

ii. 11. Many things, and these too are wondrous, are prefigured at the same time by this singular and earliest sign. For honest nuptials are sanctified, and the curse that was laid on womankind is taken away. No more shall she bring forth children in sorrow, since Christ has placed His Blessing on the beginning of human generation. And the Saviour's glory shines as the light of the sun, and His Disciples' faith is confirmed in the wonder of these things. This will suffice as regards the history of this account: and, for the purpose of contemplation, another aspect must be considered, and we must point out what is meant by these happenings.

The Word of God, therefore, has come down from the heavens, as He has elsewhere said (Jn. vi. 28), so that as a Spouse He might persuade the nature which He united with Himself, that it be filled with the seed of wisdom. And Humanity, as is befitting, is called a bride, and the Saviour the Bridegroom; divine Scripture thus taking images from the likeness of nature, to raise us to the higher understanding of that which He said.

The nuptials are celebrated on *the third day*, that is, in the last age of the world. For the ternary number signifies for us a beginning, a middle, and an end. And so do we divide any period of time. This the prophetic speech bears out: *He will*

strike and He will cure us. He will revive us after two days: on the third day he will raise us up, and we shall live in his sight. We shall know, and we shall follow on, that we may know the Lord. His going forth is prepared in the morning light (Osee vi. 3).

For He struck us because of Adam's sin, saying: *Dust thou art, and unto dust shalt thou return* (Gen. iii. 19). But on the third day He healed those who were stricken with corruption and death, that is, not in the first age, nor in the middle, but in these last times; when, becoming man, He restored all human nature, raising it in Himself from the dead. And so He is called *the first fruits of them that sleep* (I Cor. xv. 20). Therefore when the Evangelist speaks of *the third day*, upon which was celebrated the wedding feast, he means this present age.

More, the Evangelist speaks of the place of the event. In the village of Cana in Galilee, he says. Here the careful listener will notice that the celebration was not held in Jerusalem, but outside Judea, so that the gathering was celebrated in the country of the Gentiles. For *Galilee is of the Gentiles*, as the prophet says (Mt. iv. 15). For it is very plain that the Synagogue of the Jews had rejected the heavenly Bridegroom: but by the Church of the Gentiles He was received with a joyful heart.

And the Saviour came to the wedding feast, not as one uninvited, but as besought by the multitude of the voices of the saints. Then, says the Evangelist, the guests ran short of wine. *For the Law brought nothing to perfection* (Heb. vii. 19); the Mosaic code did not suffice for perfect happiness.

Neither was that inward guide of natural sobriety equal to the task of conducting us to salvation. And so of us also can it be said: *They have no wine.* But the most bountiful God does not despise us who are striving with the hunger for good things. He offers us a wine far better than we had. *For the letter killeth, but the spirit quickeneth* (II Cor. iii. 6).

Further, the Law had no completeness in good things: but the teaching of the Gospel has in it the fullness of every blessing. The Chief steward wonders at the wine. I believe that anyone among those that are raised to the pontificate, and to whom is given the care of the House of Christ Our Saviour, will wonder exceedingly at the goodness of His teaching above that of the Law. To Him Christ has ordered that the wine be brought, that he may taste it, because, according to the teaching of Paul: *The husbandman, that laboureth, must first partake of the fruits* (II Tim. ii. 6). Again, let him that hears take into his heart that which I say. Amen.

VI. St Bernard, Abbot and Doctor
The Six Watering Pots [7]

1. In the reading of today's Gospel, Brethren, we have heard that Our Lord went to a wedding feast. Let us then do that which He elsewhere admonished us to do and become as those men *who wait for their Lord, when He shall return from the wedding* (Lk. xii. 36). One does not say to a man holding a wagon in the field, or to one buying or selling at the market: whom are you expecting? Neither are we like to those who so wait, but to one whom we see standing by a door, frequently hastening out, looking out often from the windows, is it to be wondered at if we say: whom are you expecting?

They indeed are like to the men who wait for their Lord, who have heard, and not with a deaf ear; *Be still and see that I am God* (Ps. xlv. 11). For the Lord will come to those who wait for Him in truth, such as he who said: *With expectation I have waited for the Lord* (Ps. xxxix. 1). He will come as one returning from the wedding, inebriated with the wine of love, and forgetful of our offences. He will not come to those who wait, as one returning from the wedding *like a mighty man that hath been surfeited with wine* (Ps. lxxvii. 65). He will come as one inebriated, and unmindful of His own sorrows. And then, as to those others, God will forget to be merciful. He will come *in wrath, and indignation, as an angry man*; but, O Lord, *rebuke me not in thy indignation* (Ps. vi. 2). These words are spoken, not so much with reference to the present wedding feast, but rather on its occasion.

2. Let us together with His Disciples follow the Lord as He goes there, so that seeing that which He is about to do, we may also with them believe in Him. *And the wine failing, the Mother of Jesus saith to Him: they have no wine.* She, most kind and compassionate, has pity on their embarrassment. But from that source of tenderness what could flow but compassion? What wonder, I say, if that compassionate

heart should show such tender consideration? For should anyone hold sweet smelling fruit in his hand for half the day, will not the fragrance of it linger there for the remaining half? How much therefore did the power of love effect that heart where He rested for nine months? And it filled her soul before it filled her womb: and leaving the womb it departed not from her heart.

The answer of Our Lord could seem stern and unfeeling: but He knew to whom He was speaking: and Who it was that spoke she also knew. And that you may know in what manner she received His answer, or how great was her confidence in the compassion of her Son, she says: *Whatsoever he shall say to you, do ye.*

3. *Now there were there six watering pots of stone, according to the manner of the purifying of the Jews.* We now propose to set these six watering pots of stone for the purifying of those that are *Israelites indeed*, not in the letter but in the spirit, or rather that being *set there* to point them out to you. For the Church has not yet reached that perfection, when purified and made glorious, and *without spot or wrinkle, or any such thing*, Christ shall present her to Himself (Eph. v. 27). Meanwhile she has need of manifold purification, yet though sin abounds, forgiveness also abounds, and just as misery is multiplied so likewise is mercy: though not as the offence was, *so also the gift* (Rom. v. 15). For His grace not alone washes away our sins, it also bestows merit.

The six jars therefore have been placed there for those who after baptism have fallen into sin. It is of these we now speak: for to these

we belong. We put away our old stained garment, but alas, now more guiltily have we put it on again. We washed our feet: but we have soiled them worse than before. And as he who soils himself must cleanse himself, so we having soiled ourselves must wash ourselves clean. Another's water has cleansed those whom another's guilt has stained. Yet saying another's I deny not that the guilt is also ours: otherwise it would not have stained us. But it is another's, because all we unknowing have sinned in Adam; it is ours, because, though in another, we too have sinned, and to us the fault was imputed, by the hidden though just judgement of God.

Yet, that you may not have cause to complain, O man, against the disobedience of Adam, for you is offered the obedience of Christ, so that though sold to bondage for no fault of yours, yet are you freely purchased back; if unknowingly you died in Adam, unknowingly you live again in Christ. You knew not when Adam stretched forth guilty hands to the forbidden tree: neither did you know when Christ stretched forth unblemished hands upon the saving tree. From the first there flowed down to you the blemish by which you were stained: from the side of Christ the water flowed whereby you are made clean. Now by your own fault you are stained again, and washed clean, not by water that is yours, but by Him and through Him, Who alone cleanses us of our sins.

4. The first watering jar therefore, and the first purification, is that of repentance, since we read that *if the wicked do penance for all his*

sins which he hath committed, I will not remember all his iniquities that he hath done (Ezech. xviii. 21, 22). The second is confession. All things are made clean in confession. The third is almsgiving. So we read in the Gospel: *Give alms, and behold, all things are clean unto you* (Lk. xi. 41). The fourth is the forgiving of injuries, according to what we say when we pray: *Forgive us our debts, as we also forgive our debtors* (Mt. vi. 12). The fifth is mortification of the body: hence, in our prayer we ask that through abstinence in this world, we may come to sing the praises of God.[8] The sixth is obedience to such counsels as were given to the Disciples, and would that we also might merit to hear: *Now you are clean by reason of the word which I have spoken to you* (Jn. xv. 3); because they were not as those to whom He said: *My word hath no place in you:* for they hearing His word gave heed to it (Jn. xviii. 37).

These are the six water pots set for our purification, and which are empty and full of wind if they are used in vain glory. They are full of water if they are used in the fear of God; since *the fear of the Lord is a fountain of life* (Prov. xiv. 27). The fear of the Lord is, I repeat, water, which, having a simpler flavour, is yet supremely refreshing to the soul parched with evil desires. It is a water that can extinguish the fiery darts of the wicked one. Nor is it against what we are saying that water seeks the lowest level: for fear leads down to deepest reflection, and lights up the abode of darkness to our fearful mind, as we read in Isaias: *In the midst of my days I shall go down to the gates of hell* (Is. xxxviii. 10). But by divine

grace this water is changed into wine, since perfect charity *casteth out fear* (I Jn. iv. 18).

5. The water jars are described as being of stone, not so much because of hardness as because they are enduring. And as containing *two or three measures apiece.* Two measures mean a twofold fear: the fear of being cast into hell, and the fear of being shut from heaven. But since these have in mind the uncertain future, and since the soul can deceive itself, as it were, saying: after you have had a little pleasure then do penance, so you neither lose the one nor perish in the other, it is therefore expedient to join to them a third fear, one known to those that are spiritually minded, and which the more it is present to us the more we profit from it.

For those who have tasted spiritual food are ever fearful lest they be defrauded of it. They need robust food who have put their hands to difficult tasks. Let them live of the straw of Egypt who slave in *works of clay, and brick;* for us stronger nourishment is needed, since there is a long way before us, that we may journey in the strength of this food. This is the Bread of angels, the living Bread, our daily Bread. It is of this we were promised we would receive a hundredfold in this world. And since to the hired servant there is given his food while he labours and his wage at the end of the day, so also at the end the Lord shall render us eternal life, and meanwhile He promises us a hundredfold, and He fulfils His promise (Mt. xix. 29).

What wonder then that a man should fear to lose this grace who has once attained it? This is the third measure, which He has clearly set before us, but with a distinction, in that it is not for the use of all: for not to all was a hundredfold promised, but only to those who have left all things. Amen.

VII. St Bernard, Abbot and Doctor
The Spiritual Nuptials of the Gospel [9]

1. A simple consideration of the works of the Lord will nourish simpler minds; but they whose souls are more exercised find within a food more nourishing, more flavoured, and as *the fat and marrow of corn*. For the works of God are lovely in their outward seeming, and yet more lovely in their inward perfection; as He outwardly was beautiful among the sons of men (Ps. xliv. 3), but within Him possessed the splendour of eternal light, surpassing the countenances of the angels (Wisd. vii. 26). For to outward eyes He appeared as a man without stain, flesh without sin, a lamb without blemish. How beautiful are the feet of him that bringeth good tidings, and that preacheth peace (Is. lii. 7): yet more beautiful, more precious, His head; since God is the Head of Christ.

Most beautiful was He in His outward form of man, on whom sin hath not fallen, and blessed are the eyes that saw Him; yet more blessed are the clean of heart, for they shall see God (Mt. v. 8). And lastly, the Apostle, when he had come to the final inwardness of things reckoned this as but a potsherd, though beautiful indeed, saying: *And if we have known Christ according to the flesh; but now we know him so no longer* (II Cor. v. 16). And this no doubt he said because the Lord Himself had foretold: *The flesh profiteth nothing, it is the spirit that quickeneth* (Jn. vi. 64). This however is a wisdom that Paul speaks among the perfect, not among those to whom we read that he said: *For I judged not myself to know anything among you but Jesus Christ, and him crucified* (I Cor. ii. 2).

All sweet is He, All wholesome, and most lovely, as the voice of the Spouse declaims (Cant. v. 16). And as He is there shown to us, so will you find Him in His works. For as in His outward look, as seen by others, He is indeed lovely, yet should one break the nut within he will find what is yet more lovely, and still more desirable. This you find not among the Fathers of the Old Testament. For in their works what is beautiful is their mystical meaning; considered in themselves they are sometimes found less worthy; as in the deeds of Jacob, the adultery of David, and many similar things. Precious indeed the trays, but not so precious the vases. And perhaps for this it was said: *Dark waters in the clouds of the air*; since these were indeed dark clouds: while of the Lord there is added: *At the brightness that was before him the clouds passed* (Ps. xvii. 12).

2. I believe that you have now seen why I desire to say these things. For today you have heard of the miracle that was performed at the wedding feast, which was the beginning of the Lord's miracles; of which indeed the account is wonderful, yet more wondrous is its significance. It was a truly great

sign of divine power, that at the word of the Lord water is changed into wine; but there is a more perfect change wrought by the hand of the Almighty which He prefigured in this wonder. For we are all of us invited to spiritual nuptials, in which the Bridegroom is none other than Christ the Lord: for in the psalm we sing: *And He as bridegroom coming out of his bridal chamber* (Ps. xviii. 6). And we are the Spouse, and, if this does not appear incredible to you, all together we are one Spouse, and the soul of each single one of us is itself a Spouse. But when can our misery know this of its God, that He loves us as the Bridegroom loves the Spouse? This Spouse is far below Her Bridegroom, in degree, in appearance, and in dignity. Yet for this Ethiopian the Son of the Eternal King has come from afar, to espouse Her, and feared not to die for Her.

Moses also espoused an Ethiopian, but he could not change her colour; but Christ loved His Spouse, lowly and stained though She be, that He might present Her to Himself, a glorious Church, without spot or wrinkle (Eph. v. 27). Let Aaron murmur, and Mary, not the new, but the old; not the Mother of the Lord, but the sister of Moses (Num. xii); not, I repeat, our Mary, for She was anxious only that nothing be wanting at the wedding feast. But though the priests murmur, and the Synagogue murmurs, let you remember to give thanks with all your heart.

3. Whence is this to thee, O Human Soul, whence to thee? Whence to thee this immeasurable glory, that you should merit to become the spouse of Him on Whom

the angels desire to look? Whence is it to thee that He is thy Bridegroom Whose beauty the sun and moon reflect with wonder, at whose nod all things are moved? What wilt thou render to the Lord for all that He has rendered to thee (Ps. cxv. 12), who art the companion of His table, the sharer of His Kingdom, the consort of His bridal chamber, and at the end the King will bring you into His House?

Behold how much already you perceive of the Lord, how much you have already tasted of Him; see with what eagerness of love bestowed must He be embraced and loved in return, Who has deemed thee worthy of so much, nay, Who for thee has done so much? From His side He refashioned thee, when for thee He slept upon the Cross, and for thee accepted the sleep of death. For thee He went forth from His Father, departed from the Synagogue His mother, that cleaving to thee, you might become one with Him in spirit.

And hearken thou, O Daughter, and see, and reflect (Ps. xliv. 11), and consider how great is the condescension of thy God to thee, and forget thy people and thy father's house. Depart from the loves of the flesh, unlearn the ways of the world, withhold thee from thy former sins, and forget thy evil habits. And why you may wonder? Does not an angel of God stand by thee, who shall cut thee in two (Dan. xiii. 59), should you, which God forbid, accept another lover?

4. For thou art already espoused to Him, and now is the nuptial breakfast: the supper is prepared in heaven, in the eternal banquet hall. And shall wine be wanting there?

Far from it. For there we shall be inebriated with the abundance of Thy House, and drink of the torrent of Thy pleasures (Ps. xxxv. 9). For thou has prepared for Thy nuptials a torrent of wine; of wine, I say, that will gladden the heart, for the stream of the river maketh the city joyful (Ps. xlv. 5).

But now we partake of the breakfast here, for great is the way that still remains to us, but we partake not with great abundance, for fullness and satiety pertains to the eternal supper. Here the wine sometimes fails, that is, the grace of devotion, the fervour of love. How often, have I Brethren, after your miserable complainings, had to implore the Mother of mercy that she remind Her most gentle Son that you had no wine? And She, I declare to you, Beloved Brethren, if devoutly implored by us will not be wanting in our necessities: for She is merciful and the Mother of mercy. For if She had compassion on the embarrassment of those who invited her to the wedding, much more will she have compassion on us if we devoutly beseech Her. For She is pleased with our nuptials, and they concern her more closely than theirs: since it was from her womb, as from His chamber, that the heavenly Bridegroom came forth (Ps. xviii. 6).

5. But whom does it not move that at these nuptials the Lord made answer to His kind and most holy Mother, saying: *Woman, what is it to me, and to thee? My hour is not yet come.* What is it to Her and to Thee, O Lord? Does not what concerns the mother concern also the son? Why do you ask what is it to Her, since Thou art the Blessed fruit of her immaculate womb? Is it not She that with modesty undefiled conceived Thee, and without corruption brought Thee forth? Is it not She in whose womb for nine months Thou didst abide, at whose virginal breast thou hast drunk milk with whom at twelve years old Thou hast gone down from Jerusalem, and was subject to Her? Why now, O Lord, dost Thou complain to Her, saying: *What is it to Me, and to Thee?* Much indeed, and for every reason. But yet do I see that it is not as though annoyed, or as seeking to trouble the tender reserve of the Virgin Mary that Thou hast said, *What is it to me, and to thee,* since it was at the word of Mary the waiters came to Thee, and without delay Thou didst that which She had laid before Thee.

Why then, Brethren, why then did He thus reply at first? It was especially because of us, so that being given over to the service of God anxiety regarding our earthly parents might not be allowed to trouble us, and that their needs must not stand in the way of our spiritual service. As long as we are of the world it is true that we are debtors to our parents. But having abandoned our own selves, how much more are we freed from anxiety concerning them? Regarding which we read of a certain one of the brethren, who lived as a hermit, who when approached for aid by his brother in the flesh replied, that he ought rather seek aid from their other brother since he himself had died. And he who had come was so impressed that the other should answer that he had died, that he made answer that he too now died.

Perfectly therefore did the Lord teach us that we also should not be solicitous for our kindred more than religion requires, when He said to His Mother, and to such a Mother: *Woman, what is it to me, and to thee?* So also in another place, when it was said to Him that His Mother and His brethren stood without seeking to speak with Him, He answered: *Who is my mother and who are my brethren?* (Mt. xii. 48). Where then do they stand who so unspiritually and so unwisely are wont to be concerned with their kindred in the flesh, as though they were still living among them?

6. But let us see what follows? There were the Evangelist tells us, *six water pots of stone, according to the manner of the purifying of the Jews.* From this you can see that the nuptial feast was not at the stage of completion but of preparation, where there was yet need for the purifications. They were therefore the nuptials of betrothal and not of union. Far be it from us to believe that there will be water pots of purification at those nuptials where Christ will present to Himself a glorious Church, having neither spot nor wrinkle, or any such thing (Eph. v. 27). For what stain will purification be necessary? Now indeed is the time to wash one's self, now it is evident that purification is necessary for us, since no one is free from stain, not even an infant whose life upon the earth is but one day. Now the Spouse is being washed clean, now is she to be purified, so that in these celestial nuptials she may be presented without stain to Her heavenly Bridegroom.

Let us therefore seek for the six water pots of stone, in which the ablution of the Jews, that is, of those who believe, becomes a purification. For if we say that we have no sin we deceive ourselves, and there is not in us that Truth Which alone makes us free, alone redeems us, alone washes away our sins. But if we confess our sins there will not be wanting to the true Israelite vessels of purification, since God is faithful, to forgive us our sins, and to cleanse us from all iniquity (I Jn. i. 8, 9).

7. For my part I believe the six jars are the six observances which the holy Fathers laid down for the purification of the hearts of the faithful, and all of them unless I am mistaken we shall find here. The first jar is the self-restraint of chastity, by which whatsoever before was stained by sensuality is washed away. The second is abstinence: so that what gluttony has stained abstinence may now clean. Through sloth and laziness which are enemies of the soul we have defiled ourselves with much filth; against the command of God, we are bread that came from the sweat of another's brow, and not of our own (Gen. iii. 19); and for this cause also is the third jar *set there*, that these stains may be washed away by the labour of our own hands.

So likewise through excessive sleep and other works of the night and of the darkness we have offended much; therefore the fourth jar, the nightly watch, is placed there, so that by rising by night to praise the Lord we may buy back the nights of other times that were not well spent. Now indeed as to the tongue who is it that does not know how much we soil ourselves through idle talk and lies, through detraction and flattery, through malicious talk and idle boasting? For all these the fifth jar is necessary, namely silence, the safeguard of religion, and wherein is our strength. The sixth jar is discipline, whereby we live not by our own but by another's will, so that we may wipe away that of which we have been guilty through disordered living.

The jars are of stone, they are hard, but we needs must be cleansed in them, unless we wish to receive from the Lord a bill of divorce *because of our uncleanness* (Deut. xxiv. 1). Yet in this that they are said to be of stone, not alone hardness, but even more, durability may be understood; since these will not wash us unless they remain firm and steadfast.

8. Then the Lord said to the waiters: *Fill the water pots with water.* What does this mean, O Lord? The waiters are concerned with the shortage of wine, and You say to fill up the vessels with water. They are thinking of the drinking cups: and You bid them fill up the water pots of purification. So Jacob desiring the embrace of the promised Rachel was given Leah by her father. To us, Brethren, who are your waiters and servants Christ has given orders to fill up the watering pots with water, as often as wine is wanting. It is as if He says: these seek devotion, they desire wine, they crave to serve with love, but My hour is not yet come: fill the stone water pots with water. For what is the water of saving wisdom, though not so pleasant, if not *the fountain of life*, and the beginning of wisdom that is the fear of the Lord? To the servants is it therefore said: Awaken fear, and fill up not alone the watering pots but mens' hearts

with the spirit of fear: for to come to love they must begin by fear, so that they too may say: from the fear of thee have we conceived, O Lord, and brought forth the spirit of salvation (Is. xxvi. 18).

But how are the jars filled up? For the Evangelist says: *containing two or three measures apiece.* What are the two measures, and what is the third? There is indeed a common twofold fear, and known to all; and a third that is less frequent, and less known. The first is fear lest we be tormented in hell. The second is the fear of being shut out from the inestimable glory of the vision of God. The third fills every anxious soul with deepest dread: lest it be forsaken by grace.

9. As water puts out fire, so every fear of the Lord puts out the concupiscence of sin, but especially this fear, since it rises up at every temptation, lest having once lost grace a sinner may then be abandoned to himself, and day by day fall from one evil to a greater, from lesser guilt to more grievous, such as many we see, who being filthy are left in filth (Apoc. xxii. 11). For against this fear the soul cannot deceive itself, either on the grounds of the smallness of the offence, or with the hope of future amendment; for with such blandishments we may quieten the two other kinds of fear.

The Lord therefore commands us to fill the stone jars with water; for sometimes they stand empty, and filled with wind. If anyone is so foolish as to remain in this state through vanity, the holy exercises of which we have spoken to you are deprived of their enduring reward, and such are as the foolish virgins in whose vessels there was no oil (Mt. xxv. 3).

Sometimes, and this is a greater evil, they are full: but filled with the poison which is envy, murmuring, bitterness of soul, detraction. Lest therefore it should happen that these evils enter when the wine is wanting, we are ordered, so that the commandments of the Lord be obeyed in fear, to fill up the jars with water, which is then changed into wine, since fear is cast out by charity (I Jn. iv. 18), and all things are filled with fervour of spirit and joyful in their obedience, by the grace and mercy of Our Lord Jesus Christ, Who with the Father and the Holy Spirit liveth and reigneth world without end. Amen.

NOTES

[1] Now regarded as inauthentic cf. PRM 40.
[2] PG 59, Sermo 22.
[3] PG 59, Sermo 23.
[4] PL 20, Ex Serm. 8.
[5] PL 42, 684. Sermo 123.
[6] PG 73, 223 seq.
[7] PL 183, 155. Sermo 1.
[8] Hymn for Prime.
[9] PL 183, 157.

THIRD SUNDAY AFTER
THE EPIPHANY

I. Origen: The Healing of the Leper

II. St Jerome: The Healing of the Leper

III. St John Chrysostom: On the Gospel

IV. St Cyril of Alexandria: The Mystical Significance of
the Healing of the Leper

THE GOSPEL OF THE SUNDAY

Matthew viii: 1–13

At that time: When Jesus had come down from the mountain, great multitudes followed Him: and behold a leper came and adored Him, saying: Lord, if thou wilt, thou canst make me clean. And Jesus stretching forth His hand, touched him, saying: I will, be thou made clean. And forthwith his leprosy was cleansed. And Jesus saith to him: see thou tell no man: but go, shew thyself to the priest, and offer the gift which Moses commanded for a testimony unto them. And when He had entered into Capharnaum, there came to Him a centurion, beseeching Him and saying, Lord, my servant lieth at home sick of the palsy, and is grievously tormented. And Jesus saith to him: I will come and heal him. And the centurion making answer, said: Lord, I am not worthy that thou shouldst enter under my roof: but only say the word, and my servant shall be healed. For I also am a man subject to authority, having under me soldiers; and I say to this, Go, and he goeth, and to another, Come, and he cometh, and to my servant, Do this, and he doeth it. And Jesus hearing this, marvelled: and said to them that followed Him: Amen I say to you, I have not found so great faith in Israel. And I say to you that many shall come from the west and the east, and shall sit down with Abraham, and Isaac, and Jacob, in the kingdom of heaven: but the children of the kingdom shall be cast out into the exterior darkness: there shall be weeping and gnashing of teeth. And Jesus said to the centurion: Go, and as thou hast believed, so be it done to thee. And the servant was healed at the same hour.

PARALLEL GOSPELS

MARK i. 40–45

And there came a leper to Him, beseeching Him, and kneeling down said to Him: If thou wilt, thou canst make me clean. And Jesus having compassion on him, stretched forth His hand; and touching him, saith to him: I will. Be thou made clean. And when he had spoken, immediately the leprosy departed from him, and he was made clean. And He strictly charged him, and forthwith sent him away. And He saith to him: see thou tell no one; but go, shew thyself to the high priest, and offer for thy cleansing the things that Moses commanded, for a testimony to them. But he being gone out, began to publish and to blaze abroad the word: so that He could not openly go into the city, but was without in desert places: and they flocked to Him from all sides.

LUKE v. 12–15

And it came to pass, when He was in a certain city, behold a man full of leprosy, who seeing Jesus, and falling on his face, besought Him, saying: Lord, if thou wilt, thou canst make me clean. And stretching forth His hand, He touched him, saying: I will. Be thou cleansed. And immediately the leprosy departed from him. And he charged him that he should tell no man, but, Go, shew thyself to the priest, and offer for thy cleansing according as Moses commanded, for a testimony to them. But the fame of Him went abroad the more, and great multitudes came together to hear, and to be healed by Him of their infirmities.

LUKE vii. 2–10

And the servant of a certain centurion, who was dear to him, being sick, was ready to die. And when he had heard of Jesus, he sent unto him the ancients of the Jews, desiring him to come and heal his servant. And when they came to Jesus, they besought him earnestly, saying to Him: He is worthy that thou shouldst do this for him. For he loveth our nation; and he hath built us a synagogue. And Jesus went with them. And when He was now not far from the house, the centurion sent his friends to Him, saying: Lord, trouble not thyself; for I am not worthy that thou shouldst enter under my roof.

For which cause neither did I think myself worthy to come to thee; but say the word, and my servant shall be healed. For I also am a man subject to authority, having under me soldiers: and I say to one, Go, and he goeth; and to another, Come, and he cometh; and to my servant, Do this, and he doeth it. Which Jesus hearing, marvelled: and turning about to the multitudes that followed Him, He said: Amen I say to you, I have not found so great faith, not even in Israel. And they who were sent, being returned to the house, found the servant whole who had been sick.

EXPOSITION FROM THE CATENA AUREA

1. *When Jesus had come down from the mountain, great multitudes followed Him.*

JEROME: After His sermon and instruction an occasion presented itself for working a miracle; so that by means of a miracle the sermon just heard might be confirmed.

CHRYSOSTOM, *Ex. Op. Imp., Hom.* 1: Because He taught as one having power, and so that His manner of teaching might not be regarded as presumptuous, He creates the same impression by His works: as one having power to heal. Accordingly the Gospel says: *When He had come down . . .*

ORIGEN, *Hom. 5 inter collecta ex. var. Locis*: While the Lord was preaching on the mountain His Disciples were with Him, to whom it was given to know the secrets of heavenly doctrine. But now, coming down from the mountain, the multitudes who had been unable to ascend the mountain followed Him, as they on whom the burden of sin lies are not able to ascend to the heights of the sacred mysteries. But when the Lord came down, that is, stooping to the infirmity and weakness of these others, He had compassion on their imperfections. The multitudes followed Him: some out of love for Him, others because of His teaching, and many because of His healing and comfort.

HAYMO, *Ex Catena G.P.*: Or again: By the mountain on which the Lord was sitting heaven is signified; of which it is written: *Heaven is my throne* (Is. lxvi. 1). But while the Lord was sitting on the mountain only His Disciples came to Him (Mt. v. 1), because before He took upon Himself our frail humanity, God was known only in Judea (Ps. lxxv. 2). But however, after He came down from the mountain of His divinity, and assumed the weakness of human nature, a great multitude of the nations followed Him. It is thus shown to those who must teach, that their discourse should be tempered to their hearers; and that they should announce the word of God according to what they see is the capacity of each one. The Teachers go up into the mountain when they make known to the more advanced: they come down when they teach the simpler truths to the weaker ones.

2. *And behold a leper came and adored him etc.*

CHRYSOSTOM, *Ex. Op. Imp.*: Among those who had not ascended the mountain there was a leper who had been unable to ascend, carrying as it were the burthen of his sins. For the sins of our soul are a leprosy. The Lord therefore comes down from heaven, as from a high mountain, to cleanse the leprosy of our sins. And so as it were prepared beforehand the leper meets Him coming down. Hence we have: *And behold a leper came.*

ORIGEN: He runs to meet Him as He comes down; on the mountain he did not venture to speak, because there is a time for everything under heaven; a time for teaching, and a time for healing. On the mountain

He taught, He cured souls, He healed hearts. This being done, as He comes down from the heavenly mountain to redeem frail humanity, a leper comes and adores Him. Before he makes his prayer, he begins by adoring, by paying homage.

CHRYSOSTOM, *Op. Imp.*: He did not seek Him out as a skilled physician, but adores Him as God. Faith, and the confession of faith, is a perfect prayer. Hence the leper, adoring, fulfils the duty of faith; the duty of confession He fulfils by words. Hence, *he adored Him, saying etc.* ORIGEN: Lord, by thee were all things made. Therefore, *if thou wilt, thou canst make me clean.* Thy will is necessary; Thy works obey Thy will. Thou, in a former time, cleansed Namaan the Syrian of leprosy by Thy servant Eliseus: And now if Thou will it Thou canst make me clean. CHRYSOSTOM, *Hom.* 26 *in Matt.*: He did not say: if you will ask God for me; nor, if you will adore for me. But he said: if You will it, You can make me clean. Neither did he say: Lord, clean me: but defers all to Him, and calls Him Lord and attributes to Him power over the universe. CHRYSOSTOM, *Op. Imp.*: Thus he offers spiritual payment to his spiritual physician; for as physicians are paid in money, He is paid with prayer. In this that he says: *if thou wilt*, he doubts not that the will of Christ is disposed to every good work. But because corporal health is not profitable to everyone, he knew not whether this healing would be a gain to him. He says therefore: *if thou wilt*, as if he said: I believe that what is good thou wilt; I know not however if what I ask is for me a good.

3. *And Jesus stretching forth his hand, touched him, etc.*

CHRYSOSTOM, *Hom.* 26 *in Matt.*: Since He can heal by will or by word, He puts forth His Hand, and touches him. Hence we read: *and Jesus stretching forth His Hand, touched him,* that He might show that He was not subject to the Law, and that to the clean nothing is unclean. Eliseus, however, observing the Law in its detail, did not go forth and put his hand on Naaman, but sent him to wash in the Jordan. The Lord makes plain that He heals, and touches, not as a servant of the Law, but as Lord; for not by leprosy is His Hand made unclean, rather at the touch of His Hand the leprous body is made whole. He came, not alone to heal the body, but that He might guide the soul to true wisdom. So therefore as He now forbids not to eat with unwashed hands; so here does He also teach us that only the leprosy of the soul is to be feared, which is sin; and that leprosy of the body is no impediment to virtue.

CHRYSOSTOM, *Op. Imp.*: Although He undid the letter of the Law, He did not undo its purpose. The Law forbade to touch a leper; because it could not secure that leprosy would not stain the one so touching. Therefore, it forbade the touching of a leper, not that the lepers might not be healed, but so that those touching a leper might not be stained. But He is not stained in touching the leper; rather in touching him He cleanses the leper.

DAMASCENE, *de Fide Orthod. III*, 15: For He was not alone God, but also Man; hence by touch and by word He wrought divine wonders; so that divine actions might be accomplished by His Voice and also by His Body.

CHRYSOSTOM, *Hom.* 26: When He touched the leper, no one reproached Him; because His hearers were not yet possessed by envy. CHRYSOSTOM, *Op. Imp.*: If He had cured him silently, who would have known by what power he was healed? The will to heal was awakened because of the leper; the words were for those who were present. Therefore He says: *I will, be thou made clean.*

JEROME: The words (*volo mundare*) must not as many Latins think be read linked together, but separately. First I will (*volo*) is said, then as though commanding: Be thou made clean (*mundare*). The leper had said: If you will. The Lord replied: I will. The leper said: Thou canst make me clean. The Lord answered: Be thou made clean.

CHRYSOSTOM, *in Hom.* 26: Nowhere else does He appear to say this word (*volo*), though He worked many miracles. But here He added *I will* so that He might establish in both leper and people a belief in His power. CHRYSOSTOM, as above: Nature obeyed Him with fitting promptness. Hence: *And forthwith his leprosy was cleansed.* But the word *forthwith* does not convey the speed with which the miracle was accomplished.

ORIGEN: As he hesitated not to believe the healing was not delayed; because he delayed not in declaring his belief the cleansing was not delayed. AUGUSTINE, *Harmony of the Gospels, II,* 19: Luke also mentions the healing of the leper,

though not in this order, but, recalling as they who write are wont to events they had forgotten, or telling beforehand what happened later as these things were divinely brought to their minds; things known before, but remembering them afterwards and putting them down in writing.

4. *And Jesus said to him: See thou tell no man: but, go show thyself etc.*

CHRYSOSTOM: Having cured his body Jesus bids him tell no one; hence: *And Jesus saith to him: see thou tell no man.* Some say that He so commanded him so that malice might not be stirred up because of the healing, which is foolishness. For He did not heal so that the healing should remain doubtful; rather He ordered him to tell no one so that He might teach us not to be taken up with boasting and vain glory.

Why then does He order a person healed on another occasion to proclaim the fact? (Mk. v, 20; Lk. xvii. 18). In that case He was teaching men to be grateful. For there He did not command that He Himself be proclaimed but that glory be given to God. In the case of the leper He teaches us to turn from vain glory; in the other that we ought never be ungrateful, but should refer all things in the praise and glory of God.

JEROME: And indeed what need was there that he should spread abroad by word what was proclaimed by his body? HILARY, *Matt.* 7: Or, since the healing was besought rather than offered silence is imposed.

But go, show thyself to the priest: JEROME: He sends him to the priests, first because of submission, that he might be seen to be subject to the priests: then so that they seeing the leper made clean might be saved should they believe in the Saviour. If however they would not believe they would be inexcusable. And also so that He may not appear to infringe the Law, an accusation they were frequently to make.

CHRYSOSTOM: For He neither everywhere dissolved it, nor everywhere observed it; but sometimes did the one, and sometimes the other; in the one case preparing the way of the future wisdom, in the other stopping the shameless mouths of the Jews and deferring to their weakness. For this reason the Apostles seem sometimes to observe the Law and sometimes to ignore it.

ORIGEN: Or, He sent them to the priests that they might learn that not by the requirements of Law had he been made clean, but by the action of grace. JEROME: There was a precept of the Law that whoever was made clean of leprosy should offer gifts to the priests; hence: *And offer the gift which Moses commanded for a testimony unto them.* CHRYSOSTOM, *Ex. Op. Imp. Hom.* 21: Do not understand this as saying that Moses commanded this for a testimony to them, but go you and offer it for a testimony unto them.

CHRYSOSTOM, *Hom.* 21: Christ, foreseeing no fruit from this, said: not for their correction, but for a testimony or accusation against them: for what is to be done by Me, has been done. Although He foreknew that they would not amend the error of their ways, He

did not on that account neglect what was due on this occasion; they however remained in their evil dispositions. He did not say: the gift which I order, but, *which Moses commanded*, so as to remit him to the Law, and stop the mouths of the malicious. That they may not have it to say that He usurped the prestige of the priests, He Himself performed the wonder, but to them He yielded its approbation.

ORIGEN: Or, offer thy gift, so that all who see you bring it, may believe the miracle. CHRYSOSTOM, *Op. Imp. Hom.* 21: Or, He orders that the gift be offered, so that afterwards, should the priests seek to drive the man forth, he then could say to them: you accepted the gift from me, as from one made whole, how now do you drive me forth as a leper? HILARY, *in Matt. Ch.* 7: Or, we must read, *what Moses commanded for a testimony*; as meaning that what Moses laid down was in witness, not an effect, of the Law.

BEDE, *in Hom. of this Sunday*: Should anyone bring it forward, that since the Lord seems to approve the sacrifice of Moses, why does the Church also not accept it, let him keep in mind that Christ had not yet offered in His Passion His own Body as a Victim. The foreshadowing sacrifices ought not to be put away, till that which they prefigured would be confirmed, by the testimony of the Apostles' preaching, and by the faith of believing peoples. This man typifies the whole human race, for he was not alone a leper, he is described in the Gospel of Luke as being *full of leprosy*.

For all have sinned, and do need the

glory of God (Rom. iii. 23), that glory whereby, in putting forth the Hand of the Saviour, that is, of the Incarnate Word of God, and touching human nature, all men are made clean of the wound of the primeval error, so that they who were for so long considered as unclean, and cast forth from the camp of the people of God, now being at length restored to priest and temple can offer up their own bodies as a living sacrifice to Him, of Whom it was said: *Thou art a priest forever* (Ps. cix. 4).

REMIGIUS: Mystically, by the leper the sinner is signified—as sin makes the soul unclean and inconstant—who falls down before Christ, when troubled by its former sins; which it must yet confess, and for them implore pardon. For the leper shows his scars, and seeks a remedy. The Lord puts forth His hand, when He bestows the help of the divine mercy: immediately there follows the forgiveness of our sins. Neither is the sinner restored to the Church, except by the decree of the priest.

5. *And when he had entered into Capharnaum, there came to him a Centurion, etc.*

CHRYSOSTOM, *Op. Imp. Hom.* 21: After the Lord had taught the Disciples upon the mountain, and healed the leper at the foot of the mountain, He came to Capharnaum, as fulfilling a mystery; for after the cleansing of the Jews, He came to the Gentiles. HAYMO: For Capharnaum, which is interpreted as meaning *seat of abundance*, or *a field of consolation*, signifies the Church, which is gathered together from the Gentiles, and is filled

with spiritual fatness, according to the words: *let my soul be filled as with marrow and fatness* (Ps. lxii. 6). And amid the distresses of the world She is comforted from on high, as the psalmist says: *Thy comforts have given joy to my soul* (Ps. xciii. 19). Hence is said: *When he had entered into Capharnaum, there came to Him a centurion.*

AUGUSTINE, *De Verb. Dom. Serm.* 6: This centurion was from the Gentiles, for now the Jewish people had among them an army of Imperial Rome. CHRYSOSTOM, *Op. Imp.*: This Centurion was the first fruits of the Gentiles, in comparison with whose faith the faith of all the Jews is seen to be unfaith. He who neither heard Christ preaching, nor had seen the leper cleansed, having only heard about the leper, believed more than he heard. For he was a type of the future peoples, who had read neither the Law nor the Prophets concerning Christ, nor had seen Christ Himself performing miracles. He came therefore asking, and saying: *Lord, my servant lieth at home sick of the palsy, and is grievously tormented.*

6. *And saying, Lord, my servant lieth at home sick of the palsy, etc.*

See here the good heart of this Centurion, who hastened so anxiously to secure the healing of his servant, as if he were about to suffer, not a money loss by the death of his servant, but rather his own health. For he regarded not the difference between master and servant, for though in this world their dignity varies, yet are they one in nature. See too the faith of the Centurion, in that he said not: Come, and heal him; because the

Lord being in every place was present there already; see his wisdom, since he said not: Even here heal him; for he knew that He had power to do so, wisdom to understand, mercy to hear. Accordingly he makes known the sickness; the restoring of health he leaves to the power of His mercy, saying: *And is grievously tormented*; from which it is clear that he loved him. For each one thinks that the loved one suffers more than he does, even though he be but moderately ill.

RABANUS MAURUS: He mentions all these things with grief: that he is lying ill, the palsy, the fact that he is tormented; that he may show the anxiety of his soul, and move the Lord. So ought all to suffer with their servants, and seek their cure. CHRYSOSTOM: Some however say that, excusing himself, he said this as the reason for not bringing him there; for it was not possible, paralysed as he was, to bring him. Luke said: *He was at the point of death.* But I say that this was a sign of great faith, even greater than theirs who let a sick man down through the roof. For he knew with certainty that a simple word sufficed to heal him, and so it was superfluous to bring him.

HILARY *in Matt. Ch.* 27: As the infirm of this world, and as weakened by the contagion of sin, so must the Gentiles be spiritually regarded; all their members are relaxed, and unable to fulfil the tasks of standing and walking; the mystery of whose healing is prefigured in this servant of the Centurion, who is himself said to have been the first of the Gentiles to believe. Who this leader is the Canticle of Moses narrates,

where it says: *He appointed the bounds of people according to the number of the children of Israel* (Deut. xxxii. 8).

REMIGIUS: Or, by the Centurion are signified those who were the first among the Gentiles to believe, and who were perfected in virtue; for he is called a Centurion who is placed over a hundred men, and the hundred is the perfect number. Rightly therefore does the Centurion plead for his servant, because the first fruits of the Gentiles plead before God for the salvation of all the Gentiles.

7. *And Jesus saith to him: I will come and heal him.*

JEROME: The Lord seeing the faith of the Centurion, his humility and his concern, immediately promised that He will come and heal the servant; hence follows: *And Jesus saith to him: I will come and heal him.* CHRYSOSTOM, *Hom.* 27 *in Matt.*: What He never did, Jesus does here: for everywhere He follows the will of His suppliants, here He goes beyond it, and not alone promises to heal, but also to go to the house. He does this that we may learn the virtue of the Centurion. CHRYSOSTOM, *Op. Imp.*: For unless He had said: *I will come and heal him*, never would this man have replied: *I am not worthy.* Then, since he was pleading for his servant, the Lord promised to go, that He might teach us not to flatter the great, and despise the lowly; but to honour alike both rich and poor.

8. *And the Centurion making answer, said: Lord I am not worthy, etc.*

JEROME: As we praise the faith of the Centurion, in that he believes that the paralytic could be healed by the Saviour, so also he reveals his own humility, in this, that he considered himself unworthy that the Lord should enter his house. Hence: *And the Centurion making answer said: Lord I am not worthy that thou shouldst enter under my roof.*

RABANUS: Because of his awareness of what the life of the Gentile was, he considered himself shamed rather than helped by this honour; although he was endowed with faith he was yet not strengthened by the sacraments.

AUGUSTINE, *De Verb. Dom. Serm.* 6: In saying he was not worthy he showed himself worthy that Christ the Word of the Lord should enter, not into his house, but into his heart. Neither would he have said this with such faith and humility unless he bore Him in his heart, of Whom he was here apprehensive lest He enter his house: for it would be no great joy should Jesus enter his house and not enter his heart.

SEVERIANUS (or CHRYSOLOGUS): Mystically this roof is the body which covers the soul, and closes in the mind from the vision of heaven. But God does not disdain to dwell within flesh, nor to enter under the roof of our body. ORIGEN: For even now when the rulers of the Church, holy and pleasing to God, enter under our roof, then through them the Lord enters; and let you regard it as though the Lord were entering. And when you eat and drink the Body and Blood of the Lord, then the Lord enters under your roof, and then, humbling yourself, repeat: *Lord, I am not worthy.* Where He enters a place

that is not worthy, there He enters in judgement on the one so receiving Him.

JEROME: The wisdom of the Centurion is here apparent, seeing beyond the outward cloak of the Body, he discerns the veiled divinity: whence he adds: But only say the word, and my servant shall be healed. CHRYSOSTOM, *Ex. Op. Imp.* 21: For he knew that ministering angels were invisibly standing by who would turn each word of His into work, and should the angels be still, the sickness would still be cast forth by his healing words.

9. *For I also am a man subject to authority, having under me soldiers, etc.*

HILARY, *in Matt.* 7: The Centurion says that his servant could be healed by a word, because all salvation for the Gentiles is by faith, and the true life of all men is in the commandments of the Lord; and so he adds: *For I also am a man subject to authority, having under me soldiers: and I say to this, Go, and he goeth, and to another, Come, and he cometh, and to my servant, Do this, and he doeth it.*

CHRYSOSTOM, *Op. Imp.* 21: Under the inspiration of the Holy Ghost he depicts here the mystery of the Father and the Son, as though he said: Although I am under the power of another, yet I have power to order those under me; so You also, although subject to the power of the Father, that is, as man, You have yet the power to command the angels. But perhaps Sabellius will say, seeking to show that the Father and the Son are the same [*the same person*], so must this be understood:

If I, placed subject to authority, can yet command, how much more You, Who are under the power of no one? But the text does not support this interpretation. For he did not say: If I am subject to authority; but said: for I also am a man subject to authority; in which, between himself and Christ, he makes, not a distinction of contrast, but puts forward a basis of resemblance.

AUGUSTINE, as above: If I, who am subject to authority, have the power to order, what canst Thou do, to Whom all power is subject?

GLOSS: Thou canst, by the ministry of angels, and without the presence of the body, say to the infirmity that it shall depart, and it departs: and to health, that it come, and it comes. HAYMO: By the subjects of the Centurion we may understand the natural virtues, in which many of the Gentiles were strong; or even good and evil thoughts. Let us say to the evil ones, that they go, and they will go, and let us call to us good thoughts, and they will come; let us say also to our servant, that is, to our body, that it be subject to the divine will.

AUGUSTINE, *Harmony of the Gospels II*, 20: To what is here said there seems to be opposed that which Luke says: *When he had heard of Jesus, he sent unto him the ancients of the Jews, desiring Him to come and heal his servant*, and again: *and when He was not far from the house, the Centurion sent his friends to Him, saying: Lord, trouble not thyself; for I am not worthy that thou shouldst enter under my roof.* CHRYSOSTOM, *Hom. 27 in Matt.*: Some say that this is not the same reason as that other: though

they have points of resemblance. So, of the one Luke records: *he loveth our nation; and hath built us a synagogue*: and of the other the Lord Himself said: *Amen, I say to you, I have not found so great faith even in Israel*; and accordingly it would seem he was not a Jew. To me however he seems one and the same person. But when Luke says that he sent that He might come, he is hinting at the flatteries of the Jews. It is possible that the Centurion wished to come, but was prevented by the flatteries of the Jews, and by their saying, "we shall go and bring Him".

But when he is free of their importunity he then sends, saying: "do not think that it was through sloth that I have not come, but because I did not think that I was worthy to receive you under my roof". And if Matthew says that he says this, not through his friends, but himself in person, this is not contradictory; for both bear witness to the eager desire of the man, and to the belief he had regarding Christ. But it seems probable, that after sending his friends, he himself also said this to Him as He approached. And if Luke does not say this, nor Matthew the other, they do not contradict each other, rather they fill up that which either may have omitted.

AUGUSTINE, *Harmony II*, 20: Matthew wished therefore, in this compendious way, to speak of an approach which the Centurion had made through others; because the Lord had praised the faith whereby the Centurion had approached to God, that He might say: *I have not found such great faith in Israel.* Luke however has unfolded the whole incident as it happened, so that from this we are compelled to understand how Matthew, who would not lie, has said in what manner he viewed it. CHRYSOSTOM, *Hom. 27 in Matt.*: Neither is it a contradiction that he built a synagogue, as Luke records, and that he is known not to be a Jew. For it is possible for one while not being a Jew, to build a synagogue, and to love that nation.

10. *And Jesus hearing this, marvelled, etc.*

CHRYSOSTOM, *Hom. 27 in Matt.*: As that which the leper had said regarding the power of Christ: *if thou wilt, thou canst make me clean*, was confirmed by the words of Christ: *I will, be thou made clean*; so here also, Christ, not alone does not reproach the Centurion for bearing testimony to His power, He commends him. He does more; for the Evangelist, giving an indication of His praise, says: *And Jesus hearing this, marvelled.*

ORIGEN: Observe how great a thing, and what kind of thing, it is at which Jesus, the Only-Begotten of God, marvels. Gold, riches, kingdoms, principalities, in His eyes are but a shadow, or a flower that fades; in the eyes of God no single one of these is wonderful, or great, or precious, save only faith; at this He marvels, honouring it; this He regards as acceptable to Him.

AUGUSTINE, *Super Gen. Contra Manich. I*, 8:[1] Who had wrought in him that faith but He Who marvelled at it? But if another wrought it why should He marvel Who foreknew it? That the Lord marvels means that we must marvel who have need to be so moved. In

Him all such motions are signs, not of a spirit moved, but of one who gives an example.

CHRYSOSTOM, *Hom. 27 in Matt:*. And so in the presence of all the people He is said to marvel at him, and set him before others as an example that they may imitate him. For there follows: *Amen I say to you: I have not found so great faith in Israel.* AUGUSTINE, *contra Faust. 22*, 74: He praises his faith but He did not bid him give up the military life. JEROME: He said this of those living in Israel, not of former prophets and patriarchs.

CHRYSOSTOM, *Ex. Op. Imp.*: For Andrew believed, but only upon hearing John say: Behold the lamb of God; Peter believed, but upon hearing the good news from Andrew; Philip believed, but through reading the Scriptures; and before that Nathaniel received proof of His divinity, and so made a confession of faith.

ORIGEN, *Sermo 5 Ex Collectis. Var.*: Jairus the prince of Israel when he was beseeching Him on behalf of his daughter did not say, *say but the word*, but *come quickly* (Mk. v. 23). Nicodemus hearing of the mystery of faith said: *How can this be done?* (Jn. iii. 9). Mary and Martha said to the Lord that if He had been there their brother would not have died (Jn. xi. 21), as it were doubting that the power of God could be everywhere.

CHRYSOSTOM, *Ex. Op. Imp.*: Or if we wish to regard him as more believing than the Apostles, we must then understand the testimony of Christ to mean that the good which anyone does is to be praised according to the capacity of that person. For an unlettered person to say something profound is a great thing, which from a philosopher is a matter that excites no wonder. In this sense was it said of the Centurion that in no one in Israel *have I found such faith.* CHRYSOSTOM, *Hom.* 21: For it was not the same thing for a Jew to believe as for one outside that nation. JEROME: Or perhaps in the Centurion the faith of the Gentiles is praised above that of Israel. Hence He says:

11. *And I say to you that many shall come from the east and the west.* AUGUSTINE, *De Verb. Dom.* 5: He does not say *all*, but *many*, and these from the East and West; by these two parts the whole world is indicated. HAYMO, *Serm.* 61: Or they come from the East who as soon as they are baptised pass away; from the West they who have suffered persecution for the faith unto death; or from the East he comes who began from his childhood to serve God, from the West he who was converted in old age to the service of God. ORIGEN: But how does He elsewhere say that but *few are chosen?* Because throughout many generations *few* are chosen in each one; brought together in the time of visitation they are found to be many.

And shall lie down: Not in the bodily sense, but spiritually at rest; not in temporal rejoicing, but feasting eternally: *with Abraham, and Isaac, and Jacob in the kingdom of heaven*, where are light and joy and glory and length of eternal days. JEROME: Since the God of Abraham, Creator of heaven, is the Father of Christ, so all nations that have believed in Christ, the Son of the Creator, will take their rest with Abraham in the kingdom of heaven.

12. *But the children of the kingdom shall be cast out into the exterior . . .*

AUGUSTINE, *Verb. Dom.* 5: As we see Christians invited to the heavenly banquet where the Bread of heavenly Justice is dispensed, and the Drink of Wisdom, so do we see The Jews rejected. Hence follows: *The children of the kingdom shall be cast out into exterior darkness*, that is, the Jews, who received the Law, who commemorate the *figures* of the things to come, yet reject them now fulfilled. JEROME: Or, He calls the Jews the children of the kingdom, because amongst them God aforetime reigned.

CHRYSOSTOM, *Hom.* 27: Or, He means as the children of the kingdom those for whom the kingdom was prepared; because against these was He more in wrath. AUGUSTINE, *contra Faust.* 16, 24: If then Moses commended to the people of Israel no other God, but the God of Abraham, of Isaac, and of Jacob, the Same does Christ commend. He does not attempt to turn this people from their God; but He therefore warns them that they will go into exterior darkness because He sees them turn from their God, in whose kingdom the Gentiles, called from the whole world, will recline, He says, with Abraham, with Isaac and with Jacob; and for no other cause than that they held fast to the faith of Abraham, of Isaac, and of Jacob. JEROME, *Hom.* 27: The darkness is called exterior, since he who is driven forth from the Lord leaves the light behind.

HAYMO: What they will suffer there He reveals when He adds: *there shall be weeping and gnashing of teeth.* By a metaphor he describes the punishments of the tormented. For at the contact of smoke eyes are wont to shed tears, and teeth rattle in intense cold. He indicates therefore that the reprobate will suffer intolerably heat and cold in hell; as Job also says: *let him pass from the snow waters to excessive heat* (Job xxiv, 19).

JEROME: If there shall be weeping of eyes, and if grinding of teeth means bones, then it is true that there will be a resurrection of bodies, and of those members that have fallen away. RABANUS: Or gnashing of teeth indicates the disposition of an angry man, because he has repented too late, and is angry with himself, in that he continued to offend with persistent iniquity. REMIGIUS: Or, differently, He calls the outer nations *exterior darkness.* For, as regards history, Christ has in these words foretold the tragedy of the Jewish people, and that because of their infidelity they would be led captive, and scattered throughout the nations of the earth. Weeping is wont to be caused by heat, chattering of teeth by cold. The weeping therefore is ascribed to those who dwell in the hotter regions, as in India and Ethiopia; the chattering of teeth to those who live in the colder countries as in Hyrcania and Scythia.

13. *And Jesus said to the Centurion: Go, and as thou hast believed, so be it,* etc.

CHRYSOSTOM, *Hom.* 27: Lest anyone think that these were but words of flattery, that he was praised for believing, He creates confidence by a sign. Hence follows: And Jesus said to the centurion: *Go, and as thou hast believed, so be it done to thee.* RABANUS: As if to say, let this favour be done to thee in accordance with the measure of your faith. The merit of the Master can also avail the servants; not alone the merit of his faith, but his zeal for the law of God. CHRYSOSTOM, *Hom.* 27: We may marvel how speedily it was done. The power of Christ is shown in this, that not alone does He heal, but He heals swiftly, in a moment of time.

AUGUSTINE, *De Verb. Dom. Serm.* 6:[2] For as the Lord did not enter bodily into the house of the Centurion, but absent, in body, yet present in power, He heals the servant; so was He present in Body in the midst of the Jewish people: among no other peoples was He either born of a virgin, or had He suffered, or borne human afflictions, or wrought divine wonders; and yet He fulfilled what was said of Him: *A people, which I knew not, hath served me: at the hearing of the ear they have obeyed me* (Ps. xvii. 45). The Jewish people knew Him, and crucified Him; the whole earth has heard of Him, and believed.

I. ORIGEN, PRIEST AND CONFESSOR

The Healing of the Leper[3]

And when He was come down from the mountain. When Jesus was teaching on the mountain top His disciples were with Him; to whom it was given to know the secrets of His heavenly doctrine, through which the heart of the insensate world would be seasoned by the knowledge of salvation, and by means of which the eyes of the blind, obscured by the shadows of earthly indulgence, would open to the light of Truth. Hence the Lord says to us: *you are the salt of the earth. You are the Light of the world* (Mt. v. 13, 14). And now coming down from the mountain, *great multitudes followed Him.*

They could in no way ascend the mountain because, they upon whom the burthen of sin lies heavily, unless they cast off their load, are wholly unable to ascend to the heights of the divine mysteries. So neither, long ago, could the Children of Israel go up the mountain and behold the Face of the Lord, for they were hampered by the burthen of the manner of life which they had learned in Egypt, so Moses alone ascended, and with him a few among the Elders of Israel. Accordingly, as the Apostles ascended the mountain with the Lord, so now do faithful souls that fear God, that love God, desiring His heavenly kingdom, and forever following after the Lord, go up after Him unto the heavenly mountain, hearing the Apostle saying: *Mind the things that are above, not the things that are upon the earth* (Col. iii. 2).

The Lord coming down, that is, stooping down to the infirmity and helplessness of the others, and merciful towards their weakness and misery, *the multitudes followed Him*; some, because they loved Him, many because of His doctrine, and not a few because of His healing and compassion. *And behold a leper*, one of those who sought to be cured, who longed for deliverance, *came and adored Him, saying:*

Lord, if thou wilt, thou canst make me clean. Running to Him as He comes down you beg Him, O Man; but on the mountain you spoke not? Why is this? Because *all things have their season* (Ecclus. iii): a time for teaching, and a time for healing. On the mountain He taught, He enlightened, He cured souls, He healed hearts. Because of these greater things, I was reluctant to speak. I stood aside for these supreme things.

Having completed these tasks, He comes down from the heavenly mountain to heal all flesh, and there comes to Him a man, a leper, adoring Him. Before he makes his petition he begins by adoring Him; before he begs, he renders homage. He adored Him. By this action, addressing Him as Lord and God, he adored Him. As those blessed Magi first kneeling down adored Him, and then offered their gifts, so in like manner this man, falling down, adored Him, and in this way presented his petition, saying: Lord, thou who art fittingly adored and rightfully served, I adore Thee as Lord, and so as Lord I call upon Thee, confessing Thy works. By Thee are all things made, Thou, Lord, if Thou wilt, Thou canst make me clean. Thou hast willed that this unclean leprosy should come upon me, either because of my sins, that being chastised I may do penance, or because of Thy Providence, that miraculously healing me, Thou mayest be glorified. All things are done by Thy command and disposition, and Thou givest health abundantly.   Therefore, whether I am afflicted with this leprosy because of my sins, wiping out my sins, heal me: or, whether because of Thy Providence, miraculously heal me, that Thou mayest be glorified before men.

Lord, if thou wilt, thou canst make me clean. There is need here of Thy will, because creatures obey only Thy will, and so if Thou will Thou canst make me clean. I do not falter doubting, nor do I speak as he who besought the healing of his son: *if thou canst do anything help us* (Mk. ix. 21). But I know that Thou canst do all things, and here I petition not Thy power, nor seek Thy might. Men I know are weak, but I implore Thy will, and the power that follows it will immediately perform this grace for me. *Lord, if Thou wilt, Thou canst make me clean.* To me the gain, to Thee the praise; to all who behold Thy wonder an increase in knowledge of the truth.

Lord, if Thou wilt, Thou canst make me clean. Thou Who by Thy servant Eliseus didst cleanse of leprosy Naaman, the prince of Syria, bidding him wash in the Jordan, now, if Thou wilt, Thou canst make me clean.

To whom in reply the Lord says: Believing, you confess that I can, and that if I will it comes to pass; accordingly, I will: be thou made clean. Wondrously hast thou believed, and wondrously art thou healed; without measure thou hast confessed, without measure art thou made joyful. I will: be thou made clean. You faltered not in believing: I am quick to heal. You delayed not to confess your faith: I delay not to cleanse thee. I will: be thou made clean. That I may show thee great favour, I stretch forth my Hand to thee; *and stretching forth His hand, touched him, saying: I will: be thou made clean.*

And why did He touch him,

since the Law forbade the touching of a leper? For this did He touch, that He might show that *all things are clean to the clean* (Tit. i. 15). Because the filth that is *in* one person adheres not to others; neither does external uncleanness defile the clean of heart. But wherefore, in this circumstance, does He touch him? That He might instruct us in humility; that He might teach us that we should despise no one, or abhor them, or regard them as pitiable, because of some wound of their body, some blemish that is sent by God, for which it is He that will give reason, and render an account. I am the heavenly physician, He says, I can cure bodies as well as souls. And so I touch all, not that their infirmities may adhere to me, but that I may drive them from those who are afflicted. For I am the Incomparable Sun, and the Moon of Justice. And so I draw nigh to all, and I shine in all my splendour unto their salvation. I am as I was, and I abide in the beauty of My own singular holiness.

Stretching forth His hand, He touched him. I do not despise the Law, but I cure the wound. I do not dissolve the precept, but I banish and cleanse this leprosy. And so when I stretch forth My Hand, it goes away; nor can its taint come near my perfection, nor resist my power. I say therefore: *I will: be thou made clean,* and stretching forth His hand to touch, the leprosy immediately departs, and the Hand of the Lord is found to have touched, not a leper, but a body made clean!

Let us consider here, beloved Brethren, if there be anyone that has the taint of leprosy in his soul, or the contamination of guilt in his heart? If he has, instantly adoring God, let him say to Him: *Lord, if thou wilt thou canst make me clean.* Thou hast long ago cleansed Naaman who committed many crimes, and Thou hast had compassion throughout the ages on an immeasurable number of others who have besought Thee. *Thou, therefore, if Thou wilt, Thou canst make me clean.* And the Lord, swiftly stretching forth the hand of His mercy, will say: *I will: be thou made clean,* as Jesus says it to the one He cleansed of leprosy.

The Lord had compassion on this man who believed in Him, who trusted in His power. To him Jesus said: thou hast believed, you are healed; thou hast hoped, you are made clean. Forget not what you were, nor what you are now made into. Cease not to give thanks, nor cease to confess the Lord. Beloved, this also we must do, as often as He has delivered us from some peril, or comforted us in some grief, or infirmity, or sickness, or from any extremity whatsoever. Let us not be ungrateful, nor forgetful of our Benefactor, but speedily render Him thanks; and let us offer a gift according to our means, to shew Him honour. For this also the Lord commands.

But go, shew thyself to the priest, and offer the gift which Moses commanded for a testimony unto them. Jesus therefore saith to him: *see thou tell no man.* And wherefore, Lord, will he tell no one? Because of My humility, because of My hidden sweetness. And you, let this be a lesson unto you, whenever you do anything of good, do not seek to be honoured for it before men, to be extolled, to be foolishly pleased, as is the way with so many when they

do a little good, or have fasted, or given an alms to the poor, or a gift in honour of an altar or in honour of the saints. For these seek to be glorified before men, and to please themselves, losing their reward with God. *See thou tell no man*; but though thou be silent, this deed will most wondrously cry out. Though thou open not thy mouth, every member of thy body will be exultant; yesterday unclean, today clean; but a little while ago, repulsive; now, most pleasing.

See thou tell no man, but go, shew thyself to the priest. For as you go walking to the temple, all who see thee will be astonished, and the priest beholding thee will feel a sense of dread, since, according to the Law, once, and yet a second time, you were shut up by him, and then showing thyself it was found that you could not be made clean. Go, therefore, show thyself to the priest, that seeing you he may know that you were made clean, not through the observances of the Law, but by the operation of grace; not by the shadow that is the earthly priest, but by the heavenly splendour of the High Priest.

Go, shew thyself to the priest. Sent by the High Priest, show thyself to the priest, cleansed as thou art by the High Priest of God the Father. But be not seen in the presence of God, nor come not before the High Priest, with empty hands. Come not into the midst of the holy temple without fruit, but offer a gift. This that was spoken to him, is said to us all, and admonishes us that we hold not our gifts and our possessions to ourselves; but use them to give thanks: especially when delivered from some tribulation.

Offer, He says, *thy gift.* And

wherefore? That all who see thee bearing it, and offering it, may believe in this wonder; and may give thanks to God who has had compassion on you; and to the unbelieving let it be a reproach and a testimony of the hardness of their hearts. So likewise the man lying for eight and twenty years in infirmity, raising him up from his sickness, He bids him take up his bed and go into his house (Mk. ii. 11), so that the bed, being borne by him through the city, would proclaim the wonder; making known and praising Him that had healed him. So did He send the blind man to the pool of Siloe, so that others, seeing the blind man walking there, and returning cured, being struck with wonder, would believe in Him that wrought such signs and wonders, Who liveth and reigneth world without end. Amen.

II. St Jerome, Priest and Doctor
The Healing of the Leper [4]

When He was come down from the mountain, great multitudes followed Him. And behold a leper came and adored Him:

As the Lord came down from the mountain, the multitudes met Him, because they were unable to ascend to the heights. And the first to meet Him was a leper. Because of his leprosy he had been unable to hear the wondrous discourse of the Saviour spoken on the mountain. And observe that he was the first to be miraculously cured; then, secondly, the servant of the Centurion; thirdly, the mother-in-law of St Peter, of a fever, in Capharnaum; in the fourth place, those that *were brought to Him possessed with devils*, whose evil spirits He cast forth *with His word, when all that were sick He healed*. Fittingly, after His sermon and instruction, an occasion presents itself for a sign, so that the sermon they had heard might be confirmed by the power of a miracle.

Lord, if thou wilt, thou canst make me clean. He who petitions the will of the Lord, does not doubt His power. *And Jesus stretching forth His Hand,* etc., etc. Stretching forth His Hand, immediately the leprosy disappears. Consider here again how humble and unassuming the answer. The leper had said: *if thou wilt.* The Lord answers: *I will.* The leper had already said: *thou canst make me clean.* The Lord joins both requests, and says: *be thou made clean.*

Not therefore, as many Latins are of opinion, must we unite and read together these phrases, as: *I will be thou made clean*; but separately, as that He first says: *I will,* Then, as it were commanding, He says: *Be thou made clean.*

And Jesus saith: see thou tell no man. And indeed what need was there that he should boast by word of that which his body proclaimed. *But go, shew thyself to the priest.* He bids him, for various reasons, go to the priest. First out of humility, so that he will be cleansed of leprosy should make an offering to the priests. Again, that those seeing the leper now made clean would either believe in the Saviour or would not believe. If they believed, they would be saved: if they believed not, they would be inexcusable. And lastly, lest He might not seem to infringe the Law, of which they were frequently to accuse Him.

III. St John Chrysostom: On the Gospel[5]

And when he was come down from the mountain, great multitudes followed him.

1. Note that only the Disciples are said to have gone up the mountain to Jesus; but coming down from the mountain the multitude followed Him, and indeed *great multitudes*; because the mountain is the summit of virtue, the very pinnacle of the Church, on which the multitudes cannot come nigh to Christ, either because they are burthened with sin, or laden with worldly cares. They cannot draw near to Christ, nor hear the sublime discourse He spoke upon the mountain; only His Disciples can, who are free of the fevers of the vices, and unburthened by the cares of this world. Accordingly, as free and unencumbered they come unto Christ, that they may hear His more sublime discourses, becoming His imitators in all things. Yet, when from the heights of His compassion He came down to the lowly, who because of human infirmities were unable to hear Him on the mountain top, then great multitudes followed Him.

2. *And behold a leper.* You must know that both Luke and Mark tell first of the cure of the man possessed by an unclean spirit, and secondly of the woman who was freed of the bodily infirmity of fevers; because God has greater concern for the salvation of the soul than the body. First, because the soul is of a higher dignity than the body. For the soul can live without the body, but the body without the soul cannot survive. Second, in every sin it is the soul that first sins, then the body sins. Unless the soul be first overcome, the flesh could never sin. The flesh can first be moved with desire for that which is evil, but cannot sin unless the soul shall first consent; for the flesh is subject to the power of the soul, not the soul to the flesh. So it was necessary that the soul, which first had fallen, should first be raised; the soul then freed from the power of the devil would free its own flesh from sin. The flesh that is healed from infirmity cannot free the soul from its sin, but rather inclines it yet further from what is right; for the well-being of the flesh wars against the discipline of righteousness.

But Matthew begins with the account of the leper made clean in the mystery of the flesh. Why is this? Is there a reason which the other Evangelists have not disclosed? No. But he has recorded the event more fully. Where they tell of the deliverance of the possessed man, in the mystery of the soul, he, likewise because of the salvation of the soul, tells of Christ teaching on the mountain, of which the others have not written. For as the banishment of the unclean spirit freed the soul, from the power of sin, which was first committed at the prompting of the devil, so also the word of doctrine breaks down the work of the devil, and sets the soul free from the dominion of error; frees it from slavery to sin, and from the other evils which are born from the suggestion of the evil one; because not alone is he afflicted by the devil whose body is tormented by him; but all who do his will are so afflicted. He places the sign of the healed leper within the mystery of man made clean. For leprosy is a carnal affliction. But however, lest people might say: sublime and wonderful are His words, but deeds there are none: to speak sublimely is no great thing, but to work wonders matters much. Accordingly, He brought forward the leper that by the miracle of his healing He might give authority to the words. He had been speaking; so that being held wonderful in word, He might be yet more wondrous in deed.

And behold the leper, as though prepared beforehand, meets Him as He comes down from the mountain. It may be that for this cause He came down, that He might heal the leper. For sin is the leprosy of the soul. So the Lord descends from the heights of heaven, *as from a high mountain apart*, to cure the leprosy of our sins. Why think you did this man not go up with the others into the mountain to hear the divine discourse? Because he was burthened with leprosy, and bearing the weight of his sins, and unable to ascend there. Or heard you not the prophet saying, that they must be unstained that ascend the ecclesiastical mountain? *Who*, he says, *shall ascend into the mountain of the Lord: or who shall stand in His holy place? The innocent of hands, and clean of heart* (Ps. xxiii. 3, 4).

And so whosoever walks with evil cannot ascend into the Church, which is here named the mountain of the Lord, nor hearken to her spiritual instruction. And should he come there, he comes indeed in his body, in his soul he goes not up. For he who comes not with a pure heart gains nothing, for he comes only in his body. And should he hear spiritual things he will not understand: because his intelligence is corrupted by the leprosy of carnal sin. For no one can discern the flavour of good things, while revelling in what is evil. For as long as evil delights him, good cannot give him pleasure. Then only will he begin to delight in what is good, when evil begins to displease him.

. . . *Came and adored Him.* Faith, and its confession, form a perfect prayer, as the Apostle says: *for, with the heart, we believe unto justice; but, with the mouth, confession is made unto salvation* (Rom. x. 10). For as the leper, adoring, fulfilled the duty of faith, he fulfilled that of confessing with words, saying: *Lord, if thou wilt, thou canst make me clean.* He besought Him, not as a man that was skilled, but adored Him as God. And to his spiritual Physician he offered a spiritual payment. For all physicians are paid in money, he pays with prayer alone. And in truth nothing is more fittingly offered to God than trustful prayer. For whatsoever material thing we offer is not ours; but our prayer is our own.

Lord, if thou wilt, thou canst make me clean. He doubted not that the will of God is disposed to every good action, saying: *if thou wilt*: this does not imply doubt on the part of the leper, but rather the expression of his mind regarding Christ's judgement. For since Christ is good, He wills not to bestow that which is harmful, even though He be asked. Neither is bodily integrity profitable to everyone. Since therefore he knew not whether this healing was expedient for him or otherwise, he was unsure as to the divine will, although knowing it disposed to every good. For to believe good of the divine mercy is the sign of a believing man; to know the judgements of the divine mercy is beyond the power either of man or of faith, since it is plain that not even the Apostle did not know this, when he thrice besought the Lord that, *the sting of the flesh, the angel of Satan*, might depart from him; which had been given to him, lest he be exalted, and for which cause it was said to him: *my grace is sufficient for thee: for power is made perfect in infirmity* (II Cor. xii. 9).

It is as if the leper said: I believe that whatsoever is good, Thou wilt it. But I know not if what I seek is for me a good. But this I clearly doubt not, but rather believe: that if this be good for me, Thou dost will it also. The words of the leper therefore show him to be uncertain not of the mercy of God, but of the judgements of the divine mercy.

3. *And Jesus stretching forth His Hand, touched him.* Because it was laid down in the Law that he who touched a leper would be unclean until sundown, He touched the leper, not as a servant of the Law, but as its Lord. For the Law is under the Lawgiver; it is not the Lawgiver that is subject to the Law. What then? Did He do away with the Law? No, the letter of the Law He did indeed break, but its purpose He did not set aside, but rather gave added dignity to that purpose. For if the Law could have ordained that leprosy would

not taint a person touching a leper, it would not have forbidden that anyone should touch the leper. It therefore laid it down that no one was to touch a leper, because it could not secure that the leprosy would not taint the one so touching. He, therefore, Who in touching the leper was not soiled by the leprosy, did not act contrary to the Law, but even goes beyond that which the Law required; because not alone was he unstained by the leprosy, but He Himself made the leper clean.

Neither is it believable that He could be said to be stained by the leprosy, Who had healed the leprosy. For the Law forbade the touching of a leper not so that lepers might not be healed, but lest those touching leprosy be contaminated. He therefore Who in touching was not stained but rather made clean the leper, did more than the Law required. He touched the leper and so broke the letter of the Law, in order that not alone the leprosy of the body, but also that that of the soul might be taken away. We must compassionate the infirmity of the body, not despise it; the infirmity however of the soul must not be compassionated, but despised: for the infirmity of our body depends not upon ourselves as to whether it comes or does not come upon us; but the infirmity of our soul is within our own power, and, whether it comes upon us or not depends only upon ourselves.

The infirmity of our bodies holds us fast, we do not hold fast to it; the infirmity within our souls holds us not, we rather cling to it. Therefore, the one infirmity is to be compassionated, the other despised. He therefore rescinded the Law, but not the righteousness of the Law: not that Law which in creating men He inscribed upon their hearts, but that rather which He wrote upon a book, whilst the People were adoring a calf: not that Law of which it was said: *The Law of the Lord is unspotted, converting souls* (Ps. xviii. 8), but that of which it was said: *For the Law worketh wrath. For where there is no law, neither is there transgression* (Rom. iv. 15). How could that Law be worthy of being observed which brought about sins? Fittingly, therefore, being pleased, He put away that which in His wrath He had ordained. For if the Law were not taken away, the leprosy of the soul would never be healed; because each one who lives under the Law is a leper.

I will, be thou made clean. And forthwith his leprosy was cleansed. Not from this that He touched the leper did the leprosy depart, but because He commanded it to go; so that it might be seen that He touched the leper, not so as to drive away the leprosy, but so as to undo the Law. For as to the leprosy a word would have sufficed. Not even a word was necessary, but only His will to heal. He used His will therefore for the leprosy, His voice because of those who were witnesses. For had He cured him in silence with so many standing about the person of Christ, who then could know by what power he had been healed? Accordingly He said: I will, be thou made clean, so that all present might know that it was by His power the man was healed Who had laid down the laws of health. That He said: I will, indicated His will in response to what the leper had said: If thou

wilt. That He said, be thou made clean, is a command proceeding from His power in response to what was begged by the other: Thou canst make me clean.

4. *And Jesus saith to him: see thou tell no man: but go, shew thyself to the priest, and offer the gift which Moses commanded for a testimony unto them.* Do not understand this as meaning that Moses had ordered this gift in testimony to the priests, but as meaning: Go you and offer a gift for a testimony unto them. He did not say either: Go, show yourself to the priests and tell no one; but, first: *Tell no one*, and then, *Go, show thyself.* For He did not bid keep silent for always, but only until he had shown himself to the priests; lest perhaps in telling it to someone else the news passing from mouth to mouth the priests would come to hear of it, and because of their hate and enmity towards Christ they might seize the man on the pretext of his leprosy, and drive him forth, and not accept him as made clean.

Accordingly He bids him offer them gifts, so that if they should afterwards try and drive him forth He could then say to them: You have taken the gifts from me, as from one made clean, and how then do you now drive me forth as a leper? If I am still a leper you should not have taken my gifts, as though I were made clean; for if I were made clean, you cannot then drive me forth.

Or considering the same thing in another way. All the works of healing wrought by Christ contain within them mysteries of the hidden purposes of God. The bodily benefits of His healing were theirs then, now they are ours; the spiritual gains are perhaps ours alone. This leper therefore, who, immediately after the Sermon of Enlightenment comes forward as though prepared, was a figure of the Jewish People, standing below as the People stood: hearing the word of God spoken from above, and believing it, and adoring it, and embracing it. For everyone who adores the Word of God, believing it to be divine, and embracing it with all his heart, the Word of God has without doubt touched his soul. For it is not possible that a soul which embraces the word is not touched by it. When however the word has touched it, it cleans it of the leprosy of unbelief, as is written: *Now you are clean by reason of the word, which I have spoken to you* (Jn. xv. 3): and Peter also says: *Purifying their hearts by faith* (Acts xv. 9).

For which reason the people who had grown up under the harsh rule of the Law, and had not yet come to know the Dispensation of Mercy, believed firmly according to the tradition of their fathers in the divine power, but being uncertain regarding His mercy they said: *If thou wilt, thou canst make me clean.* For the Law spoke full of the Might of God, but of His mercy in a veiled manner. And so the Lord makes up to them, who knew the power of the Christ according to the Law, what was wanting in their knowledge, so that they might also come to learn of the mercy of His grace, and said: I will, be thou made clean.

And he saith to him: Go, offer the gift which Moses commanded.

What gifts? *Two turtles or two young pigeons* (Lev. xiv. 22). For all righteousness is contained within those two: in abstinence from evil-doing, and in the doing of good works. By a turtle, therefore, He orders that the people cleansed from unbelief offer holiness to God by abstaining from evil; since the spiritual chastity of the soul consists in absence of evil, so that it commingles not with an alien spirit, nor receives the seed of its inspiration, lest it bring forth works similar to the evil spirit. By the dove is signified every good work that arises out of charity; since it is charity that begets every good work. Whosoever, therefore, loves his neighbour as himself, takes from his neighbour nothing of good, nor from himself. When therefore anyone has fulfilled this twofold righteousness, he will keep himself from evil, which is the work of chastity, and doing whatsoever good he may, which is the work of charity, he manifestly becomes such a person as *shall be rightly cleansed* from the leprosy of unbelief.

So does a people *rightly cleansed*, and offering to God such sacrifices become a witness against the unbelieving priests, who, glorying in the letter of the Law, have rejected the Author of the Law, Who washes away the sins of the people whom the Law was unable to make clean.

And if you have embraced the Word of God with all your heart, the Word will touch your soul also, since *He loves them that love Him*, as is said in the Proverbs of Solomon (Prov. viii. 17), and will cleanse thee of every leprosy of unbelief. When however He will have made thee clean, He will command thee that thou wilt show thyself to the priests, as one made clean; restraining thyself from every contamination of evil-doing, and unfolding in good works your charity to all men, so that through these sacrifices you *may learn from the priests that you are made clean* (Lev. xiii); since they see thee not doing to another that which you are yourself unwilling to endure; but rather doing to all men that which you would wish them to do unto you. But if thou wilt not offer these sacrifices to God, it is plain to the sight of all men that you are not yet made clean; but that you still abide a leper in your former faithlessness. Amen.

IV. St Cyril, Bishop and Doctor
The Mystical Significance of the Healing of the Leper[6]

Behold a leper came. The faith of this man who came to Jesus is indeed worthy of all our praise. He testified that Emmanuel can do all things perfectly, and He pleads with Him that by His divine command He might be delivered of his leprosy, although it was an incurable disease. For leprosy is not wont to yield to the remedies of the physicians. For, he says, have I not seen unclean spirits driven forth by divine power, and other men freed from other diseases. I know that this has been done by some divine and invincible hand. I see also that Thou art both good and most kind, and that You show compassion to all that come to Thee. Why then should I not also seek Thy mercy?

What did Christ say to this? He confirmed him in his faith, and by this miracle showed that He approved it. He receives his prayer, and reveals that He can do this, saying to him: I will: be thou made clean. He also bestows on him the touch of His holy and omnipotent hand, and immediately the leprosy leaves him, and his sickness departs.

Let you join with me in awe, beholding Christ at work as both God and man. For it belongs to His divinity so to will that all things are as He wills; it is a human act to stretch forth the hand. In both the one and the other Christ is perceived, since the Word became flesh.

And Jesus saith to him: see thou tell no man. The character of the wonder that was performed, even though the leper remained silent, was enough to reveal to all who had known the leper the power of the One Who had healed him. Nevertheless He bids him tell no man. Why? That they who have received from God the gift of healing may learn that they are not to look for applause from those they heal, nor accept praise from others, lest they fall into pride, which is the wickedest of all sins.

But, Go, show thyself to the priest, and offer . . . Prudently therefore He counsels the leper to offer a gift to the priests, according to the law of Moses. For though without any doubt He intended to take away the shadows, and to change the figures of the law into the pure spiritual worship, yet, because the Jews did not believe in Him, but still clung to the precepts of Moses, as though the old law still endured, He permits the leper to do this for a testimony unto them.

Why did He do this? The Jews at all times were proclaiming their zeal for the law, and declaring that the great prophet Moses was the minister of the will of heaven, and they strove to belittle Christ the

Saviour of all men. And so they said openly: *We know that God spoke to Moses: but as to this man, we know not whence he is* (Jn. ix. 29). It was therefore necessary to convince them by these signs that the dignity of Moses was below the glory of Christ. Moses was but a faithful servant in the house of God: Christ was the Son in the house of His Father.

And so from the healing of the leper it was clearly evident that Christ, in an incomparable manner, far transcended the law of Moses. For Mary the sister of Moses, because she had murmured against him, was stricken with leprosy. And Moses at this affliction of his sister was profoundly grieved; but since he was unable to banish the disease from the woman, falling down before God he besought Him, saying: *O God, I beseech thee heal her* (Num. xii. 13).

Now observe carefully. In the one case there is entreaty: with prayer he sought to obtain the divine clemency; but the Saviour of mankind, with authority that was truly divine, says, I will: be thou made clean. This healing of the leper served therefore as a warning to the priests, that from it they should learn that those who gave precedence to Moses were wandering from the truth. Without doubt they should reverence Moses as the minister of the Law, a helper of the grace made known by angels (Gal. iii. 19), but much more is Emmanuel to be praised and glorified, as the true Son of God and the Father.

It may be that someone would like to see here the great and profound mystery concerning Christ, which is related to us in Leviticus.

The Law of Moses declared that a leper shall be condemned of uncleanness, and ordered to be driven forth from the camp as unclean. Afterwards, should the sickness leave him, it prescribed that he be received back into the camp. It lays down in what manner he shall be regarded as made clean, saying: *This is the rite of a leper, when he is to be cleansed: he shall be brought to the priest: who going out of the camp when he shall find that the leprosy is cleansed, shall command him that is to be purified, to offer for himself two living sparrows, which it is lawful to eat, and he shall command one of the sparrows to be immolated in an earthen vessel over living waters; but the other that is alive he shall dip in the blood of the sparrow that is immolated, wherewith he shall sprinkle him that is to be cleansed seven times, that he be rightly purified. And he shall let go the living sparrow in the field* (Lev. xiv). There were accordingly two sound, that is, clean birds, free according to the Law of every defect; of which one is slain over living waters; the other, exempt from slaughter, being sprinkled with the blood of the one that was slain, is then set free.

This figure truly designates the great and ever to be adored mystery of Our Saviour; for He, the Word, was from above, that is, from the Father and from heaven: and so is appropriately compared with the bird. By His Incarnation He came down in the likeness of our nature, and took upon Himself the form of a slave. But even in this He was from above. For which reason, speaking with the Jews, He said openly to them: *You are from beneath: I am from above* (Jn. viii. 23). And again: *And no man hath ascended* into heaven, *but he that descended from heaven, the Son of man* (Jn. iii. 13).

For as I have just now said, being made flesh, that is, truly man, He yet was not of the earth, nor of clay like us, but heavenly and supramundane, as God is understood to be. Nevertheless it is truly lawful to see Christ in the figure of the birds, having suffered in the flesh, as the Scripture says (I Pet. iv), yet remaining beyond the reach of suffering; humanly dead, divinely living: for the Word is life. Wherefore it is that the most wise Disciple says of Him, that *being put to death indeed in the flesh, but enlivened in the spirit* (I Pet. iii. 18).

But though the Word could not suffer in His own divine nature, nevertheless He truly made His own the passion of His Body. For the living bird was sprinkled with the blood of the one that was slain: and so dyed with its blood, and becoming almost a sharer of its suffering, was sent forth into the desert. For the Only-Begotten Word of the Father has returned to heaven, and with Him the flesh of our lowliness, and there was a strange spectacle in heaven. For the family of heaven were astonished at seeing the King of the earth, the Lord of all powers, appearing as one of us. And they exclaimed: *Who is this that cometh from Edom,* that is, from the earth? *With dyed garments from Bosra,* which is interpreted as meaning, *flesh,* or straitness or *affliction.* Then shall they say to Him: *What are these wounds in the midst of thy hands? And he shall say: with these I was wounded in the house of them that loved me* (Zach. xiii. 6).

For as after His resurrection, Christ, showing His hands, most prudently bade the doubting Thomas touch in them the marks of the nails, and likewise the opening in His side; so also returning to heaven He makes known to the holy angels that Israel had deservedly fallen from His favour and friendship. And for this He shows them His garments dyed with blood, and the wounds in His hands, not because He could not obliterate them, for, risen from the dead He had put off corruptibility, and with it whatsoever arose from it, but that according to the divine plan of the Incarnation the manifold *wisdom of God may be made known to the principalities and powers in heavenly places through the Church, which he made in Christ Jesus Our Lord* (Eph. iii. 9–11).

But someone may say: why do you speak of one and the same Christ, since there were two birds offered? Does not the Law here obscurely imply by this that there were two sons and two Christs? They would indeed fall into grievous irreverence who would believe and profess that one is the Christ above, the Word of God the Father, and another He that was born of the house of David. We however here declare to those who because of ignorance believe that this is so: we say, I repeat, what the divine Paul wrote: *One Lord, one Faith, one Baptism* (Eph. iv. 5). If therefore you should say that there are two Sons, there will then be two faiths, and as many baptisms. He will therefore proclaim what is false who has Christ so speaking in him, as the same Paul says (II Cor. xiii. 3). These things are not true. Far from it. Therefore we know but One Lord the Only-Begotten Incarnate Word of the Father, making no separation between man and God, but declaring that the

Word of God the Father became man, continuing in His Godhead at the same time.

Moreover, for argument's sake, let the adversaries of the truth say: if there are two sons, one born of the stock of David, the other the Word of God the Father; will not the latter then be higher in nature than the son that is born of the family of David? But note what follows. When we were speaking of the two birds, they were in no way different in nature from each other, but rather similar, and without any difference, each exactly as the other. Therefore they must concede that because of the uniform nature of the birds, the Word of God should differ in no way from the man. But here they make no headway; for humanity profoundly differs from the divinity. The figures then must be understood in a manner that confirms with reason. Furthermore we say that even the Law was but a shadow, a figure, and as it were a picture which showed the future to those who were looking towards it.

The Law therefore was a picture, a type, of the things which brought forth truth; so that even though there were two birds, yet by them but one Christ was prefigured, both as suffering and as not suffering; dying, yet above all dying; finally also ascending to heaven, as a second beginning of humanity, reborn to immortality. He in truth has prepared for us a new way to heaven, and we in due time shall follow Him. That one of the birds was slain, and that the other was sprinkled with the blood of the one that was slain, and that being free it escaped slaughter, must all be considered as a figure of the things that now are true. For Christ died for us, and we are baptised in His death, and He by His blood redeemed us, Who with the Father and the Holy Ghost liveth and reigneth world without end. Amen.

NOTES

[1] Now considered as possibly the work of a later writer, cf. PRM 42.

[2] PL 38, Sermo 62.

[3] Translated from the Latin rendering of Combefis: Ex Diversis Hom. in Matthaeum BPC, III, 245.

[4] PL 29, 550.

[5] PG 56, 747. The *Opus Imperfectum* from which this sermon, the twenty-first on Chapter eight of Matthew, is taken, is an erudite and acute commentary, which is incomplete, generally associated with the name of St John Chrysostom; though it is not and cannot be regarded as his work. It appears to have been used for reading in churches in exposition of the Gospel.

According to G. Moran it was written by an Arian bishop of northern Italy about A.D. 559. This seems a common opinion. Learned opinions for and against its integrity are to be found, vide *Diatriba Ad Opus Imperfectum*, PG LVI, 601. One significant comment—that of Johannes Mahusius, 1537—points out that the oldest copy of the work then extant had not a trace of any error, *sed alia manu omnia adscripta in marginibus*; which appears to agree with an approval of the work of Paul IV, excepting certain errors inserted against the mind of the author.

The decision to include this instructive and discerning homily is based, not on any personal opinion relative to this question, but solely because St Thomas Aquinas makes use of it so extensively in the Catena Aurea. Had there been errors of doctrine in the text used by the author of the Catena Aurea it is impossible that they could have escaped the discernment of the Angel of the Schools, or that if there were that he would have made such use of it as he has.

It is of interest to recall that many of the Goths—very many—were not Arians. They had their own national church in Constantinople, at the opening of which St John Chrysostom preached; and his memory appears to have been held in great veneration among them (Cf. Life of St John Chrysostom, by Fr. Chrysostom Baur, O.S.B., Vol. I, 50, 69). Apart from the fact that the Goths had as yet no literature of their own at the time, it is hard to imagine any other than Greek origins for this work, so closely woven in texture, and so subtle and acute in its reflections. The question of the integrity of the Opus Imperfectum is not easily disposed of.

[6] PG 72, 555–563.

FOURTH SUNDAY AFTER
THE EPIPHANY

I. Origen: The Testing of the Apostles

II. St Jerome: On the Gospel

III. St Augustine: On Anger

IV. St Cyril of Alexandria: On the Gospel

THE GOSPEL OF THE SUNDAY

Matthew viii. 23–27

At that time: When Jesus entered into the boat, His disciples followed Him: and behold a great tempest arose in the sea, so that the boat was covered with waves, but He was asleep. And they came to Him, and awaked Him, saying: Lord, save us, we perish. And Jesus saith to them: Why are you fearful, O ye of little faith? Then rising up He commanded the winds, and the sea, and there came a great calm. But the men wondered, saying: What manner of man is this, for the winds and the sea obey Him?

PARALLEL GOSPELS

Mark iv. 35–40

And He saith to them that day, when evening was come: Let us pass over to the other side. And sending away the multitude, they take Him even as He was in the ship: and there were other ships with Him. And there arose a great storm of wind, and the waves beat into the ship, so that the ship was filled. And He was in the hinder part of the ship, sleeping upon a pillow; and they awake Him, and say to Him: Master, doth it not concern thee that we perish? And rising up, He rebuked the wind, and said to the sea: Peace, be still. And the wind ceased: and there was

Luke viii. 22–25

And it came to pass on a certain day that He went into a little ship with His disciples, and He said to them: Let us go over to the other side of the lake. And they launched forth. And when they were sailing, he slept; and there came down a storm of wind upon the lake, and they were filled, and were in danger. And they came and awaked Him, saying: Master, we perish. But He arising, rebuked the wind and the rage of the water; and it ceased, and there was a calm. And He said to them: Where is your faith? Who, being afraid, wondered, saying one to another: Who made a great calm. And He said to them: Why are you fearful? Have you not faith yet? And they feared exceedingly: and they said one to another: Who is this, thinkest thou, that both wind and sea obey Him?

is this, think you, that He commandeth both the winds and the sea, and they obey Him?

EXPOSITION FROM THE CATENA AUREA

MATTHEW viii. 23–27

23. *And when he entered into the boat, his disciples followed him . . .*

ORIGEN, *Hom. 6 Ex. Var. locis*: When Christ had performed many and wondrous miracles upon the land, He crossed over the sea that there also He might reveal the wonders of His works, whereby He showed to all He was Lord of both land and sea. Hence there is written: And when He entered into the boat His Disciples followed Him; and they were not weak men, but robust, and firm of faith. They follow Him not so much walking in His footsteps as keeping close to Him in holiness.

CHRYSOSTOM, *Hom. 29 in Matt.*: He took His Disciples with Him, and in a ship, to prepare them for two things: one, that they might learn not to let themselves be carried away by fear in dangers, and next that they should learn that when honoured they should comport themselves with modesty. And so that they would not think highly of themselves for this that having sent all others away He took them with Him, He permits them to be buffeted by the sea. When there was a manifestation of miracles He allowed the people to be present, but when terror and dangers are approaching He takes with Him only His Disciples, they who had to combat the world, whom He now wished to exercise in fortitude.

24. *And behold a great tempest arose in the sea, so that the boat was . . .*

ORIGEN, as above: Having gone up into the ship, He caused the sea to become stormy. Hence: *And behold a great tempest arose in the sea, so that the boat was covered with waves.* This storm did not arise of itself, but in obedience to the power Who had commanded it, *Who bringeth forth winds out of his stores* (Ps. cxxxiv. 7). A great storm arose so that a great sign might be given; and the more the waves beat against the little ship, the more did fear assail the hearts of His Disciples, and consequently the greater was their desire to be delivered through the power of the Saviour.

CHRYSOSTOM, as above: For though they had seen others receive favours from Christ, yet no one regards in the same way things done in the persons of others and those done to themselves, so it was necessary that through personal experience they should receive a clear understanding of the benefits which Christ had conferred on others. Accordingly He wills that this storm arise, so that being delivered from it they might have a clear sense of benefit received.

The storm was a foreshadowing of their future trials, of which Paul says: *For we would not have you ignorant, brethren, of our tribulation, that we were pressed out of measure above our strength* (II Cor. i. 8). And to give time for their fear to grow,

there follows: *But he was asleep.*
Had He been awake while the storm
was on, either they would not have
been afraid, or they might not have
besought His help, or it might not
have occurred to them that He
could work such a wonder.

25. *And they came to him, and
awakened him, saying: Lord, save us.*

ORIGEN: It is an astonishing thing,
that He Who never sleeps nor
grows weary, is here said to sleep.
He slept in His Body, but in the
Godhead He keeps watch: showing
that He bore a true human body,
that He had clothed Himself with
what was perishable. In His Body
therefore He slept, to make the
Apostles keep watch, and lest we
should also slumber in our souls.
The Disciples were fearful, and so
nearly out of their senses that they
rushed upon Him; they did not beseech Him modestly or quietly, but
rather awakened Him violently;
hence follows: *And they came to him,
and awakened him, saying: Lord, save
us, we perish.*

26. *And Jesus saith to them: Why
are you fearful?*

JEROME: In Jonah we read of a figure
of this kind; while the others are in
peril he is safe, and sleeps, and is
awakened. ORIGEN: O trustful
Disciples, you have with you the
Saviour, and you are fearful of
danger? With you is Life, and you
are apprehensive of death? But
hear them answering: We are as
children, and we are still weak; and
so we are fearful. Hence follows:
*And Jesus saith to them: why are ye
fearful, O ye of little faith?* As if He
said to them: Since you have known
me upon the land as possessing

power, why do you not believe I
have power also upon the sea? And
though death assail you, ought you
not meet it courageously? He that
is of little faith, let him be reproved;
he that is without faith, let him be
despised.

CHRYSOSTOM, as above: Should
anyone say that it was not an indication of little faith to come and
waken Him, I say that this was a
sign that they had not a fitting
belief regarding Him. For they
knew that being wakened He could
command the sea, but that this He
could do also while sleeping they
did not yet know. For this reason
also He did not perform this sign in
the presence of the multitude, lest
they be accused of little faith, but
taking only the Disciples with Him,
He first corrects them, and then
calms the tempest of the waters.
Hence follows: *Then rising up He
commanded the winds and the sea, and
there came a great calm.*

JEROME: From this occasion we learn
that all creatures hearken to the
voice of the Creator. For they that
here were commanded heard Him
commanding; not in the sense of
those heretics who believe that all
things are living, but, by reason of
the Majesty of the Creator, the
things which to us appear unper-
ceiving, are to Him perceiving.

ORIGEN: He commanded the wind
and the sea, and from a great tempest there came a great calm. It is
fitting that He that is mighty should
do great things; and so He Who
a while before had stirred the deeps
of the sea, now orders that there
shall be a great calm: so that the
Disciples, who had been grievously

troubled, will now be wondrously made glad.

27. *But the men wondered, saying: What manner of man is this?*

CHRYSOSTOM: In this recital it is also shown that the entire storm was at once put to rest: no trace of its violence remaining, which was unusual. For when a storm comes naturally to its end, the waves continue for some time to be disturbed: but here at once all is made calm. What before was spoken of the Father: *He said the word and there arose a storm of wind* (Ps. cvi. 25) Christ fulfils in this miracle: and by His word and command alone He calms and restrains the sea. From His appearance, and from His sleeping, and because He makes use of the ship, those that were present regarded Him as a man; now they are astonished, and so we have: *But the men wondered, saying: what manner of man is this? For the winds and the sea obey him?*

GLOSS: Chrysostom cites the comment: *what manner of man is this?* For sleep, and His outward appearance, showed Him to be man: but the sea and the calm proclaim Him God.

ORIGEN: But *what* men wondered? You do not think that the Apostles are here referred to? For nowhere do we find the Lord's Disciples spoken of without due respect; but always referred to either as the Apostles or as the Disciples. The men therefore who wondered are they who owned the boat and were sailing it for Him.

JEROME: If anyone, contentiously, will have it that those who were wondering were the Disciples, we

shall reply that they are rightly referred to as men, since they knew not as yet the power of their Saviour.

ORIGEN: Not as questioning do they say, what manner of man is this, but as asserting that He is so great that the winds and the seas obey Him. *What manner* therefore *of man is this,* signifies, how great, how strong, how wonderful? He commands all creatures and they pass not one step beyond His command. Only men disobey Him, and so they are condemned in judgement. Mystically, all we who are united with the Lord in the bark of Holy Church float above this stormy world. The Lord however sleeps quietly, lovingly awakening our fearfulness, and our turning to Him from evil.

HILARY, *Ch. 7 in Matt*: Or He sleeps in the sense that in our sleeping He is put to sleep in us. It especially happens that in time of danger we hope for help from God. Would that serene and tranquil hope should ever confide in the power of Christ watching within us to deliver us from danger!

ORIGEN: Let us turn quickly to the Lord, saying with the prophet: *Arise, why sleepest thou, O Lord?* (Ps. xliii. 23). And He will command the winds, that is, the demons who stir up the waves; that is, the princes of this world who persecute the saints, and He will make a great calm round about body and soul, and He will give peace to the Church, and tranquillity to the world.

RABANUS: Or again: The sea is the unrest of the world; the little boat into which Christ ascends signifies the tree of the Cross, by whose aid the faithful in Christ, crossing the waves of the world, reach to the heavenly city as to a safe shore, on which with Christ they land; whence later He says: *If any man will come after me, let him deny himself, and take up his cross, and follow me* (Mt. xvi. 24).

When therefore Christ was placed upon the Cross, a great storm arose: because His Disciples were fearful by reason of His passion, and the little boat *was covered with waves*; for the whole fury of the persecution was around the Cross of Christ, where He slept in death; hence is it said: *But he was asleep.* His sleep was His death. The Disciples awakened the Lord when, terrified at His death, they

plead in earnest prayer for His resurrection, saying: *Save us*, by rising again, *for we perish*, by reason of the tempest of Your dying. He rising up reproves the hardness of their hearts, as is elsewhere read. But He commanded the winds, for He laid low the power of the devil; He commanded the sea, because He brought to nothing the rage of the Jews; and there came a great calm, when the minds of His Disciples were comforted by the vision of His resurrection.

Gloss: Or, *the little boat* is the Church on earth, in which Christ with His own crosses the sea of this world, and calms the waves of persecutions. Whence we wonder, and we give thanks.

I. Origen: The Testing of the Apostles[1]

The Lord going into the boat His Disciples follow Him. They were not weak men, but strong and steady in faith, kind, good, and unworldly: nor were they two-faced, but simple of heart. They followed Him, not alone in His footsteps, but also walking with Him in holiness of life, striving after justice.

And behold a great tempest arose upon the sea. For since the Lord had wrought great and wondrous signs upon the land, He now crosses over the sea that here also He may show yet greater wonders, that He might make plain to all that He was Master both of the sea and of the land. Entering therefore into the little boat He caused a storm to arise upon the sea, and caused the winds to blow and the waves to swell up. Why did He do this? That He might awaken fear in the hearts of His Disciples, that they be

compelled to seek His help, and to make manifest His power to those that sought it. For this storm arose not of its own accord, but in obedience to His power: *Who bringeth forth winds out of his stores* (Ps. cxxxiv. 7); *Who set the sand a bound for the sea* (Jer. v. 22); *and said: hitherto thou shalt come, and shall go no further, and here thou shalt break thy swelling waves* (Job. xxxviii. 11).

By His command, therefore and precept the tempest has risen in the sea, for the reasons we have already said. There was then a great tempest raging, not a little one, that He might put forth a great wonder, not a little one; and the greater the battering of the waves against the little boat, the more the fear of the Disciples mounted, and the more they desired to be delivered by the wonders of the Saviour.

But the Lord was asleep. O great and wondrous thing! Does

He Who never sleeps now sleep? Does He now sleep that rules both heaven and earth? Is it He Who never wearies, or falls asleep, that here is said to fall asleep? Yes, in His Human Body He sleeps, but in His Godhead He keeps watch. He sleeps in this Body of flesh, yet He causes the storm to arise on the sea, and the waves to mount up, and fear to come upon the Disciples, so that He may reveal to them His Power. He sleeps in this Body, as at the well by the wayside He sat tired and weary; showing that He bore a Body that was truly human: that He had clothed Himself with what was perishable.

In this Body He slept; in His Godhead He troubled the sea, and again restored it to tranquillity. He thus slept in His Body that He might awaken His Disciples, and make them keep vigil; and we likewise, so that we too sleep not in our souls, nor in our understanding, nor in wisdom; but that at all times we keep watch, and give praise to the Lord, and eagerly seek from Him our salvation. For He Who now sleeps in the Body has spoken these holy words: *I sleep, and my heart watcheth* (Cant. v. 2).

And they came to Him, and awakened Him, saying: Lord, save us we perish. So fearful were they, and almost out of their minds, that they rushed to Him, and roused Him, not modestly and gently, but violently awakening Him, they cried: *Lord save us, we perish.* O blessed and truthful Disciples of the Lord! You have with you the Lord our Saviour, and you are in fear of danger? With you is Life, and you are fearful of death? Fearful of the tumult of the sea, you thus waken its Creator, Who is beside you, as

if, while sleeping in His Body, He could not calm the waves or hush them to rest?

But what answer do they give, these beloved Disciples? We are, they say, but as children, still weak, nor yet grown to our strength. And so we fear, so we tremble. Nor have we yet beheld the Cross, nor has the Passion of Christ yet strengthened us, nor has His resurrection, nor His ascent into heaven, nor the sending and the coming of the Holy Ghost the Comforter. For this reason we waver in our weakness; for this reason have we heard from the Lord the oft repeated chiding of our littleness of faith. But we bear up, we readily endure, we eagerly look forward. Hence says the Lord: *Why are ye fearful. O Ye of little faith?* Why have ye not courage? Why have you no confidence, no trust, among you? and though death should threaten you, ought you not courageously to stand your ground? For against that which you shall meet courage is necessary. We must cling steadfastly to courage of soul in the face of every danger, or suffering, even to the giving up of life, and likewise against earthly delights, riches, honours, so that, O Man, you be not blown up, or raised above yourself in pride: so that you despise not your enemy: nor look down upon the lowly: nor be unmindful of the Lord: nor forget thy Creator: nor become an unprofitable servant. If then fortitude is necessary in trial and in danger so as to bear up manfully against whatever may assail you, how much more is it needful, as I have said, against allurements, against luxuries, lest you be caught in the devil's mousetrap?

Why therefore are ye troubled, O ye of little faith? If you have known me to have power on the land, why do you not believe that I have power also upon the sea? If you believe me to be God, the Creator of all things, why do you not also believe that the things which I have made are subject to my power? Why do ye doubt, O ye of little faith? He that is of little faith is reproved, he that believeth not will be condemned; the weak in faith will be gathered in, those wholly estranged from the faith will be punished. Such were the Jews and the Pagans, and in their evils they have vanished. Such are the heretics, and so in the day of judgment will they be condemned.

Then rising up He commanded the winds and the sea, and there came a great calm. It was written: *and the Lord was awakened as one out of sleep, and he smote his enemies on the hinder parts* (Ps. lxxvii. 66); and now rising up He commands, and there comes a great calm. He commands the winds and the sea as their Lord, and, for the first time, in the presence of the Disciples, so that hearing Him command them they would be confirmed in their faith. And he here commands by the veiled power of the Godhead; and He commanded as it was also written: *thou rulest the power of the sea: and appeasest the motion of the waves thereof* (Ps. lxxxviii. 10). Upon a sea tossed about and swollen by a great wind, and a great tempest, there comes a great calm. It was befitting that He that is Mighty should do great things. And so, girt with mighty power, he shakes the sea to its depths: and again, showing the splendour of His might, He commands that there shall arise a great calm, so that the Apostles, who had feared exceedingly, being now delivered might rejoice.

By means of all these happenings the Lord gave us a figure and image of His teaching, so that we might be patient in the face of every storm and persecution; that we may be steadfast; that we betray not our faith. And if all this world should boil up as the sea, and rise in fury against us: though on every side there should rage the winds and the whirlpools of the demons: though, as we have said, every menace of the sea, that is, every principality and power of this world, be roused against us, foaming with the swelling of their wrath, so as to torment the sanctified: and though like to the sea they whip up wickedness and treacheries to the very skies, stirring up against you the murmuring of the evilminded: yet, be not afraid; be not troubled: do not tremble: do not yield.

For as many as are in the little ship of faith are sailing with the Lord; as many as are in the Bark of Holy Church will voyage with the Lord across this wave-tossed life; though the Lord Himself may sleep in holy quiet, He is but watching your patience and endurance: looking forward to the repentance, and to the conversion, of those who have sinned.

Come then to Him eagerly, instant in prayer, saying with the prophet: *Arise, why sleepest thou, O Lord? Arise, and cast us not off to the end*; and again: *Arise, O Lord, help us and redeem us for thy name's sake* (Ps. xliii. 23, 26). And He rising up *commanded the winds*, that is, the spirits among the demons that dwell in the air. For they stir up the tempests of the sea, that is, they provoke the evil swollen waves who are the rulers of this world, to wage persecutions against the sanctified; to inflict torments on the faithful in Christ. But the Lord commands all things, rebukes all things, lays upon each what they must do, tempers all things; and then brings a great calm around soul and body, gives back peace to the church, restores serenity to the world.

For how often have *the counsels of the wicked*, sometimes from among the pagans, sometimes from the heretics, plotted against the faithful steadfast church? As the waves of the sea have risen, so have the rulers of this world, to threaten and terrify, and thinking in this way to exterminate the children of the Church. But the Lord has reproved the rising winds, which are the demons, and scattered these impudent adversaries, and given a great peace to the church.

But the men that were in the boat wondered. Which men? Those who were the owners of the boat, or those who were only sailing in it? Do not believe that it is the Apostles that are here referred to. For nowhere do we find the Apostles referred to without due respect; always they are spoken of either as the Apostles, or as the Disciples. Those men therefore wondered who were sailing the ship with Him; they to whom it belonged, and others who were also crossing over in the same ship: these it was who wondered. And it was truly a cause of wonder; to quieten a sea that was shaken to its depths, calm the stormy waves, and check the fury of the winds. They wondered therefore, saying: *What manner of man is this?* They say this:

what manner of man is he, not as questioning but as affirming that he is such that the sea and the winds obey Him. What manner of man is this? As much as to say: how great, how strong, how wonderful? What manner of man is this? Greater than Moses, mightier than Elias. For of these two, one by the instrument of the rod stretched forth above the sea crossed over on dry ground (Ex. xiv. 16), the other needed with his mantle to strike the waters so as to cross the bed of the Jordan (IV Kgs. ii. 8); while He with a word speaks to those that are without words, and they obey Him, to those that hear not, and they hearken to Him: to the things that are without sense or understanding, and they bow to Him that commands them: to them that have neither speech nor words, and they obey His voice. But in their substance, in their nature, they are set in motion and obey His command; to the confusion of men, to the condemnation of our disobedience.

He commands the sea, and it disobeys not: He speaks to the winds, and to the storm, and Lo! they are still: He commands every creature, and they move not beyond what He commands. Only the race of men, which alone is honoured in being made in His likeness, to whom speech and understanding has been given, only these, only men, resist; they alone obey Him not: they alone despise Him. And for this cause they alone will be condemned at the judgement, and punished by His justice; in this being lower than the dumb beasts, or than the things of the world that are without sense or without feeling.

They wonder at Him because He restrained the sea, and quietened the winds. Let us wonder at Him too, when He shows kindness and generosity towards us; when He comes down to deliver us from dangers; when He delivers us from manifold trials and pains; when He rescues us from the snares of our enemies. Let us wonder, and wondering give thanks; let us be responsive to His grace, and being obedient, let us also fear Him; and fearing Him, let us love Him, so that we become inheritors of eternal love.

They wondered, saying: what manner of man is this? He appears as man, but as God He shows forth His power. For while we see that He is of our flesh, He manifests signs and wonders that are above the power of all flesh. As man He sleeps, as God He commands the winds and the seas. He rests in the little ship, yet where He wills all creatures bow down before His Majesty, Jesus Christ Our Lord, Who with the Father and the Holy Ghost, liveth and reigneth world without end. Amen.

II. St Jerome: On the Gospel[2]

And when he entered into the boat, his disciples followed him: and behold a great tempest arose in the sea, so that the boat was covered with waves. Jesus performed His fifth miracle when, entering into a boat at Capharnaum, He commanded the winds and the sea. The sixth, when in the country of the Gerasenes He gave the swine into the power of the demons. The seventh, when going into His own city He cured a second paralytic, who was lying upon a bed. For the first paralytic healed was the servant of the Centurion.

But he was asleep. And they came to him, and awakened him, saying: Lord, save us, we perish. And Jesus saith to them: Why are you fearful, O ye of little faith? We read a foreshadowing of this sign in Jonah (Jn. i), who, while the others were in danger, he being safe, both slept and was awakened; and at his command and by the mystery of

what he suffered, delivered his awakeners.

Then rising up he commanded the winds, and the sea, and there came a great calm. From this account we understand that all creatures hearken to their Creator. For that which He rebukes, and which He commanded, hear Him commanding; not in the sense of those heretics who believe that all things are living, but by the power of the Creator, those things are responsive to Him, which to us appear without perception.

But the men wondered, saying: what manner of man is this, for the winds and the sea obey him? It was not the Disciples, but the sailors, and the others who were in the ship that wondered. Unless someone should contentiously hold that it was the Disciples who wondered then we reply that they are fittingly called simply men, who had not yet learned the power of the Saviour.

III. St Augustine, Bishop and Doctor
On Anger[3]

1. *Voyaging in this world.* I shall with God's help speak to you upon the portion of the Gospel that has just been read, and in its light I

exhort you, that you sleep not in your hearts amid the storms and distresses of this world. Perhaps the Lord had not power over death, nor had He sleep within His power? And it may be that sleep overpowered the Omnipotent, as He sailed upon the water? If you have so believed, then He sleeps in you: if Christ keeps watch in you, your faith keeps watch.

The Apostle says: *That Christ may dwell by faith in your hearts* (Eph. iii. 17). Therefore the sleep of Christ is also a sign of mystery. Those in the boat are those crossing the world upon the Wood. Even this ship prefigures the Church. And each soul is itself a world of God, and each one voyages within his own heart; nor is he shipwrecked, if he dwells on the things that are worthy.

2. *Christ must be awakened in the storms of anger.* Have you received an insult, it is the wind: are you provoked to anger, it is the buffeting of the waves. As the wind rises, and the waves mount up, your ship is in peril; your heart is buffeted by waves, your soul is endangered. Swift on the insult you are eager for revenge: and lo! you are revenged, and yielding to a new disaster, you are shipwrecked. And why? Because in thee Christ sleeps. What does this mean: in thee Christ sleeps? It means you have forgotten Christ. Then awaken Christ, bring Him to mind; let Christ keep watch in thee: look upon Him.

What was it you desired? To be revenged. Has it gone from your memory what He said while they crucified Him: *Father, forgive them for they know not what they do* (Lk. xxiii. 34)? He Who was sleeping in your heart sought not to be revenged. Awaken Him, remember Him. Remembrance of Him is remembrance of His words: and to remember Him is to obey Him. And should Christ awaken in you, you will say to yourself: What kind of man am I that I should seek to be revenged? Who am I that I should utter threats against another?

It may be that I shall die before I can be revenged. And when breathing my last, on fire with anger, thirsting for revenge, I go forth from this body, He shall not receive me Who desired no revenge: He shall not receive me Who said: *Forgive, and you shall be forgiven. Give, and it shall be given unto you* (Lk. vi. 37, 38). Therefore shall I bridle my anger, and return to the peace of my heart. Christ commanded the sea, and there came a great calm.

3. *At the command of Christ there is calm.* What I have said to you regarding anger, observe in every temptation. A temptation arises, it is the wind: you are troubled, it is the waves. Awaken Christ, let Him speak with thee. Who is this, for *the winds and the sea obey him?* Who is this whom the sea obeys? *the sea is his, and he made it* (Ps. xciv. 5). *All things were made by him* (Jn. i. 3). Be then as the winds and the sea: obey thy Creator. When Christ spoke, the sea gave ear: and wilt thou be deaf? The sea hearkens to His voice, and the winds cease: and wilt thou keep blowing? What mean you? I keep on talking, I keep on doing, I keep on contriving: what is this but to keep on blowing, and refusing to be still at the command of Christ?

Let not the sea master you in this tempest of the heart. Yet, since we are men, should the wind beat hard against you, and should it awaken passion in the soul, let us not lose hope. Let us awaken Christ that we may sail on in peace, and come safely home. Turning then to the Lord Our God, the Father Almighty, in pureness of heart, let us as best we can give thanks with all our hearts; beseeching Him that in His goodness He will graciously hear our prayers, and by His power drive evil from our thoughts and actions, increase our faith, guide our minds, grant to us His holy inspirations, and bring us to unending joy through His Son Our Lord and Saviour Jesus Christ, Amen.

IV. St Cyril: On the Gospel[4]

And when He entered the boat. As Christ together with His holy Disciples crossed over the sea or lake of Tiberias, a sudden fierce storm struck the ship, and the waves swelling under the breath of the wind cast the fear of death upon the hearts of the Disciples. For this great disturbance troubled all of them, though they were not ignorant of the ways of the sea, and indeed were long familiar with its storms and dangers. Now their danger became so acute that they were filled with a fear they became unable to support, and as there remained no other hope of escaping the danger they awakened the Lord of all power Himself, Who is Christ, with these words: *Master, save us: we perish.* For the Evangelist relates that He had fallen asleep. Mark adds to the account, *upon a pillow;* offering an example as well as teaching simplicity of life.

It seems to me that all this was arranged with profoundest wisdom, so that they might not ask His aid as soon as the storm had begun to beat against the ship, but only when the danger would be at its highest, that the might of the divine power might thus be the more evident, checking the fierce sea and bringing such a great calm that of a sudden not a vestige of the storm remained. For had it risen while He was awake, either they would not have been afraid, or they would not have besought His help, or they might have thought in a circumstance of this kind that He could do nothing.

And so He sleeps, leaving them in fear, in which their senses would be sharpened to perceive the significance of what was to come. For no one feels what takes place in another's body as acutely as that which happens in his own. Before, they had seen others receive favours, while they as yet had received none, and so in this way they were without experience: and since in their peril they would receive help from Him, He permits them for their instruction to be tossed and shaken about by the storm. Fittingly too it was a storm that had taken place, so the miracle would stand out more vividly, and a clear enduring memory of what had happened would remain. For since at first they were certain that they were about to perish, and were then saved, being made aware how great was their danger, they came to learn the greatness of the miracle.

Once again let us draw near unto the Lord, that as with the harp of David we may praise Him: *I will praise the Lord at all times, his praise shall always be in my mouth* (Ps. xxxiii. 2): *Who doth great things and unsearchable and wonderful things without number* (Job v. 9); for His wonders are without ceasing, and give us cause without end to praise Him, yet no word of ours suffices to describe His Power or Majesty, which rises above all created things. It is true that *the glory of the Lord conceals the word* (Prov. xxv. 2); but we must not neglect the glory that is due to Him, and offer joyfully what gifts are in our power. Let us then come together and praise Him, Christ the Saviour of all men. Let us contemplate His perfection, and the majesty of His rule.

But as I have said they awaken Him, saying: *Save us, we perish.* Note here with me their faith, and how weak it is. They believe He can save them, yet having little faith they cry: *We perish.* It could not happen that they would perish, since He Who can do all things was with them. Christ Who has power over every creature immediately awakens; forthwith He restrains the storm, checks the fury of the winds, calms their fears, and by this shows that He is God. Let us sing with the psalmist: *Thou rulest the power of the sea: and appeasest the motion of the waves thereof* (Ps. lxxxviii. 10).

Calming the storm upon the sea, at the same moment He changed the faith of the holy Disciples which had been shaken, with their little ship; changing its wavering to constancy, and He wrought in them also a great calm: smoothing the waves of their little faith. And so together with the tumult of the waves, He quietens the fear within their souls, chiding them while He teaches them, that the cause of their fears was not the assault of the tempest, but their own timidity of soul. For He said to them: *Where is

your faith?* (Lk. viii. 25). Another Evangelist, Matthew, affirms that He said: *Why are you fearful, O you of little faith?*

But it will happen even to steadfast courageous minds to be shaken by the fear of death. It is for this reason that some of them came to Christ praying Him: *Lord, increase our faith* (Lk. xvii. 5). He falls short of the fulness of faith, who continues to offend through weakness of faith. For as gold is tested in fire, so is faith by temptation. But the mind of man is weak and needs help from above, so that he may with courage face the dangers of the way. And this Our Saviour teaches when He says: *Without Me you can do nothing.* And the most wise Paul confesses also: *I can do all things in Him who strengthened me* (Phil. iv. 13).

Then having calmed the storm, and by His command restored the sea to serenity and peace, His Disciples wondering at this extraordinary happening whisper to each other: *What manner of man is this, for the winds and the sea obey Him?* Did they say these words because they knew Him not? Who does not see that this is wholly unlikely? For they knew that Jesus was the Son of God and God; but they were awe-stricken at the sublimity of the power that was in Him, and at the glory of His divinity. But since He still dwelt among men, and they beheld Him clothed in the flesh, it is for this reason they use these words: *What manner of man is this?* It is as if they said: How great He is! Of what nature? With what power and majesty is He clothed, that He commands the very winds and the sea and they obey Him!

His manner of acting on this

occasion was not that of a suppliant, but of one who rules. This is a great sign; an inspiration to all who hear it. For creation is obedient to every command of Christ. Also, as Mark relates it, the manner in which He reproves the winds is in accord with the divine dignity. For He says that the Lord spoke to the sea: *He threatened the wind and said to the sea: Be silent.* And as soon as He had spoken there follows that which He commands, and the sea foaming in angry waves hears the Incarnate Word and ceases from its fury; acknowledging Him Who at the beginning of the world had *gathered together the waters into one place* (Gen. i. 19): and *set a bound which they shall not pass over* (Ps. ciii. 9).

In this sign Almighty God shows forth His splendour, for, says one of the Prophets, in a certain place where He is reproving those who had sinned shamelessly: *Will you not then fear me, saith the Lord: and will you not repent at my presence? I have set the sand a bound for the sea, an everlasting ordinance, which it shall not pass over* (Jer. v. 22). He signifies the same thing in the Book of Job regarding the sea: *I set my bounds around it, and made its bars and doors, and I said: Hither thou shalt come, and shall go no further, and here thou shalt break thy swelling waves* (Job xxxviii. 10, 11). The blessed psalmist plucking his harp of the Spirit also sings: *Thou rulest the power of the sea: and appeasest the motion of the waves thereof* (Ps. lxxxviii. 10).

Since however it belongs to the divine nature, that it has power and rule over the sea, and gives a rule unto its waters, and places every element under the dominion of the Lord: and since the Son shows

forth with mighty power that He does this, how does He not share in the nature of God? How was He created Who can with a word perform these wonders, that may alone proceed from God the Father? For if we say that a thing of nothing can impose its command upon the sea, and set bounds to it: why does God and the Father glory in these things as proclaiming His majesty? But if on the contrary such things proceed alone from the divine power and glory, there is no reason whereby we may attribute to a created being what is due to God alone. The Son will not therefore be a created being, Who enters into the sphere of the Godhead, since He can of Himself do those things which are recognised as proper to It alone.[5]

The storm was likewise a figure of the things that were later to happen to the Disciples. For the lake signified Judea, upon which there arose a great storm of anger among the Jews against our Lord. The Disciples became so fearful that they fled. But the Saviour arose as it were from sleep, and again to the Disciples there came a great calm. And standing in their midst He said: *Peace be to you* (Lk. xxiv. 36).

In yet another way the sea is for us a figure of the visible world, and the Church is the little ship, and the rowers are the Just, who because they have received the faith have Christ always present with them. And frequently it is assailed by violent storms, and the waves of many persecutions beat against the holy Bark, and countless trials agitate it, and the cruelty of unclean spirits rage against it, and fill it with the fear of death.

But Christ is among His chosen servants, and while in His holy wisdom He permits that they suffer persecution, He seems to sleep. But when the storm is at its fiercest, and those in the Bark can endure no more, then ought we cry out: *Arise, why sleepest Thou, O Lord* (Ps. xliii. 23). Without delay He will awaken, and take away all thy fear.

He will reprove them that afflict us, and change our mourning into joy, unfolding to us a shining and untroubled sky. For He averts not His Face from those that trust in Him, Who liveth and reigneth with the Father and the Holy Spirit world without end. Amen.

NOTES

[1] BPC 2, Hom. 6 in diversis in Matthaeum.

[2] PL 26, 53. Book I in Mt.

[3] PL 38, 424.

[4] GF 72, 627.

[5] This paragraph is not found in Migne, and is taken from Combefis's translation of the original. Cf. BPC for this Sunday.

FIFTH SUNDAY AFTER
THE EPIPHANY

I. St John Chrysostom: On the Gospel

II. St Augustine: The Tares and the Wheat

III. St Isidore of Pelusium: On Evil Thoughts

THE GOSPEL OF THE SUNDAY

MATTHEW xiii. 24–30

At that time: Jesus proposed to the multitude this parable, saying: The Kingdom of heaven is likened to a man that sowed good seed in his field. But while men were asleep, his enemy came and oversowed cockle among the wheat and went his way.

And when the blade was sprung up, and had brought forth fruit, then appeared also the cockle.´ And the servants of the good man of the house coming said to him: Sir, didst thou not sow good seed in thy field? Whence then hath it cockle? And he said to them: an enemy hath done this. And the servants said to him: wilt thou that we go and gather it up? And he said: No, lest perhaps gathering up the cockle, you root up the wheat also together with it. Suffer both to grow until the harvest, and in the time of the harvest I will say to the reapers: gather up first the cockle, and bind it into bundles to burn, but the wheat gather ye into my barn.

EXPOSITION FROM THE CATENA AUREA

MATTHEW xiii. 24–30

24. *Another parable he proposed to them, saying: the kingdom of heaven ...*

CHRYSOSTOM, *Hom. 47 in Matt.*: In the preceding parable the Lord speaks of those who do not receive the word of God; here He speaks of those who receive corrupted teaching; for it is characteristic of the cunning of the devil always to intermingle his falsehoods with the truth. Hence: And *another parable He proposed to them*, etc.

JEROME: He puts forward another parable, as a rich man feasting his guests with many dishes, so that each according to his taste may partake of the varied foods of his table. He did not say *the other* parable, but *another*. For if He had said *the other*, we could not have expected a third. He said *another* since several follow. Which parable it is He shows when He adds: The kingdom of heaven is likened to a man. REMIGIUS: He calls the Son of God

328

the kingdom of heaven; since the kingdom is said to be like to a man who sowed good seed in his field.

25. *But while men were asleep, his enemy came, etc.*

CHRYSOSTOM: Then He makes known to them the method of the devil's guile: *while men were asleep, his enemy came and oversowed cockle among the wheat and went their way.* He here shows us that error appears *after* truth, as events proved. For after the Prophets there were pseudo-prophets; and after the Apostles pseudo-Apostles; and after Christ anti-Christ. For unless the devil has seen what to imitate, or against whom to plot, he does not try to tempt. Because however he sees that one has brought forth fruit a hundredfold, that other sixty-fold, and another thirty-fold, and that as he cannot carry off or choke the seed that has taken root, he plots against it by means of another deception, commingling his own evil seed with the good seed, tinting it with a number of resemblances, so that he easily deceives those who are susceptible to deception. For this reason the Lord says that he sowed not any other seed except tares which in some ways outwardly resemble wheat. The malice of the devil also reveals itself in this, that he sowed his seed when the whole work of the sowing was completed, so as the more thoroughly to undo the work of the husbandman.

AUGUSTINE, *Liber Unus Quaest.* XVII *in Matt.* 11: He says: *While men sleep*; for when the pastors of the Church are negligent, or when the Apostles succumbed to the sleep of death, the devil came and oversowed those whom the Lord later interprets as signifying *the children of the wicked one.* But it may be asked if these are the heretics, or those Catholics who live wickedly? But since He says they were sown among the wheat they appear to be here meant who are all of one communion. Yet since the Lord Himself interpreted the field as meaning, not the Church, but the world, they are more correctly interpreted as signifying the heretics who in this world are mingled with the good, so that the wicked who also dwell in the bosom of the Church are rather more like straw than tares; because the straw has the same root and stalk as wheat.

Schismatics however seem more like the spoiled wheat, withered, or split in the ear and discarded from the yield. But it does not follow that every heretic or schismatic is corporally separated from the Church: since the Church contains many of them, for as they do not so defend the falseness of their teaching as to make the people watchful; for if they did they would be cast forth. When therefore the devil has scattered about his wicked errors and false teaching he has in this way oversown tares, that is, he has oversown heresy upon the implanted name of Christ; and the more he conceals his own hand the more secretly has he done this. For this is what He means by, *and went his way*, although in this parable, as He implies in his later explanation, the Lord is understood to have meant that by tares are signified, not some, but *all scandals* (verse 41), and all who work iniquity.[1]

26. *And when the blade was sprung up, and had, etc.*

CHRYSOSTOM, as above: In what follows He accurately describes the character of heretics: *And when the blade was sprung up, and had brought forth fruit, then appeared also the cockle.* At first heretics conceal themselves. When however they have acquired a certain security, should anyone enter into conversation with them, they then begin to pour out their poison. AUGUSTINE, as above: Or again: when a man begins to be spiritual, looking carefully into all things, then errors begin to reveal themselves to him. For he recognises in what he hears or reads, that which is opposed to the rule of faith; and until he has become strengthened in these same spiritual things error will have power over him. It is for this reason that so many of the falsities of the heretics come out from under the Christian name. Hence follows:

27. *And the servants of the good man of the house coming said to him: Sir, didst thou not sow good seed in thy field? whence then hath it cockle?*

Whether these servants are the same as those whom He afterwards calls reapers, or whether, because in the exposition of the parable He says that *the reapers are angels*, let no one venture to say that the angels did not know who it was that had oversown the tares. And we ought rather understand here that by the name of *servants* is signified believing men. Nor is it to be wondered at if they are also called *good seed*, for many figures of speech may be used of the same thing: just as He speaks of Himself as a Door, and also as a Shepherd.

28. *And he said to them: An enemy hath done this.*

REMIGIUS: *Coming said to him.* Not in the body, but in their hearts, in the desires of their mind do they come to God: and by His teaching they perceive that this has been done by the evil craft of the devil: an enemy hath done this. JEROME: An evilly disposed person is called a devil, because God has abandoned him. And in the twentieth verse of the ninth psalm we read: *Arise, O Lord, let not man be strengthened.* For which reason let he that is a bishop of the Church not sleep, lest through his neglect some man who is an enemy oversow tares, that is, the doctrines of the heretics.

CHRYSOSTOM: He is called an enemy because of the injuries he inflicts on men: for the ill will of the devil is directed against us. The beginnings of that will however arise not from his enmity towards us, but from his enmity against God.

AUGUSTINE, as above, XII: When the servants of God learn that the devil has contrived this fraud, that he might cloak his errors by this Name (of Christ) since he knew he could himself do nothing against the authority of so great a name, they may feel the impulse to remove such men from human affairs, if the opportunity presents itself; but whether they should do so let them take counsel of the divine justice, as to whether He commands this, or permits it, or if it be the duty of men? Hence the servants say: *Wilt thou that we go and gather it up?*

29. *And he said: No, lest perhaps gathering up the cockle . . .*

CHRYSOSTOM: Here we must note the zeal and affection of the servants, for they are eager to root out the tares, showing their anxiety for the good seed. They are concerned only with this, not that someone be punished, but that the seed which was sown may not perish. Then follows the answer of the Lord: *and He said: No.* JEROME: For time is allowed for repentance; and here we are warned lest, before due time, we cut off a brother. For it may happen that he who today is infected by some poisonous teaching, may tomorrow come to his right mind, and begin to defend the truth. Hence is added: *lest perhaps gathering up the cockle, you root up the wheat also together with it.*

AUGUSTINE: as above, XII: In this way he restored them to complete tranquillity and patience. For here it is made clear that even the good, since they too are still weak, have need in some things of mixing with sinners, either that through them they may be tested, or that by the contrast of their own way of life they may be a help to them, and attract them to the better things. Or lest perhaps the wheat be uprooted, while they try to remove the tares. Because many in the beginning are tares, and afterwards they become wheat, who, unless patiently endured while they are sinners, do not arrive at this meritorious transformation. And so, if they had been uprooted, then at the same time the wheat would have been uprooted which they would have become had they been spared.

30. *Suffer both to grow until the harvest, etc.*

Accordingly He says that such are not to be removed from this life, lest in attempting to destroy those who are wicked, the good they might have become are also killed; or lest the good suffer loss, to whom the others, though unwillingly, are profitable. This will be done in due time, when, at the end, there is left neither time to change their manner of life, nor time to learn the truth, either by some favourable opportunity, or by comparing it with false teaching. And so He said: *suffer both to grow until the harvest*, that is, until the time of judgement.

JEROME: But this seems to be contrary to the precept: *Put away the evil one from among yourselves* (I Cor. v. 13). For if we are forbidden to uproot, and if we are to wait in patience until the harvest time, how then are we to cast out certain persons from amongst us? But, between the true wheat and the tares (which we call *lolium*), while the latter is still green, and the stalk not yet come into ear, there is a great similarity, and little or no difference between them so as to tell one from the other. The Lord therefore warns us that in the beginning we are not to be too ready to deliver judgement, where anything is uncertain; but that we leave judgement to God, so that when the day of the Judge shall come, He shall exclude the wicked from the company of the blessed, not on the mere suspicion of having committed an offence, but because of manifest guilt.

AUGUSTINE, *Contra Ep. Parmen.*, 3, 2; *pars.* 13–16: In this I state something that is neither new or singular, but which the sound sense of the Church observes, namely: that when one of the Christians in full standing in the Church is taken in a fault of such a kind that he is deemed worthy of anathema, let this be done, providing there is no danger of schism, with love, so as not to uproot but to correct. But should he not come to acknowledge his fault, or amend it by repentance, then let him go forth, and let him, of his own will, be cut off from the communion of the Church. Hence was it the Lord said: *suffer both to grow until the harvest*, he added the reason of this: *lest perhaps gathering up the cockle, you root up the wheat also together with it*, wherein He makes it sufficiently plain that, where this fear is absent, and where there is no anxiety as to the safety of the wheat, that is, when the crime of someone is so well known, and appears to everyone so execrable that he is entirely without defenders, or at least without such defenders as might cause a schism, then let the severity of the discipline not sleep; in which the more charity is observed the more efficacious will be the correction of error.

When however the same disease has attacked very many, then nothing of good remains, only grief and pain. So therefore let man correct as mercifully as he can. What he may not correct, let him endure with patience, and in Christian love let him grieve and deplore, until He on high emends and corrects; and let him leave until the harvest time the uprooting of the tares, and the sifting of the chaff. Who ponders these things will not, in preserving unity, neglect the strictness of discipline; nor sever the bond of union, by excess of coercion.

When however an occasion offers of preaching to all the people, then let the disorder of the evil-doers be smitten hard by a general reproof. And this particularly when some visitation from the Lord on high provides the occasion; when it may seem that He is scourging them in chastisement. For then the misfortunes of those who are listening, will render their ears humble to the words of Him who corrects them, and thus more readily move their grieving hearts to tears of repentance, than to murmurs of opposition. And should there be no such calamity, then whenever the occasion arises, let the multitude be profitably reproved, as a multitude; for where as single individuals they are apt to rage against correction, gathered together they will receive them contritely.[2]

CHRYSOSTOM: The Lord said this, forbidding that anyone be killed. For a heretic must not be put to death; for this would lead to interminable war throughout the world; and accordingly he says: *lest perhaps gathering up the cockle, you root up also the wheat together with it*; that is, if you take up arms and kill heretics, then many of the saints will also perish. He does not therefore forbid us to restrain heretics, or to prevent their free discussion and propagation of error, or to close their schools and places of assembly. But He forbids that they be killed, or caused to perish.

AUGUSTINE, *Ep. ad Vincent*, 48: Formerly I was of opinion, that no one must be forced into the unity of Christ; that we must rather strive by word, wage war by disputation, overcome by reason, so that we may not have among us, as pretended Catholics, those whom we had known as open heretics. But this opinion of mine has been overcome, not by the arguments of those opposing it, but by proofs from those who favoured it. For the terror of these laws (Imperial Laws and punishments against heretics), in promulgating which *Kings shall serve God in fear* (Ps. ci. 16), was so profitable, that now some say: for a long time we wished to do this: now let thanks be given to God who has given us the opportunity, and made an end of trifling with delays. Others say: we knew this to be the true church, but we were held back by I know not what ties, but thanks be to God Who has broken our bonds. Others say: we did not know that this was the truth, neither did we desire to learn, but fear has made us eager to learn. Thanks be to God Who has shaken us out of our negligence by the stimulus of dread. Yet others say: we were fearful of entering because of lying rumours, which we would never know were false had we not entered; and we would not have entered had we not been compelled. Thanks be to God Who removed our trepidation with the scourge, and taught us, whom He now has approved, how vain and empty were the things that lying rumour had spread concerning the Church. Still others say: we thought it mattered nothing where we practised our faith in Christ. But thanks be to God Who has brought us together out of division, and shown us that it is truly fitting that the One God be in unity adored. Let then the kings of the earth serve Christ, by proclaiming laws in favour of Christ.[3]

AUGUSTINE, *Ep.* 185, *to Count Bonifat*: Who amongst you would

wish that anyone from among the heretics should perish, or even suffer any loss? But if in no other way could the House of David be in peace, unless that in the very war he had stirred up against his father, Absolom his son be destroyed, though with anxious care he had bidden his men that as far as they could they should preserve him alive and untouched, so that paternal love might pardon him in repentance. But what was left to him save to grieve for the lost one, and to take comfort in his grief in the peace now restored to his kingdom? So likewise does the Catholic Mother the Church, if by the loss of some she gathers in many others, soothe the pain of her maternal heart, and heal it with the salvation of so many peoples.

Where in the Scriptures do we find what they are so ready to cry out: "is not man free to believe, or not to believe? Against whom has Christ used violence? Whom has He compelled?" Behold have they not Paul the Apostle? Let them see there Christ first compelling, then later teaching; first smiting him, afterwards comforting him. Is it not a wondrous thing that he who through chastisement of the body was compelled to accept the Gospel, *has laboured more abundantly than all they* (I Cor. xv. 10) that were called by word alone? Why therefore should not the church compel her lost children to return, if these same wayward children use violence against others so that they are lost?[4]

Then follows: *and in the time of the harvest I will say unto the reapers: gather up first the cockle, and bind it into bundles to burn, but the wheat gather ye into my barn.* REMIGIUS:

The harvest means the time of the reaping; by the harvest here is meant the day of judgement, in which the good shall be separated from the bad. CHRYSOSTOM: But for what reason does He say *gather up first the cockle?* That the good may not be fearful, as though the wheat was to be carried off with the tares. JEROME: Because He said the *bundles* of cockle are to be burned, and the wheat to be gathered into the barn, it is manifest that heretics and hypocrites of every sort shall be burned in the fires of hell; but the good, they who are called the wheat, shall be gathered into barns, that is, into the heavenly mansions.

AUGUSTINE, *Liber Quaest. XVII in Matt.* XII, 3: It may be asked why He did not bid them to make one bundle, or one heap of the tares? It may be because of the variety of the heresies, which differ not alone from the wheat but also from one another, that he gave to the assemblies of each single heresy, by which they are set apart within their own communion, the name of bundles; so that even then they began to be prepared for the fire, when, separated from Catholic communion, they began to have their own as it were particular churches; as though their burning is to be at the end of the world, but not their binding into bundles.

But if this were so then not so many by returning to their senses, and coming back to the Catholic Church, would depart from error. Accordingly the binding into bundles will take place in the future, so that obstinacy in error may be punished, not in a confused way, but in the exact measure of each single man's perversity in his error.[5]

RABANUS MAURUS: And note that where He says *a man sowed good seed,* He is pointing out the good will which is in the elect. Where He says *his enemy came,* He wishes to teach us that we are to be on our guard. When however, as the tares were growing up, He says, as if bearing the misfortune in patience, *an enemy hath done this,* He is commending to us an example of patience. Where He says, *lest perhaps you root up the wheat also,* He gives us an example of discretion. When He goes on to say, *suffer both to grow until the harvest,* He is commending longanimity. Lastly, He speaks of strict justice when He said, *gather it into bundles to burn.*

I. ST JOHN CHRYSOSTOM, BISHOP AND DOCTOR

On the Gospel[6]

Synopsis:
   I. The difference between the two parables concerning the good seed.
   II. The artifice of the devil in leading men into error.
   III. Heretics should not be put to death.

1. What is the difference between this and the preceding parable? In the first He speaks of those who hearkened not to Him, turning away, and rejecting the good seed. Here He speaks of heretics. He foretold this also lest later His Disciples might be troubled

regarding this very matter. The parable that precedes this refers to those who did not receive His Word. This speaks of those who receive the corruptors of His Word. For it is the guile of the spirit of evil to commingle his own errors with the sowing of the truth, so that they have the shape and colour of truth, and so deceive the trusting. He then here speaks not of any seed, but only of tares, which resemble wheat.

Then He speaks of the manner of this guile, *while men are asleep.* Here lies no small danger of headlong disaster for the rulers of the Church, to whom has been confided the care of the field; and not only to the rulers, but to the subjects as well. He shows here very clearly that wherever the seed of truth has been sown, error follows after, as events have truly confirmed. For after the Prophets have come the pseudo-prophets; after the apostles the pseudo-apostles; and after Christ anti-Christ. For the devil, except he sees what he can imitate, or against whom he may plot, knows not what to do, and neither does he attempt anything. But since he has learned that of the seed that was sown some brought fruit a hundredfold, some sixty, and some thirty, he tries yet another stratagem. Not being able to carry off what has taken firm root, nor choke it, nor wither it, he conspires against it by oversowing it with his own evil seed.

But what difference, you may ask, is there between those that sleep, and those who are signified by the wayside? There is this. That in the latter case the devil immediately snatched away the seed, not permitting it to take root. But

in this case he has need of greater cunning. And Christ tells us this in order to teach us of the need for unsleeping vigilance. For though, He says, you escape these snares, you are not yet safe and secure; yet others remain. For as in the preceding parable disaster came to some by the wayside, to others because of stony ground, to others through being smothered by thorns, so here it came because of sleep. There is need therefore for continual watchfulness. Because of this He has said: *he that shall persevere unto the end, he shall be saved* (Mt. x. 22).

Something of this evil happened in the beginning of the Church. For many among the bishops, not being vigilant, received into the Church men who were evil and unworthy, secretly heretics, and gave them authority and opportunity to lay snares of this kind. The devil has no further need to labour after he has planted in our midst such men as these. But, you may ask, how is it possible that we are never to sleep? As to natural sleep, it is indeed impossible; but it is otherwise with the sleep of the will. So Paul has said: *watch ye, stand fast* (I Cor. xvi. 13).

He shows that this artifice of the devil is not alone injurious, but wanton. For when the tilling of the field is completed, and no more toil remains, then last of all he sows his seed, which also the heretics do, who for no other cause than vain glory scatter abroad their poison. That this the manner of their acting appears not alone from His words, but also from what follows. *And when the blade was sprung up,* He says, *and had brought forth fruit, then appeared also the cockle.* This undoubtedly is the method of the heretics; at first concealing their true selves, then, having acquired boldness, and after being entrusted with the teaching of the word, they boldly pour out their poison.

But why does He here bring in the servants, hastening to tell what has happened? That He may thus have an opportunity of declaring that such heretics are not to be killed. He calls the devil an enemy because of the injuries he ever strives to inflict on all men. Though the ill will of the devil is directed against us, in its beginning it was not directed against us, but against the divine majesty. Hence it is apparent that we are loved more by God than we are loved by ourselves. See likewise the craft of the devil. For he did not sow his seed before, when there was nothing he could destroy, but only when he saw that the work of the sowing was completed, so as the more thoroughly to undo the work of the Husbandman. And with such malevolence of mind has he ever worked against Him.

Note in the parable also the zeal and affection of the servants. They are eager to root out the tares, though in this they are not wise, yet their concern for the good seed is very manifest, and they have thought only for this, not that someone be punished, but that the seed that was sown be not lost. And so they hasten to find out how the evil may be undone. Neither do they themselves decide what to do, but they look to the word of the Lord, asking: *Wilt Thou that we go and gather it up?* But the Lord forbids them, *lest you root up the wheat also*; which He also said in order to forbid wars and slaughters. For if men were to be killed for

heresy it would lead to interminable war throughout the world.

2. *How we are to act regarding heretics—The Forbearance of Christ.*

The Lord forbade this for two reasons. First, lest the wheat be injured; second, because whoever has a disease that is not cured, will not escape punishment. Therefore if you desire to see them punished without injury to the wheat, then you must wait for the due time. What else does He mean when He says *lest you root up the wheat also together with it*, unless that if you take up arms, and kill heretics, it must also follow that many of the sanctified will fall with them. And even of many from among the tares it is likely that they will be converted into wheat. If therefore you now uproot them, you will also destroy the wheat they would become, should they be converted. He did not however forbid us to reprove heretics, to silence their mouths, to restrict their liberty of speech, to scatter their assemblies; but He forbade that they should be killed.

But observe His gentleness and forbearance. He not alone forbids, but He also gives His reasons. What if the tares continue till the end? Then He says *I will say to the reapers, gather up first the cockle, and bind it into bundles to burn.* He recalls to their minds the words of John speaking of Him as the Judge (Mt. iii. 10), and says: we must spare the tares as long as they stand close to the wheat in the field, for it is possible that they too may become wheat. But when they have been cut down, and have not profited from the forbearance of the Lord, then must they receive their inevitable chastisement. For *I will say to the reapers*, He says, *gather up first the cockle*. Why first? Lest the good be anxious, fearing that the wheat will be carried off with the cockle. Let the cockle first be burned, He says, and then let the wheat be gathered into my barn. Amen.

II. St Augustine, Bishop and Doctor

The Tares and the Wheat[7]

1. Both yesterday and today we have listened to the words of Our Lord Jesus Christ, recounting the parables of the Sower. You who listened yesterday, will today recall them to mind. Yesterday we read of the Sower who while he scattered the seed some fell by the wayside, and the birds seized it; and some fell upon stony ground, and it withered in the heat; and some fell among thorns, and was choked, and did not reach to bearing fruit. And some fell on good ground and bore fruit: some a hundredfold, some sixtyfold, and some thirtyfold.

Today the Lord relates another parable, again relating to the Sower, who sowed good seed in his field. While men slept an enemy came and oversowed it with tares. While the tares were yet green they were not detected, but when the fruit of the good seed began to appear, then the tares revealed themselves. The master's servants were angry, seeing the weed standing thick amid the true grain, and they desired to uproot it at once, but were not permitted. But it was said to them, *suffer both to grow until the harvest*. The Lord Christ also explained this parable, saying, that He was the Sower of the Good Seed, that the devil was the enemy, the sower of tares, the harvest was the end of time and His field the world.

But hear what He says: *In the time of the harvest I will say to the reapers: gather up first the cockle, and bind it into bundles to burn, but the wheat gather ye into my barn*. Why hasten then, zealous servants, He says? See you not that the tares stand in the midst of the good growth, and you wish to uproot the bad? Remain quiet, it is not yet the time of harvest. Let it come, and let it reveal to you the true wheat. Why need you be angry? Why are you impatient that the bad should now be mixed with the good? They may be among you in the field, but in My barn they shall not be with you.

2. Recall the three places that were spoken of yesterday, where the seed grew not, the wayside, the stony ground, the thorny ground. The tares are the same as these. In another similitude they receive but another name. Because when one speaks in parables it is not an attempt to describe the properties of a thing, or some truth, but to convey a likeness of a truth. What I am here saying I know that few have understood, but we must speak for the good of all. In the visible things a wayside is a wayside, stony places are stony places, thorny places are thorny places. What they are, they are; because they are spoken of according to their literal meaning. But in parables and figures one thing can be called by many names. And so it is not out of place for me to say to you that the wayside, the stony places, the thorny places, are

weak Christians; and that they are likewise tares. For is not Christ a Lamb? And is He not also a Lion? Among wild animals and domestic that which is a lamb is a lamb, and a lion is a lion. Christ is both. They are what they are by nature. He is both in figure.

It happens also in a similitude that things widely dissimilar are called by the same name. What is so widely dissimilar as Christ and the devil? Yet Christ is called a lion, and so also is the devil. Of Christ the Lion it is written: *Behold the Lion of the tribe of Juda* (Apoc. v. 5); and of the devil: *your adversary the devil, as a roaring lion, goeth about seeking whom he may devour* (I Pet. v. 8). Therefore the One is a Lion, and the other is a lion. The One is a Lion in strength, the other a lion in ferocity. The devil likewise is a serpent, *that old serpent* (Apoc. xii. 9). Are we bidden to imitate the devil when Our Shepherd said to us, *Be ye therefore wise as serpents and simple as doves* (Mt. xii. 16)?

3. And yesterday I spoke of the wayside, I spoke of the stony ground, and of the thorny ground, and I said, be ye changed while ye may: break up the hard ground with the plough, cast the stones from the field: root out the thorns. Keep not your hearts hardened within you, where the word of God quickly perishes. Be not shallow soil, where charity takes no deep root. Smother not the good seed, sown among you with our labour, with the cares and the greed of this world. For it is the Lord who sows, we are but His labourers. But be ye good ground. We said yesterday, and we say it again today, to you all: let one man bring forth fruit a hundredfold, another sixty-fold, another thirty. In one man there is greater fruit, in another there is less: but all shall enter into My barn.

Yesterday I spoke to you in these words. Today I speak to the tares; but the sheep of the flock are themselves the tares. O unworthy Christians! You that fill the Church and at the same time torment it by the wickedness of your lives. Correct your ways before the time of the harvest! Be not like those who said: *I have sinned, and what harm hath befallen me?* (Ecclus. v. 4). God has not lost His power but He requires of you repentance. This I say to the wicked, who are likewise Christians; this I say to the tares. For they are yet standing in the field: and it may be that they who today are tares may tomorrow become good wheat. And now I address myself to the wheat.

O you Christians whose lives are worthy. You weep, few amid the multitude: you mourn, few among the many. But the winter will pass, and the summer will come, and lo! it will be harvest time. The Angels will come, who can divide the one from the other, and they will not err. We at this time are like to the servants, of whom it is written: *Wilt thou that we go and gather it up?* For we are anxious that, if it were possible, nothing that was evil should remain among the good. But it was said to us: *Suffer both to grow until the harvest.* Why so? Because such as you are liable to error. Listen: *Lest perhaps gathering up the cockle, you root up the wheat also with it.* What good can you do? Will you not rather destroy my crop with your rashness? The reapers will be coming: and He explains who the reapers are: *The reapers are angels.* We are but men, but the reapers are Angels. We too, if we finish our course, shall be like unto the angels: but now, though we are angry with the wicked, we are ourselves still men. And we should remember this: *He that thinketh himself to stand, let him take heed lest he fall* (I Cor. x. 12).

And do you think, my Brethren, that the tares do not reach to these high seats?[8] Do you think they are all down among you, and none here above? That we may not be such! *But to me it is a small thing to be judged by you* (I Cor. iv. 3). But I tell Your Charity, that in these high seats there are good wheat, and there are tares; as among the people there are good wheat, and there are tares. Let the good be patient with the wicked; let those who do evil change their ways, and become as the good. Let us all, if possible, come unto God. May we all through His mercy escape the wickedness of this world. Let us *seek good days,* for we are in the midst of days that are evil: but in these wicked days let us not blaspheme, that we may reach unto the good days.

Turning then with contrite hearts to the Lord our God, the Father Almighty, let us as best we can give thanks with all our hearts beseeching Him that in His goodness He will graciously hearken to our prayers, and by His power drive evil from our thoughts and actions, increase our faith, guide our minds, grant unto us His holy inspirations, and bring us to joy that is without end, through His Son Our Lord and Saviour Jesus Christ. Amen.

III. St Isidore of Pelusium: On Evil Thoughts[9]

Whence is it that evil thoughts come forth from the heart, and defile a man? (Mt. xv. 19). Doubtless, because the labourers are asleep who should be keeping watch, so as to safeguard and preserve the fruits of the good seed that is growing up. For unless we have weakened in our vigilance, by gluttony and by sloth, defiling the divine image, that is, corrupting the good seed, the sower of tares would not have found a way to creep up on us, nor would he have sown within us tares worthy of the fire; that is, *evil thoughts which come forth from and which defile a man.*

Wilt thou that we go and gather it up? Thus speak the angels, ever prepared with eager devotion to serve the divine will, as they see our inactivity and sloth, and the infinite forbearance of God. But they are forbidden, lest they uproot the good wheat together with the tares, that is, so that the sinner may not be cut off while in his mind there is yet a possibility of repentance; lest innocent children be destroyed together with their parents, who though perhaps yet in their parents' loins, nevertheless with God, Who sees all things, they already are.

For the ranks of the Angels, fellow servants of creation, know not the things that as yet exist not. But God both knows and has wrought because of these very circumstances. For He did not cut off the evil-doing Esau, who had not yet begotten; lest together with him Job might also perish, who from him took descent. Nor did he slay Matthew, who had given himself to the exacting of the tribute, so that He might not thus impede the preaching of the gospel. Neither did He destroy the harlots who served lust and immodesty, lest models of repentance might be wanting. He avenged not Peter's denial, because already He beheld his burning tears of repentance. Nor did he strike down with death the persecuting Saul, lest the ends of the earth be deprived of salvation.

All tares therefore that await the time of the harvest, and do not change themselves into fruits of repentance, are being got ready for the great fire, since they have flowered wholly unto fruitlessness. But they whose roots are deep, whose ears of corn are abundant, who are bending over at harvest time with the weight of fruit and all but calling for the sickle of the harvesters, these Christ orders to be carried by the angels to the heavenly seats, to share their joy, to reign with Him, and be sharers of His immortal happiness, Who with the Father and the Holy Ghost liveth and reigneth world without end. Amen.

NOTES

[1] PL 35, 1365–1378, II. This work is now considered inauthentic: cf. Portalie DTC Art. Augustine. PRM 35.

[2] Cf. PL 43, cols. 92–95.

[3] Cf. PL 43, 329.

[4] Cf. PL 33, Ep. 185, to Count Boniface, now not regarded as authentic. *De rebus gestis Boniface* (1941); *Clavis* 367.

[5] PL 35, 1370; *inauthentic*, cf. footnote 1.

[6] PG 58, 475.

[7] PL 38, Sermo 73.

[8] He is here referring to the *apsidas*, the raised semi-circular part of the chancel, where the Bishop sat in the midst of his Presbyters.

[9] PG 77, 184–185.

SIXTH SUNDAY AFTER
THE EPIPHANY

I. St Aphraates: Against Envy and Discord

II. St Ambrose: The Grain of Mustard Seed

III. St John Chrysostom: The Leaven of Holiness

IV. St Maximus of Turin: Christ our Leaven

THE GOSPEL OF THE SUNDAY

Matthew xiii. 31–35

At that time: Jesus proposed to the multitude another parable, saying: The kingdom of heaven is like to a grain of mustard seed, which a man took and sowed in his field. Which is the least indeed of all seeds; but when it is grown up, it is greater than all herbs, and becometh a tree, so that the birds of the air come, and dwell in the branches thereof.

Another parable He spoke to them: The kingdom of heaven is like to a leaven, which a woman took and hid in three measures of meal, until the whole was leavened.

All these things Jesus spoke in parables to the multitudes: and without parables He did not speak to them. That it might be fulfilled which was spoken by the prophet, saying: I will open my mouth in parables, I will utter things hidden from the foundation of the world.

PARALLEL GOSPEL

Mark iv. 26–34

And he said: So is the kingdom of God, as if a man should cast seed into the earth. And should sleep, and rise, night and day, and the seed should spring, and grow up whilst he knoweth not. For the earth of itself bringeth forth fruit, then the blade, then the ear, afterwards the full corn in the ear. And when the fruit is brought forth, immediately he putteth in the sickle, because the harvest is come.

And he said: To what shall we liken the kingdom of God? Or to what parable shall we compare it?

It is as a grain of mustard seed: which when it is sown in the earth, is less than all the seeds that are in the earth. And when it is sown, it groweth up, and becometh greater than all herbs, and shooteth out great branches, so that the birds of the air may dwell under the shadow thereof.

And with many such parables, he spoke to them the word, according as they were able to hear. And without parable he did not speak unto them; but apart, he explained all things to his disciples.

EXPOSITION FROM THE CATENA AUREA

MATTHEW xiii. 31–35

31. *Another parable he proposed unto them, saying: The kingdom of heaven . . .*

CHRYSOSTOM, *Hom. 47 in Matth.*: Because the Lord had said that three parts of the seed would be lost, and another saved, and of that saved some again would be lost, because of the tares that were sown among it, lest anyone might then say: Who then, and how many, are the believers, He takes away this anxiety by the parable of the grain of mustard seed. Accordingly, it is written: *Another parable he proposed unto them, saying: The kingdom of heaven is like to a grain of mustard seed, which a man took and sowed in his field.*

JEROME: The kingdom of heaven is the preaching of the Gospel, and the knowledge of the Scriptures, which leads to the true life: concerning which He said to the Jews: *The kingdom of heaven shall be taken from you and shall be given to a nation yielding the fruits thereof* (Mt. xxi. 43).

AUGUSTINE, *Liber Primus Quaest., Evang. XI*: For the grain of mustard seed relates to the fervour of faith, in this, that it is said to drive out poison.

There follows: *Which a man took and sowed in his field.* JEROME: The man who sowed seed in his field is by many interpreted as the Saviour, Who sows in the souls of the believing; by others he is believed to represent man himself, sowing in his own field, that is, within his own heart. Who indeed is it that sows save our own mind and soul, which receiving the grain of the word of God, nourishes the seed sown with the moisture of faith, and causes it to grow in the field of his heart? The Gospel goes on:

32. *Which is the least indeed of all seeds.*

The preaching of the Gospel is the least indeed of the sciences. For as to its primary teaching, it has not even the credibility of ordinary truth: proclaiming that God became man, that God died, the scandal of the Cross. Compare doctrines of this kind with the discussions of the philosophers, with their books, the splendour of their eloquence, the elaboration of their discourses, and you will see how small is the seed of the Gospel, compared to other seeds.

CHRYSOSTOM: Or the seed of the Gospel is the least of all, because its Disciples were more backward than all others; yet because there was a great power in them, their preaching has spread across the whole world; accordingly there follows: *But when it is grown up it is greater than all herbs,* that is, than all dogmas. AUGUSTINE, *as above XI*: Dogmas are the teaching of the sects, that is, that which is the opinion of the sects.

JEROME: When the teaching of the philosophers grows up, it reveals nothing virile, nothing vital: everything is flaccid, soft, abounding in leaves and stalks that quickly wither and vanish. But the Gospel preaching, which seemed so inconspicuous in the beginning, when it is sown within the soul of a believer, or spread throughout the world, does not come up as a shrub, but as a tree: so that the birds of the air come and dwell in its branches, that is the souls of believers, or the powers dedicated to God's service. *And becometh a tree.* I believe that the branches of the Evangelical tree, sprung from the grain of mustard seed, are the varieties of sacred instruction in which each of the birds we have spoken of find rest. Let us also, taking wings like a dove, fly upwards, that we may dwell in the branches of this tree, and make ourselves nests in its doctrines; leaving behind earthly things, and hastening to those that are heavenly.

HILARY: The Lord compares Himself to a grain of mustard seed, a bitter seed, and the least of all seeds: whose virtue is revealed by crushing it. GREGORY, *Moralium*, 19, 1: He indeed is the grain of mustard seed, which in the garden of the sepulchre grew into a great tree. He was but a seed when He died, a tree when He rose again. A seed in the lowliness of the flesh, a tree in the power of His majesty.

HILARY: This seed after it was sown in the field, that is, when it was seized by the multitude and betrayed unto death, was as it were buried in a field in a kind of a sowing of His Body, and grew up in a manner exceeding the measure of all growing plants, and exceeding all the glory of the prophets. To the sick Israel, in the place of a

medicinal herb, there was given the preaching of the prophets. Now the birds of the air dwell in the branches of the tree, which are by us interpreted as the Apostles: stretching out their arms in the power of Christ, and by their branches giving shade to the world. To which the peoples of the world, harassed by the turmoil of the winds, that is, by the voice and by the breath of the devil, fly in the hope of life, taking refuge as in the branches of a tree.

GREGORY, *Moral.* 19: In these branches birds take their rest, for devout souls, raising themselves on wings of grace, find repose in their words from earthly anxieties, and consolation from the wearinesses of the present life.

33. *Another parable he spoke to them: The kingdom of heaven is like to a leaven.*

CHRYSOSTOM: To confirm His teaching the Lord then goes on to the parable of the Leaven. Hence it is written: *Another parable he spoke to them: The kingdom of heaven is like to a leaven, which a woman took and hid in three measures of meal:* as if to say: as the leaven imbues a large quantity of dough with its own virtue, so shall you transform the world. And observe the prudence of Christ. He speaks of things having their due place in the order of nature, showing that as it happens undoubtedly with regard to them, so shall it happen with regard to the Apostles. He did not say that the woman simply *put* the leaven in the dough, but that she *hid* it; as if to say: so you also, when you shall be overwhelmed by your oppressors, it is then that you shall overcome them. And as the leaven, buried beneath the dough, and not destroyed, gradually changes all about it into its own nature, so shall it be with your preaching. Fear not because I have said that many tribulations shall come upon you: for in that way shall you shine forth, and conquer all men. Here He speaks of *three* measures, in place of several, using this determinate number to signify an indefinite multitude.

JEROME: A measure (*satum*) is a unit of measure proper to the province of Palestine, and is about three gallons. AUGUSTINE, *Quaest. Ev. Lib.*, I *XII*: Or leaven means love, in that it creates and inflames fervour. The woman means wisdom. By three measures of meal are understood either: these three things in man: with his whole heart, with his whole soul, with all his mind (Mt. xxii. 37): or, the three degrees of fruitfulness, a hundredfold, sixtyfold, and thirtyfold (Mt. xiii. 8, 23): or, these three types of men: Noah, Daniel, Job (Ezech. xiv. 14).

RABANUS: He says however, until the whole was leavened, because the charity that is *hidden* in our mind ought so to increase that it transforms the whole man into its own perfection: and what is begun here will be perfected hereafter. JEROME: Or again, the woman who received the leaven and *hid it* appears to me to represent the preaching of the Apostles, or the Church, assembled from diverse peoples. She takes the leaven, that is, the knowledge and understanding of the Scriptures, and hid it in three measures of meal, so that spirit,

body, and soul, being made one, might be in harmony. Or, again: we read in Plato that there are three passions in the soul: the *rational,* the *irascible,* the *concupiscible*; and we therefore, if we have received the leaven of the evangelical writings, shall possess prudence in our reason, hatred against the vices in our anger, and in the place of concupiscence a longing for the virtues; and all this will be done through the teaching of the Gospel which Mother Church bestows on us. May I recount a third interpretation that some have offered so that the curious reader may choose at will. The woman these interpret as the church, which has mixed together the faith of man in three measures of flour, namely into belief in the Father, Son, and Holy Ghost; when they shall be leavened into one mass, it will lead him, not to a threefold God, but to the knowledge of a single Godhead. A pious interpretation, doubtless, but never can parables, and the doubtful interpretation of mysteries, give support to the authority of dogmas.[1]

HILARY: Or again, The Lord compares Himself to a leaven, for the leaven is from the dough, and returns the power it has received to the mass of its own kind. This leaven being received, the woman, that is, the Synagogue, hid it by the sentence of death. This however being buried in three measures of flour, that is the commingling of the Law, the Prophets, and the Gospels, makes of all three one: so that what the Law laid down, and the Prophets announced, the same is now fulfilled by the progress of the Gospel; although bear in mind that many think that the three measures of flour refers to the vocation of the three peoples sprung from Sem, Cham, and Japhet. But I know not if reason permits us so to believe, for though all peoples are called, in this Christ is not hidden, but revealed to all; and with the vast multitude of the unbelieving, the *whole* is not *leavened*.

34. *All these things Jesus spoke in parables to the multitudes.*

CHRYSOSTOM: After recounting the parables, and so that no one would think that Christ was giving utterance to novelties, the Evangelist here introduces also a prophet, as foretelling this very manner of teaching; and so he says: *these things Jesus spoke in parables . . . that it might be fulfilled which was spoken by the prophet, saying: I will open my mouth in parables.* Mark however says: *with many such parables He spoke to them the word, according as they were able to hear* (Mk. iv. 33). Hence, do not wonder, if in speaking of a kingdom He makes mention of seed and of wheat; for He was speaking to unlettered men, who needed to be instructed in this way.

35. *That it might be fulfilled which was spoken by the prophet . . .*

REMIGIUS: The Greek word *parabola* in Latin is rendered by similitude, by means of which a truth is made evident. For in the similitude He uses certain word-pictures and likenesses of the truth. JEROME: He spoke to the multitude in parables, not however to the Disciples: and even to this day the people are instructed in parables; and so it is said: *And without parables He did not speak to them.* CHRYSOSTOM: For although a few things He did speak to the multitudes without parables,

on this occasion He spoke nothing without them.

AUGUSTINE, *Liber Unus Quaest. XVII in Matt. XV*:[2] And this is not said as meaning that He conveyed nothing to them in its literal sense, but as meaning that He scarcely gave a discourse without explaining some portion of it by a parable, although He taught some things in a literal manner; accordingly, sometimes a whole discourse is unfolded in parables, but nowhere did He unfold a whole discourse in a purely literal way. I mean that His discourses are explained when He speaks, by making use of the natural circumstances at hand in the order of nature until He has made clear whatever pertains to the subject, then passing on to something else.

Sometimes it will happen that one Evangelist joins together in one narrative discourses which another Evangelist records as spoken upon different occasions. But the first sets down the narrative he is composing, not according to the actual order of the events, but according to his recollection of them. The Evangelist makes clear why it was that He would speak in parables when he adds: *That it might be fulfilled which was spoken by the prophets saying: I will open my mouth in parables, I will utter things hidden from the foundation of the world.*

JEROME: This testimony is taken from the seventy-seventh psalm. Where we in the Vulgate edition have put, *spoken by the prophet*, in some codices you will read, *spoken by the prophet Isaias*. REMIGIUS: Whence Porphyrius objected to the faithful: your Evangelist was so foolish that what he found in the psalms he attributed to Isaias. JEROME: And since it is not at all to be found in Isaias, I think that it was afterwards removed by discreet men. But my opinion is, that in the beginning it was written: *Which was written by the prophet Asaph, saying:* for the seventy-seventh psalm, from which this testimony was taken, is inscribed with the name of the prophet Asaph, and the first copyist did not know of Asaph and reckoned that this was a slip of the writer's, and accordingly changed the name to Isaias, a name more known to him. For we must know that not alone David, but others as well, whose names are inscribed upon the psalms and hymns and canticles of God, are to be called Prophets: Asaph, namely, and Ididthun, Eman the Ezrahite and Ethan, the Sons of Core, and others whom the Scriptures commemorate.

And because it is said in the Person of Our Lord: *I will open my mouth in parables, I will utter things hidden from the foundation of the world,* we should carefully reflect on this, and we shall find that here is described the going forth of Israel from Egypt, and that all the signs are narrated which are contained in the history of the Exodus. From which we are to understand that everything there written is to be interpreted parabolically; containing not alone a literal meaning, but likewise mysteries that are hidden. For by this the Saviour promises that He will reveal Himself, saying: *I will open my mouth in parables.*

GLOSS: As though He were saying: I Who before have spoken by the mouth of the Prophets, now, in My own Person, will open My mouth in parables, and I shall bring forth from the treasury of My mystery, I will give utterance to mysteries that have been concealed since the foundation of the world.

I. ST APHRAATES, BISHOP AND MARTYR

Against Discord and Envy[3]

Dearly beloved, it is not enough to read and to study the Sacred Scriptures, we must fulfil them also. For to me it seems that if anyone is involved in contentions and in quarrels, his prayers are not acceptable, his supplications are not answered, his gift rises not upwards from the earth; and neither does the giving of alms avail him for the forgiveness of his sins. And wheresoever there is no peace and tranquillity, the door is left open to the Evil One. Where correction and right order are also absent, then the Christian manner of living, and earnest striving after righteousness

are also absent. Then the wheat is mixed with the tares, thorns flourish, the disorderly multiply, mockery is everywhere, there is neither correction nor amendment of life, nor any right order. The salt then loses its flavour, mens' minds become obscured, and the body walks clothed in darkness. The ordinary things of life are thrown into confusion, and there is peace neither for the one coming, nor for the one going. Such are the fruits of discord.

In times such as these, those who are worthy reveal themselves, those who are truly wise are now seen to be so, the good are shown forth, they who follow after peace, who foster tranquillity among men. Their reward is enduring, and their fruit abundant. These are the men who, *set up a defense and stand in the gap before me, that I may not destroy the land* (Ezech. xxii. 30); who give themselves to toil on behalf of the people, and receive their reward with *the good and faithful servants* of holy memory.

But envy and discord throw even kingdoms into disorder; lay waste great cities, devour peoples; betray mighty fortresses. They provoke endless tragedies, and because of them destruction is multiplied. Through envy and discord brothers are separated from brothers, driven from place to place, made into wanderers, driven forth from their homes. And while these poor wanderers live, they are looked upon as dead by their own kindred.

Envy comes between husbands and wives. It makes children rise in disobedience against their parents. It separates friend from friend, making one who was loved before now an object of hatred to those who are dearest to him. It leads men to violence and disorders, setting them against their own brothers. It puts two against three, and three against two. By it one man slays another with his tongue, and with his mouth drives another mercilessly to ruin. Day by day envy brings sorrow among men.

In those that love strife and discord evil thoughts take deep root; in them the old leaven ferments, and grows yet older. A man of this kind conceives evil in his heart, and brings forth fruit of the most bitter kind. There is no sleep or rest for

such a one; and the friend is so changed that he prepares iniquities against him he loved. Should a good thought overtake him, and find entry in his heart, the Evil One uproots it, and casts it forth from his mind. But he sends his own roots down deep into the heart, and secures himself firmly within the thoughts of the mind. He gathers together a multitude of images, and drives them towards him, and entering in they take possession of the mind.

What the Evil One has begotten, when it is scattered about it is sown over him; but he is a stranger to the wisdom of the wise: the good seed is suffocated in him, and the wheat is choked amid the thorns. From the mind of the envious no good fruit comes forth, and from his heart the Evil One plucks out the good seed and casts it away.

The Evil One now places his own guards at the door of the soul and disturbs the mind with manifold allurements. Gradually like water they seep inwards, and the soul is overcome. The heart becomes like rock underneath, and when the good seed is scattered it is immediately received, but its roots will wither, and bear no fruit.

Such a man, given to envy and discord, will stand and pray as is his daily habit: he will begin his prayer, continue on with it, and bring it to an end. But his heart takes no heed of what his lips are saying, His mouth fulfils its usual office, but his heart is empty of every good work. He keeps far from his soul the teaching of the Spirit, and from his mind has departed the memory of that which he learned but yesterday. Or should his mind recall anything of it, he will grieve over each single fault, but the Evil One will goad him on, and again possess his heart. The memory of evil lingers, and the heart fluctuates as the waters of a deep lake. His nature is dark, his mind clouded, his intellect is blind; he gropes and stumbles. Then the Evil One takes his hand and hurries him along his way, the pathless way of deceit. He takes away from him and casts out whatsoever worthy thoughts are within him, and leads in his own shameful ones, and thus he urges him on his way: Pay no heed to good advice, do not inflict on yourself the humiliation of seeking forgiveness.

But the Evil One while he caresses him is but mocking him, since he himself has acquired a slave that obeys his will. The man devoured by envy does not know that he has been purchased, and almost for nothing, and neither is he aware of the blindness of his own mind. The Evil One astutely flatters him, beguiles him with every trick and allurement. He throws a fish towards him, as one throws it to a bird. The unwary bird, as soon as it sees the piece of fish set upon the edge of the trap, rejoices in its heart, and in its simplicity approaching to seize it is suddenly struck. It struggles to free itself, but it is caught. It is the clever hunter that rejoices, at his own good fortune: because his wait was not without gain.

Such is the lot of a man who loves discord and envy. The Evil One blows him up, and inflates him with his own bitter fruits. As with the bird he allures him, beguiles him, throws him a fish, and he falls into the trap. When by the sweetness of his enticements he has caught him, he gives him counsel such as he has never before heard; he learns of injustice, he is smothered with words, and gathers into his mind the most evil dispositions.

It will happen then that the good things he had learned will vanish from his memory; what thoughts were his own remain deep down in him, like a treasure hidden; but the roots of evil gather strength in his mind, and then it is only by the greatest labour that its claws, like those of a lion fastened on its prey, are drawn forth. But a wise physician will draw forth these claws with many remedies. But yet while evil thoughts still linger in the man, from day to day his heart will bring forth evil fruits, and his tongue foster counsels of discord.

Suave is the enticement of the Evil One, and flattering to the mind, but its end is more bitter than a serpent's venom. But to any man who has the will to oppose him, there is no remedy that will heal him other than to follow after peace, to be reconciled with his brother, to put up with injury from his friend, and, until the fruits of peace shall come, to let all envious thoughts depart. Neither let him keep them in his memory, nor permit them to creep back into the heart. Amen.

II. St Ambrose, Bishop and Doctor

The Grain of Mustard Seed[4]

To what is the kingdom of God like, and whereunto shall I resemble it? It *is like a grain of mustard seed, which a man took and cast into his garden, and it grew and became a great tree, and the birds of the air lodged in the branches thereof.*

This Gospel lesson teaches us that it is the *nature* of the figures which are taken as examples that we must consider, and not their *appearance.* And so let us see for what reason is the sublime kingdom of heaven likened to a grain of mustard seed: for the Lord, you will remember, spoke in another place of the grain of mustard seed as having faith: *For if you have faith as a grain of mustard seed, you shall say to this mountain: Remove from hence hither, and it shall remove* (Mt. xvii. 19). Not small, but truly great, is that faith which can bid a mountain move itself; and so neither did the Lord demand that the Apostles have but a moderate faith; for He knew that they must enter into combat with the might of the spirit of iniquity, now rearing itself up against them. Would you like to learn that great faith is required? Read the Apostle: *If I should have all faith, so that I could remove mountains* (I Cor. xiii. 2).

There if the kingdom of heaven is like to a grain of mustard seed, and faith is like to a grain of mustard seed: faith is then truly the kingdom of heaven, and the kingdom of heaven is faith. He therefore that has faith, possesses the kingdom of heaven. And the kingdom of heaven is within us, and faith is within us; for we read: *For lo, the kingdom of God is within you* (Lk. xvii. 21). And elsewhere: *Have in you the faith of God* (Mk. xi. 22). Then Peter, who had all faith, received the keys of the kingdom of heaven, that he might open it to others.

Now let us, from the nature of the mustard seed, estimate the force of this comparison. Its seed is indeed very plain, and of little value: but if bruised or crushed it shows forth its power. So faith first seems a simple thing: but if it is bruised by its enemies it gives forth proof of its power, so as to fill others who hear or read of it with the odour of its sweetness. Our martyrs, Felix, Nabor, and Victor, possessed the sweet odour of faith; but they dwelt in obscurity. When the persecution came, they laid down their arms, and bowed their necks, and being stricken by the sword they diffused to all the ends of the earth the grace of their martyrdom; so that rightly may it be said that: *Their sound hath gone forth into all the earth* (Ps. xviii. 5).

At one time the faith is bruised, at another time oppressed, at other times it is sown. The Lord Himself is the grain of mustard seed. He was without injury; but the people were unaware of Him as a grain of mustard seed of which they took no notice. He chose to be bruised, that we might say: *For we are the good odour of Christ unto God* (II Cor. ii. 15). He chose to be crushed; whence also Peter said: *The multitudes throng and press thee* (Lk. viii. 45). He chose to be planted in the earth as *a seed which a man took and cast into his garden.* For it was in a garden that Christ was taken prisoner, and likewise buried: He sprung up in a garden, where He also rose from the dead, and became a tree; as it is written: *As the apple tree among the trees of the woods, so is my beloved among the sons* (Cant. ii. 3).

You also then sow Christ in your garden—for a garden is a place that is full of flowers and various fruits

—in which by virtue of your labour He may grow and breathe forth the multiple sweetness of His many virtues. There where fruit is, let Christ be found. Plant ye the Lord Jesus. He is a seed when *a man takes hold of Him*: He is a tree when He rises again, a tree that gives shade to the world; He is a seed when He is buried in the earth: He is a tree when raised to heaven.

Press close to Christ, and sow faith. We follow close and sow faith when we adore Christ crucified. Paul followed close in faith when he said: *And I, brethren, when I came to you, came not in loftiness of speech or of wisdom, declaring unto you the testimony of Christ. For I judged myself not to know anything among you, but Jesus Christ, and him crucified* (I Cor. ii. 1, 2). And because he taught us to follow in faith, he also taught us to raise it upwards, saying: *For now we no longer know Christ Crucified* (II Cor. v. 16).

We sow the faith when from the prophetical and apostolical writings and from the Gospel we believe in the passion of the Lord. We therefore sow the faith when we as it were bury it in the soft and tender soil of the Lord's flesh, so that from the embrace and warmth of the sacred Body, faith spreads itself abroad. For he that has believed that the Son of God became man, believes that He died for us, believes that He rose again. I therefore sow the faith when I plant it in His sepulchre.

Would you know Christ the seed, Christ the sown? *Unless the grain of wheat falling into the ground die, itself remaineth alone. But if it die, it bringeth forth much fruit* (Jn. xii. 24). Therefore we err not when we say that which He had already

said. He is also the grain of wheat, because *He strengthens the heart of man* (Ps. ciii. 15), and He is the grain of mustard seed, because He sets fire to the heart of man. And though either figure may be applied to all things, yet He appears as the grain of wheat when we speak of His resurrection: *For he is the bread of God, which cometh down from heaven* (Jn. vi. 33), in this, that the word of God, and the proof of His resurrection, nourish our minds, whet our hope, and confirm our love. He is the grain of mustard seed, in that the narrative of the Lord's passion is most bitter and most grievous: most bitter unto tears, most grievous unto compunction. And so when we hear and when we read that the Lord fasted, the Lord thirsted, the Lord wept, the Lord cried out, and hear Him saying close to the hour of His passion: *Watch ye, and pray that ye enter not into temptation* (Mt. xxvi. 41), reproached by the bitter taste of this chronicle we justly moderate the more agreeable delights of our body's pleasures. He therefore who sows the grain of mustard seed sows the kingdom of heaven.

Do not despise this grain of mustard seed: *It is the least indeed of all seeds; but when it is grown up, it is greater than all herbs, and becometh a tree.* If Christ be the grain of mustard seed, in what manner is He *the least of all seeds*, and how does He grow up? Not indeed in His nature does He grow, but in outward appearance. Would you know Him as *the least of all? We have seen him and there was no beauty in him, nor comeliness* (Is. liii. 2). And behold Him, *greater than all: Thou art beautiful above the sons of men* (Ps. xliv. 3). For He that had neither beauty nor comeliness is become more beautiful than the angels, above the glory of the prophets: they whom weak Israel consumed as though they were pot herbs; for that other bread by which *hearts are strengthened* it hath rejected, that other bread it hath not received.

But Christ is a seed, because He is the seed of Abraham: *To Abraham were the promises made and to his seed. He saith not, And to his seeds, as of many: but as of one, And to thy seed, which is Christ* (Gal. iii. 16). Not alone is Christ the seed, but *the least of all the seeds*, because He came not in power, nor in wealth, nor in the wisdom of this world. But suddenly He unfolds as a tree the soaring eminence of His might, that we may say: *I sat under his shadow, whom I desired* (Cant. ii. 3). And frequently, as I believe, He appears as both seed and tree. For He is a seed when it is said: *Is not this the carpenter's son?* But in the midst of these words of a sudden He grows, as the Jews, because they could not see the branches of the veiled tree, bear witness, saying: *How came this man by this wisdom and miracles?* (Mt. xiii. 55, 54).

The seed therefore is a figure, the Tree is wisdom, in whose leafy branches that night raven in the house (Ps. ci. 7, 8), that solitary sparrow on the housetop, he that was caught up to paradise (II Cor. x. 4), he that *shall be taken up in the clouds*, into the air (I Thess. iv. 16), now take their rest in safety. There also rest the Angels and Powers of heaven, and whosoever by the deeds of the spirit merit to fly up there. There rested the holy John when he leaned on the breast of Jesus (John xiii. 25; xxi. 20): nay, from the sap of the Tree he is also spread forth as a branch. Peter is a branch, a branch likewise is Paul, *forgetting the things that are behind, and stretching towards those that are before* (Phil. iii. 13): into whose bosom, in the security so to speak of whose teaching, we *who were afar off* (Eph. ii. 13), we that are gathered from the nations, whom the confusion of the spirit of iniquity, and the distress of this world, have long vainly tossed about, now, taking to ourselves the wings of holiness, hasten to fly, so that the protecting shadow of the saints may defend us from the heat of this world: dwelling happily in the peace of this sure haven, since *our soul* which before was like that woman in the Gospel *laden* with sins *hath been delivered as a sparrow out of the snare of the fowlers* (Ps. cxxiii. 7), and hath flown to the mountains, and to the branches of the Lord (Ps. x. 1).

And so we who before were idle, flying hither and thither in futile disputation, now with hands unbound through faith in Christ, and freed of the shackles of the sabbatical observance, give ourselves to good works: and even in our very rejoicings we have liberty, and shut out intemperance, lest being made free of the Law we become slaves of our desires. For the Law bound us to itself, that it might free us from desires. Grace which has taken away the lesser servitude, imposes yet more serious obligations. *All things are lawful to me, but not all are expedient* (I Cor. vi. 12); for it is a grave thing to use our liberty so as to fall back under dominion. Cease to be subject to the law, so that by reason of your virtues you shall be above the law. Amen.

III. St John Chrysostom, Bishop and Doctor
The Leaven of Holiness[5]

Another parable He spoke to them: The Kingdom of heaven is like to a leaven.

Since He had said that of the seed three parts would be lost and one part saved, and again that of that which would be saved much again would be lost, because of the tares that were sown among it, lest then anyone might say: Who then and how many will be saved, He takes away their anxiety bringing them to confidence through the parable of the grain of mustard seed. By this similitude He foretold that the preaching of the Gospel would resound throughout the whole earth.

For which reason He makes use of the figure of this plant as being above all others the most suited to symbolise these events: *Which is indeed the least of all seeds, but when it is grown up, it is greater than all herbs, and becometh a tree, so that the birds of the air come and dwell in the branches thereof.*

For He wished to give an indication of greatness. Thus, He as it were says, shall it also be in the preaching of the Gospel. For though His Disciples were more timid and more unlettered than all others, yet, since there was in them great power, the Gospel was preached throughout the whole world.

He then proceeds to include the simile of the Leaven in this view of what was to come, saying: *The kingdom of heaven is like to a leaven, which a woman took and hid in three measures of meal, until the whole was leavened.* For as the leaven gives its own strength to the great mass of the dough, so shall you change the world. And observe the Lord's wisdom, how He speaks of things that have their simple place in the order of creation, in this way showing that since these things happen so shall this. Let you not therefore say to Me: What can we do, twelve men against so great a multitude? For it is this that makes your power so striking, that amid the multitudes of the world your influence is not lost. For the leaven, when placed in the dough, and not simply placed there but thoroughly kneaded into it, ferments the whole mass; for which reason He did not say simply placed in the dough but *hid in it.* So likewise, when you shall be one with, and commingled with, your attackers, then shall you overcome them. And as the leaven hidden in the dough is not destroyed, but rather changes the dough into its own nature, so shall you also do in the preaching of the Gospel.

Be not therefore fearful if I have foretold that tribulations will come: for your light no man will extinguish, but will rather overcome all men. The three measures here stand for a great number: for Scripture is wont to use this number to convey the idea of a multitude. And do not wonder that in speaking of the kingdom of heaven He speaks of a grain of mustard seed, and of leaven: for He was speaking to unlettered men, men who were accustomed to be instructed in this way, and who were so simple that oftentimes even these figures required to be explained for them. Where now are the disciples of the Gentiles? Let them learn of salvation from that which has happened, and how wondrous is the power of Christ, and let them believe that He must be adored for either of these two reasons: either because He foretold this unbelievable happening, or because that which He foretold has been fulfilled as He had foretold it.

For He it is Who has given such power to the leaven; He it is Who has mingled those who believe in Him with the multitude, so that they might share with it their knowledge of Him. Let none of you therefore, He says, be troubled because of your fewness: for great is the power of the Gospel, and that which is once leavened becomes in turn a leaven for the remainder. And just as the glowing ashes when dry wood is thrown upon them change again to flame which can then set fire to green wood, so shall it be with your preaching.

But He spoke not of fire but of leaven. Why? Because the whole effect in the case of fire is not caused by the fire but by wood and fire, but the leaven of itself brings about the leavening of the whole mass.

And if twelve men could leaven the whole world, how unprofitable are we that though so great a number, yet we cannot convert those that remain: we who should be enough to leaven a thousand worlds? But, you will say, they were Apostles? But what of that? Were they not men such as you are? Did they not dwell among men? Did they not have the same interests as you? Did they not do the same things? Perhaps you think they were angels? That they came down from heaven? No. But, again you will say, they worked miracles. It was not because of their miracles that they were remarkable. How long must we speak of miracles

to cover up our own laziness? Look upon the number of the saints. They shone forth, but not because of their miracles. For many who even cast out devils are not honoured, because they did evil, and for this were punished.

What then you may ask was it that made them great? Their rejection of wealth, and their contempt of vain glory, their turning away from the things of this world. Because had they been wanting in this regard, or had they indulged their passions, then even though they had raised thousands from death to life they would have been not merely worthless, but would have been held as deceivers and frauds. Behold then that it is their life which shines forth on every side, and draws down on them the graces of the Spirit.

What miracles did John work, he who drew to himself so many from out the cities? That he wrought no miracles the Evangelist tells us: *John indeed did no sign* (Jn. x. 41). And wherefore was Elias honoured? Was it not for the courage with which he rebuked a king? Was it not for his zeal for God? Was it not for his poverty, his poor sheepskin garment, his cave, and the solitude. For it was after all this he wrought miracles. And at what miracles wrought by Job was the devil astonished? Wonders there were none: but he beheld in him an upright honourable life, and a patience more enduring than adamant.

What miracles had David wrought in his youth that the Lord should say of him: *I have found David a man according to my own heart* (Acts xiii. 22). And Abraham, and Isaac, and Jacob, what dead did they bring back to life? What leper did they cleanse? Do you not know that miracles, unless we are watchful, generally do harm? So many among the Corinthians were divided among themselves because of miracles; and because of this many among the Romans were filled with pride; for this likewise Simon was cast forth. Finally, he who desired to follow Christ, heard as one reproved the words: *The foxes have holes, and the birds of the air nests.* Each of these fell away and perished because both the one and the other sought either profit or glory from their miracles. But scrupulous sanctity of life, and the love of the virtues, so far from provoking such a desire, they rather uproot it entirely, if it be there.

Christ Himself, when He was laying down laws for His Disciples, what did He lay upon them? Certainly not that they should perform wonders, that men might behold them. No. But what did He say? *Let your light shine before men, that they may see your good works, and glorify your Father who is in heaven.* To Peter likewise He did not say: *if you love me* work miracles, but: *Feed My sheep* (Jn. xxi. 17). And since on all occasions He singles him out from the rest, together with James and John, I ask why did He so single them out? Because of their miracles? But all the Apostles cleansed the lepers, and raised the dead. To all alike He gave this power. Why then were these three preferred? Because of the virtue of their lives, and the magnanimity of their souls. See then the need of a good life and the need of fruitful works. *By their fruits you shall know them* (Mt. vii. 16).

What is it that commends our own life? Is it miracles, or is it a life scrupulously and uprightly lived? It is rather from the latter that miracles arise, and to that they tend. For he that lives a worthy life, draws this grace upon himself; and whosoever received such graces receives them that he may help others to amend their lives. For even Christ wrought miracles that He might the more be accepted as worthy of belief, and so might the more attract men to Himself, and by this means bring sanctity into their lives. Therefore we observe in Him the greatest solicitude, the most earnest anxiety, in this regard. And He makes use not merely of signs and wonders, but threatens with the pains of hell, and promises the Kingdom of heaven; and He gives us wondrous laws and counsels, and tries all other means to the end that in our lives we shall be like the angels.

And why do I say that Christ does all things for this one end? Were anyone to give you the power of choosing, between raising the dead in His Name, or dying in His Name, tell me which would you choose? Is it not plain that you would choose the second? Yet the first is a miracle, the second but a good work. And should someone offer you the choice of either turning grass into gold, or of regarding all gold as grass, would you not choose the latter? And rightly so. For the first would draw all men, above every other thing. For should they see grass become gold, they would seek this power, as Simon did, and the love of wealth would be increased in them; but should all men see you despise gold, as though it were grass, they would in part themselves be healed of the disease of craving for it.

See you not how the beauty of a good life can help others more? I mean by a good life not simply fasting, nor lying down in sackcloth and ashes; but to despise riches as they should be despised, to have charity towards your neighbour, to give of your bread to the hungry, to control your anger, to seek not after vain glory, and to turn away from envy. This has He taught us Who said: *Learn of me, because I am meek and humble of heart* (Mt. xi. 29). He did not say: learn of me, because I fast, although He could put forward His fast of forty days, not because *I am meek and humble of heart.* Again, when He sent forth His Apostles to preach He did not say: *Fast ye,* but: *Eat such things as are set before you* (Lk. x. 8). But when it came to money, He laid upon them a severe injunction: *Do not possess gold nor silver; nor money in your purses.*

All this I say, not to deprecate fasting. Far from it. Rather do I praise it greatly. But it grieves me when I behold you neglecting other good works, believing that to be sufficient for salvation which holds but the least place in the choir of the virtues. These are the supreme virtues: charity, forbearance (*epieikeia*), and almsgiving, which even surpasses virginity.

And so if you desire to imitate the virtues of the Apostles, there is nothing to prevent you. All that is needed is your own fervent will, and a most tender love of virtue. Let not the expectation of miracles hold you back. The devil is indeed angered when cast forth from a human body; but much more so, if he sees a soul freed from sin. For this is his greatest power, the spreading of sin. Because of this Christ died, that He might break this power. This has brought death. Because of sin the whole world is turned upside-down. If you destroy sin you have broken the nerves of the devil, you have *bruised his head,* you have destroyed his power, you have defeated his army, you have wrought a sign greater than all miracles. This is not my word, but that of the Blessed Paul, for when he said: *Be zealous for the better gifts. And I show unto you yet a better excellent way* (I Cor. xii. 31), he did not then go on to speak of miracles, but of charity, the root of every good work, and its foundation. If we observe this, and all the wisdom that flows out from it, we have no need of miracles; but if we observe it not, then miracles will avail us nothing.

Dwelling on these things let us rather strive after that by means of which the Apostles became so great. How have they become great? Hear Peter answering: *Behold we have left all things, and have followed thee.* And hear also Christ answering them: *you shall sit on twelve seats judging the twelve tribes of Israel.* And then: *And everyone that left house, or brethren, or sisters, or father, or mother, or wife, or children, or lands, for my name's sake, shall receive an hundredfold, and shall possess life everlasting* (Mt. xix. 27, 28, 29).

For which cause therefore, withdrawing ourselves from all the anxieties of this world, let us give ourselves instead to Christ, so that according to His promises we may receive, as the Apostles have received, and enjoy, life eternal, to which may we all together come, by the grace and mercy of Our Lord Jesus Christ, to whom be glory and empire for ever. Amen.

IV. St Maximus, Bishop of Turin
Christ Our Leaven[6]

It is well known to you all that from the beginning, Brethren, from the day I came to you, I have ceased not to bring to your mind all that the Lord has taught, seeking always to root deep within you, partly by exhortation and partly by reproaches, His Divine precepts; so that while to many I have been as it were a father, to not a few I have seemed a stern master. As a father he has regarded me who willingly has embraced what I have taught him, as a stern teacher he who has felt his conscience aggrieved because of my preaching. But it matters little to me, provided that, either by kindness or by sternness, Christ be made known to you: though even sternness is a kindness used towards children who are neglectful, so that they may learn by fear what they have neglected to love. Not that a father does not love all his children with equal affection, but the tenderness of a father is shown according to the disposition of each one, arousing the well-disposed by exhortation and the wayward by sternness, so that by the correction of the one and the other he is sure of both; for the one he urges on with love, the other by harshness; just as the Blessed Apostle says: *Now all chastisement for the present indeed seemeth not to bring with it joy, but sorrow, but afterwards it will yield, to them that are exercised by it, the most peaceful fruit of justice* (Heb. xii. 11).

Since I believe that you have been the gainers from my discourse to you, it gives me happiness to speak with you regarding certain parts of the Holy Writings, as I see that what I have said you accept with a lively faith. Says the Lord in to-day's holy gospel: *The kingdom of heaven is like to leaven, which a woman took and hid in three measures of meal, until the whole was leavened.*

I do not doubt that the power and virtue of leaven is known to all. That while small in quantity, simple in appearance, and everywhere common in nature, it possesses such power that when hidden in the dough, its vigour changes the whole mass, so that it gradually becomes what it is itself; and it continues to permeate the whole mass by its energy until every portion of the dough becomes itself a leaven; as if a thing acquires from its own resources an amount of new energy. This women do each day so as to provide wholesome bread and beneficial food for their families. But since the Law of the Gospel is spiritual, and since the Gospel meaning is specially contained within the parables, let us see what is the meaning of the leaven, and who is the woman, and what is the flour?

We read in the holy Gospel, where the Lord speaking of Himself says: *Amen I say to you, unless the grain of wheat falling into the ground die, itself remaineth alone.* Therefore if the Lord is wheat, the Lord is also leaven, for the leaven is wont to be made only from flour. Rightly therefore is the Lord compared to leaven, Who since He appeared in the likeness of man, is become small in His lowliness, insignificant in His mortal weakness, yet within possesses such a power of wisdom that the whole world itself could scarcely contain all that He has taught, and Who, since He began to diffuse Himself throughout the world by the power of His Divinity, immediately drew into his own substance men of every race, that He might lay on all the yoke of His Holy Spirit, that is, that all Christians may become even as Christ is. For the Lord Jesus as Man, and He alone in this world, as a leaven hidden in the mass, makes it possible that all men be as He is. Whosoever therefore will adhere to the leaven of Christ, becomes himself a leaven, as profitable unto himself as he may be to all others: without fear for his own salvation, and a sure means of gaining others.

And as the leaven, when it is to be mixed in a heap of dough, is broken up and crushed into little pieces, and sprinkled through the mass until it is itself lost, so that it may bind together the scattered multitude of the grains of flour by its vigour, reducing to a solid mass what was inert and powerless when it was but powder, making this unity a potent whole of what had before seemed unprofitable, so the Lord Jesus Christ, since He is the Leaven of the whole world, was broken by manifold torments, was wounded and pierced, and His sap, which is His Precious Blood, poured out for our salvation, so that mingling with Him all mankind would be made into one body, they who before His passion were prostrate and divided.

So as to a Leaven we cling to Him: we who before were but dust of the Gentiles. We, I repeat, who before lay wholly scattered and broken in pieces, have by the power of His passion been kneaded into the Body of Christ, as the blessed Apostle says: *We are members of His Body, of His Flesh, and of His Bones* (Eph. v. 30). We therefore who were cast away like dust among the nations (Osee ix. 17), by the sprinkling of the Blood of the Lord, are joined into the Body of His Oneness.

The woman who is said to hide the leaven in three measures of meal, who is she but the Holy Church, which each day strives to hide the doctrine of Christ in our hearts? She, I repeat, is the woman who in another place is said to be grinding at a mill, as the Lord says: *Two women shall be grinding at the mill: one shall be taken and one shall be left* (Mt. xxiv. 41). For the Holy Church grinds at the mill through her law, through the Apostles, through the Prophets, when she makes catechumens, and when she breaks down the hardness of paganism, and grinds it into little pieces, and being ground, as flour. She makes them ready to be joined together by the Blood of the Lord.

For I have said that the whole passion of Christ is a leaven. And the leaven is the symbol of our salvation, and without which symbol or leaven no one can merit the substance of life eternal. And because the Gospel describes two women grinding at the mill, and the one we have said is the Church grinding unto our salvation, who is the other if not the Synagogue? For it also ground through Moses and the Prophets; but it ground to no gain, as the Apostle says of the Jews: *They have a zeal of God, but not according to knowledge* (Rom. x. 2).

To no profit, I repeat, does the Synagogue stand grinding at the mill, because it does not leaven its mass with the doctrine of Christ. And so the Lord bids us to avoid the leaven of the Synagogue: *Beware of the leaven of the Pharisees* (Mt. xvi. 6, 11). For it has been prepared from the bloodshed and from the cruelties of the Jews, who said of the Lord: *His Blood be upon us and upon our children* (Mt. xxvii. 25). Whence is it the Gospel says:

Two women shall be grinding at the mill; one shall be taken and one shall be left. The Holy Church shall be taken up into eternal rest, She who has ground the food of holiness unto the Lord; the Synagogue, stained with blood, shall be left at the mill, to endure for ever the round of its own unfaithfulness. Amen.

NOTES

[1] Cf. PL 26, 91.

[2] PL 35, 1373; inauthentic; cf. PRM 35.

[3] St Aphraates, Bishop and Abbot (A.D. 280–350), of a region near Mosul of modern Mesopotamia. This homily is translated from a Latin version of Dom Parisot: Graffin, Patrologia Syria, Paris 1894. Against Envy and Discord, paragraph 43.

[4] CSEL 32, 360–366.

[5] PG 58, 479, hom. 47 in Matt.

[6] PL 57, hom. 111.

SEPTUAGESIMA SUNDAY

THE GOSPEL OF THE SUNDAY

Matthew xx. 1–16

At that time: Jesus spoke to His Disciples the following parable: The kingdom of heaven is like to an householder, who went out early in the morning to hire labourers into his vineyard. And having agreed with the labourers for a penny a day, he sent them into his vineyard.

And going out about the third hour, he saw others standing in the market place idle. And he said to them: Go you also into my vineyard, and I will give you what shall be just. And they went their way. And again he went out about the sixth and the ninth hour, and did in like manner. But about the eleventh hour he went out and found others standing, and he saith to them: Why stand you here all the day idle? They say to him: Because no man hath hired us. He saith to them: Go you also into my vineyard.

And when evening was come, the lord of the vineyard saith to his steward: Call the labourers and pay them their hire, beginning from the last even to the first.

When therefore they were come, that came about the eleventh hour, they received every man a penny. But when the first also came, they thought that they should receive more: and they also received every man a penny. And receiving it they murmured against the master of the house, saying: These last have worked but one hour, and thou hast made them equal to us, that have borne the burden of the day and the heats.

But he answering said to one of them: Friend, I do thee no wrong: didst thou not agree with me for a penny? Take what is thine, and go thy way: I will also give to this last even as to thee. Or, is it not lawful for me to do what I will? Is thy eye evil, because I am good? So shall the last be first, and the first last. For many are called, but few chosen.

EXPOSITION FROM THE CATENA AUREA

The kingdom of heaven is like to an householder, who went out early in the morning to hire labourers into his vineyard . . . REMIGIUS: Because the

359

Lord had just said: *Many that are first, shall be last: and the last shall be first,* so that He might confirm this saying, He adds a similitude, saying: *The kingdom of heaven is like to an householder . . .*

CHRYSOSTOM, *Super Matthaeum, Hom.* 54 *ex Op. Imperfecto*: Christ is the householder, and the heavens and the earth are as it were His house, His family is made up of the creatures of both heaven and earth, and those that are beneath. The vineyard is the life of justice in which the various virtues are planted, like vines in a vineyard; as for example: mildness, chastity, patience, and the other virtues; all of which are called by the name *justice.* The labourers in the vineyard are men; hence He says: *Who went out early in the morning to hire labourers into his vineyard.* God has planted His justice in our hearts, not for His own profit, but for ours. Learn therefore that we are hired servants. And as no one hires a servant whose sole service is to feed himself, so likewise we are not called by Christ that we may do only the things that are for our personal benefit, but those that pertain to the glory of God.

And just as the servant first has mind for the task he has to do, then afterwards for his daily bread, so must we also look first to what belongs to the glory of God, then to that which is to our own profit; and as the hired servant gives the whole day to the work of his master, and but one hour to his own nourishment, so ought we devote all the days of our life to God's glory, reserving but a little portion to our earthly needs. And as the servant is ashamed, upon a day in which he has not laboured, to enter the house of the master and ask for bread, ought you not be ashamed to enter the Church and stand before the face of God, when in His sight you have not laboured unto good?

GREGORY. *Hom.* 19 *in Evang.*: The householder, that is, our Creator, has a vineyard, namely, the universal Church, which from Abel the Just until the last of the Elect that shall be born into this world, has brought forth as many saints as it sends forth shoots. And at no time has the Lord failed to send labourers to work in His vineyard, that is, to instruct His people unto justice. This He first did by means of the Patriarchs, then through the Teachers of the Law, then by the Prophets, and last of all He has cultivated His vineyard by the Apostles, His labourers; though whosoever has performed, with a right intention any good action, the same has been a worker in this vineyard.

ORIGEN, *Tr.* 10 *in Matt.*: We may describe this whole present world as but one day, which is great indeed to us, but as nothing in the sight of God. GREGORY, as above: The morning of the world was the time from Adam until Noah; therefor is it said: *Who went out early in the morning to hire labourers into his vineyard.* And He also describes the form of the contract, saying: *And having agreed with the labourers for a penny a day.* ORIGEN: I believe that the word *denarius* (penny) stands for salvation. REMIGIUS: A *denarius* is the coin which formerly was reckoned as equal to ten *nummi* (pence), and had on it the effigy of the king. Rightly therefore is a *denarius* used to indicate the reward of the observance of the Decalogue;

and rightly is it said: *Having agreed with the labourers for a penny a day*, because in the field of the holy Church each one labours for a reward that is promised.

GREGORY: The third hour was from Noah to Abraham: of which it is said: *And going out about the third hour he saw others standing in the market place idle*. ORIGEN: The market place is anywhere that is outside the Catholic Church. CHRYSOSTOM, *Super Matth.*: For in this world men live by buying and selling: and by defrauding each other they sustain their own lives. GREGORY: He who lives for himself, who gratifies himself with the pleasures of the flesh, is rightfully considered as one standing idle, because he is not seeking after the fruits of labouring for God.

CHRYSOSTOM, as above: Or those *standing idle* are sinners: for they are said to be dead; for that man is idle who does not the work of the Lord. Do you wish then not to be idle? Then do not take what is another's, and give of your own: and thus you shall labour in the vineyard of the Lord, cultivating the vine of mercy. Then follows: *And he said to them: go you also into my vineyard*. Note here that it was only with the first hired that he agreed upon a particular wage, the others he hired with an undefined agreement, saying only: *I will give you what shall be just*. For the Lord, knowing that Adam would sin, and that all would later perish in the flood, made with him a certain agreement: lest he might afterwards say that he had departed from justice because he knew not what reward he would receive. With the workers who

were called later he made no agreement, for He was resolved to give them an amount such as they had no expectation of receiving.

ORIGEN: Or He did not call the labourers of the third hour to a whole day's work: whatever they were able to do He reserved to His own judgement to reward accordingly. For they could do an amount of work equal to that done by those who had worked from the early morning, were they willing, in the shorter space of time, and not sparing their toil, to put forth a greater effort to the work in hand.

GREGORY: The sixth hour is from Abraham to Moses; the ninth from Moses to the coming of the Lord; hence follows: *And he went out about the sixth and the ninth hour and did in like manner*. CHRYSOSTOM, as above: He unites the sixth and ninth hour in this manner, because in the sixth and ninth hour He called the Jewish people, and frequently visited mankind, in order to establish His covenants with them as the time drew near for the salvation of all men.

GREGORY: The eleventh hour is from the coming of the Lord until the end of the world. The workers in the morning, at the third, the sixth, the ninth hour, stand for the ancient Jewish people, which, in its Elect, and from the beginning of the world, while it served God with an upright heart, has scarcely ceased from labour in the divine vineyard. At the eleventh hour the Gentiles were called: *About the eleventh hour he went out and found others standing, and saith to them: why stand you here all the day idle?* They who for so long a period of the world's time neglected to labour for their livelihood were standing as it were all the day idle. But note what those who were so questioned made answer: *They say to him: because no man hath hired us.* No Patriarch had come to them, and no Prophet. What means no man hath hired us if not that no man hath preached to us the way of life?

CHRYSOSTOM, as above: What is our hiring, and what is the wage of our engagement? The promise of life eternal. The Gentiles alone knew not God nor His promises. HILARY, *in Matth.* 20: These therefore are sent into the vineyard; hence follows: *He saith to them: go you also into my vineyard.* RABANUS: At the computation of the day's work, a time suitable for payment, the Gospel says: *And when the evening was come,* that is, when the day of the world had inclined towards the evening of its ending.

CHRYSOSTOM, as above: Observe that He gave payment at evening time, not on the following morning: therefore while the world endures judgement is yet to come, and to each must his reward be given, and this for two reasons. The first is because happiness is itself the future reward of justice: therefore not in the next world is judgement given, but prior to it. Then, judgement will be given before the Coming of the Lord, lest sinners see that day's happiness. The Gospel continues: *The Lord said to his steward,* that is, the Son says to the Holy Spirit.

GLOSS: Or if you will, the Father says to the Son: because the Father worketh through the Son, and the Son through the Holy Spirit; but not because of any difference of substance or of dignity.

ORIGEN: Or the Lord saith to His steward, that is to one of the angels who have the duty of bestowing rewards; or to one of the many *governors,* according to that which is written: *As long as the heir is a child he is under tutors and governors* (Gal. iv. 2). REMIGIUS: Or the Lord Jesus Christ is Himself the householder and the steward of the vineyard just as He is both the Door and the Doorkeeper. He therefore calls the workers, and gives them their wage, when all shall be gathered together at the judgement, so that each may be seen to receive according to his works.

ORIGEN: For the first workers being *approved by the testimony of faith, received not the promise. God,* the householder, *providing some better thing for us* who were called at the eleventh hour, so that *they should not be perfected without us* (Heb. xi. 39). And because we have obtained mercy, for the reason that we stood the whole day idle, we hope to be the first to receive reward, because we are Christ's; and after us He will pay those who have laboured before us; and therefore is it said: *Call the labourers and pay them their hire, beginning from the last even to the first.*

CHRYSOSTOM, as above: We give more readily to those to whom we give something freely, because we give only for our own honour. Therefore God in rendering reward to all the saints appears as just: but in giving to the Gentiles He is seen as merciful, as the Apostle says: *But the Gentiles are to glorify God for his mercy* (Rom. xv. 9). And so is it said: *Beginning from the last even to the first.* That the Lord may make known His inestimable mercy, He first renders payment to the late-comers, and the least deserving; afterwards to the first: for boundless mercy has not regard to order.

AUGUSTINE, *De Spir. et Litt.* 24: Or the lesser are found to be first, because the lesser have been made rich. The Gospel continues: *When therefore they were come, that came about the eleventh hour, received every man a penny.* GREGORY: They received the same coin who had laboured at the eleventh hour (for which they had longed with all their soul), and they who had laboured from the first: since, equally with those who were called from the beginning of the world, they received the reward of eternal life who had come to God at the end of the world.

CHRYSOSTOM, as above: And not unjustly: for he that was born in the first time of the world, lived no longer than his allotted time. And what loss would it be to him if after going forth from the body the world then stood still? And those born at the end, they lived no less than the days assigned to them: and what would it profit them if, after receiving their wage, the world should come to an end, since they had finished their life's task before the world had ended? Then also it rests not within man's power that he be born either before or after, but with the power of God. Neither can he claim to be first in order who was born first, nor is he

to be held as the lesser who was born later.

And receiving it they murmured against the master of the house. If that be true which we have said, that the first as well as the last shall each live their allotted time, and neither more nor less, and that for each one death is his own consummation, what then does this mean: *We have borne the burthen of the day and the heats?* Because to us is given a great power to fulfil justice, and to know that the end of the world is near. Whence Christ also, warning us, has told us: *The kingdom of heaven is at hand.* But to them it was a grievous thing to know that there were yet to be prolonged tracts of time. Though they did not live all through this time, yet they seem to have borne the weight of all the years of it. Or again *the burthen of the day* means the onerous precepts of the Law: the *heats*, the burning trials of error which the evil spirits kindled against them, urging them to be as the Gentiles. From out all this the Gentiles came forth as children believing in Christ, and fully redeemed by the shorter way of grace.

GREGORY, as above: Or to bear the burthen of the day and the heats signifies to be wearied by the heats of the flesh borne through the years of a longer life. But it might be asked: how may they be said to murmur who are called to the kingdom of heaven? For no one who murmurs will receive this kingdom, and no one murmurs who receives it. CHRYSOSTOM, *Hom. 65 in Matth.*: We ought not to search into the parables so as to scrutinise literally whatever is contained there, but seek rather to understand its purpose and search no further. He does not therefore introduce this remark in order to show that certain individuals were stirred to envy, but to show that some attained to such honour that they awakened envy in others.

GREGORY: Or because the ancient Fathers, up to the Coming of Christ, although they lived just lives, were not brought into the kingdom, and so this murmuring was theirs. But we who have come at the eleventh hour murmur not at the end of the day's toil, because, coming into this world after the Advent of our Mediator, we are conducted into the kingdom as soon as we leave the body. JEROME: Those of each earlier calling all envy the Gentiles, and their calling is changed in favour of the Gentiles. HILARY: This murmuring of the servants of the vineyards is like to the arrogance of a stubborn people under Moses.

But he answering said to one of them: Friend, I do thee no wrong. REMIGIUS: This *one* may stand for all who believed among the Jews, and whom, because of their faith, He calls friend. CHRYSOSTOM, *Super Matthaeum*: They were not grieving as though defrauded of their wages, but because, these later ones received more than they merited. So do the envious grieve when to another something is given, as though it were taken from themselves: from which it is apparent that envy arises from vainglory. For he who is envious grieves that he is second when he desired to be first; accordingly the Lord takes away their motive for envy, saying: *Didst thou not agree with me for a penny?*

JEROME: The *denarius* bears the effigy of the king; you have received therefore the reward which I promised, that is, My image and likeness: what further do you seek? Or do you desire, not that you yourself received more, but that another receive nothing?

Take what is thine, and go thy way. REMIGIUS: That is, receive thy reward and enter into glory. *I will also give to this last,* that is, to the Gentiles, according to their merit *as to thee.* ORIGEN: Perhaps it was to Adam He said: *Friend, I do thee no wrong,* etc. The *denarius,* which is salvation, is yours: *I will give to the last as to thee.* It is not unbelievable that *this last* is the Apostle Paul, who in one hour *laboured more abundantly than all they* (I Cor. xv. 10).

AUGUSTINE, *De San. Virg.* 26: Because eternal life will be equally the possession of all the blessed, the *denarius,* which is the wage of all, is given to each alike. But because in the life eternal the brightness of each one's merits shall shine forth differently, there are many mansions in the Father's House. But with a *denarius* one does not live more richly than another; but with manifold mansions one may be honoured more evidently than another. GREGORY: And because to enter the kingdom comes only from the goodness of His will rightly does He add: *Is it not lawful for me to do what I will?* For the question of one who is murmuring against the will of God is foolish. One may murmur if that is not given which is due, but not if that is not given which is not due: hence is simply added: *Is thy eye evil, because I am good?*

REMIGIUS: By *eye* He desires to signify the state of the mind. For the Jews had an evil eye, that is, they were of an evil disposition of mind, and therefore they were grieved because of the salvation of the Gentiles. He then makes clear what is the aim of the parable, when He finally adds: *so shall the last be first, and the first last*; this, namely, that from being at the head the Jews are moved around to the tail, and we, from the tail, are changed to the head.

CHRYSOSTOM, *super Matth*.: Or He calls the first last, and the last first, not so that the last may be more honoured than the first, but that they may become co-equal; and that between them there is no difference by reason of time. That He said: *Many are called, but few chosen*, refers not to the saints who are gone before, but to the Gentiles; since of many who are called from these same Gentiles few shall be chosen.

GREGORY: For many come to faith, but few are brought into the heavenly kingdom. And many serve God with their tongue, but turn from Him in their lives. From this we should reflect on two things. The first is that no one should presume concerning his own salvation; for though he is called to the faith, he knows not whether he will be chosen to enter the kingdom of heaven. The second is, that no one should take it upon himself to despair of his neighbour, whom he sees steeped in vice, because no one knows the richness of the divine mercy.

Or again: our morning is childhood; by the third hour we may understand the time of adolescence, because as at that time the sun is mounting up so also is the heat of growing life; the sixth hour stands for young manhood, because the sun is then at its zenith, so is man then at the fullness of his strength. The ninth hour stands for mature age, in which as the sun recedes from the full noon day heat, so does later age decline from the heats of youth. Lastly the eleventh hour is that time which is called infirmity, or old age.

CHRYSOSTOM, *Hom. 65 in Matt*.: That He did not hire them all together, but some in the morning, some at the third hour, and so on, proceeds from their varying states of mind. He called them when they were ready to obey; as He called the Good Thief when he was ready to rsepond. If however they say: *Because no man hath hired us*, as was said, we must not search into all that is said in the parables. Besides, it was not the Lord, but the labourers, who say this. For that He, in what relates to Himself, calls all from their first beginning is signified when it is said: *He went out early to hire labourers*.

GREGORY: They therefore who fail to live for God until their old age stand idle in the market place until the eleventh hour: yet these also the Master hires, and for the most part rewards earlier, for they depart from this life for the kingdom of heaven before those who seemed to have been called from childhood.

ORIGEN: *Why stand you idle* is not said to those who began living in the Spirit, but were overcome by the flesh, so that they may live again in the Spirit if they desire to return. This we do not say so as not to dissuade those wicked children who, living riotously, have consumed the substance of the Gospel teaching, from returning to their Father's House; since they are not as those who sinned in youth, while yet untaught in the things of faith.

CHRYSOSTOM, *Hom. 65 in Matt.*: That He said: *The last shall be first,* *and the first last,* refers obliquely to those who at first were conspicuous in virtue, and afterwards despised it; and to those likewise who, being converted from evil, then surpassed many who were already in grace. This parable therefore was composed so that they who were converted in their later years might have confidence, and be not fearful that they will receive less than the rest.

I. ORIGEN: EXPOSITION OF THE PARABLE[1]

The Kingdom of heaven is like to an householder . . .
It seems as if the whole parable was uttered that we might learn that those coming last to work receive the same wage as those that were first called, and that they who first were called were placed last by the master of the vineyard, and were accordingly the last to receive payment. But we must know that if this parable of Jesus, *in Whom are hid all the treasures of wisdom and knowledge* (Col. ii. 3), be carefully studied, so much wisdom will be found hidden in its depths, by those who have the gift to discover it; so that it must be this parable especially the Saviour had in mind when He said: *I will open my mouth in parables, I will utter things hidden from the foundation of the world* (Mt. xiii. 35).

It is necessary for whosoever desires to understand this parable that he first knows what is the day that is here spoken of, and what is the meaning of its hours; and that it was not by chance that the master of the vineyard entrusted the care of his vineyard to five different orders of labourers. Then he must seek out, he that is able to seek, why some of the labourers were hired in the morning; and, after this, not a the second hour, but about the third hour, yet others were hired; and after this again the next hiring was not at the fourth, or the fifth hour, but at the sixth, and so on; not at the seventh or eighth hour, but at the ninth? Lastly, not at the tenth hour, but at the eleventh. For there should be a reason worthy of Jesus why between the morning and the next hour there is but a brief interval and not such as there is between the third and sixth hour, and between the sixth and ninth? And then why is there but one hour between the ninth and the eleventh, such as there was between the morning and the third hour?

Neither must we pass over the question as to why the householder made a contract of a *denarius* a day with those labourers he had hired in the morning, while to those he hired about the third hour he made no mention of a fixed sum, saying merely: *I will give you what shall be just.* He acted likewise with those he called about the sixth and ninth hours, and to those who had given a reason why they stood all day idle He said likewise: *go you also into my vineyard.* Since the master of the vineyard was standing outside his vineyard, and finding there the labourers, he sent the first into his vineyard, to the second he said: *go you also into my vineyard*, using the same words to those he called even up to the eleventh hour: *go you also into my vineyard*; let him strive to understand who can what is the market place, which in Greek is called *nundinae* or ninth day, in which Jesus found men standing idle. Again he must likewise seek to learn who they are whom he found standing there, and to whom he said: *why stand you here all the day idle?* And let him ponder who can the significance of their reply who had stood there the whole day idle; and the pain of standing there idle, and the promptness of their answer: that they were ready to work but no one had hired them; as there were many to be hired, but few to hire them.

And also we must carefully reflect upon what it was that the lord of the vineyard said to his steward when evening was come: *Call the labourers, and pay them their hire, beginning from the last even to the first.* We must try to understand what was it moved the lord of the vineyard to tell his steward to call the labourers, bidding him pay them their hire, beginning with the last to arrive and then going to the first, so they received payment first who were hired about the eleventh hour, then those that were hired at the ninth hour, in the third place those who were hired about the sixth hour, fourthly, they who were hired about the third hour, and, last of all, they were paid who were hired in the morning early. This is plainly shown from this that he

said: *Pay them their hire, beginning from the last even to the first.*

But who is it, apart from the lord who owns the vineyard, that is steward of the vineyard, and who pays the wages according to the lord's bidding? And if they who were called about the ninth hour did not therefore bear the burthen of the day and the heats, then manifestly it was not they who murmured against the householder, saying: *These last have worked but one hour, and thou hast made them equal to us, that have borne the burthen of the day and the heats.*

Neither did they who were called about the sixth hour bear the burthen of the day and the heats, unless perhaps of half a day. And they who were called about the ninth hour did not sustain the burthen of the whole day, but, if one must speak with accuracy, the half of the day and also its quarter. Only they who were hired in the morning, bore the burthen of the whole day and the heat. The rest endured only according to the measure of the time they had laboured in the vineyard.

Since also there are different parables concerning the vineyards, we must inquire whether the vineyard is here employed in its literal sense, or in different senses. I believe that we should also seek to understand why it was he said, not to *all* of those who came first, and who thought that they should receive more, but only *to one* of them: *Friend, I do thee no wrong: didst thou not agree with me for a penny?*

These and similar questions I find contained in the parable before us, to be answered by someone; and it is not for anyone to speak in a manner

befitting the parable, other than
he who may in strict truth say: *But
we have the mind of Christ* (I Cor. ii.
16). This I shall confidently make
clear to you. For who indeed has
the mind of Christ in this parable,
save he that submits himself to the
Holy Spirit, of Whom the Saviour
says: *He will teach you all things, and
bring all things to your mind, whatsoever I shall have said to you* (Jn. xiv.
26). For unless the Paraclete had
taught all that Jesus said, as also this
parable, nothing worthy of Jesus
could be said concerning it. And if
they that search into the Gospel
according to John have sought these
things from the Paraclete, according to the words of Jesus, some have
given heed, not indeed to the Paraclete, but *to spirits of error, and doctrines of devils, speaking lies in hypo-
crisy, and having their conscience
seared* (I Tim. iv. 1), so that they
call the spirit of error, and demons,
by the great name of the Paraclete,
Whom the Saviour had promised
to the Apostles, and to whosoever
is as it were the equal of the
Apostles.[2]

And I am of opinion that
Matthew knew all the mysteries
throughout this parable, and also
those contained in those of the
Sower of the Seed, and of the Tares
sown among the Wheat, but he did
not consider it practical, as in the
case of the others, to write about
them, for fear that in committing
to writing the full meaning, to a
certain degree, of this parable, he
would be writing as it were an
entire record of the whole. If
Matthew is wisely reserved in
regard to the unfolding of the
parable, it is evident that, if anyone,
even in part, can discern this, he is
perhaps to be praised; indeed to

make known what is disclosed to
him, and to put it in writing, will
in no way be a hindrance to the
exposition of the mysteries.

Now we are far from penetra-
ting to the depths of the things
hidden in the parable, but the few
that have been made clear to us we
venture, and not without earnest
prayer, to put before you, setting
out briefly some things we have
learned, and then having fittingly
meditated on the parable we shall
go on to other things. Let us therefore first consider what is the meaning of that *day* of which the parable
speaks; let us see also whether we
can speak of the whole of this
present time as a kind of day, great
indeed to us, but of little duration
in relation to the life of God the
Father, of Christ, and of the Holy
Spirit. And this present time has
the same relationship to the life of
the blessed Powers and Virtues,
brought together out of many
generations. For as one single day
is in relation to the life of all long-
living things, so is this present span
of time in comparison with the life
of the heavenly beings. And if it is
such in relation to the life of the
heavenly creatures, see then of what
little moment is this life in comparison with the life of the Father,
Son, and Holy Ghost.

Whether such a mystery is referred to in the Canticle of Deu-
teronomy: *Remember the days of old*
(Deut. xxxii. 7), let him seek out
who can. And if such are the days
of the world, it follows that a similar meaning is to be given to the
words of Psalm 76, verses six and
seven: *I thought upon the days of old:
and I had in mind the eternal years. I
meditated in the night with my own
heart: and I was exercised and swept in*

spirit. Will God then cast off forever? And perhaps God, if I may speak boldly, will not cast off for ever, for it is a grave thing for the Lord to cast off in one world; but in the other world He may perhaps cast off, when a certain sin shall not be forgiven either in this world or the next (Mt. xii. 32).[3]

Who therefore can relate the six days and the seventh of resurrection to days of this kind, or the sabbath days, and the days of the new moon, and the festival days of the first month, and the fourteenth day of the Pasch, and the other days of Azymes? He who follows reason in this matter will fall into an abyss of opinions, regarding a *day* of this kind after the manner of festival days, or after the manner of that sabbatical year in which God bestowed the fruits which remained from the precious cultivation upon the poor and the stranger, and upon the beast of the field while he is yet suffered to rest (Ex. xxiii). Who is able to scrutinise the number of the days in that sea of fifty years; (I say sea because of the profundity of the teaching here) so that he may know and truly understand the fiftieth year, and what is there laid down to be filled (Lev. xxv).

But in seeking to investigate this one *day* of the parable before us, and thinking that it is to represent the whole of this present world, we here enter into the deeps, and have need of the Spirit of God *that searcheth all things, yea, the deep things of God* (I Cor. ii. 10). I however believe, that as in the end of any year it is said that certain things are to be done, so at the end of many ages, or of ages that complete a certain space of time, Jesus *hath appeared for the destruction of sin*

(Heb. ix. 26), so that at the end of ages, as after the days of a year, a new beginning may then follow on so *that he might show in the ages to come the abundant riches of his grace,* to those to whom He thinks they should be shown (Eph. ii. 7).

These things we have said because of the *day* commemorated in the parable, which you may confirm from the Epistle of John where he says: *Little children, it is the last hour: and as you have heard that Anti-Christ cometh, even now there are become many Anti-Christs: whereby we know that it is the last hour* (I John ii. 18). For the last hour is after the eleventh hour of the parable that is here before us, for it was *about the eleventh hour,* according to the parable, that the householder, *going out found others standing there, and said to them: why stand you here all the day idle?*

After this let us inquire whether it was by chance that the lord gave the work of his vineyard to the five orders of labourers? To the first order, when *going out in the morning early to hire labourers into his vineyard.* To the second, when *going out about the third hour he saw others standing idle in the market place.* To the third and fourth, when *going out about the sixth and the ninth hour he did in like manner.* And to the fifth, when *about the eleventh hour going out he found others standing, and said to them: why stand you here all the day idle?*

Observe if you can that the first order stands for Adam, and for the creation of the world: for the Householder going out in the morning early as it were hired Adam and Eve to work in the vineyard of His justice. The second order of workers means Noah, and the

Covenant which He established with him. The third order signifies Abraham, and those who, following him, were Patriarchs, until the time of Moses. The fourth order is Moses, and all who went with him out of the land of Egypt, and the Law that was given in the desert. The last order, about the eleventh hour, means the Coming of Jesus Christ. The Householder was but one, as the parable records: He went forth five times, and He went forth that He might send into His vineyard *workmen that needeth not to be ashamed, rightly handling the word of truth* (II Tim. ii. 15), who would labour in His service. And One is Christ coming frequently among men, ever providing what is needed for the calling of His workers.

Let him that can see if it be not that the five orders of workers form as it were a certain symbol of the visible world, and of that which is perceived by our outward senses. Let him try though he may not wish to accept our notion or opinions. Someone will say that perhaps touch is implied in the first calling, because of which the woman said to the serpent: *God hath commanded us that we should not eat; and that we should not touch* (Gen. iii. 3); the sense of smell is the second, hence in the days of Noah *the Lord smelt a sweet savour* (Gen. viii. 21); taste was signified in Abraham, for when he received the angels at his table he set before them cakes made on the hearth and a calf which he boiled (Gen. xviii. 6, 5); hearing by the age of Moses when, namely, he could hear the Voice of the Lord spoken from on high. Lastly, sight, which is the noblest of the senses is signified by the advent of Christ, when their eyes that behold Christ shall be called blessed (Mt. xiii. 16). I have mentioned these things as a kind of pleasant exercise of the reason or if you wish as a sort of reflection on the five vocations.

I believe that the various tasks of the vineyard needed particular workers for the various hours. For certain things were to be done in the vineyard in the morning early, and the Master of the vineyard saw the workers that were most suitable to the task. In the third hour a work needed to be done, this is the time of Noah, when God made His Covenant with him. Then the ten generations from Noah to Abraham, and ending with Abraham, gave rise to another calling, and the worker of the vineyard now beginning his task was Abraham. And after him came Moses and those who together with him were brought into the vineyard. There remained one last work to be done in the vineyard, one which required a fresh and vigorous vocation, to do opportunely and with expedition that work which remained to be done. This task was the work of the New Dispensation.

The intervals between the third, the sixth, and the ninth hour were equal. And the time between the morning and third hour was similar to that between the ninth hour of Moses and the eleventh of the appearance of Christ Jesus in the flesh. The master of the vineyard agreed to pay a *denarius* to these hired in the morning; which, I am of opinion, is the token simply of salvation, and not to be reckoned with the case of those who were rewarded with degrees of glory; the word *denarius* seems to me but the name of salvation: that which is over and above the *denarius*, wherever it is mentioned, is the coin of the one who multiplied fivefold, and even tenfold, the talent that was given to him.

In saying to those called at the third hour: *I shall give you what shall be just*, he encouraged the workers of the third hour to work as best they could, reserving to himself to judge the payment fitting the work done. He did the same with those called at the sixth and ninth hour, saying also to them: *I will give you what shall be just*. And indeed if they put strength and energy into the work, even though the time should be shorter, they would accomplish as much as those hired in the morning early, but who had become sparing of effort, as happened to those who had been called very early.

Someone may ask, why did the master of the vineyard, going out about the eleventh hour, say, not to those who were simply idle, but to those standing idle all the day, that is for the whole time before the eleventh hour, *why stand you here all the day idle?* I suspect that there is here some deep hidden meaning, concerning the soul, in this idleness of the whole day until the eleventh hour. For though prompt and ready for work, they were not brought into the vineyard; and they pleaded with confidence on their own behalf, saying: *No man hath hired us.* We shall therefore endeavour, depending on certain words of Holy Writ, and from this parable that we are now considering, to show for what reason they stood the whole day idle, who were called at the eleventh hour.

Let those to whom our teaching is not acceptable then teach us the significance of this *whole day*, and the meaning of those who while prepared to work yet stood the whole day *idle*, and were not brought into the vineyard, and dared to answer that accusation by saying: *No man hath hired us.* For if the soul was together planted with the body how did they stand the whole day idle? Or, let them tell us what means this *whole day*, and what mean the various hours of the various callings of the labourers; and whether these latter are the blessed whom according to the parable the Householder has hired; and whether there were other labourers hired, either by other householders or by the same; and whether they are the blessed, or not the blessed, because of the sublimity of the question can it become known by the mind, or if known can it be written down?

I would also desire to discover the place, outside the vineyard, in which the workers were found by him who went forth to hire them; and I would like to reflect upon whether the place outside the vineyard is not the same as that of the souls not yet united to bodies, or; whether the vineyard signifies not alone the things of this life, but those outside the body, where, I believe, the labourers continue to do their work; for the souls of the labourers employed to cultivate the fields of the householder are not idle after they leave the body. For Samuel, though separated from his body, laboured prophesying (I Kgs. xxviii) and Jeremiah likewise, praying for the people (II Mac. xv. 14).[4]

Let us labour with great zeal in the cultivation of the vineyard, whether we dwell in the body, or have gone forth from it, and we shall be given a just wage. For, according to the parable, no one who is not prepared to do the work of the vineyard is sent into it; for no one does the householder reprove for work not done, though he has reproved one as to his hope of a greater or lesser reward.

And perhaps that place outside the vineyard is the market place, in which they lingered who stood idle. And they who said that *no man hath hired us*, used a good argument for being considered worthy of receiving the wage of the whole day; on which account he did hire them, and, if I may say so, made a return to them for this that they had stood there patiently the whole day, and had waited until evening for someone who might hire them. And then as the evening drew nigh, that is, the end of the world and of *the day* spoken of in the parable, the Lord speaks to His steward, or to the one among the angels whose duty it was to bestow rewards, or to one among the many governors, since while the heir is a child he *is under tutors and governors until the time appointed by the father* (Gal. iv. 2).

According to the command of the master, the steward calls the labourers, that he may pay those first who came last: since the first labourers *being approved by the testimony of faith, received not the promise, God providing some better thing for us*, who were called at the eleventh hour, *so that they should not be perfected without us* (Heb. xi. 39, 40). And because we stood there the whole day, and hoped that someone would come to hire us, and because we were idle, and because of

the reason we gave we were held worthy that we be given something to do, and accordingly, have awakened mercy, and receiving mercy we hope to receive the reward first, as we expect to become disciples of Christ. Then, moving on, he will give their wage to those who have laboured before us; and then to those who laboured before them, and so on to the first. Should someone look to the place where Samuel dwelt (I Kgs. xxviii. 15), and reflecting on that which was done by those called in the eleventh hour, he will see in what manner they bore the burden of the day and the heats who first were called, and that they who were called at the eleventh hour did not, as they, bear the burden of the day and heat, but they bore the burden of standing idle.

Before the coming of the Master Who said to us: *Come to me, all you that labour and are burdened, and I will refresh you* (Mt. xi. 28), it was a burden to be idle, and not to be judged worthy to be called to work in the vineyard. And the heats they endured who were called before the eleventh hour, each according to the time of his hiring. The first called not knowing the dignity of the Master of the vineyard, and that they ought not to murmur against Him, believed that they should receive more of salvation than the last come; and they murmured against the Householder, envious of those who came last, who worked but one hour until the evening, and were made equal to those who were called from the beginning into the divine vineyard. To one of them, perhaps it was Adam, the Master said: *Friend I do thee no wrong: didst thou not agree with me for a penny? Take what is thine, and go thy way.*

By *what is thine* is meant your salvation, which is the *denarius*. *I will also give to this last as to thee,* He says. He did not say *to these last,* but to *this last,* indicating one, eminent and outstanding; whom, it would be imprudent to say: but they would not be far from the truth who guess that this is Paul the Apostle, who in his *one hour* laboured more abundantly than all the others before him (I Cor. xv. 10). If one must speak as to the meaning of the vineyard, then relying on what was said by Him Who made plain in another parable what is the vineyard, we say that here also the vineyard is the kingdom of God. For as He said in that place: *The kingdom of heaven shall be taken from you, and shall be given to a nation yielding fruits thereof* (Mt. xxi. 43). All therefore who do the work of the vineyard are doing the work of the kingdom of God, and are worthy of salvation, and will be paid the *denarius*.

Having placed before you these reflections on the present parable, there come to our mind certain others which may be of profit to those who seek a deeper and more mystical exposition. It may be said that the whole life of men is but one day, according to the parable, and that they who are called by the Master of the vineyard in the morning early, are they who from their childhood were called to do the things of the kingdom of God. They who, after they had come to adolescence, begin to serve God are they who are called about the third hour. They who begin as men fully grown are they who were called at the sixth hour. They who

in mature age are converted to the work of God are those of the ninth hour, who after the heat of youth, and before the burden of old age, take on themselves the word of the Lord. And the old, who are near to death, are signified by those called at the eleventh hour to labour in the vineyard.

Since it is the purpose that governs life and not the time, which is scrutinised, and in which a man labours in hope: therefore, to every man who labours earnestly, from the time of his calling, an equal reward will be given. Hence they who were faithful from their childhood, who have laboured much, enduring the temptations and difficulties of youth, are grieved at seeing themselves receive an equal reward of salvation with those standing idle from their childhood till old age: standing as it were idle in unbelief, they have come now for but a brief while to believe and to labour.

The vineyard interpreted in this way is the Church of God. The market place that is outside the vineyard means that which is without the Church. Then the Word takes hold of those that are called, and sends them into the vineyard, the Church. According to this interpretation they will not be numbered among the labourers of the vineyard, who though called first to work in the vineyard, did not remain faithful to its teaching, and being overcome by their passions, they went forth from it; even if after they have had their fill of pleasure they should desire, having done penance, to return again to the vineyard. For they will not be able to say to the Master of the vineyard: *No man hath hired us.* For they were hired when they were first called to the faith. Nor will it be said to these: *Why stand you here all the day idle,* and especially if, *having began in the spirit,* and then afterwards *being delivered of the faith,* they desire to rise again, and to seek afresh the life of the spirit.

But we do not say this, lest we frighten those who are fearful and who desire to rise again, or make more difficult the return to their father's house of those who have consumed the substance of the Evangelical teaching by living riotously; but because of their repentance, and through turning back to a new way of life, they possess better things than those who are still held by their sins; but they are not as those who sinned in their youth, while yet untaught in the things of the faith.

To the last therefore as to the first the Master of the Vineyard wishes to give equally a *denarius,* that is, salvation: since it is lawful for Him to do as He wishes with what is His, and He reproves the *one* that is envious because the Master is good. There will be many of the last first; and some from the first will be last: *For many are called, but few chosen.*

He however that is truly more learned, and has been adjudged by God worthy of more enlightened and more abundant grace in *the word of wisdom, through the Spirit of God,* and in *the word of knowledge according to the same Spirit* (I Cor. xii. 8), and with every help to study this parable, will find in it greater and more sublime things, and expounding the revealed word, will pour out upon it yet more abundant meanings. We however, having delivered to you what we have grasped of the meaning of the parable, if we have failed here in our purpose to explain the meaning of the Scriptures, ask pardon of our readers: and because of our earnest will, and of our not wanting in effort, may we at least be deemed worthy of your approbation. Amen.

II. St John Chrysostom: On Preparing for Salvation[5]

What does this parable mean? For that which is said at the end is not in agreement with what is said in the beginning, but announces something wholly contrary. For in the first part He shows all men as receiving the same rewards; not some being excluded, and others admitted to enter. And both before the parable and after, the Lord has said something that is contradictory: *The first shall be last, and the last first;* that is, that those who came later shall be placed before the very first; these now ceasing to be first, and being placed after those others.

What this may mean He then makes known, saying: *For many are called, but few are chosen,* so that He may at one and the same time urge onwards the former, and comfort and console the latter. But the parable however does not say this: but that the chosen ones shall be made equal with those who have been proved just, and have laboured much: for these latter say: *Thou hast made them equal to us, that have borne the burden of the day and the heats.*

What then is the meaning of this parable? This we must first make clear; then we shall consider the other question. The vineyard, He says, is the particular injunctions of God, and His Commandments: the time of labouring is our present life; the labourers are all those who, in different ways, are called to the fulfilment of these commands. The morning early, the third hour, the sixth, the ninth, the eleventh, hour stand for those who at different periods of their lives have drawn near, and have done a good work.

But now the question arises: if those first called were so worthy in their lives and pleasing to God, and have shone out in the midst of all their trials throughout their days, how is it that they now have turned to evil feelings, namely: to envy and to jealousy? For seeing the others profiting equally with themselves they say: *These last have worked but one hour, and thou hast made them equal to us, who have borne the burden of the day and the heats.*

And even though they would lose nothing, nor would their own wage be lessened, from envy and jealousy they were resentful of what the others received. And furthermore, the Master of the vineyard answering in regard to these latter, and, as it were, justifying Himself to those who had so spoken, adjudged them guilty of envy and jealousy by these words: *Didst thou not agree with me for a penny? Take what is thine and go thy way: I will also give to this last even as to thee. Is thy eye evil because I am good?*

What is to be understood from these words? For the same appears in other parables also. For the son that was worthy is shown to have fallen into the same evil state of mind, when he saw his prodigal brother about to receive more and greater honour than he had ever received (Lk. xv. 28). For as the last were more honoured in being paid the first, so was he more honoured by this abundance of gifts; and to this the older brother gives testimony. What then are we to say? In the kingdom of heaven there is no one disputing or accusing in this manner. Far from it. For there is neither envy nor any jealousy. For if in this life the sanctified give up their lives for sinners how much more will they rejoice when they behold them dwelling amid the joys of heaven, which they believe to be equally the possession of all.

Why then did He use this form of speech? His discourse was a parable, and accordingly it is not fitting to take literally every word spoken. But when we have learned the purpose of the parable, we should gather in this, and not be too concerned as to the rest. Why was this parable composed, and what does He mean to lay down for our instruction? He wishes to make more eager those converted in later life, and to convince them that they should not think that their reward will be less. So he shows others as taking badly their good fortune; not that He may show the former as touched by envy; far from it, but that He may make plain that these who came last enjoy such honour that it can cause envy to others. Just as we sometimes say: he criticised me because I so honoured you. Not that we wish to accuse this person of a fault, but to show how great was the courtesy shown.

But why did He not hire them all together immediately? As to His own will, He has done so; and if all have not obeyed, it was the will of those called that made the difference. And so some are called early in the morning, some at the third hour, some at the sixth and the ninth, some at the eleventh: when they would be disposed to answer the call. This Paul also says: *When it pleased him, who separated me from my mother's womb, and called me by his grace* (Gal. i. 15). When did it please Him? When he was ready to obey. For the Lord willed it from the beginning, but because Paul would not have been obedient, then *it pleased Him* only when Paul was disposed to obey. In like manner He called the Good Thief, though He could have called him earlier; but he would not then have answered the call. For if Paul would not have obeyed earlier, much less would the Good Thief.

And that these say: *No man hath hired us*; here, as I have said, we must not examine with too close scrutiny all that may be included in the parable. It is they, not the Master of the vineyard, that say this. Neither does He go into that with them, as He seeks not to confuse them, but to bring them to Himself. That He, for His part, has called all, and from the first hour, the parable itself declares, saying: that he went out *early in the morning to hire*.

From everything that is said it seems to us therefore, that the parable is directed to those who have embraced the way of virtue in their early youth, and to those who embraced it in later age. To the former so that they might not become proud, nor scornful of those coming in later life, to the latter that they may learn that it is possible in a brief while to earn the whole wage. Because, prior to this, He had been speaking (Mt. xix) of great fervour, and of rejecting riches, and of contempt of the world. For this there was need for great courage of soul, and of youthful fire. To kindle a flame of eager love, and form in them the will to endure, He showed that it is possible, even for these last come, to receive the wage of the whole day. But He does not say this, lest they be tempted to pride, but He shows that the whole wage comes from His own kindness and bounty, and that by His help they will not be lost, but will attain to ineffable joys. And this principally is what He means to lay down for our instruction in this parable.

That He adds: *So shall the last be first, and the first last*, and, that: *many are called, but few chosen*, need not cause wonder. For this is not something which He, as it were, inferred from the parable, but means this: as the former has happened, so shall the latter; for in the parable the first did not come last, but all, beyond hope and expectation, received the same wage. And as that happened contrary to hope and expectation, and they who came late were made *equal* to the first comers, so shall this which is yet more wonderful come to pass, namely: that the last comers shall be placed even *before* the first, the first being placed after the last. Here we are speaking of two different things. To me He here seems to be hinting at the Jews, and at those believers who first shone forth in virtue, and then, turning aside from doing good, fell away, and also to those who, having risen up from evildoing, soon outstripped others in virtue. For daily we see many transformations of this kind, both in believing and in the conduct of life.

Accordingly, Dearest Brethren, I entreat you, let us use all diligence that we may remain steadfast in our holy faith, and show ourselves worthy in our daily lives. Unless we lead a life that is in harmony with our faith we shall be grievously punished. And this the Blessed Paul declared from the beginning, when he said: *And did all eat the same spiritual food, and all drank the same spiritual drink*, but adding that not all were saved, but many of them *were overthrown in the desert* (I Cor. x. 3–5). And in the Gospel Christ has declared this same truth for He made reference to many that had cast out devils, and had prophesied, and yet were dismissed into darkness (Mt. vii. 22, 23). And all these parables, such as that of the virgins, that of the fisherman's net, that of the thorns, of the tree that failed to bring forth fruit, demand the virtue that comes from good works.

Of Doctrine He speaks rarely, for the subject needs not to be laboured; but of life He speaks frequently, nay, at all times; for in this the battle is unending, and so also the toil. And why do I speak of the whole of life? Because, even a part neglected leads on to great evils. For example, failing to give alms casts into Gehenna those who are neglectful regarding it, though it is not the whole of virtue, but a part of it. Yet the virgins that were not adorned with this virtue are punished; for this the rich man was tormented: and they that gave not food to the hungry are themselves given over to the company of the demons. Again, to rail at others is but a small part of our lives, and yet it will shut out those who do not abstain from it. For He says:

And whosoever shall say to his brother, Thou fool, shall be in danger of hell fire (Mt. v. 22).

Again, continence is likewise but a part of virtue. Yet without it no man shall see God: *Follow peace with all men*, says Paul, *and holiness: without which no man shall see God* (Heb. xii. 14). Humility also is but a part of righteousness: yet he that does the other works of justice but does not strive for humility is not made clean before God, as is plain from the Pharisee who, though laden with good works, because of this lost all.

But I have a greater thing to say to you. For even one part of virtue despised closes heaven to us. And should we fulfil this, but without love or reverence the result is the same. For He says: *Unless your justice abound more than the Scribes and Pharisees, you shall not enter the kingdom of heaven* (Mt. v. 20). And so if you give alms, but not more than they gave, you shall not enter there. And what alms did they give? This I wish to tell you here, so that they who give not may be moved to give, and that they who give may not be proud, but give yet more. What did they give? A tenth of all they possessed. And after this another tenth, and after this another; so that in all they gave away a third of their substance: the three tenths together making up this. And together with this, the first fruits; the firstborn; and many other things, as for instance, sin offerings, those made at purifications, those given in times of festival, those of the jubilee, those given in payment of debts in the freeing of servants, and in the giving of loans without interest. But if he who gives a third of his goods, or rather the half, for all this together would make up the half, if then he who gives a half of all he possesses does nothing great, what merit shall he have who gives not even a tenth? So rightly is it said that few are chosen.

Be not therefore contemptuous of keeping a careful accounting of all your life. For if one portion of a just life neglected shall merit such punishment, how shall we escape justice and judgement, or what penalties shall we receive, should we neglect all of it? You may ask, what hope of salvation have we, if each of those things I have spoken of can lead us to hell? This then I shall also say to you. If we fully apply ourselves we can attain to salvation, preparing for ourselves the medicine of almsgiving, and so attending with care to our wounds. For oil does not more strengthen the body, than almsgiving strengthens the soul, making it impregnable against the devil. For wherever he lays hold his hold must slip, since the oil of almsgiving does not permit him to grip our shoulders so as to hold us fast. With this oil let us anoint ourselves generously. For just as oil gives light and cheerfulness, so also is it a means of salvation.

But you may say, such and such a one has so much, so very much money, and yet gives nothing. What is that to you? And so shall you be the more worthy of merit, if out of your poverty you are more generous than he. For this Paul praised the Macedonians (II Cor. ix. 2), not because they gave, but because they gave from great poverty. Take no heed therefore of such people, but of the common Teacher of all, Who had not whereon to lay

His head. And why you will say, does this man or that man not do these things? Do not concern thyself with anyone else, but rather free thyself from blame: for the punishment is greater if, while doing nothing yourself, you yet blame others; since while you are sitting in judgement on another you yourself are as guilty as he is. For He permits not the just to judge others and much less those who are sinners.

Let us then not judge others; neither have your eyes on those that take life carelessly, but upon Jesus; and from Him let us take our model. Was it I who gave you what you possess? Was it I who redeemed thee, that thou shouldst look up to me? It is Another who has placed all these things before thee. Why turn from the Master, and look to thy fellow servant? Have you not heard Him say: *Learn of Me, because I am meek, and humble of heart?* (Mt. xi. 29.) And again: *Whosoever shall be the greater among you, let him be your minister.* And again: *even as the Son of Man is not come to be ministered unto, but to minister* (Mt. xx. 26, 28). And yet again, lest you should take some offence at your fellow servants who are idle, and cut yourself off from them, He says: *For I have given you an example, that as I have done to you, so you do also* (Jn. xiii. 15).

But you have no teacher in your midst who might direct you to this end? More honour and glory will then be yours, that without a teacher you become worthy of reward. And that this can be, and, with readiness, if we will it, can be proved from those of old who have done so, such as Noah, as Abraham, Melchisedech, Job, and those other just men, towards whom we should daily lift our mind, and not to those whom men are continually praising, and whom you talk about when you come together. For everywhere I can hear such talk as this: such a one owns so many and so many acres of land; this other one has great wealth: this other is putting up great houses. Why always, O Christian, must you look to what is outside? Why look to others? If you must look at others, look to those who are worthy of your regard; men that are just and upright whose whole life is lived according to the law of God, not to those who are breaking it, and live unworthily. For if you look to these last you will draw from them only much that is evil; and fall into indifference to good, and into vanity, and you will be critical of others. But if you turn your attention to those whose lives are worthy; towards humility, towards loving earnestness, to compunction, you will be preparing for yourself a multitude of good things.

Hearken to what was said of the Pharisee who despised others, who were upright men, and saw only the sinner (Lk. xviii. 11). Hear and take warning! Behold how admirable was David in that he reverenced the just who went before him: *I am a stranger with thee, and a sojourner as all my fathers were* (Ps. xxxviii. 13). For he and such as are like unto

him turning away from sinners, regarded only men that were conspicuous for worthy living. So do you also. For you are not to sit as judge upon the crimes of others. You are commanded to judge yourself, not others: for *if we would judge ourselves, we should not be judged. But while we are judged by the Lord we are chastised* (I Cor. xi. 31, 32).

But you have perverted the right order of things when you exact no account from yourself for your own sins great and small, but instead search carefully into the sins of others. Make an end of this; and, putting from us this perversion of right order, let us set up a tribunal within ourselves, and become in it the accuser, the judge, and the punisher of our own crimes. But if you are still eager to investigate that which others may have done, then search not into their sins, but into their good actions: so that from the memory of our own evil-doing, and from the desire to imitate their good lives (and from the presence of an incorruptible Judge, each day goading the conscience onwards as with a spur)[6] we shall become more humble, and more earnest, and reach at length to the joy of eternal happiness through the grace and mercy of Our Lord Jesus Christ, to Whom with the Father and the Holy Ghost be honour and glory and empire for ever and ever. Amen.

III. St Gregory: On the Gospel[7]

Given to the People in the Basilica of the Blessed Laurence on Septuagesima Sunday

1. Many things need to be said in the explanation of this Gospel reading, which I wish, if I can, to set out briefly, lest you be wearied

both by the long-drawn out procession, and by a too prolonged explanation.[8] The kingdom of heaven is like to a man, a householder, who hires labourers to cultivate his vineyard. Who more truly resembles the householder than Our Creator, Who rules the world He has made, and governs His elect in this world, as a master cares for the subjects of his household? He too possesses a vineyard, namely, the Universal Church, which, from the time of just Abel until the last of the elect that shall be born at the end of the world, has brought forth as many saints, as it has sent forth shoots.

This Householder therefore, in the morning early, at the third hour, the sixth, the ninth, and the eleventh, hires labourers to till His Vineyard; because from the beginning of this world until the end He ceases not to gather together preachers to instruct the multitude of the faithful. For the morning of the world was from Adam to Noah: the third hour from Noah to Abraham: the sixth from Abraham to Moses: the ninth from Moses till the Coming of the Lord: the eleventh from the Lord's Coming till the end of the world. In which last hour the holy Apostles were sent as preachers, who, though they came late, yet received the full wage.

At no time therefore has the Lord failed to send workers to cultivate His Vineyard, which is to say, they instruct His people; as from the beginning by means of the Patriarchs, then the Doctors of the Law and the Prophets, and lastly by means of the Apostles, He has attended to the care of His Vineyard, when as it were by His labourers He has formed worthy dispositions in His people. The workers of the early morning, and of the third hour, the sixth, and the ninth, signify the ancient Jewish people, who, in their

elect have from the beginning of the world endeavoured to serve God in true belief, and have not as it were ceased to labour in the cultivation of the Vineyard. But at the eleventh hour the Gentiles were called, and it is to them it was said: *Why stand you here all the day idle?*

They who during so long a period of time had neglected to labour for their true life, have been standing *all the day idle*. But consider what they answered when questioned: *They say to him: because no man hath hired us*; since no Patriarch had come to them, and no Prophet. What does this mean: *No man hath hired us*, if not, that no man hath preached to us the way of true life? What excuse therefore shall we make for neglecting to do good, who have come almost from our mother's womb into the light of faith, who have heard the words of life from our cradle, who together with our mother's milk have drunk in heavenly teaching from the breasts of holy Church?

2. We may also see in these same varying hours the changing of the years in the life of every man. For the morning is the childhood of our reason. The third hour can be interpreted as adolescence, because while the heat of youth increases, it is as though the sun mounts higher in the sky. The sixth hour is young manhood, because as the sun is now as it were in its zenith, so now is the full strength of manhood attained. Mature age is signified by the ninth hour, in which the sun descends from its highest point, because in that age man already declines from the heat of youth. The eleventh hour is that time of life which is called senility or old age;

concerning which the Greeks are wont to describe those that are advanced in years, not simply as old men, but as *elders* (presbyters), that in this way they may show that they are more than old men who are regarded as advanced in years.

Because therefore one man is called to the good life in boyhood, another in youth, another in manhood, another in later life, another in old age, the labourers are as it were called at different hours to the Vineyard. Therefore, dearly Beloved Brethren, look to your manner of living, and see whether even now you are labourers of God. Let each one look to what he is doing, and let him consider whether or not he labours in the Vineyard of the Lord. For they who in this life seek the things that are their own, have not yet entered the Lord's Vineyard. For they work for the Lord who think upon the Master's gain and not upon their own; who serve Him with eagerness of love and the fervour of devotion; who are watchful to gain souls, and hasten to bring others with them to the true life. But he who lives for himself, who feeds on the pleasures of his own flesh, is rightly rebuked as idle, because he seeks not for the fruit of divine labour.

3. He that has failed till his latest years to live for God, has truly been standing idle till the eleventh hour. Whence was it rightly said to those who were inert till the eleventh hour: *Why stand you all the day idle?* As if he said openly to them: And if you have been unwilling to serve God in youth and in manhood, at least in your old age come to your senses, and though it is late come yet to the ways of true life, since

little time is left you wherein to labour. And such as these, therefore, the Householder calls to Him; and for the most part gives them their wage earlier, since they go forth from the body to His Kingdom earlier than those that appear to be called from their childhood. Did not the Good Thief come at the eleventh hour, though he came late, not through age but through punishment, and he confessed God from the cross, and almost with the words of his confession yielded up the breath of life. The Householder began indeed from the last to pay the *denarius* that was due, for even before Peter He leads the Thief into the repose of paradise.

How many Fathers were there before the Law, how many lived under the Law, and yet without any delay they entered the Kingdom who were called at the Coming of the Lord. They received who came at the eleventh hour that same wage which they desired with all their heart who had laboured from the first; because they who came to the Lord at the end of the world received the wage of eternal life equally with those who were called from the beginning of the world.

Because of this they who had preceded them in labour murmuring said: *These last have worked but one hour, and thou hast made them equal to us, that have borne the burden of the day and the heats.* They have borne the burthen of the day and the heats, because they to whom it befell to have lived from the beginning of the world, must also suffer more prolonged trials of the flesh. For to each one to bear the burthen of the day and the heats means, to be wearied by the heats of his own flesh throughout the days of a long life.

4. But you may ask how can it be said that they murmured who were called, though at evening time, to enter the Kingdom? For no one who murmurs enters the Kingdom, and no one murmurs who enters there. But because the Fathers, however justly they lived until the Coming of Our Lord, were not brought into the Kingdom until He had descended Who would open the gates of Paradise by the intervention of His death, they it was who murmured, because they had lived justly in order that they might enter the Kingdom, and yet they suffered long delay before they entered the Kingdom. It was they who had laboured in the Vineyard, and it was they who murmured, whom the abodes of hell, however peaceful, had received after their just lives. It was therefore, as it were after their murmuring, that they receive the *denarius*; they who after the long ages of hell reached at length the joys of the Kingdom. We however who have come at the eleventh hour, we murmur not after our labour, and we also receive the *denarius*, because coming into this world after the Coming of the Mediator, we are brought into the Kingdom almost as soon as we depart from our body; and we receive without any delay that which the ancient Fathers merited to receive after prolonged delay.

For which reason the Householder says: *I will give to this last as to thee.* And since to enter heaven is due to the goodness of His will, He rightly adds: *Is it not lawful for me to do what I will?* Foolish is the

questioning of man against the goodness of God. He should not complain if He does not give what He owes not, but if He does not give what is due. Whence He aptly questions: *Is thy eye evil because I am good?* Let no one exalt himself because of his work, or because of his time: for having completed the last sentence Truth then proclaims: *So shall the last be first, and the first last.* For though we know what or how much good we have done, we know not with what exactness the heavenly judge will weigh it. And it is certain that every man must greatly rejoice to be in the Kingdom of God at last.

5. But after these words, truly terrible is that which follows: *For many are called but few are chosen*: because they are many that arrive at faith, but few that are led into the heavenly kingdom. Behold how many are here gathered for this day's festival: we fill the church from wall to wall, yet who knows how few they are who shall be numbered in that chosen company of the elect? Behold the voices of all proclaim Christ, but the lives of all do not proclaim Him. And many keep company with God in word, but shun Him in deed. And it was with this in mind that Paul said: *They profess that they know God: but in their works they deny him* (Tit. i. 16). For this reason also James says: *That faith without good works is dead* (Jas. ii. 20, 26). And says the Lord Himself by the mouth of the psalmist: *I have declared and I have spoken: they are multiplied above numbers* (Ps. xxxix. 6). At the call of the Lord the faithful are multiplied without number, because not a few come also to faith

who do not belong to the elect. Here below they are mingled with the faithful, through confession, but because of their reprobate way of life they shall not merit to be partakers of the lot of the faithful. This sheepfold of the Church receives young goats with the lambs; but, as the Gospel bears witness, when the judge shall come, He shall separate the good from the bad, as the shepherd separates the sheep from the goats (Mt. xxv. 32).

Nor can they who are here slaves to the pleasures of their bodies, be there numbered in the flock of His sheep. There the judge shall separate from the lot of the humble those that now exalt themselves upon the horns of pride. Neither shall they receive a kingdom, who though formed in heavenly faith, with all their hearts seek the things of earth.

6. And within the Church, dearest Brethren, you will see many such persons, but you must neither imitate them, nor despair of them. What a man is today you can see, but what each one will be tomorrow no man knows. Often he that was seen to be behind us, has in his zeal in doing good come to outstrip us: and he whom today we excel, tomorrow we may scarce follow. We know indeed that while Stephen was dying for the faith, Saul held the garments of those that stoned him. Therefore did he by the hands of those who stoned also cast stones, since he encouraged them all to stone him. And yet this same person, within the holy Church, surpassed in labours the one whom, by persecuting him, he made a martyr.

Two things there are therefore upon which we should carefully reflect. Because many are called and but few chosen, the first is: let no one presume on his own salvation; for though he be called to faith, whether he is worthy of the eternal kingdom he knows not. The second is: let no one presume to despair of his neighbour, whom perhaps he sees lying in sin; for he knows not the riches of the divine mercy.

7. I shall now, Brethren, relate to you something which has happened recently, and if from your heart you look upon yourselves as sinners, you will then love yet more the omnipotent mercy of God. In this very year, in my monastery, which is situated close to the church of the blessed martyrs John and Paul, a certain brother, turned to repentance, entered the monastery, was devoutly accepted, and became himself yet more devoutly changed in life. His brother followed him into the monastery: in the flesh, not in the spirit. For though detesting the monastic dress, and the monastic life, he remained in the monastery as a guest; and he was unable to discontinue living there, though he shunned the life of the monks, because he had neither occupation nor the means to live.

His evil conduct was a burthen to all; yet all endured him with patience out of love for his brother. And though he knew not what followed after this present life, yet, arrogant and uncertain, he scoffed if anyone wished to instruct him in this. And so, flippant in speech, restless in movement, empty in mind, disorderly in dress, dissipated in behaviour, he lived on in the monastery, but in the dispositions of the world.

During the month of July last, he was stricken down in that epidemic of the pestilence that you remember; and as he was approaching his end he was urged to put his soul in order. The power of life now remained only in his heart and in his tongue, his extremities were already dead. The brethren stood by him, helping him in his end by their prayers, as far as God permitted. Suddenly, beholding the demon coming to take possession of him, he began to cry out in a loud voice, "Look, I am delivered over to the dragon to be devoured; but he cannot devour me because of your presence. Why do you delay me? Go away that he may finish me!"

And when the brethren exhorted him to sign himself with the sign of the Cross, he answered as well as he was able: "I want to bless myself but I cannot, because I am held fast by the dragon: my throat is held in his jaws, and the foam of his mouth has smeared my face. Look! My arms are imprisoned by him who has my head in his jaws!"

While he was saying this, trembling, pale, and dying, the brethren began ever more earnestly to pray for him, to help by their intercession this man here tormented by the presence of an evil spirit. Then of a sudden he was delivered, and began to cry out aloud, "thanks be to God. See, he has gone, he has fled: the dragon who already had me in his grip, has fled before your prayers." There and then he vowed to serve God, and to become a monk; but from that moment until now he lies oppressed by fever and

weakened by pain. He was truly snatched from death, yet not fully restored to life. For he is afflicted by tedious infirmities, and tormented with grievous weakness: the severe fire of purification burning away the hardness of his heart; for it has pleased divine Providence that prolonged illness shall cleanse him of even more prolonged habits of evil-doing.

Who would have believed that this man would have been preserved and converted? Who can fathom the so great depths of the mercy of God? An evil-living young man sees in death the evil spirit he has served in life; nor did he see him that being brought down he might lose his life, but that he might learn who it was that held him in bondage, and knowing might resist him, and resisting would overcome him; and he saw him by whom, unseen, he was held a slave, that he might afterwards be free.

What tongue can speak of the bowels of the divine mercy? What soul is not awed at the richness of the divine kindness? It was this treasure of the divine mercy the psalmist had in mind when he said: *Unto thee, O my Helper, will I sing, for thou art God my defence; My God My mercy* (Ps. lviii. 18). Here reflecting on the labours of which man's life is made up, he calls God his helper. And because He lifts us out of present tribulation into eternal peace, he calls Him also his defence. But remembering that He sees our evil-doing, and suffers it in patience, that He is unmindful of our offences, and with all this brings us through repentance to final reward, he wished not to say that God was merciful, but called

Him mercy itself, saying: *My God my mercy.*

Let us keep before our minds the evil we have done: and let us think of the great kindness with which we are suffered in patience; and let us consider what are the deep sources of the mercy of God, that not alone forgives our offences, but having forgiven our sins, promises an eternal kingdom to those that repent of evil-doing. And from the depths of every heart let us cry out, let us all together cry: *My God my mercy,* Who livest and reignest, Three in One, and One in Three, for ever and ever. Amen.

NOTES

[1] PG 13, 1337–1362.

[2] Παραπλήσιος.

[3] This is a reference to the error, attributed to him, of an end to the punishment of the damned; according to BPC.

[4] Souls separated from their bodies are not idle; but they neither merit nor demerit, as Origen elsewhere clearly teaches.

[5] PG 58, 612–618, hom. 64 in Mt.

[6] The words within brackets are, according to some authorities, opposed to the sense and structure of the homily, and are not found in all codices.

[7] PL 76, 1153–1159.

[8] A reference to the great procession of people, clergy, and pontiff, which about this time began to mark the celebration of the Holy Sacrifice at "Stational" churches.

SEXAGESIMA SUNDAY

I. St John Chrysostom: On Temperance

II. St Cyril of Alexandria: On the Gospel

III. St Gregory the Great: Christian Moderation

THE GOSPEL OF THE SUNDAY

Luke viii. 4–15

At that time: when a very great multitude was gathered together, and hastened out of the cities unto Him, He spoke by a similitude. The sower went out to sow his seed. And as he sowed some fell by the wayside, and it was trodden down, and the fowls of the air devoured it. And other some fell upon a rock: and as soon as it was sprung up, it withered away, because it had no moisture. And other some fell among thorns, and the thorns growing up with it, choked it. And other some fell upon good ground; and being sprung up, yielded fruit a hundredfold. Saying these things, He cried out: he that hath ears to hear, let him hear. And His Disciples asked Him what this parable might be. To whom He said: to you it is given to know the mystery of the kingdom of God; but to the rest in parables, that 'seeing they may not see, and hearing may not understand. Now the parable is this: the seed is the word of God. And they by the wayside are they that hear; then the devil cometh, and taketh the word out of their heart, lest believing they should be saved. Now they upon the rock, are they who when they hear, receive the word with joy: and these have no roots; for they believe for a while, and in time of temptation, they fall away. And that which fell among thorns, are they who have heard, and going their way, are choked with the cares and riches and pleasures of this life, and yield no fruit. But that on the good ground, are they who in a good and perfect heart, hearing the word, keep it, and bring forth fruit in patience.

PARALLEL GOSPELS

Matthew xiii. 1–9

The same day Jesus going out of the house, sat by the sea side. And great multitudes were gathered together unto Him, so that He went

Matthew xiii. 18–23

Hear you therefore the parable of the sower. When any one heareth the word of the kingdom, and understandeth it not, there cometh up into a boat and sat: and all the multitude stood on the shore. And He spoke to them many things in parables, saying: Behold the sower went forth to sow. And whilst he soweth some fell by the way side, and the birds of the air came and ate them up. And other some fell upon stony ground, where they had not much earth: and they sprung up immediately, because they had no deepness of earth. And when the sun was up they were scorched: and because they had not root, they withered away. And others fell among thorns: and the thorns grew up and choked them. And others fell upon good ground and they brought forth fruit, some an hundred fold, some sixtyfold, and some thirtyfold. He that hath ears to hear, let him hear.

the wicked one, and catcheth away that which was sown in his heart: this is he that received the seed by the way side. And he that received the seed upon stony ground, is he that heareth the word, and immediately receiveth it with joy. Yet hath he not root in himself, but is only for a time: and when there ariseth tribulation and persecution because of the word, he is presently scandalised. And he that receiveth the seed among thorns, is he that heareth the word, and the care of this world and the deceitfulness of riches choketh up the word, and he becometh fruitless. But he that received the seed upon good ground, is he that heareth the word, and understandeth, and beareth fruit, and yieldeth the one an hundredfold, and another sixty, and another thirty.

MARK iv. 1–9

And again He began to teach by the sea side; and a great multitude was gathered together unto Him, so that He went up into a ship, and sat in the sea; and all the multitude was upon the land by the sea side. And He taught them many things in parables, and said unto them in His doctrine: Hear ye: Behold, the sower went out to sow. And whilst he sowed, some fell by the way side, and the birds of the air came and ate it up. And other some fell upon stony ground, where it had not much earth; and it shot up immediately, because it had no depth of earth. And when the sun was risen, it was scorched; and because it had no root, it withered away. And some fell among thorns, and the thorns grew up, and choked it, and it yielded no fruit. And some fell upon good ground; and

MARK iv. 13–20

And He saith to them: are you ignorant of this parable? And how shall you know all parables? He that soweth, soweth the word. And these are they by the way side, where the word is sown, and as soon as they have heard, immediately Satan cometh, and taketh away the word that was sown in their hearts. And these likewise are they that are sown on the stony ground: who when they have heard the word, immediately receive it with joy. And they have no root in themselves, but are only for a time: and then when tribulation and persecution ariseth for the word, they are presently scandalised. And others there are who are sown among thorns: these are they that hear the word, and the cares of the world, and the deceitfulness of riches, and the lusts after other things entering brought forth fruit that grew up, increased and yielded, one thirty, another sixty, and another a hundred. And He said: He that hath ears to hear, let him hear.

in choke the word, and it is made fruitless. And these are they who are sown upon the good ground, who hear the word, and receive it, and yield fruit, the one thirty, another sixty, and another a hundred.

EXPOSITION FROM THE CATENA AUREA

THEOPHYLACTUS, *in hoc loco*: That which David had foretold, speaking in the person of Christ: *I will open my mouth in parables*, the Lord here fulfils; hence is it said: *And when a very great multitude was gathered together, and hastened out of the cities unto him, He spoke by a similitude.* The Lord speaks in parables, in the first place so as the better to secure the attention of his listeners; for men are wont to be drawn to things that are obscure, and turn from what is readily obvious to the mind; in the second place so that those who were unworthy might not comprehend that which was mystically unfolded.

ORIGEN, *in Catena G.P.*: And therefore is it significantly recorded: *When a very great multitude was gathered together*; for they are few, not many, who enter in at the narrow gate, and find the strait way that leads to life eternal (Mt. vii. 14). Hence Matthew says, that *outside* He taught in parables, but that *when He came into the house* He expounded them to His Disciples. EUSEBIUS, *in Catena G.P.*: Fittingly did Christ speak the first parable to the multitude, not alone of those who were standing about Him, but to all who in the future would come after them; awakening their minds to attend to His words, when He said: *The sower went out to sow his seed.*

BEDE, *in Lucam*: We can imagine no greater sower than the Son of God, Who, coming forth from the bosom of the Father, to which no creature hath access, enters this world to give testimony of truth.

CHRYSOSTOM, *Hom. 45 in Matt.*: He went forth Who is everywhere, yet unconfined in space, and came to us in the garment of our flesh. Christ aptly speaks of His approach to us as a going forth; for we were shut out from God, as those who are condemned and rebellious are cast forth by a king. But he that wishes to reconcile them to the king, going forth, speaks with them outside the kingdom. Then they being made worthy he brings them into the royal presence. Thus did Christ also act.

THEOPHYLACTUS: He goes forth now, not to kill labourers, or lay waste fields, but to show His seed. EUSEBIUS: There were others that came forth from the heavenly home and came down among men, not however that they might sow, for they were not sowers, but spirits who were sent as governors. Even Moses and the prophets who came after him did not sow the mysteries of the kingdom of God in the minds of men, but from afar they prepared their souls, withdrawing the foolish from the folly of their error, and from the worship of idols, and got ready the ground for the sowing. The Word of God is alone the Sower of all things, Who shall announce the New Seed, namely, the mysteries of the kingdom of heaven.

THEOPHYLACTUS: The Son of God ceases not to sow the word of God in our soul; for not alone when He teaches, but even when He creates us, He sows good seed in our hearts. TITUS: He went forth that He might sow His own seed; since He spoke not borrowed words, for of His own nature He is the Word of the Living God. The seed sown by Paul, or by John, is not their own; they have it because they received it. The seed Christ possesses is His own; He utters wisdom that is of His very nature. Hence the Jews declared: *How did this man know letters, having never learned?* (Jn. vii. 15).

EUSEBIUS: He teaches therefore that there are two degrees among the receivers of the seed. First, they who were made worthy of their heavenly vocation, but because of sloth and neglect fell from grace. The second kind are those who have multiplied the seed with abundance of fruit. He lays down according to Matthew three kinds in each degree. For they who spoil the seed do not all do so in the same way; and they who bring forth fruit do not all receive in equal measure. The seed reveals the actions of those that lose it. For there are some who, without having sinned, lose the implanted life-giving seed within their own souls: for it becomes hidden from their mind and memory by evil spirits and demons, who fly through the air, or also by deceitful lying men, whom He here calls *fowls of the air.*

The Gospel continues: *And as he sowed, some fell by the way side.* THEOPHYLACTUS: He does not say that in sowing the seed the sower cast it by the way side, but He says that *some fell.* For He Who is sowing preaches true doctrine: but His words fall with varying effect among His hearers; as some of them are called a *way side. And it was trodden down, and the fowls of the air devoured it.*

CYRIL, *Catena G.F.*: For they are dry and untilled as is every way side; for it is trodden on by everyone, and nothing of this seed is buried therein. So to those who have an unteachable heart the divine counsel does not enter in, to grow unto the praise of virtue: rather such are as a *way side* that is haunted by unclean spirits. Some there are who hold the faith lightly within them, as though it were a matter of words; their faith lacks root, and concerning such as these He goes on: *And other some fell upon a rock: and as soon as it was sprung up, it withered away, because it had no moisture.*

BEDE: A heart that is hard and stubborn He calls a rock. What is here spoken of as moisture for the root of the seed, in another parable is called the oil that is to nourish the virgins' lamps, namely: love, and perseverance in virtue. EUSEBIUS: There are some who because of their greed and appetite for pleasure, and because of their earthly cares, which here are called thorns, cause the seed that is sown among them to be smothered; and of these He says: *And some other fell among thorns, and the thorns growing up with it, choked it.*

CHRYSOSTOM, as above: For as the thorns do not let the young wheat grow up, but, pressing against them, smother the growing shoots, so do the cares of this present life prevent the spiritual seed from coming to fruit. A farmer would be chided who would sow seed among thorns, and upon rock, and upon the way side. For it is not possible for rock to become earth, or for a road to cease to be a road, or for thorns to cease to be thorns. But it is otherwise with reasoning beings. For here it is possible for rock to be changed into good earth, and for a way to cease to be trodden on, and for thorns to be rooted out.

CYRIL, in *Catena G.P.*: Rich and fertile earth is the good and honest souls who receive deep within them the seed of the Word, and keep it, and nourish it. And regarding such as these there is added: *And other some fell upon good ground, and being sprung up, yielded fruit a hundredfold.* When the divine word is infused into a soul that is freed from every disorder, it there takes deep root, bringing forth as it were ears of corn, and is thus brought to the desired end. BEDE: Perfect fruit He calls *fruit a hundredfold.* For the denary number is always accepted as the number of perfection; for the observance of the Law is contained within ten precepts. Ten multiplied by itself is a hundred: so by a hundred great perfection is signified.

CYRIL: What the parable means we learn from Him Who composed it; hence follows: *Saying these things, he cried out: He that hath ears to hear, let him hear.* BASIL, in *Catena G.P.*: To hear relates to the intellect. So by this saying He arouses their interest so that they attend to what is being said.

BEDE: As often as this admonition is inserted in the Gospel or in the Apocalypse of John, it is indicated to us that what is said is something mystical, and that we are to seek carefully the meaning of it. Accordingly, the Disciples, not understanding Him, ask the Saviour; for there follows: *And his disciples asked him what this parable might be.* No one is to imagine that as soon as the parable was spoken the Disciples put their question, but only *when,* as Mark says, *He was alone, the twelve asked him* (Mk. iv. 10).

ORIGEN: A parable is a discourse about something as though it had happened, which nevertheless, though it is possible, has not happened in reality, and signifying certain things by their analogy with the things spoken of in the parable. An enigma is a form of speech in which certain things are related as facts, which however have neither taken place, nor can take place, but which yet signify something hidden; as was said in the Book of Judges: *The trees went to anoint a king over them* (Judg. ix. 8). What is here written did not actually take place, namely, that a sower *went out to sow his seed,* yet it was possible for it to happen.

EUSEBIUS: The Lord did teach them why He spoke to the multitudes in parables. For there is added: *To you it is given to know the mystery of the kingdom; but to the rest in parables.* GREGORY NAZIANZEN: When you hear this, do not begin to invent different natures, like certain heretics, who are of opinion that the one are of a ruined, the others of a sound nature; that some are so constituted that their own will leads them either to what is good or what is bad. But add to this the words: *To you it is given*; that is, to those who are willing, and plainly worthy.

THEOPHYLACTUS: But to those who are not worthy of such mysteries, they were spoken in a veiled manner; so there follows: *But to the rest in parables, that seeing they may not see, and hearing may not understand.* They think they hear, but they do not; they do hear, but they understand not all. Christ concealed His meaning from them for this reason, lest a greater peril be made for them, if having understood the teaching of Christ they should despise it. For he that has understood it, and then rejected it, shall be punished more severely.

BEDE: Rightly therefore are they instructed in parables, since the ears of their hearts being closed, they give no thought to learning the truth, unmindful of what the Lord had said: *He that hath ears to hear, let him hear.* GREGORY, *Hom.* 15 *in Evang.*: The Lord deigned to explain to them what He had been saying, so that we may learn to ask the meaning of those things also which He has willed not to explain. For he continues: *Now the parable is this: The seed is the word of God.*

EUSEBIUS: He says that there are three causes that destroy the seed implanted in the souls of men. For some destroy the seed buried within themselves, lightly giving ear to those who seek to deceive them; of

whom He says: *And they by the wayside are they that hear: then the devil cometh, and taketh the word out of their heart, lest believing they should be saved.* BEDE: They, namely, who do not consider the word which they hear as being worthy of any belief, any understanding, or of using to any profit.

EUSEBIUS: Some, since they have not received the word of God deeply into their souls, are easily overcome when adversity arises: of whom He goes on to say: *Now they upon the rock, are they who when they hear, receive the word with joy: and these have no roots; for they believe for a while, and in time of temptation, they fall away.* CYRIL: For these when they enter a Church, joyfully take part in the divine mysteries, but without a serious mind, so when they are outside the church again they forget about the sacred rites. And while the Christian faith is left in peace, they will remain with us: but should persecution arise, they will not stand fast, because their faith lacks root.

GREGORY: Many make a start upon some good work, but speedily grow weary, because of temptations and tribulations, and abandon what they have begun. The rocky ground had not therefore the moisture whereby to bring to fruition that which it had germinated. EUSEBIUS: Some smother the seed implanted with them, through riches and pleasures, as though smothering it among thorns; of whom He says: *And that which fell among thorns, are they who have heard, and going their way, are choked with the cares and pleasures and riches of this life, and yield no fruit.*

GREGORY: It is remarkable how the Lord interprets thorns as meaning riches, since the first wound, while the latter delight. Yet thorns they are, because they wound the mind with the stings of anxiety: and since they lead men on to sin, they stain, as with the blood of a wound received. There are two things which He links with riches: cares, and pleasures; because riches oppress the mind through care, and undo it through abundance. They choke the seed, because they strangle the throat of the mind with burthensome thoughts; and as long as they keep good desires from entering the mind, they as it were shut out the life-giving air.

EUSEBIUS: These things were described by the Saviour from foreknowledge. For events have shown that so it was to be. For not otherwise have some men fallen away from faith than in one or other of the ways which He foretold.

CHRYSOSTOM: That I may put many things in a few words: some hear His words carelessly; some are soft and weak; and some, becoming slaves of their appetites and of the things of this world, fall from goodness. The succession of *way side*, and *rock*, and *thorns*, is good; for there is need in the first place of remembering, and of caution; then we need fortitude; lastly, indifference to the things of the present. Finally He describes the *good ground* as the very opposite of the *way side*, or the *rock*, or the *thorns*, when He goes on: *But that on the good ground, are they who in a good and perfect heart, hearing the word, keep it, and bring forth fruit in patience.* For they who are by the way side do *not keep* the word, for the devil steals it from them; they who are on rocky ground, do not ensure *in patience* the onset of temptation, since they are weak: they who are among thorns bear no fruit and *are choked.*

GREGORY: Through patience therefore the good ground yields fruit; because the good we do is undone, unless we also bear in patience the evil-doing of our neighbour. Through patience therefore is it that men bear fruit, because when tribulations are humbly endured, after tribulation they are received on high with joy, into eternal rest.

I. ST JOHN CHRYSOSTOM, BISHOP AND DOCTOR

On Temperance[1]

The Sower went out to sow his seed. What is the meaning of this parable? He went out to sow His seed. From where did He go out, Who is present everywhere, and fills all places? He went out, not into a place, but into a life and into a dispensation of things wherein He saved us, being brought close to us, by reason of becoming clothed in our flesh. Since we could not enter in, for our sins had shut the door to us, He came out to us. And why did He come out? Was it to destroy the earth that brought forth thorns? To punish the husbandmen? No. He came to till and to take care of the earth: to sow the word of compassion. For here He calls His teaching seed; the souls of men a ploughed field; and Himself the Sower.

What happened to this seed? Three amounts of it were lost and one saved. *And as He sowed, some fell by the way side, and was trodden down, and the fowls of the air devoured it.* He does not say that He threw it, but that if *fell. And other some fell upon a rock: and as soon as it was sprung up, it withered away, because it had no moisture. And other some fell among thorns, and the thorns growing up with it, choked it. And other some fell upon good ground; and being sprung up, yielded fruit a hundredfold, and some sixty, and some thirty. He that hath ears to hear, let him hear.*

A fourth portion is saved: and this again not in equal measure, for here there is a greater variation. He speaks in this manner to show that He is teaching all men alike, without any distinction. For as the sower makes no distinction in his field, but scatters his seed broadcast, so neither does He distinguish between rich and poor, between wise or unwise, the slothful or the diligent, the courageous or the timid, but addresses His words to all; fulfilling what was His to do, though He foreknew that which was to come to pass: that He might be able to say: *What is there that I ought to do more to my vineyard that I have not done to it?* (Is. v. 4). For the Prophets spoke of their people as a vineyard. For Isaias says: *My beloved had a vineyard in a fruitful place*; and says the psalmist: *Thou hast brought a vineyard out of Egypt* (Ps. lxxix. 9).

But here He speaks only of seed. What does this mean? That obedience will now be more easy, more prompt, and will bring forth more speedily. When you hear that *the sower went out to sow his seed,* do not regard this as expressing the same idea twice; for the sower often goes forth for other reasons, such as to plough his fields, to kill weeds, to uproot the thorns, and for similar reasons. But here the sower went out to sow his seed.

But why, tell me, is the greater part of the seed lost? Because of the earth that receives it, not because of the sower. It was because of the soul that heeded not. And why then does He not say: the careless received the remaining seed, and lost it; the rich, and they choked it; the self-indulgent, and they betrayed it? He did not wish to reprove them sharply, lest He throw them into despair but left the reflection to the consciences of those who would hear Him. He permitted this, not alone in the figure, of the seed, but also in that of the net. For that too yielded many that were unprofitable. But He desired in this parable to form and to educate His disciples, so that should many of those who would receive the preaching of the Apostles be lost, they should not lose heart. For this happened also to their Teacher; Who, though knowing what was yet to be, ceased not from sowing.

But, you may say, what sense can there be in sowing among thorns and upon rock, and upon the wayside? As to seeds, and to the earth, there is no sense. But in the cultivating of men's souls, and in their instruction, it has much to commend it. A farmer would rightly be reproved for doing this; for rock cannot become earth, nor a way cease to be a way, nor can thorns cease to be thorns. But in the things of the mind it is far otherwise. For the rock can be changed, and become rich and fruitful soil; and the way may cease to be trampled on, and to lie open to all that comes, and become a fertile field. Thorns can be uprooted, and the young plants, being freed of them, allowed to come to maturity. For unless this could be, He would not have sown.

That this transformation has not taken place in all is not the fault of the Sower, but of those who were unwilling to be changed. He has done His part, and if they have wasted the seed they received from Him, He that has shown such goodness, in this also is without blame. But note with me that the way of destruction is not one only, but manifold, and each one differs from the rest. For they that are like to the *way side* are the depraved, the slothful, and the indifferent. They that are compared to the *rock* are those that fall from weakness alone, for He says: *some fell upon a rock, and as soon as it was sprung up it withered away*, or refers to *he that heareth the word, and immediately received it with joy, yet hath he no root . . . etc.* (Mt. xiii. 20). Now it is not the same thing, that the word of doctrine should wither, when no one is either tempting or persecuting you, as when a man is under the pressure of temptations. They that resemble the thorns are less worthy of forgiveness than these last.

Lest we suffer any of these things, let us bury safe in our memory what has been taught to us. For though the devil may steal it, we are the masters as to whether or not he shall steal. And if the young shoots of the wheat wither, that is not because of the heat, for He did not say that it withered because of the heat, but *because it had no roots*. And if that which He has taught us is choked, neither is it the fault of the thorns,

but of those who allow them to grow. For you can, if you will, oppose their evil growth, and make fitting use of your wealth. For this reason He says: not *the world*, but: *the care of this world*; not *riches*, but *the deceitfulness of riches*. Let us put blame, not on created things, but on the corrupted will.

For it is possible to be rich, and not to be deceived by riches; to be in this world, and not to be oppressed by its cares. For the rich man has two opposing disadvantages; the one: care, wearying and overclouding the mind; the other: luxury, making it soft. Rightly therefore does he speak of *the deceitfulness of riches*, for all that pertains to riches is a deceit to man. For they are but a name, merely, and not something inherent in the things themselves. Similarly pleasure, and praise, and the love of display, and all such things, are a sort of make believe, not the reality of things.

When He had spoken of the various ways of destruction, He then speaks of *the good earth*, so as not to allow them to become despondent; giving them the hope of a change of heart, and showing them how they can turn away from the paths now mentioned, to this one. And if the earth be rich and fruitful, and if the Sower be one, and the Seed the same, for what reason, therefore, have some brought forth fruit a hundredfold, and some sixty and other thirty? Here obviously the difference depends upon the nature of the earth; and even where the ground is good, there is a great variety here likewise. You see then that the Sower is not the cause of this, nor the seed, but the earth which receives it. The difference therefore arises not from our nature, but from our will. Observe here the divine goodness, which does not expect from all an equal measure of perfection, but cheerfully receives those that are the first, likewise those that come second, and for those that are third He also finds a place. All this He said, so that those who were listening to Him, might not think that merely to listen sufficed for salvation.

And why, you may ask, did he not mention the other vices, such as the desires of the body, and vanities of various kinds? In saying *the cares of the world*, and *the deceitfulness of riches*, He recounted all of them. For both vain glory and all the other things, are a part of the care of this world, and pertain to the *deceitfulness of riches*. Such are pleasure, gluttony, envy, vanity and all similar things. But He added both the *way side* and the *rock*, showing that it is not sufficient to free ourselves from the cares of riches, but that we must also cultivate the remainder of justice. For what if you are free of riches, if at the same time you are worthless and weak? And if you be not worthless in character, what if you are neglectful and contemptuous of listening to the word? For not one part of justice alone suffices for salvation; for first we must listen carefully; then be constantly mindful of what we hear; then steadfast in courage; then possess contempt of riches, and detachment from the things of the present life.

He put in the first place, careful attention to the word: then the other things; because this is the first task: *How shall they believe him, of whom they have not heard?* (Rom. x. 14). And we also unless we pay careful attention to what has been taught to us, shall not learn what it is that we must do. He places next, courage of soul; and after this detachment from the things of the present life.

Hearing all this, let us strengthen ourselves in every direction: attending to what He teaches, sending down deep the roots of our faith, and clean ourselves from worldliness. But should we do but one of the things He has taught us, and forget the rest, then we shall gain nothing. For if we do not lose ourselves in that way, we shall then in some other way. And what difference does it make should we lose our soul, not through riches, but through sloth; and if not through sloth, then because of sensuality. For the farmer grieves whether he loses the good seed by this means or that. Neither let us comfort ourselves that we shall not lose our souls by any one of these means; rather let us be in fear of losing our souls by any means whatever.

Let us burn the thorns that choke the word. And let certain rich persons be mindful of this: that those who are worthless in this respect, are the same in regard to other things. For being slaves and captives to pleasures, they are without value also in public or civic affairs; and if valueless in this respect, how much more unprofitable are they in the things of God? For a twofold defilement has entered into their minds: that of softness, and that of care; either of which is sufficient to sink the boat; and when both join together, then how mightily do the waves mount up?

Wonder not that He should call wantonness thorns. You that are intoxicated with passion will not

understand this; but they that are
free of it, know that it pierces more
sharply than thorns; that all self-
indulgence wounds the soul, even
more than care, and causes more
grief, to body as well as soul. For
no one is wounded more by care
than by bodily excess. And when
sleeplessness, and throbbing of the
head and temples, and torments of
the body, have fast hold of you,
think then how much more deeply
than thorns it wounds.

And as thorns, however you may
grasp them, draw blood from the
hand that seizes them, so likewise
does self-indulgence injure the
hands and the feet and the head and
the eyes and all the members. And
it withers the body, making it like
to the thorn, and unfruitful; and
hurts far more sharply than the
thorn, and in a manner more vital.
It brings old age before its time. It
dulls the senses, and puts a darkness
upon the mind. The intelligence
that was clear becomes clouded. It
slackens the whole body, and increases only the store of the body's
waste, multiplying our miseries,
making the burthen of life too
heavy, the load too great, so that
our falls are frequent, and our misfortunes multiplied.

Why then, will you tell me, why
then do you fatten the body? Are
we going to offer you in sacrifice?
Are you being prepared for the
table? Rightly do you fatten birds;
and even them not too much, for
when they are too fat they are
worthless as healthy food. So great
a perversion is gluttony, that the
evil of it is shown even in the brutes.
For in them excessive fat is worthless, and from this grossness there
arises only a moist rottenness.
Animals that are not fed in this

way, but as it were live sparingly,
are profitable both to themselves
and to us, for food and for other
uses. They who live on them are
healthier. They who eat the other
kind become like them, becoming
dull and sickly, and bearing a
heavier halter. For nothing is so
injurious, nothing so damaging, to
the body as self-indulgence; nothing so rends it asunder, overloads
it, corrodes it, as profligacy.

The folly of men in this regard is
truly astonishing; that they should
treat themselves with less regard
than others have for their wine-
skins. For the wine-sellers do not
allow the skins to be filled more
than is right, lest they burst. But
the self-indulgent do not regard
their own miserable bodies as
worthy of such consideration, but
when they have already been filled
and distended, they fill them yet
more, to the very ears, to the nostrils, to the throat, with wine; in-
flicting a double strain, upon the
soul, and upon the power that
governs the active living body.
Was it this thy throat was given to
thee, that by means of it you might
be filled to the very mouth with
wine and with other corruptions?
No! Not for this, O Man, but that
you may above all things else give
praise to God, that you use it in
holy prayers, that you may proclaim His holy laws, and that you
may give to your neighbour the
aid of your counsel.

But you put it not at all to this
sacred use, but, as though it were
bestowed upon you for this alone,
you degrade it throughout your
life to a vile servitude. As if a man
receiving a lyre, with strings of
gold and wondrously made, instead of awakening it to the sweetest

music, should cover it with dung and mire. I use the word dung, not of plain living, but of wanton living and licentiousness. For that which is over and above what is needful is no longer nourishment but poison.

The stomach was given for the reception of food alone; but the mouth, the throat, the tongue, for purposes that are still more necessary; and indeed the stomach was given not simply for the reception of food, but for the reception of moderate food. And this it shows clearly by complaining when injured through excess. Nor does it merely complain; it avenges the injury, and exacts severe punishment. First it punishes the feet that sustain and guide it to the evil festivities: then the hands that ministered to it so many and such a variety of delights. How many have through this cause disfigured their own mouths, their eyes, their heads? And just as a servant who receives commands that are beyond his power to obey, will, becoming desperate, sometimes turn on the one who orders him; so too the stomach, because of being strained to excess, will turn and rend and destroy, not alone the members of the body, but even the governing brain.

And God Himself has fittingly decreed that excesses should be visited with such grievous punishment, so that, since of your own will you were not temperate, you would learn to be temperate in spite of your will, through the fear of such a dreadful end. Since we know these things, let us turn away from all self-indulgence. Let us take thoughts and strive to learn moderation, so that we may enjoy health in our bodies, and deliver our souls from sickness; that we may come to the enjoyment of the future happiness of heaven by the grace and love of Our Lord Jesus Christ, to Whom be glory and honour, now and for ever. Amen.

II. ST CYRIL: ON THE GOSPEL[2]

The blessed prophets have spoken in various ways concerning Christ; for they foretold He was the Light that was to come; some proclaimed He was endowed with royal dignity and excellence. And a certain one among them has said: *Blessed is he that hath seed in Sion, and friends in Jerusalem. Behold a king shall reign, and princes have preceded him with judgement. And he shall be a man that hides his words, and he shall hide himself as from water rushing down* (Is. xxxi. 9; xxxii. 1, 2). That the words of the Saviour were for the most part hidden is plain to us. It is so that the psalmist also brings Him speaking before us: *I will open my mouth in parables* (Ps. lxxvii. 2).

Now you may see that what was foretold has come to pass. For a great multitude stood about Him, gathered from all Judea, to whom He spoke, and in parables; but since they were unworthy to understand the mysteries of heaven His words were obscure to them. Neither had they the will to believe in Christ: more, they blasphemously opposed His teaching. And for this reason they also began to denounce those that followed Him, impiously declaring: *He hath a devil, and is mad: why hear you Him?*

Accordingly, it was not *given to*

them, to know the mysteries of the kingdom of heaven; but to us who are ready to believe, it has been given. For he has given us *to understand a parable, and the interpretation; the words of the wise, and their mysterious sayings* (Prov. i. 6). We must also tell you that parables are as it were images, not of visible things, but rather of things of the mind and of the spirit. That which cannot be seen with the eyes of the body, a parable will reveal to the eyes of the mind, informing the subtlety of the intellect by means of things perceivable by the senses, and as it were tangible. Let us see of what kind is the enlightenment the word of the Lord prepares for us.

What is the scope of this parable, and what its hidden profundity aims at, let us learn from the One' composing it. For even before our time the blessed Disciples did not grasp its meaning, and they came to the Saviour, asking Him: *What this parable might be?* Let us consider the reason why the seed on the *way side* was seized. A way side is almost always hard and unbroken, because it is trodden on by the feet of all who pass, and seed is never sown there. Into whosoever therefore that have minds that are hard and unyielding, no divine or sacred word will enter, by whose aid the joyful fruits of virtue might grow. Men of this kind are a highway that is trodden by unclean spirits, and by Satan himself, and they shall never be yielders of holy fruit, because their hearts are sterile and unfruitful.

Again there are others who carry the faith indifferently within them, a faith that is simply a matter of words. They have a religion that is without root; for entering a church they take a delight in seeing so many assembled there, and they readily take part in the sacred mysteries; but they do so from no serious purpose, and from a certain levity of will. And when they go out of the churches such people straightaway consign to forgetfulness the holy teachings. And as long as Christians are left in peace, they keep the faith; but should persecution arise, they will be of a mind to seek safety in flight. To such as these the prophet Jeremiah says: *Prepare ye the shield and buckler, and go forth to battle* (Jer. xlvi. 3). For the hand of the Lord our Defender cannot indeed be overcome; as the most learned Paul says: *God is faithful, who will not suffer you to be tempted above that which you are able: but will make also with temptation issue, that you may be able to bear it* (I Cor. x. 15).

Yet if it should happen that we must endure suffering for the sake of the religion of Jesus Christ, then in every way and everywhere we are blessed. For the Saviour has said to the holy Apostles: *Be not afraid of them who kill the body, and are not able to kill the soul* (Mt. x. 28). And this lesson He gave us, not by words alone, but by deeds. For He laid down His own life for us, and repurchased all men by His blood. We are therefore not our own possession: we are His Who purchased us, and redeemed us, to Whom we owe our life. For as the holy Paul has said: *To this end Christ died and rose again; that He might be Lord both of the dead and of the living* (Rom. xiv. 9).

Let us consider next, what do the thorns mean, by which the divine seed is choked? What does the

Saviour say here? For it is He that scatters the seed which, remaining in the ground of the souls of those that receive it, and being absorbed by them, and beginning to put forth shoots, is choked by the cares of this world, and as Jeremiah says, becomes *a bud that shall yield no meal.*[3] *Break up anew,* says another prophet, *your fallow ground, and sow not upon thorns* (Jer. iv. 3). Therefore, that the divine seed may germinate in us, let us first drive forth from our minds all worldly cares.

They are rich and fruitful soil who yield fruit a hundredfold; and good and beautiful are the souls that take deeply into themselves the seeds of the Word, and keep them, and tend them with care. Of these it may be said, as was said by the Lord by the mouth of one of the prophets: *And all nations shall call you blessed: for you shall be a delightful land, saith the Lord of hosts* (Mal. iii. 12). For when the divine word falls upon a soul purified of the things that afflicted it, then it takes deep root, and comes forth as an ear of corn, and yields fruit abundantly.

I consider that this also will profit those seeking what is profitable. For Matthew when also relating this parable tells us, that the *good ground* brought forth fruit in three different degrees. For he says: *Some brought forth fruit an hundredfold, some sixtyfold, and some thirtyfold* (Mt. xiii. 8). Note that Christ has recounted three ways of disaster, and that three likewise are the grades of glory. For the seed that fell upon the *way side* was seized by the birds. That which sprang up on *stony ground* quickly perished. That which grew amid *the thorns* was choked. But the desirable *good earth* brought forth fruit, and with a threefold difference, as I have said; some *a hundredfold,* some *sixty,* and some *thirtyfold.*

As the most learned Paul writes: *Everyone hath his proper gift from God; one after this manner, another after that* (I Cor. vii. 7). And we do not find the good actions of holy men to be all of equal merit. But it behoves us to strive earnestly after their better actions, and rise above the less worthy: so shall we be rewarded bountifully by Christ, to Whom, with the Father, and the Holy Ghost, be praise and glory for ever. Amen.

III. St Gregory: Christian Moderation[4]

Given to the People in the Basilica of Blessed Paul on Sexagesima Sunday

1. The lesson of the holy Gospel, Dearly Beloved Brethren, which you have heard, requires not an exposition but a friendly warning. Let human frailty not presume to explain what the divine Truth has made clear. But you should carefully reflect, that if in this Sunday exposition I had presumed to say to you, that the seed signified the word of God, that the field signified the world, that the birds signified the demons, and the thorns riches, your minds would have hesitated to believe us.

And so the Lord Himself has deigned to explain the meaning of what He said, so that you may earn to seek the meaning in those things which He has not willed to explain. In explaining here that which He said, He lets it be known that He spoke in figures, so that you might have no doubt when our own human limitations would attempt to unfold to you the figures of speech which He used.

For who would ever have believed me had I wished to convince you, that riches were as thorns; seeing that the latter wound, while the former give delight? And yet thorns they are; for they wound the soul with the stabbings of anxiety regarding them; and when they lead us into sin, they stain as with blood from a wound received. For which reason also the Lord, elsewhere, as another Evangelist bears witness (Mt. xiii. 22), uses, not the word *riches*, but the phrase *the deceitfulness of riches*. For they are deceitful. They deceive because we may only have them for a time. They are deceitful because they do not relieve the real poverty of the soul.

Those riches are true riches, which enrich us in virtue. If then, Brethren, you desire to be truly rich, love the riches that are true. If you aim at the summit of true honour, strive upwards towards a heavenly kingdom. If you love the glory of great dignity, strive to be enrolled in the heavenly court of the angels.

2. The words of God which you receive by your ear, hold fast in your heart. For the word of God is the food of the soul. And when the instruction you hear is not retained in the stomach of the memory, it is as when good food is rejected by an ailing stomach. He who cannot retain food is in danger of losing his life. Be you then fearful of everlasting death, if you receive indeed the food of holy doctrine, but its

words of life, which is the food of justice, you cannot retain in your memory.

Behold everything that you do comes to an end, and day by day you are hastening, whether you will or not, and without the halting of a moment, to final judgement. Why then is that loved which is left behind? Why is that neglected by which the end is attained? Keep before your minds what He has said: *He that hath ears to hear, let him hear.* All who were then standing about Him had indeed bodily ears. But He Who said to them, all of whom possessed the ears of the body, *He that hath ears to hear, let him hear,* without doubt spoke of the ears of the soul. Strive then that the words you hear, may remain in the ear of your soul. Strive that the seed fall not by the way side; lest an evil spirit should come and steal the word out of your memory. Take care that the seed fall not on stony ground sending forth fruit of good works, but without the roots of perseverance. For what they hear in instructions is indeed pleasing to many people, and they set about the beginning of good works: but soon being wearied by the afflictions that come to them, they abandon the good they have begun.

The stony ground had not the moisture wherewith to bring to maturity that which it had germinated. Thus, many when they hear, for example, a sermon against avarice, begin to detest avarice, and to praise contempt of all material things. But as soon as the mind sees something it craved for, that which it praised is forgotten. Again many when they hear a sermon against wanton living, not alone do they no longer desire the works of the flesh, but they are ashamed of what they have already done. But as soon as the vision of some carnal temptation comes before their bodily eyes, the mind is drawn to desire as if it had never resolved deliberately against all such temptations; and thus a man is led on to do that which he has condemned: and that for which, he remembers, he condemned himself.

Oftentimes we grieve over our sins, and yet after repentance we turn again to the same faults. So did Balaam; looking down upon the tents of the Israelites he wept and prayed that in death he might become like to them, saying: *Let my soul die the death of the just, and my last end be like to them* (Num. xxiii. 10). But scarcely had the moment of repentance passed, than he burns again with the evil of greed; for he gave counsel, because of the gifts that were promised him, towards the death of this same people whom he had prayed to become like in his own death; and he forgot whom he had wept over, since he sought not to put out the fire which greed had kindled in him.

3. Observe that Our Lord when explaining the parable said that cares and riches and pleasures choked the word. They choke it because by their burthensome pre-occupations they as it were strangle the throat of the soul; for as long as they do not allow entry to any good desires, they cut off the entry of the life-giving air. Observe also that there are two things that He links with riches: *cares*, and *pleasures*; because they both burden the mind with anxiety and weaken it through over-abundance of delights. But because pleasure and anxiety do not blend, now they are tormented with concern for their possessions, and again they are softened by self-indulgence to excess.

4. The good ground *brings forth fruit in patience*; because the good we do is without value, unless at the same time we bear in patience the evil-doing of our neighbour. And the higher anyone ascends in virtue, the harder will this world bear down on him; for the more the love of the heart turns from the present life, the more the opposition of this same world mounts up. Hence it is that we see so many strive after, and do, that which is good; yet they sweat under the burden of afflictions. For though they have turned away from earthly things, they are yet harassed with increasing tribulations. But, according to the word of the Lord, they shall bring forth fruit in patience, and after their time of tribulation they shall be received into rest above; because they have borne their cross in patience.

For the grapes must be treaded so that the preciousness of wine may flow. So must the virtue of the olive, pressed out by crushing, leave the husk and become the fatness of oil. So likewise is the grain, beaten out on the threshing floor, separated from the chaff, and being cleaned is brought into the barn. Whosoever then is desirous of wholly overcoming his defects, must bear with pleasure the pain of being made clean; and the more he is now purified in the fire of tribulation, the more worthy shall he be to appear at the judgement seat of God.

5. Under the portico by which you enter the church of the Blessed Clement there used to be a certain man of the name of Servulus, whom many among you, like myself, will remember; a man poor in the things of this world, but rich in merit, whom long illness had enfeebled. From an early age until he died he lay completely paralysed. Not alone could he not stand, he could not even sit up in his bed, nor raise a hand to his mouth, nor turn from one side to the other. He was cared for by his mother and his brother, and by their hands he distributed to the poor whatever he would receive in alms.

He could not read; but he purchased for himself codices of the Sacred Scriptures, and he was wont to ask religious-minded persons who came to see him to read them to him. And in this way he became fully acquainted with the Word of God, in as far as it was possible to him; for as I have said he was wholly illiterate. In the midst of his continuous infirmity he strove fervently at all times to give thanks to God, and to fill his days and nights with hymns and praise of God. As the time drew near for his great patience to be rewarded, pain returned to the vital parts of his body. When he knew himself near to death he would exhort all who came to visit him to stand and recite with him the psalms in expectation of his going forth.

And as he lay dying, and while they were reciting the psalms, of a sudden he hushed the voices of the singers, and they were awed at the strength of his voice as he said to them: "Be silent. Can you not hear what glorious praises are resounding from heaven?" And while he

lay there listening to these same praises, which he was hearing within his own heart, this sanctified soul was delivered from the weariness of the flesh. And at his going forth, such was the fragrance of the odour that was diffused about him, that all who were present were filled with its wondrous sweetness; and by this sign they understood that the praises heard by him had greeted his soul as it entered paradise. One of our monks, who is still with us, was present at this happening, and is still wont with tears to tell us, that until the body was placed in the grave the fragrance of the odour was never absent from their nostrils.

Behold in what manner he departed this life, who while in it bore his afflictions with patience. And so, according to the word of the Lord, the good earth has *brought forth fruit in patience*; which having being broken up by the ploughshare of trial, came at length to the reward of the harvest. But, dearest Brethren, I ask you, look and see what excuse shall we have to offer at the solemn hour of judgement, slothful as we are in every good work, and possessing both goods and health, when he that was poor and helpless has thus fulfilled the teaching of the Lord?

Grant that the Lord may not then, in witness against us, point to the Apostles, who by their preaching have brought with them into His Kingdom a multitude of believers; may he not bring forth to our condemnation the martyrs who have reached the heavenly home through the shedding of their blood. And what shall we say when we see this Servulus, of whom I have been speaking, whose arms were held fast in long sickness, yet this did not withhold him from doing good? Reflect upon these things, Brethren, and by this means awaken in yourselves a zeal for what is good, so that keeping before you the good example of the just, you may become sharers in their reward, through Jesus Christ Our Lord, Who with the Father and the Holy Ghost liveth and reigneth world without end. Amen.

NOTES

[1] PG 57, 467–472.
[2] PG 72, 623–627.

[3] Rather, Osee viii. 7.
[4] PL 74, 1131.

QUINQUAGESIMA SUNDAY

THE GOSPEL OF THE SUNDAY

Luke xviii. 31–43

At that time, Jesus took unto him the twelve, and said to them: Behold, we go up to Jerusalem, and all things shall be accomplished, which were written by the prophets, concerning the Son of man. For he shall be delivered to the Gentiles, and shall be mocked, and scourged, and spit upon: and after they have scourged him, they will put him to death; and the third day he shall rise again.

And they understood none of these things, and this word was hid from them, and they understood not the things that were said.

Now it came to pass, when he drew nigh to Jericho, that a certain blind man sat by the way side, begging. And when he heard the multitude passing by, he asked what this meant. And they told him, that Jesus of Nazareth was passing by. And he cried out, saying: Jesus, son of David, have mercy on me. And they that went before, rebuked him, that he should hold his peace: but he cried out much more: Son of David, have mercy on me.

And Jesus standing, commanded him to be brought unto him. And when he was come near, he asked him, saying: What wilt thou that I do to thee? But he said: Lord, that I may see. And Jesus said to him: Receive thy sight: thy faith hath made thee whole. And immediately he saw, and followed him, glorifying God. And all the people, when they saw it, gave praise to God.

PARALLEL GOSPELS

MATTHEW XX. 17–19

And Jesus going up to Jerusalem, took the twelve disciples apart, and said to them: Behold we go up to Jerusalem, and the Son of man shall be betrayed to the chief priests and the scribes, and they shall condemn him to death. And shall deliver him to the Gentiles to be mocked, and scourged, and crucified, and the third day he shall rise again.

MATTHEW XX. 29–34

And when they went out from Jericho, a great multitude followed him. And behold two blind men sitting by the way side, heard that Jesus passed by, and they cried out, saying: O Lord, thou son of David, have mercy on us. And the multitude rebuked them that they should hold their peace. But they cried out the more, saying: O Lord, thou son of David, have mercy on us. And Jesus stood, and called them, and said: What will ye that I do to you? They say to him: Lord, that our eyes be opened. And Jesus having compassion on them, touched their eyes. And immediately they saw, and followed him.

MARK X. 32–34

And they were in the way going up to Jerusalem: and Jesus went before them, and they were astonished; and following were afraid. And taking again the twelve, he began to tell them the things that should befall him. Saying: Behold we go up to Jerusalem, and the Son of man shall be betrayed to the chief priests, and to the scribes and ancients, and they shall condemn him to death, and shall deliver him to the Gentiles. And they shall mock him, and spit on him, and scourge him, and kill him: and the third day he shall rise again.

MARK X. 46–52

And they came to Jericho: and as he went out of Jericho, with his disciples, and a very great multitude, Bartimeus the blind man, the son of Timeus, sat by the way side begging. Who when he had heard, that it was Jesus of Nazareth, began to cry out, and to say: Jesus son of David, have mercy on me. And many rebuked him, that he might hold his peace; but he cried a great deal the more: Son of David, have mercy on me. And Jesus, standing still, commanded him to be called. And they call the blind man, saying to him: Be of better comfort: arise, he calleth thee. Who casting off his garment leaped up, and came to him. And Jesus answering, said to him: What wilt thou that I should do to thee? and the blind man said to him: Rabboni, that I may see. And Jesus saith to him: Go thy way, thy faith hath made thee whole. And immediately he saw, and followed him in the way.

EXPOSITION FROM THE CATENA AUREA

GREGORY, *Hom. 2 in Evang.*: The Saviour foreseeing that because of His passion, the minds of His Disciples would be troubled, told them well beforehand of the chastisements of His passion, and of the glory of His resurrection; accordingly we are told: *Then Jesus took unto Him the twelve, and said to them: Behold we go up to Jerusalem, and all things shall be accomplished which were written by the prophets concerning the Son of man.*

BEDE: Foreseeing there would be certain heretics, who would say that Christ taught that which was contrary to the Law and the Prophets, He shows that His passion, and later glory, would be perfect fulfilment of what the prophets had foretold concerning His death.

CHRYSOSTOM, *Hom. 66 in Matt.*: He spoke of His passion apart with His Disciples; it was unnecessary that His words be made known to the people, lest they be troubled. But He foretold it to His Disciples, so that they being awakened through expectation would more readily meet it; CYRIL: and also that they might know that He foreknew of His passion, and of His own will went towards it, so that afterwards they might not say: How came it that He fell into the hands of His enemies Who promised to save us? And so He foretells the order of His passion, adding: *For he shall be delivered to the Gentiles, and shall be mocked, and scourged and spit upon.*

CHRYSOSTOM: This Isaias had foretold, saying: *I have given my body to the strikers, and my cheeks to them that plucked them: I have not turned away my face from them that spit upon me* (Is. l. 6; liii. 12). And the yoke of the Cross the prophet also foretold when he says: *He hath delivered his soul unto death, and was reputed with the wicked.* Then Our Saviour continues: *And after they have scourged him, they will put him to death.* And David foretold His resurrection, saying: *Thou wilt not leave my soul in hell* (Ps. xv. 10). Accordingly, He then here adds: *And the third day he shall rise again.*

ISIDORUS PELUS, II 212: I am astonished at the madness of those who question why Christ arose before the third day. For had He risen later than He foretold, it would be a sign of lack of power; but if earlier, it is a sign of supreme power. For if we see a man, who has promised to pay a debt after three days, pay it on that same day, we look on him, not as a deceiver, but rather as a very truthful man. I affirm that He did not say that He would rise again after three days, but *on the third day.* So you have the sabbath eve, the sabbath till sunset, and after the sabbath He rose from the dead.

CYRIL: The Disciples however had not yet come to know precisely what the prophets had foretold. But after He arose their minds *were opened,* so that they understood the Scriptures. And so there follows: *And they understood none of these things.*

BEDE: For since the Disciples supremely desired that He might live, they could not listen to anything concerning His death; since they knew He was not alone an innocent man, but truly God, they could not conceive that He would die. And as they were accustomed to hear Him speak in parables, they believed that as often as He said anything concerning His passion, that this must be applied allegorically to something else. And so there follows: *And this word was hid from them, and they understood not the things that were said.* But the Jews, who were plotting against His life, knew that He was speaking of His passion when He said: *The Son of man must be lifted up* (Jn. iii. xiv). Because of which they said: *We have heard out of the Law, that Christ abideth for ever; and how sayest thou: the Son of man must be lifted up?* (Jn. xii. 34).

GREGORY, as above: Because the Disciples were yet carnal men, they could not understand words of mystery, and so a miracle is performed. Before their eyes a blind man receives sight, so that their faith might be made firm through signs from heaven. Hence it is narrated: *Now it came to pass, when he drew nigh to Jericho, that a certain blind man sat by the way side, begging.*

THEOPHYLACTUS: And that His entry might not be without profit, He wrought on the way the miracle of the blind man, giving His Disciples by this a lesson, that we must turn all things to profit, and be never wholly idle.

AUGUSTINE, *de Quaest. Evang. II*, 48: We could understand regarding those approaching Jericho in this manner, that they had already left it, but were still close to that city; which is not a usual manner of speaking. But it seems that it can be said, since Matthew says, that as they were going out from Jericho, two blind men who sat by the way side were given sight. There is indeed no question as to the number, if another of the Evangelists is silent concerning one and mentions the other. For Mark also speaks of one blind man, since he says that he was healed of his blindness as they were going out from Jericho; and mentions his name, and also his father's, so we may believe the man was well known, and that the other was unknown, and so it was reasonable that only the one who was known should be commemorated. But since the events which follow, in the Gospel according to Luke, very plainly show that what he describes took place while they were yet approaching Jericho, there is no alternative but to believe that this miracle took place twice: once for a single blind man, whilst they were yet going into that city, and again for two blind men when He was going out from it; and that Luke records one event, and Matthew another.[1]

CYRIL: There were many people around Jesus, and the blind man had not known Him, but he felt His presence, and laid hold of Him with his heart whom his eye could not see: and so there follows: *And when he heard the multitude passing by, he asked what this meant.* And those who could see were speaking of Him according to common report; for there follows: *And they told him, that Jesus of Nazareth was passing by.* But the blind man cried out that which was true. Told one thing, he proclaims another: *And he cried, saying: Jesus Son of David, have mercy on me.* Who has taught you to speak thus, O man? Have you, though deprived of sight, read the Scriptures? How have you discerned the Light of the world? Truly *the Lord enlighteneth the blind* (Ps. cxlv. 8).[2]

CYRIL: Nurtured in Judaism, he knew that God would be born, according to the flesh, from the family of David; and so he speaks to Him as to God, saying: *Have mercy on me.* Let them imitate him who divide Christ in two: for he comes to Christ as to God, and calls Him *Son of David.* Let them admire the urgency of his confession: for while he proclaims his faith, some rebuked him. Then follows: *And they that went before, rebuked him, that he should hold his peace.* But his courage was not hindered by their rebukes, for faith learns to withstand all things, and to overcome all things; and in the service of God it is profitable to put aside timidity. For if many thrust themselves forward for the sake of gain, should not a man put timidity aside for his soul's salvation? Hence: *But he cried out much more: Son of David, have mercy on me.*

The voice of the man crying out in faith causes Christ to stand, and He looks back to those crying to Him in faith: and He calls the blind man, and bids him come to Him; so there follows: *And Jesus standing, commanded him to be brought to Him,* so that he who had drawn nigh to him in faith, might now come near to Him in body. The Lord questions him as He comes near; for there follows: *And when he was come near, He asked Him, saying:*

What wilt thou that I do to thee? He asked him for a purpose, not as though He were ignorant, but so that those who stood about Him might learn that the blind man was seeking, not money, but a divine remedy, as from God; and so there follows: *But he said: Lord, that I may see.*

CHRYSOSTOM: Or because the Jews being betrayers of the truth, might say, as they said of the man born blind: it was not this man, but one like him (Jn. ix). He desired the blind man might first show the nature of his infirmity, and then learn the greatness of the favour. And when the blind man had made evident the nature of his petition then, with supreme power He commanded him to see: so there follows: *And Jesus said to him: receive thy sight*; a sign which recoiled on the deceitfulness of the Jews; for who among the prophets had said a thing of this kind?

Note what the Physician claims from him to whom He has given health; for there follows: *Thy faith hath made thee whole.* Favours are given in exchange for faith. Grace is poured out, which faith receives. And as from a fountain some draw a little water in little vessels, and others draw more in bigger vessels, the fountain not distinguishing between the one vessel and the other, since it is the vessels, not the fountain, that measures the water, and each draws according to his measure; and as the splendour of light enters to a greater or less degree according to the dimensions of the window, so is grace received according to the measure of our desire. The voice of Christ, becomes now the light of the blind, for it is the word of the true light; and so there follows: *And immediately he saw.* And as the blind man showed a vigorous faith before he received this favour, so afterwards he failed not to give thanks; for the Gospel relates: *And he followed Him, glorifying God.*

CYRIL: From which it appears that he was delivered of a twofold blindness; one corporal, the other intellectual; for he would not have glorified Him as God unless he truly saw. To others he became a reason for giving glory to God; for there follows: *And all the people, when they saw it, gave praise to God.* BEDE: Not alone for the gift of sight for which he had prayed, but also and with reason for the faith of the man who had prayed.

CHRYSOSTOM: Here we must ask why it was that Christ forbade the man from whom He had cast out a devil to follow Him, yet does not so forbid the man now cured of blindness? I do not believe that either decision was without purpose. For He sent the one as His herald, so that in his new delivered state he may proclaim his Benefactor. For it was a striking miracle, to see one who before was raging mad now made sound in mind. But He permitted the blind man to follow Him as He was going up to Jerusalem, to complete by means of the Cross, His profound *mystery*, so that His Disciples having before them this reminder of the miracle would not think that He suffered through infirmity, and not through compassion.

AMBROSE: But in the blind man we see a figure of the Gentiles, who,

under the rule of the Lord, received back the brightness of the lost light. It matters not whether the healing was wrought in one blind man or in two; since, descending from Chem and Japhet, the two sons of Noah, in the two blind men they reached back to the two authors of their generation.

GREGORY: Or the blind man is the human race which, in its first parent, turned from the brightness of the heavenly light, and suffered the darkness of its own banishment. Jericho however is interpreted as the moon, which, diminishing in its monthly course, symbolises the eclipse of our mortality. As our Saviour therefore draws nigh to Jericho, the blind man returns to the light; because when divinity assumed to itself the failing of our flesh, mankind received back the light it had lost. He therefore that knows not the brightness of the eternal light is blind. But if he believes in the Redeemer Who said *I am the way* (Jn. xiv. 6), *he is sitting by the way side*; if he has believed, and now earnestly implores that he may receive the eternal light *he is sitting by the way side, begging.*

They who walked in front of Jesus, signify the crowds of carnal desires, and the tumult of the vices, which, before Christ makes entry to our heart, scatter our thoughts, and torment us even in our prayer. *But he cried out much more*; because the more we are afflicted by the excessive troubling of our thoughts, the more earnestly ought we to persevere in prayer. But when in our prayer we still suffer the thronging images of the senses, we are in a manner hearing Jesus passing by. But when we are earnestly insistent in our prayer, God is held fast in our heart, and the lost light is restored.

Or again; it pertains to His Humanity that He passes by, and to His Divinity to be still. And so the Lord when passing by heard the blind man crying out, and standing He gave him sight; for suffering with us in His own humanity He hears with compassion the cries of our blindness; but it is by His Divinity that the light of His grace is poured into our souls. For this however He asks the blind man what he wishes: that He may waken our hearts to prayer.

AMBROSE: Or, He asked the blind man, so that we may believe that unless a man confesses his faith he cannot be saved. GREGORY: The blind man wishes from the Lord, not gold, but light; and let us pray,

not for *deceiving riches*, but for that light which we alone with angels may see; and to this light the way is by faith. So rightly did He say to the blind man: *Receive thy sight, thy faith hath made thee whole.* He who sees and follows Him, is he who does the good he understands.

AUGUSTINE, *De Quaest. Evang. II*, 48: If however we interpret Jericho as the moon, and accordingly as mortality, the Lord approaching death, commands that the light of the Gospel be preached to the Jews alone, for whom this blind man stands, of whom Luke speaks; but rising from the dead, and departing from it, He commands that it be preached to both Jews and Gentiles, who are signified by the two blind men, of whom Matthew speaks.

I. ST JOHN CHRYSOSTOM, BISHOP AND DOCTOR

On Jesus ascending to Jerusalem[3]

1. He did not go up at once to Jerusalem from Galilee, but after He had performed certain miracles, and had rebuked the Pharisees, and spoken with His Disciples of the need for renunciation. For, He says: *If thou wilt be perfect, go sell what thou hast, and give to the poor* (Mt. xix. 21); and of virginity: *He that can take, let him take it* (Mt. xix. 12); and of humility: *Unless you be converted, and become as little children, you shall not enter the kingdom of heaven* (Mt. xviii. 3); and of reward in this life: *And everyone that hath left house, or brethren, or sisters, or father, or mother, or children or lands for my name's sake, shall receive an hundred fold*; and of reward in the future life: *And shall possess ternal life* (Mt. xix. 29).

Then at length He approaches the city, and since He is about to go up there, He speaks again of His passion. For since it was very likely, seeing they wished these things would not happen, that they would put them from their memory, He frequently recalls them to their mind; strengthening their spirit, and softening their grief, by frequent references to what is to happen.

Of necessity He speaks to them apart: for it was not fitting that these things be made common knowledge, or be clearly described: for no good could come of it. For if the Disciples were troubled at hearing these things, much more would the people be troubled. What then, you will ask, was it not told to the people? It was in fact announced to them; but not clearly. For said He: *Destroy this temple, and in three days I will raise it up* (Jn. ii. 19); and again: *An evil and adulterous generation seeketh a sign; and a sign shall not be given it, but the sign of Jonas the prophet* (Mt. xii. 39); and again: *Yet a little while I am with you: you shall seek me, and you shall not find me* (Jn. vii. 33, 34).

But not in this manner did He speak to His Disciples, but more clearly: as in other matters, so also did He speak to them in this. But if the people understood not the significance of His words, why did He pronounce them? So that after these events had come to pass they might come to learn that He went forth to meet His passion with knowledge and deliberation, being neither ignorant of it nor compelled to it.

And not for this reason only did He foretell His passion to His Disciples, but, as I have said, so that they being roused by expectation, would the more readily confront His passion, and so that it would not overwhelm them by coming upon them unprepared. And for this reason, at the beginning, He foretold only His death; afterwards, when they had reflected on this, and when they were prepared for them, He also told them of the other things; for example: that they would deliver Him to the Gentiles, that they would mock Him and scourge Him; and for this reason likewise, that when they came to behold these sorrowful events, they would then look also for His resurrection. For He Who had not hidden the sorrowful things from them, and what would appear as shameful, must then with

reason be believed concerning what was joyful.

But observe how He seeks for a fitting moment of time. For He did not tell them this in the beginning, lest they be frightened; nor at the actual time of the events, lest they be thrown into confusion; but after they had received adequate proof of His power, when He had given them great promises of eternal life, then He spoke of this: once, and twice, and mingling it frequently with His teaching and His miracles.

Then one of the Evangelists says that He brought forward the prophets as witnesses (Lk. xviii. 31). Another says the Disciples understood not His words, that they were hidden from them, and that *they were astonished; and following were afraid* (Mk. ix. 31; x. 32). Then, you will say, the value of the prediction was taken away? For if they knew not, as He said, what that meant which they were hearing, they could not then look out for what was to come: and not expecting it, neither could they be aroused by expectation.

And so I shall say another thing that is more difficult. If they knew not, how then were they grieved? For another Evangelist says that they were sorrowful. If then they do not know what is to come, why are they grieving? How came it that Peter said: *Lord, be it far from thee, this shall not be unto thee?* (Mt. xvi. 22). What then are we to say? They knew He was to die, although the mystery of His Plan they could not clearly see. Neither did they know clearly of His resurrection, nor what great events were to follow it.

And this too was hidden from them. And this also they grieved over. They had known that some persons had been raised to life by others: but never had they known of one who raised himself from the dead, and had so raised himself that he would not die again. This, though often told to them, they did not understand: nor did they know clearly what kind His death would be, nor how it would come to Him. And so they were *astonished* and *followed Him in fear*; and not for this alone, but, as it seems to me, because He in speaking of His Passion filled them with terror.

2. Yet none of these warnings gave them courage, even though they heard frequently of the resurrection. For besides the prophecy of His death, this especially afflicted them: to hear that He would be mocked and scourged, and endure other things of this nature. For when they thought about His miracles, and of the possessed persons He had delivered, and of the dead who were raised to life, and of other wondrous happenings, they were stupefied that He who could work such wonders should undergo such indignities. And so they were in great perplexity, now believing, now disbelieving, and neither could they understand these things.

So far were they from having a clear understanding of them, that the Sons of Zebedee came to Him at the same time, and began to speak to Him of advancement for themselves. *Master*, they say, *we desire that whatever we shall ask, thou wouldst do it for us* (Mt. xx. 21; Mk. x. 35, 37). But how then, you will say, did another Evangelist say that it was their mother who approached Him? It is possible that both happened, and that they took their mother with them to strengthen their pleading, so that in this way they might the more move Christ. That it was their own request, and that through shame they brought their mother, Christ directing His answer to them now proves.

But let us first see what it is that they ask: and with what disposition of mind, and for what reason were they stirred up to this? From whence were they moved to this? They had seen that they were treated with more honour than the rest, and because of this they expected to secure what they were asking. But what did they ask for? Listen to another Evangelist telling it clearly: *Because*, he says, *he was nigh to Jerusalem, and because they thought that the kingdom of God should immediately be manifested* (Lk. xix. 11), they asked for these things. For they thought that this kingdom was now close, and could almost be seen, and that once having secured what they sought, they would not suffer grievously: for not alone for the favour itself did they make their request, but that they might escape hardships.

And so Christ first draws them away from such notions, bidding them rather look for slaughter, dangers, and extremities of every kind. For said He: *Can you drink the chalice that I shall drink?* (Mt. xx. 22). Let no one be troubled at seeing the Apostles so imperfect. For the Cross had not yet come, the grace of the spirit was not yet given. If you would know of their true virtues, look at them after these things had come to pass, and you will see them rise above every infirmity of the soul. And for this does He make known their imperfections, that you may afterwards know what they become because of grace.

That they were seeking nothing spiritual, and that they had no thought of a heavenly kingdom, is here very evident. But let us see how they come to Him, and what they say: *We desire that whatsoever we shall ask, thou wouldst do it for us?* (Mk. x. 35). And Jesus asked them: *What would you that I should do for you?* Not because He did not know, but that He might compel them to answer and so lay bare the ulcer, that He might apply a remedy to it. But they were feeling ashamed, because from a purely human desire they had come to this state of mind, and because they had asked Him when they had taken Him a little apart from the others. For they had gone ahead, lest they be observed by the others, and in this way had said what they wished to say.

Because they had heard Him say: *You shall sit on twelve seats* (Mt. xix. 28), they wished to ask Him for the first seats. They knew that they would precede the others: but they were afraid as to Peter, and so they say: *Say that one may sit on thy right hand, and the other on thy left*; and they urge Him with this word, *Say*. What does He say? That He may show that they are asking for nothing spiritual, and that if they had known what it was they asked, they would not have ever dared to ask it, He says: *You know not what you ask.* How great is He, how wonderful: how He surpasses the heavenly powers!

Then He adds: *Can you drink of the chalice that I drink of: or be baptized of the baptism wherewith I am baptized* (Mk. x. 38). Observe how

He immediately draws them away from this notion, speaking to them of the very opposite kind of things. For you speak to me, He seems to say, of crowns and of honour: I speak of struggles, of the sweat of toils. This is not the time for rewards, neither shall my glory be now revealed; the present hour is one of slaughter, of wars, and of dangers.

And observe with me, from the manner in which He questions them, with what end in view He both exhorts them, and encourages them forward. For He did not say: Can you endure slaughter? Are you prepared to shed your blood? How did He speak? *Can you drink of this Chalice?* Then, drawing them on, He says: *That I shall drink*; so that in His company they might be more willing. And this He calls a baptism, showing that from it the whole world would receive a great purification.

Then they say to Him: *We can.* In the fervour of their spirit they promise immediately, not knowing what they said, but looking to obtain that which they were asking. What then does He say? *You shall indeed drink of the chalice that I drink of: and with the baptism wherewith I am baptized, you shall be baptized* (Mk. x. 39). He foretold great things for them; that is, you shall be held worthy of martyrdom, you shall suffer the things I have suffered, you shall end your life with a death from violence, and in this also you shall be sharers with Me. *But to sit on my right hand, or on my left, is not mine to give to you, but to them for whom it is prepared* (Mk. x. 40). After he had lifted up their hearts, and made of them nobler men, He then reproves them. See how imperfect they all were, both these two who had tried to obtain precedence over the other ten, and the ten who were displeased with them. But, as I have said, show them to me after this, and you will see them free of every passion. And hear how this same John, who now comes for this purpose, at all times yields the primacy to Peter, in preaching and in miracles, as is recounted in the Acts of the Apostles, and describes his great deeds, and the confession which he made when all the others were silent.

Let us then be humble, that we may be exalted. For arrogance lowers us completely. It was pride cast Pharao down: *Who is the Lord? I know not the Lord*, he says; and then he was made lower than flies and frogs and locusts; and afterwards was drowned with all his horses and armies. But Abraham was the opposite of this: *I will speak to my Lord, whereas I am dust and ashes* (Ex. v. 2; Gen. xviii. 27), and he overcame many thousands of the barbarians, and being come into the midst of the Egyptians, he returned, bearing a more glorious trophy than before, and remaining steadfast in virtue was raised

ever higher. And for this he is everywhere celebrated, everywhere honoured and spoken of; but Pharao is dust and ashes, or whatever is lower than they are.

For God is opposed to nothing so much as to pride. And because of this there is nothing He has not done, and from the beginning, to overthrow this evil disposition. Because of it we are subject to death, and live in grief and pain; because of it we labour in sweat and toil, and in afflictions without end. Through pride the first man sinned, because he aspired to become equal to God. And so did not even keep what he already had, but fell from everything.

For it is the nature of pride, that not alone does it add nothing to our life, but it takes from us that which we have. But humility takes from us nothing of what we have, but rather adds that which we have not. Let us then form ourselves in this virtue, let us beg that we may obtain it, that we may have joy in this our present life, and attain to future glory, by the grace and mercy of Our Lord Jesus Christ, to Whom with the Father and the Holy Ghost be glory and empire for ever and ever. Amen.

II. St John Chrysostom

On the Gospel[4]

Many and various are the teachings of the Scriptures, one however is the grace that shines in all of them: the source of their inspiration: the Holy Spirit. And whatsoever it be the Law declares, whatsoever the prophets foretold, whatsoever the Apostles teach, and the Gospel of justice lays down, all flow from the Holy Spirit, as from one

single breast, one abundant fountain. Neither is it possible to utter any noble thought, or to conceive anything in wisdom, or to do what is worthy of men's admiration, unless what is said and what is done is confirmed by the Holy Spirit.

However much anyone may glory in human wisdom, and abound in it, and possess a mind that is equipped and fortified with human reasonings, but which turns away from the word of God, rejecting it, he is as nothing, and shall be accounted as nothing. It is because of this the Prophet says: *They have cast away the word of the Lord, and there is no wisdom in them* (Jer. viii. 9). But for us the Scriptures of righteousness are the flower of truth: many indeed are the flowers, but one the field that grows them: many the lamps of doctrine, but One is the True Light: many the stars, but one the sky that brings them forth: many the fingers, but one the hand that records the works of the fingers: many the strings, but one the harp of the Spirit: many the teachings, but one the fountain of righeousness.

To me it is a source of wonder to reflect, by what inspiration did this blind man, who had not read the Law, nor scanned the Prophets, neither had he yet read the Gospels nor had he been confirmed by the Apostles, should so address the Saviour of mankind, and say to Him: *Jesus Son of David, have mercy on me*. Where have you learned so to address Him? You have not read books, since you are without the use of your eyes; you have not given your years to study since you must sustain life by begging your bread from door to door; where then have you learned that this is the Light of the world, Whom, being without sight you have never seen either in heaven or on earth? Truly in this there was fulfilled what was said by the prophet David: *The Lord enlighteneth the blind* (Ps. cxlv. 8).

There was a multitude of people round about the person of Jesus:

the blind man could not see the Light of Truth, but in his soul he could feel His Presence, and with the desire of his heart he laid hold of what his eye could not see. What is the meaning of all these people, he asks? They tell him that Jesus of Nazareth is passing by. O wondrous event! He is told one thing, and cries out another. He hears them saying it is Jesus of Nazareth, but he cries out, not Jesus of Nazareth, but Jesus Son of David. They who could see made answer from what was known by common report, but the blind man makes known what he had learned from Truth Itself; for he cries out: *Jesus Son of David, have mercy on me*.

It is here as when many have assembled at the grave of one about to be committed to the earth, and looking upon the body of the dead, and seeing him wept over by his family, all weep together; some because they grieve for the same reason as the bereaved family; others because they are thinking again of their own griefs. Often a woman will weep and mourn, not for the one now being made ready for the grave, for he is a stranger to her, but for her own departed husband: so another's loss becomes a reminder of her own sorrow. So any one among you Brethren, when he has heard this account from the words of the Gospel will apply it to himself, and for the healing of his own afflictions let him cry out: *Jesus Son of David, have mercy on me*.

Let every heart cry out aloud from its own miseries: this one because he is blind in his heart: this other because he is deaf in his soul: this other because his reason has become blinded; another because he has lost the power of true judge-ment. For the infirmities that Christ healed in the bodies of men have their counterpart in the soul, and need remedies that are divine. Blind is the soul that needs to have the use of its eyes restored to it: blind is the soul that cannot discern the wonders of the Law: blind is the soul that cannot see that there is a world to come: blind is the soul that beholds the Body of Christ, but cannot discern His divinity. Isaias bears witness that the soul is blind which ignores the things of God: *Who is blind but the servant of the Lord? Thou that seest many things, wilt thou not observe them? Thou hast ears open, wilt thou not hear? And who is blind, but my ser-vant? or deaf, but he to whom I have sent messengers?* (Is. xlii. 19, 20).

And the Saviour, desiring to point out their blindness of mind, reproached the Pharisees for obscur-ing the truth; saying of them: *Let them alone: they are blind, and leaders of the blind. And if the blind lead the blind, both fall into the pit* (Mt. xv. 14). The soul is deaf which does not listen to the word of God, which despises the teaching of the Lord: deaf, not by nature, but deaf in the purposes of the mind: for which reason the Saviour said: *He that hath ears to hear, let him hear* (Mt. xi. 15). It was not that some of those who were present had not ears: for how should they know of His teaching if they had not organs of hearing? He here says that the ear that is seen was given for hear-ing: but this hearing is not of use to understand the meaning of the divine law. The external sense avails nothing, if the inner under-standing and the heart have become deaf.

And leprous is the soul, not of him whose body is discoloured and corrupt, but of him whose soul is smothered in darkness: for what is leprosy of the body but a diversity of colour? What is leprosy of the soul? A twofold mind. *Woe to them that are of a double heart* (Ecclus. ii. 14), as when one now believes, and now is unbelieving; now dis-posed to mercy, now towards in-humanity. The soul is leprous, not in being blemished and discoloured, but in being as it were two-faced. As leprosy sunders the body, so evil purposes divide the mind. Let every man therefore cry out for the healing of his wounds, and call upon the Physician of souls, and of bodies as the blind man called out: *Jesus Son of David have mercy on me.*

And they that went before, rebuked him. But his courage in speaking was not stayed by their rebuke. Faith renews in man the strength to withstand all things, to triumph over all. Men shouted at him to be silent, but the man of faith abated nothing of his eagerness, but sought the Lord, as one who well knows that honest presumption may serve the cause of righteousness. For if there be many who thrust them-selves forward for the sake of gain, should a man not put bashfulness aside, when it is a question of his soul's salvation?

Jesus commanded him to be brought unto him. He had brought it about that Jesus stood. The voice of the man who cried out in faith had caused Jesus to stand still. He orders him to be brought before Him, *and He asked him, saying: What wilt thou that I do to thee?* He does not ask idly: for He could have healed him as he sat by the way side. But because the Jews might say, as they said of the man born blind: *it is not this man but one like to him* (Jn. ix. 8). He therefore calls the blind man into their midst, that He first might make evident to them the defect in his nature, and then show the power of His grace. *What wilt thou that I do to thee?* He questions the man, and in this way instructs those about Him. *But he said: Lord, that I may see.* Observe what testimony He requires of this man, to whom He gave health, so as to thwart the falsehoods of the evil-minded. He thereupon says to him: go, *Thy faith hath made thee whole.* See how, as we said in this regard yesterday, His works give testimony of Him: and these are not venal favours; they are sold for faith alone. Jesus bestows His favours, not for gold, but sells them for faith. Unless you pay the coin of faith, you shall not receive His favour.

Was the favour bestowed, then grace preceded it. And as the fountain is one, yet many draw from the fountain: this one with a little vessel, this other with a larger; the first draws but little water, the second draws much; and it is not the fountain that determines the measure of the water drawn forth; for each draws according to the capacity of his vessel. So grace is placed before us as a fountain. The will of each man who draws from it, becomes the vessel, the pitcher, of the grace he receives. If therefore you put in but a little faith, as with the vessels, you will draw forth but a little grace. But if you dip in a soul that is great in faith, you draw forth a great return.

Accordingly the Saviour says: *Do you believe that I can do this to you?* He says to Him, *Yea, Lord.*

Then says the Saviour: *According to your faith be it done unto you* (Mt. ix. 28, 29). For this reason also the Apostle exhorts the Corinthians, saying: *Be enlarged in your hearts* (II Cor. vi. 13), in order to show that the more abundant gifts of grace will enter the larger, the more generous soul. So too the Prophet: *Open thy mouth wide, and I will fill it* (Ps. lxxx. 11). No barrier save our own neglect comes between us and the divine favour.

Jesus the Sun of Justice has arisen. The rays of this spiritual Sun spread out in all directions; and one indeed receives less grace, and another more; not that grace so gives itself; it is our own disposition that supplies the measure. For as the sun is one which gives light to the whole universe, and its ray is one, and its splendour, yet it does not shine with equal light upon all the world. Here is wondrous and abundant sunshine, here there is less. This house has little sunlight, this has it more abundantly; not because the sun gives more to this house, and less to that, but according to the windows which were opened to it by those who built the houses, it has more room to enter, and pours in accordingly. And since our thoughts and purposes are the windows of our soul, when you open wide your heart you receive a larger, more generous, divine favour; when you narrow your soul, you can but receive a less abundant grace. Open wide and lay bare your heart and soul to God, that His splendour may enter into you. Because of this Paul says of himself: *But we all beholding the glory of the Lord with open face, are transformed into the same image from glory to glory* (II. Cor. iii. 18). According to this narrative one blind man is healed by faith; through instruction the eyes of many are opened. *According to your faith be it done unto you* (Mt. ix. 29).

The blind man *followed, glorifying God*, and neither did Jesus forbid him. And here it is worth while to consider why it was that Christ, when He had delivered a man that was tormented by a devil, and when this man upon whom He had bestowed so great a favour asked that he might follow Jesus, for *he besought Him that he might be with Him* (Lk. xviii. 38), He did not permit it, but said to him: *return to thy house, and tell how great things God hath done to thee*. For what reason did He forbid this man who desired to follow Him, and did not forbid the other? Why did He permit this latter to accompany Him, and not permit the former? The one He did for a useful end, the other for a fruitful end.

To the one He denied permission to follow Him for another reason than that he had been possessed by a devil. Now it is characteristic of anyone possessed by a devil that their speech and tongue is disordered, and perverted. He sends him therefore as His herald, so that in his new delivered state he might make known Who was his benefactor. For it was a truly striking miracle to see one who before was out of his mind, now well, and speaking in the full possession of his senses; thus making use, as His herald, of that very member of the man's body upon which He had bestowed such a favour. And see here also another admirable thing: behold the humility of the Saviour: and behold also the grateful soul of the man who was possessed by a

demon. The Saviour says: *Go, and tell how great things God hath done to thee*. He does not say: what great things I have done to thee, but, speaking not of Himself, He attributes this work to the Name of God.

He that was possessed by a demon went about declaring what great things Jesus had done to him. This man He sends forth, that from his very restoration to health he may show the greatness of the favour granted him. But He permits the blind man to follow Him. Why so? Because He was about to go up to Jerusalem to fulfil there His profound mystery, and take upon Himself His plan for the redemption of the world; and it was to be that the Cross would follow, and humiliations, and all that was later done to Him by the impious, and by the enemies of God, in their unheard-of wickedness. And so He willed that the blind man should follow Him, so that the constant reminder of this miracle would confirm and steady the minds of those who might falter. He saw to it that the blind man followed Him, so that no one might deny the miracle that took place before all; because the minds of the Apostles were to be shaken and tossed as by a storm, and the soul and the steadfastness of all beholding these events would be grievously perturbed, when they beheld the Only-Begotten Son of God upon a cross. Lest they should give way when they beheld His passion, He permits the blind man to follow Him, so that having before their eyes this proof of His recent miracle, they would preserve an unshaken hold upon His truth.

Christ did many such things, because He had in mind that He had come to fulfil this task for all men. But lest any man might think that He suffered in this way because of infirmity, and not because of compassion, seeing a certain fig tree by the way side, just before He entered Jerusalem, *He came to it,* says the Gospel, *and found nothing but leaves,* and not finding fruit on it *He saith to it: May no fruit grow on thee hence forward and for ever. And immediately the fig tree withered away* (Mt. xxi. 19).

In what had the fig tree offended? Was it through the power of its own intelligence that it suffered fruitlessness? Or is it not only when the Creator so wills that it has power to bring forth fruit? Then again, it was not *the time for figs.* To this the Gospel bears witness. Who among men, not to speak of God, would look to gather fruit out of due season? Was it not Thee, O Creator, who ordered the years? Was it not Thee Who laid down the times and the seasons for bearing fruit? Why then do You seek it outside the time You have

appointed? If it were the time of figs, and the fig tree had borne no fruit, it would then have been the fault of nature. Does it bear fruit when it pleases? Or rather, does it bear only when commanded?

Why then did He reproach the fig tree? Since He was about to undergo His passion, lest they might think He suffered because He was without power, He showed them the power of His might upon this inanimate thing, so that He might also show them that He could so wither all who had contradicted Him, and destroy all who were enemies of His divinity. But since He came not to judge the world but to save it, as He has Himself declared, He showed His power upon a thing that lacked a soul, and reserved His tenderness for men. And for this cause He allowed the blind man to follow Him, that the so recent memory of the shining miracle of his healing, would take from their minds the scandal of the Cross, through Jesus Christ Our Lord. Amen.

III. St Augustine, Bishop and Doctor
On the Love of God, and the Illumination of the Blind Man[5]

Love God. You will not find anything more worthy of love. You love silver, because it is more precious than iron or bronze. You love gold still more, because it is more precious than silver. Still more precious stones, for they are prized above gold. Last, you love this light; which all who dread death fear to leave. You love light, I say, as he loved it, with deep longing, who cried to Jesus: *Son of David, have mercy on me.*

The blind man cries out, as Jesus was passing by. He heared He

might pass by, and not heal him. And how earnestly he cried? Though the crowd rebuked him, he would not be silent. He overcame his rebukers, and held our Saviour. While the crowd clamoured against him, and forbade him cry out, Jesus stands, and called him, and said: *What wilt thou that I do to thee? Lord,* he said, *that I may see. Receive thy sight: thy faith hath made thee whole.*

Love Christ: Seek ye the light that is Christ. If he longed for the light of the body, how much the more ought you to long for the light of the soul? Let us cry out to Him, not with words, but with virtuous living. Let us live in virtue, and esteem not the world: all that is transitory to us is nothing. They will rebuke us should we live as worthy men, and lovers of ourselves, and lovers of the earth, delighting in the games, drawing nothing from heaven, unbridled in heart, and testing all delights: they will, and without any doubt, rebuke us; and should they see us despise what is human, what is earthly, they will say: why do you wish to suffer? Why are you foolish?

The crowd clamours, that the blind man shall not cry out. There are not a few Christians who seek to hinder us from living as Christians: like the crowd that walked with Christ, and hindered the man crying out to Christ, and hungering for light from the kindness of Christ. There are such Christians: but let us overcome them, and live in virtue: and our life shall be the voice of our cry to Christ. He will stand; because He stands.

For here is a great mystery. He was passing by when this man began to cry out: when He healed him He stood still. Let Christ's passing by make us prepared to cry out. What is Christ's passing by?

Whatsoever He has endured for us here is His passing by. He was born, He passed by: for is He yet being born? He grew up, He passed by; is He yet growing up? He was suckled: is He yet suckled? When weary He slept: does He yet sleep? He ate and He drank: does He yet do this? At the last He was seized, He was bound with ropes, He was beaten, He was crowned with thorns, He was struck by blows, He was defiled with spittle, He was hung on a Cross, He was put to death, He was pierced by a lance, He was buried, He rose again. Till then He passes by.

He ascended into heaven, He sits at the right hand of the Father: He stands still. Cry out all you can: now He will give thee light. For that in Him the *Word was with God*, He has of a surety stood still; since He was not changed. And *the Word was God: and the Word was made Flesh*. The Flesh has wrought many things through passing by, and suffered many. The Word has stood still. By this Word the soul is enlightened; as by this Word the flesh which He took on is adorned. Take away the Word, what then of the flesh? It is as yours. That the flesh of Christ be honoured, *the Word was made flesh, and dwelt amongst us*. Let us live virtuously, and so cry out to Him.

IV. St Cyril: On the Gospel[6]

Our Blessed Lord, by foretelling to His Disciples the events that were now about to come to pass, anticipated both wrongful judgements and any ground for taking scandal. For these men who had beheld the wonders He had wrought, and had been made strong in courage by His words, were now

to see Him mocked by the Jews, crucified, and dishonoured. It was therefore possible, that scandalised by this mockery they might think to themselves: He that possessed such mighty power, working wonders by as it were a simple nod of His head, and Who has been wont to say that the providential care of

His Father reached even to the sparrows, this the Only-Begotten and the First-Born, how is it He has not known what was about to happen? How is it that He was seized by His enemies, Who had promised He was about to deliver us?

That therefore they might learn that He both foreknew the coming of His passion, and that when He could easily have avoided it, of His own will, He went forth to meet it, He now makes known what is to come to pass. And of necessity He also told them that all these things had been foretold by the holy prophets, God having disposed that when these things should come to pass no one should be scandalised. For beyond any doubt He was free to avoid the passion He had foreknown was to come. No one compelled Him: He suffered of His own free will; knowing fully that His passion would be salutary for the whole world. He suffered death, in His flesh; overcoming corruption, He rose again; and by His resurrection from the dead, He poured His own life into the bodies of men; for in Him the whole nature of man is turned back towards immortality.

And the common Saviour of all men foretold these things to the holy Apostles; but they did not, as the Evangelist says, *understand the things that were said.* For they did not yet know precisely what the prophets had foretold. For which reason the Prince of the Apostles, not yet perceiving the depths of the mystery, had so withstood the Master as to say: *Lord, be it far from thee, this shall not be unto thee* (Mt. xvi. 22). Which saying was chastised with a rebuke. But after He rose from the dead, Christ opened

their eyes, as one of the holy Evangelists says (Lk. xxiv, 31); since their minds were enlightened through having received an abundant sharing of the Holy Spirit, they could say: *And we have the more firm prophetical word: whereunto you do well to attend, as to a light that shineth in a dark place, until the day dawn, and the day star arise in your hearts* (II Pet. i. 19).

This man draws near to Him, as to the Omnipotent God: Whom however he calls Son of David. for being reared in Judaism, and a native of the country, he could not have been ignorant of what was Foretold concerning Him in the Law, and by the holy prophets, and that He could be born, according to the flesh, of the House of David. Therefore, already believing that this was the Word of God, Who, of His own will, had been born according to the flesh from the holy Virgin, he comes before Him as God, saying: *Son of David, have mercy on me.* And that it was in this belief he offered up his prayer, Christ Himself bears witness, Who said to him: *Thy faith hath made thee whole.*

Let those who divide Christ in two imitate this blind man, for he drew near to Christ, the Saviour of all men as unto God, and called Him both Lord and Son of David. He bears testimony to His power, when he asks of Him an act that only God can perform. Let them admire likewise the steadfastness with which the blind man proclaimed his belief, for there were some who, while he confessed his faith, cried out to him to be silent. But he did not cease, nor lessen the confidence of his prayer, because of those who strove to forbid him.

For faith knows how to combat all things, and to overcome all. They indeed rebuked him; but in him faith did not waver, but steadfastly pursued the Lord; believing that courage was desirable in defence of belief. For if there are many who are daring in the cause of gain, ought not a man be courageous for the cause of his soul's salvation?

At the voice of the man crying out in faith, the Lord stands, and the faith of the blind man was well rewarded. The Lord stands, and He called him to come to Him, so that he who had already drawn close to Him in his heart through faith, might now come near to him in his body. Faith brings us likewise into the very presence of Christ, so that by it we also become worthy to hear His voice.

And when the blind man was standing in His presence, He asked him, saying: *What wilt thou that I* do to thee? Was the petition of the blind man unknown to him? How can we think this? Foreknowing, and of purpose, He questions him, so that those who stand about and were accompanying Him, might know, that the blind man was not seeking money, but rather a manifestation of divine power, as from God.

And Jesus said to him: receive thy sight: thy faith hath made thee whole. And being delivered of his blindness, did the blind man fail to give fitting thanks? By no means, He was therefore healed of a twofold blindness; being delivered of the blindness both of the eye, and of the heart and soul. For he could not have honoured Him as God, unless he could truly see. And to others also he became an occasion of giving praise to God, *for all the people, when they saw it, gave praise to God.* Amen.

V. St Gregory: Steadfastness in Prayer

Given to the People in the Basilica of the Blessed Peter the Apostle on Quinquagesima Sunday[7]

1.   Our Redeemer foreseeing that the minds of His Disciples would be troubled because of His passion, foretold to them from afar both the humiliation of His passion, and the glory of His resurrection: so that when they would behold Him dying, as He had predicted, they would not doubt He would also rise again. But since His Disciples, still carnal men, could not grasp the meaning of the words of the *mystery*, He wrought a miracle. Before their eyes a blind man receives sight, so that they who could not grasp the words of the heavenly mystery, would be strengthened in faith through heavenly deeds. But the miracles of Our Lord and Saviour, Dearly Beloved Brethren, are so to be received, that they are believed as true, and that they teach us something by a similitude. His works proclaim one thing by their power, another in their mystery.

For who this blind man was as regards his personal history we know not, yet whom he mystically represents we do know. For this blind man is truly humanity, which driven out from the joys of paradise in our first parent, not knowing the brightness of eternal light, suffers the darkness of its own condemnation: but through the presence of its Redeemer it is given sight, so that it may behold in desire the joy of the inward light, and *set its steps in the way* of a life of good works (Ps. lxxxiv. 14).

2. We must note that it is when Jesus is said to be approaching Jericho, that the blind man is given sight. For Jericho is interpreted as the moon: and the moon in sacred speech is used as a figure of the mortality of man, because, diminishing in its monthly courses, it typifies the eclipse of our mortality. While Our Saviour therefore draws nigh to Jericho, the blind man is restored to sight; because when divinity took on the infirmity of our nature, mankind received back the light it had lost. For the reason whereby God endures what is human, by this same is man raised to what is divine: who fittingly is represented as a blind man sitting by the way side, and begging: for He that is the Truth has said: *I am the way.*

He who therefore does not know the brightness of the eternal light is blind indeed; but if he does believe in the Redeemer, he *is sitting by the way side*; and if he believes in Him, but neglects to pray that he may receive the light eternal, and ceases from prayer, then is he a blind man *sitting by the way side* who does not beg. If however he has believed, and has seen the blindness of his own heart, and prays that he may receive the light of truth, then he is a *blind man sitting by the way side, begging.*

Whosoever therefore acknowledges the darkness of his own blindness: whosoever sees within himself the need of the eternal light, let him cry out from the depth of his heart, let him cry out and with the voice of his soul, saying: *Jesus son of David, have mercy on me.* But what is it we hear added concerning the blind man: *And they that went before, rebuked him, that he should hold his peace.*

3. Whom do they signify, who went before Jesus as He came, if not the crowd of carnal desires, and the tumult of the vices, which, before Christ makes entry into our hearts, scatter our thoughts with their temptations, and confuse the pleadings of the soul in prayer? For often when we desire to turn again to the Lord, after we have committed many sins against Him, and while we struggle in prayer against these same vices to which we have yielded, the images of the sins we have committed rise against us, they war against the fervour of our soul, they darken the spirit, and strive to silence the voice of our supplication. They who went before rebuked him that he hold his peace; and so do the sins to which we have consented mock our pious aspirations by their evil memory, because before Jesus enters the heart, the sins we have committed mock our desires with their wicked images, and bring confusion into our very prayer.

4. But let us hear what answer the blind man, who was about to be cured, made to this. The Gospel says: *But he cried out much more: Son of David, have mercy on me.* See how he whom the crowd rebukes, to make him be silent, cries out more and more; and so the more we are tormented by the crowd of carnal thoughts within us, so much the more let us steadfastly persevere

in prayer. This crowd torments us, lest we cry out: for it is generally in prayer that we have to suffer the images of our former sins. But it is necessary that the more they oppose the cry of our heart, the more courageously let it be steadfast, until it has overcome the tumult of the evil thoughts, and broken upon the sacred ears of the Lord by the force of its importunity.

I think, that each will understand within himself, that of which we speak; for when we turn our souls from this world unto God, when we give ourself to the task of prayer, the things that before delighted us, afterwards we carry as heavy and importunate burthens in our prayer. Only with difficulty is the thought of them brushed from the eyes of the soul by the hand of holy desire: only with effort are their images wiped away by our tears of repentance.

5. But when we are earnestly steadfast in prayer, we hold Jesus, Who is passing by. For which reason there is added: *And Jesus standing, commanded him to be brought unto him.* Behold He now stands, Who before was passing by; for while yet we suffer the thronging images of the senses in our prayer, we are as it were hearing Jesus passing by. When however we are firmly steadfast in prayer, Jesus stands, that He may bring back the light: for God is held fast in the heart, and the lost sight is restored.

6. In this the Lord indicates something to us which can with profit be understood, concerning both His divinity and His humanity. Jesus passing by hears the blind man crying out, but standing still He brings forth the miracle of restoring sight. It belongs to His humanity to pass by: to His divinity to be still. Since it was through His humanity He came to be born, to grow up, to die, to rise again, to go from place to place. And because in His divinity there is no change; and to pass by is itself to be changed: plainly then His passing by is of the flesh, not of the divinity. In His divinity he is forever still, because He is everywhere present, and neither does He come through motion, nor through motion depart. The Lord therefore passing by hears the blind man crying out; standing, He gives him sight; for by suffering with us in His humanity, He hears with compassion the cries of our blindness: but it is by the power of His divinity He pours the light of His grace into our souls.

7. And we should also carefully note what He says to the blind man: *What wilt thou that I should do to thee?* Does this mean that He Who has power to give sight to the blind does not know what the blind man craves? No. But He wishes to be asked for that for which He foreknows we shall pray, and He will grant. For He Himself, in season and out of season, exhorts us to pray, yet at the same time He tells us: *Your father knoweth what is needful for you, before you ask him* (Mt. vi. 8). But for this He requires that we ask Him: for this He requires that our hearts be moved to prayer. And so the blind man forthwith replies: *Lord, that I may see.* Behold the blind man prays, not for money, but for light. He reckons nothing worth the asking compared with this light; for even should he be given whatsoever

He wishes, without sight he cannot see what it is he has.

Let us, Dearly Beloved Brethren, imitate this man whom we have heard was healed in body and mind. Let us seek from the Lord, not deceiving riches, not earthly gifts, not fleeting honours, but light. And not that light which may be enclosed in space, and is measured by time, and changes with the coming of night, and which is enjoyed in common by sheep and men; but let us seek for the light that we and the angels alone may see; which no beginning commences, and no end encloses. To this light the way is through faith alone. Fittingly then does He answer the man who is now about to be given sight: *Receive thy sight, thy faith hath made thee whole.*

To all this the mind of the carnal man makes answer: how shall I seek for a spiritual light, which I cannot behold? And how shall I know that which shines not on mortal eyes? To which reflection each one may answer, that the very things he sees, he considers, not with his body, but by means of his soul. Yet no one sees his own soul; neither does anyone doubt that he has that soul, which he sees not. For the visible body is governed by the invisible soul. And if that which is invisible be taken away, that immediately collapses which appeared to endure of itself as visible. It is by this invisible substance therefore that man lives in this visible life; and is it to be doubted that there is an invisible life?

8. But let us hear what happened to the blind man, or what he himself did. The Gospel goes on: *And immediately he saw and followed him.*

He sees, and follows, who does the good He understands. He sees, but does not follow, who knows what is good, but despises the doing of good works. If, therefore, Dearest Brethren, we perceive the blindness of this our earthly sojourn; if, believing in the mystery of our Redeemer, we sit by the way side; if by daily prayer we beg for light from our Creator; if we have been enlightened after our blindness, seeing now that light by our understanding, Jesus Whom we see in our soul, we follow in work.

Let us look and see whither He is going, and let us find our way by following His footsteps. He follows Jesus who imitates His example. For He says: *Follow Me, and let the dead bury their dead* (Mt. viii. 22). Follow here means imitate. Again He warns us, saying: *If any man minister to me, let him follow me* (Jn. xii. 26). Let us consider then whether He goes, that we may merit to follow.

Behold, though He is the Lord and Creator of the angels, He comes to take upon Himself, in the womb of the Virgin, that nature which He created. Nor did He will to come into the world in wealth, but chose parents that were poor. And so it was for want of the lamb which should have been offered for Him (Lk. ii. 24), that His mother procures a pair of young doves for the sacrifice. He willed not to be prominent in the world, and submitted to its scorn and derision. He endured to be spat upon, the scourging, blows, a crown of thorns, and the Cross. And because we fell from eternal joy through bodily delights, He shows us through what pain we return there.

What then should a man suffer

in his own behalf, if God has suffered so much for men? He therefore who already believes in Christ, but still pursues the gains of avarice, he that is still puffed up with earthly pride, he that burns with the flame of jealousy, he that soils himself with the uncleanness of lust, he that seeks only the world's good fortune, despises to follow Jesus in Whom he has believed. He to whom his Guide has shown the way of self-denial, walks by another way, if he craves only delight and pleasures.

Let us recall to our minds the sins we have committed, and think well how stern is the judge that comes to avenge them. Let us dispose our hearts to repentance. Let us taste in due season the sharp flavour of repentance, lest we taste for ever the bitterness of retribution. We are told on the word of Truth, that through tears shall we come to everlasting joy: *Blessed are they that mourn: for they shall be comforted* (Mt. v. 5). But the same truth bears witness that through delights also we come to sorrows: *Woe to you that now laugh, for you shall now weep* (Lk. vi. 25).

If then we hope for the reward of joy on our arrival, let us hold fast to self-denial on the way. In this way our life shall be not alone a journey to God, but the manner in which we ˙ live will encourage others unto the praise to God. For this reason there was added: *And all the people, when they saw it gave praise to God*, Who liveth and reigneth, world without end. Amen.

VI. THEOPHYLACTUS: ON THE GOSPEL[8]

Then Jesus took unto Him the twelve . . .

He foretold His passion for these two reasons. First, that He might show that not against His own will, or as a mere man not knowing death, was He crucified, but that He had foreseen His own suffering, and gone to meet it of His own free will. For if He had not wished to suffer, He could have avoided that which He foreknew. It is only the unaware who are captured. Secondly, to prepare them to meet calmly the events that were about to follow, and which, since they would have heard concerning them beforehand, would not now come on them unexpectedly.

Since these things were to be done to Thee, which were spoken of by the prophets, why then dost thou go up, O Lord? For this alone: that I may accomplish your salvation. And so of His own will He goes. Thus spoke the Lord but, the Disciples at this time *understood none of those things. For the word was hid from them*, and most of all they understood nothing of the word *resurrection*. And other words which they did not understand were: *He shall be delivered to the Gentiles*. But the word *resurrection* was in no way understood by them, for it was not a word in common use. And neither did all the Jews, particularly the Sadducees, believe in the resurrection of the body.

But you may ask why, if they understood none of these things, why does He foretell them to His Disciples? What comfort could they be to them in the hour of the Cross, if they understood not the things which were now said?

That they would be of no small value to them, when, at the time they took place, they remembered that these were the things which they had not understood, when the Lord was foretelling them, is plain from many things, and especially from that which was said by John: *These things His Disciples did not know at first; but when Jesus was glorified, then they remembered that these things were written of Him* (Jn. xii. 16). And the Holy Spirit *brought all these things to their mind* (Jn. xiv. 26), imparting to them the securest testimony concerning Christ. It was abundantly attested to by the other Evangelists who wrote concerning Him, and that He was for three days in the sepulchre.

Now it came to pass, when He drew nigh to Jericho . . .
The Lord wrought this miracle of the healing of the blind man by the way side, that His *passing by* as well as His teaching might be profitable to us, as disciples of Christ; and so that we also might always and everywhere and among all peoples be profitable servants, and never be slothful. The blind man, believing that this was the Christ whose coming was looked for, for it was unlikely that reared as a Jew he did not know that He was to be of the seed of David, cries out with a loud voice: *Son of David, have mercy on me.* By saying: *have mercy on me,* he openly declares that he believes Him to be divine, and does not think Him a mere man.

And admire with me the steadfastness of his confession, and how though many rebuked him that he be silent, he would not hold his peace, but cried out all the more. An interior ardour urged him, and,

accordingly, Jesus, since the man was so deserving of approaching Him, commanded that He be brought before Him. He then asks him: *What wilt thou that I do to thee?* He does not ask as one not knowing, but for fear, with others standing by, the blind man might appear to them to be asking for one thing, and He grant another; as should the blind man ask for money and He, as if desiring to make a display, should instead heal his blindness. For malice and envy might readily invent such things. Accordingly when He had asked and when He had ascertained that the blind man was fervently praying for his sight, He gave him this.

Observe here also how far from arrogance was the Lord's manner. *Thy faith,* He says, *hath made thee whole,* for you have believed that I am that Son of David Who is called the Christ, and you have shown such fervour, that though they tried to silence you, you would not hold your peace. From this we may learn that when we ask with faith for some favour, He bestows upon us, not something other than we ask for, but that which we asked for. And as often as we ask for one thing, and receive another, it is evident that either we did not ask worthily, or with faith. *You ask, and receive not; because you ask amiss* (Jas. iv. 3).

Observe yet further His divine power: *Receive thy sight,* He says . . . And which of the prophets has healed in this manner, I ask you, and with such power? And thereupon, the word that came forth from the True Light, became the light of the eyes of the man that was blind. Behold also the gratitude of the man who was healed. For he followed Jesus, *glorifying God*, being made also a cause why others when they saw this wonder *gave praise to* God, to Whom, with the Son and Holy Ghost, be honour and glory for ever and ever. Amen.

NOTES

[1] Cf. PL 35, 1360.

[2] Cf. PG 72, 863, note.

[3] PG 58, 617; Hom. 65 in Matthaeum.

[4] This homily is certainly not authentic. It is given among the *Spuria* in PG 59, 599–610. It is also cited under the name of St Cyril of Alexandria; cf. PG 72, 863, footnote. It is filled with pious and instructive reflections on this Gospel, and is without doubt of ancient composition, and, was probably read in the churches under one of the great names, as frequently happened. It is included in this homiliary because of its approval by St Thomas Aquinas, who cites it abundantly (under Chrysostom's name) in the Catena Aurea, in the exposition of this portion of the Gospel.

[5] PL 39, 1539–32.

[6] PG 72, 863–866.

[7] PL 76, 1081–1086.

[8] PG 123, 1017.

INDEX

The following abbreviations have been used: Aph: Aphraates; Alc.: Albinus Alcuin; Amb.: Ambrose; Amph.: Amphilochius; Aug.: Augustine; Bd.: Bernard; Chr.: Chrysostom; Cyl. of A.: Cyril of Alexandria; Eph:. Ephraem; Gau.: Gaudentius; Gy. Ny.: Gregory of Nyssa; Gy. Gt.: Gregory the Great; Isi. of Pel.: Isidore of Pelusium; Jer.: Jerome; L. Gt.: Leo the Great; Max.: Maximus; Or.: Origen; Ptk.: Patrick; Theo.: Theophylactus.